SHORTER EDITION

OF WESTERN
MUSIC

BY DONALD JAY GROUT

PROFESSOR OF MUSIC, CORNELL UNIVERSITY

W · W · NORTON & COMPANY · INC · New York

Contents

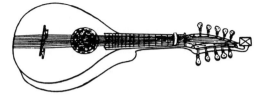

sonatas. Concertos. Bach's orchestral suites. Concertos for solo instruments with orchestra. Other works. Bach at Leipzig. Bach's church cantatas. Cantata No. 21. Cantatas No. 4 and No. 80. Bach's secular cantatas. Bach's motets. Bach's *Passions*. The *Mass in B minor*. Handel's instrumental music. Handel's suites and sonatas. Handel's concertos. Handel's operas. Handel's oratorios. Handel's choral style.

Aspects of eighteenth-century life. The ideal eighteenth-century music. Rococo and expressive styles. New concepts of melody and harmony. Domenico Scarlatti. Sonata form. Pre-Classical symphonies and chamber music. The *empfindsamer Stil*. C. P. E. Bach. German symphonic composers. Chamber music. Italian *opera seria*. The aria. Beginnings of opera reform. Christoph Willibald Gluck. Comic opera. Italy. France. England. Germany. The Lied. Singspiele. Church music.

Haydn's symphonies. The symphonies of 1771-1774. The quartets of 1760-1781. The symphonies of 1775-1788. The quartets of the 1780's. The *London* symphonies. The last quartets. The sonatas. Haydn's church music. Haydn's oratorios. Mozart's career. Mozart's early works. Mozart's Italian and German traits. Piano and violin sonatas. Serenades. Violin concertos. Vocal music. The *Haydn Quartets*. The concertos for piano and orchestra. Mozart's operas.

Beethoven's character. Characteristics of Beethoven's music. The sonatas. The quartets. The First Symphony. The Second Symphony. The *Eroica* Symphony. *Fidelio*. The *Rasumovsky* quartets. The Fourth to Eighth Symphonies. The sonatas and concertos. Characteristics of Beethoven's late style. The Mass in D. The Ninth Symphony. Beethoven and the Romantics.

Traits of Romanticism. The Romantic dualities. Music and words. The crowd and the individual. Man and nature. Science and the irrational. Materialism and idealism. Nationalism and internationalism. Tradition and revolution. Franz Schubert. Schubert's *Lieder*. Schumann's *Lieder*. Brahms's *Lieder*. Part songs and cantatas. Church music. Other music on liturgical texts. The Romantic oratorio.

General features. The early Romantic composers. Franz Schubert. Felix Mendelssohn-Bartholdy. Robert Schumann. Frédéric Chopin. Franz Liszt. Johannes Brahms. Other composers. Schubert's chamber music. Schumann's chamber music. Brahms's chamber music. César Franck's chamber music. Schubert's symphonies. Mendelssohn's symphonies. Schumann's symphonies. Berlioz's symphonies. The *Symphony fantastique*. Berlioz's other symphonic works. Liszt's symphonic poems. Brahms's symphonies. Franck's symphony. Bruckner's symphonies. Other composers.

Grand opera. *Opéra comique*. Lyric opera. Hector Berlioz. Gioacchino Rossini. Gaetano Donizetti. Vincenzo Bellini. Giuseppe Verdi. Early works. Late works. Weber. Other German opera composers. Richard Wagner. Earlier works. The *Ring*. The leitmotif. Formal structure. Late works. Wagner's influence.

Illustrations

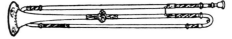

Preface

This shorter edition of *A History of Western Music* has been designed
for those who prefer or need a more compact presentation of the
material. Based as it is on the regular edition, it concentrates on style
analysis and musical examples. The changes made have been a matter
of compression; no vital aspect of the subject has been slighted.

A generation ago this book would have been called simply a "History of Music." Today's view is different, and the word *Western* in
our title reflects the realization that the musical system of Western
Europe and the Americas is but one of several among the civilizations
of the world. Two further limitations should be stated here: this
book is concerned only with art music; and it emphasizes certain
composers, works, and historical relationships. Fashions in history
change with the generations, like fashions in musical taste. Of course
a historian tries to be objective; but any general history of music is
bound to reflect its writer's judgment as to which of the music of
the past that he happens to know, and which aspects of the historical
development of that music, are most worth attending to in the present.

The history of music is primarily the history of musical style, and
cannot be grasped except by first-hand knowledge of the music itself. It is therefore essential to become acquainted with the *sound*
of the musical examples cited in this book and to hear them *in their
context;* for this reason, most of the examples have been selected from
works which are conveniently accessible in standard editions or in
anthologies of music, and these are listed in the Appendix to each
chapter.

An elementary knowledge of musical terms and of harmony—
equivalent perhaps to a first-year course in theory—has been assumed.
The Glossary contains brief definitions of terms not elsewhere defined in this book; but many of these are terms which a student who
is ready to begin the study of the history of music should not need
to look up, unless by way of reminder.

The Appendixes also contain suggestions for further reading.
These lists are not intended as bibliographies. Most of the titles are

in English, since many university undergraduates are not able to read a foreign language.

Particular thanks are due to Professor Otto Kinkeldey and Professor Paul Henry Lang. Both read all the chapters in manuscript and gave me much excellent advice, most of which I have followed. Other colleagues as well have given me the benefit of their specialized knowledge from time to time. I want to thank Dr. Emanuel Winternitz and Professor Carl Parrish for help with the illustrations; Mrs. Brian McGuinness for special assistance; and Mr. Harold Samuel, Music Librarian of Cornell University, for his quiet efficiency and never-failing patience.

DONALD JAY GROUT
Ithaca, N. Y.

I The State of Music at the End of the Ancient World

Anyone living in a province of the Roman Empire in the fifth century of the Christian era might have seen roads where people used to travel and now travelled no more, temples and arenas built for throngs and now falling into disuse and ruin, and life everywhere becoming with each generation poorer, more insecure, and more brutish. Rome in the time of her greatness had imposed peace on most of western Europe as well as on considerable parts of Africa and Asia; but Rome had grown weak and unable to defend herself. The barbarians were pouring in from the north and east, and the common civilization of Europe was splintering into fragments which only after many centuries began to coalesce gradually into the modern nations.

The grand events of Rome's decline and fall stand out so luridly in history that it is hard for us even now to realize that, along with the process of destruction, there was quietly going on an opposite process of creation. This came to be centered in the Christian Church, which until the tenth century was the principal—and oftentimes the only—bond of union and channel of culture in Europe. The earliest Christian communities, in spite of three hundred years of sporadic persecution, grew steadily and spread to all parts of the Empire. After his conversion in 312, the Emperor Constantine adopted a policy of toleration and, what is more, made Christianity the religion of the imperial family. In 395 the political unity of the ancient world was formally broken up by the division into Eastern and Western Empires, with capitals at Byzantium and Rome. When after a terrible century of wars and invasions the last Western Emperor finally stepped down from his throne in 476, the foundations of the Papal power were already so firmly laid that the Church was ready to assume the civilizing and unifying mission of Rome.

1

I. The State
of Music at
the End of
the Ancient
World

The Greek Heritage

The history of Western art music properly begins with the music of the Christian Church. But all through the Middle Ages and even to the present time men have continually turned back to Greece and Rome for instruction, for correction, and for inspiration in their several fields of work; this has been true in music—though with some important differences. Roman literature, for example, never ceased to exert influence in the Middle Ages, and this influence became much greater in the fourteenth and fifteenth centuries when more Roman works became known; at the same time, too, the surviving literature of Greece was recovered. But in literature, as well as in some other fields (notably sculpture), medieval or Renaissance artists had the advantage of being able to study and, if they so desired, imitate the models of antiquity. The actual poems or statues were before them. In music this was not so. The Middle Ages did not possess a single example of Greek or Roman music—nor, it may be added, are we today much better off. About a dozen examples—half of them mere fragments—of Greek music have been discovered, nearly all from comparatively late periods, but there is no general agreement as to just how they were meant to sound; there are no authentic remains of ancient Roman music. So we, as well as the men of medieval times, derive nearly all our knowledge of this art in the ancient civilizations at second hand from a few rather vague accounts of performances and from theoretical treatises.

There was a special reason for the disappearance of the traditions of Roman musical practice at the beginning of the Middle Ages: most of this music was connected with social occasions on which the early Church looked with horror, or with pagan religious exercises which the Church believed had to be exterminated. Consequently every effort was made not only to keep out of the Church music which would recall such abominations to the minds of the faithful, but, if possible, to blot out the very memory of it. How much may have slipped in and been preserved, and how much may have survived outside the Church over the centuries, no one knows; certainly it could have been but little, if any.

Yet there were some features of ancient musical practice that lived on in the Middle Ages if only for the reason that they could hardly have been abolished without abolishing music itself; furthermore, ancient musical theory was the foundation of medieval theory. So in order to understand medieval music, we must know something about the music of ancient peoples, and in particular about the musical practice and theory of the Greeks.

Greek mythology ascribed to music a divine origin and named as its inventors and earliest practitioners gods and demigods, such as Apollo, Amphion, and Orpheus. In this dim prehistoric world, music had magic powers: people thought it could heal sickness, purify the body and mind, and work miracles in the realm of nature. Similar powers are attributed to music in the Old Testament: we need only recall the stories of David curing Saul's madness by playing the harp (I Samuel xvi: 14–23), or of the trumpet-blasts and shouting that toppled the walls of Jericho (Joshua vi: 12–20). In the Homeric Age, bards sang heroic poems at banquets (*Odyssey* VIII, 72–82).

From earliest times music was an inseparable part of religious ceremonies. In the cult of Apollo the lyre was the characteristic instrument, while in that of Dionysus it was the aulos. Both these instruments probably came into Greece from Asia Minor. The lyre and its larger counterpart, the kithara, were instruments with five to seven strings (later as many as eleven); both were used for solo playing and to accompany the singing or reciting of epic poems. The aulos, a double-pipe reed instrument (not a flute) with a shrill piercing tone, was used in connection with the singing of a certain kind of poetry (the dithyramb) in the worship of Dionysus, out of which it is believed the Greek drama developed. As a consequence, in the great dramas of the classical age—works by Aeschylus, Sophocles, Euripides—choruses and other musical portions were accompanied by, or alternated with, the sounds of the aulos.

From at least as early as the sixth century B. C. both the lyre and the aulos were played as independent solo instruments. There is an account of a musical festival or competition held at the Pythian games in 586 B. C. at which one Sakadas played a composition for the aulos illustrating the combat between Apollo and the dragon—the earliest known piece of program music, and one which remained famous for centuries. Contests of kithara and aulos players, as well as festivals of instrumental and vocal music, became increasingly popular after the fifth century B. C. As instrumental music grew more independent the number of virtuosos multiplied; at the same time the music itself

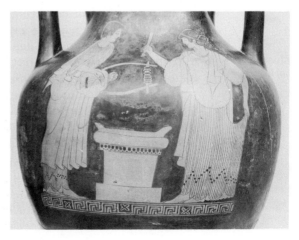

Vase painting of Apollo playing a lyre and Artemis holding an aulos before an altar. The lyre was a loosely constructed instrument with a body made from a tortoise shell or wooden bowl over which was stretched a skin. Two horns or wooden arms projected upward from the bowl and supported a horizontal crosspiece to which strings were attached; the other ends of these arms were fastened to the underside of the sounding bowl after passing over a bridge. The lyre was played by plucking the strings either with the fingers or a plectrum. (Courtesy Metropolitan Museum of Art, Rogers Fund, 1907)

I. The State
of Music at
the End of
the Ancient
World

became more complex in every way. In the fourth century Aristotle warned against too much professional training in general music education:

The right measure will be attained if students of music stop short of the arts which are practised in professional contests, and do not seek to acquire those fantastic marvels of execution which are now the fashion in such contests, and from these have passed into education. Let the young practise even such music as we have prescribed, only until they are able to feel delight in noble melodies and rhythms, and not merely in that common part of music in which every slave or child and even some animals find pleasure.[1]

Sometime after the classical age (about 450 to 325 B. C.) a reaction set in against technical complexities, and by the beginning of the Christian era Greek musical theory, and probably also its practice, had become simplified. Most of our surviving examples of Greek music come from relatively late periods. The chief are: two Delphic hymns to Apollo from about 150 B. C., a *skolion* or drinking song from about the same time or perhaps a little later, and three hymns of Mesomedes of Crete from the second century A. D. (see HAM, No. 7 for examples).

Although we do not know much about Greek music or its history, we can say that in two fundamental respects it was the same kind of music as that of the early Church. In the first place, it was primarily monophonic, that is, melody without harmony or counterpoint. In the second place, Greek music was almost always associated with words or dancing or both; its melody and rhythm were most intimately bound up with the melody and rhythm of poetry, and the music of the religious cults, of the drama, and of the great public contests was performed by singers who accompanied their melody with the movements of prescribed dance patterns. To say, however, that the music of the early Church resembled Greek music in being essentially monophonic and inseparable from a text is not to assert a historical continuity. There doubtless was some connection, but it cannot be clearly demonstrated.

We do not know whether any significant contributions to either the theory or the practice of music were made by the Romans. They took their art music from Greece, especially after that country became a Roman province in 146 B. C., and it is possible that this imported culture replaced an indigenous Etruscan or Italian music of which we have no knowledge. The Romans invented or developed, chiefly for military purposes, some brass instruments of the trumpet and horn types. Many passages in the writings of Cicero, Quintilian, and others show that familiarity with music, or at least with musical terms, was considered a part of the education of a cultivated person, just as such a person was expected to be able to speak and write Greek.

During the great days of the Roman Empire (the first two centuries of the Christian era), music, philosophy, new religious rites, and many

*Music in
ancient Rome*

A Roman matron playing a kithara is depicted in this Roman fresco of the first century A.D. The kithara had a heavy body solidly joined together with a wooden sounding board and strong arms supporting a crossbar around which the strings were wound. (Courtesy Metropolitan Museum of Art, Rogers Fund, 1903)

other luxuries were brought to Rome from the Hellenistic world. There are numerous reports of the popularity of famous virtuosos, of the prevalence of large choruses and orchestras, and of grandiose musical festivals and competitions. Many of the emperors were patrons of music; Nero even aspired to personal fame as a musician. With the economic decline of the Empire in the third and fourth centuries, the production of music on the large and expensive scale of earlier days ceased. Music-making there undoubtedly was, even in those troubled times, but little record of it has been preserved; after the fifth century, practically all traces of secular musical practice disappear. This, of course, does not mean that there was no secular music in the early Middle Ages. As for the ancient Romans, it is difficult to believe that the countrymen of Cicero, Virgil, and Horace could have been completely unoriginal in the field of music; yet we can only say that, if they did make any significant original contributions to the art, no evidence of the fact has so far come to light.

Although there is much uncertainty about the details, we do know that the ancient Roman world bequeathed to the Middle Ages certain fundamental ideas about music: (1) a conception of music as consisting essentially of pure, unencumbered melodic line; (2) the idea of melody intimately linked with words, especially in matters of rhythm and meter; (3) a philosophy of music which regarded the art not as a play of beautiful sounds in a spiritual and social vacuum of art for art's sake, but rather as an orderly system interlocked with the system of nature, and as a force capable of affecting human thought and conduct; (4) a scientifically founded acoustical theory; (5) a system of scale-formation based on tetrachords; and (6) a musical terminology.

Part of this heritage (Nos. 4, 5, and 6) was specifically Greek. The rest was common to all ancient nations, but the knowledge of it and ideas about it in the Middle Ages came from Greek writers—in some cases, by way of the works of Arabic scholars.

5

I. The State
of Music at
the End of
the Ancient
World

The Early Christian Church

It is impossible for us to know exactly how much, and what, music of the Greeks or of the mixed Oriental-Hellenistic societies around the eastern Mediterranean was taken into the Christian Church during the first two or three centuries of its existence. Certain features of ancient musical life were definitely rejected—for example, the idea of cultivating music purely for enjoyment as an art, or as an essential part of common education. Above all, the forms and types of music connected with the great public spectacles such as festivals, competitions, and dramatic performances, as also the music of more intimate convivial occasions, were regarded by many as unsuitable for the Church, not so much from any dislike of music itself as from the need to wean the increasing numbers of converts away from everything associated with their pagan past. This attitude involved at first even a distrust of all instrumental music. Yet the break could not have been complete. Just as early Christian theology and literature were more or less consciously influenced by the philosophy and literature of antiquity, so early Christian music must have taken over much from non-Christian sources.

In addition to its inescapable cultural environment, early Christianity had a specific heritage in the music and ritual of the ancient Jewish temple. The first Christian congregations naturally adopted the Jewish organization of the daily prayer hours as well as the custom of singing

The Judean heritage

psalms in the services. Among the Hebrews, psalms were sung in alternation between a soloist and the congregation; in one form of alternation, which later became important in Christian liturgy under the name of *responsorial psalmody*, the leader sang the first line of each psalm verse and the congregation responded by singing the second line. Such a method is particularly appropriate to the psalms, so many of which have verses with two parallel phrases, the second restating or continuing or amplifying the thought expressed in the first:

> Bless the Lord, O my soul,/ and forget not all his benefits:
> Who forgiveth all thine iniquities;/ who healeth all thy diseases.

A related form of singing, not peculiar to the Jewish temple but found all over the ancient world, was *antiphonal psalmody*, in which the two parts of the verse, or alternate verses, were sung in turn by two choruses. Still another usage inherited by the early Church from the Jewish service was the reciting of prescribed passages of Scripture by a soloist, using certain melodic formulas the essential outlines of which could be retained while details were varied to suit the requirements of a particular text.

As the early Church spread through Asia Minor and westward into Africa and Europe, it accumulated musical elements from diverse national sources. Hymn singing is the earliest recorded musical activity of the Christian Church (Matt. xxvi: 30; Mark xiv: 26). It is likely that some of the hymns of the early Church were sung to what would now be called folk melodies, and it is possible that some of these melodies eventually found their way into the official chant books. The oldest surviving example of Christian church music is a hymn of praise to the Trinity, with Greek words and in Greek vocal notation, found, in 1896, on a papyrus at the site of the ancient Egyptian town of Oxyrhynchos. The date of the papyrus is toward the end of the third century. It contains only the last few lines of the hymn and is so mutilated that even these cannot be completely reconstructed.

The city of Byzantium (or Constantinople, now Istanbul) was rebuilt by Constantine and designated in 330 as the capital of his reunited Roman Empire. After the permanent division in 395 it re- mained the capital of the Eastern Empire for over a thousand years, until its capture by the Turks in 1453. During much of this time Byzantium was the seat of the most powerful government in Europe and the center of a flourishing culture which blended Hellenistic and Oriental elements. The music of the Byzantine Church continued to have some influence in the West until the final schism of the Eastern and Western Churches in 1054. Byzantine Chant is also the ancestor of the music of the modern Greek Orthodox, the Russian, and other Eastern Churches.

The melodies of the Hebrew Synagogue and the Byzantine Church (as also those of the Western Church) were handed down by oral tradition for centuries before being reduced to written form. Comparison of the oldest available records and consideration of other evidence by modern scholars have left no doubt that the melodies sung in both the ancient Jewish temple and the earliest Eastern Christian churches were constructed according to the system of *echoi*, that is, by combining certain melodic formulas in improvisatory fashion. In some cases it has been possible to reconstruct with a high degree of probability the ancient melodic formulas. The importance of these discoveries for the history of early Western Church music is twofold:

(1) Many of the oldest Western chants are constructed according to the method used in Eastern melodies—that is, by combining and varying a number of established melodic motives. In a few instances the resemblances between Western and Eastern chants are so close as to suggest that either the Western melody was taken directly from the Eastern, or else both were variants of one earlier common formula. Isolated melodic similarities, however, are less important than the basic similarity of the method and principles of melodic construction used in both Eastern and Western chant. From this similarity we can conclude that the earliest Western Church music incorporated a great many Eastern elements, some probably from Hebrew song, and some from Syria, Byzantium, Greece, Egypt, and other centers.

7

I. The State
of Music at
the End of
the Ancient
World

(2) The Byzantine system of eight *echoi* had an important influence on the Western medieval theory of the eight church modes. Like the Western Church modes, the *echoi* were grouped in four pairs, and the four pairs had as their final tones respectively the four notes d, e, f, and g.

In the West, as in the East, local churches at first were relatively independent. Although they shared, of course, a large area of common practice, yet it is likely that each region of the West received the Eastern heritage in a slightly different form; these original differences combined with particular local conditions to produce several distinct liturgies and bodies of chant. Eventually all these local versions except one (the Ambrosian) either disappeared or were completely absorbed into the single uniform practice for which the central authority was Rome. From about the ninth to the sixteenth centuries, in theory and for the most part also in practice, the liturgy and music of the entire Western Church were established by the Church of Rome.

Ambrosian Chant, from a twelfth-century Manuale Ambrosiano. *This folio contains portions of the Office and Mass of the Feast of the Beheading of St. John the Baptist.*

The most important Western Church center outside Rome was Milan, a flourishing city with close cultural ties to Byzantium and the East; it was the chief residence of the Western emperors in the fourth century, and later was made the capital of the Lombard Kingdom in northern Italy, which flourished from 568 to 744. The Bishop of Milan from 374 to 397 was St. Ambrose, who first introduced antiphonal psalmody and hymns to the west. Owing to the importance of Milan and to the energy and high personal reputation of St. Ambrose, the Milanese liturgy and music exerted a strong influence not only in

France and Spain but also at Rome, where antiphonal psalmody was adopted early in the fifth century. The songs of the Milanese rite later came to be known as Ambrosian Chant, though it is doubtful whether any of the music that has come down to us was composed by St. Ambrose himself. The Ambrosian liturgy with its complete body of chants has been maintained at Milan to the present day, in spite of various attempts to suppress it. Many of the chants are very similar to those of the Roman Church, indicating either an interchange or a derivation from a common source.

The most important contributions of St. Ambrose to the Western liturgy were hymn texts. Since the hymns constitute one of the two basic divisions of Western church music, we must define their essential character. Probably at first no distinction was made among the "hymns, psalms, and spiritual songs" of which St. Paul speaks (Col. iii: 16) and which are mentioned by other writers of the first three centuries. All the surviving hymn texts from these three centuries are Greek; one of them, *O gladsome light*, by an unknown author of (probably) the third century, is still sung at Vespers in the Greek church. Gradually, and especially in the Latin West, the meaning of *hymn* was narrowed to denote a poem in strophic form, all the stanzas of which were intended to be sung to the same melody; the setting was mostly *syllabic* (one note to a syllable), and comparatively simple and tuneful—music originally for the congregation or the individual worshiper rather than for a trained choir or soloist. As to subject matter, the hymn is limited only by its general purpose of "celebrating Christian truths or events";[2] thus it need not be Scriptural —though there was a considerable struggle before the Church finally admitted non-Biblical hymns. In general, it may be said that hymns, in both form and content, are apt to express personal, individual sentiments, whereas other parts of the liturgy are by comparison more objective, public, and formal.

As the liturgy developed, and especially after the singing of hymns in the service was entrusted to the choir instead of the congregation, many of the earlier tunes were enriched by the addition of ornamental notes; also, new melodies of a sometimes quite ornate character were composed. Beside the versified hymns there are a few with prose texts, among which the best known is the *Te Deum laudamus* (*We praise Thee, O God*), written probably in the latter part of the fourth century and sung now to a melody compounded of formulas from different historical periods. According to legend, at the moment when St. Ambrose baptized St. Augustine the two spontaneously improvised the *Te Deum* in alternate verses. This legend is thought to refer to what was undoubtedly a practice in the early Church, namely the creation of hymns under the inspiration of strong religious feeling, somewhat the way today new phrases of text and new melodic variations spontaneously arise during the enthusiasm of a camp meeting.

I. The State
of Music at
the End of
the Ancient
World

In addition to the main outlines of the liturgy, the body of responsorial and antiphonal psalmody, the reciting formulas, and the hymns, one other Eastern element became important in Western church music: the class of songs originally used in the Hebrew Synagogue as refrains, for example on the word "amen" or "alleluia." The refrains were chanted responsively after each verse or after the last verse of a psalm, and some of them developed into independent song types, losing their primitive simple character and becoming more or less elaborate solo melodies. The Alleluias were especially noteworthy because of their florid (melismatic) style, in which the last syllable was drawn out in ecstatic melody, soaring phrase after phrase "in gladness of heart outflowing, joy too full to be expressed in words."[3] Alleluia melodies were introduced at Rome by Pope Damasus about 380, and were finally incorporated in the music for the Mass on every Sunday except during the fasting or penitential seasons.

Another species of Western chant that grew out of the synagogue songs with refrains was the *antiphon*. At first the antiphon, a verse or sentence with its own melody, probably was repeated after every verse of a psalm or canticle, like the phrase "for His mercy endureth forever" in Psalm 135/6. In later practice, the refrain was usually sung only at the beginning and end of the psalm; at the present day only the "intonation" or opening phrase of the antiphon is sung first, and the entire antiphon is heard after the psalm (examples, HAM, No. 11, MM, No. 1). The four *Marian antiphons* (so called, although they are really independent compositions rather than antiphons in the strict liturgical sense) are especially beautiful melodies (see Example 1, page 16).

A form akin to the antiphon is the *responsory* or *respond*, a short verse which is sung by soloist and repeated by the choir before a prayer or short sentence of Scripture, and repeated again by the choir at the end of the reading. The responsory, like the antiphon, was originally repeated by the choir, either wholly or in part, after each single verse of the reading; this early practice survives in a few present-day *responsoria prolixa* or Long Responsories (see HAM, No. 14).

Although the manner in which the various elements of Eastern chant were adopted by the West during the first three Christian centuries is not altogether clear, one thing is certain: as far as the music is concerned there was no evolution from a simple to a more complex musical style. Many of the chants that were brought from the East were undoubtedly ornate, full of melismatic passages with opportunities for improvisation; and at least some of them were based on Oriental scale patterns with chromatic and enharmonic intervals. The course in the West was, in general, toward order and relative simplicity, a course made the more imperative by events of the early fourth century.

The dominance of Rome

In 313 Constantine recognized the Christians as entitled to equal rights and protection along with other religions in the Empire; the Church at once emerged from its underground life, and during the fourth century Latin replaced Greek as the official language of the liturgy at Rome. As the prestige of the Roman Emperor declined, that of the Roman Bishop increased, and gradually the predominant authority of Rome in matters of faith and discipline began to be acknowledged.

With ever greater numbers of converts and ever growing riches, the Church began to build large basilicas, and services could no longer be conducted in the comparatively informal manner of early days. From the fifth to the seventh centuries many popes were concerned with revising the liturgy and music, a work in which they were

S. Apollinare Nuovo, built by Theodoric at Ravenna between 493 and 525, is a simple three-aisle basilican church of the early Christian church-building period. These magnificent mosaics are on the nave walls.

greatly aided by the monks of the Order of St. Benedict (founded in 529). The post of Cantor, or chief solo singer (an institution inherited from the synagogue) was officially established; boy choirs, common at Jerusalem by the beginning of the fifth century, were introduced in the West; a singing school (*Schola Cantorum*) was founded at Rome in the fifth century for training both men and boys as church musicians. In all these steps the original basic distinction between solo and choral singing was retained, and as a consequence, to this day Roman chant preserves a division between the music of responsorial and solo psalmody on the one hand and that of antiphonal psalmody and hymnody on the other—the former being rhythmically flexible and melodically elaborate, the latter by comparison strict and simple.

The culminating reform of the liturgy and chant seems to have been in large part the work of Gregory I (The Great), Pope from 590 to 604. St. Gregory's achievement was so highly regarded that

I. The State
of Music at
the End of
the Ancient
World

in the Middle Ages a legend grew up that he had himself composed all the melodies in use by the Church; he was often depicted as receiving these from the Holy Spirit, as a dove, and dictating them to a scribe (see illustration). His actual contribution was probably much less than that which medieval tradition ascribed to him; so great a work could not have been accomplished in fourteen years. He recodified the liturgy and reorganized the Schola Cantorum. He caused a collection of chants to be compiled from those already in use, retaining as many as were serviceable, revising where necessary; he assigned particular chants to the various services throughout the year in an order that remained essentially untouched until the sixteenth century; in short, he brought all the music of the Western Church for

St. Gregory receiving the Chant melodies from the Holy Spirit and dictating them to his scribe.

the first time into a systematic and well-proportioned whole. In his honor this music is called Gregorian Chant, a name apparently in common use as early as the ninth century; it was given also, in the twelfth and thirteenth centuries, the designation *cantus planus* (*plainsong*) to distinguish it from the *cantus figuralis* or *mensuratus* (figural or measured song), the measured polyphonic music of the Middle Ages. What changes took place in the chant between the time of St. Gregory and the beginning of the ninth century (the earliest date to which the present form of the melodies can be traced with certainty) we do not know. It is possible that the Roman forms were overlaid with Frankish elements. In any event, the Gregorian chants are one of the great treasures of Western civilization. Like Romanesque architecture, they stand as a monument to medieval man's religious faith; they were the source and inspiration of a large proportion of all Western music up to the sixteenth century. They constitute one of the most ancient bodies of song still in everyday use, and include some of the noblest artistic works ever created in pure melody.

The principal events and tendencies in the history of Western music to the time of Gregory the Great (making allowance for incomplete knowledge due to the lack of evidence on many points) may be summed up as follows: During the first three centuries of the Christian era the earliest forms of worship and their musical concomitants, taken over from the Hebrew Synagogue, were variously modified and expanded in different regions of the East. There was no uniform practice, and individual improvisation seems to have played a certain role. There were three main types of chant: the reciting formulas, the melismatic songs, and the refrains sung by the choir or congregation. The melodies of all these were built up according to the Oriental fashion of combining traditional standard melodic formulas within a given mode. There were three ways of performing: direct (without alternation), responsorial (alternation of soloist and chorus), and antiphonal (alternation of two choruses).

From the fourth to the sixth centuries all this system was assimilated by the Western churches; but the Western trend was toward a uniform practice, which eventually emanated from Rome. Probably the extremes of Oriental chant were modified, the melismatic tunes made somewhat plainer and the simple tunes somewhat more ornate. More and more of the performance was handed over to an officially constituted body of trained singers. The culminating reforms under Gregory I and his successors aimed to organize the whole body of chant in a uniform manner for the entire Western Church, embracing diverse types and practices in one orderly system. So the first stage of Western music seems to have been one in which an early emphasis on ecstasy and individual liberty was succeeded by emphasis on order and discipline. Thus the Gregorian age may be called the first "classical period" in the history of Western music.

This was the main stream of history. Parallel with it through these six centuries ran another: the musical practice of the dying world of antiquity. We know little about this, and even less about how much of it may have found its way into the Church. As for the musical theory of antiquity, it was maintained—after a fashion—in a few encyclopedic manuals, and was gathered up—imperfectly—early in the sixth century by Boethius in a treatise *De institutione musica*, a work which became the principal, indeed almost the sole, authority for medieval writers when eventually they undertook to formulate a theory for the music of their own times.

13

II Gregorian Chant and Secular Song in the Middle Ages

Gregorian Chant and the Roman Liturgy

In studying the history of music it is of course necessary to learn certain facts about musical forms and styles in the different historical periods; but it is even more necessary to get to know the music itself. When we hear Gregorian Chant for the first time, we are apt to have a negative impression of it. We are struck not so much by what is there as by what is not there. We feel the lack of supporting harmony or accompaniment; we miss clearly defined time values and regular accents; we notice that the melodic line sometimes turns strangely and often does not cadence on the expected note; and we are perhaps resentfully conscious that the music makes no attempt to thrill our senses or entangle our emotions. We may incorporate these impressions in a definition: Gregorian Chant is the official liturgical music of the services of the Roman Catholic Church; it consists of single-line melody sung to Latin words by unaccompanied men's voices, in a flexible rhythm articulated by means other than regular accentuation, in a scale system different from our major or minor; and it has an impersonal, objective, otherworldly quality in which sensuous beauty and emotional appeal are largely subordinate to expression of the religious content of the text. Gregorian Chant is not to be listened to for its own sake; as an adjunct to worship, it is strictly functional music. Consequently, in order to understand the music it is essential to know something of the liturgy within which it has its place. We shall therefore first consider the modern Catholic liturgy, which, although not identical with the medieval, is close enough in all essential points to serve our purpose.

The nature of Gregorian Chant

The two principal classes of services are the *Office* and the *Mass*.

14

There are eight Offices, or *Canonical Hours*, which are celebrated every day at stated times in a regular order, though their public recitation is generally observed only in monasteries and certain cathedral churches: *Matins* (before daybreak), *Lauds* (at sunrise), *Prime, Terce, Sext, Nones* (respectively at about 6 a.m., 9 a.m., noon, and 3 p.m.), *Vespers* (at sunset) and *Compline* (usually immediately after Vespers). From the musical point of view the most important Offices are Matins, Lauds, and Vespers. Vespers has the canticle *Magnificat anima mea Dominum* ("My soul doth magnify the Lord," St. Luke 1: 46–55); and inasmuch as this Office is the only one that admitted polyphonic singing from early times, it is especially important to the history of sacred music. A feature of the Offices is the singing of one of the four antiphons of the Blessed Virgin Mary, the so-called "Marian" antiphons: *Alma Redemptoris Mater* ("Sweet Mother of the Redeemer"), *Ave Regina caelorum* ("Hail, Queen of the Heavens"), *Regina caeli laetare* ("Rejoice, Queen of Heaven"), or *Salve Regina* ("Hail, O Queen"; see Example 1, and illustration

Salve Regina *as it appears in modern Gregorian notation in the* Liber Usualis.

Antiphon: *Salve Regina*

MODE 1

Sal - ve*† Re- gi - na, ma-ter mi - se - ri - cor-di - ae:

Vi - ta, dul - ce - do, et spes nos - tra, sal - ve.

Ad te cla - ma - mus, ex - su - les, fi - li - i He - vae.

Ad te sus - pi - ra - mus, ge-men - tes et flen - tes in hac

la - cri - ma - rum val - le. E - ia er - go, Ad-vo-ca - ta

no - stra, il - los tu - os mi - se - ri - cor - des o - cu - los

ad nos con - ver - te. Et Je - sum, be - ne - di - ctum fructum ven -

tris tu - i, no - bis post hoc ex - si - li - um os - ten-de.

O cle - mens: O pi - a:

O dul - cis *Vir- go Ma - ri - a.

Example 1

† The asterisk indicates where the chant alternates between soloist and choir, or between the two halves of the choir. The straight lines under some pairs of notes are extensions of the sign for *poco tenuto*.

Hail, O Queen, Mother of mercy, our life, our sweetness, and our hope! To thee we cry, banished children of Eve; to thee we send up our sighs, mourning and weeping in this vale of tears. Turn then, our Advocate, thine eyes of mercy toward us; and after this our exile, show unto us the blessed fruit of thy womb, Jesus. O clement, O loving, O sweet Virgin Mary.

above). The Gregorian music for the Offices is collected in a liturgical book called the *Antiphonale* or *Antiphonar*.

The Mass, although its liturgy was developed later than that of the Offices, is the principal service of the Catholic Church. In its present form the liturgy of the Mass begins with the *Introit;* originally this was an entire psalm with its antiphon, chanted during the entrance of the priest (the *antiphona ad introitum,* or "antiphon for the entrance"), but later was shortened to only a single verse of the psalm with an antiphon. Immediately after the Introit the choir sings the *Kyrie,* to the Greek words *Kyrie eleison* ("Lord have mercy upon us"), *Christe eleison* ("Christ have mercy upon us"), *Kyrie eleison,* each invocation being sung three times. Next follows (except in the seasons of Advent and Lent) the *Gloria,* begun by the priest with the words *Gloria in excelsis Deo* ("Glory be to God on high") and continued by the choir from *Et in terra pax* ("And on earth peace"). Then come the prayers (*Collects*) and the reading of the *Epistle* for the day, followed by the *Gradual* and Alleluia, both sung by a soloist or soloists with responses by the choir. In penitential seasons the Alleluia is replaced by the more solemn *Tract.* After the reading of the *Gospel* comes the *Credo,* begun by the priest *Credo in unum Deum* ("I believe in one God") and continued by the choir from *Patrem omnipotentem* ("the Father Almighty"). During the preparation of the bread and wine the *Offertory* is sung. This is followed by various prayers and the *Preface* which leads into the *Sanctus* ("Holy, holy, holy") and *Benedictus* ("Blessed is He that cometh"), both sung by the choir. Then comes the *Canon* or prayer of consecration, followed by the *Agnus Dei* ("Lamb of God"). After the bread and wine have been consumed, the choir sings the *Communion,* which is followed by the singing of the priest's *Post-Communion* prayers. The service then concludes with the dismissal formula *Ite missa est* ("go, [the congregation] is dismissed") or *Benedicamus Domino* ("Let us bless the Lord"), sung responsively by the priest and choir.

Certain parts of the Mass are invariable; others change according to the season of the year or the dates of particular feasts or commemorations. The variable portions are called the *Proper of the Mass* (*Proprium missae*). The Collects, Epistle, Gospel, Preface, and the Post-Communion and other prayers are all part of the Proper; the musical portions of the Proper are the Introit, Gradual, Alleluia, Tract, Offertory, and Communion. The invariable parts of the service are called the *Ordinary of the Mass* (*Ordinarium missae*), and include the Kyrie, Gloria, Credo, Sanctus, Benedictus, and Agnus Dei. The Gregorian music for the Mass, both Proper and Ordinary, is published in a liturgical book, the *Graduale.* The *Liber Usualis,* another book of Gregorian music, contains a selection of the most frequently used chants from both the *Antiphonale* and the *Graduale.*

The melodies of Gregorian Chant are preserved in hundreds of manuscripts dating from the ninth century and later. These manuscripts were written independently at different times and in widely separated areas. Very often the same melody is found in many different manuscripts: and it is a remarkable fact that these manuscripts record the melody in almost identical form. This suggests not only that the melodies must have come originally from one source but also that, if they go back to the age of Pope Gregory, they must have been transmitted with surprising accuracy, either by purely oral tradition or with the help of some early notation of which no specimens have survived. Whether the agreement among the manuscripts proves that the chants they contain actually have come down unchanged from Gregorian times is another question.

Classes, Forms, and Types of Gregorian Chant

All chants may be divided into those with *Biblical* and those with *non-Biblical* texts; each of these divisions may be subdivided into chants with *prose* texts and those with *poetical* texts. Examples of Biblical prose texts are the lessons of the Office, and the Epistle and Gospel of the Mass; of Biblical poetical texts, the psalms and canticles. Non-Biblical prose texts include the *Te Deum*, many antiphons, and the four Marian pseudo-antiphons; chants with non-Biblical poetical texts are the hymns and sequences.

Chants may also be classified according to the manner in which they are (or were, in earlier times) sung as *antiphonal* (alternating choirs), *responsorial* (alternating soloist and choir), or *direct* (without alternation).

Still another classification is based on the relation of notes to syllables. Chants in which most or all of the syllables have a single note each are called *syllabic;* those characterized by long melodic passages on a single syllable are called *melismatic*. This distinction is not always clear-cut, since chants that are prevailingly melismatic usually include some syllabic sections or phrases, and many chants otherwise syllabic have occasional short melismas of four or five notes on some syllables. This type of chant is sometimes called *neumatic*.

In Gregorian Chant there is hardly ever any repetition of the text; word-painting or similar pointed reflection of single words or images is exceptional. The melody is adapted to the rhythm of the text, to its general mood, and to the mood of the liturgical situation in which a chant is used; no attempt is made to adapt the melody to special emotional or pictorial effects. This is not to say that Gregorian Chant is inexpressive, but only that it does not have that quality musicians call *espressivo*.

We shall now examine some of the more important categories of chants used in the Mass and Office, beginning with syllabic and proceeding to melismatic types.

The chants for the recitation of prayers and readings from the

Bible are on the border between speech and song. They consist of a single *reciting note* (usually a or c′), to which each verse or period of the text is rapidly chanted. This reciting note is also called the *tenor*, or (in later times) the *dominant*; occasionally the upper or lower neighboring note will be introduced to bring out an important accent. The reciting note may be preceded by a two- or three-note introductory formula called the *initium*; at the end of each verse or period there is a short melodic cadence. Similar to these recitation tones, but slightly more complex, are standard formulas called *psalm tones;* there is one tone for each of the eight church Modes and an extra one called the *Tonus peregrinus* or "foreign tone." The psalm tones and recitation tones are among the oldest chants of the liturgy. All the psalms are sung antiphonally in the Offices to one or another of the tones, and this same general type of melodic formula also occurs in many other chants. A psalm tone consists of the *initium* (used only in the first verse of the psalm), *tenor, mediatio* (semicadence in the middle of the verse), and *terminatio*, or final cadence. Usually the last verse of a psalm is followed by the *Doxology* or *Gloria Patri* ("Glory be to the Father"); in the chant books the closing words of the Doxology are indicated by vowels below the last notes of the music, thus: *euouae*. These vowels are an abbreviation for the last six syllables of the phrase *et in secula sEcUlOrUm, AmEn* ("world without end, Amen").

Antiphons are more numerous than any other type of chant; about 1250 are found in the modern *Antiphonale*. However, many antiphons are sung to the same melody, with only slight variations to accommodate the text, a practice which goes back to the Eastern origins of early Church music.

Moderately ornate forms of antiphonal psalmody are found in the Introit and Communion of the Mass. The Introit, as noted above, was originally a complete psalm with its antiphon. In the course of time this part of the service was very much shortened, so that today the Introit consists only of the original antiphon, a single psalm verse with the customary *Gloria Patri,* and the repetition of the antiphon. The Communion, coming at the end of the Mass as a counterpart to the Introit at the beginning, is a short chant, often consisting of only one verse of Scripture. In contrast to the Introit, which is apt to be comparatively animated, the Communion usually has the character of a quiet close to the sacred ceremony.

The most highly developed chants, musically, of the Mass are the Graduals, Alleluias, Tracts, and Offertories. The Tract was originally a solo song. The Gradual and Alleluia are responsorial; the Offertory was probably at first an antiphonal chant, but today no trace of the original psalm remains, and what must have been the original antiphon is performed now as a responsorial chant by soloist and choir.

The Tracts are the longest chants in the liturgy, partly because they have long texts and partly because their melodies are extended

Tracts

Graduals

Alleluias

Offertories

by the use of melismatic figures. The musical form of the Tracts is a complex variation of a simple formula very like a psalm tone; each verse of the Tract is divided by a mediatio as in a psalm tone, and the characteristic reciting notes or tenors of psalmody are present. There are certain recurring melodic formulas which are found in many different Tracts, and regularly in the same place—at the mediatio, at the beginning of the second half of the verse, and so on. These features—the form (a psalm recitation ornamented with melismas) and the presence of standard melodic formulas—suggest that in the Tracts we have a survival, probably in elaborated form, of some of the most ancient music of the Church.

The Graduals are more florid than the Tracts, and their structure is essentially different. A Gradual in the modern chant books is a shortened responsory; it has an introductory refrain or *respond*, followed by a single verse of the psalm. The refrain is begun by a soloist and continued by the choir; the verse is sung by a soloist with the choir joining in on the last phrase. A well-known example of this form is the Easter Gradual *Haec dies quem fecit Dominus* ("This is the day which the Lord hath made"; Example 2).

Alleluias consist of a refrain, on the single word "alleluia," and a verse, followed by repetition of the refrain. The present manner of singing is as follows: the soloist (or soloists) sings the word "alleluia"; the chorus repeats this and continues with the *jubilus,* a long melisma on the final "a" of "alleluia"; the soloist then sings the verse, with the chorus joining on the last phrase, after which the entire Alleluia with jubilus is sung by the chorus. The "alleluia" is moderately florid; the jubilus is, of course, melismatic. The verse usually combines shorter and longer melismas; very often the last part of the verse repeats part or all of the refrain melody. The Alleluias thus have a design different from that of any other type of chant: their musical form is outlined by systematic repetition of distinct sections. The repetition of the Alleluia and jubilus after the verse results in a three-part (*ABA*) pattern; this is subtly modified when melodic phrases from the refrain are incorporated in the verse. Moreover, both refrain and verse are often related in some kind of *AAB* form; and within the general schemes, the melody is always skilfully organized by the repetition or echoing of motives, musical rhyme, combination and contrast of melodic curves, and similar devices, all evidence of a highly developed sense of musical continuity.

The Offertories are similar in melodic style to the Graduals. Originally, Offertories were very long chants sung by both congregation and clergy during the ceremony of presentation of bread and wine; when this ceremony was curtailed, the Offertory also was shortened, but curious traces of its original use are evident in the occasional text repetitions.

The chants for the Ordinary of the Mass were originally quite simple syllabic melodies sung by the congregation. The syllabic style is still maintained in the Gloria and Credo, but the other parts of the Ordinary generally now have somewhat more ornate settings. The Kyrie, Sanctus, and Agnus Dei, by the nature of their texts, have

Classes, Forms, and Types of Gregorian Chant

Gradual: *Haec dies*

MODE 2

Example 2

† The symbol ℣ is the customary abbreviation for "versus" ("verse"), that is, a single verse from a psalm, Canticle or other scriptural text, sung by a soloist.

This is the day which the Lord hath made; we will rejoice and be glad in it. O give thanks unto the Lord; for he is good: for his mercy endureth for ever.

21

three-part sectional arrangements. The Kyrie, for example, suggests the following setting:

> A *Kyrie   eleison*
> B *Christe   eleison*
> A *Kyrie   eleison*

Since each exclamation is uttered three times, there may be an *aba* form within each of the three principal sections. More sophisticated versions of the Kyrie may have the pattern *ABC*, with motivic interconnections: part *A* and *B* may be similar in outline and have identical final phrases (musical rhyme); the last repetition of part *C* may be expanded by repeating the initial phrase, the last section of which will be similar to the first phrase of part *A*. In an analogous fashion, the Agnus Dei may have the form *ABA*, though sometimes the same music is used for all the sections:

> A *Agnus Dei . . . miserere nobis* ("Lamb of God . . . have mercy upon us")
> B *Agnus Dei . . . miserere nobis*
> A *Agnus Dei . . . dona nobis pacem* ("Lamb of God . . . grant us peace")

The Sanctus likewise divides naturally into three sections; a typical distribution of musical material is as follows:

> A   *Sanctus, sanctus, sanctus* ("Holy, holy, holy")
> B   *Pleni sunt caeli et terra* ("Heaven and earth are full")
> B′ *Benedictus qui venit* ("Blessed is He that cometh")

Later Developments of the Chant

Between the fifth and the ninth centuries the people of western and northern Europe were converted to Christianity and the doctrines and rites of the Roman Church. At the same time, various important centers of culture were arising in the northern part of Europe. Changes in the style of Gregorian Chant took place: the range of expression was enlarged; the melodic line became modified by the introduction of more skips, especially by the interval of a third; and new forms of chant, or forms growing out of the chant, were created, chiefly the *trope*, the *sequence*, and the *liturgical drama*.

A trope is an addition—originally of music alone, later of words as well—to an established liturgical chant; a trope may come at the beginning, in the midst, or at the end of the chant, or in any combination of these places. Tropes of all kinds flourished from the tenth to the twelfth centuries; but the custom of troping various chants of the Mass and Office apparently began in France at least as early as the eighth century. An important center of troping was the Monastery of St. Gall, where the monk Tuotilo (d. 915) was distinguished for compositions in this form. Why the custom of troping arose, other than from the desire to amplify and embellish the regular liturgy, we do not know. Certainly a phrase such as "Lord, have mercy upon us" invites amplification—for example:

Lord, *omnipotent Father, God, Creator of all*, have mercy upon us.

All parts of the Mass, except Graduals and Tracts, and of the Office, except the psalms, could be, and were, embellished. The Kyrie tropes, such as the one quoted, were most common.

It is obvious that troping could easily be overdone, and that the liturgy might be smothered under a growth of accretions. This threat led to a reaction against troping after the twelfth century; the few that remained in use were finally officially abolished by the Council of Trent about 1560. A single trace of their existence survives in the modern chant books: the titles of certain Kyries, such as *Kyrie fons bonitatis*, indicate the troped words that were once sung to these melodies.

A sequence is a special kind of trope, one that seems to have orig-inated in connection with the Alleluias of the Proper of the Mass. The early history of sequences is obscure, and there are conflicting theories about how they arose. The most generally accepted explanation has been that in the monasteries of France or England, after about the eighth century, monks began writing words for the ornate melodies of Alleluias—either because they did not care for the melismatic style, or because they found the long florid chants difficult to memorize without some aid—and these words were adapted to the melodies syllabically. The result of this practice, according to the traditional explanation, was a new form which in France was called a *prosa*, in Germany (and eventually elsewhere) a *sequentia* or *sequela* (from the Latin *sequor*, to follow). Recent scholarship, however, suggests that both the purely melodic versions and the versions consisting of melodies with words originated at the same time, and that the two were used alternatively in church services.

The formal organization of the sequence is based on melodic and textual segments: each strophe of the text is immediately followed by another with exactly the same length and metre; these two strophes are sung to the same melodic segment, which is repeated for the second strophe. The only exceptions are the first and last verses, which usually do not have parallels. Although any two paired strophes are identical in form, the form of the next pair may be quite different. The sequence pattern may be represented thus: *a bb cc dd . . . n; bb, cc, dd . . .* represent an indefinite number of strophic pairs and *a* and *n* the unpaired verses. Sequences soon became separated from Alleluias, and blossomed forth as independent compositions. Hundreds of se-quences were produced all over Western Europe from the eleventh to the thirteenth centuries and even later. Popular sequences were imitated and adapted to secular uses; considerable mutual influence was exercised between sequences and contemporary forms of semi-sacred and secular vocal music, as well as of instrumental music, in the late Middle Ages.

One of the most celebrated sequences is *Victimae paschali laudes* ("Praises to the Paschal Victim"), ascribed to Wipo, chaplain to the Emperor Henry III in the first half of the eleventh century; in it the classical sequence form of paired strophes is plainly evident, as is also the common device of unifying the different melodic segments by similar cadential phrases. The twelfth-century proses of Adam of St. Victor illustrate a later development in which the text was regularly versified and rhymed.

Like tropes, most sequences were abolished from the Catholic service by the liturgical reforms of the Council of Trent, and four only were retained in use: *Victimae paschali laudes*, at Easter; *Veni Sancte Spiritus* ("Come Holy Ghost"), on Whitsunday; *Lauda Sion* ("Zion, praise") by St. Thomas Aquinas, for the festival of Corpus Christi; and the *Dies irae*. A fifth sequence, the *Stabat Mater* ("By the Cross the Mother Standing," ascribed to Jacopo da Todi, a Franciscan monk of the thirteenth century) was added to the liturgy in 1727.

Just as in ancient Greece the drama had grown out of religious rites, so in the West the earliest musical dramas grew out of the liturgy—or, to be exact, out of tropes. One of the earliest of these liturgical dramas was based on a tenth-century trope preceding the Introit of the Mass for Easter. The original trope, in dialogue form, represents the three Marys coming to the tomb of Jesus. The angel asks them, "Whom seek ye in the sepulchre?" They reply, "Jesus of Nazareth," to which the angel answers, "He is not here, He is risen as He said; go and proclaim that He has risen from the grave" (Mark 16:5–7). Contemporary accounts indicate not only that this dialogue was sung responsively, but also that the singing was accompanied by appropriate dramatic action.

Liturgical dramas

Similar little scenes were performed in connection with the Christmas liturgy, and on other occasions, and in time the action was expanded to include incidents preceding and following the original scene. As the scope of the plays was enlarged and acting grew more realistic, spoken dialogue was introduced. Eventually the plays were detached from the regular church services; hymns and songs of a popular nature were introduced in addition to the liturgical chants, and the texts became a mixture of Latin and the vernacular. Songs for the congregation to sing were frequently incorporated. Many of the Easter plays used the familiar sequence *Victimae paschali laudes*, and the performance usually concluded with the singing of the *Te Deum*. The liturgical drama at its height in the twelfth and thirteenth centuries was extremely popular. Its mixture of sacred and secular elements illustrates the interpenetration of these two areas in late medieval times.

Medieval Musical Theory and Practice

There were two types of musical treatises in the Middle Ages: theoretical and practical. Medieval practical teaching put much emphasis on the training of pupils to read notes and sing melodic intervals; the medieval writers usually went on to the study of intervals in combination, and the correct use of consonance and dissonance in composition. In connection with all these matters, the treatises also discussed musical notation and the system of the eight modes (or, as medieval writers called them, the *tones*) of music.

The development of the medieval modal system was a gradual process, not all the stages of which can be clearly traced. In its complete form, achieved by the eleventh century, the system recognized eight modes, differentiated according to the position of the tones and semitones in a diatonic octave scale built on the *finalis* or *final;* in practice this note was usually—not invariably—the last note in the melody. The modes were identified by numbers, and grouped in pairs; the odd-numbered modes were called *authentic* ("original"), and the even-numbered modes *plagal* ("derived"). A plagal mode always had the same final as its corresponding authentic mode. The authentic modal scales were notated as white-key octave scales rising from the notes *d* (mode I), *e* (mode III), *f* (mode V), and *g* (mode VII), with their corresponding plagals a fourth lower (Example 3). It must be remembered, however, that these notes do not stand for a specific "absolute" pitch—a conception foreign to Gregorian Chant and to the Middle Ages in general—but were chosen simply so that the distinguishing interval patterns could be notated without the use of accidentals.

The Church modes

The finals of each mode are shown in Example 3 as ♮. In addition to the final, there is in each mode a second note, called the *tenor, reciting tone,* or *dominant* (shown in Example 3 as ○), which sometimes functions as a secondary tonal center. The finals of the corresponding plagal and authentic modes are the same, but the dominants are different. A handy way to identify the dominants is to remember these facts: 1) in the authentic modes the dominant is a fifth above the final; 2) in the plagal modes the dominant is a third below the dominant of the corresponding authentic mode; 3) whenever a dominant would fall on the note B, it is moved up to C.

A mode is identified by its final, its dominant, and its range. A plagal mode differs from its corresponding authentic mode by having a different dominant and a different range: in the authentic modes the entire range lies above the final, whereas in the plagal modes the final is the fourth note from the bottom of the octave. Thus modes I and VIII have the same range, but different finals and dominants.

The only accidental properly used in notating Gregorian Chants is B-flat. Under certain conditions the B was flatted in modes I and II, and also occasionally in modes V and VI; if this was consistently done, 25

The Medieval Church Modes

Example 3

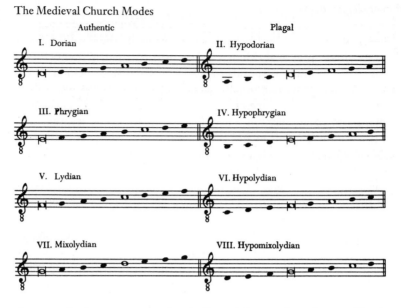

these modes became exact facsimiles of the modern "natural" minor and major scales respectively. Accidentals were necessary, of course, when a modal melody was transposed; if a chant in mode I, for example, were written on G, a flat would be required in the signature.

Some chants remain entirely within the range of a fifth above the final and one note below; others use the entire octave range with perhaps one note beyond in either direction; still others, like the sequence *Victimae paschali laudes*, cover the entire combined range of the authentic mode and its corresponding plagal. Some chants even combine the characteristics of two modes that have different finals; such chants cannot be definitely assigned to either one mode or the other. In short, the correspondence of theory and practice is no more exact for medieval modal melodies than for any other type of actual music in any period.

Modes I and II are now often called Dorian and Hypodorian, modes III and IV Phrygian and Hypophrygian, modes V and VI Lydian and Hypolydian, and modes VII and VIII Mixolydian and Hypomixolydian. The modes on *a* and *c*, which correspond to our minor and major, have been recognized theoretically only since the middle of the sixteenth century.

Sight singing also received attention in medieval musical writings. An eleventh-century monk, Guido of Arezzo, perfected a method of teaching sight singing which had as its basis the memorizing of six tones in the pattern *c-d-e-f-g-a;* in this pattern a semitone falls between the third and fourth steps and all other steps are whole tones. Guido pointed out, as an aid to memorizing the pattern, that in a familiar hymn, *Ut queant laxis,* six phrases each began with one of the notes of the pattern in regular ascending order—the first phrase on *c,*

*The hexachord
system*

Hymn: *Ut queant laxis*

Ut que - ant la - xis *re* - so - na - re fi - bris Mi - ra ge - sto -

rum fa - mu - li tu - o - rum, *Sol* - ve pol - lu - ti

La - bi - i re - a - tum, San - cte Jo - an - nes.

That thy servants may freely sing forth the wonders of thy deeds, remove all
stain of guilt from their unclean lips, O Saint John.

the second on *d*, and so on. (See Example 4.) The initial syllables of
the words of these six phrases became the names of the notes: *ut, re,
mi, fa, sol, la.* We still learn them this way today, except that we say
do for *ut* and add a *ti* above *la*. The semitone, it will be noticed, is
always the interval *mi-fa.*

This *hexachord,* or pattern of six notes, could be found at different
places in the scale: beginning on C, on G, or (by flatting the B) on F.
The hexachord on G used the B-natural, for which the sign was   ,
"square b" (*b quadrum*); the F hexachord used the B-flat, which had
the sign ♭, "round b" (*b rotundum*). These two signs are, of course,
the originals of our ♮, ♯, and ♭. Because the square form of the B was
called "hard" and the rounded form "soft," the G and F hexachords
were called respectively the "hard" (*durum*) and "soft" (*molle*)
hexachords; the one on C was called the "natural" hexachord. The

*Guido of Arezzo and Bishop Theo-
bald of Arezzo with the mono-
chord. From a twelfth-century
German manuscript.*

whole of the musical space within which medieval composers worked and with which medieval theorists were concerned extended from G (which was written as the Greek letter Γ, and called *gamma*) to e″; within this range every note was named not only by its letter, but also according to the position it occupied within the hexachord or hexachords to which it belonged. Thus gamma, which was the first note of its hexachord, was called *gamma ut* (whence our word *gamut*); e″, as the top note of its hexachord, was *e la*. Middle c′, which belonged to three different hexachords, was *c sol fa ut* (see Example 5).

Example 5   The System of Hexachords

One task that occupied the theorists of the Middle Ages was developing an adequate musical notation. As long as the chants were transmitted by oral tradition, and a certain latitude was tolerated in the application of the texts to the traditional melodic formulas, all that was needed was an occasional reminder of the general outline of the melody. Signs (neumes) were used above the words to indicate an ascending melodic line (╱), a descending one (╲), or a combination of the two (∧). These neumes probably were derived from grammatical accent marks like those still used in modern French and Italian. As the repertoire of chant melodies grew, a more precise way to notate a melody was required, and by the tenth century scribes were placing neumes at varying heights above the text to indicate more exactly the course of the melody; these are called "heighted neumes." Sometimes dots were added to the solid lines to indicate the relationship of the individual notes within the neume, and thus make clearer what intervals the neume represented. A decisive advance was made when a scribe drew a horizontal red line to represent the pitch f, and grouped the neumes about this line; in time a second line, usually yellow, was drawn for c′. By the eleventh century Guido of Arezzo was using a four-line staff on which letters indicated the lines for f, c′ and sometimes g′—letters which eventually evolved into our modern clef signs.

The invention of the staff made it possible to notate precisely the relative pitch of the notes of a melody, and freed music from its hitherto exclusive dependence on oral tradition. The staff notation with neumes was still imperfect, however; it conveyed the pitch of

A page containing several Alleluia verses from the earlier of the two Winchester Tropers, a late tenth-century Anglo-Saxon service book.

the notes, but did not indicate their relative durations. Signs showing rhythm do exist in many medieval manuscripts, but modern scholars have not been able to agree about what they meant. Today, the general practice is to treat the notes of a chant as if they all had the same basic value; notes are grouped rhythmically in twos or threes, these groups being in turn flexibly combined into larger rhythmic units. This method of interpretation has been worked out in detail by the Benedictine monks of the Abbey of Solesmes and has been adopted by the Catholic Church as being in conformity with the spirit of her liturgy.

Nonliturgical and Secular Monody

The oldest preserved specimens of secular music are songs with Latin texts. The earliest of these form the repertoire of *Goliard songs* from the eleventh and twelfth centuries. The Goliards—named after a probably mythical patron, Bishop Golias—were students or foot- 29

loose clerics who migrated from one school to another in the days
before the founding of the great resident universities.

Another kind of monophonic song written in the period from the
eleventh to the thirteenth century is the *conductus*. Conducti are
outstanding illustrations of how vague the dividing line was between
sacred and secular music in the Middle Ages. They originally may
have been sung at moments when an actor in a liturgical drama or a
celebrant in the Mass or some other service was formally "conducted"
in procession from one place to another. Their texts were metrical
verses, like the texts of sequences of the same period; but their connection with the liturgy was so tenuous that by the end of the twelfth
century the term *conductus* was applied to any nonliturgical Latin
song, generally of a serious character, with a metrical text, on either
a sacred or a secular subject. One important feature of the conductus
was that, as a rule, its melody was newly composed, instead of being
borrowed or adapted from Gregorian Chant or some other source.

The characteristic aspects of the secular spirit of the Middle Ages
are of course, most clearly reflected in the songs with vernacular texts.
One of the earliest types of vernacular song was the *chanson de geste*
—an epic narrative poem recounting the deeds of national heroes,
sung to simple melodic formulas, a single one of which might serve
unchanged for each line throughout long sections of the poem. The
most famous of the *chansons de geste* is the *Song of Roland*, the
national epic of France, which dates from about the second half of the
eleventh century.

The people who sang the *chansons de geste* and other secular songs
in the Middle Ages were the *jongleurs*, a class of professional musicians
who first appear about the tenth century.

The jongleurs were neither poets nor composers; they sang and
danced to the songs that others had created. But their professional
traditions and skill played a part in an important development of
secular music in Western Europe—the music of the troubadours and
the trouvères. These two words mean the same thing: finders, or
inventors; *troubadour* was the term used in the south of France,
trouvère the term used in the north. Troubadours flourished in the
twelfth and early thirteenth centuries in Provence, the region now
comprising southern France; they wrote in Provençal, the *langue d'oc*.
Their art spread quickly to northern France, to the trouvères; the
latter were active throughout the thirteenth century, especially in the
provinces of Champagne and Artois. The trouvères wrote in the
langue d'oïl, the dialect of medieval French that became modern
French. The troubadours and trouvères were, at least in the beginning,
noblemen, "gentlemen amateurs." Most of them were both poets and
composers, but not performers; having written a song, they hired a
jongleur or kept a minstrel to sing it. Troubadours and trouvères
could afford to have their compositions copied out in song collections
(*chansonniers*), and many of these manuscripts still exist; some of the

collections have been published in modern facsimile editions. Altogether, about 2600 troubadour poems and 260 melodies have been preserved, and about 4000 trouvère poems and 1400 melodies.

The poetic and musical substance of the troubadour and trouvère songs is often not profound, but the formal structures employed show great variety and ingenuity. There are simple ballads and ballads in dramatic style, some of which require or suggest two or more characters. Some of the dramatic ballads evidently were intended to be mimed; many obviously call for dancing. Often there is a refrain which, at least in the older examples, must have been sung by a chorus. In addition, they wrote love songs—the subject par excellence for troubadour song. There are songs on political and moral topics, and songs whose texts are debates or arguments, frequently on an abstruse point of courtly love.

A favorite genre was the *pastourelle*, one of the class of dramatic ballads. The text of a pastourelle always tells the following story: a knight makes love to a shepherdess who usually, after due resistance, succumbs; alternatively, the shepherdess screams for help, whereupon her brother or lover rushes in and drives the knight away, not without blows given and received. In the earliest pastourelles, all the narration was monologue; it was a natural step, however, to make the text a dialogue between the knight and the shepherdess. Later, the dialogue came to be acted as well as sung; if one or two episodes were added, and if the rescuing shepherd appeared with a group of rustic companions, and the performance were decked out with incidental songs and dances, the result was a little musical play. One such play, in fact, is the famous *Jeu de Robin et de Marion*, written by Adam de la Hale, the last and the greatest of the trouvères, about 1284.

Adam de la Hale, also called the Hunchback of Arras, was born in Arras about 1230 and died at Naples about 1288. Gifted as both poet and composer, he is depicted here in a miniature from the Chansonnier d'Arras.

31

The melodic settings of both troubadour and trouvère songs were generally syllabic with occasional short melismatic figures; it is probable that in performance melodic ornaments were added and that the melody was varied from stanza to stanza. The range is narrow, frequently no more than a sixth and hardly ever more than an octave. The modes used were chiefly the first and seventh, with their plagals; certain notes in these modes were probably altered chromatically by the singers in such a way as to make them almost equivalent to the modern minor and major. There is some uncertainty about the rhythms of the songs, especially with regard to the oldest extant melodies, which are notated in a way that does not indicate the relative time values of the notes.

In trouvère songs the phrases are almost always clear cut, fairly short (three, four, or five measures in a modern transcription in 3/4 time), and with a definite, easily retained melodic profile. The troubadour melodies are less sectional and often suggest a relatively free rhythmic treatment.

The repetition, variation, and contrast of short, distinctive musical phrases naturally produce a more or less distinct formal pattern. Many of the troubadour and trouvère melodies repeat the opening phrase or section before proceeding in a free style. But on the whole the melodies in the original manuscript sources do not fall so neatly into categories as the designations in modern collections suggest. Many of the trouvère songs have *refrains*, a recurring line or pair of lines in the text which usually also involve the recurrence of the corresponding musical phrase.

The art of the troubadours was the model for a German school of knightly poet-musicians, the *Minnesinger*. The love (*Minne*) of which they sang in their *Minnelieder* was sometimes even more abstract than troubadour love, and had a distinctly religious tinge. The music is correspondingly more sober and is closer to music written in the ecclesiastical modes. The rhythmic pulse is generally slower and more of the tunes are in duple meter. A common Minnesinger form is what is called in German a *Bar—AAB*—in which the same melodic phrase, *A*, is repeated for the first two units, called *Stollen*, of a stanza, and the remainder, *B*, called the *Abgesang*, has new melodic material.

In France toward the end of the thirteenth century the art of the trouvères came to be carried on more and more by cultured middle-class citizens instead of predominantly by nobles as in earlier times. A similar movement took place in Germany in the course of the fourteenth, fifteenth, and sixteenth centuries; the eventual successors of the Minnesinger were the *Meistersinger*, stolid tradesmen and artisans of German cities, whose lives and organization have been accurately portrayed by Wagner in his opera *The Mastersingers of Nuremberg*. Hans Sachs, the hero of this opera, was a real Meistersinger who lived in the sixteenth century. The art of the Meistersinger was so hedged about by rigid rules that their music seems stiff and inexpressive in comparison with that of the Minnesinger.

In addition to monophonic secular songs, there were also in the Middle Ages many monophonic religious songs not intended for use in church. These songs were expressions of individual piety; they had vernacular texts and were written in a melodic idiom that seems to be derived about equally from church plainchant and popular folk song. The few surviving English songs of the thirteenth century show a variety of moods and suggest a much more extensive musical life than is now possible to reconstruct. Spanish monophonic songs include a large number of *cantigas*, hymns to the Virgin; these have been preserved in a large late thirteenth-century collection, and resemble in many ways the music of the troubadours. Contemporary Italian monophonic songs were the *laude;* they were sung by processions of penitents, and have music of a vigorous, popular character.

Medieval Instrumental Music and Instruments

Dances in the Middle Ages were accompanied not only by songs but by instrumental music as well. The *estampie*, of which several English and Continental examples exist from the thirteenth and

King David holds his harp while musicians below play the bell chimes, recorder, vielle, and positive organ. A miniature from a late eleventh-century Bible.

fourteenth centuries, was a dance piece, sometimes monophonic and sometimes polyphonic, in several sections (*puncta*), each of which was repeated (compare the sequence); the first statement ended with an "open" (*ouvert*), or incomplete, cadence; the repetition ended with a "closed" (*clos*), or full, cadence. In some *estampies* the cadences of all the *puncta* are identical or similar.

Estampies happen to be the earliest known examples of an instrumental repertoire that doubtless goes back far beyond the thirteenth century. It is unlikely that the early Middle Ages had any instrumental music other than that associated with singing or dancing, but it would be completely incorrect to think that the music of this period was exclusively vocal.

Perhaps the oldest characteristically medieval instrument was the *harp*, which was imported to the Continent from Ireland and Britain some time before the ninth century. The principal bowed instrument of medieval times was the *vielle* or *fiedel*, which had many different names and a great variety of shapes and sizes; it is the prototype of the viol of the Renaissance and the modern violin. The thirteenth-century vielle had five strings, one of them usually a drone. This is the instrument with which jongleurs are most often depicted, and with which they probably accompanied their singing and recitations. Another stringed instrument was the *organistrum;* described in a tenth-century treatise, it was a three-stringed vielle played by a revolving wheel turned by a crank, the strings being stopped by a set of rods instead of by the fingers. In the early Middle Ages the organistrum was apparently a large instrument requiring two players, and was used in churches; after the thirteenth century it degenerated into a smaller form, from which the modern hurdy-gurdy is descended.

An instrument that appears frequently in the Middle Ages is the *psaltery*, a type of zither played either by plucking, or more often by striking, the strings—the remote ancestor of the harpsichord and clavichord. The *lute* was known as early as the ninth century, but did not come into common use, outside of Spain, until the time of the Renaissance. There were *flutes*, both the recorder and the transverse types, and *shawms*, reed instruments of the oboe variety. *Trumpets* and *horns* were used only by the nobility; the universal folk instrument was the *bagpipe*. *Drums* came into use by the twelfth century, chiefly to beat time for singing and dancing.

In the Middle Ages there were, in addition to the great organs in churches, two smaller types, the *portative* and the *positive*. The portative organ was small enough to be carried (*portatum*), perhaps suspended by a strap around the neck of the player; it had a single rank of pipes, and the keys were played by the right hand while the left worked the bellows. The positive organ also could be carried but had to be placed (*positum*) on a table to be played and required an assistant for the bellows.

Angel musicians playing the zither, timbrels or drums, and bagpipe. Early fourteenth-century marbles by Giovanni Balduccio da Pisa. (Courtesy Duveen Brothers, Inc.)

III The Beginnings of Polyphony and the Music of the Thirteenth Century

Historical Background of Early Polyphony

We are accustomed to regard all the music of the ancient Greek and Roman world, all Gregorian Chant, and the music of most non-European peoples as monophonic, that is, a single melodic line without harmonic support. Yet the music of ancient times was not always strictly monophonic; a melody was frequently doubled at the octave and ornamented by heterophony—that is, by performing the same melody simultaneously in plain and ornamented form. As for non-European music, both primitive and civilized, its basically monophonic structure is usually overlaid, deliberately or incidentally, by polyphonic complications in the form of drone basses, parallel fourths, fifths, or thirds, heterophony, and canonic imitation.

Polyphony as such—that is, the systematic sounding of two or more tones at the same time—is not exclusively Western or European; what is distinctive about Western music is that Western composers have specialized in writing polyphony. What in other musical systems is an optional or incidental factor, in Western music is an essential one. We have developed polyphony to a unique degree, and, it must be admitted, at the expense of certain melodic and rhythmic subtleties that are characteristic of the music of other civilizations, those of India and China, for example.

Early Organum

There are good reasons to believe that polyphony existed in Europe long before it was first unmistakably described. It was probably used chiefly, if not exclusively, in nonliturgical music; it probably consisted of melodic doubling at the third, fourth, or fifth, and a more or less systematic practice of heterophony. There are no surviving musical documents of this early European polyphony. But the first clear description of music in more than one voice, dated about the end of the ninth century, manifestly refers to something already being practiced, and is not a proposal of something new. In this treatise, *Musica enchiriadis* ("Handbook of Music") and in a contemporary commentary on it, the *Scholia enchiriadis*, two distinct kinds of "singing together" are described, both being designated by the name *organum* (pronounced or'-gan-um). In one style of organum, a plain-song melody in one voice, the *vox principalis*, is duplicated at a fifth or a fourth below by a second voice, the *vox organalis;* either voice or both may be further duplicated at the octave and at other intervals, as shown in Example 6.

Parallel Organum Example 6

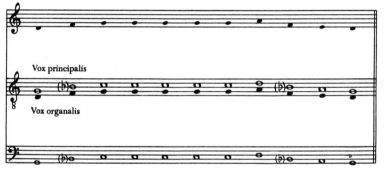

In the second kind of organum the two voices start at the unison; the *vox principalis* moves upward until it forms the interval of a fourth with the *vox organalis*, whereupon both proceed in parallel fourths until they come together again on a unison at the cadence (Example 7). Duplication of the voices is possible in this as in the first type.

Organum Cadence Example 7

Despite the fact that no theorist in the tenth century and only one in the eleventh so much as mentions organum, during this time it was undoubtedly being sung—improvised—and the idea of two simultaneous independent voices seems to have gradually caught on. The first type of organum—purely parallel organum—was hardly susceptible of development, and its mention in the theory books may have been no more than an attempt to account theoretically for certain examples of

III. The
Beginnings of
Polyphony
and the
Music of the
Thirteenth
Century

its use in contemporary musical compositions. Extant musical examples of the eleventh century show important progress toward melodic independence: contrary and oblique motion become regular features. These are illustrated in Example 8; a complete transcription appears in HAM, No. 26a. As a rule the *vox organalis* sings above the *vox principalis* instead of below, though the parts frequently cross; and rudimentary rhythmic diversity is shown by the *vox organalis* occasionally singing two notes against one of the *vox principalis*. In all eleventh-century organa the consonant intervals are the unison, octave, fourth, and fifth, all others occur only incidentally and are treated as dissonances requiring resolution. The rhythm is that of plainsong, on which the pieces are always based.

Example 8   Eleventh-century Organum

Vox organalis

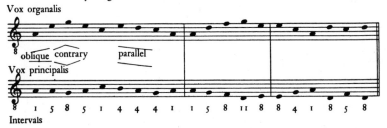

Vox principalis

Intervals

The oldest large collection of pieces in organum style is in the Winchester Troper (that is, a liturgical book containing tropes) used at Winchester Cathedral, dated in the first half of the eleventh century. The music, in two voices, is notated in heighted neumes without staff lines, so that the precise intervals cannot be determined, but the general style is that described above.

By the end of the eleventh century, polyphony had developed to a point where composers were able to combine two *melodically* independent lines by using the devices of oblique and contrary motion. Harmonic intervals had been stabilized by the invention of precise pitch notation on a staff. Two other essentials had still to be achieved: the ability to combine two or more *rhythmically* independent melodies; and a precise method of notating rhythm.

It should be stressed that the development of a precise notation depended on and was a consequence of the growth of polyphony. As long as there was only one melody, a certain leeway in pitch and rhythm could be permitted; but when two or more melodies had to be played or sung together, the pitch and the rhythmic relationships had to be definitely fixed.

St. Martial Organum

The first distinct step toward rhythmically independent melodies is evident in a kind of organum that was sung in the early part of the

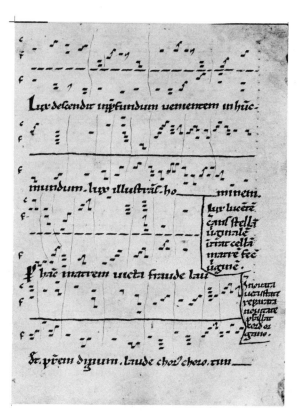

A manuscript page containing the polyphonic St. Martial organum, Lux descendit. (Courtesy of the British Museum)

twelfth century, called variously "sustained-tone organum," "melismatic organum," or "St. Martial organum." Examples of this type survive in four manuscripts from the Abbey of St. Martial in southwestern France (hence the "St. Martial" name), and in one manuscript from Santiago de Compostela in northwestern Spain. The style is unmistakable: the given melody—a portion or the whole of a chant—is sung by a lower voice or voices in sustained tones; above each of the long lower voice notes a second solo voice sings fairly long melismatic phrases in Gregorian melodic style and (probably) free rhythm.

The St. Martial style

The phrases in medieval organum usually begin and always end with one of the consonant intervals (unison, octave, fifth, and rarely, fourth), and throughout each phrase these intervals are the most prominent. Thirds and sixths, seconds and sevenths, are used as supplementary tones, seconds and sevenths especially being often treated as sharply dissonant "appoggiaturas." Example 9 (given completely in HAM, No. 27b) shows this use of intervals. It should be said, however, that the rhythmic interpretation of the original notation is not certain, and consequently the points at which the voices came together may not have been exactly those shown in modern transcriptions.

The texts of the St. Martial organa are like the texts of the eleventh-century organa; tropes of the *Benedicamus Domino* are especially

Example 9   Melismatic St. Martial Organum, *ca.* 1125

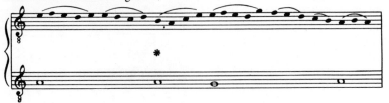

frequent. As a rule the two voices sing the same words; occasionally the lower voice sings the original plainsong text, while the upper voice sings the melismatic melody to the words of a trope. As in the earlier organum, sections of unison chant are alternated with sections of polyphony; further variety is obtained by contrasting sections in the older note-against-note style with sections in the new or sustained-tone style. The lower voice, because it sustained or held the principal melody, came to be called the *tenor*, from the Latin *tenere*, to hold; and this word was used to designate the lowest part of a polyphonic composition until after the middle of the fifteenth century.

Organum in the St. Martial style could be sung from a notation that did not specify the relative time values of the notes in the two voices. The two parts were written one above the other—*score notation*—fairly well-aligned vertically, and with vertical lines on the staff to mark off the phrases; two singers, or one soloist and a small group, could not easily go astray. But in pieces whose rhythmic structure was more complicated, some way had to be found of distinguishing between long and short notes and indicating their relative durations.

By the middle of the thirteenth century, a simple set of signs had been evolved for the notation of rhythm. In the meantime, eleventh- and twelfth-century composers and singers of polyphonic music devised a system in which the prevailing rhythmic pattern of a melody, called the *rhythmic mode* (not to be confused with melodic modes), was specified by certain conventional combinations of notes and note-groups.

The Rhythmic Modes

There were in theory six rhythmic modes, identified as a rule simply by number:

I. ♩ ♪   IV. ♪ ♩ ♩.
II. ♪ ♩   V. ♩. ♩.
III. ♩. ♪ ♩   IV. ♪ ♪ ♪

In theory, a melody in a given rhythmic mode consisted of an indefinite number of repetitions of the pattern, usually ending with the first note followed by a rest; then another series of repetitions ending in the same way; and so on. In practice, the rhythmic monotony which this suggests was mitigated by occasionally breaking up a longer note into shorter ones or by combining two shorter notes into a longer one. Thus, for example, the upper voice of a twelfth-century *Benedicamus Domino* in the first rhythmic mode (Example 10a) is modified at the third and fifth "measures" (there is, of course, no division by barlines in the original score) by combining the notes ♩ ♪ into ♩. ; and at "measure" seven the ♩ ♪ becomes ♫. Later in this same piece there is a shift to the second rhythmic mode, illustrated in Example 10b (the entire piece is transcribed in HAM No. 28c). Thus in practice the system of rhythmic modes admitted considerable flexibility within a prevailing pattern, as well as the possibility of changing from one pattern to another in the course of a piece, not to mention the contrasts obtainable by writing the several voices in different rhythmic modes.

Upper Voice of Twelfth-Century Organum, *Benedicamus Domino*   Example 10

The required rhythmic mode was indicated to the singer by the choice and order of the notes. *Ligatures,* compound signs derived from the compound Gregorian neumes, denoting a group of two or three tones, were important in conveying this information. For example, if a melody were notated as in Example 11a—a single three-note ligature followed by a series of two-note ligatures—a singer would sing it in a rhythm that can be expressed in the modern notation of Example 11b; in other words, the particular series of ligatures in Example 11a indicated to the singer that he was to use the first rhythmic mode. The other rhythmic modes could be shown in equivalent ways. Departures from the prevailing rhythmic mode—for example the substitution of ♩. or ♫ for ♩ ♪—a change of rhythmic mode, or repeated tones (which could not be indicated in a ligature) necessitated modifications of the notation which we shall not describe here.

Use of Ligatures to Indicate a Rhythmic Mode   Example 11

III. The
Beginnings of
Polyphony
and the
Music of the
Thirteenth
Century

Notre Dame Organum

It must not be supposed that the system of rhythmic modes was invented at one stroke, or that the system was invented first and the music written to conform to it. The opposite is true: the system and its notation were developed gradually during the twelfth and thirteenth centuries to fill the needs of a school of polyphonic composers whose activities were centered at Paris. Two composers in this school —the first composers of polyphony whose names are known to us— were Leonin, who lived in the third quarter of the twelfth century, and Perotin, who lived perhaps in the last part of the twelfth century and the first part of the thirteenth (1183?–1238?). Both men apparently were choirmasters at the Church of Notre Dame (predecessor to the cathedral now known by that name). Their compositions, together with those of their anonymous French contemporaries, are known collectively as the music of the Notre Dame school.

The Leonin style

Three principal styles or types of composition are represented in the music of the Notre Dame school and the later thirteenth century: organum, conductus, and motet. Leonin wrote a cycle of two-part Graduals, Alleluias, and responsories for the entire church year, called the *Magnus liber organi* ("The Great Book of Organum"). The *Magnus liber* no longer exists in its original form, but its contents have survived in various manuscripts at Florence, Wolfenbüttel, Madrid, and elsewhere. As an example of Leonin's style of composition, let us take the setting of the Easter Gradual *Haec dies quam fecit Dominus* ("This is the day which the Lord hath made"; a reproduction of the first part of this piece in the original notation is illustrated below, on page 45). A comparison of the plainsong Gradual (see Example 2) with the polyphonic setting shows that the original chant, approximately two and one-half minutes long, has been expanded to about six minutes of music. Only the solo portions of the chant, however, have been expanded; the chorus sections have been left in simple plainsong. This contrast of solo voices in polyphony alternating with chorus voices in unison is the principal formal characteristic of the piece. But within the polyphonic sections themselves there is further contrast.

The first section, through the words "haec dies" (given in Example 12; the entire piece is transcribed in HAM, No. 29), is like the older St. Martial style of organum; the original melody, stretched out into indefinite unmeasured long notes, forms the tenor. Could this actually have been sung by one soloist? It would seem more likely that it was played on a stringed instrument or on the organ, or at least carried by several singers, who could take breaths at different times. Above the long notes of the tenor, a solo voice sings expressive textless melismatic phrases, broken at irregular intervals by cadences and rests.

The exact note values of this upper voice in a modern transcription are not to be taken too literally; in some instances the interpretation of the signs in the original notation is doubtful, and in any event the desired effect seems to be a flexible delivery of which the modern notes give only an approximate indication.

First Section of Organum Duplum, *Haec dies*

Example 12

III. The
Beginnings of
Polyphony
and the
Music of the
Thirteenth
Century

Example 12
(cont.)

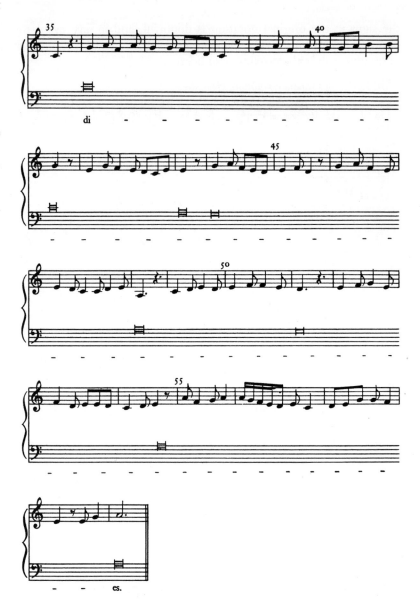

After a choral unison interlude, consisting of the original plainsong
chant from the words "quam fecit" through "laetamur in ea" ("let us
rejoice in it"), the two-voice texture is resumed. But beginning with
the word "Domino" a quite different style is heard (Example 13).
The tenor now sings many short notes in strictly measured rhythm;
the upper voice, which moves in still faster notes, likewise takes on a
distinct rhythmic character. Both parts sing in notes of definitely
measured duration, in contrast to the comparatively flexible rhythm
of the previous section. This new contrapuntal style in which all the

Organum [*Leonin*], Haec dies quam fecit Dominus, *from Wolfenbüttel manuscript 677.*

parts are in measured rhythm came to be called *discant;* it did not exclude occasional short melismas, particularly at cadential points, but for the most part the two voices moved strictly according to the rhythmic modes. A section written in discant style was called a *clausula.*

The choice of whether to use organal or discant style was not a matter of caprice. It was based on the general principle that in those portions of the original chant which were syllabic or only slightly florid—in other words, in the portions where there were comparatively few notes to a syllable—the organal style with long sustained tones in the tenor was appropriate; but in those portions where the original chant was itself highly melismatic, it was necessary for the tenor to move along more quickly in order not to lengthen the whole piece unduly. Clausulae, therefore, as a rule correspond to those parts of the chant that were florid or melismatic. Each clausula was kept distinct, with a definite final cadence. The *Haec dies* organum of Example 12 has in all three clausulae, with a contrasting section in organal style between the second and third. After the last discant section the chorus   45

III. The
Beginnings of
Polyphony
and the
Music of the
Thirteenth
Century

Beginning of Clausula from *Haec dies*

Example 13

Do — — — — — — — mi — —

etc.

— — — — no

finishes the piece with the last few phrases of the plainsong Gradual on which the organum is based.

One of the distinctive features of the Leonin style was the juxtaposition of old and new elements, passages of organum of the St. Martial type alternating and contrasting with the livelier rhythmic discant clausulae. As the thirteenth century went on, *organum purum* was gradually abandoned in favor of discant; in the course of this development, clausulae first became quasi-independent pieces, and eventually evolved into a new form, the *motet*.

The work of Perotin and his contemporaries may be regarded as a development of that done by Leonin's generation. The basic formal structure of the organum—an alternation of unison chant with polyphonic sections—remained unchanged by Perotin, but within the polyphonic sections there was a continuing tendency toward greater rhythmic precision. Not only were the older rhapsodic portions of St. Martial organa often replaced with discant clausulae; many of the older clausulae were replaced with faster movements in definite and stylized patterns. The tenor of Perotin's organum was characteristically laid out in a series of reiterated identical rhythmic motives, corresponding usually to the fifth or third rhythmic mode; these tenors, in modern transcription, give the effect of distinct binary grouping in two, or multiples of two, measures—see Example 14. Moreover, the tenor melody, which in Perotin's style was in shorter notes than the tenors of Leonin, often had to be repeated wholly or in part in order to bring a section out to the length the composer desired. Both these kinds of repetition—of rhythmic motive and of melody—were also part of the formal structure of the later motet.

Perotin organum

An important innovation made by Perotin and his contemporaries was the expansion of organum from two voices to three or four voices. Since the second voice was called the duplum, by analogy the third and fourth were called respectively the *triplum* and *quadruplum*.

These same terms also designated the composition as a whole; a three-voice organum was called an *organum triplum*, or simply *triplum*, and a four-voice organum a *quadruplum*.

The three-voice organum, or triplum, became standard in the Perotin period and remained in favor for a long time; examples have been found in manuscripts dating from the second half of the thirteenth century. Two fairly distinct styles are usually present in a long organum triplum, either intermingled or alternated. Most tripla begin with long-held notes of the chant in the tenor, and two voices moving above in measured phrases. This style corresponds to the sustained-note portions of Leonin organum, differing only in the more regular rhythmic quality of the upper voices. In a typical Perotin organum, an opening section of this sort will be followed by one or more discant sections in which the tenor is also measured, though it moves less rapidly than the upper voice. As the composition proceeds, sections in sustained-tone style blend and alternate with sections in discant style; the latter as a rule correspond to the melismatic parts of the original chant, and the sections in sustained-tone style to the more syllabic parts of the chant.

The sustained-note sections, which sometimes involve as many as a hundred or more measures of a modern transcription in 6/8 time over one unchanging bass tone, form great blocks of fundamentally static harmony, markedly different from the quick-moving harmonic rhythm of the discant sections. Yet even the latter do not have the quality of harmonic movement to which we are accustomed in music of the eighteenth and nineteenth centuries, organized around clearly related tonal centers and working with dominant-tonic relationships; one cannot properly speak of chord *progressions* in Perotin, but only of chord *successions*.

The musical shape of a Perotin organum is defined by the design of the Gregorian Chant on which the piece is built, much as the plan of a Gothic cathedral is defined by the form of a Cross; in both arts the basic sacred symbol has almost unlimited possibilities for expansion and enrichment, depending on the creative fantasy of the artist. A melody used in this way as the basis of a polyphonic composition was called a *cantus firmus* or "fixed song"; if the melody was taken from some already existing source, that fact might be indicated by calling it a *cantus prius factus*, or "song previously made."

Polyphonic Conductus

The tripla and quadrupla of Perotin and his generation are the summit of purely ecclesiastical polyphony in the early thirteenth century. The conductus, which also flourished chiefly before 1250, developed from quasi-liturgical sources such as the hymn and the sequence, but was extended to include secular words. Its texts were like those of the eleventh- and twelfth-century monophonic conduc-

III. The
Beginnings of
Polyphony
and the
Music of the
Thirteenth
Century

Example 14

Tenors on "Domino" from *Haec dies*

1. Gregorian (*Graduale*, p. 241)

2. Two-voice clausula (Leonin? *HAM* 29)

3. Two-voice clausula (Perotin? *HAM* 30)

4. Three-voice clausula (Perotin? *HAM* 31)

5. Motet (*HAM* 32c; *cf.* Las Huelgas Ms., No. 131)

6. Motet (Montpellier Ms., No. 190)

7. Motet (Montpellier Ms., No. 193)

8. Motet (Montpellier Ms., No. 221)

† e′ in original

tus: they were metrical Latin poems, hardly ever liturgical, though often on sacred themes; if they were secular, they dealt seriously with moral questions or historical events.

The polyphonic conductus written by Perotin and by other composers of the Notre Dame era had a less complex musical style than organum. The music of the polyphonic conductus was written in two, three, or four voices which, as in organum, were held within a comparatively narrow range, crossing and recrossing, and were organized harmonically around the consonances of the octave, fourth, and fifth.

As usual with music of this period, the basis of the rhythm was a triple division of the beat; but in conducti all the voices moved in practically the same rhythm, so that the effect was—to use a modern term—chordal, in contrast to the greater rhythmic variety of the voices in organum. This thirteenth-century chordal manner of writing

† c′in original

is often referred to as "conductus style," and sometimes was used in compositions other than conducti: for instance, two-part or three-part settings of hymns, sequences, ballades, and rondeaux were written in this style throughout the twelfth and thirteenth centuries, as were also some early thirteenth-century motets. Example 15 (transcribed completely in HAM, No. 39) illustrates the conductus style.

The Motet

The motet originated in France in the thirteenth century, and most of the manuscripts containing examples of organum and conductus of the Notre Dame period also contain motets. After 1250, however, the organum and conductus gradually dropped out of favor, and during the second half of the thirteenth century the motet became the most important type of polyphonic composition.

III. The
Beginnings of
Polyphony
and the
Music of the
Thirteenth
Century

Early Thirteenth-Century Conductus

Example 15

At this opening of the year, in this January, let us turn to our labors, supported
by our virtues.

Motets have a singular and fascinating musical structure. The composer of a motet began by selecting a passage of Gregorian Chant—
for example, a portion of one of the Graduals, Alleluias, or responsories that formed the repertoire of the Notre Dame organum compositions. He arranged the notes of this theme in a certain pattern
based on one or more of the rhythmic modes, in such a way that the
melody proceeded from beginning to end in a series of repeated, short,
rhythmically identical motives, usually separated by rests (compare
Example 14, Nos. 5, 7, 8); the entire melody was repeated as many
times as might be necessary to stretch out the composition to the
required length. Against the theme or *cantus firmus* so arranged, the

*Origins and
general features*

composer wrote one, two, or three counter melodies, making a motet of two, three, or four voices.

The reader will notice that this description of the structure of a motet would serve equally well to describe a discant clausula in organum; as a matter of fact, the first motets were probably nothing other than discant clausulae with words added to the upper voice or voices. Indeed, the term *motet* comes from the French *mot*, meaning "word," and was originally applied to the text added to the duplum of a clausula; by extension it came to signify the composition as a whole. The Latin form, *motetus*, is customarily used to designate the second voice (the original duplum); the third and fourth voices have the same names (triplum, quadruplum) as in organum.

Thus the motet, like the sequence, began from the practice of adding a text to an originally melismatic vocal melody. In the earliest motets, this text was usually a trope on the text of the tenor, in the form of rhymed metrical Latin verses; if there were two upper voices—that is, if it were a three-voice motet—both sang the same words. A motet like this would have been sung in church as equivalent to a clausula in organum.

This early type of motet was soon modified in various ways. (1) Motets were written to be sung outside the church services; the upper voice of these motets was given a vernacular secular text. Motets with French secular texts in the upper voice still used a plainsong melody as *cantus firmus;* but as the *cantus firmus* served no liturgical function, there was no point in singing the original Latin text, and probably these tenors were played on instruments. (2) It was a natural step to discard a discant clausula over a given tenor, and instead of putting words to one or more pre-existing upper-voice melodies, to keep only the tenor and write one or more new melodies to go with it. This practice gave the composers much more freedom in the selection of texts, since they were able to set to music the words of any poem instead of having to choose one that would fit a given musical line. (3) It had become customary, before 1250, to use a different text for each of the two upper voices in a three-voice motet; both texts might be in Latin, or both in French, or (in some instances) one in Latin and the other in French. This kind of three-part motet with different texts (but not necesarily in different languages) in the upper voices became standard in the second half of the thirteenth century.

The admixture of sacred and secular elements in a motet, however incongruous or even irreverent it may appear to us, must be understood from the medieval point of view, which recognized no such gulf between those two realms as exists in modern thought. A motet was not one piece, but many, like a garment which serves different purposes according to the weather or the occasion. Any of the upper voices might be sung by itself as a solo melody. A motet like *Quant voi—Virgo—Haec dies* (Example 16) could, by omitting the triplum, be performed as a sacred duet; by playing the tenor and motetus on

III. The
Beginnings of
Polyphony
and the
Music of the
Thirteenth
Century

Example 16

Motet: *O mitissima (Quant voi)—Virgo—Haec dies*

Triplum, upper line (from the Bamberg Codex):
O sweetest Virgin Mary, beg Thy Son to give us aid and relief against the deceiving wiles of the demons and their wickedness.

Triplum, lower line (from the Montpellier Codex):
When I see the summer season returning and all the little birds make the woods

vielles, it could be transformed into a secular solo with accompaniment.

In early motets, the motetus and triplum were essentially alike in character: they intertwined in a moderately lively movement with similar slight modifications of a basic rhythmic mode, but remained practically indistinguishable as far as melodic style was concerned. In the later period, composers often sought to introduce distinctions in style not only between the upper voices and the tenor, but also between the two upper voices themselves. This kind of later motet is sometimes called *Franconian*, after Franco of Cologne, a composer and theorist who was active from about 1250 to 1280. The triplum had a longer text than the motetus, and was given a rather fast-moving melody with many short notes in short phrases of narrow range; against this triplum, the motetus sang a comparatively broad, long-breathed, lyrical melody. A charming example of a Franconian-style motet is *Pucelete—Je languis—Domino* (Example 17). Each voice in this motet is in a different rhythmic mode. The tenor is in the fifth mode; the motetus moves for the most part in the ♩ ♩ pattern of the second mode; the triplum moves in a version of the sixth mode, with the first note broken into two shorter ones (♩ ♩ ♩ = ♫ ♩ ♩).

The Franconian motet

The musical contrast between the two upper voices in this piece is supported by the texts. The triplum is a chatty description of a lady's attractions, and the motetus a conventional plaint by her despairing lover. The tenor text, *Domino*, simply refers to the source of this melody (the setting of the word "Domino" in the chant *Benedicamus Domino*—see *Liber Usualis*, p. 124 or HAM, No. 28a) and has nothing to do with either motetus or triplum, since this part would have been played rather than sung.

Another development in the rhythm used in motets involved the tenor. In the early and middle thirteenth century, one of the most conspicuous traits of the motet was the tenor's rigid rhythmic scheme; indeed, much of the effect of freedom and freshness in the unsymmetrically phrased triplum depended on its contrast with the more regularly laid out motetus and especially with the persistence of a strongly marked and unvarying tenor motive. Toward the end of the thirteenth century, however, even the tenor was sometimes written in a more flexible style approaching that of the other two parts. *Pucelete —Je languis—Domino* is an early example of the use of a freer tenor;

---

resound, then I weep and sigh for the great desire which I have for fair Marion, who holds my heart imprisoned.

Motetus:
Virgin of virgins, Light of lights, restorer of men, who didst bear the Lord: through Thee, O Mary, let grace be given as the angel announced: Thou art Virgin before and after.

Tenor:
This is the day [which the Lord hath made].

III. The
Beginnings of
Polyphony
and the
Music of the
Thirteenth
Century

Example 17

Motet: *Pucelete—Je languis—Domino*

Triplum

Pu - ce - le - te bele et a - ve - nant, Jo - li - e - te, po - lie et plai -

Motetus

Je lan - gui des maus d'a - mours; Mieuz aim

Tenor

Do - [mino]

sant, La sa - de - te que je de - sir rant Mi fait liés,

as - sez qu'il m'o - ci - e Que nul

jo - lis, en - voi - siés et a - mant. N'est en mai ein - si gai rous -

au - tre maus; trop est jo -

si - gno - let chan - tant. S'a - me - rait de cuer en - tie - re - mant

li - e la mort; A - le -

Triplum: The fair maid, pretty, polite and pleasing, the delightful one whom I desire so much, makes me joyful, gay, and loving. No nightingale in May sings so gaily. I shall love with all my heart my sweetheart, the fair brunette. Fair friend, who hast held my life in thy command so long, I cry you mercy, sighing.

Motetus: I languish with the sickness of love; I had rather that this kill me than any other illness; such death is very pleasant. Relieve me, sweet friend, of this sickness lest love kill me.

the (instrumental) lowest voice, with its diversified phrasing and quiet movement, is assimilated into the texture, instead of standing out in aggressive isolation after the fashion of the earlier motet tenor.

The two tendencies just described—the one toward greater diversity and the other toward greater homogeneity of texture—were to a certain extent contradictory. By the late thirteenth century, they were not ordinarily found together in the same composition. Rather, 55

III. The
Beginnings of
Polyphony
and the
Music of the
Thirteenth
Century

the trend at this time was toward the emergence of two distinct types of motets: one with a fast, speech-like triplum, a slower motetus, and a Gregorian (though instrumentally performed) tenor in a strict rhythmic pattern; and the other, usually on a French secular tenor, in which all voices proceeded in more nearly equal rhythm, although the triplum was frequently most important melodically.

The first type of motet is often called after Petrus de Cruce (Pierre de la Croix), one of the few identifiable thirteenth-century composers, who was active from about 1270 to 1300. He wrote motets in which the triplum attained an unprecedented speed in comparison with the

Example 18   Motet: *Aucun—Lonc—Annun[tiantes]*, Petrus de Cruce

Triplum: Some invent their song from habit, but it is love that gives me incentive, rejoicing my heart so that I must make a song.

Motetus: Long time have I refrained from singing.

lower voices, becoming almost like a patter song (see Example 18; the entire piece is in HAM, No. 34). It is probable that in these pieces both tenor and motetus were played on instruments.

The motet with similar rhythm in all voices is illustrated in Example 19, *On parole—A Paris—Frèse nouvele* (a complete transcription is in HAM, No. 33b). As is usual with French tenors, the lowest voice of this motet is to be sung, not played. The piece is a vocal trio celebrat-

Motet: *On parole—A Paris—Frèse nouvele*   Example 19

Triplum: They speak of beating and winnowing and of digging and plowing, but these pastimes do not please me; for there is no life so good as to be at ease.

Motetus: At Paris, night and morning, one finds good bread and good clear wine, good meat and good fish, and all sorts of company.

Tenor: Fresh strawberries! Wild blackberries!

57

III. The
Beginnings of
Polyphony
and the
Music of the
Thirteenth
Century

ing the joys of life in the city of Paris; the tenor theme, repeated three times, may be a couple of Parisian street cries.

Changes in the rhythmic structure of the motet in the course of the thirteenth century were more extensive than changes in its harmonic vocabulary. In 1300, as in 1200, the fifth and octave were the accepted correct consonances for strong beats. The fourth had come more and more to be treated as a dissonance. Thirds were beginning to achieve theoretical status as consonances, though they were not actually being used much more often at the end of the century than they had been at the beginning. The harmonic rhythm of a motet was, at least after the middle of the century, that of the tenor part; that is to say, each note of the tenor carried its own chord, so that in works in the style of Petrus de Cruce, where the tenor notes were extremely long in comparison with those of the triplum, a characteristic contrast existed between a rapid melodic movement and long-drawn-out harmonic changes. After 1250, cadences began to be written more often in forms that were to remain standard for the next two centuries; these are given in Example 20.

Example 20   Cadence Forms

Musicians and audiences of the thirteenth century gave much less attention than we do to the harmonic or vertical dimension of music. Provided the ear was satisfied by the recurrence of consonance at the proper points, any degree of dissonance was tolerated between. Passages like that in Example 21 were not uncommon in motets of four voices around the middle of the century; the strong-beat dissonances (marked by asterisks) were justified by Franco's rule that "he who shall wish to construct a quadruplum . . . ought to have in mind the melodies already written, so that if it be discordant with one it will be in concord with the others." Even in three-part writing it was thought sufficient to make the triplum consonant with *either* the motetus or the tenor on strong beats. Moreover, the dissonant clashes practically always occurred casually as a result of the uninhibited progression of the various melodic lines.

Notation in the thirteenth century

The progress toward rhythmic flexibility in the thirteenth century was paralleled by developments in notation. As was explained above, the rhythmic organization of music in the first half of the century was based on the system of rhythmic modes; the particular rhythmic mode in each voice was indicated either by the form of the ligatures in melismatic passages or by the meter of the text. Modifications of the

normal modal formulas, such as the division of a longer note into two
or more shorter ones, were indicated by various other devices. Before
the middle of the thirteenth century, however, none of the notation
symbols—whether ligatures, single notes, or signs for melodic ornamentation—had a fixed value; the meaning of a given sign varied
according to the context, so that the same sign might indicate a long
duration in one situation and a short duration in another. As long as
the rhythmic patterns of the music stayed close to those of the
standard rhythmic modes, however, ambiguity in the notation was not
a serious defect, since the context was usually a sufficient guide; but
as composers began to introduce more rhythmic variety and thus
depart from the simple modal formulas of earlier times, the older
notation became inadequate.

The main requirement was to stabilize the relative duration values
of the written notes, so that a performer could always easily tell what
rhythm was demanded. Various ways to approach this ideal were   *Franconian*
proposed, but the codification of a practicable system was the work of   *notation*
Franco of Cologne, who in his *Ars cantus mensurabilis* (*The Art of
Mensurable Music*), written sometime between 1250 and 1280, established rules for the time values of single notes, ligatures, and rests.
Franco's system of notation remained in use through the first quarter
of the fourteenth century and many of its features survived until the
middle of the sixteenth century.

Franconian notation was based on the rhythmic modes; its principle
of division was ternary. There were four single-note signs: the double
long: ▬ ; the long: ▮ ; the breve: ■ ; and the semibreve: ♦. The
basic time unit, the *tempus* (plural, *tempora*), was the breve. A double
long always had the value of two longs; a long might be perfect (three
tempora) or imperfect (two *tempora*); a breve normally had one
tempus, but might under certain conditions have two, in which case   **59**

III. The
Beginnings of
Polyphony
and the
Music of the
Thirteenth
Century

it was called an *altered* breve; similarly the semibreve might be either *lesser* (1/3 of a *tempus*) or *greater* (2/3 of a *tempus*). Three *tempora* constituted a *perfection,* equivalent to a modern measure of three beats.

The Franconian system allowed the breve to be divided into not more than three semibreves. When Petrus de Cruce began writing music in which four or more notes were to be sung within the time value of one breve, he simply used as many semibreves as he needed for the syllables of the text, sometimes indicating their grouping by dots. Thus, although values shorter than a lesser semibreve were actually in use by the end of the thirteenth century, there were no specific notational signs to represent them; but the complicated rhythms used in the triplum of a Petrus de Cruce motet were carried into the music of the fourteenth century, and before many years an adequate notation was invented for them.

One further notational change came about as a result of the evolution of thirteenth-century motet style. The earliest motets were written in score, like the clausulae from which they were derived. As the upper voices acquired longer texts, and as each syllable had to have a separate note-sign, composers and scribes soon found that these voices took a great deal more room on the page than did the tenor, which had fewer notes and which, being melismatic, could be written in the compressed notation of ligatures. To write all the parts in score would mean that there would be long vacant stretches on the tenor staff, a waste of space and costly parchment (see Example 18). Since the upper voices sang different texts, it was natural to separate them; and so in a three-voice motet, the triplum and the motetus came to be written either on facing pages or in separate columns on the same page, with the tenor on a single staff extending across the bottom. This arrangement may be seen in the illustrations given below, which show the motet En non Diu—Quant voi—Eius in oriente in the original notation of the Montpellier and Bamberg Codices. (This piece is transcribed in MM, No. 10.) The writing of the voices in different places on the same or facing pages is called *choirbook* format, and was the usual way of notating polyphonic compositions after 1230 until the sixteenth century.

Other Late Thirteenth-Century Forms

A number of thirteenth-century forms, styles, or technical devices of composition deserve a brief review. An important type was the *cantilena*, a term applied to both polyphonic and monophonic secular song settings. Like the polyphonic conductus, cantilenas have a single text and all the voices move in uniform phrases; unlike the conductus, the principal melodic interest lies in the upper parts, and the tenor has

(Left) *Two facing pages of the motet* En non Diu—Quant voi—Eius in oriente *as it appears in the Montpellier manuscript.*

(Right) *The same motet as it appears in the Bamberg Codex.*

III. The
Beginnings of
Polyphony
and the
Music of the
Thirteenth
Century

the character of a supporting bass line rather than of an independent melody.

Another type of composition mentioned by some theorists was the *hocket* (Latin *ochetus*, literally, "hiccup"). In a hocket, the flow of melody is interrupted by the insertion of rests, generally in such a way that the missing notes are supplied by another voice so that the melody is divided between the voices (compare Webern's orchestration of the Ricercare from Bach's *Musical Offering*. The device also occurs in the music of primitive peoples). Hocket was used occasionally in conducti and motets of the thirteenth century, but it was especially frequent in the music of the fourteenth century. Pieces of the late thirteenth century in which hocketing was used extensively were themselves called "hockets." Such compositions might be either vocal or instrumental. A fast tempo is implied in an instrumental hocket; indeed, theorists distinguished three tempi: slow for motets in which the breve in the triplum was subdivided into many shorter notes (the Petrus de Cruce-style motets); moderate for those in which there were not more than three semibreves in a breve (the Franconian motets); and fast, for hockets.

Two other forms of composition being written around 1300 were the *rota* and *rondellus*. The rota was simply a round or canon: the most famous example is *Sumer is icumen in*, which probably dates from about 1240. This piece, of English origin, shows many traits characteristic of English medieval music, especially its full chordal texture, its free use of thirds as consonances, and its distinct major tonality. Below the canon two tenors sing a *pes* ("foot," i.e. a repeated bass motive) with continuous interchange of the voices.

The *rondellus* was a song in which all parts were systematically interchanged by each voice singing every phrase in turn; in effect, therefore, each section was like a round, except that all the voices began together instead of entering one after another:

a	b	c	d	e	f
b	c	a	e	f	d
c	a	b	f	d	e

Summary

The period from the middle of the twelfth to the end of the thirteenth century may be regarded as a distinct epoch in the history of music. It is commonly known under the name of *ars antiqua*—the "old art" or manner of composing, so called by modern scholars in contrast to the *ars nova* or "new art" of the fourteenth century—and is chiefly remarkable for the rapid growth of polyphony and the rise of three types of polyphonic composition: organum and conductus in the Notre Dame period, to about 1250, and the motet in the second half of the thirteenth century. All this activity was centered at Paris, so that for one hundred and fifty years all Western European polyphonic music was dominated by French composers. The principal technical achievement of these years was the invention of an unambiguous notation to convey a measured rhythm.

At the beginning of the thirteenth century practically all polyphonic music was sacred; by the end of the century, although there was yet no clear distinction between sacred and secular musical styles, polyphonic settings were being written for both sacred and secular texts. The principal polyphonic form was the motet, which toward the end of the century was evolving toward greater rhythmic flexibility and toward emphasis on the topmost voice as a melody against the background of the lower voices. These developments prepared the way for the *ars nova* of the fourteenth century.

IV French and Italian Music of the Fourteenth Century

General Background

Ars nova—the "new art" or "new technique"—was the title of a treatise written about 1325 by the French composer, poet, and theorist, Philippe de Vitry (1291–1361). Though the only novelty in this particular work was Philippe's description of a new way of dividing and measuring time, the term *ars nova* was so apt that it has come to be used to denote the musical style that prevailed in France during the first half of the fourteenth century, and is often extended to cover the music of the entire century in both France and Italy.

Naturally, many tendencies and traits characteristic of the fourteenth century had appeared before 1300, and many features of the thirteenth century persisted for a long time after that date. The chief differences between the older and the newer styles were (1) the acceptance in the fourteenth century of duple or "imperfect" division of time values in addition to the traditional triple or "perfect" division; and (2) the rhythmic and notational complexities of the newer music which resulted from the use of both perfect and imperfect division and from the use of a multitude of short note-values.

Rhythmic subtlety, sometimes carried to fantastic extremes, was indeed the most obvious point in which the music of the fourteenth century differed from that of the earlier period; but other and equally important contrasts emerged. Thirds and, to a lesser degree, sixths occurred more often in consonant positions (that is, on strong beats), though the final sonority was still always a unison, octave, or open fifth; parallel thirds and sixths appeared, while parallel fifths, unisons, and octaves became rarer; chromatic alteration was used; and the range of the voices was gradually extended upward.

The motet continued and was further developed in the fourteenth century; but the characteristic new musical forms were purely secular compositions without *cantus firmus* and having most often the texture of a solo song with accompaniment. Far more secular music than sacred was composed; a number of composers are known by name, in contrast to the typical anonymity of the thirteenth century. The abstract linear style of the thirteenth-century motet lost its dominance, and was overshadowed by a more harmonic idiom in which sensuous appeal and emotional expressiveness were sought. The thirteenth century was the last great unified medieval musical period: organum, conductus, and motet were different manifestations of one fundamental style. The fourteenth century, though still medieval, was an era of relatively rapid change; much of its music sounds experimental, tentative; some of it seems affected and over-refined, like the manners of its knightly patrons. Most of what has come down to us in the manuscripts was composed for the pleasure of aristocratic and cultivated listeners or amateurs, but contemporary pictures and writings show that the practice of music, both vocal and instrumental, was widespread among all social classes.

Giotto's art marks the beginning of the realistic movement in Italy. This fresco (dated 1350) in the Arena Chapel, Padua, shows Joachim and Anna at the Golden Gate.

The Ars Nova *in France*

The earliest fourteenth-century musical document from France is a beautifully decorated manuscript, dating from 1316, of a satirical poem, the *Roman de Fauvel*, in which are interpolated about 130 musical compositions of various types; they constitute, in effect, an anthology of the music of the time. The thirty-three motets of this collection include, among other examples of the late thirteenth-century style, several that introduce the new duple division of the breve. Many of their texts are denunciations of the clergy, and there are many allusions to contemporary political events. Such allusions were characteristic of the motet in the fourteenth century, as they had been of the conductus in an earlier period; and the motet in the fourteenth century came to be used as the typical form of composition for the musical celebration of important ceremonial occasions both ecclesiastical and secular, a function it retained through the first half of the fifteenth century.

The most important novelty of the Fauvel motets, however, was a method of construction, the so-called *isorhythmic* ("same rhythm") principle. In an isorhythmic motet the tenor (usually a Gregorian melody) was written as a series of repetitions of an unchanging rhythmic pattern called a *talea*. Later in the fourteenth century, motets were written in which isorhythm was applied, usually somewhat freely, to the upper voices as well. The isorhythmic principle was not entirely new, since it was an extension of thirteenth-century practice; the essential difference was that in the fourteenth-century isorhythmic motet the fundamental pattern was longer and more complex, and had shed most traces of its original derivation from the simple formulas of the old rhythmic modes.

Isorhythmic structure was a way of giving unity to long compositions which had no other effective means of formal organization; yet the repetitions of the pattern, extended over many long sections, were anything but obvious to the ear, especially since the composers often

A miniature depicting a charivari; from the Roman de Fauvel, *an early fourteenth-century musical manuscript. Fauvel was a symbolic horse or ass whose name was made up from the first letters of Flaterie, Avarice, Vilanie, Variété, Envie, and Lascheté. (After Gérold)*

added complications to the basic design. For instance, the *talea*, after two or three repetitions, might by compressed into shorter note values, or be begun on a different part of the "measure." As a rule the entire melody (called the *color*) was repeated at least once, and the beginning of the new *color* coincided with the beginning of a new *talea;* but sometimes the two overlapped, with the result that when the melody was repeated it would sound in a different rhythm. In general style and especially in harmonic procedures the motet—isorhythmic or otherwise—remained conservative, and during the fourteenth century came to be treated more and more as a consciously archaic form.

The leading composer of the *ars nova* in France was Guillaume de Machaut (1304?–1377), whose works were preserved in excellent manuscripts and have been published in a modern edition. Machaut was born in the province of Champagne in northern France. He was educated as a cleric and took holy orders; at about the age of twenty he became secretary to King John of Bohemia, whom he accompanied on military campaigns over many parts of Europe. After King John's death at the battle of Crécy in 1346, Machaut entered the service of the French court and eventually ended his days in retirement as a Canon at Rheims. Machaut was famous not only as a musician but also as a poet. His musical works include examples of most of the forms that were current in his time, and show him as a composer of mingled conservative and progressive tendencies.

Machaut's monophonic songs comprise *lais* (in a form similar to that of the sequence) and *chansons balladées*. The latter term was used by Machaut to designate a form more commonly known as the *virelai*. A typical *chanson balladée* or *virelai* had the pattern *AbbaA*: a refrain (*A*) at both the beginning and end of the stanza, the repetition of the first phrase of the verse (*b*), and the use of the refrain melody for the last phrase of the verse (*a*). Machaut also wrote a few polyphonic *chansons balladées*, with an accompanying instrumental tenor part below the vocal solo; in these he occasionally introduced the device of a musical rhyme between the endings of the two melodic sections.

Most of Machaut's 23 motets were based on the traditional pattern of construction: an instrumental liturgical tenor melody and different texts in the two upper voices. New features characteristic of the fourteenth century in Machaut's motets were their isorhythmic structure (which sometimes involved the upper voices as well as the tenor), greater length, and much greater rhythmic complexity. Considerable use was made of hocket in these motets, but the only work of Machaut's specifically called a "hocket" is an apparently instrumental three-part motet-like piece with an isorhythmic tenor whose melody came from the Gregorian intonation of the word "David" in an Alleluia verse.

It was in his polyphonic virelais, *rondeaux,* and ballades that 67

*Guillaume de Machaut in his study. Amour is presenting to him his three
children Doux Penser, Plaisance, and Espérance. A miniature by the Maître
aux Bouqueteaux in a manuscript of Machaut's works.*

Machaut showed most clearly the progressive tendencies of the *ars
nova*. The rondeau, like the virelai, made use of only two musical
phrases, combined typically in the pattern *ABaAabAB* (capital letters
indicate the refrain of the text). Machaut's rondeaux have a highly
sophisticated musical content, and one of them is an often cited example of ingenuity. Its enigmatic tenor text—"Ma fin est mon commencement et mon commencement ma fin" ("My end is my beginning and my beginning my end")—means that the melody of the
tenor is that of the topmost voice sung backward; the melody of the
contratenor also illustrates the text, because its second half is the
reverse of its first half.

One of Machaut's most important achievements was the perfection
of the "ballade style." This style is exemplified in his polyphonic
virelais and rondeaux, as well as in the forty-one *ballades notées,*
so called to distinguish them from his poetic ballades without music.
Machaut's ballades, whose form was in part a heritage from the
trouvères, normally consisted of three or four stanzas, each sung to
the same music and each ending with a refrain. Within each stanza
the first two lines (or first two pairs of lines) had the same music,
although often with different endings; the remaining lines within each
stanza, together with the refrain, had a different melody, the ending

of which might correspond to the ending of the first section. The formula for the ballade is thus *AAB*, in which *B* is understood to include the refrain.

Machaut wrote ballades with two, three, and four parts and for various combinations of voices with instruments; but the typical setting was for high tenor solo voice with two lower, more slowly moving instrumental parts. These instrumental parts, the tenor and the contratenor, were similar in melodic style and moved within the same range, constantly crossing; in effect they constitute a kind of accompaniment and support for the solo (see Example 22; the entire composition is transcribed in HAM, No. 45).

The music is organized in relatively distinct phrases, each ending with a definitive cadence. Most of the principal cadences take the form illustrated in Example 20, with various melodic and rhythmic ornamentations of the basic pattern; one such ornamental cadence formula, in which the leading tone (to use modern terminology) moves down to the sixth before rising to the tonic, became almost a mannerism in the music of the late fourteenth and early fifteenth centuries (see Example 23). This figure is sometimes called the *Landini cadence* after its supposed inventor, the fourteenth-century Italian composer Francesco Landini.

Although we still hear many parallel fifths and many pungent dissonances in Machaut, the total effect is less strange to our ears than that of thirteenth-century music, owing to the pervading milder sonorities of the third and sixth and to the general sense of harmonic order. Most admirable is the finely-wrought, flexible melodic line in the solo voice, in which the new lyricism of the fourteenth century speaks with an accent of sincerity that often imparts warmth even to the stilted language of chivalric verse. Machaut himself declared that true song and poetry could come only from the heart (*Qui de sentiment non fait/son dit et son chant contrefait*), and once he sent a new composition to a friend with the message "I have *listened* to it several times and it pleases me right well."

The most famous musical composition of the fourteenth century is Machaut's *Messe de Notre Dame* (*Mass of Our Lady*), a four-part setting of the Ordinary of the Mass together with the dismissal formula *"Ite, missa est."* This work is historically important because it is one of the first known complete and musically unified settings of the Ordinary. (An earlier example, the *Mass of Tournai*, though complete, appears to be a compilation.) In the twelfth and thirteenth centuries composers of polyphonic music had been chiefly interested in texts from the Proper of the Mass, for example the Graduals and Alleluias in Leonin's and Perotin's organa; they sometimes set parts of the Ordinary too, but when and if these pieces were ever performed together in one service, their selection and combination were fortuitous. No one seemed to care particularly whether the Kyrie, Gloria, Credo, Sanctus, and Agnus Dei were in the same mode or the same

Machaut's Messe de Notre Dame

IV. French
and Italian
Music of the
Fourteenth
Century

Example 22

First Section of Ballade: *Je puis trop bien*, Guillaume de Machaut

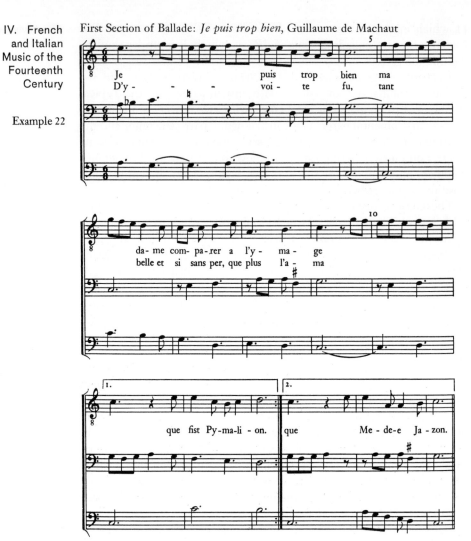

All too well can I compare my lady to the image Pygmalion made: it was of ivory, so beautiful, so peerless, that he loved it more than Jason did Medea.

style or based on the same thematic material or musically unified in any way. This attitude prevailed until about the second quarter of the fifteenth century; although fourteenth- and early fifteenth-century composers did write music for the Ordinary, they did not as a rule attempt to relate the different movements musically. In the manuscripts the different parts of the Mass were usually separated, all the Glorias being placed together, followed by all the Credos, and so on; the choirmaster would select from these collections what he considered appropriate individual items for the complete Ordinary to be performed. Machaut's *Messe de Notre Dame*, therefore, insofar as he seemed to regard the five divisions of the Ordinary as one musical composition rather than five isolated pieces, was exceptional not only

The Landini Cadence

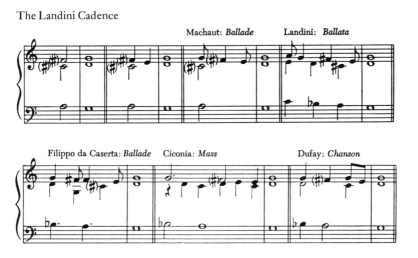

Machaut: *Ballade*   Landini: *Ballata*

Filippo da Caserta: *Ballade*   Ciconia: *Mass*   Dufay: *Chanson*

for its time but for the next seventy-five years as well. The means by which musical unity is achieved in this work are not easy to define; the relationship between movements is based on similarity of mood and general style rather than obvious thematic interconnections, although some commentators have called attention to the recurrence of a certain musical motive throughout the work:

Motive of Machaut Mass

Example 24

The Kyrie, Sanctus, and Agnus Dei are based on Gregorian tenors and are wholly or partly isorhythmic. Both the Gloria and the Credo, probably because of the length of their texts, are given a straight conductus-like setting in syllabic style; their extraordinarily austere music, full of parallel progressions, strange dissonances, chromatic chords, and abrupt pauses, is organized in a free strophic form, a series of musical "stanzas" articulated by conspicuous similar cadences.

It is impossible to tell with certainty just how Machaut's Mass was meant to be performed. It seems likely that the contratenor part, in view of its general melodic style and the fact that in some of the manuscript sources it has no text, was played rather than sung; in the isorhythmic movements, at least, the tenor voice may have been doubled by an instrument. In the Gloria and Credo there are numerous short interludes, always for tenor and contratenor, that are almost certainly instrumental. But what instruments were used, and to what extent, we cannot say. Nor do we know for what occasion the work was written, despite a persistent but unfounded legend that it was for the coronation of the French King Charles V in 1364.

Church Music in the Fourteenth Century

Machaut was a typical fourteenth-century composer in that his sacred compositions formed only a small proportion of his total output. The relative decline in the production of sacred music in this period was due partially to the weakened prestige of the Church and to the ever increasing secularization of the arts. In addition, the Church itself had become critical of the use of elaborate musical settings in the service. From the twelfth century on, there had been numerous ecclesiastical pronouncements against complicated music and against displays of virtuosity by the singers. The burden of these complaints was twofold: it was objected, first, that such practices distracted the minds of the congregation and tended to turn the Mass into a mere concert; and second, that the words of the liturgy were obscured and the liturgical Gregorian melodies made unrecognizable. Such objections undoubtedly had some effect in discouraging the composition of polyphonic church music during the fourteenth century. Nevertheless, composers in this period continued to write motets and Masses, though without ever developing a distinctive church style. Sometimes a particular section in a Mass would be written in the style of a motet with an instrumental tenor, sometimes as a chordal conductus-like movement with text in all the voices. In addition to these two styles, both of which had been used by Machaut, composers of the later fourteenth and early fifteenth centuries wrote Masses and hymns in ballade style—that is, for solo voice, usually with two accompanying instrumental parts. A few of these Masses and hymns made use of a liturgical *cantus firmus;* for example, a Gregorian Kyrie might be adapted as the tenor of a polyphonic Kyrie in motet style, or a Gregorian hymn, more or less ornamented, might appear as the upper voice in a ballade-like setting of the same text.

Fourteenth-Century French Secular Music

At the Papal Court of Avignon and at other courts in southern France a brilliant chivalric society flourished, providing a congenial environment for the work of many late fourteenth-century French and Italian composers. Their music consisted chiefly of ballades, virelais, and rondeaux for solo voice with supporting instrumental tenor and contratenor parts. Many of these pieces are works of refined beauty, with sensitive melodies and delicately colored harmonies, examples of aristocratic art in the best sense of the word. Most of the texts were probably written by the composers themselves. Some of the ballades include reference to contemporary events and personages, but the majority of all the pieces are love songs.

One feature of French secular music of this period is a remarkable rhythmic flexibility. The solo melody in particular exhibits the most subtle nuances: the beat is subdivided in an infinite variety of ways, and the line of the phrase is broken by pauses in hocket, or held in suspense through long-continued syncopation—as though the composers had tried to capture and fix in notation the free, rubato-like delivery of a singer. This flexibility is illustrated in Example 25; the leisurely melodic line reflects the opening words of the ballade text: "En attendant"—"While waiting." (The entire piece appears in HAM, No. 47.)

Beginning of Ballade: *En attendant*, Jacob de Senleches

Example 25

Rhythmic complexity penetrates the very texture of all this late fourteenth-century French music: voices move in contrasting meters and in contrasted groupings within the beat; harmonies are refracted and purposely blurred through suspensions and syncopations. No doubt sometimes the fascination of the technique caused it to be carried to extremes that degenerated into mannerism; but, properly used, it was an indispensable element of the style. Example 26 (the two lowest staves are merely a reduction of the parts, not an accompaniment) shows a typical phrase from a rondeau by Antonello da Caserta in which the syncopation gives the effect of a delayed entrance by the soloist; the rhythmic complexity of the passage is of an order not to be matched in any other music before the twentieth century, yet everything falls logically into place. Noteworthy is the delightful effect of the sixth at measure 2, the coquettish hesitation between B-flat and B-natural after the first rest in the solo part, and the way in which the contratenor sounds now above, now below the tenor, so that the real bass of the harmony is in first one then the other of these voices, and is sometimes revealed in one by the cessation of the other (marked in the example by an asterisk). We may imagine the sheer variety of sonorities resulting from these two lower parts being played on instruments of contrasting timbres—say a trombone for the tenor and an English horn or a viola for the contratenor, with a recorder doubling the voice in the superius.

Since most of the phrase quoted in Example 26 is a melisma, the text has been omitted. The entire composition may be found in Apel's *French Secular Music of the Late Fourteenth Century*, No. 29.

Example 26   Rondeau: *Dame gentil*, Antonello da Caserta

Vous [estes tout mon bien]

Accidentals below or above the notes are not in the original. The so-called "partial signatures"—different signatures in different voices —were common in the fourteenth and fifteenth centuries.

Italian Music of the Fourteenth Century

Italian music in the fourteenth century differed from French music chiefly in that the Italians did not use the *cantus firmus* technique and

Italian Music
of the
Fourteenth
Century

Example 26
(cont.)

were little interested in the structural complexities and extreme rhythmic subtleties that characterized the art of their northern colleagues. The Italian spirit expressed itself rather in spontaneous, flowing melodies and comparatively simple textures.

Although polyphonic secular music was undoubtedly being written in Italy soon after the beginning of the fourteenth century, few examples have been preserved which can be dated earlier than about 1330. After this date, however, and continuing through the first two decades of the fifteenth century, we have a large number of compositions. Three distinct types are found: *madrigal, caccia,* and *ballata.* The fourteenth-century madrigal, one of the first polyphonic genres   *The madrigal* to be cultivated in Italy, has many traits that suggest some historical connection with the French thirteenth-century polyphonic conductus. Madrigals were usually written for two voices; their texts were idyllic, pastoral, amatory, or satirical poems of two or three three-line stanzas. The stanzas were all set to the same music; at the end of the stanzas an additional pair of lines, called the *ritornello,* was set to different music with a different meter. Both voices had the same text and both apparently were meant to be sung, perhaps with instrumental doubling. Although the two melodic lines flowed in similar smooth vocal style, the upper was embellished with melismatic passages; the longest of these were placed—as in the conductus—at the beginning and just before the principal cadences, though similar shorter passages might occur elsewhere too.

The caccia, which seems to have been most popular from 1345 to   *The caccia* 1370, was a lively piece for two equal voices in canon at the unison, with a free supporting instrumental part in slower movement below. Its poetic form was irregular, though many *cacce,* like madrigals, had   75 a ritornello, which was not always in canonic style. The word *caccia* means "hunt" or "chase"; as the name of a type of composition it was a pun, alluding both to the canon (Latin *fuga*, "flight") and to the subject matter of the text, which described a hunt or some other scene of animation, such as a fishing party, a bustling market-place, a party of girls gathering flowers, a fire, or a battle. Vivid and realistic details —shouts, bird songs, horn calls, exclamations, dialogue—all are brought out with spirit and humor in the music, often with the aid of hocket and echo effects.

Composers in the fourteenth century had what seems to us a strange attitude toward the use of imitation as a technique. They either wrote strict canons or eschewed systematic imitation almost entirely. Canons are found sporadically in Italian madrigals and *ballate*, but continuous systematic free imitation, which was to be so fundamental in the style of the sixteenth century, did not exist in the fourteenth. Occasional short passages of imitation were written, however, and these became more numerous in works of the early fifteenth century, though without ever forming a prominent element in the style of that period.

The polyphonic ballata, the third type of Italian secular fourteenth-century music, flourished later than the madrigal and caccia, and showed some influence of the French ballade style. Originally the word *ballata* signified a song to accompany dancing (Italian *ballare*, to dance); the thirteenth-century ballate (of which no musical examples have survived) were monophonic dance songs with choral

The ballata

refrains. A few early fourteenth-century monophonic ballate have been preserved, but most of the examples in the manuscripts are for two or three voices, and date after 1365. These purely lyrical, stylized, polyphonic ballata resemble in form the French virelai. They have a two-line refrain (*ripresa*) which was sung at both the beginning and the end of a six-line stanza. The first two pairs of lines in the stanza (which were called the *piedi*) had their own musical phrase, while the last pair (the *volta*) used the same music as the refrain.

The leading composer of ballate was Francesco Landini (1325–1397), the foremost Italian musician of the fourteenth century. Blind

*Francesco
Landini*

from boyhood as a result of smallpox, Landini nevertheless became a well-educated man and a master of the theory and practice of music; a virtuoso on many instruments, he was especially known for his skill at the organetto, a small portative organ, which he played "as readily as though he had the use of his eyes, with a touch of such rapidity (yet always observing the measure), with such skill and sweetness that beyond all doubt he excelled beyond comparison all organists who can possibly be remembered."[1]

Landini's extant works comprise 87 two-part and 54 three-part ballate, besides one caccia and a dozen madrigals. The two-part ballate are evidently early works; their style in general resembles that of the madrigals, save that the melodic line is more ornate. Many of the three-part ballate are, like the French ballades, for solo voice with two accompanying parts. The ripresa of a Landini ballata is given in Example 27; the entire piece appears in HAM, No. 53.

Ripresa of Ballata: *Amor c'al tuo suggetto*, Francesco Landini

Example 27

Love, who to thy slave now givest life, under thy yoke I live without suffering.

One of the charms of Landini's music, in addition to the graceful vocal melody, is the suavity of the harmonies. There are no parallel seconds and sevenths, such as abounded in the thirteenth century, and few parallel fifths and octaves. Full triad sonorities are plentiful, though they are never used as either first or final chords. Landini's three-part madrigal *Sy dolce non sonò* is exceptional in being constructed on an isorhythmic tenor, and one senses that the composer was not entirely at ease with this difficult technique. On the other hand, in *De dimmi tu* a canon at the fifth between tenor and contratenor does not constrain him in the least; this madrigal, in fact, is one of Landini's most beautiful compositions.

Chromaticism and Musica Ficta

A special flavor is imparted to much fourteenth-century music, both French and Italian, by the use of chromatically altered notes. Chromatic alteration was common at cadences in which otherwise there would have been a whole step between the seventh note of the modal scale and its upward resolution to the final, as for instance at a cadence on D, illustrated in Example 28a and b. This species of chromatic alteration was enjoined by a rule that the interval of a third contracting to a unison must be made minor, and a sixth expanding to an octave must be made major. Sometimes in cadences of the type shown in Example 28b, *both* the upper two notes of a penultimate three-note chord would be raised, thus making what might be called a double leading tone—Example 28c. Cadences on G and C were altered similarly to those on D (see Example 23, and compare Example 22, measures 8 and 15). Cadences on E, however, usually remained in their unaltered modal form—Example 28d.

Example 28   Chromatic Alteration at Cadences

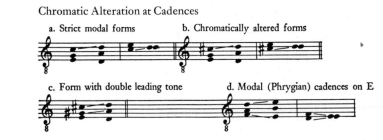

Elsewhere than at cadences, chromatic alteration was used in order to avoid sounding a diminished fifth or an augmented fourth above the lowest note of a chord, and especially to avoid in a melody the tritone interval F-B♮, which was sometimes called by medieval musicians *diabolus in musica*, the devil in music. Chromatics might also be introduced to make a smoother melodic line, or for no other reason than *causa pulchritudinis*, simply because they sounded well—

literally, "for the sake of beauty." Since in thus raising or lowering certain notes on their own responsibility the performers were making sounds different from those shown on the page, the result was called *musica ficta* or *musica falsa*—"fictitious" or "false music."

Notation

By the end of the thirteenth century a notation had been developed that showed the exact relative durations of the long, the breve, and the semibreve, on the basis of triple division. The task of the fourteenth century was to develop a notation that could indicate duple as well as triple division of these notes, and to provide signs for notes shorter than a semibreve, which in the older system was never less than one-third of a breve. Italian composers used dots, supplemented by various letter signs, to show the subdivision of long notes, and also invented new signs for the shorter note values. By the end of the fourteenth century, however, Italian notation was generally superseded by French notation.

The French system was an extension of Franconian principles. The long, the breve, and the semibreve could each be divided into either two or three notes of the next smaller value. The division of the long was called *mood*, that of the breve *time*, and that of the semibreve *prolation;* division was *perfect* if it was triple, *imperfect* if duple. Two new note forms were introduced to indicate values shorter than the semibreve: the *minim* ♩ , one-half or one-third of a semibreve; and the *semiminim* ♪ , one-half of a minim. The essentials of the system thus were as follows:

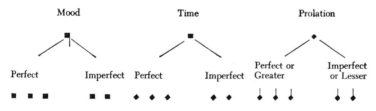

Eventually the original signs for perfect and imperfect mood were dropped and simplified signs for time and prolation were combined: a circle indicated perfect time and a half-circle imperfect time; a dot inside the circle or half-circle indicated greater prolation, and the absence of a dot lesser prolation, thus:

⊙ ■ = ♦ ♦ ♦ = ♩♩♩ ♩♩♩ ♩♩♩ perfect time and greater prolation, equivalent to 9/8 time

₡ ■ = ♦ ♦ = ♩♩♩ ♩♩♩ imperfect time and greater prolation, equivalent to 6/8 time

○ ■ = ♦ ♦ ♦ = ♩♩ ♩♩ ♩♩ perfect time and lesser prolation, equivalent to 3/4 time

C ■ = ◆ ◆ = ♩ ♩ ♩♩ imperfect time and lesser prola-
    tion, equivalent to 2/4 time

The last sign, ⊂ , has come down as the modern sign for 4/4 time. About 1450 the notes pictured above began to be written as "white" notes, that is with black outlines unfilled (ᛃ ▫ ◇ ♭); the semiminim became ♩ , and shorter notes were devised *ad libitum* by adding flags to the semininim (♪ ♪ ♪ etc.). These are essentially the forms of present-day notes; the change from diamond-shaped to rounded heads took place toward the end of the sixteenth century.

Instruments

A full and accurate account of instrumental music in the fourteenth and fifteenth centuries is impossible, for the simple reason that the music manuscripts practically never tell even whether a given part is instrumental or vocal, let alone specify the instruments. If composers had had in mind some particular combination of voices and instruments, there was no reason why they should not have marked it clearly on the page. The fact that they did not do so probably means that they were content to rely on custom or tradition for the manner of performing their music, and did not feel that specific directions were needed.

We know from pictorial and literary sources that the most usual way of performing polyphonic music in the fourteenth and early fifteenth centuries was with a small vocal and instrumental ensemble, normally with only one voice or one instrument to a part. We can be fairly sure that certain parts, such as the Latin tenors in isorhythmic motets and the textless tenors in Landini's three-part ballate, were instrumental rather than vocal. But beyond a few general principles like these we can discern no uniform rules; apparently performances varied according to circumstances, depending on what singers or players happened to be at hand, or on the taste or caprice of the performers. The prevailing quality of tone was clear, bright, or shrill; instruments, if one may judge from the art of the time, were grouped not in families of homogeneous timbre (like a string quartet, for example), but in contrasting colors, such as viol, lute, harp, and trombone; or viol, lute, psaltery, flute, and drum.

The earliest keyboard instruments of the clavichord and harpsichord type were invented in the fourteenth century, but do not seem to have come into common use until the fifteenth century. In addition to the portative organ or organetto, there were positive organs; and large organs were being installed in an increasing number of churches. A pedal keyboard was added to organs in Germany toward the end of the fourteenth century. A mechanism of stops enabling the player to select different ranks of pipes at will, and the addition of a second keyboard, were achievements of the early fifteenth century.

V Music at the Close of the Middle Ages: the English and Burgundian Schools

English Music to the Early Fifteenth Century

England had an active musical life in the twelfth and thirteenth centuries. The fourteenth century, as far as can be ascertained, was a time of comparatively small production; but after about 1400 English music again came to the fore, and English composers exercised considerable influence on the Continent during the first half of the fifteenth century.

English music, like that of northern Europe generally, had been characterized from earliest times by a rather close connection with folk style and, by contrast with Continental developments, a certain *Gymel* disinclination to carry abstract theories to extremes in practice. Thus there had always been a tendency in English music toward major tonality (as opposed to the modal system), toward greater harmonic unity (as opposed to the independent lines, divergent texts, and harmonic dissonances of the French motet), toward greater fullness of sound, and toward a freer use of thirds and sixths than in the music of the Continent. It was in the writings of English theorists around 1300 that the third was first recognized as a consonant interval, and a twelfth-century example of parallel thirds occurs in a *Hymn to St. Magnus*, patron saint of the Orkney Islands. The practice of writing in parallel thirds or parallel sixths, which was later given the name *gymel* ("twin [voices]"), was common in English polyphonic compositions of the thirteenth century.

Three-part conducti and motets were composed in England in the thirteenth century and were also known on the Continent; for instance, the English motet *Alle psallite—Alleluia* is found in the Montpellier Codex. (The tenor is given in Example 29; the entire piece in   81

V. Music
at the Close
of the
Middle Ages:
the English
and
Burgundian
Schools

HAM, No. 33a.) This motet illustrates the freedom with which
English composers adapted the form of the French motet. The tenor,
instead of being cramped into an unvarying rhythmic formula, is
organized in such a way as to present three phrases, each repeated,
which seem to grow organically one out of another while the duplum
and triplum interchange their melodies at each repetition of the tenor
phrase—a favorite device in English music of this period. As shown in
Example 29, the tenor is related to a Gregorian Alleluia and was
perhaps inspired by it; similar melodies occur in other contemporary
motets of this type. The fresh, folklike quality of all the melodic lines
and the harmonious blending of the voices are other English traits,
such as may be heard also in the famous *Sumer* canon.

Example 29   Tenor of *Alle psallite—Alleluia*

The chief sources of our knowledge of English fourteenth-century
music are a number of manuscript fragments containing works that
point to the existence of a school of composition centering at
Worcester Cathedral. These works comprise chiefly tropes of various
sections of the Ordinary of the Mass, selections from the Proper of
the Mass, motets, and·conducti. Most of the motets are oldfashioned,
but a few closely resemble in spirit and technique *Alle psallite—
Alleluia.*

The conducti and some of the conductus-like tropes of the Ordinary exhibit a new stylistic feature, one that was to be of great importance in the music of the early fifteenth century: the melodic line
is accompanied by two other voices in generally parallel motion, in
such a way as to produce successions of chords that would be described in modern terms as first-inversion triads or sixth chords
(marked with brackets in Example 30; the complete piece is given in
HAM, No. 57b). This kind of writing, so different from the thirteenth-century motet and the fourteenth-century ballade styles, reflects the English national predilection for thirds and sixths and for

English discant

82

full, harmonious sounds. Its Continental counterpart of English discant was called *fauxbourdon* (literally, "false bass"), a term whose exact significance has not yet been satisfactorily explained. The important practical consequence of fauxbourdon was the emergence of a fauxbourdon *style* in three-part pieces in which the two lower voices moved relatively freely below an embellished treble. Faux-

Gloria from Fourteenth-Century English Mass

Example 30

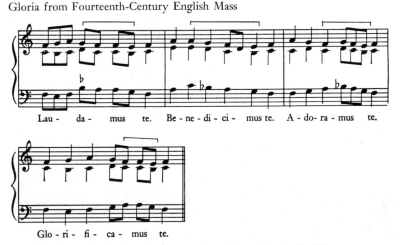

Lau - da - mus te. Be - ne - di - ci - mus te. A - do- ra - mus te.

Glo - ri - fi - ca - mus te.

We praise Thee. We bless Thee. We adore Thee. We glorify Thee.

bourdon style exercised a strong influence on all types of composition —an influence in the direction of homophonic texture, full triad sonority, and acceptance of the sixth chord as a conspicuous element in the harmonic vocabulary.

The chief collection of English music of the early part of the fifteenth century is the Old Hall Manuscript. It contains 148 compositions dating from about 1400 to 1430, of which approximately four-fifths are settings of various sections of the Ordinary of the Mass and the remainder are motets, hymns, and sequences.

The majority of the twenty-four composers in the Old Hall collection seem not to have been known outside the British Isles. However, there was in the first half of the fifteenth century a group of English composers whose works are found in Continental manuscripts of the period, and who may therefore be presumed to have been the representatives of English music abroad. Their influence is attested by a French poem of about 1440 which speaks of the *contenance angloise* (English countenance, or qualities) which contributed to making contemporary Continental music so "joyous and notable" with "marvelous pleasantness." Allusion is made particularly to the leading English composer of the time, John Dunstable (*ca.* 1385–1453). Part of Dunstable's life was probably spent in the service of the English Duke of Bedford, Regent of France from 1422 to 1435 and

V. Music
at the Close
of the
Middle Ages:
the English
and
Burgundian
Schools

commander of the English armies that fought against Joan of Arc; the extensive English possessions and claims in France in this period partly explain the presence of Dunstable and many other English composers on the Continent as well as the spread of their music.

Most numerous and most important historically among Dunstable's works are the three-part sacred pieces—settings of antiphons, hymns, and other liturgical or Biblical texts. These are composed in various ways: some are like English discant, with a *cantus firmus* in the tenor part; others are in a style apparently derived from gymel, with a florid treble line and a borrowed melody in the middle voice, which moves for the most part in thirds and sixths above the tenor; others have an ornamented liturgical melody in the treble (see Example 31); and still others are freely composed, without borrowed thematic material. A piece of this last type is the antiphon *Quam pulcra es*, Example 32, a work we shall analyze in some detail, since it not only exemplifies Dunstable's style but also illustrates some important historical developments.

Dunstable's three-part sacred works

In *Quam pulcra es* the three voices are similar in character and of nearly equal importance; much of the time they move in the same rhythm and usually pronounce the same syllables together: in sum, the texture is that of conductus, and the short melisma at the end on the word "alleluia" is in accordance with the ornamented conductus style. A composition like this one was not limited by a *cantus firmus*, nor by any prescribed scheme of structure, as in an isorhythmic motet, nor by any prescribed pattern of repetitions or sections, as in a ballata

Example 31   Treble of Motet: *Regina caeli laetare*, John Dunstable

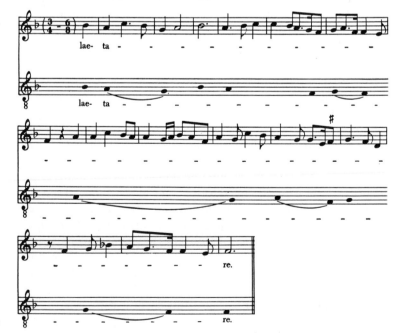

or rondeau. The form of the music, therefore, was a matter for the composer's free choice, limited only insofar as he might wish to follow any suggestions of a formal outline that were implicit in the text. In this instance Dunstable has divided the piece into two sections. Section one (measures 1–38) comprises, in shortened form, verses 6, 7, 5, and 11 of Chapter vii of *The Song of Solomon;* section two, beginning with "et videamus," is on verse 12, with an added "alleluia." The longer first section is punctuated near the end by the held notes on the word "veni" ("come"); its pattern of subdivision is 9 +9 + 11 + 8 measures, with cadences on C, C, D, and G. The second section subdivides, though less neatly, into (4 + 3) + (6 + 3) + 4 measures, with cadences on F, D, C, D, and C. The musical subdivisions of the first section correspond to the modern divisions of the text into verses; those of section two are less distinct, just as the subdivisions of the text are less clearly marked than in section one, but the "alleluia" is definitely set off by its melisma and the livelier melodic and harmonic rhythm as the final cadence is approached.

Not only is the musical form in its main outlines determined by the text; the outline of many phrases also is molded to the rhythm of the words, as may be noted in the declamation by repeated notes of "statúra túa assimiláta est," "mála Púnica," and "íbi dábo tíbi." Other details to be noted are: the conspicuous melodic intervals of a third in the topmost voice, and the occasional outlining of a triad in the melody (for example, measures 1–5, 43, 55); and the use of fauxbourdon style, particularly at the approach to a cadence (as in measures 12–15).

Although English music after the death of Dunstable no longer held a leading position on the Continent, its development at home continued without interruption. One form of English composition *The carol* that flourished in the fifteenth century was the *carol*. Originally the carol, like the rondeau and ballata, was a monophonic dance song with alternating solo and chorus portions. By the fifteenth century it had become stylized as a two-part setting of a religious poem in popular style, often on a subject of the Incarnation, and frequently written in a mixture of English and Latin rhyming verses. In form the carol

Quam pulcra es, John Dunstable

Example 32

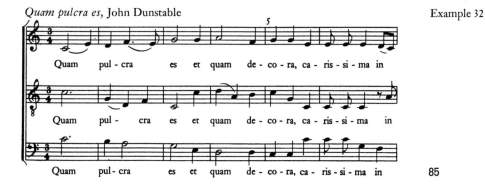

V. Music
at the Close
of the
Middle Ages:
the English
and
Burgundian
Schools

Example 32
(cont.)

V. Music
at the Close
of the
Middle Ages:
the English
and
Burgundian
Schools

Example 32
(cont.)

How fair and how pleasant art thou, O love, for delights! Thy stature is like to a palm tree, and thy breasts to clusters of grapes. Thine head upon thee is like Carmel: thy neck is as a tower of ivory. Come, my beloved, let us go forth into the field . . . and see whether the tender grapes appear, and the pomegranates bud forth: there will I give thee my loves.[1]

consisted of a number of stanzas all sung to the same music, and a *burden* or refrain with its own musical phrase, which was sung at the beginning and then repeated, usually in three-part settings, after every stanza. The carols were not folk songs, but their fresh, angular melodies and lively triple rhythms give them a distinctly popular character and an unmistakably English quality. The Incarnation carols were probably used to accompany religious processions and other religious ceremonies at the Christmas season.

The Evolution of Musical Style in the Late Middle Ages

We may summarize the course of musical evolution from 1225 to 1425 as a movement from the *motet* principle to the *conductus* principle: from the French Gothic motet with its stylized liturgical *cantus firmus*, highly independent melodic lines, multiple texts, rigidly logical abstract structure, and relative indifference to harmonic progression or suavity of effect, to the secularized style of the early fifteenth century with its fusion of French, Italian, and English qualities. In this new international style, a liturgical *cantus firmus* is either altogether absent or, if present, is incorporated into the musical ensemble without dominating it; the melodic lines move within a harmonically planned framework; the form is determined either by the musical device of repeated and contrasted sections or by the literary form of the single text; and the harmonies, enriched by the employment of thirds and sixths as consonant intervals, begin to assume significance in the shaping of the phrase and of the work as a whole. Dunstable's *Quam pulcra es* is an example of this new style, which had favorable soil for growth in fourteenth-century England because English composers continued to cultivate the conductus and conductus-like style of composition after these had largely fallen out of use on the Continent.

Quam pulcra es is classified in the standard edition of Dunstable's works as a "motet." This word, which we have hitherto used to denote the French form of the thirteenth century and the isorhythmic form of the fourteenth and early fifteenth centuries, began in the fifteenth century to take on a broader meaning, being applied generally to settings of liturgical or even secular texts in the newer musical style of the time. From the sixteenth century onward, the word was also applied to sacred compositions in languages other than Latin. This broader meaning of the term has prevailed up to the present day: a motet, in this usage, means almost any polyphonic vocal composition on a sacred text other than the Ordinary of the Mass, and thus includes such diverse forms as antiphons, responsories, and other texts from the Proper and the Office or from the Scriptures.

The fifteenth-century motet

The Burgundian School

The court of Philip the Good, Duke of Burgundy from 1419 to 1467, was the most resplendent in Europe, and his influence as a patron of music was so extensive that the name "Burgundian" has been given both to the style of music and the school of composers which flourished during his reign. The term does not connote a particular region or nationality. The Dukes of Burgundy in the fifteenth century had no fixed principal residence, but sojourned at various places in their dominions, which comprised most of present-day Holland, Belgium, northeastern and east central France, Luxembourg, and Loraine. Their *chapel*, or permanent corps of composers and per-formers, numbered fifteen to twenty-seven persons, recruited from different countries of Europe. The cosmopolitan atmosphere of such a fifteenth-century court was accentuated by numerous visits from foreign musicians and by the fact that the members of the chapel themselves were continually on the move, migrating from one service to another in response to "better offers." Under such circumstances a musical style could not be other than international; the prestige of the Burgundian court was such that the kind of music cultivated there

V. Music
at the Close
of the
Middle Ages:
the English
and
Burgundian
Schools

A fête champêtre *at the court of Duke Philip the Good (1396–1467) of
Burgundy. The musicians, ever present on these occasions, serenade the
Duke's party, which is at the center. Hunters are chasing game in the
background. This painting, dated 1430–31, is ascribed to Jan Van Eyck.*

influenced other European musical centers, such as the chapels of the
Pope at Rome, the Emperor in Germany, the kings of France and
England, and the various Italian courts, as well as cathedral choirs—
the more so because many of the musicians in these other places either
had been at one time, or hoped some day to be, in the service of the
Duke of Burgundy himself.

Guillaume Dufay is commonly named as one of the chief figures of
the Burgundian School, although he was perhaps never a regular

member of the ducal chapel. Dufay was born about 1400 in the Burgundian province of Hainaut (the present Franco-Belgian border region). He travelled much, and was a welcome guest at many European courts. Already before his death in 1474, and for a generation after, he was celebrated as one of the greatest composers of his time and the teacher of many famous musicians.

The principal types of composition of the Burgundian School were Masses, Magnificats, motets, and secular chansons with French texts. The prevailing combination of voices was the same as in the French ballade and the Italian ballata: tenor and contratenor both moving within the range c to g′, and a melodic treble or *discantus* normally not exceeding the compass of a tenth (a to c″ or c′ to e″). As in the fourteenth century, the intention was for each line to have a distinct timbre and the whole a transparent texture, with decided predominance of the discantus as the principal melody. The style in general may be regarded as a combination of the homophonic suavity of fauxbourdon with a certain amount of melodic freedom and contrapuntal independence, including occasional points of imitation. The typical discantus line flows in warmly expressive lyrical phrases, breaking into graceful melismas at the approach to important cadences —see Example 33.

The Burgundian cadence formula was still for the most part that of the fourteenth century (Example 20), and the Landini embellishment figure was very common (Example 23); but along with this older type of cadence, another began to appear which was in effect a dominant-tonic progression and which, in three-part writing, nearly always involved crossing of the two lower voices; see Example 34a and b.

The feeling for chord progressions of a dominant-tonic or tonic-dominant character became continuously more marked throughout

Guillaume Dufay (ca. *1400–1474*) *and Gilles Binchois* (ca. *1400–1460*), *the leading Burgundian composers, are shown together in this miniature from* Le Champion des Dames. (*Bettmann Archive*)

V. Music
at the Close
of the
Middle Ages:
the English
and
Burgundian
Schools

Example 33

Chanson: *Franc cuer gentilx*, Guillaume Dufay

the first half of the fifteenth century; and after about 1460 the normal cadence formula was one that would be described in modern terminology as V–I. The great majority of the compositions of the Burgundian School were in some form of triple meter, with frequent cross rhythms resulting from the combination of the patterns ♩ ♩ ♩ and

Cadential Formulas

Example 34

♫ ♫ ; see Example 34c and d. Duple meter was used principally in subdivisions of longer works as a means of contrast.

In the fifteenth century, *chanson* was a general term for any polyphonic setting of a secular poem. The Burgundian chansons were, in effect, accompanied solo songs. Their texts—nearly always love poems —were most often in the pattern of the rondeau, sometimes the traditional form with a two-line refrain, sometimes an expanded form; in the latter type, often only a portion of the poem would be used for the musical setting, perhaps only the refrain, which might consist of four or five lines. The chansons were the most characteristic productions of the Burgundian School. The chief center of their cultivation was the Burgundian court itself, and the outstanding master of the genre was Gilles Binchois (ca. 1400–1460).

The Burgundian chanson

Binchois's chansons excel in the expression of a tender melancholy, just touched with sensuous longing. The moving charm of the melodies, the clear, bright-colored sound of the ensemble, and the miniature proportions of the whole contrive to suggest to our minds the picture of a visionary world, remote yet strangely familiar, standing at the threshold between the Middle Ages and the modern era. So strong was the spell of this Burgundian musical style that the tradition of it lingered in Europe long after the downfall of the Duchy of Burgundy as an independent political power.

Gilles Binchois

In their church music the Burgundian composers at first developed no distinctive sacred style, but wrote both motets and Masses in the

V. Music
at the Close
of the
Middle Ages:
the English
and
Burgundian
Schools

manner of the chanson, with a freely melodic solo treble supported by tenor and contratenor parts in the usual three-voice texture. The treble might be newly composed, but in many cases it was an embellished version of a Gregorian chant (for example, Dufay's *Alma Redemptoris Mater*). The influence of fauxbourdon style on the Burgundian motet may be recognized in the prevailing homophonic texture and relatively frequent sixth chords of Dufay's *Alma Redemptoris Mater*, his *Veni Creator Spiritus*, and, in a simpler form quite close to strict fauxbourdon, his setting of the hymn *Aures ad nostras deitatis*.

*Burgundian
motets*

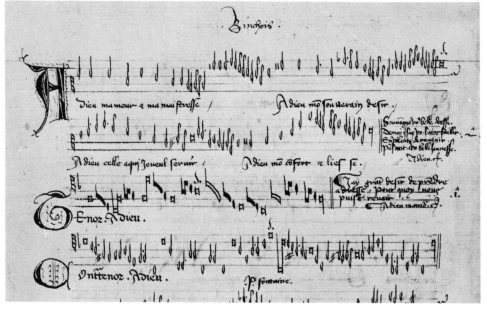

The first four staves of this manuscript page show Adieu m'amour *by Binchois. A transcription is given in MM, No. 16. (Courtesy Bodleian Library, Oxford)*

It was in settings of the Mass that composers of the Burgundian period first developed a specifically sacred musical style, and moreover began an evolution which by the end of the century made this form the principal vehicle for the thought and effort of composers. We have already noted the increased number of polyphonic settings of the Mass in the late fourteenth and early fifteenth centuries. Previous to about 1420 the various sections of the Ordinary were composed as separate pieces (Machaut's Mass being practically the sole exception), though occasionally such separate items might be brought together by a compiler into a unified cycle. A central achievement of the fifteenth century was to establish as regular practice the polyphonic composition of the five divisions of the Ordinary—Kyrie, Gloria, Credo,

*Burgundian
Masses*

Sanctus, and Agnus Dei—as a musically unified whole. The motive for this development was the desire of musicians to give coherence to a large and complex musical form; the most practical way of achieving a definite, perceptible musical interconnection of the various sections of a Mass was to use the same thematic material in each. At first the connection consisted only in beginning each movement with the same melodic motive, usually in the treble; but this technique was soon superseded by or combined with another, namely the use of the same *cantus firmus* in every movement. The resulting cyclical musical form is known as a *cantus firmus Mass* or *Tenor Mass*. The earliest cyclical Masses of this kind were written by English composers, but the form was quickly adopted on the Continent and by the second half of the fifteenth century had become the customary one.

The tradition of the medieval motet suggested the placing of the borrowed melody in the tenor; but the new conception of music in the fifteenth century required that the lowest voice be free to function as a foundation for the desired harmonic progressions, particularly at cadences. To use as the lowest voice a given melodic line which could not be essentially modified would have limited the composer's freedom and possibly have led to harmonic monotony. This difficulty was resolved by making the tenor the next-to-lowest voice, placing below it a part at first called *contratenor bassus* ("low contratenor"), later simply *bassus;* placing above the tenor a second contratenor called *contratenor altus* ("high contratenor"), later *altus;* and retaining in the highest position the treble part, called variously the *cantus* ("melody"), *discantus* ("discant"), or *superius* ("higher" part). These four voice parts came into being about the middle of the fifteenth century, and this distribution has remained, with few interruptions, the standard one to our own day.

Another heritage from the medieval motet was the custom of writing the tenor of a *cantus firmus* Mass in longer notes than the other parts and in isorhythmic fashion—either imposing a certain rhythmic pattern on a given plainsong melody and repeating it with the same pattern, or keeping the original rhythm of a given secular tune and altering the succesive appearances of the melody by making them now faster, now slower, in relation to the other voices. Thus, as in the isorhythmic motet, the identity of the borrowed tune might be quite thoroughly disguised, the more so that it lay now in an inner voice and not in the lowest one as in the fourteenth century; nonetheless its regulative power in unifying the five divisions of the Mass was undeniable. The melodies used as *cantus firmi* were taken from the chants of the Proper or the Office, or else from a secular source, most often the tenor part of a chanson; in neither case did they have any liturgical connection with the Ordinary of the Mass. The name of the borrowed melody was given to the Mass for which it served as a *cantus firmus;* in Dufay's Mass *Se la face ay pale* (*If my face is pale*), the tenor is taken from one of the composer's own chansons.

V. Music
at the Close
of the
Middle Ages:
the English
and
Burgundian

A favorite tenor was the song *L'homme armé* (*The Armed Man*), on which nearly every composer of the late fifteenth and sixteenth centuries wrote at least one Mass.

L'homme armé, Example 35a, was perhaps a folk song. Example 35b shows how Dufay used it as the tenor of the first Agnus Dei in a Mass.

L'homme armé

Example 35a

L'hom-me, l'hom-me, l'homme ar - mē, l'homme ar - mé, L'homme ar - mé doibt

on doub - ter, doibt on doub - ter. On a fait par - tout cri - er

Que chas - cun se viengue ar - mer D'un hau - bre - gon de fer.

The armed man is to be feared; everywhere it has been proclaimed that everyone should arm himself with an iron coat of mail.

(Other parts of this Mass using the same tune are in HAM, No. 66.) In Example 35b, the text is given as it appears in the original manuscript. Evidently the exact adjustment of the syllables to the notes was left to the singer; the tenor may have been played rather than sung. The rhythmic complication of measures 22–23 is notable. (For a different interpretation of the *musica ficta* accidentals see Gustave Reese's *Music in the Renaissance*, p. 74.)

A *cantus firmus* was not necessarily used continuously throughout a Mass. For example, in Dufay's Mass the *L'homme armé* tune is absent from a long section of the Osanna and does not appear at all in the Benedictus. Also, the prevailing four-part texture in a Mass was frequently replaced by duet or trio sections, which usually were composed freely, without a *cantus firmus*. The *cantus firmus* itself might be subjected to various rhythmic modifications, or elaborated melodically, or be inverted, or sung backwards (*cancrizans*, literally "crabwise"; this device is used by Dufay in the third Agnus Dei of his *L'homme armé* Mass).

Dufay's four-part *cantus firmus* Masses are relatively late works, dating for the most part after 1450. It is clear that in such compositions as these we are no longer dealing with typically Burgundian music in the style of the chansons and chanson-like motets and Masses of the first part of the century. The new features in the *cantus firmus* Masses of Dufay are, in fact, indicative of a new musical style which rose to a dominating position after 1450, and which in some respects seemed to signalize a revival of medieval ideals of church music. In the following chapter we shall examine this new style in more detail, and

Agnus Dei from the Mass *L'homme armé*, Guillaume Dufay

V. Music
at the Close
of the
Middle Ages:
the English
and
Burgundian
Schools

Example 35b
(cont.)

Lamb of God that takest away the sins of the world, have mercy [on us].

seek to understand the conditions that favored its rise and growth in
the Renaissance world of the late fifteenth and early sixteenth centuries.

VI The Age of the Renaissance: Ockeghem to Josquin

General Features

The period from 1450 to 1600 in the history of music is now generally known as "the Renaissance," a term which, like "Gothic" for the late Middle Ages or "Baroque" for the seventeenth and early eighteenth centuries, has been borrowed from art history. Its literal meaning is "rebirth," and many writers and artists of the fifteenth and sixteenth centuries viewed the achievements of their own time as a revival of the glories of Greece and Rome, a revival stimulated in part by discoveries of many ancient works of art and literature. But no comparable discoveries of ancient music were made; and although a few innovations in sixteenth-century music were ascribed by theorists to Greek or Latin doctrines, the connection was mostly illusory. *Renaissance*, then, in the sense of a rebirth of ancient art, is all but meaningless when applied to music of this period.

There remains the more general meaning of Renaissance as a rebirth of the human spirit, a revival of standards of culture. Renaissance men were convinced that theirs was an age both different from and better than immediately preceding times: "The world is coming to its senses as if awaking out of a deep sleep," Erasmus said. The whole temper of the age was optimistic and buoyant.

Social conditions

Of course it is impossible to date precisely any such momentous and far-reaching change in human attitudes, habits, and institutions as is implied in the idea of the Renaissance. From our own vantage point in time, we can see that certain historical and cultural events of the late fifteenth and early sixteenth centuries appear to signal the end of the Middle Ages and the beginning of the modern era. In 1453, the year of Dunstable's death, the Turks captured Constantinople, the

Historical events

capital and last stronghold of the eastern Roman Empire, thereby severing the last visible link with the world of antiquity; many Byzantine scholars fled to Italy, where their presence stimulated the study of the Greek language and of ancient Greek literature and philosophy. The invention of printing from movable type was made at about the same time. The discovery of America by Columbus in 1492 was followed by other voyages of discovery and the eventual colonization of the western hemisphere. Finally, the two great universal medieval institutions—the Catholic Church and the Holy Roman Empire—were both splintered. The Reformation begun by Martin Luther in 1517 divided the Church into Catholic and Protestant branches.

*Music
printing*

One of the most important factors in the growth of music during the Renaissance was the rise of music printing. Isolated examples of printed music appeared in the late fifteenth century, but the first collection of polyphonic music printed from movable type was brought out in 1501 by Ottaviano dei Petrucci at Venice. By 1523 Petrucci had published fifty-nine volumes (including reprints) of vocal and instrumental music. Regular publication of music in printed form began in France in 1527 (or possibly 1520), in Germany about 1534, and in the Netherlands in 1538; Venice, Rome, Nuremberg, Paris, Lyons, Louvain, and Antwerp became the principal centers. The application to music of the newly invented art of printing was obviously an event of far-reaching consequence. Instead of a few precious manuscripts laboriously copied by hand and liable to all kinds of errors and variants, a plentiful supply of new music was now made

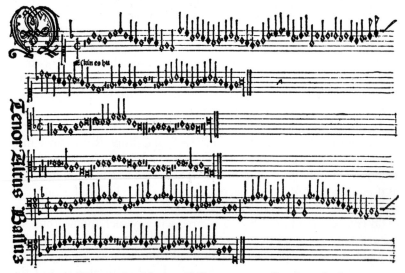

A page from Harmonice Musices Odhecaton, *a collection of 96 part-songs by Netherlands composers, the first such book to be printed from movable type. Ottaviano dei Petrucci (1466–1539) published it at Venice in 1501. Petrucci's editions are highly prized for their neat presswork.*

possible—not exactly at a low price, but still less costly than equivalent manuscripts, and of uniform accuracy.

Insofar as it is possible to define a Renaissance musical style, the following general features may be noted.

The characteristic "ideal" sound was that of four or more voice lines of similar character and equal importance in a homogeneous tone color, instead of three more or less dissimilar lines in contrasting timbres as in the Middle Ages. The various voice parts more and more came to be conceived as a sonorous whole rather than as separate melodic lines; composers began to write all the parts simultaneously instead of successively, as in the Middle Ages. The units of harmony were the triad and the 6/3 chord, which tended to progress according to the principles of major-minor tonality, although these principles had not yet been explicitly formulated and indeed were not consciously present in the composers' minds. The bass was gradually given the function of a harmonic foundation, even when it was imitating the other voices.

With respect to the rhythm, two distinct tendencies were apparent: (1) the music might move with fluid rhythm either in a contrapuntal texture with systematic free imitation involving all the voices, or in a freely improvisatory style, as in certain types of lute and keyboard pieces; or, (2) the movement might be by strongly marked rhythmic patterns in a predominantly chordal texture, as in instrumental dance

In this sixteenth-century painting, The Musicians *by Michelangelo Caravaggio (1565–1609), three partbooks are shown. The instruments are a lute, a fiddle, and a curved cornett. (Courtesy Metropolitan Museum of Art)*

pieces and certain kinds of secular vocal compositions. These two tendencies represent two different traditions; they interact to some extent in the sixteenth century, but on the whole they remain differentiated.

Music became both more closely united with words and more independent of words. On the one hand there was a constant and successful effort throughout the sixteenth century to make the texts in vocal music more easily understandable and to make the music immediately and strikingly express the images and especially the feelings suggested by the text; at the same time the rise of instrumental music bears witness to the urge to create musical forms which should be complete and satisfying as purely musical entities, not needing the support of words.

Finally, although the typical *ars nova* and Burgundian texture of a solo voice with instrumental accompaniment was not entirely dropped during the Renaissance, for a long time it was neglected. The fundamental nature of most Renaissance music suggests equal importance of the voices, yet many pieces in this style were actually performed by a vocal soloist with instruments playing the other parts. Also, a certain number of pieces were frankly written as solos with accompaniment; but it was not until near the end of the sixteenth century that this particular type of composition rose to special prominence.

For convenience we may distinguish two main overlapping periods in the history of Renaissance music. Until well into the sixteenth century the prevailing style was international, relatively uniform, and still somewhat under the influence of medieval ideas. As the sixteenth century progressed, diverse national styles arose; and after about 1550, the progress of music was marked by the growing dominance of these styles and by new departures that foreshadowed the Baroque era.

In this and the next two chapters we shall divide the complex history of Renaissance music in the following way: the present chapter will deal with the principal composers and musical forms from the middle of the fifteenth century to about 1520. Chapter VII will be concerned with the Catholic church music of the period from 1520 to 1550, with the beginnings of national styles and of instrumental music, and the flowering of the madrigal and related forms in the middle and late sixteenth century. In Chapter VIII we shall follow the growth of sacred music in the Lutheran and other Protestant churches in the sixteenth century, the Catholic church music of the latter half of the sixteenth century, the instrumental music of the same period, and the rise of the Venetian school, the immediate predecessor of the Baroque.

The Netherlands Composers

The period between 1450 and 1550 in the history of music has been called "the age of the Netherlanders." Other terms sometimes used are "Flemish" and "Franco-Flemish." The name used is of little consequence, as long as it is understood to be simply a geographical expression.

The period after the middle of the fifteenth century is represented by the later works of Dufay and the compositions of Johannes Ockeghem. As is true of many other Netherlands composers, the exact date (1430?) and place of Ockeghem's birth are unknown. We first hear of him as a singer in the choir of the Cathedral at Antwerp in 1443. In 1452 he entered the chapel of the King of France, and in 1465 was made its leader (*maître de chapelle*), which post he held until his death in 1495. He was celebrated not only as a composer but also as the teacher of many of the leading Netherlanders of the next generation. A miniature in a French manuscript of about 1530 shows Ockeghem and eight other singers of his chapel singing a Gloria from a large manuscript choirbook on a lectern (see p. 104), in the usual fashion of the time

Johannes Ockeghem

Ockeghem does not seem to have been an exceptionally prolific composer. His known works comprise about twelve Masses, ten motets, and some twenty chansons. The relatively large number of Masses reflects the fact that in the second half of the fifteenth century this was the principal form of composition, in which the composer was expected to demonstrate most fully his skill and imagination. Most of Ockeghem's Masses are similar in general sonority to Dufay's *Se la face ay pale*, with four voices of like character in a contrapuntal texture of independent melodic lines. However, the bass, which before 1450 rarely sang below c, is now extended downward to G or F, and sometimes as much as a fourth lower in special combinations of low voices, otherwise the ranges normally are the same as in the early part of the century. Example 36 shows the ranges used; the compass of the superius corresponds to that of the modern alto; the tenor and contratenor (the "tenor altus") are in nearly the same range, and frequently cross each other in the part-writing. The result, as compared with Burgundian style, is a fuller, thicker texture, a darker and at the same time a more homogeneous sound. This effect is reinforced by the character of Ockeghem's melodic lines, which are spun out in long-breathed phrases, in an extremely flexible rhythmic

Ockeghem's style

Normal Ranges of Voice Parts in the Late Fifteenth Century

Example 36

Agnus Dei II from the Mass *Mi-mi*, Johannes Ockeghem

Example 37

flow much like that of melismatic plainchant, with infrequent cadences and few rests (see Example 37).

Although Ockeghem's harmonic vocabulary is founded solidly on
diatonic triads and sixth chords, the harmonic organization of his
phrases and sections is by no means oriented toward the modern tonal
system. In fact, the sound of his church music is more austerely modal,
and thus closer to the spirit of Gregorian Chant, than that of the
Burgundians. This is one sign of a general tendency on the part of
composers in the second half of the fifteenth century to create a style
of church music distinctly different from that of secular music, instead of, as in the earlier period, writing Masses and motets in a style
practically indistinguishable from that of the chanson.

*Johannes Ockeghem and the singers
of his chapel.*

The
Netherlands
Composers

*The
Netherlands
canon*

In general, Ockeghem did not rely heavily on imitation in his Masses; there are many imitative passages, but these seldom involve all the voices, and the technique is used only incidentally, not continually and systematically as it later was in the sixteenth century. One class of compositions, however, the *canons*, are a conspicuous exception to this general rule. Ockeghem, in common with his contemporaries, took delight in writing music in which the audible structure was supported on another, concealed structure of a theoretically rigid nature; it was the same propensity as that which led medieval composers to write isorhythmic motets, partly for sheer pleasure in the exercise of technical virtuosity, and partly as a public demonstration of professional skill. With the Netherlanders these displays of technique took the form of canons.

The method of writing canon is to derive one or more additional voices from a single given voice. The additional voices may be written out by the composer, or they may be sung from the notes of the given voice, modified according to certain directions. The additional voice may be derived in various ways. For example, the second voice may start at a certain number of beats or measures after the original one; the second voice may be an inversion of the first—that is, move always by the same intervals but in the opposite direction; or the derived voice may be the original voice backward—called a *retrograde* canon, or *cancrizans* ("crab") canon.

An outstanding example of canonic writing is Ockeghem's *Missa prolationum*, every movement of which is constructed as a double canon making use of various intervals and various combinations of time signatures. Example 38 shows the beginning of the second Kyrie from this Mass. Each of the two parts in the original notation has two mensuration signatures— ○ and ⊂ in the superius, ⊙ and ⊆ in the contra—and two C clefs, one with each signature. In the transcription (Example 38b) the two top voices represent the superius and the lower voices the contra, with appropriate reduction of the original note values.

The importance of this and similar flights of virtuosity can easily be exaggerated. It is less important to know that Ockeghem wrote canons than to realize that the use of such artifices does not in the least inhibit Ockeghem's ability to communicate to the listener untutored in the "science" of musical composition, though when the underlying scheme of the work is known, one must admire all the more the smooth melodic lines, the harmonious proportions, and the apparent ease with which the music moves despite the formidable technical problem which the composer has set himself.

In the fifteenth and sixteenth centuries, Masses without a *cantus firmus* took their titles from the mode in which they were written (for example, *Missa quinti toni*, "Mass in Mode V") or from some peculiarity of structure. A Mass having neither a *cantus firmus* nor any other identifying peculiarity, or one whose source the composer

VI. The Age
of the
Renaissance:
Ockeghem to
Josquin

Example 38

Kyrie II from the *Missa prolationum*, Johannes Ockeghem

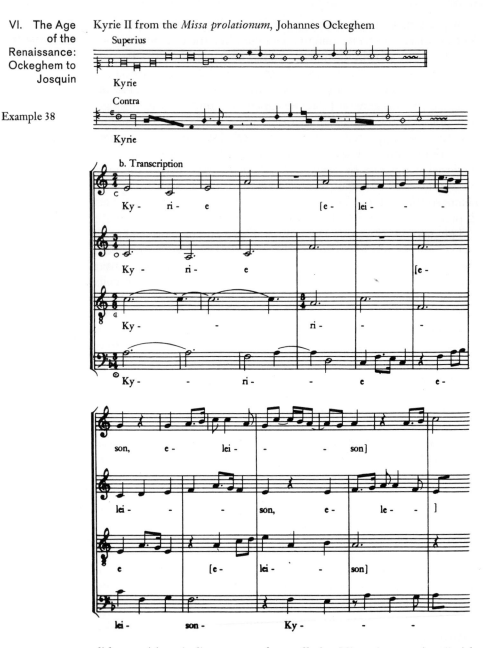

did not wish to indicate, was often called a *Missa sine nomine*, "with-out a name."

The essential quality of Ockeghem's church music is difficult to describe. The low range, the nonpulsatile rhythms, the prevailing texture of nonimitative counterpoint, the seemingly random harmonic progressions, and especially the long-breathed, winding melodies, unarticulated either by regular cadences or melodic sequences—all combine to produce an effect of vastness and mystery, a suggestion

Ockeghem's church music

of inward rapture rising from the contemplation of thoughts embodied in the sacred text.

Ockeghem's Masses show an extreme reaction against the Burgundian chanson-style Mass and motet of the early fifteenth century; a more even balance between mystic withdrawal on the one hand and articulate expressiveness on the other was restored in the next generation of Netherlands church composers, many of whom directly or indirectly were pupils of Ockeghem. The three most eminent figures of this generation were Jacob Obrecht, Henricus Isaac, and Josquin des Prez, all born about 1450—Obrecht near Antwerp, Isaac perhaps at Bruges, and Josquin probably somewhere in the territory of Hainaut. All received their earliest musical training and experience in the Netherlands. All traveled widely, working in various courts and churches in different countries of Europe. The careers of these three composers, like those of most of their contemporaries, well illustrate the lively continual interchange in musical matters that went on in the fifteenth and sixteenth centuries between northern and southern Europe, between the French and Netherlandish centers and those of Italy and (somewhat later) Spain. It is natural, therefore, that we should find in their music a diversity, a mixture, and to some extent a fusion, of northern and southern elements: the serious tone, the leaning toward rigid structure, the intricate polyphony, the smoothly flowing rhythms of the Netherlands; and the more spontaneous mood, simpler homophonic texture, more distinct rhythms, and more clearly articulated phrases of the Italian style.

Few details are known of the life of Jacob Obrecht (1452–1505). His works include some two dozen Masses, about an equal number of motets, and a number of chansons and instrumental pieces. Most of his Masses are built on *cantus firmi*, either secular songs or liturgical Gregorian melodies; but there is much variety in the treatment of these borrowed themes. Obrecht's Masses and motets differ from those of Ockeghem first of all by reason of the more spontaneous, impulsive quality of his musical imagination. His melody is typically Netherlandish in its smoothly vocal curves and its richly melismatic character; but unlike the long, winding, rapt, unbroken line of Ockeghem, Obrecht's melody is organized into relatively short though perfectly proportioned phrases with periodical cadences, supported always by clear and appropriate harmonies.

Jacob Obrecht

Obrecht's style

An excellent example of Obrecht's style is the three-voice motet *Parce Domine*. (Example 39; the entire motet appears in MM, No. 18.) The two upper voices are pervaded by the motive of a stepwise-descending fourth, a motive like a gesture of supplication, which unifies these two parts without much obvious imitation and likewise binds them thematically to the lowest voice, which has the same descending interval as its underlying structural feature. This lowest voice, with its longer note-values, frequent pauses, and plain syllabic text setting, contrasts with the other two parts and moreover generates the form of the entire composition, serving both in the manner of a *cantus firmus* melody (its only "harmonic" interval is the fifth e-A at the end) and as the foundation of the harmonic scheme.

Motet: *Parce Domine*, Jacob Obrecht

Example 39

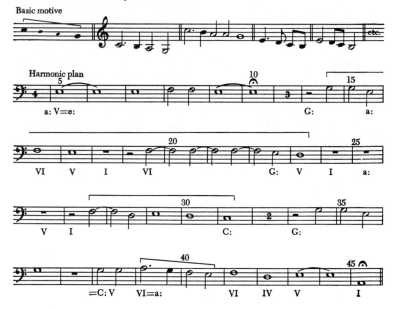

Although polyphonic church music, especially settings of the Ordinary of the Mass, had achieved greater prestige in the second half of the fifteenth century than at any time in the previous two hundred years, there was no lack of secular composition in this period. Furthermore, it was in the chansons—polyphonic songs with texts in the vernacular—that most of the progressive style tendencies of the period were first worked out. During this time also the miniature proportions typical of the early Burgundian school were being expanded into larger musical forms; fixed patterns, such as the rondeau, were gradually being abandoned in favor of freely composed songs.

The late Burgundian chansons of 1460–80 show a gradually increasing use of imitative counterpoint, involving at first only the superius and tenor voices, then later all three. Binchois's *Filles à marier* has a sustained tenor and contratenor (possibly instrumental) supporting two soprano voices written in free imitation and a vivacious syllabic style that obviously derives from a tradition quite different from the usual courtly Burgundian chanson.

This concise, syllabic, strongly rhythmic type of melody is also found in the middle section of Ockeghem's *Ma maîtresse* (Example 40a; entire piece in HAM, No. 74); here it makes a striking contrast to the first section, which is in the most elegant Burgundian courtly manner. The melody of *Ma bouche rit* also begins in this strongly rhythmic way, but as the chanson goes on the simple tune tends to be lost in melismatic cadences and rhythmic subtleties (Example 40b; entire piece in HAM, No. 75). Evidently in this latter work Ockeghem was seeking to amalgamate two distinct styles, to capture a markedly rhythmic, periodically cadencing tune in a contrapuntal web of three similar voices with considerable use of imitation; but in the interest of a continuous musical flow he was constrained to minimize and obscure the cadential implications of the melody.

The inherent conflict between a markedly rhythmic tune on the one hand and the requirements involved in a continuous contrapuntal three-part texture on the other preoccupied Netherlands composers throughout the second half of the fifteenth century. It was most happily resolved, perhaps, in the chansons of Antoine Busnois (d. 1492), a contemporary of Ockeghem.

Chanson Melody: *Ma maîtresse*, Johannes Ockeghem

Example 40

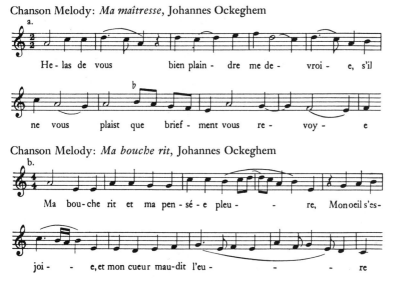

He-las de vous   bien plain - dre me de -   vroi -   e, s'il

ne vous   plaist que   brief - ment vous   re -   voy -   e

Chanson Melody: *Ma bouche rit*, Johannes Ockeghem

Ma bou-che rit et   ma pen - sé - e pleu -   -   re, Mon oeil s'es-

joi -   - e, et mon cueur mau-dit l'eu -   -   -   re

The chanson in the generation of Obrecht, Isaac, and Josquin may be studied in one of the most famous of all music anthologies, the *Harmonice Musices Odhecaton A*, which was published by Petrucci at Venice in 1501—the first printed collection of polyphonic music. The title means "One hundred songs [actually there are only ninety-six] of harmonic [that is, polyphonic] music"; the letter "A" indicates that this is the first of a series of such collections, of which the other volumes, the *Canti B* and *Canti C* were in fact issued in 1502 and 1504. The *Odhecaton* is a selection of chansons written between about 1470 and 1500; it includes pieces ranging from late Burgundian composers to the "modern" generation. Somewhat more than half of the chansons are for three voices, and these in general are written in the older styles. Among the composers represented in the collection are Isaac, Josquin, and two of their contemporaries, Alexander Agricola (*ca.* 1446–1506) and Loyset Compère (*ca.* 1455–1518).

The blending of learned counterpoint with popular melody in the Netherlands chanson came to the height of its development in the early part of the sixteenth century. The Netherlands chanson in this period approaches in many respects the style of contemporary church music; or rather, we may say that the church music, especially the motet, approaches the style of the chanson. It was undoubtedly the chanson that influenced Obrecht and his contemporaries toward greater use of imitation, more distinct phraseology, a more easily grasped melody, and in general a more human, down-to-earth quality in their Masses and motets as compared with those written by the previous generation of Netherlanders. Yet the secular and churchly styles never quite coalesced. The typical chanson theme was derived from popular music, had a marked duple rhythm, a positive, angular stride, repeated notes, and syllabic declamation; such a theme did not easily lend itself to the churchly style of counterpoint that had evolved in the later fifteenth century—a style based on plainchant and marked by long, smoothly flowing melodic lines, many melismas, and flexible rhythms. Yet many of the Netherlands composers of the early sixteenth century successfully accomplished a fusion of the two styles. Side by side with the elaborately contrapuntal chanson of the Netherlanders in the early sixteenth century, however, there existed a simpler, more homophonic chanson; and after about 1520, this type partly displaced the older one.

Josquin des Prez

Throughout the history of Western music, periods of exceptionally intense creative activity have occurred, during which the curve of musical production rises to a notable peak. The early sixteenth century was such a period. Out of the extraordinarily large number of first-rank composers living around 1500, one, Josquin des Prez (*ca.* 1440–1521), must be counted among the greatest of all time. Few musicians have enjoyed higher renown while they lived, or exercised more profound and lasting influence on those who came after them. Josquin was hailed by contemporaries as "the best of the composers of our time," the "Father of Musicians." "He is the master of the notes," said Martin Luther. "They must do as he wills; as for the other composers, they have to do as the notes will."

The early Netherlands chanson reached the climax of its development at Josquin's hands. He was unmatched in the skill of combining the hearty, colorful quality of secular popular song with the intricacies of counterpoint. Thus his five-voice chanson *Faulte d'argent* takes for its framework a canon at the lower fifth between the contratenor and the *quinta pars* ("fifth voice"; see Example 41), around which the other three voices play in a continuous network of close imitation, but without ever sacrificing clarity of texture (the entire chanson is given in HAM, No. 91).

The high proportion of motets in Josquin's output is noteworthy. In his day the Mass was still the principal vehicle by which a composer was expected to demonstrate mastery of his craft; but because of its liturgical formality, unvarying text, and established musical conventions, the Mass offered little opportunity for experimentation. The motets were freer; they could be written for a wide range of texts, all relatively unfamiliar and hence suggesting interesting new possibilities

Josquin des Prez

Canon from Chanson: *Faulte d'argent*, Josquin des Prez   Example 41

VI. The Age
of the
Renaissance:
Ockeghem to
Josquin

*Josquin's
Masses*

for word-music relationships. In the sixteenth century, therefore, the motet, rather than the Mass, came to be the most progressive form of sacred composition.

Josquin's Masses illustrate many of the techniques and devices that were commonly used in the sixteenth century. The theme of the Mass *Hercules dux Ferrariae* offers an example of what the sixteenth century called a *soggetto cavato*,[1] a "subject [or theme] carved out" of a word or sentence by letting each vowel indicate a corresponding syllable of the hexachord, thus:

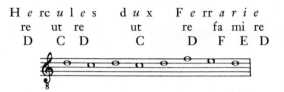

Hercules, or Ercole I, Duke of Ferrara from 1471 to 1505, from whose name this theme was derived, was a patron for whom Josquin wrote at least two other works in addition to this Mass.

Josquin's Mass *Malheur me bat* is an early instance of a procedure that became more common later in the sixteenth century. This Mass is based on a chanson by Ockeghem; but instead of only a single voice, the entire chanson is employed as a basis for free fantasy and expansion. A Mass which thus takes over not merely a single voice, but several—including (to varying degrees) the characteristic progressions, cadences, or even the whole musical substance and general structure—of some pre-existing chanson, Mass, or motet, is known as a *parody Mass* (the word "parody" is simply a technical term for the manner of composition and has no pejorative meaning). Instances of the parody Mass have been found as early as the fourteenth century, although the practice does not seem to have been common before the early sixteenth century.

In another of Josquin's Masses, *Faysans regres*, there is a fascinating mixture of motives from secular and sacred sources. This Mass takes its theme from the second part of a rondeau by Walter Frye, an English composer of the first half of the fifteenth century who was perhaps associated with the Burgundian court. (The same theme was used in a chanson by Alexander Agricola, published in Petrucci's *Canti C* of 1504.) Josquin, taking over only a single phrase of the melody, constructs the tenor of his Mass from beginning to end on nothing but this four-note motive, transposed to different scale degrees and subjected to a myriad of rhythmic variations; in the Agnus Dei it is combined with another motive (in the altus) from the first part of the original chanson. In addition, in the Kyrie, Gloria, and Credo Josquin introduces appropriate Gregorian melodies. The superius uses only these liturgical motives and figures derived from them; the melodic material of the altus comes chiefly from the superius, and that of the bassus from either the superius or the tenor. Example 42 shows how expertly Josquin worked.

Although Josquin's individuality is apparent in his Masses despite their adherence to traditional forms and practices, it was in the motets that he made his most original contributions; a good example is the beautiful four-voice *Ave Maria* based in part on the Gregorian antiphon (in MM, No. 19). This work illustrates the style which came to be characteristic of the entire sixteenth century. Each phrase of the text has its own musical motive, which is first presented in imitation by each voice in turn; the musical sentence thus initiated comes eventually to a cadence, and a similar sentence, on the next phrase of the text and with its own musical motive, begins. But the cadences are

Kyrie from the Mass, *Faysans regres*, Josquin des Prez   Example 42

Example 42
(cont.)

concealed by overlapping, so that while some of the voices are still finishing one sentence, others are beginning the next, and the music continues without obvious division into sections. This was the basic plan of a sixteenth-century motet. However, the plan was subject to various modifications in order to avoid the danger of monotony arising from the same kind of texture too long continued and in order to achieve clear formal outlines and proportioned structure in the work as a whole.

*Motet
structure*

Some of the means that Josquin used to attain this ideal balance and formal articulation were: (1) the repetition of phrases, either literally or with added voices; or—frequent with Josquin and not uncommon with other composers of the time—with contrasting pairs of voices. (2) Division of the work into large sections, set off by simultaneous cadencing of all voices and by the introduction of changes in meter and tempo. (3) A rounded three-part form, resulting from the similarity of sections one and three and their contrast with section two. (4) A purposive approach to cadences: the cadence of one part may be signalized by a long preparation on the dominant with threefold repetition of the bass motive and the coming together of all voices in a chordal ensemble at the end; or by a similar piling-up of voices and a marked quickening of the harmonic pulse as well as of the movement of the individual voice-parts. This "drive to cadence" was characteristic of all Netherlands polyphony between 1480 and 1530.

Another example of Josquin's three-part structure is found in *Tu pauperum refugium* (Example 43; also, HAM, No. 90) which is itself the second half of a complete motet. The peculiar character of the third mode (Phrygian) and the effective use of chordal style in phrases fitted closely to the accent of the words contribute toward the somber, deeply moving quality of this music. The hymn-like middle section with its slightly lilting triple rhythm (Example 43b) is typical of many passages in Josquin's work, and offers a suitable foil, appropriate also to the text, to the first and third sections. The

voice pairing at the beginning of section three on the words "in Thee
I hope—in Thee I trust" (Example 43c) is an exceptionally fine use of
this device, suggested naturally by the parallelism of the words.

The closing measures of this motet of Josquin illustrate another
common early sixteenth-century usage, the prolongation of the
cadence by a pedal point in one or more voices while the others
oscillate gently back and forth before coming finally to rest. The last

Motet: *Tu pauperum refugium*, Josquin des Prez

Example 43a-c

a. Thou refuge of the poor

b. And now, Redeemer, Lord

c. In Thee I hope, in Thee I trust

chord, as is usual in this period, is an open fifth, which was still regarded as more perfect and final-sounding than a full triad.

In Josquin's music, more than in that of any previous composer, we
become aware of a consistent organization of the harmonies along the
lines of our own common practice. Though they are still rooted in the
modal system, the chord progressions and the general harmonic plan
in most of Josquin's works are to a large extent governed by dominant-
tonic relationships. One sign of this organization is the conduct of the
bass line: more and more it has begun to be distinguished from the
primarily melodic nature of the other voices and has begun to assume
the function of a harmonic support; consequently it often moves by
fourths and fifths (see Example 43). This kind of harmonic organization and this type of bass movement become increasingly prevalent in
the course of the sixteenth century.

Text and music

Josquin was particularly praised by his contemporaries for the care he took to suit his music to the text. His concern for correct declamation is most apparent in the syllabic pasages (especially those in familiar style) of his motets. *Tu pauperum refugium* is particularly instructive because it has a mixture of syllabic and melismatic styles. In the syllabic passages the setting of the Latin words is faithful both to the grammatical accent and to the emotional sense as well. But Josquin sometimes abandons the strictly syllabic setting for the sake of depicting the words even more graphically: at "laborantium" (the "heavy-laden"), by poignant suspensions; and at "errantium" (the "erring," or wandering ones; those who have lost the track) by a deliberately halting, directionless line in the altus. Among the wonderful tonal pictures in this motet is one at the words "ne unquam obdormiat in morte" ("lest ever [my soul] sleep the sleep of death"), where the drooping, descending lines of the voices going down one

Example 43d

116   *d.* Lest ever my soul sleep the sleep of death.

after another to the low dark tones of their register seem to bring the image of Death itself before us (Example 43d).

"Suiting the music to the meaning of the words, expressing the power of each different emotion, making the things of the text so vivid that they seem to stand actually before our eyes..."—these words are from a famous description of the music of another Netherlands composer,[2] but they apply equally well to Josquin. The author adds: "This kind of music is called *musica reservata.*" This strange term (literally, "reserved music") seems to have come into use shortly after the middle of the sixteenth century to denote the advanced or "new" style of those composers who, motivated by a desire to give strong and detailed reflection of the words, introduced chromaticism, harmonic freedom, ornaments, and contrasts of rhythm and texture in their music to a degree hitherto unknown. Insofar as "musica reservata" refers to vivid musical expression of moods and images suggested by the text, one may justly call Josquin its originator, or at least its precursor.

Compositions in syllabic chordal style, like *Tu pauperum refugium,* are a minority of his total production; but expressive rendition of the text is common in his more conventional contrapuntal style as well. The ending of the motet *Absalon fili mi* ("O my son Absalom": David's lament, II Samuel 18: 33) has an extraordinary passage of tone-painting on the words "but go down weeping to the grave" (Example 44). Here the voices descend not only melodically but also harmonically, taking the music through the circle of fifths from G to E-flat. In one manuscript of this motet the music lies a major sixth lower than in our example, so that the extreme key becomes G-flat. If this is the original form of the work, it shows Josquin as a bold

Motet: *Absalon fili mi,* Josquin des Prez

Example 44

experimenter, for the early sixteenth century as a rule never went beyond E-flat, and even this note occurred only rarely.

Josquin excelled as a tone-painter not only of death and gloom, however; apart from the chansons, which are anything but gloomy, there are passages like the tender lyric interlude in triple rhythm from the second part of the Christmas motet *Mittit ad Virginem*, that "combination of cradle song, pastorale, and angelic hymn"; or the playful musical punning on the last two words of the motet *Virgo prudentissima*, which ends *electa ut sol* ("clear as the sun"; Song of Solomon, 6: 10), giving occasion for a procession of *ut-sols* to stalk through the four voices in turn;

or the incomparable prayer for peace to the Lamb of God at the end of the Mass *Pange lingua*.

Josquin was a composer of the period of transition between medieval and modern times, as Monteverdi was between the Renaissance and Baroque, Handel between the Baroque and Classical periods, and Beethoven between the Classical and Romantic. Josquin and Beethoven resemble each other in many ways. In both, the strong impulse of personal utterance struggled against the limits of the musical language of their time. Both were tormented by the creative process, and worked slowly and with numerous revisions. Both had a sense of humor; both, because of their independent attitude, had trouble with their patrons. Both, in their best works, achieved that combination of intensity and order, individuality and universality, which is the mark of genius. It may be added that both annoyed fastidious critics for the same reasons: "He lacked moderation, and the judgment that comes from sound learning, so that he did not always properly curb the violent impulses of his imagination." This was said by the Swiss theorist Glarean[3] about Josquin, whom he nevertheless admired above all other composers.

Some Contemporaries of Obrecht and Josquin

A general history of music must, for lack of space, renounce all hope of doing justice to the many excellent composers of the early sixteenth century who were contemporary with Obrecht and Josquin. *Henricus Isaac* Henricus Isaac (*ca.* 1450–1517), a Netherlander by birth, was a prolific composer in all the forms current in his time; he absorbed into his own style musical influences from Italy, France, Germany, and the Netherlands, so that his output is more fully international in character than that of any other composer of his generation. He wrote a large number of songs with French, German, and Italian texts, and many other short chanson-like pieces which, since they occur without words in the sources, are usually regarded as having been composed for instrumental ensembles. The melody of one of his German polyphonic songs, *Isbruck, ich muss dich lassen* ("Innsbruck, I now must leave thee"), was later adapted to sacred words and became widely known under the title *O Welt, ich muss dich lassen* ("O world, I now must leave thee").

Isaac's sacred compositions include some thirty settings of the Ordinary of the Mass and a cycle of motets based on the liturgical texts and melodies of the Proper of the Mass (including many sequences) for a large portion of the church year. This monumental cycle of motets was commissioned by the church at Constance, and is known as the *Choralis Constantinus*. Its musical style is representative of the Netherlands practice of Isaac's time: a prevalent texture of imitative counterpoint is clarified by repetitions and melodic sequences, and it is often evident that Isaac took particular care to emphasize important or dramatic words. Many of the melodic lines, especially in the altus and bassus voices, have a rather unvocal character which is not uncommon in the works of this period, and which may or may not indicate that the composer had instrumental performance in mind.

One of the foremost Netherlands composers of the early sixteenth century was Pierre de la Rue (*ca.* 1460–1518), whose numerous Masses and motets still await a comprehensive modern edition. The supreme example of his technical skill is the Mass *Ave Sanctissima*. This is a parody Mass based on a motet which is perhaps by La Rue himself although it is also attributed to another Netherlander, Philippe Verdelot (d. *ca.* 1540). La Rue's *Ave Sanctissima* is thought to be the earliest Mass for six voices, and is written entirely in canon: from three notated voices three others are derived by canonic imitation at the fourth above, at various distances in each movement. The miracle, however, is not the technique but the music itself, for within this rigid and extremely difficult technical framework La Rue created one of the most beautiful settings ever made of the Mass.

VII New Currents in the Sixteenth Century

The Netherlands Generation of 1520-1550

The thirty years between 1520 and 1550 witnessed a constantly growing diversity of musical expression. In every country new types and forms of vocal music began gradually to modify the dominant cosmopolitan style of the Netherlands; the amount and importance of instrumental music also increased. In the Mass the parody method of composition gradually replaced the older technique of a single *cantus firmus*. Liturgical chants were still commonly used as the melodic substance of both Masses and motets, but in general they were treated quite freely. In both motets and Masses, composers were beginning to write for five or six voices in preference to the earlier standard four.

The classical Netherlands motet style of the period 1520–50 is found in the works of Nicolas Gombert (*ca.* 1490–1556), supposedly a pupil of Josquin. His motet *Super flumina Babilonis* (HAM, No. 114) exemplifies this style: a continuous series of imitative sentences with interlocking cadences, save for a single short contrasting section in triple meter and fauxbourdon harmonies; a generally smooth and uniform texture, without many rests, with all dissonances carefully prepared and resolved—quite undramatic in effect as compared with many of the works of Josquin, though not without a sensitive feeling for the rhythm and general mood of the text. The majority of Gombert's 160 motets are divided into two approximately equal parts or sections; and in some instances these are thematically connected by the use of closing portions identical in both text and music.

Another important Netherlands composer of this period was Jacob Clement or, in Latinized form, Jacobus Clemens (*ca.* 1510–*ca.* 1556); he was called "Clemens non Papa," probably to distinguish him from a poet named Jacobus Papa who lived in the same city of Ypres. Clemens's Latin motets are similar in style to those of Gombert.

The most notable Netherlander in Italy near the middle of the

Nicolas Gombert

Jacobus Clemens

sixteenth century was Adrian Willaert. Born around 1490 in Flanders, Willaert in 1527 was appointed director of the music in St. Mark's Cathedral at Venice. Here he remained until his death in 1562, conducting, composing, and training many eminent pupils, through whom his fame and influence spread all over Italy. He was the principal founder of the Venetian school of composition for two or more choruses, a school which was pre-eminent during the second half of the sixteenth century.

The majority of Willaert's motets were rooted in the Netherlands style, although the traditional contrapuntal texture frequently shaded over into a more homophonic, chordal sound. An example is *Victimae paschali laudes* (HAM, No. 113), in which the melodic life of the individual lines seems cramped because of the full, rather opaque texture of six voices; in place of the freely flowing long melismas of the early Netherlanders, Willaert's phrases are shorter and move in a narrower compass, mostly syllabically and with many repeated notes; the bass has lost nearly all melodic character, and functions as the foundation of a harmonic structure. The plainsong *cantus firmus* is retained in the old-fashioned manner in long notes in the quintus of this motet, after having been first introduced in the sextus; yet it is all but lost in the full rich sound of the surrounding harmonies.

The Rise of National Styles

Although Netherlands composers were scattered all over Western Europe in the early sixteenth century, and their idiom was a common international musical language, each country also had its own distinctive music which was certainly better known and probably better enjoyed by most people than the learned art of the Netherlanders. Gradually in the course of the sixteenth century these various national idioms rose to prominence and eventually caused the Netherlands style to be modified in varying degrees. The process was most clearly marked in Italy. When Petrucci started to print music at Venice in 1501, he began with chansons, Masses, and motets; but then, from 1504 to 1514, he published no fewer than eleven collections of strophic Italian songs, set syllabically to music in four parts, having marked rhythmic patterns and a definitely harmonic style with the melody in the upper voice. These songs were called *frottole* (singular, *frottola*).

Italy

The frottola

The religious counterpart of the frottola was the polyphonic *lauda* (pl. *laude*), a popular nonliturgical devotional song. The texts were sometimes in Italian, sometimes in Latin; these were set to four-part music, the melodies being often taken from secular songs. Two books of *laude* were published by Petrucci in 1507 and 1508. *Laude* were commonly sung in semi-public devotional gatherings, either *a cappella* or possibly with instruments playing the three lower voices. Like the *frottole*, the *laude* were syllabic, homophonic, and regularly rhythmic,

The lauda

with the melody practically always placed in the highest voice. In their simple harmonic settings they were often remarkably expressive.

France

French was always the language of the chanson as Latin was of the Mass. But although French composers of Masses and motets in the first half of the sixteenth century continued to write in a slightly modified version of the international style of the Netherlands, French chanson composers during the long reign of Francis I (1515–47) took a new direction. The result was a type of chanson quite different from those of Josquin and his Netherlands contemporaries, which were French in language and spirit, but Netherlandish in technique.

*The new
French chanson*

Chansons of the new type were light, fast, strongly rhythmic songs for four voices, syllabic, with many repeated notes, predominantly in duple meter with occasional passages in triple meter, and predominantly homophonic although not excluding short points of imitation; one is illustrated in Example 45. They had distinct short sections which as a rule were repeated so as to form an easily grasped pattern, such as *aabc* or *aaba*. The texts covered a considerable range of verse forms and subjects, a favorite topic being some amatory situation that might allow the poet occasion for all sorts of pleasant comments and equivocal allusions. Not all the texts, however, were frivolous.

The two principal composers of chansons around 1530 were Claudin de Sermisy (*ca.* 1490–1562) and Clément Janequin (*ca.* 1485 –*ca.* 1560). Janequin was particularly celebrated for his descriptive chansons in free form, songs not unlike the Italian fourteenth-century caccia, introducing imitations of bird calls, street cries, and the like. The most famous of Janequin's descriptive chansons was one entitled *La Guerre*, traditionally supposed to have been written about the Battle of Marignan (1515); it is the ancestor of innumerable "battle" pieces in the sixteenth century and afterward. The leading composer of chansons at Paris after Sermisy and Janequin was Pierre Certon (*ca.* 1510–1572) whose works ably continue the style founded by Sermisy.

Germany

Polyphony developed later in Germany than in the other countries of Western Europe. A distinctive type of German polyphonic song came into existence during the fifteenth century. The *Lochamer Liederbuch* (*Lochamer Songbook*) of 1452, one of the earliest collections of such songs, contains both monophonic melodies and three-part settings with the leading melody in the tenor part. Similar three-part settings are found in the *Glogauer Liederbuch* of about the same date.

*The German
polyphonic song*

Song composers skilfully combined German melodic material with a method of setting and a contrapuntal technique derived from the Netherlands. The first real masters of the polyphonic song were Isaac and his contemporary Heinrich Finck (1445–1527). In Isaac's *Zwischen Berg und tiefem Tal* ("Between Mountain and Deep Valley") a characteristically German melody—perhaps original, perhaps borrowed, perhaps even a folk song—is presented, phrase by phrase,

Chanson: *Fy, fy d'amours*, Claudin de Sermisy

Bah! Their love and their alliance are nothing but abuse, torment, and hardship, blows, mourning, boredom, labor, and mistrust; in fact, all they do is harm the soul and the body. Several have seen foolish people destroy and abandon God in order to devote themselves to love.

in canon by the bass and tenor; the other two voices anticipate each phrase with brief imitations in quicker rhythm. Part of this song is given in Example 46; the entire piece appears in HAM, No. 87. In performance possibly only the tenor was sung, the other parts being taken by instruments.

Polyphonic song: *Zwischen Berg und tiefem Tal*, Henricus Isaac

Example 46

Between mountain and deep valley lies an open road.

Another excellent composer of songs was Paul Hofhaimer (1459–1537), court organist of the Emperor Maximilian. With Ludwig Senfl (*ca.* 1490–1543), the polyphonic song reached a climax of artistic perfection; some of his songs are, in all respects except the language of the text, full-fledged motets of the Netherlands type, and most beautiful examples of that style. Senfl also wrote many shorter songs on folklike tenor tunes, filled with picturesque or humorous touches, yet always exhibiting a certain earthy, serious quality that seems inseparable from the German musical feeling.

Collections of German songs continued to be published during the first half of the sixteenth century, chiefly at Nuremberg, which was a leading center of German culture at this time. After 1550, German taste veered to Italian madrigals and villanelle, and consequently the song declined in importance or took on Italianate characteristics. Meanwhile, however, it had provided the musical model and a great deal of the musical material for the chorales or hymns of the Lutheran church.

Spanish sacred polyphony, like that of all continental Europe in the late fifteenth and early sixteenth centuries, was strongly under the influence of the Netherlands style. Gombert, Manchicourt, Crécquillon, and other Netherlanders worked from time to time in Spain, and Spanish manuscripts of the period include many works by Netherlands masters. Within its basic framework of Netherlands technique, however, Spanish sacred music was marked by a particular sobriety of melody and moderation in the use of contrapuntal artifices, together with a passionate intensity in the expression of religious emotion. These qualities may be heard in the music of Cristóbal de Morales (*ca.* 1500–1553), the most eminent Spanish composer of the early sixteenth century and one who had acquired fame in Italy during his residence at Rome from 1535 to 1545 as a member of the Papal chapel. Morales was one of a large number of Spanish composers in the sixteenth century; some of these men worked entirely in their own country, while others, like Morales and Victoria, were closely associated with the music of the church at Rome. As in Germany and Italy, so also in Spain: after the middle of the sixteenth century the traditional Netherlands technique was gradually absorbed into a new style of both sacred and secular music, a style determined in large part by national characteristics.

Spain

The greatest English composer of the first half of the sixteenth century was John Taverner (*ca.* 1495–1545). His Mass on an English melody *The Western Wind* is one of the exceptional instances of the use of a secular *cantus firmus* by an English composer. Toward the middle of the century, three other distinguished composers appeared: Christopher Tye (*ca.* 1500–*ca.* 1572), Thomas Tallis (*ca.* 1505–1585), and Robert White (*ca.* 1530–1574). All three wrote music for both the Roman and the Anglican churches, but their Latin motets are superior to their compositions with English words.

England

Tallis's *Lamentations* are among the most eloquent of all settings of these verses from the prophet Jeremiah, texts which first attracted the attention of composers shortly after the middle of the fifteenth century and which in the sixteenth century formed a distinct type of church composition. Tallis's motet *Audivi vocem de caelo* ("I Heard a Voice from Heaven") is an excellent specimen of mid-sixteenth-century English style; by that time the principle of systematic imitation had been thoroughly assimilated by English composers. One remarkable feature of the work (and it is a feature of much English music of the sixteenth century) is the essential vocality of the melodies; one senses on hearing or singing them that they have been conceived not as an interplay of abstract melodic lines, but as an interplay of *voices*—so closely is the melodic curve wedded to the natural cadence of the words, so imaginatively does it project their content, and so naturally does it lie for the singer. For instance, note the extraordinary effect of Tallis's apparently simple closing measures on the word "venit," given in Example 47; the entire motet is in HAM, No. 127.

Example 47   Closing Measures of Motet: *Audivi vocem de caelo*, Thomas Tallis

The Rise of Instrumental Music

Although the period from 1450 to 1550 was primarily an era of vocal polyphony, the same hundred years witnessed a growth of interest in instrumental music on the part of serious composers and the beginnings of independent styles and forms of writing for instruments. This statement does not imply that there was no instrumental music before 1450. As we have already seen, instruments took part with voices in the performance of every type of polyphonic music in the Middle Ages, although we cannot be certain of the extent or the exact manner of their participation. Moreover, a great deal of music

The walls of the private study of the Duke of Urbino in his palace at Gubbio are of intarsia in trompe-l'oeil. This corner displays a portative organ, what may be a viol, a lute, and two cornetts. This remarkable room was probably designed in the late fifteenth century by the Sienese Francesco de Giorgio. (Courtesy Metropolitan Museum of Art, Rogers Fund, 1939)

was performed purely instrumentally, including on occasion many of the compositions we customarily regard as at least partly vocal; medieval manuscripts that include keyboard arrangements and elaborations of cantilenas and motets undoubtedly represent only a fraction of the music that was transcribed in this way; and in addition independent instrumental music, in the form of dances, fanfares, and the like, has not come down to us apparently for the reason that it was always either played from memory or improvised. So the seeming increase in instrumental music after 1450 is to a considerable degree an illusion; it means only that now more of this music began to be written down and that consequently we are in a position to know something definite about it.

One sign of the sixteenth century's growing regard for instrumental music was the publication of books which describe instruments or give instructions for playing them. The first such publication was in 1511; others followed in increasing numbers throughout the century. It is significant that from the outset most of these books were written not in Latin but in the vernacular; they were addressed not to theorists, but to practical musicians. From them we can learn some of the problems of pitch, temperament, and tuning in this period, and can 127

VII. New
Currents
in the
Sixteenth
Century

Instruments

observe the importance that was attached to improvising ornaments on a given melodic line.

In Sebastian Virdung's *Musica getutscht und ausgezogen* (*A Summary of* [*the science of*] *Music in German*) of 1511, and much more fully in the second volume of Michael Praetorius's *Syntagma musicum* (*Treatise of Music*) of 1618, there are descriptions and woodcuts of

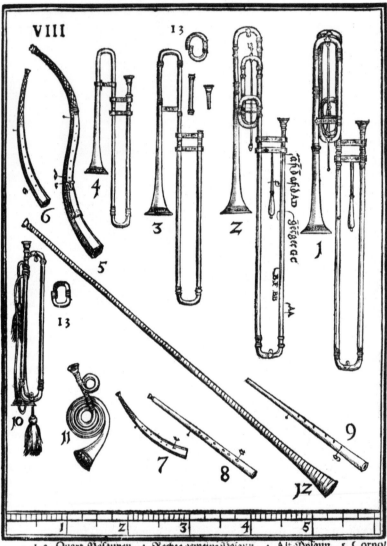

1. 2. Quart-Posaunen. 3. Rechte gemeine Posaun. 4. Alt-Posaun. 5. Cornol Groß Tenor-Cornet. 6. Recht Chor Zinck. 7. Klein Discant Zinck / so ein Quint höher. 8. Gerader Zinck mit eim Mundstück. 9. Still Zinck. 10. Trommet. 11. Jäger Trommet. 12. Hölzern Trommet. 13. Krumbbügel auff ein gantz Thon.

A plate from Michael Praetorius's Syntagma musicum, *showing sets of Renaissance horns: trombones (Nos. 1, 2, 3, and 4); cornetts (Nos. 5, 6, and 7, curved; Nos. 8 and 9, straight); trumpets (Nos. 10, 11, and 12); and (No. 13) a crook by the use of which a horn player could achieve extra tones.*

the various instruments in use during the sixteenth century. Two
things are of particular interest: the extraordinary number and variety
of wind instruments, and the fact that all instruments were built in
sets or families, so that one uniform timbre was available throughout
the entire range from bass to soprano. This is in keeping with the
Renaissance ideal of a homogeneous sound mass; the "chest" or "consort"—the complete set—of three to eight recorders or viols, for example, corresponded to the complete "family" of voices ranging from
bass to soprano.

Besides recorders, the principal wind instruments were the shawms
(double-reed instruments), cromornes (also with a double reed, but
softer than the shawms), and cornetts (made of wood or ivory, with
cup-shaped mouthpieces); the trumpets and trombones were softer in

*A shop for the manufacture of musical instruments. Among those shown
are the organ, harp, a harpsichord-type instrument, drums, kettledrum,
lute, trumpet, viol, flute, cromorne, recorders, and trumscheit. (Courtesy
Metropolitan Museum of Art)*

tone than their modern counterparts. The viols differed in many details of construction from the present-day violin family of bowed instruments: the neck was fretted, there were six strings tuned a fourth apart with a major third in the middle (as A-d-g-b-e'-a'), and the tone was more delicate, finer, less *espressivo*—because without vibrato—than that of modern instruments of the violin type.

Another indication of the Renaissance ideal was the rise to prominence of solo instruments which could by themselves cover the entire compass of tones with a uniform sonority. The tone of the organ began to be varied by the addition of solo stops and stops of softer sound, which could be combined with the unvariable principals and mixtures of the medieval instrument. By about 1500 the large church organ was similar in essentials to the instrument as we know it today,. although the pedal keyboard was employed in Germany and the Netherlands long before it was adopted in other countries. The medieval portative organ did not survive beyond the fifteenth century, but the sixteenth century had small positive organs, including the regal, which had reed pipes of a rather strident tone.

There were two types of stringed keyboard instruments, the clavichord and the harpsichord. In the clavichord, the tone was produced by a metal tangent which struck the string and remained in contact with it; the tone was delicate, but within narrow limits its volume could be controlled by the performer and a slight vibrato could be imparted. Instruments of the harpsichord type were built in different shapes and sizes, and were known under various names (virginal, spinet, clavecin, clavicembalo, among others); in all these the sound was produced by a quill plucking the string. The tone was more robust than that of the clavichord, but could scarcely be shaded by varying the pressure on the key; different timbres and degrees of loudness were possible only by a special mechanism of stops. The clavichord was essentially a solo instrument for use in small rooms; the harpsichord was used for both solo and ensemble playing.

By far the most popular household solo instrument of the Renaissance was the lute (see illustration below). Lutes had been known in Europe for over five hundred years; before the end of the sixteenth century they were being built in various sizes, often of costly materials and with exquisite workmanship. A Spanish type of lute, the *vihuela de mano*, had a guitar-like body; but the standard lute was pear-shaped. It had one single and five double strings, tuned G-c-f-a-d'-g'; the neck was fretted and the pegbox turned back at a right angle. The usual method of playing was to pluck the strings with the fingers. Chords, melodies, runs and ornaments of all kinds, even contrapuntal pieces, could be performed on the lute; it was used as a solo instrument, to accompany singing, and in ensembles, and a skilled player could produce a great variety of effects. A special kind of notation was invented for lutenists, called *tablature*, the principle of which was to show, not the pitch of each sound, but the point at

The lute

which the finger had to stop the strings in order to produce the required pitch. (See illustrations pages 151, 206.) Tablatures were devised also for viols and keyboard instruments.

The adaptation of vocal pieces to instrumental performance led naturally to certain species of instrumental compositions which, while not necessarily derived from any particular vocal piece, were obviously patterned on vocal prototypes. Such were the imitative *ricercar* and the *canzona*, instrumental counterparts respectively of the motet and chanson. The word *ricercar* comes from an Italian verb meaning both "to seek" or "search out," and "to attempt" or "try." Both of these meanings are reflected in the different types of instrumental pieces which in the first half of the sixteenth century are called *ricercari*. Most of these consist of a succession of themes without marked individuality or contrast, each of which was developed in imitation and interlocked with the next by overlapping the cadence— in effect, a textless imitative motet. Ricercari of this kind were usually intended for ensemble playing, but after about 1540 they were written also for keyboard instruments and for the lute; they differ from strict vocal style simply by freer voice leading and by the addition on the printed pages of typically instrumental embellishments.

Canzona is the Italian word for "chanson." An instrumental canzona in Italy was called a *canzon da sonar* ("chanson to be played") or *canzona alla francese* ("chanson in the French style"). Canzonas were written for both ensembles and solo instruments. The development of the canzona as an independent instrumental form in the second half of the sixteenth century had important historical consequences.

A considerable part of the instrumental music of the sixteenth century consists of dance pieces for lute, keyboard, or ensembles; as befits their purpose, these pieces usually have clearly marked and

Portrait of a Young Lute Player, *painted about 1522 by Francesco Ubertini Bacchiacca (1494?–1557). (Courtesy Isaac Delgado Museum of Art, New Orleans, Louisiana)*

131

quite regular rhythmic patterns, and are divided into distinct sections. There is little or no contrapuntal interplay of lines, though the principal melody may be highly ornamented or *colored*. Commonly the dances were grouped in pairs or threes, and these groups are the historical precursors of the instrumental dance suite of later times. A favorite combination was a slow dance in duple meter followed by a fast one in triple meter on the same tune, the second dance thus constituting a variation of the first. One instance of this kind of pairing of dances is the combination, frequently found in French publications of the sixteenth century, of *pavane* and *gaillarde*.

Compositions in improvisatory style, not based on any given *cantus firmus* but unfolding freely, often in a somewhat rambling fashion, with varying textures and without continued adherence to a definite meter or form, are found among the earliest specimens of music for solo players (this style being obviously unsuited to ensembles). Such pieces appeared under various names: prelude or *preambulum*, *fantasia*, or ricercare. The last name is strictly a misnomer; the true ricercare is the imitative type described above. But ricercari were often introduced by, or alternated with, sections in free improvisatory style, and hence the name ricercare came sometimes to be applied to compositions which consist in large part of such improvisatory sections.

One other important new form of composition, the *theme and variations*, probably began with the Spanish lute and keyboard composers in the first half of the sixteenth century. Here, as in other instrumental forms, the works of the great Spanish organist and composer Antonio de Cabezón (1510–1566) were outstanding. His keyboard variations on the *Song of the Cavalier* (HAM, No. 134) present the complete theme successively in the uppermost voice (twice), the tenor, the alto, and the bass, accompanied each time by a different contrapuntal network in the other parts—a basically simple scheme which is worked out with admirable taste and a satisfying sense of continuity from beginning to end. A form related to the theme with variations was the composition on a short ostinato pattern, the prototype of the later chaconne and passacaglia.

The Madrigal and Related Forms

The Italian madrigal of the sixteenth century had nothing in common with the madrigal of the *ars nova* except the name. The *ars nova* madrigal was a strophic song with a refrain (ritornello); the early sixteenth-century madrigal was a musical setting of a short non-strophic poem with no refrain. Those madrigals composed in the first period of madrigal production, from about 1530 to 1550, were usually set for four voices; after the middle of the century, five voices became the rule, although six-part settings were not infrequent. The word "voices" is to be taken literally: the madrigal was a piece of vocal chamber music intended ideally for performers with one singer to a part, although as always in the sixteenth century instrumental doubling or substitution was possible and indeed common.

A madrigal resembled a motet in that all the voice parts had equal importance; like a motet also, a madrigal was constructed as a series of overlapping sections, some contrapuntal and some homophonic, each based on a single phrase of the text. The artistry of the composers was shown in their ability to infuse this quasi-sectional form with a sense of continuity and proportioned climax, always reflecting and enhancing the spontaneous flow of the poetry. There are no more perfect examples in music of art concealing art. One important means of continuity was the harmonic organization, which in most madrigals is a fascinating blend of modern major tonality and ancient modality.

Although essentially similar in form to the motet, the madrigal was usually more varied and vivid. Of course it was not subject to the restrictions of style that prevailed in church music; and the free atmosphere of the secular surroundings in which madrigals were sung encouraged experimentation. Consequently, madrigal composers developed pictorial and expressive writing to an extraordinary degree, and particularly experimented with harmonic boldness. The madrigal was the most progressive form of composition in the late sixteenth century, as the motet had been in the earlier part of the century and the Mass before that.

Madrigals were sung in all sorts of courtly social gatherings; in Italy they were sung especially at meetings of the academies, societies organized in many cities for the study and discussion of literary, *Madrigal texts* scientific, or artistic matters. The output of madrigals and similar polyphonic songs in Italy was enormous: some two thousand collections (counting reprints and new editions) were printed between 1530 and 1600, and the flood of production continued well into the seventeenth century.

The leading early composers of Italian madrigals were Philippe Verdelot (*ca.* 1480–*ca.* 1540), a Fleming who worked at Venice and Florence; Costanzo Festa (ca. 1490–1545) of Rome, one of the few *Early madrigal* Italians in the Papal chapel in the early sixteenth century and one of *composers* the first Italian composers to offer competition to the Netherlanders; Adrian Willaert, the Netherlands master at Venice; and Jacob Arcadelt (*ca.* 1505–*ca.* 1560), a Netherlander who for a time was head of the Pope's chapel and later became a member of the Royal Chapel at Paris. Verdelot and Arcadelt composed French chansons as well as Italian madrigals, and Festa was also noted for his motets and Masses.

Festa's madrigal *Quando ritrova* (Example 48; the entire piece is in HAM, No. 129) is known in English translation as *Down in a Flow'ry Vale*. This piece illustrates a stage at which the madrigal form is still similar to the frottola. The homophonic setting suggests that such madrigals were performed by solo voice with instrumental accompaniment; as in the frottola, the symmetrical phrasing and occasional

Madrigal: *Quando ritrova*, Costanzo Festa

Example 48

When I find my shepherdess in the meadow, with the sheep in the pasture, I approach her and greet her.

repetitions in the music closely follow the structure of the poetry.

In the madrigals of Arcadelt, written a quarter of a century later than Verdelot's, the style has become more contrapuntal and the texture and spirit more refined; the voice parts are more nearly equal in melodic interest, and the music does not follow quite so rigidly the scheme of the verses. The delicacy of the pictorial effects in *Voi ve n'andat' al cielo* (Example 49; the entire piece appears in HAM, No. 130) is noteworthy: for example, the rising line at "cielo" ("heaven," Example 49a), echoed at "levarmi a volo" ("rise in flight," Example 49b); the suggestion of helpless struggle by the repeated "struggendo mi torno" ("but, striving, I fall back," Example 49b); and the allargando-like repeated closing cadence with the E-flat, reserved until this point in the piece to underline the important "in voi chiuso" ("enclosed within thee," Example 49c).

Important innovations in the madrigal were made with the publication in 1542 of the first book of five-part madrigals by Cipriano de Rore (1516–1565). Rore was a Netherlander who worked in Italy chiefly at Ferrara and Parma, although he also for a short time held the post of music director at St. Mark's in Venice as successor to his master Willaert. Rore's publications included five books of madrigals for five voices and three books for four voices; these and other works

*Cipriano
de Rore*

Madrigal: *Voi ve n'andat'al cielo*, Jacob Arcadelt

VII. New
Currents
in the
Sixteenth
Century

Example 49c

Guar - da - t'il mio ch' in voi chiu - so te - - ne - - te.

a. Thou risest to heaven
b. I would gladly rise in flight but, struggling, I fall back in pain and tears
c. Behold my [heart] which thou holdest enclosed within thee.

were issued repeatedly in new printings and editions throughout the second half of the sixteenth century.

Beginning with Rore, the normal setting of the Italian madrigal is for five voices, the fifth voice (*quinta pars*) being usually paired with one of the other four as a second tenor or second soprano. But the expansion of the form in this period was not alone a matter of sonority. All the dimensions were enlarged; in contrast to the regularity of the frottola and early madrigal in which each line of text was set to its own line of music, the text of the later sixteenth-century madrigal was handled freely, almost capriciously, the music now moving ahead, now lingering over a particular phrase or word to give it a special intensity: this point is illustrated in Rore's *Da le belle contrade*, Example 50, with the realism of the exclamations beginning at "t'en vai" ("thou goest"); the obvious but effective device of using a single voice for the words "sola mi lasci" ("thou leavest me solitary"); the dramatic pause before the climax at "ahi, crud'amor" ("ah, cruel love"); and the long, mournful descent of this phrase to "finisc'in pianto" ("end in tears"). Yet with all this detail the larger proportions of the piece are not neglected. The agitated rhythms and wayward harmonies of the middle portion (the entire piece appears in HAM, No. 131) are inclosed by two sections of clear F-major tonality in phrases of regular length, with a symmetrical repetition of the closing phrase.

Chromaticism

One result of the composers' desire to depict vividly the emotions of the text was their use of venturesome harmonic progressions, of which Example 50 furnishes instances. Chromatic passages were always written in a homophonic style, so that emphasis was given to the striking character of the chord successions; effect like the juxtaposition of the A major and C minor triads (Example 50, measures 11 and 12) became common expressive devices.

Netherlands madrigalists

Among the many Netherlanders who shared in the development of the Italian madrigal after the middle of the century, three in particular must be mentioned: Orlando di Lasso, Philippe de Monte, and Giaches de Wert. Orlando di Lasso (1532–1594) is most important as a church composer, but his was a universal genius equally at home with the madrigal, the chanson, and German song. Philippe de Monte (1521–1603), like Lasso, was prodigiously productive in both the sacred and

136

Madrigal: *Da le belle contrade*, Cipriano de Rore

137

Example 50
(cont.)

Thou goest, alas! Farewell! Thou leavest me solitary. Farewell! What will become of me here, forgotten and sorrowing? Ah, cruel Love! Uncertain and brief are Thy pleasures, and it pleases Thee that the highest joy should end in tears.

secular fields; he began writing madrigals in his youth in Italy and continued uninterruptedly through the many years of his service under the Hapsburg Emperors in Vienna and Prague. He published thirty-two collections of secular madrigals, in addition to three or four books of *madrigali spirituali* on texts of religious devotion. Giaches de Wert (1535–1596), though of Netherlands birth, spent nearly his entire life in Italy; he further developed the style of madrigal composition begun by Rore and exercised an important influence on Monteverdi.

The leading madrigalists toward the end of the century were Italians. Luca Marenzio (1553–1599) was a composer of remarkable *Luca Marenzio* artistry and technique, in whose works contrasting feelings and visual details were depicted with utmost virtuosity. As was typical of madrigal composers of the late sixteenth century, Marenzio mainly used pastoral poetry as his texts. One of the most celebrated of his madrigals is a setting of a Petrarchan sonnet in which the mood of the opening lines

Solo e pensoso i più deserti campi	Alone, thought-sick, I pace where none has been,
Vo misurando a passi tardi e lenti	Roaming the desert with dull steps and slow[1]

is suggested by means of a slow chromatic scale in the topmost voice, rising without a break from g' to a'' and returning to d'', while the other voices form a background of expressively drooping figures for the first line and all but come to a dragging halt for the second—a masterpiece of sensitive musical imagery, harmonic refinement, and skilful contrapuntal writing.

The height of chromaticism in the Italian madrigal was reached not in the works of Marenzio but in those of Carlo Gesualdo, Prince of Venosa (*ca.* 1560–1613), a picturesque character who was both musician and murderer. In some of his later madrigals Gesualdo carries chromatic harmony to a point that almost suggests Wagner. Sometimes with Gesualdo the chromaticism is mere mannerism, style for style's sake; but at its best it is a sincerely felt and deeply moving response to the text (see Example 51; the entire madrigal appears in HAM, No. 161).

Carlo Gesualdo

The musician who served as a transition figure from the sixteenth century to the seventeenth—that is, from the Renaissance to Baroque —was Claudio Monteverdi (1567–1643), one of the major composers in the history of Western music. In 1590 Monteverdi entered the service of Vincenzo Gonzaga, Duke of Mantua, and from 1613 until his death in 1643 he was choirmaster at St. Mark's in Venice.

Claudio Monteverdi

The works of Monteverdi with which we are concerned at present are the first four books of madrigals, published respectively in 1587, 1590, 1592, and 1603. In these madrigals Monteverdi, without going to such extremes as Gesualdo, demonstrated his mastery of the madrigal technique of the late sixteenth century, with its smooth combination of homophonic and contrapuntal part-writing, its faithful reflection of the text, and its freedom in the use of expressive harmonies and dissonances. But there were certain features—not altogether absent in the music of his contemporaries—which showed that Monteverdi was moving swiftly and with remarkable assurance toward the new style of the seventeenth century. For example, many of the musical motives are not melodic but declamatory, in the manner of recitative; the texture often departs from the Renaissance ideal of equal voices and becomes a duet over a harmonically supporting bass; and certain formal practices characteristic of the Baroque are foreshadowed. As an example of the flexible, animated, vivid, and variegated style of Monteverdi's sixteenth-century madrigals, rich in musical invention, humorous and sensitive, audacious yet perfectly logical in harmonies, the five-voice madrigal *Ohimè, se tanto amate*, first published in Book IV in 1603, will repay study. (Example 52; the entire piece is in HAM, No. 188.) A work like this represents the limits of the *a cappella* madrigal style, the culmination of a century of development.

The madrigal was not the only type of Italian secular polyphony in the sixteenth century. Among the lighter varieties of song was the *canzon villanesca* (peasant song) or *villanella*, which first appeared around Naples in the 1540's and flourished chiefly in the Neapolitan

area. The villanella was a three-voice, strophic, lively little piece in
homophonic style, in which composers often deliberately used parallel
fifths—originally to suggest its supposedly rustic character, later perhaps to caricature the suave correctness of the madrigals, which were
often parodied in both the words and music of the villanella. Neither
the villanella nor any of the other lighter types of Italian song are to
be regarded as distinctively popular or nationalistic; they were written
by the same Italians and Netherlanders who composed serious madrigals, and were meant for the same sophisticated audiences. In the
course of time the villanella became like the madrigal and gradually
lost its own identity.

*Other Italian
secular vocal
forms*

Example 51   Madrigal: *Io pur respiro*, Gesualdo

...give an end [at once] to life and to [my] great pain.

Claudio Monteverdi (1567–1643).
(Fratelli Bocca, Milan)

By the end of the sixteenth century the most important lighter forms of Italian vocal polyphony were the *canzonetta* ("little song") and the *balletto*. These two forms are very similar; they are written in a neat, vivacious homophonic style, with clear major-minor harmonies and distinct, evenly phrased sections which are often repeated. *Balletti*, as the name suggests, were intended for dancing as well as singing or playing; a "fa-la-la" refrain is one of their characteristics. The leading

Madrigal: *Ohimè, se tanto amate*, Monteverdi   Example 52

141

Example 52
(cont.)

a. Alas! If you love so much to hear me say "Alas!" why do you cause to die him who says "Alas"?

b. ... then you will have from me thousands and thousands of sweet "alas's".

composer of canzonette and balletti was Giacomo Gastoldi (d. 1622). Both forms were extremely popular in Italy, and were imitated by German and English composers.

The chief figure among the international composers in Germany in the sixteenth century was the Netherlander, Orlando di Lasso, who entered the service of Duke Albrecht V of Bavaria in 1556 or 1557, became head of the ducal chapel in 1560, and remained in that post at Munich until his death in 1594. Among the vast number of Lasso's compositions were seven collections of German polyphonic songs. The song *Ich armer Mann* has somewhat uncouth verses which Lasso matched with appropriate music (see Example 53; the entire piece is given in GMB, No. 125). Lasso's setting no longer surrounds a familiar tune in the tenor by a web of counterpoint, as was done in earlier German songs; instead, he sets the text in the manner of a madrigal, with all the parts having equal importance in the variegated interplay of motives, bits of imitation, echoes, and mock-pathetic melismas at the phrase "muss ich im hader stahn" ("I must always be bickering").

A union of Italian sweetness with German seriousness was achieved in the music of the greatest German composer of the late sixteenth century, Hans Leo Hassler. Born at Nuremberg in 1564, Hassler was studying in 1584 with Andrea Gabrieli at Venice; from 1585 until his death in 1612 he held various positions at Augsburg, Nuremberg, Ulm,

Orlando di Lasso

and Dresden. His works comprise instrumental ensemble and keyboard pieces, canzonets and madrigals with Italian texts, German songs, Latin motets and Masses, and settings of Lutheran chorales. The two songs, *Ach Schatz* (HAM, No. 165) and *Ach, süsse Seel'* (GMB, No. 152), are good examples of Hassler's music, and show his suave melodic lines, sure harmonic structure, and clearly articulated form with its varied repetitions and balanced echoing of motives. Hassler's work stands nearly at the end of the age of German Renaissance polyphony for equal voices. The only notable German composers in this style after Hassler were Johann Hermann Schein (1586–1630) and Heinrich Schütz (1585–1672); but their German songs and madrigals in Italian style were youthful works, and both men were more important for the Baroque than the Renaissance.

France

In France and the Netherlands the chanson continued to flourish in the second half of the sixteenth century. The old polyphonic tradition remained alive longest in the north, as may be seen from two books of chansons published by the Netherlands composer Jan Sweelinck (1562–1621) in 1594 and 1612. In France, however, the tradition was modified by a lively interest in the Italian madrigal, the effects of which on French music were particularly evident in the period from 1560 to 1575. One of the principal mediators of the Netherlandish-Italian influence in France was Orlando di Lasso, whose powerful musical personality impressed itself on the chanson as on every other type of vocal composition in the later sixteenth century. Many of Lasso's chansons with French texts are written in a tight polyphonic texture with close imitations and sudden changes of pace in tense, delightfully humorous settings; others are in the homophonic style of the Parisian chanson, with fascinatingly varied rhythms which seem to spring spontaneously from each nuance and accent of the text. An example of a homophonic chanson, which also illustrates Lasso's uncanny gift for penetrating to the essential qualities of a style, is *Bon jour, mon coeur* (Example 54; the entire chanson is given in HAM, No. 145a).

Note the way in which both the harmonic progressions and the

Example 53   Song: *Ich armer Mann*, Orlando di Lasso

I, poor man, what have I done? I have taken a wife. [It would be better if I had never done it; how often I have rued it you may well imagine:] all day long I am being scolded and nagged, [at bedtime and at table].

145

Johann Hermann Schein (1586–1630).

melodic lines of the three upper voices bring out the correct accentuation of the first four words:

Bon jóur mon coéur
C: V   IV   I   V

It is obvious that no system of regular barring can accurately indicate the changing rhythmic patterns of this music, though they may be suggested by barring somewhat as in Example 54.

Other chanson composers in France in the latter part of the sixteenth century were Claude Le Jeune (1528–1600), Guillaume Costeley (1531–1606), and Jacques Mauduit (1557–1627). Many of Le Jeune's chansons are serious polyphonic works in several sections for five or more voices, and have other points of similarity to the Italian madrigals of the Rore period. The later Italian madrigal experiments (for example, those of Marenzio and Gesualdo) were not favorably received in France; on the other hand, the villanella and balletto had many French imitators.

Along with the polyphonic chanson, a different type of chanson appeared in France about 1550. These new chansons were strictly homophonic, short, strophic, often with a refrain, and usually performed as a solo with lute accompaniment. They were at first called *vaudevilles*, a word whose etymology and precise meaning are obscure; later this type of song was known as an *air* or *air de cour* ("court tune"). The forms taken by these compositions in homophonic style with a musical meter bound to the meter of the text reflected the experiments of some poets and composers who in 1570 formed an *Académie de Poésie et de Musique* (Academy of Poetry and Music) under the patronage of King Charles IX. The poet Jean-Antoine de Baïf wrote strophic French verses in ancient classical meters (*vers*

**Musique
mesurée**

146

mesurés à l'antique), substituting for the modern accentual principle the ancient Latin usage of long and short syllables; and composers (Le Jeune, Mauduit, and others) set these verses to music for voices *a cappella*, strictly observing the rule of a long note for each long syllable and a note half as long for each short syllable. The variety of verse patterns thus produced a corresponding variety of musical rhythms in which duple and triple groupings were freely alternated. This *measured music* (*musique mesurée*), as it was called, was too artificial a creation to endure for long, but it did serve to introduce

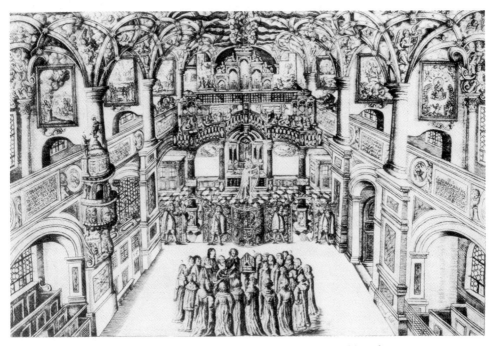

Heinrich Schütz (1585–1672) surrounded by his singers in the Chapel of the Elector of Saxony in Dresden; he was master of the Chapel from 1617 to his death.

nonregular rhythms into the later air de cour, a feature which remained characteristic of this form as it was developed by a school of French composers in the first half of the seventeenth century; and after about 1580, the air de cour was the predominant type of French vocal music.

The golden age of secular song in England came later than in the Continental countries. In 1588 (the year of the Spanish Armada), Nicholas Yonge published at London *Musica transalpina*, a collection *England* of Italian madrigals in English translation; many of these madrigals had doubtless been circulating in manuscript for several years before Yonge's book came out. Four more collections of Italian madrigals appeared in the next decade, and these publications gave the initial 147 impulse to the brief but brilliant period of the English madrigal and the solo air (or *ayre*, in the usual Elizabethan spelling) with lute accompaniment. Within the short space of about thirty years were published the works of composers whose names will always be honored in the history of British music; of these, Thomas Morley (1557–

Example 54   Chanson: *Bon jour, mon coeur*, Orlando di Lasso

Good day, my heart; good day, my sweet life; good day, my eye; good day, my sweetheart. Ah! good day, my pretty one, my sweet one; good day, my delight, my love, my gentle springtime, my sweet new flower, my sweet pleasure, my dove.

1602), Thomas Weelkes (*ca.* 1575–1623), and John Wilbye (1574–1638) are the most illustrious among the madrigalists, and John Dowland (1562–1626) and Thomas Campion (1567–1620) among the lutenist song writers, although there were several other masters of almost equal rank with those named. William Byrd (1543–1623), the greatest English composer of this period, wrote excellent madrigals, but his genius, on the whole, is less evident in this field than in that of keyboard and church music.

A comprehensive idea of the English madrigal may be obtained from *The Triumphes of Oriana*, a collection edited and published by Thomas Morley in 1601, and doubtless suggested by a similar Italian anthology called *Il Trionfo di Dori*, published in 1592. Each of the twenty-five madrigals in Morley's collection is by a different composer; all the pieces presumably acclaim Queen Elizabeth I (reg. 1558–1603), and each madrigal ends with the words "Long live fair Oriana," a name from the conventional vocabulary of pastoral poetry often applied to Elizabeth. A large proportion of English madrigal texts are pastoral poems, for the most part anonymous. An example of a madrigal with a pastoral text is John Bennet's *Thyrsis, sleepest thou?* (MM, No. 28). The different pictorial suggestions in the text—as at the words "holla," "hold up," "cuckoo," "sighed," "drive him back"—are wittily taken up in Bennet's music.

The expressive and pictorial traits in the music of the madrigals are combined with a wonderfully accurate, nimble declamation of the English texts. The accents of the words are maintained independently in each voice (to appreciate this feature fully, remember that the barlines of modern editions did not exist in the original), so that the ensembles produce sparkling counterpoint of endless rhythmic vitality. Moreover, with all the sharpness of detail, the long line of the music is never obscured. Bennet's *Thyrsis* reflects the madrigal's blend of major and medieval tonalities: despite its signature of two flats, for the most part it is written in F major; but it also is strongly attracted toward the subdominant key of B-flat because of the flatted seventh degree characteristic of the Mixolydian mode. On the other hand, Morley's *My bonny lass* (HAM, No. 159) is clearly in G major, with a nice balance of tonic and dominant harmonies.

There is little chromaticism of an extreme sort in English madrigals; composers occasionally resorted to chromatic harmonies for the special purpose of expressing distress or grief, as in the remarkably beautiful opening of the second part of Weelkes's *O Care, thou wilt despatch me* (Example 55) or the ending of his *Cease sorrows now*; but such passages are not frequent.

In addition to madrigals properly so called, a few composers—notably Morley and Weelkes—wrote songs in a predominantly homophonic four-part texture with a tune in the topmost voice, in dance-like meter, and with distinct sections set off by full cadences; some of the sections were repeated, resulting in formal patterns such as *AABB*,

Madrigal: *O Care, thou wilt despatch me,* Thomas Weelkes

Example 55

and the entire composition usually consisted of two or more strophes
sung to the same music. These songs were called *balletts* or *Fa-las*
(from the refrain syllables); both the name and the style, and sometimes even the musical themes, were taken from Italian *balletti,* particularly those of Gastoldi. Some of the balletts, for example Morley's
My bonny lass and Weelkes's *Hark, all ye lovely saints,* are among
the most charming and best-known productions of the English madrigal composers. Both madrigals and balletts were written primarily for
unaccompanied solo voices, although many of the published collections of partbooks indicate on the title page that the music is "apt for
voices and viols," presumably in any available combination. Indeed,
the ability to read a part, either vocally or instrumentally, in the performance of such pieces was expected of an educated person in
Elizabethan England.

The solo song with lute accompaniment, popular on the Continent
since the early part of the sixteenth century, was taken up in England

in 1597 with the publication of Dowland's *First Book of Songs or Ayres,* the first of many such collections issued throughout the following twenty years. These songs are fully equal in artistic quality to the madrigals; the poetry, in fact, is usually considerably better, and the composers' perception of the rhythms of the text is just as sensitive. However, the ayres have none of the madrigalesque pictorial touches, and their mood is uniformly lyrical. The accompaniments are completely subordinated to the voice, with no independent contrapuntal interest. The voice and lute parts are usually printed on the same page in vertical alignment, evidently so the singer could accompany himself. In some collections the songs are printed both this way and in an alternative version with the lute part written out for three voices and the staffs so arranged on the page that singers or players sitting around a table could all read their parts from the same book (see illustration below). These vocal and instrumental versions rarely differ except in slight details.

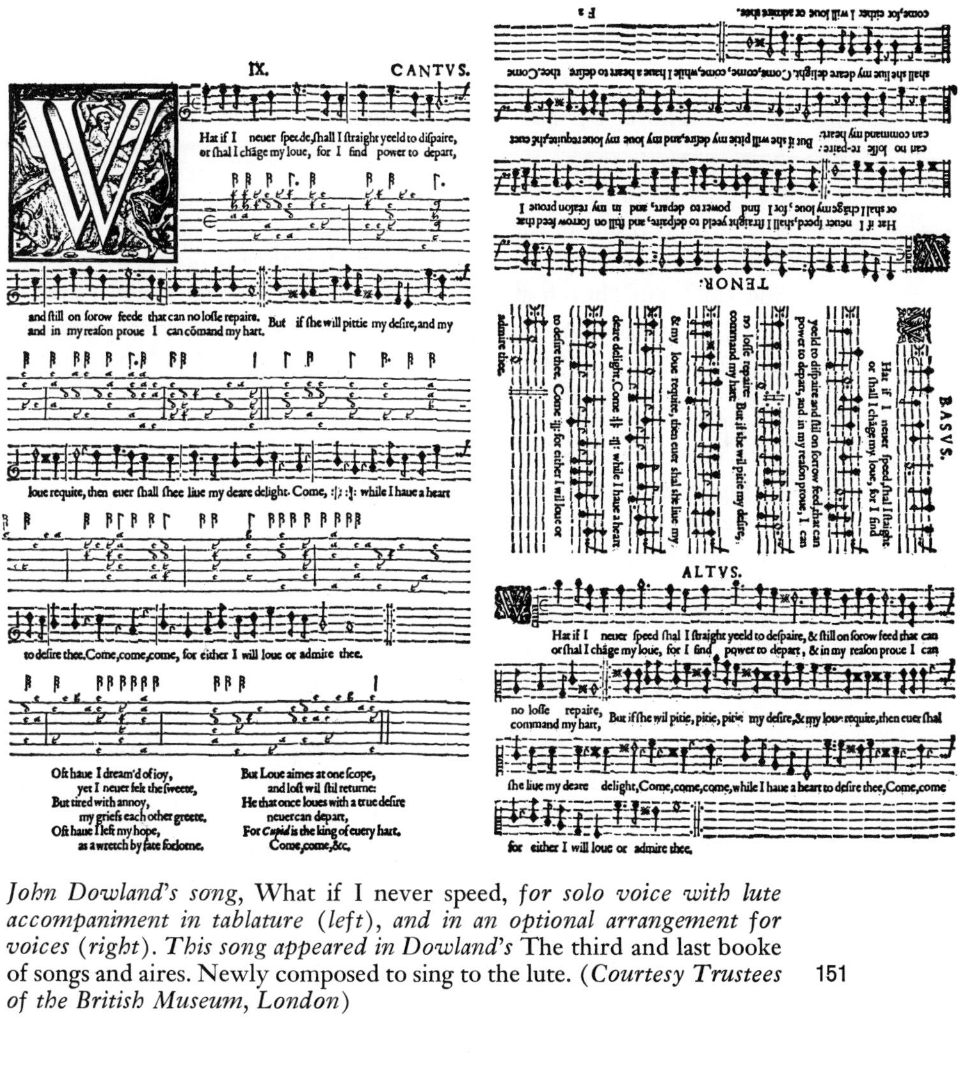

John Dowland's song, What if I never speed, *for solo voice with lute accompaniment in tablature (left), and in an optional arrangement for voices (right). This song appeared in Dowland's* The third and last booke of songs and aires. Newly composed to sing to the lute. (*Courtesy Trustees of the British Museum, London*)

VIII Church Music and Instrumental Music in the Late Renaissance

The Music of the Reformation in Germany

Martin Luther

When Martin Luther posted his ninety-five theses on the church door at Wittenberg in 1517, he had no intention of initiating a movement that would result in the formation of organized Protestant churches completely separate from Rome. Even after the break was irreparable, the Lutheran church still retained much of the traditional Catholic liturgy, along with a considerable use of Latin in the services; and similarly, much Catholic music, both plainsong and polyphony, was kept, sometimes with the original Latin text, sometimes with the original text translated into German, or sometimes with new German texts adapted to the old melodies (called *contrafacta* or parodies).

The position of music in the Lutheran church, especially in the sixteenth century, reflected Luther's own convictions on this subject. He was a lover of music, a singer, a composer of some skill, and a great admirer of Netherlands polyphony and of the works of Josquin des Prez in particular. He published as early as 1526 a *German Mass* (*Deutsche Messe*), which followed the main outlines of the Roman Mass, though with many changes of detail: the Gloria was omitted; new recitation tones were used, adapted to the natural cadence of the German language; several parts of the Proper were omitted or condensed, and for the remainder, as well as for most of the Ordinary, German hymns were substituted. But Luther never intended either this formula or any other to prevail uniformly in the Lutheran churches, and almost every imaginable combination and compromise between the Roman usage and the new ideas could be found somewhere in Germany sometime in the sixteenth century. Latin Masses and motets continued to be sung, and Latin remained in the liturgy at some places even into the eighteenth century: at Leipzig in Bach's time, for example, considerable portions of the services were still sung in Latin.

The most distinctive and important musical contribution of the Lutheran church was the strophic congregational hymn called in German a *Choral* or *Kirchenlied* ("church song") and in English a *chorale*. Since most people today are acquainted with these hymns chiefly in four-part harmonized settings, it must be pointed out that the chorale, like plainsong and folk song, consists essentially of only two elements, a text and a tune; but—also like plainsong and folk song —the chorale lends itself to enrichment through harmony and counterpoint and can be expanded into large musical forms. As most Catholic church music in the sixteenth century was an outgrowth of plainsong, so much Lutheran church music of the seventeenth and eighteenth centuries was an outgrowth of the chorale.

For a long time the demand for suitable songs in the Lutheran church far exceeded the supply. Luther himself wrote many chorale verses, for example, the well known *Ein' feste Burg* ("A mighty fortress"); it has never been definitely established that Luther wrote the melody of this chorale (first printed in 1529), though the music is generally ascribed to him. Many chorale tunes were newly composed, but even more were made up entirely or partly from songs already existing. Thus the Gregorian hymn *Veni Redemptor gentium* became *Nun komm' der Heiden Heiland* ("Come, Saviour of the nations"); familiar nonliturgical spiritual songs were taken over, for example, the mixed Latin-German Christmas hymn *In dulci jubilo* or the German Easter song *Christ lag in Todesbanden* ("Christ lay in death's dark prison"), later rearranged by Luther on the model of the Easter sequence *Victimae paschali laudes*.

A particularly important class of chorales were the *contrafacta* or parodies of secular songs, in which the given melody was retained but the text was either replaced by completely new words or else altered so as to give it a properly spiritual meaning. The use of secular songs and the parodying of secular compositions for church purposes was common in the sixteenth century, as we have already seen in the history of the Mass. Perhaps the most famous and certainly one of the most beautiful of the parodied chorales was *O Welt, ich muss dich lassen* ("O world, I now must leave thee"), adapted from Isaac's song, *Innsbruck, I now must leave thee*. A later and somewhat startling example was the tune from Hassler's song *Mein Gmüt ist mir verwirret* ("My peace of mind is shattered" [by a tender maiden's charms]), which about 1600 was set to the sacred words *Herzlich thut mich verlangen* ("My heart is filled with longing") and later to *O Haupt voll Blut und Wunden* ("O sacred head now wounded"). The transfiguration of the opening phrase of this song from Hassler's original version into one of the settings in Bach's *Passion according to St. Matthew* is shown in Example 56.

VIII. Church
Music and
Instrumental
Music in the
Late
Renaissance

Lutheran composers early began to write polyphonic settings for chorales. In 1524 Luther's principal musical collaborator, Johann Walter (1496–1570), published a volume of thirty-eight German chorale settings together with five Latin motets; this collection was expanded, with a larger proportion of Latin motets, in subsequent editions, of which the fifth and last appeared in 1551. A more important collection of 123 polyphonic chorale arrangements and motets was issued at Wittenberg in 1544 by Georg Rhaw (1488–1548), the leading music publisher of Lutheran Germany. Unlike Walter's work,

*Polyphonic
chorale settings*

Example 56a

Hassler, *Mein Gmüth ist mir verwirret*

Example 56b

J. S. Bach, *Passion according to St. Matthew*

At the time of my departing, forsake me not; when I shall suffer death, be thou my help.

this was a compilation of pieces by all the leading German and Swiss-German composers of the first half of the sixteenth century, including Ludwig Senfl, Thomas Stoltzer (*ca.* 1475–1526), Benedictus Ducis (*ca.* 1490–1544), Sixtus Dietrich (*ca.* 1490–1548), Arnold von Bruck (*ca.* 1470–1554), and a Netherlander, Lupus Hellinck (*ca.* 1495–1541). The chorale settings in these and other sixteenth-century collections naturally varied considerably in style; some used the older technique of the German polyphonic song, with the plain chorale tune in long notes in the tenor, surrounded by three or more parts in free-flowing polyphony, with independent motives and little use of imitation; others were like the Netherlands motets, with each phrase of the chorale being developed imitatively through all the voices; still others were in a simple, almost chordal style. Through the first half of the century there was a general trend toward this last style of simplified writing.

In the last third of the century chorales began to be published in *cantional* style, that is, in plainly chordal, hymn-like, rhythmically

154

straightforward settings with the tune in the topmost voice. The chief composers of cantional settings in the early seventeenth century were H. L. Hassler, Michael Praetorius (1571–1621), and Johann Hermann Schein (1586–1630).

By the end of the sixteenth century many Lutheran regions of Germany had returned to the Catholic faith, and the line between Protestant north and Catholic south was fixed substantially as it has remained to this day. With this definitive separation, a new and distinctive kind of Lutheran polyphonic church music emerged. Composers began to use the traditional melodies as the basic material for free artistic creation, to which they added individual interpretation and pictorial details. These new settings were called *chorale motets.*

An example of the Lutheran chorale motet is the *bicinium* (two-part song) based on the chorale *Our Father*, by Michael Praetorius (Example 57; see also HAM, No. 167a, and GMB, No. 160).

Composers of chorale motets could, and did, break away altogether from the traditional chorale tunes, though they still used melodic material related to the chorale or song style. The appearance of these motets confirmed the division which has existed ever since in Protestant church music between simple congregational hymns and more elaborate music for a trained choir. The leading composers of German motets at the turn of the sixteenth century were Hassler, Johannes Eccard (1553–1611), Leonhard Lechner (*ca.* 1550–1606), and Michael Praetorius. Their work established the Lutheran church music style in Germany and opened the road to a development that culminated over a hundred years later in J. S. Bach.

Reformation Church Music Outside Germany

The effect that the Reformation had on music in France, the Netherlands, and Switzerland was quite different from developments in Germany. Jean Calvin (1509–1564) and other leaders of the reformed Protestant sects opposed much more strongly than did Luther the retention of elements of Catholic liturgy and ceremonial. To a general distrust of the allurements of art in services of worship was added a particular prohibition of the singing of texts not found in the Bible. As a consequence, the only notable musical productions of the Calvinist churches were the psalters, rhymed metrical translations of the Book of Psalms, set to melodies either newly composed or, in many cases, of popular origin. The principal French Psalter was published in 1562, with psalm texts translated by Clément Marot and Théodore de Bèze set to melodies selected or composed by Loys Bourgeois (*ca.* 1510–1561).

The most important French composers of psalm settings were Claude Goudimel (*ca.* 1505–1572) and Claude Le Jeune; the most important Netherlands composer was J. P. Sweelinck. Translations of

VIII. Church
Music and
Instrumental
Music in the
Late
Renaissance

the French Psalter appeared in Germany, Holland, England, and Scotland, and many of the French tunes were taken over by the Reformed churches in those countries. In Germany many psalter melodies were adapted as chorales (see Example 58a). In Holland the translation of 1566 replaced an earlier Dutch Psalter, the *Souter-*

Example 57   Bicinium: *Vater unser,* Michael Praetorius

Our Father in Heaven, who dost bid us all alike to be brothers and to call upon thee, and desirest prayers from us.

liedekens of 1540, the melodies of which had been taken from contemporary popular songs and were later given three-part settings by Clemens non Papa.

The French model also influenced the most important English Psalter of the sixteenth century, that of Sternhold and Hopkins (1562), and was even more influential for the Scottish Psalter of 1564. A combination of the English and the French-Dutch traditions was embodied in the psalter brought out by Henry Ainsworth in Amsterdam in 1612 for the use of the English Separatists in Holland; this was the psalter which was brought to New England by the Pilgrims in 1620, and it remained in use many years after the appearance of the first American Psalter, the *Bay Psalm Book* of 1640.

The French Psalter melodies on the whole are suave, intimate, and somewhat austere in comparison with the forthright, aggressive, vigorous quality of most of the German chorales. Since the Calvinist

Melodies from the French Psalter of 1562, with Some Later Adaptations   Example 58a

The transgression of the wicked saith within my heart that there is no fear of God [before his eyes].

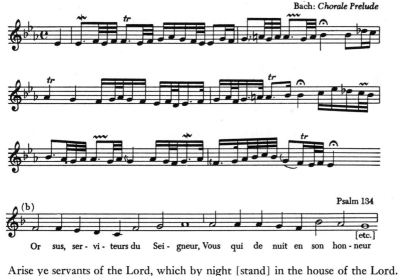

Example 58b

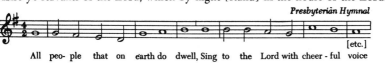

Arise ye servants of the Lord, which by night [stand] in the house of the Lord.

VIII. Church
Music and
Instrumental
Music in the
Late
Renaissance

churches discouraged musical elaboration, the psalter tunes were seldom expanded into larger forms of vocal and instrumental music, as were the Lutheran chorales; and consequently they are much less conspicuous in the general history of music. Yet as devotional music they are excellent; their melodic line, which prevailingly moves by step, has something of the quality of plainsong, and the phrases are organized in a rich variety of rhythmic patterns. It is surprising that so few of the melodies from the French Psalter of 1562 are found in modern hymnals: the best-known example is the tune sung orginally to Psalm 134, used in the English Psalters for Psalm 100 and hence known as "Old Hundred" (Example 58b).

*Anglican
church music*

The Church in England was formally separated from the Roman Catholic communion in 1534; by the middle of the century the English liturgy of the Book of Common Prayer was adopted. With this change, a demand arose for a simplified musical style that would permit the words to be clearly understood, and hence a new body of Anglican church music began to be created. William Byrd, though a Roman Catholic, wrote five Services and about sixty anthems for Anglican use; some of this music is equal in quality to his Latin motets and Masses. Orlando Gibbons (1583–1625) is often called the father of Anglican church music; his works, despite the fact that they derive their technique from the Latin tradition, are thoroughly English in spirit. Thomas Weelkes and Thomas Tomkins (1572–1656) should also be mentioned among the early composers of English church music.

The principal forms of Anglican music are the *Service* and the *anthem*. A complete Service consists of the music for the unvarying portions of Morning and Evening Prayer (corresponding respectively to the Roman Matins and Vespers) and of that for Holy Communion, which corresponds to the Roman Mass but which had a less important place in the Anglican musical scheme—often only the Kyrie and the Creed were composed. A Service is either a "Great Service" or a "Short Service"; these terms refer not to the number of items composed but to the style of the music used, the former being contrapuntal and melismatic, the latter chordal and syllabic. One of the finest examples of Anglican church music is the *Great Service* of Byrd.

The English anthem corresponds to the Latin motet. There are two types of anthems. One, which later came to be called a "full" anthem, was for chorus throughout, usually in contrapuntal style and (ideally) unaccompanied; an example is Tomkins's *When David Heard* (HAM, No. 169), an extraordinarily moving and beautiful setting of this emotional text. The "verse" anthem was for one or more solo voices with organ or viol accompaniment, and with brief alternating passages for chorus; it was most popular in England during the seventeenth century.

The Counter Reformation

From 1545 to 1563, with numerous intermissions and interruptions, a Council was held at Trent in northern Italy to formulate and give official sanction to measures for purging the Roman Catholic Church of abuses and laxities. As far as Church music was concerned, the final pronouncement of the Council of Trent was extremely general: it merely stated that everything "impure or lascivious" must be avoided in order "that the House of God may rightly be called a house of prayer." The implementation of this directive was left to the diocesan Bishops, and a special commission of Cardinals was appointed to oversee its enforcement in Rome. The Council touched on no technical point whatever: neither polyphony nor the parodying of secular models was specifically forbidden.

The essential effect of the Council's decrees was to recognize and sanction stylistic tendencies in church music which were already established, particularly at Rome, by the middle of the century. The consequence was a style of composition whose greatest representative was Giovanni Pierluigi da Palestrina (*ca.* 1526–1594).

By far the greatest part of Palestrina's work was sacred: he wrote 102 Masses, about 450 motets and other liturgical compositions, and 56 spiritual madrigals with Italian texts. His 83 secular madrigals are not particularly outstanding examples of their kind, and in later life he "blushed and grieved" to have written music for profane love poems.

No other composer before Bach is so well known by name as Palestrina, and no other composer's technique has been subjected to more minute scrutiny. He has been called "the Prince of Music" and his works the "absolute perfection" of church style. It is generally recognized that, better than any other composer, he captured the essence of the sober, conservative aspect of the Counter Reformation in a polyphony of utter purity, completely detached from any secular suggestion. The Palestrina style is exemplified most clearly in his Masses; its objective, coolly impersonal quality is most appropriate to the formal and ritualistic texts of the Ordinary. There can be no doubt that he had thoroughly studied the works of the Netherlands composers and made himself master of their technical accomplishments. A more significant reflection of Palestrina's churchly attitude is the fact that of his 102 Masses no fewer than 79 are built on themes from Gregorian Chant; this figure includes those parodied on motets or similar pieces which themselves were based on plainsong, such as the Mass *Veni sponsa Christi*. This matter is more than one of mere statistics. Gregorian Chant is the very earth out of which Palestrina's music grows, the only background against which his music can be properly heard and understood. Palestrina not only uses melodic substance from the Chant; its essential spirit and its entire body of technical procedures he takes up and transfigures in his polyphony.

VIII. Church
Music and
Instrumental
Music in the
Late
Renaissance

*Palestrina's
harmony*

For example, take the melodic line of any individual voice-part of a typical piece such as the first Agnus Dei from the famous *Mass of Pope Marcellus* (Example 59; the entire piece appears in HAM, No. 140): long-breathed, flexibly articulated in rhythmic measures of varying length; prevailingly stepwise, with few repeated notes, moving for the most part within the range of a ninth, easily singable, the few skips greater than a third never dramatically treated but smoothed over by returning to a note within the interval of the skip—in all, an even, natural, elegant curve of sound. The harmony matches the purity of the melody: the piece is clearly in C, with passing modulations to D, G, and A; over half of the root movements are by the interval of a fourth or fifth, that is, of dominant-tonic or tonic-dominant character.

Another characteristic of Palestrina's harmony is the complete—one might say, studied—avoidance of chromaticism, that new expressive resource which was being so thoroughly exploited by the more progressive contemporary composers. Even in his secular madrigals Palestrina was conservative in this respect; the more so in his sacred works, and above all in the Masses, where the peculiarly intense, personal, carnal quality of chromatic harmonies would have been for him an unthinkable secular intrusion. Only the essential alterations required by the rules of *musica ficta* are tolerated.

The elements of Palestrina's harmony are the same as those of all sixteenth-century composers: triads and chords of the sixth. But the absence of chromatic progressions and especially the discreet handling of dissonance give Palestrina's music a consistent serenity and transparency not matched by any other composer's.

The rhythm of Palestrina's music, like that of all sixteenth-century polyphony, is compounded of the rhythms of the various voices plus a collective rhythm resulting from the harmonic and contrapuntal combination of the lines. In Example 60, the opening of the first Agnus Dei of the *Pope Marcellus* Mass, each voice is barred in accordance with its own natural rhythm; this example shows graphically how independent the individual lines are. However, the collective rhythm, heard when all the voices are sounding, gives the impression of a fairly regular succession of 2/2 or 4/4 "measures," set off not by stress accents but mostly by the changes of harmony and the placing of suspensions on "strong" beats, (see Example 59). This gently marked regularity of rhythm is characteristic of the Palestrina style.

Most of Palestrina's church compositions, and especially the Masses, are in the Netherlands contrapuntal style, with a texture consisting of several rhythmically independent and equally important voice parts. However, Palestrina also used the more modern homophonic or chordal conception of texture in his litanies and lamentations, and in one of his most celebrated works, the *Improperia* (*Reproaches;* the words of Christ on the Cross, sung on Good Friday). This composition is written entirely in chordal style, and was designed to be chanted in the manner of the harmonized Psalm tones that were widely used in Italian and Spanish churches during the sixteenth century. There are also a number of short motets by Palestrina written entirely in chordal style. The *Stabat Mater*, for double chorus, is almost completely homophonic. More typically, however, Palestrina used a mixture of contrapuntal and homophonic textures in varying proportions within the same piece.

Palestrina shows his sensitiveness to the text not only in his use of

Agnus Dei I from the *Pope Marcellus* Mass, Palestrina

Example 59

VIII. Church
Music and
Instrumental
Music in the
Late
Renaissance

Example 59
(cont.)

the stock pictorial touches (ascending passages on "ascendit" and the like) of the period, but also in the care he takes to give each word its correct accentuation. Moreover, the emotional connotation of the words does not go unmarked. It is only that in the Masses and, for the most part, in the motets as well, this matter is treated so delicately, with such reserve, is held so strictly within the bounds of liturgical proprie- ty, that it may easily escape an ear attuned to the grosser language of the madrigalists or even of other church composers of Palestrina's time. Yet in such a passage as the "Crucifixus" of the *Missa brevis*

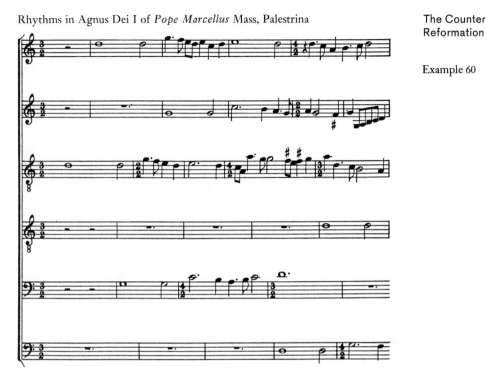

Example 60

(Example 61) the emotional tone of the words "crucifixus" ("He was crucified"), "passus" ("He suffered"), and "resurrexit" ("He rose again") is conveyed perfectly, though by the simplest possible technical means. In some of his later motets, especially the cycle from the *Song of Songs* (1584), Palestrina permitted himself somewhat richer colors and more full-bodied sonorities—but these are always held in restraint, never used for mere dramatic or external effect. His art is

Crucifixus from the *Missa brevis*, Palestrina

Example 61

VIII. Church
Music and
Instrumental
Music in the
Late
Renaissance

*Contemporaries
of Palestrina*

the expression of medieval mysticism in an intentionally restricted, and in some respects archaic, Renaissance musical vocabulary.

Some contemporaries of Palestrina whose musical style was related to his must be only briefly mentioned. Giovanni Maria Nanino (*ca.* 1545–1607), Palestrina's pupil and his successor at Santa Maria Maggiore and later director of the Papal Chapel, is to be counted among the foremost composers of the Roman school. Felice Anerio (1560–1614) was a pupil of Nanino who in 1594 succeeded Palestrina as official composer to the Papal Chapel. Giovanni Animuccia (*ca.* 1500–1571) was Palestrina's predecessor at St. Peter's. He is noted chiefly for his *laude* written for the Congregation of the Oratory at Rome. This Congregation grew out of meetings organized by a priest (later canonized), Filippo Neri, for religious lectures and spiritual exercises, which were followed by the singing of laude; the name came from the original place of meeting, the "oratory" (prayer chapel) of one of the Roman churches. The laude and similar devotional songs—Palestrina himself contributed a few pieces to this repertory—later were occasionally given in the form of dialogues or otherwise dramatized.

Next to Palestrina, however, the most important composer of the Roman school was the Spaniard, Tomás Luis de Victoria (*ca.* 1549–1611). As the career of Morales indicated, there was a close connection between Spanish and Roman composers throughout the sixteenth century. Victoria came to Rome in 1565, probably studied with Palestrina, and followed him as teacher at the Seminary in 1571; returning to Spain about 1595, he became chaplain to the Empress Maria, for whose funeral services he wrote a famous Requiem Mass in 1603. His compositions are exclusively sacred. Though his style is like that of Palestrina, Victoria often infuses his music with a mystical intensity, a dramatic quality which makes it both thoroughly personal and typically Spanish. A good example of his work is the motet *O vos omnes:* instead of the gentle, even rhythm of Palestrina, the lines are broken as if into sobbing ejaculations; arresting vivid phrases with repeated notes ("attendite"—"behold") give way to cries of lamentation, underlined by poignant dissonances ("sicut dolor meus" —"like unto My sorrow"). Palestrina's art may be compared to that of Raphael; Victoria's, with its passionate religious fervor, is like that of his contemporary, El Greco. Even in his more conventional motets this fervent spirit is always immanent in Victoria's music.

The last of the illustrious line of sixteenth-century Netherlands composers were Philippe de Monte and Orlando di Lasso. Unlike Palestrina and Victoria, a large part of their work was secular. Nevertheless, Monte produced 38 Masses and over 300 motets in which he demonstrated his mastery of contrapuntal technique and his faithfulness to the Netherlands musical tradition, although not without some more modern touches.

Orlando di Lasso ranks with Palestrina among the great composers of sacred music in the late sixteenth century. But whereas Palestrina was above all the master of the Mass, Lasso's chief glory is his motets. His settings of the penitential psalms[1] (about 1560), though perhaps the best known of his church works, are not fully representative. In both his career and his compositions, Lasso was one of the most cosmopolitan figures in the history of music. By the age of twenty-four he had already published books of madrigals, chansons, and motets, and his total production eventually amounted to over 2000 works. The principal collection of his motets, the *Magnum opus musicum* (*Great Work of Music*) was published in 1604, ten years after his death. In contrast to Palestrina's considered, restrained, and classic nature, Lasso had an impulsive, emotional, and dynamic temperament. In his motets both the over-all form and the details are generated from a pictorial, dramatic approach to the text; a vivid example of this may be heard in the motet *In hora ultima*, where a portentous announcement of the Day of Judgment is followed by abrupt musical depictions of those worldly vanities which in that hour "shall perish":

...tuba, tibia, et cythara,	...trumpet, flute, and harp,
jocus, risus, saltus,	joking, laughing, and dancing,
cantus et discantus.	song and descant.

Even in motets of a more conventional type, Lasso's attention to details of the text is evident. The distinctive technical features of his musical style seem to be an outgrowth of this attitude: the melodic movement is frequently by leap; phrases are uneven in length; texture is freely varied to suit the emotional or pictorial suggestions in the words; the harmonic rhythm is often rapid and irregular; and the dramatic values of harmonic combinations are exploited.

In the latter years of his life Lasso devoted himself wholly to setting sacred texts, particularly spiritual madrigals, renouncing the "gay" and "festive" songs of his youth for music of "more substance and energy." However, one cannot properly speak of a "Lasso style"; the man is too versatile for that. Netherlands counterpoint, Italian harmony, Venetian opulence, French vivacity, German gravity, all are to be found in his work, which more fully than that of any other sixteenth-century composer sums up the achievements of an epoch and in many ways looks forward to the age of the Baroque.

The last of the great Catholic Church composers of the sixteenth century was William Byrd of England (1543–1623). His works include madrigals, keyboard pieces, and music for the Anglican Church; *William Byrd* undoubtedly his best vocal compositions are his Latin Masses and motets. Inasmuch as there was no possibility of Latin church music being sung at public services in England, it is not surprising that Byrd wrote only three Masses (respectively for three, four, and five voices); yet these have been considered the finest settings of the Mass written by an English composer.

VIII. Church
Music and
Instrumental
Music in the
Late
Renaissance

Byrd's earlier motets were doubtless intended for private devotional gatherings; but the two books of *Gradualia* (1605, 1607) were designed for liturgical use, and they contributed to the spread of Byrd's fame on the Continent.

Byrd's music is remarkably free from the clichés that permeate even the best Continental works of his time. His melodies have a strongly individual profile, and the texture is pervaded by the same essentially English quality of vocality that we have already noticed in the music of Tallis. Byrd's treatment of dissonance is sometimes unconventional, and often extraordinarily beautiful in effect. A particular feature of his music, found also in that of other English composers of the period, is the use of the same note in both its diatonic and chromatically altered form in close juxtaposition, or even simultaneously (Example 62). This usage, of course, must be understood in its proper context of unaccompanied vocal music, although similar clashes are common also in contemporary English string and keyboard writing.

Example 62   *Ave verum*, William Byrd

O sweet, gracious Jesus, son of Mary, have mercy on me.

The Growth of Instrumental Music

Late sixteenth-century instrumental music can best be surveyed by dividing it into four classes: compositions derived from vocal models, dances, improvisatory pieces, and variations. This classification is of course imperfect, since the categories are not of the same order; they relate respectively to source, function, style, and form of compositions. Consequently, any given work may belong to more than one class, as, for example, a dance in the form of variations. It is therefore essential to regard these four classes not as so many pigeon-holes but rather as *basic principles of procedure* which are operative in the composition of instrumental music in the late sixteenth century, and one or another of which can be regarded as the *main* principle in any actual work of that period.

Of the compositions derived from vocal models a large number are nothing more than transcriptions of madrigals, chansons, or motets, decorated by turns, trills, runs, and other embellishments. Many instrumental compositions are based on *cantus firmi* of vocal origin; others make use of a favorite *cantus firmus* consisting of the six notes of the hexachord (*ut, re, mi, fa, sol, la*), around which English composers wrote many ingenious counterpoints. In the course of these compositions the hexachord might be transposed to different degrees of the scale; one celebrated "hexachord fancy" for virginals by John Bull (*ca.* 1562–1628) modulates through all twelve keys, a procedure which strongly suggests that some approximation to equal temperament must have been known in England by the end of the sixteenth century.

Compositions derived from vocal models

Keyboard and ensemble ricercari in the manner of vocal motets were composed throughout the sixteenth century, but more important historically was the development of the canzona. Originally, the canzona was an instrumental composition with the same general style as the French chanson—that is, light, fast-moving, strongly rhythmic, and with a fairly simple contrapuntal texture. The composers of instrumental canzonas took over these characteristics from the chanson, as well as the typical opening rhythmic figure ♩ ♪♪|♩ or ♩ ♫|♩, which occurs in nearly all canzonas. More lively and entertaining than the sober and somewhat abstruse ricercar, the canzona became in the late sixteenth century the leading form of contrapuntal instrumental music. The earliest Italian examples (apart from mere transcriptions) were for organ; about 1580, Italian composers began to write ensemble canzonas as well. The organ canzonas were the forerunners of the fugue; these two terms were used synonymously in Germany as early as 1607. The ensemble canzonas, on the other hand, eventually developed into the *sonata da chiesa* ("church sonata") of the seventeenth century.

The canzona

The essential step in this development was the division of the canzona into a number of more or less distinct sections. Many of the

VIII. Church
Music and
Instrumental
Music in the
Late
Renaissance

earliest canzonas had a single theme, or perhaps several themes very similar in character, treated contrapuntally in one continuous and unchanging movement. Others, however, introduced themes of somewhat contrasting character, each theme in turn going through its contrapuntal working-out and then yielding to the next. Since the themes themselves were noticeably different from each other in melodic outline and rhythm, the piece as a whole began to take on the aspect of a series of contrasting sections—even though the divisions between sections were usually concealed by overlapping of the cadences. Example 63 shows the four themes in a canzona of this type written by the Netherlander Jean de Macque (*ca.* 1550–1614; the entire piece is given in EE, No. 25).

A further stage in the direction of independent sections is illustrated in Example 64, themes from an instrumental piece by the Venetian composer, Andrea Gabrieli (*ca.* 1520–1586). (The entire piece is given in HAM, No. 136. Although it was called "ricercare," it is of the canzona type, an indication of the looseness of terminology in this period.) The themes are more contrasting than those in de Macque's canzona, and moreover the second section of the piece is set off from the others by being written in a predominantly homophonic style. The opening section is repeated in its entirety after section four.

This composition of Gabrieli's thus illustrates also an important structural principle—repetition. Of course, the ideas of contrast and repetition were not new; both are basic in musical composition, and both appear in Western music from its earliest beginnings. But before the sixteenth century the use of repetition and contrast was dictated largely by liturgical requirements, or by the poetic form of the text, or by the nature of a dance pattern. In independent instrumental pieces, such as the canzonas, the decision to use these devices is made for purely musical reasons: to give coherence and variety to polyphony intended only to be listened to, without the distractions or support of ritual, dancing, or text. This new approach embodied in the late sixteenth-century canzona, and in similar contemporary forms with other names—capriccio, ricercare, fantasia, fancy, and the like— was important, for in it was implicit the later development of independent instrumental music.

In the latter half of the sixteenth century, dance music for lute, keyboard instruments, and ensembles was published in increasing *Dance pieces* amounts. Some dances were simple arrangements of tunes for popular

Example 63   Themes from a Canzona, Jean de Macque

use, but the majority seem to have been written for social occasions. The tendency already present in the early sixteenth century to group dances in pairs or threes continued, as did the writing of stylized dance music; an excellent example of the latter is Orlando Gibbons's *Pavane Lord Salisbury*. Often a stylized dance movement was used as the subject for a set of variations. The favorite pairs of dances in the late sixteenth century were the *pavane* (*padovano, paduana*) and *galliard;* or the *passamezzo* and *saltarello*. In either pair the first dance was slow and stately and in duple time, and the second dance was a more lively movement in triple time, usually on the same melody or a variation thereof.

Themes from a Ricercare, Andrea Gabrieli

Example 64

Example 65

Toccata Sections, Claudio Merulo

a.

[etc.]

VIII. Church
Music and
Instrumental
Music in the
Late
Renaissance

Example 65
(cont.)

*Improvisatory
pieces*

The chief form of keyboard music in improvisatory style in the latter half of the century was the *toccata*. This word comes from the Italian verb *toccare* (to touch), and carries the suggestion of an organist improvising at the keyboard. As an example we may take a toccata by the Venetian organist Claudio Merulo (1533–1604; Example 65; the entire composition is in HAM, No. 153).

Merulo begins by taking advantage of the organ's power to sustain tones indefinitely; the first section is a succession of broadly conceived harmonies in F major (Example 65a) cadencing first on the tonic and then moving to a half cadence on the dominant. The numerous suspensions and other long-held dissonances are quite idiomatic to the organ. The harmonic structure is animated in all the voices by embellishments and scale passages in freely varied rhythms—ornaments probably played with a rather free rubato-like delivery. A contrasting middle section is, in effect, a short ricercare with three themes, each in turn developed by imitation (Example 65b). The last ricercare theme soon dissolves into ornamental work followed by rapidly changing harmonies that lead to a cadence on the tonic. After this middle section comes a passage similar to the opening but with harmonies more broadly laid out and with even more fantastic play of brilliant running passages. The majestic slowing down of the harmonic rhythm in the coda, coupled with the increasing animation and ever wider sweep of the runs, makes a most impressive climax (Example 65c).

The toccata was a specialty of the Venetian organ composers. Merulo, publishing at the very end of the century (1598 and 1604), was the first to introduce the ricercare-like middle section as described in the above example. Most sixteenth-century toccatas were simply in one movement, in straight improvisatory style. Various names were used for pieces of this sort: *fantasia, intonazione, prelude,* and others.

A rather different kind of improvisatory writing is found in some keyboard pieces toward the end of the sixteenth century, pieces in which the composer seems to wander dreamily through a maze of strange harmonies, as an organist might when quietly improvising. Example 66 shows a passage from a work of this sort, appropriately entitled *Consonanze stravaganti* ("Roving Harmonies"), by Jean de Macque. (The entire composition is in HAM, No. 174.) The peculiar chromaticism of this example is reminiscent of Gesualdo, with whom de Macque was associated for a time at Naples. The style is a forerunner of the beautiful chromatic toccatas of the seventeenth-century Roman organist, Frescobaldi.

The extraordinary flowering of the variation form in the late sixteenth century was due primarily to a school of English keyboard composers called the *virginalists* from the name of the principal keyboard instrument of the time. The leading composers of this group were William Byrd, Giles Farnaby (*ca.* 1560–1640), John Bull, Thomas Morley, and Orlando Gibbons. The largest collection of English keyboard music is the *Fitzwilliam Virginal Book,* a manuscript compiled about 1620, which contains nearly 300 compositions written in the late sixteenth and early seventeenth centuries. Among these pieces are madrigal transcriptions, fantasias, dances, preludes, and many sets of variations. *English keyboard music*

Most of the variations in the *Fitzwilliam Virginal Book* are on slow dance tunes or familiar song melodies; Bull's *Spanish Paven* is an example of the former, Munday's *Goe from my window* of the latter.

The tunes used as the basis for the variations as a rule were short, simple, and song-like, regular in phrasing, with a clear binary or ternary pattern set off by distinct cadences. The variations follow in uninterrupted sequence, sometimes a half-dozen of them, sometimes as many as twenty or even more. Each variation preserves the structure of the theme: the same articulations, the same cadences, the same harmonic plan. Sometimes the original melody is presented intact throughout an entire set of variations, passing occasionally from one voice to another. More often, in some of the variations the melody is broken up by figuration, so that its original profile is only suggested. 173

VIII. Church
Music and
Instrumental
Music in the
Late
Renaissance

Example 66

Consonanze stravaganti, Jean de Macque

* So in original; delete *a*?
** So in original; delete *d*?

Sometimes this decorative figuration is derived from some phrase of the melody itself, but as a rule it is freely invented. Some of the passage work, particularly in the variations by Bull, has a high order or virtuosity, if not always important musical content; evidently fast scale-playing and similar feats of technical skill had the same fascination for composers then as in the nineteenth century.

In most English virginal music, however, mere technical display is not a prominent feature. Each variation commonly makes use of one main type of figuration; and sometimes the two halves of a variation, or two successive variations, will be paired by the use of the same figure in the right hand for one and in the left hand for the other, as in the third and fourth variations of Bull's *Spanish Paven*. Apart from such pairing, the only comprehensive plan in most sets of variations was to increase the animation as the work progressed—although with intermittent quieter interludes. Changes of meter were sometimes introduced, and once in a while a composer would show off his learning by writing a variation using two or three different meters simultaneously. Quite often the last variation was slower, a broadened restatement of the theme with fuller sonority and richer harmonization. The technique may be studied with pleasure in the charming set of variations by Farnaby on *Loth to depart*.

A seventeenth-century double spinet or virginal, with an ornamented and painted case, made by Lodovicus Grovvelus of Flanders. The righthand instrument can be removed from the case and used as a portable virginal. (Courtesy Metropolitan Museum of Art, the Crosby Brown Collection of Musical Instruments, 1889)

Toward the Baroque: The Venetian School

In the sixteenth century, Venice was (next to Rome) the most important city of the Italian peninsula. The heart and center of her 175

VIII. Church
Music and
Instrumental
Music in the
Late
Renaissance

musical culture was the great eleventh-century cathedral of Saint Mark. Most of the exalted civic ceremonies of Venice took place in the Cathedral and in the vast *piazza* which it faced. Thus most Venetian music was conceived as a manifestation of the majesty of both State and Church, and was designed to be heard on solemn and festive occasions when that majesty was publicly displayed with every possible array of sound and pageantry—as the illustration below indicates.

Music in the Cathedral of Saint Mark was supervised by officials of the State, and no pains or expense were spared to keep it worthy of Venice's high traditions. The position of choirmaster at the Cathedral was the most coveted musical post in all Italy. There were two organs, and the organists, chosen after stringent examination, were always renowned artists. Choirmasters in the sixteenth century were Willaert,

Procession of the Guild of St. John the Evangelist in St. Mark's Square in 1496, a painting by Gentile Bellini (1427?–1507). The white-robed members in the foreground carry a gold reliquary holding the guild's prized possession, a fragment of the True Cross. Musicians follow along the right side of the square. (Alinari)

Rore, Zarlino, and Baldassare Donati; organists included Jacques Buus, Annibale Padovano, Claudio Merulo, Andrea Gabrieli, and his nephew, Giovanni Gabrieli (*ca.* 1557–1612). All these men were not merely conductors and players, but famous composers as well; and it will be seen that as the century went on the Netherlanders (Willaert, Rore, Buus) were succeeded by native Italians.

Many Venetian composers of the sixteenth century contributed notably to the madrigal, and Venice produced the best organ music of all Italy. Venetian music was characteristically of full, rich texture, homophonic rather than contrapuntal, varied and colorful in sonority.

In the motets, massive chordal harmonies were the rule, rather than the single intricate polyphonic lines of the Netherlanders.

Toward the
Baroque:
The Venetian
School

*Venetian
polychoric
motets*

From the time of Willaert, and even before that, the Venetian church composers had often written for double chorus, the two separate choirs which in Saint Mark's were placed with the organs on opposite sides of the church. The use of such *cori spezzati* ("divided choirs") was not original with Venice or peculiar to it (Palestrina's *Stabat Mater*, for example, is written for double chorus); but the practice was congenial to, and further encouraged, the homophonic type of choral writing and the broad rhythmic organization which the Venetian composers preferred. Moreover, Venice was not committed, as was Rome, to the ideal of *a cappella* performance. Not only the organ, but many other instruments as well—trombones, cornetts, viols—sounded with the voices. In the hands of Giovanni Gabrieli, the greatest of the Venetian masters, the motet was expanded to unheard-of proportions: two, three, four, even five choruses were employed, each with a different combination of high and low voices, each intermingled with instruments of diverse timbres, answering one another antiphonally, alternating with solo voices, and joining for massive sonorous climaxes. An example is Gabrieli's motet *In ecclesiis*. In such works a new principle of composition was established, namely the contrast and opposition of sonorities; this principle later became a basic factor in the *concertato* style of the Baroque period.

The famous *Sonata pian' e forte* of Gabrieli is essentially nothing else than a double-chorus Venetian motet for instruments. This composition owes its prominent place in music history books less to its intrinsic musical worth than to the fact that it is one of the first instrumental ensemble pieces printed which designates particular instruments for each part: the first orchestra consists of a cornett and three trombones, the second of a viol (*violino*) and three trombones.

Another innovation in Gabrieli's sonata was the indication, both in the title and in the score itself, of "*pian[o]*" and "*forte*"; the former rubric is used when each orchestra is playing alone and the latter when both are playing together. This is one of the earliest instances of dynamic markings in music. As for the term *sonata*, it was used occasionally in the sixteenth century in a very general way for almost any kind of ensemble instrumental composition, and implied nothing about form. The only connection of the sixteenth-century "sonatas" with the sonata of the Baroque and Classical periods is nominal.

The Venetian school, universally admired as the most progressive in Italy, exercised wide influence in the late sixteenth and early seventeenth centuries. Pupils and followers of Gabrieli were numerous in northern Italy and were scattered all over Germany and Austria. Jacob Handl (1550–1591), a Slovenian by birth—known also by the Latin form of his name, Jacobus Gallus—worked at Olmütz and Prague; most of his works, particularly his motets for double chorus, show a close affinity with Venetian style. The motets of Hans Leo Hassler, a

VIII. Church
Music and
Instrumental
Music in the
Late
Renaissance
German pupil of Andrea Gabrieli, are prevailingly polychoric, with typical Venetian fullness of sound and richness of harmony.

Summary

This discussion of music in the second half of the sixteenth century has many times overstepped the arbitrary boundary of the year 1600 which we set as the limit of the Renaissance period. The reason, of course, is that changes in musical style occur gradually, in complex ways, and at different times in different places. Nearly the entire development of the English madrigal school, for example, took place in the seventeenth century, but it has been dealt with in this chapter because the style of the English madrigal is more closely allied to Renaissance music than to Baroque. Certainly, late Renaissance traits persisted well into the seventeenth century; and many features of the early Baroque began to be manifest long before the end of the sixteenth.

To speak of "traits" or "features" of Renaissance or Baroque music, however, implies that there are certain characteristics by which we can identify a given piece as at least predominantly one or the other, regardless of the date of its composition. In discussing Renaissance music, we listed five general features; let us now see how each of these was affected by the changes that took place between 1450 and 1600.

Texture

The characteristic texture of similar and equal voice parts was still the rule in the work of Palestrina, Lasso, Byrd, and Gabrieli, at the end of the sixteenth century, as it had been in the music of Ockeghem and Josquin. This texture, more than any other single feature, separates Renaissance music from Baroque. On the other hand, homophony, both in its pure form and as a centripetal tendency curbing the independence of contrapuntal lines, had begun to invade all forms of polyphonic writing. Its dominance in the Venetian school is one sign of the approaching Baroque. The outlines of major-minor tonality were already plain in much of the music of Palestrina, Lasso, Byrd, and Gabrieli.

Rhythm

Rhythm, supported by systematic harmonic progressions within an incipient tonal system, had become comparatively steady and predictable by the end of the century, even in the contrapuntal style of Palestrina and in such apparently free compositions as the Venetian organ toccatas. The barline in the modern editions of Palestrina, Gabrieli, and Byrd is no longer the intrusion it sometimes seems to be in modern editions of Ockeghem and Josquin. The Baroque begins with a conspicuous revolt against rhythmic regularity; but it ends by embracing this regularity completely, within the framework of a perfected tonal system.

The pictorial and expressive touches in the madrigal, Gesualdo's chromatic aberrations, and the splendorous sonorities of the Venetian massed choruses, are all signs of the sixteenth-century drive toward vivid outward expression in music. The Baroque carries this drive to still greater lengths, and embodies it in the new dramatic forms of cantata and opera. With the rise of pure instrumental forms (the ricercare, canzona, and toccata), Renaissance music had already begun to transcend words; this line of development also continues without a break through the Baroque and beyond. Finally: whereas the solo songs of the Renaissance were lyrical pieces, hardly different in style from madrigals, one of the chief innovations of the Baroque was the discovery that the solo song could be used as a vehicle for dramatic expression. The violent states of feeling expressed by Gesualdo and Gabrieli in an ensemble of voices are by the Baroque composers expressed in a solo with instrumental accompaniment.

IX Early Baroque Music

General Features of Baroque Music

The music of the Baroque era (roughly 1600–1750) was dominated largely by Italian ideals. Independent national styles flourished for a time in France, Germany, and England during the seventeenth century, but by 1750 the music of Europe had become in effect an international language with Italian roots. Despite continuous evolution, certain musical features remained constant throughout the Baroque era. One of these was a distinction drawn between two styles of composition. In 1605 Monteverdi called these opposing styles *prima prattica* and *seconda prattica*, or the first and second "practices." By the first he meant the style of the Netherlanders; and by the second he meant the style of the modern Italians. The basis of the distinction for Monteverdi was that in the first practice music dominated the text, *The two* whereas in the second practice the text dominated the music; hence it *practices* followed that in the new style the old rules might be modified and, in particular, dissonances might be used freely to make the music conform to the expression of feeling in the text. Other writers called the two practices *stile antico* and *stile moderno* (old and modern style), or *stylus gravis* and *stylus luxurians* (sober and ornamented style); this last designation implied the use of fast notes, unusual skips, and a well-marked melody, as well as dissonances. In short, the difference came to about what we today call "strict style" and "free style." The older style was considered appropriate for church, although not all church compositions were by any means written in it. Nor were the two styles always kept separate in practice.

Another characteristic of Baroque music was that composers began *Idiomatic* to be attracted by the idea of writing music specifically for a particu- *writing* lar medium, such as the violin or the solo voice, rather than music that might be either sung or played or performed by almost any combination of voices and instruments, as could many pieces composed in the sixteenth century. The violin family began to replace the older viols, and composers developed an idiomatic violin style; also the art of

The Abbey Church of Amorbach in Odenwald looking toward the great Baroque organ. The architecture of this rich German Baroque interior incorporates painting, sculpture, carving, and metal work. (German Tourist Information Office, New York)

singing, promoted by famous teachers and virtuosi, advanced very rapidly in the seventeenth century; instrumental and vocal styles began to be differentiated.

One trait common to all Baroque composers was the effort they made to express, or rather represent, a wide range of ideas and feelings with the utmost vividness and vehemence by means of music. Composers struggled to find musical means for the expression of *affections* or states of the soul, such as rage, excitement, grandeur, heroism, lofty

The affections

181

contemplation, wonder, or mystic exaltation, and to intensify these musical effects by means of violent contrasts. In Baroque architecture, sculpture, and painting the normal forms of objects were sometimes distorted, as though past the natural limits of the medium, to reflect the passionate intensity of the artist's thought; in Baroque music, also, the limits of the old order of consonance and dissonance, of regular and equable rhythmic flow, were being broken down. In the seventeenth century this was an important stimulus both to the development of music itself and also to its increasing importance relative to the other arts.

The music of the Baroque was not primarily written to express the feelings of an individual artist, but to represent affections; these were conveyed by means of a systematic, regulated vocabulary, a common repertory of musical *figures* or devices. Figures were suggested by or borrowed from other arts, particularly rhetoric and poetry; they were of diverse sorts and were diversely combined, but their use meant that the music of the Baroque was a language capable of depicting not only affections, but even to some extent also images and objects of the external world. This depictive intention in many Baroque compositions must not be disregarded; but neither must it be over-emphasized.

Diversity of styles and idioms, together with the effort made to represent vividly and precisely ideas and feelings, brought into Baroque music factors that were somewhat incompatible. Baroque music shows conflicts and tension between the centrifugal forces of freedom of expression and the constructive forces of discipline and order in a musical composition. This tension, always latent in any work of art, was eventually made overt and consciously exploited by Baroque musicians; and this acknowledged dualism is the most important characteristic which distinguishes between the music of this period and that of the Renaissance. The dualism is apparent in the existence of the two practices. It is also evident in the two ways the Baroque treated rhythm: (1) regular metrical barline rhythm on the one hand; and (2) free unmetrical rhythm, used in recitative or improvisatory solo instrumental pieces, on the other.

Dualism:
Rhythm

Regular dance rhythms were, of course, known in the Renaissance; but not until the seventeenth century did most music begin to be written and heard in *measures*—definite patterns of strong and weak beats. At first these patterns were not regularly recurring; the use of a single time signature corresponding to a regular succession of harmonic and accentual patterns, set off by barlines at regular intervals, was common only after 1650. By the late Baroque, it had become customary for a composer to establish a distinctive rhythmic pattern at the beginning of a composition or movement, and to hold predominantly to this basic pattern throughout; the piece thus represented a single "basic affection," and made only sparing use of contrasting material.

Along with strictly measured rhythm, Baroque composers also used

an irregular, inconstant, flexible rhythm in writing instrumental toccatas and vocal recitatives. Obviously the two rhythms could not be
used simultaneously; but they were frequently used successively for
deliberate contrast, as in the customary pairing of toccata and fugue
or recitative and aria.

The basic sound ideal of the Renaissance was a polyphony of equal
independent voices; the sound ideal of the Baroque was a firm bass and
a florid treble, held together by unobtrusive harmony. The idea of a
musical texture consisting of a single melody supported by accompanying harmonies was not in itself new; something like it had been used
in the ballade style of the *ars nova*, in the Burgundian chanson, in the
early frottola, in the sixteenth-century lute songs, and in the Elizabethan ayre. The ideas that were new in the Baroque were the emphasis on the bass, the isolation of the bass and treble as the two essential lines of the texture, and the seeming indifference to the inner voice
lines. This indifference was perfectly pictured in a system of notation
used during the Baroque, called the *thoroughbass* or *basso continuo*:
the composer wrote out the melody and the bass; the bass was played
on one or more *fundament* or *continuo* instruments (clavier, organ,
lute), usually reinforced by a sustaining instrument such as a bass
gamba or violoncello or bassoon; and above the bass notes the keyboard or lute player filled in the required chords, which were not
otherwise written out. If these chords were other than common triads
in root position, or if nonharmonic tones (such as suspensions) or
added accidentals were to be played, the composer could so indicate
by little figures or signs placed above or below the bass notes (see the
piece by Caccini in the illustration below).

*Sound ideal:
the basso
continuo*

The *realization*—the actual playing—of such a *figured bass* varied
according to the nature of the composition and the taste and skill of
the player; he might play simple chords, introduce passing tones, or
incorporate melodic motives in imitation of the treble or bass parts.
(A modern edition of compositions with a figured bass usually indicates in smaller notes the editor's conception of a proper realization.) The realization of the basso continuo was not always essential:
that is to say, many pieces were provided with a continuo even though
all the notes necessary for the full harmony were already present in
the notated melodic vocal or instrumental parts. In motets or madrigals for four or five voices, for example, the continuo instrument
actually did no more than double or support the voices. But for solos
and duets the continuo was usually necessary to complete the harmonies as well as to produce a fuller sonority.

It might seem that the Baroque basso continuo implied a total rejection of the kind of counterpoint written in the sixteenth century and
earlier. As a matter of fact, this was true when the continuo was used
alone as accompaniment to a solo, unless the composer chose to give
the bass line itself some melodic significance, for the thoroughbass *was*
a radical departure from all previous methods of writing music. But it

*The new
counterpoint*

183

Part of an aria, "Sfogava con le stelle," by Giulio Caccini (ca. 1546–1618). This piece was printed in Le nuove musiche, *a collection of Caccini's madrigals published at Florence in 1602.*

must be remembered that a firm bass and florid treble was not the only kind of musical texture in the Baroque. For a long time, composers continued to write unaccompanied motets and madrigals; some instrumental ensemble pieces, as well as all solo keyboard and lute music, made no use of the basso continuo; most important, even in ensembles where the continuo was used, counterpoint did not disappear. But the new counterpoint of the seventeenth century was different from that of the Renaissance. It was still a blending of different melodic lines, but the lines all had to fit into the regulative framework of a series of harmonic chord progressions explicitly defined and sounded by the continuo: it was, in short, a harmonically governed counterpoint, whose melodies were subordinated to the harmonic scheme.

The major-minor system

Within the harmonies thus defined, composers eventually were able to use dissonance and chromatic alterations quite freely, just because the underlying harmonies were so clear. Music came to be organized according to the system of major-minor tonality familiar to us in the music of the eighteenth and nineteenth centuries. This particular tonal organization had long been foreshadowed; it was implicit in much

184

music of the Renaissance, especially that written in the latter half of the sixteenth century. Rameau's *Treatise on Harmony* (1722) completed the theoretical formulation of the system, but it had existed in practice for at least forty years before.

The basso continuo was important in the later stages of this theoretical development because it emphasized the harmonic progressions by isolating them, as it were, in a special notation different from the notation of the melodic lines. The basso continuo was the road over which music travelled from counterpoint to homophony, from a linear-melodic to a chordal-harmonic structure. After the middle of the eighteenth century, when the system of harmonic relationships had become so firmly established that there was no further need to make it explicit by continually sounding the basic chord progressions, the basso continuo gradually disappeared.

Early Baroque Opera

Various experiments in combining music with drama were made in the sixteenth century, but the creation of genuine opera had to await the discovery of an appropriate style of solo singing. This occurred around 1590 with the invention of *monody*, a kind of singing supposedly based on ancient Greek practice. In monody, the vocal line aimed chiefly to intensify the natural accents of speech; accompaniment consisted of a few simple, inconspicuous chords. The earliest surviving examples of monody are some songs written by Giulio Caccini (*ca.* 1546–1618) and published in 1602 under the title of *Le nuove musiche* (*New Music*).[1]

The monodic style quickly made its way into all kinds of music, both secular and sacred, in the early years of the seventeenth century. It was the one thing needed to make opera possible, for it provided a medium by which both dialogue and exposition could be conveyed in music clearly, quickly, and with all the necessary freedom and flexibility for truly dramatic expression. In 1600 Caccini and Iacopo Peri (1561–1633) jointly set to music a pastoral-mythological drama, *Euridice*, which was publicly performed in that year at Florence. In the following year each composer published a version of his own, and these two are the earliest surviving complete operas. *The first opera*

Euridice was the well-known myth of Orpheus and Euridice, treated in the currently fashionable manner of the pastoral and modified so as to have a happy ending. The music of both Caccini and Peri consists for the most part of recitative over a generally slow-moving bass; such unvarying monodic declamation without vocal ornaments was called *stile rappresentativo* ("representative" or perhaps "theatre style"). This recitative, which is liable to seem to us thin and formless, is said to have made an extraordinary impression on listeners in 1600. Their interest was probably partly due to the novelty of the style and 185

Beginning of Orfeo's aria "Possente spirto" from Act III of Monteverdi's Orfeo.

partly to the sensitive way in which the composers and singers were able to interpret the inner melody of the words in the vocal line while the shifting emotions of the poetry were mirrored in the changes of harmony. In addition, the monotony of the recitative was broken with occasional passages of a more melodic character or by short simple choral refrains.

Opera thus began as an experimental attempt to revive Greek music for the delectation of a little circle of learned amateurs. It might have died an early death had not the poets and composers realized that the form had to have a richer musical content. The composer who first wrote operas with this richness, and who therefore is perhaps best entitled to be called the creator of opera, was Claudio Monteverdi.

Orfeo, the first of Monteverdi's operas, was performed at Mantua in 1607. Its subject matter is the same as that of the Florentine *Euridice* operas, but expanded into full five-act length. The music likewise may

be said to take the Florentine *stile rappresentativo* as its point of departure, but it soon leaves its model behind. The representation of emotions is stronger and more varied; the harmonies are more expressive; the recitatives no longer depend solely on the words for continuity but are organized into perceptible musical forms. Moreover, Monteverdi introduced many solo airs, duets, madrigal-like choruses, and dances, which together make up quite a large proportion of the work and furnish a needed contrast to the recitative. One of the arias, Orfeo's "Possente spirto" in Act III, shows us how singers embellished a melody; in this aria Monteverdi wrote out the desired ornaments on an extra staff below the melodic line, furnishing a different set of ornaments for each strophe of the air. Consequently, we have a rare and probably quite authentic picture of how the Baroque singers ornamented melody, although we are still uncertain how to translate some of Monteverdi's notes into actual performance.

Monteverdi's treatment of the orchestra in *Orfeo* is especially interesting. Florentine operas had used only a few lutes or similar instruments for accompaniment; in conformity with the monodic ideal, these were placed behind the scenery and kept as inconspicuous as possible. Monteverdi's orchestra in *Orfeo*, on the other hand, numbered about forty instruments, including flutes, cornetts, trumpets, trombones, a complete family of strings, and several different continuo instruments. In many places the composer, in order to make the dramatic situation more vivid, specified exactly which instruments were to play. Furthermore, the score contains twenty-six orchestral numbers; these include an "overture" (a short fanfare-like movement twice repeated) and several *ritornellos*, that is, short interludes which recur between stanzas of a song or at other places, and thus contribute to the musical unity of the work.

The large orchestra of *Orfeo* was not an innovation of Monteverdi's, but an attempt to organize the traditional large performing groups of sixteenth-century stage productions. The attempt was not followed up in the later operas of Monteverdi or those of other seventeenth-century composers; for a long time after *Orfeo*, the opera orchestra consisted only of strings and harpsichord.

Apparently little progress was made in opera during the twenty years after Monteverdi's *Orfeo*, for the next important school of composers is found at Rome in the 1630's. Here, as might be expected, operas were written on sacred subjects and the ensembles held a prominent place. The most important early Roman opera was *Sant' Alessio* (1632), based on the life of the fifth-century Saint Alexis, with music by Stefano Landi (*ca.* 1590–*ca.* 1655). Roman composers also produced a number of pastoral operas and, strangely enough, it was at Rome that the comic opera began its independent career; the first writer of comic opera librettos was a nobleman of the church, Giulio Rospigliosi, who later became Pope Clement IX.

Roman composers of opera

In the music of the Roman operas we can observe the separation of solo singing into two clearly defined types, recitative and aria. The monodic declamation of Monteverdi's *Orfeo* (and this remained true also of his later operas) was semimelodic; in Landi's work, and still more in the Roman comic operas, this original semimelodic recitative became a rather dry, quick movement with many repeated notes, lacking definite musical contour and supported by thin and musically insignificant harmonies in the continuo—became, in short, more like the recitative in the Italian operas of Mozart and Rossini, a mere vehicle for the rapid delivery of words. Melody and all other elements of musical interest gradually were concentrated in the songs or arias, which now began to assume rather definite shapes: strophic arias, arias over a ground bass, and (most often) arias in a loose two-part form with the sections framed by orchestral ritornellos. The many concerted vocal pieces in the Roman operas are derived from the madrigal tradition, modified of course by the presence of a continuo and by the more regular rhythm of the seventeenth century.

The chief later Roman opera composer was Luigi Rossi (1597–1653). His *Orfeo* (Paris, 1647), on a libretto by Francesco Buti, is based on the same subject as the earlier operas of Caccini, Peri, and Monteverdi. This work illustrates the change that had come over the opera libretto during the first half of the seventeenh century. The antique simplicity of the myth is almost totally buried under a mass of irrelevant incidents and characters, spectacular scenic effects, and incongruous comic episodes. The intrusion of the comic, the grotesque, and the merely sensational into a supposedly serious drama was a common practice of Italian librettists during most of the seventeenth century. It was an indication that the integrity of the drama was no longer of first importance, as it had been with the early Florentines and Monteverdi, and that the ancient Greek and Roman myths had come to be regarded merely as conventional material to be elaborated upon in any way that promised to provide entertainment and offer good opportunities to the composer and singers. The decline of the libretto coincided with the development of an imposing style of theatre music. Rossi's *Orfeo* is, in effect, a succession of beautiful arias and ensembles well calculated to make the hearer forgive its faults as a drama.

In part, the deterioration of the opera libretto and the changes in the character of the music were the consequences of presenting opera *Venetian opera* in public performance rather than to private audiences. This step was taken when the first public opera house was opened at Venice in 1637. Before many years Venice had become the operatic capital of Italy, a position she retained until the end of the seventeenth century. Venetian composers, or composers trained in the Venetian school, were also responsible for the spread of Italian opera to the cities of southern Germany in this period.

Monteverdi wrote his two last operas for Venice: *Il ritorno d'Ulisse* (*Ulysses' Homecoming*) and *L'incoronazione di Poppea* (*The Coronation of Poppea*), performed respectively in 1641 and 1642. *Poppea* is in many respects Monteverdi's operatic masterpiece. It lacks the varied orchestral colors and the large orchestral and scenic apparatus of *Orfeo*, but excels in the depiction of human character and passions through music, being in this respect far in advance of any other seventeenth-century opera. The recitative is wonderfully concentrated and expressive, and is smoothly combined with more definitely outlined musical forms such as arias and duets. Modern revivals have proved that *L'incoronazione di Poppea*, far from being an opera of merely historical interest, is a masterpiece of living art, as able now as in the seventeenth century to stir the deepest emotions of those who listen to it.

One of the leading Venetian opera composers was Monteverdi's pupil, Pier Francesco Cavalli (1602–1676). The steady demand for new works at Venice is reflected in the quantity of Cavalli's output. Of his forty-one operas, the most celebrated was *Giasone* (1649), a full-blown score with scenes in which arias and recitatives alternate, though the two styles are always kept carefully distinct. Cavalli's music has neither the fine construction nor the penetrating psychological insight of Monteverdi's: it aims at broad striking effects and is best in scenes of violence and passion, as in the celebrated "Incantation" sung by the sorceress Medea in the first act of *Giasone*.

The operas of Marc' Antonio Cesti (1623–1669) are more polished but less forceful in style than those of Cavalli; Cesti excels in lyrical arias and duets. His opera best known today is *Il pomo d'oro* (*The Golden Apple*), which was written for and performed at Vienna in 1667 on the occasion of the wedding of the Emperor Leopold I. As a festival opera, it was staged without regard to expense and therefore includes some features that were not common at Venice, such as an unusually large orchestra and many choruses. *Il pomo d'oro* was remarkable also for its lavish scenic effects.

By the middle of the seventeenth century Italian opera had assumed the form it was to maintain without essential change for the next two hundred years. The principal features of this form were: (1) concentration upon solo singing with a concomitant neglect of ensembles and of instrumental music; (2) separation of recitative and aria; and

"The Palace of Paris," a sumptuous scene for the first act of Marc' Antonio Cesti's Il pomo d'oro. *This typically Baroque setting was designed by Lodovico Burnacini, an important seventeenth-century theatre architect.* 189

(3) introduction of distinctive styles and patterns for the arias. This development was accompanied by a complete reversal in the relation of text and music: the Florentines had considered music accessory to poetry; the Venetians treated the libretto as hardly more than a conventional scaffolding for the musical structure.

Vocal Chamber Music

At the opening of the seventeenth century composers were confronted with some disturbing questions. The first involved monody: could the rhythmic flexibility and the lifelike dramatic power of the solo recitative be absorbed into a system of vocal music based on counterpoint of several equally important parts? If so, what means of formal coherence could be devised? Then there was the basso continuo: within the bare texture of a supporting bass and one or two high voices could any resources be found to equal the ample sonority of the older contrapuntal music? The way in which composers of the early seventeenth century proceeded to reconcile the new ideas with the older tradition can perhaps be most clearly understood by regarding it as a process of gradual enrichment and formal stabilization of the monodic style. Many different means were employed, of which two were of particular importance: (1) the use of the bass, as well as the entire harmonic structure, to give formal coherence to a composition; and (2) the use of the *concertato* principle to supply variety of texture and contrapuntal interest.

In the many collections of monodies that were published during the early part of the seventeenth century one of the most important means of obtaining unity was to keep the same bass for every stanza of the text while varying the melody of the solo part at each repetition of the bass pattern. Such an arrangement is called *strophic variation*. The bass might not be identical in every repetition, but its outline was maintained so that the same succession of harmonies occurred in every strophe. This is the scheme, for example, of the coloratura aria "Possente spirto" from the third act of Monteverdi's *Orfeo;* in simpler form, it also occurs in the strophic arias of Caccini's *Nuove musiche.*

The bass as a unifying force

For such songs the bass might be freely invented, in which case it was ususally a mere series of notes without any particular melodic shape. There were, however, traditional bass patterns or *grounds*, many of them inherited from sixteenth-century dances or improvisatory practices, which composers might use instead of inventing a bass of their own. These traditional bass grounds were quite short and with easily recognizable outlines. If they were not long enough to accommodate an entire stanza of poetry, they were repeated over and over again, either unchanged (*ostinato bass*), transposed, or varied by rhythmic and melodic elaboration of the essential few notes. These repeated bass patterns of one kind or another served as unifying devices in hundreds of compositions, both instrumental and vocal, of the Baroque period.

One important kind of ostinato bass appearing early in the seventeenth century was commonly called a *chaconne* or *passacaglia* bass; the original melodic kernel of these basses was apparently a series of four notes descending diatonically by step from tonic to dominant (Example 67: 1). The chaconne bass in minor or in a chromatic variant was especially favored for laments and other songs of a mournful character (Example 67: 1c, 3). Other popular bass forms of the period were the *romanesca* (Example 67: 2), the *ruggiero*, and the *passamezzo moderno;* the last two were really chord progression schemes, not merely bass melodies.

A widespread development of the early seventeenth century was the rise of the *concertato* style. This adjective comes from the same root as *concert* and *concerto;* it connotes not only "sounding together," but also the idea of competition or emulation. The *concertato* style, then, is one in which different musical elements are engaged in a manner which deliberately emphasizes the contrast of one voice or instrument against another, or of one group against another, or of a group against a solo. The origins of the *concertato* style of the Baroque lie in the polychoral works of the Venetian school and in the many polyphonic madrigals of the late sixteenth and early seventeenth centuries in which two or three voices, or a solo voice, are brought into prominence against the background of the ensemble.

The growth of the *concertato* style, along with other developments, can be followed in the fifth, sixth, seventh, and eighth books of Monteverdi's madrigals, published respectively in 1605, 1614, 1621, and 1638. It is fascinating to observe the greatest composer of his time succeed in fusing the heterogeneous musical elements of the early seventeenth century into an eloquent language, firm in structure, varied in color, alternately joyous and sad, robust and tender, warlike and peaceful, responsive to every suggestion of the text.

All these madrigals, beginning with the last six of Book V, have a basso continuo, and many call for other instruments as well. Solos, duets, and trios are set off against the vocal ensemble; there are instrumental introductions and recurring instrumental interludes (ritornellos). The seventh book is entitled *Concerto* and is described as consisting of "madrigals and other kinds of songs." Book VIII, *Madrigals of War and Love*, is especially noteworthy for the variety of forms and types, including madrigals for five voices; solos, duets, and trios with continuo; and large works for chorus, soloists, and orchestra. Among the finest compositions in this volume is the madrigal *Hor ch'el ciel e la terra* ("Now that Heaven and Earth") for six voices, two violins, and continuo, a masterpiece of moods and sonorities, of abundantly varied harmonies and vivid dramatic contrasts.

In the eighth book also are two *balli* (semidramatic ballets) and another work in the *genere rappresentativo* or theatre style, the *Com-*

Bass Patterns

1. Chaconne or Passacaglia

(a) major form   (b) minor form   (c) chromatic form

2. The Romanesca bass

(a)   (b)

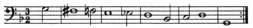

3. Purcell: *Dido and Aeneas*

4. Buxtehude: *Ciacona*

5. Bach: *Passacaglia*

6. Reger: *Introduction, Passacaglia, and Fugue* for two pianos, Op. 96

battimento di Tancredi e Clorinda ("The Combat of Tancred and Clorinda"), which had been performed at Venice in 1624. The instruments (string quartet with bass gamba and continuo), in addition to accompanying the voices, play interludes in which various parts of the action are imitated or suggested: the galloping of horses, the clash of swords, the excitement of combat. For such purposes Monteverdi invented a kind of music which he called the *stile concitato* or "excited style"; one device prominent in the *stile concitato* was the rapid reiteration of a single note, either with quickly spoken syllables in the voice or instrumentally as a string "tremolo" in rhythm. (An example of one of the *concitato* sections from the *Combattimento* appears in HAM, No. 189.) The *stile concitato*, born of the urge for a more perfect musical representation of the text, was one of Monteverdi's many contributions to the ever-expanding language of music in the early seventeenth century.

The complex Baroque musical style thus was achieved by the interaction of diverse elements. Monody and madrigal were combined; formal articulation was approached through the organization of the bass and the harmonies and through systematic use of ritornellos; texture was varied by use of the *concertato* style. As a result, the representational and pictorial power of music was enlarged and in-

The salon of the Mocenigo Palace, Venice, where The Combat of Tancred and Clorinda *was first performed before a gathering of the nobility.*

tensified. All these developments coincided with a reaction, especially strong after 1630, against considering the text the only or chief unifying factor in serious vocal composition; the innate requirements of the music became more important to composers as they began to discard the original concept of music as merely a transparent veil for text. The gradual separation of recitative and aria left the composer free to write aria melody unhampered by the necessity of following every nuance of the text; and arias began to unfold in graceful, smoothly flowing phrases supported by simple harmonies, most often in slow triple meter with a persistent single rhythmic motif (Example 68). This *bel canto* style of vocal writing was a creation of Italian composers; it was imitated in all countries and was influential in both vocal and instrumental music throughout the Baroque and after.

Italian vocal chamber music in the first half of the seventeenth century was published in collections of madrigals, arias, dialogues, duets, and the like. The form that eventually came to engage the chief attention of Italian composers was the *cantata* (literally, a piece "to be sung"). This word, like its counterpart, *sonata*, has been used to designate many different types of composition. In a collection published before 1620 it was applied to arias in the form of strophic variations. Neither that form nor any other was consistently followed by cantata composers during the next two or three decades. Toward the middle of the century *cantata* came to mean a composition usually for solo voice with continuo accompaniment, in several sections which often intermingled recitatives and arias, on a lyrical or sometimes quasi-dramatic text. Yet the Roman, Luigi Rossi, the first eminent master of this particular type of cantata, also wrote others which

Forms of vocal solo music

193

had simpler forms—either plain strophic songs, strophic variations, arias with ostinato bass, or arias in an *ABA* (called *da capo*) pattern. Other leading Italian cantata composers of the middle seventeenth century were Giacomo Carissimi (1605–1674)—whose chief field, however, was the sacred oratorio—and the opera composer, Marc' Antonio Cesti.

Church Music

Sacred music, although by nature conservative, was affected as soon and almost as strongly as secular music by the innovations of the late sixteenth and early seventeenth centuries. Monody, the basso continuo, and the *stile concertato* were all applied to sacred texts. There was, of course, some opposition to the new styles, and indeed, in the Roman Catholic Church, Renaissance polyphony of the Palestrina

Example 68   Aria from *Giasone*, Pier Francesco Cavalli

Delightful pleasures that bless the soul, remain in my heart; delay no more the joys of love. O my dear pleasures, remain.

type was never completely abandoned. Thus throughout the seventeenth century two distinct styles, one conservative (*stile antico*) and one progressive (*stile moderno*), were opposed. Many times both tendencies were manifest in one and the same composer. Before the middle of the seventeenth century Palestrina had become the supreme model for the conservative style. All composers were trained to write counterpoint based on Palestrina's practice, though in the course of time the details were modified: a basso continuo was often added, rhythms became more regular, and the older modes gave way to the major-minor system.

*The Baroque
polychoric style*

The conservative Roman counterpoint, although invaluable for study and discipline, was less important in actual early seventeenth-century composition than the style, stemming from the polychoric works of Giovanni Gabrieli and the Venetian school, which is today called the "colossal Baroque." Many composers in this period wrote sacred music for huge aggregations of singers and players, but the master of this style, and one of the major figures in seventeenth-century Catholic Church music, was Orazio Benevoli (1605-1672). His festival Mass written for the consecration of the cathedral at Salzburg in 1628 calls for two eight-part choruses with soloists; each chorus is associated with three different instrumental combinations and each has its own basso continuo; there is, in addition, a third basso continuo for the whole ensemble. This formidable score takes up fifty-three staves. Benevoli's later works, written mostly for St. Peter's in Rome during the 1640's, give a more adequate idea of his true stature than does the somewhat unwieldy Salzburg Mass; these later works include psalms, motets, and Masses for three, four, or more choruses, which are provided with a figured bass for the organ but which may equally well be sung unaccompanied. The choruses were stationed at separate places on different levels within the ample basilica of St. Peter's, so that the listeners felt they were enveloped in music from all directions—a truly grandiose and typically Baroque conception.

*Other styles in
church music*

One of the first composers to adopt the *stile moderno* in church music was Lodovico Grossi de Viadana (1564-1645), who in 1602 published a collection called *Cento concerti ecclesiastici* (*One Hundred Church Concertos*) for solo voice, or various combinations of solo voices, with basso continuo. This arrangement was of great practical significance: it allowed a work to be performed, if necessary, with a small number of singers, and so eliminated the necessity for doubling or replacing vocal parts by instruments as had often been done in the sixteenth century.

Settings of sacred texts in monodic or in *concertato* style became common during the first half of the seventeenth century. The *stile concertato*—in the form of solos, duets, dialogues, trios, choruses, and diverse small or large combinations of voices and instruments—was applied to both motets and Masses. In this field as in others Monteverdi was a notable pioneer. His *Vespers* of 1610 is a magnificent setting of a complete liturgical office incorporating traditional Gregorian Chants as *cantus firmi* but making use of all the new musical resources of the time—recitative, aria, and all varieties of solo, choral, and instrumental groupings—in a unified artistic whole. The sacred compositions of Monteverdi's Venetian period are for the most part in the *concertato* style, but treated in a completely free and sometimes operatic manner.

Not only the monodic and *concertato* styles but also the specific dramatic methods of opera were turned to sacred uses. In 1600 Emilio del' Cavalieri (*ca.* 1550–1602), a Roman nobleman associated with the Florentine Camerata, produced on the stage at Rome a morality play with music—in effect, a sacred opera with allegorical characters—entitled *La rappresentazione di anima e di corpo* (*The Representation of the Soul and Body*).

Apparently this first experiment with sacred opera was not considered successful enough to be imitated; but during the first three or four decades of the century a number of semidramatic dialogues on sacred themes were produced, as well as similar works involving solos and choruses with orchestra and continuo; these compositions combined elements of narrative, dramatic dialogue, and meditation or exhortation, and were not usually intended for stage performance. Toward the middle of the century works of this kind were called *oratorios*, though the word did not at first have any very precise connotation as to musical form. The libretto of an oratorio might be in Latin (*oratorio latino*) or Italian (*oratorio volgare*). The principal master of the oratorio in the mid-seventeenth century was Giacomo Carissimi at Rome.

The oratorio was distinguished from the contemporary opera by its sacred subject matter, by the presence of the *testo* or narrator, by the use of the chorus for dramatic, narrative, and meditative purposes, and by the fact that oratorios were seldom if ever meant to be staged. Action was narrated or suggested, not presented. Both oratorio and opera used monodic recitative, arias, duets, and instrumental preludes and ritornellos.

In Austria and the Catholic southern cities of Germany, sacred music during the Baroque remained wholly under Italian influence. Italian composers were particularly active at Munich, Salzburg, Prague, and Vienna. Composers in the Lutheran central and northern regions began early in the seventeenth century to utilize the new monodic and *concertato* techniques, sometimes with chorale tunes as melodic material, but often also without reference to traditional chorale melodies. The new methods were best adapted to compositions for a small number of performers. An important collection of such pieces was published in 1618 and 1626 at Leipzig by Johann Hermann Schein (1586–1630), entitled *Opella nova* [literally, *New Little Works*] *Geistliche Konzerte ... auff jetzo gebräuchliche Italiänische Invention* (*Sacred Concertos in the Nowadays Customary*

Italian Manner). In many respects the pieces are like Lutheran counterparts of some of Monteverdi's *concertato* madrigals. These sacred
concertos of Schein were followed by a long series of similar works
by Lutheran composers of the seventeenth century until the form
reached its height in the church cantatas of J. S. Bach.

The greatest German composer of the middle seventeenth century,
and one of the most important musical figures of the Baroque, was

Heinrich Schütz (1585–1672). After beginning university studies for
the law, Schütz was sent to Venice, where he studied with Giovanni
Gabrieli from 1609 to 1612 and brought out his first published work,
a collection of five-part Italian madrigals. From 1617 to the end of his
life, Schütz was Master of the Chapel of the Elector of Saxony at
Dresden, although during the disturbed times of the Thirty Years'
War he spent several years as Court Conductor in Copenhagen.
Schütz renewed his acquaintance with Italian music when he went to
Venice in 1628 especially to see Monteverdi, whom he greatly ad-
mired.

As far as is known, Schütz wrote no independent instrumental
music; our knowledge of him rests almost entirely on his church
compositions, which we possess in considerable quantity and variety,
dating from 1619 to the latest years of his life. The simplest of these
works are plain four-part harmonic settings of a German translation
of the Psalter (1628). Contrasting with the Calvinist plainness of the
psalm settings are the Latin motets of the *Cantiones sacrae* (1625);
in these motets a basically conservative Catholic contrapuntal style is
enlivened by harmonic novelties and by traits derived from the madrigal, such as the musical representation of sleep and waking at the
beginning of *Ego dormio et cor meum vigilat* ("I sleep, and my heart
waketh"; Example 69).

Venetian magnificence and color appear frequently in Schütz: for
example, in the *Psalmen Davids* (1619) for multiple choruses, soloists,
and *concertato* instruments, where the massive colorful sonority of
the colossal Baroque is combined with sensitive treatment of the
German texts. Indeed, the fusion of Italian and German styles, begun
by Hassler and others toward the end of the sixteenth century, was
carried to completion by Schütz, who thus established the fundamental characteristics of German music for the remainder of the
Baroque age. Only one significant element of the fully developed
Lutheran Baroque style was lacking in his works: he seldom made
use of traditional chorale melodies, although he set many chorale texts.

In 1636 and 1639, during years when war had sadly reduced the
Electoral Chapel, Schütz published his *Kleine geistliche Konzerte*
(*Little Sacred Concertos*), motets for one to five solo voices with
organ accompaniment. Another collection of German motets, written
in a severe contrapuntal style, was the *Geistliche Chormusik* (*Spiritual
Choral Music*) of 1648. Most important of Schütz's *concertato* motets

are the *Symphoniae sacrae* (*Sacred Symphonies*), which were pub-

Example 69

lished in three series in 1629, 1647, and 1650. The first two of these are for various small combinations of voices and instruments, up to a total of five or six parts with continuo. All the motets of the *Symphoniae sacrae* are remarkable for vigorous melodic invention and strong rhythms; they frequently alternate duple and triple meter, the latter often being used for ritornello ensemble sections whose recurrence provides one element of formal unity. These motets also abound, as does all of Schütz's music, in striking pictorial motives suggested by the text; for example, the figure ♫♫ ♫♫, which is used with the word *fahren* (to march, go, walk, journey).

The last part of the *Symphoniae sacrae*, published after the end of the Thirty Years' War when the full musical resources of the Dresden chapel were again available, calls for as many as six solo voices and two instrumental parts with continuo, supplemented by a full choral and instrumental ensemble. Many of these works are broadly laid out as dramatically conceived "scenes," sometimes with a closing chorus of pious reflection or exhortation; they thus approach the plan of the later church cantata.

Schütz's compositions of the oratorio type include his most famous work, *The Seven Last Words* (?1645). Here the narrative portions are set as solo recitative (in two instances, for chorus) over a basso

continuo, while the words of Jesus, in free and highly expressive
monody, are always accompanied by continuo and strings. There is a
short introductory chorus and sinfonia; after the seventh Word the
sinfonia is repeated, followed by another short closing chorus. The
quality of this music seems to sum up in itself a quiet yet deeply felt
piety, a personal, ardent, yet infinitely respectful devotion before the
figure of the Saviour.

The *Christmas Oratorio* (1664) is on a larger scale. The narrative
portions are given in rather rapid recitative over a continuo, while the
"scenes" are treated separately with arias, choruses, and instrumental
accompaniment in *concertato style*. Schütz's three Passions, written
toward the end of his life, are by comparison austere, hieratical works:
narrative and dialogue are both in a style of unaccompanied recitative
which, in spirit although not in technical details, is like Gregorian
Chant. The *turba*, that is, the chorus that represents the disciples, the
priests, and other groups, is given motet-like unaccompanied settings.
Schütz's *Seven Last Words*, oratorios, and Passions are the most significant examples of Lutheran music in these quasi-dramatic forms
before J. S. Bach.

Instrumental Music

Instrumental music in the early seventeenth century was in a different stage of development from vocal music. Vocal music had to
assimilate the new technique of monody, which brought about profound changes from the style of the sixteenth century; but instrumental music for the most part had only to continue along the paths
that had already been well marked out before the end of the Renaissance. The transference of the monodic principle to instrumental
music, as for example in sonatas for solo violin with continuo, was not
complicated by consideration of a text. The basso continuo was easily
adapted to instrumental ensembles; moreover, there was a small but
steady production throughout the Baroque of ensemble pieces in
imitative counterpoint which dispensed with the continuo or admitted it only optionally; while for solo keyboard and lute music, of
course, the question of continuo did not arise at all.

Instrumental music in the first half of the seventeenth century was
gradually becoming the equal, in both quantity and content, of vocal
music. Forms were still far from being standardized, however, and
designations were still confused and inconsistent. Nevertheless, certain
basic ways of proceeding, resulting in certain general types of composition, may be distinguished in instrumental music of this period:

1. The ricercare type: pieces in continuous (that is, nonsectional)
imitative counterpoint. These were called *ricercare, fantasia, fancy,
capriccio, fuga, verset,* and other names; they lead eventually to the
fugue.

2. The canzona type: pieces in discontinuous (that is, sectional) imitative counterpoint, sometimes with admixture of other styles. These pieces lead to the Baroque *sonata da chiesa*, the most important line of development in seventeenth-century instrumental music.

3. Pieces based on a given melody or bass: principally the *theme and variations* (or *partita*), the *passacaglia* or *chaconne*, the *chorale partita*, and the *chorale prelude*.

4. Pieces in more or less stylized dance rhythms, either strung loosely together or more closely integrated: the *suite*.

5. Pieces in improvisatory style for solo keyboard instrument or lute: called *toccata, fantasia,* or *prelude*.

These classifications are useful as an introduction to a somewhat complex field; but it must be remembered that the categories are neither exhaustive nor mutually exclusive. For example, the procedure of varying a given theme is found not only in compositions specifically called "variations" but often in ricercari, canzonas, and dance suites as well; toccatas may include short ricercare-like sections; canzonas may have interludes in improvisatory style; in short, the various types interact and interlock in many ways.

Girolamo Frescobaldi (1583–1643).

In its purest form the seventeenth-century ricercare is a fairly short, serious composition for organ or clavier in which one theme is continuously developed in imitation. One example is the *Ricercar dopo il Credo* by Girolamo Frescobaldi (1583–1643), who was organist of St. Peter's in Rome from 1608 until his death. Frescobaldi published it in 1635 in a collection of organ pieces called *Fiori musicali* (*Musical Flowers*) intended for use in the church service; this ricercare was to be played, as the title says, "after the Credo." It is remarkable for the skilful handling of the chromatic lines and the subtle use of shifting harmonies and dissonances, producing the typically Baroque effect of quiet intensity that characterizes much of Frescobaldi's organ music.

Fantasia

On a larger scale than the simple ricercare, and with a more complex formal organization, is a type of early seventeenth-century keyboard composition usually called a *fantasia*. The leading fantasia composers in this period were the Amsterdam organist Jan Pieterszoon Sweelinck (1562–1621) and his German pupils, Samuel Scheidt (1587–1654) of Halle and Heinrich Scheidemann (*ca.* 1596–1663) of Hamburg. An example of the fantasia is the magnificent *Chromatic Fantasia* of Sweelinck, the form of which is a continuous development of the initial chromatic subject; this subject always remains melodically unchanged, although rhythmically it is both augmented and diminished and several times treated in stretto. As the piece proceeds, different countersubjects and scale passages are combined with the principal theme, and the whole works up to an imposing climax. The music does not flow in absolutely unbroken continuity; despite the unifying power of the unchanging theme, the piece is plainly divided into sections, set off from one another by contrasting rhythms and textures. Moreover, the general plan—one theme presented in successive diverse aspects—has an obvious relation to the variation principle.

Titles like ricercare, fantasia, fancy, capriccio, sonata, sinfonia, and canzona were applied to polyphonic instrumental composition in the early seventeenth century rather indiscriminately. In general it may be said that the ricercare and fantasia were built on a theme or themes of sustained legato character. The tendency was to develop the themes in such pieces in continuous imitative counterpoint, as in the fugue; and, as has already been mentioned, *fuga* was the name used for pieces of this sort in Germany from the earliest years of the seventeenth century. The canzona, on the other hand, had livelier, more markedly rhythmic melodic material and composers tended to emphasize division of this material into sections.

Canzona

The continuous, monothematic ricercare gradually evolved toward the fugue; the multisectional canzona evolved toward the Baroque sonata. As in the sixteenth century, canzonas were written both for keyboard instruments and ensembles. Some distinctive features of the seventeenth-century canzona may be described by citing a series of examples. The first, an anonymous keyboard canzona (MM, No. 26), has three sections in contrasting rhythms, each developing a different theme in fugal imitation, with a closing cadenza-like flourish to round off the whole. In another keyboard canzona, by G. M. Trabaci (*ca.* 1580–1647), the contrasts between the five sections are more marked, but on the other hand a single theme is used throughout (Example 70; also see HAM, No. 191), as in the Sweelinck *Chromatic Fantasia* discussed above. A piece of this type is sometimes called a *variation canzona*. A similar structure is used in many of the keyboard canzonas by Frescobaldi and in those of his most distinguished German pupil, the Viennese organist Johann Jakob Froberger (1616–1667). Some keyboard canzonas, however, and the majority of ensemble canzonas, dispensed with the variation technique and were cast in thematically

unrelated sections—sometimes with many short periods only a few
measures long, put together like a patchwork; and sometimes with
fewer but longer sections, one or more of which might be repeated
either literally or varied after intervening material and thereby serve
as an element of unity. Ensemble canzonas of this kind were written
by Tarquinio Merula (b. *ca.* 1600).

Merula himself called these pieces *canzonas.* A later composer
would probably have called them *sonatas.* This term, the vaguest of all
designations for instrumental pieces at the beginning of the seventeenth century, gradually came to mean compositions whose form
was like the canzona but with special features. Pieces called sonatas
in the early seventeenth century were often for one or two melody
instruments, usually violins, with a basso continuo; whereas the true
ensemble canzona was traditionally written with four parts which
could almost always be played just as well without a continuo. Moreover, sonatas were frequently written for a particular instrument and
hence took advantage of the idiomatic possibilities of that instrument;
they were likely to have a somewhat free and expressive character,
whereas the typical canzona had more of the formal, abstract quality
of instrumental polyphony in the Renaissance tradition.

By the middle of the seventeenth century the canzona and the
sonata had thoroughly merged, and the term *sonata* gradually replaced *canzona;* sometimes the name was expanded to *sonata da chiesa,*
since many of such pieces were intended for use "in church." Sonatas
were written for many different combinations of instruments; a common medium was two violins with continuo. The texture of two
treble melodic parts, vocal or instrumental, above a basso continuo
had a particular attraction for composers throughout the seventeenth
century. Sonatas of this type are usually called *trio sonatas,* and the
two canzonas of Merula mentioned above may be regarded as early
examples.

The seventeenth century has been called "the age of the variation"
because the variation principle permeates so many of the instrumental
forms of the period. In a more specific sense, the *theme and variations*
is the continuation of a favorite type of keyboard composition of the
late Renaissance. Three techniques were used in such pieces: 1) The
melody could be repeated with little or no change, although it might
be transferred from one voice to another and surrounded with different contrapuntal material in each variation. This type is sometimes
called the *cantus firmus variation.* The leading seventeenth-century
composers were, in addition to the English virginalists, Sweelinck and
Scheidt.

2) The melody itself could be ornamented differently for each
variation; as a rule it remained in the topmost voice, with the underlying harmonies essentially unchanged. This type of variation was
written by Sweelinck's pupil, the Hamburg organist Jan Adams
Reinken (1623–1722). Incidentally, the word *partite* ("divisions")

IX. Early
Baroque
Music

Keyboard Canzona, G. M. Trabaci

Example 70

204

was used in the early seventeenth century to designate sets of variations; only later did it come to be applied to sets or suites of dances.

3) In a third type of variation, the bass or the harmonic structure, not the melody, is the constant factor. This is the most flexible of all Baroque variation forms, and was used for many important compositions of the late seventeenth and early eighteenth centuries. An early example is the set of *partite* by Frescobaldi on the "romanesca" theme, one of the favorite variations subjects of the seventeenth century. The outline of the romanesca bass is given in Example 67: 2. In actual composition this outline was usually filled in and ornamented in various ways; the constant element in the variations was thus not the melodic line but rather a series of harmonies. The same method of composition was sometimes used in instrumental pieces called chaconnes or passacaglias (there was apparently no clear distinction between these two in the Baroque), though on the other hand many such works do have a short clearly defined ostinato bass melody or continuously repeated ground.

An important class of Baroque organ compositions from middle and northern Germany were works based on chorale melodies. These pieces were produced in large numbers and in a great variety of forms after the middle of the seventeenth century, but there are examples already in the works of Sweelinck and Scheidt. In 1624 Scheidt published a large collection of compositions for the organ under the title *Tabulatura nova*"—"new," because instead of the old-fashioned German organ tablature Scheidt adopted the modern Italian practice of writing out each voice on a separate staff. Among the chorale compositions of the *Tabulatura nova* are a notable fantasia on the melody *Ich ruf' zu dir* ("I Call to Thee") and several sets of variations on other chorale tunes. There are also shorter organ settings of plainsong melodies, many variations on secular songs, and several monumental fantasias. The works of Scheidt, and his influence as a teacher, were the foundation of a remarkable development of North German organ music in the Baroque era.

Stylized dance music was important in the seventeenth century not only in itself but also because of the extent to which dance rhythms permeated other music, both vocal and instrumental. The characteristic rhythm of the sarabande, for example, and the lively movement of the gigue appear in many compositions that are not called dances at all. As in the sixteenth century, dances were written both for solo instruments and for ensembles. *Dance music*

The early seventeenth century is especially remarkable for the production in Germany of *suites* of dances for instrumental groups, commonly a set or consort of viols, although with the usual understanding that other instruments, such as violins or cornetts, might be substituted. The stimulus for the suites seems to have come largely from English composers living in Germany; probably it was the English influence also that led the Germans to extend the technique *Suites* of thematic variation—already established in the pavane-galliard combination of the sixteenth century—to all the dances of a suite. One of the most important collections of dances was J. H. Schein's *Banchetto musicale* (*Musical Banquet*), published at Leipzig in 1617.

French lute and keyboard music

The conception of the suite as a musical entity, as one composition in several movements rather than a mere succession of short pieces each in a certain mood and rhythm, was a German contribution. In France, the great achievement of the early and middle seventeenth century was to establish a characteristic idiom and style for the individual dances. This achievement was a reflection of the fact that most French suites were not written for an ensemble but for a solo instrument—first the lute and later the clavecin (the French term for harpsichord). Lute music flourished in France during the early seventeenth century, culminating in the work of Denis Gaultier (*ca.* 1600–1672). A manuscript collection of Gaultier's compositions entitled *La Rhétorique des dieux* (*The Rhetoric of the Gods*) contains twelve sets (one in each mode) of highly stylized dances. Each set includes an allemande, courante, and sarabande, with other dances added apparently at random; each suite is thus actually a little anthology of short character pieces, many of which were given fanciful titles.

Since the lute was incapable of sustained tone, it was necessary to sketch in the melody, bass, and harmony by sounding the appropriate tones now in one register, now in another, leaving it to the imagination of the hearer to supply the implied continuity of the various lines (see HAM, No. 211). This was the "broken style" which other French composers adapted to the harpsichord, together with certain features of the variation technique derived from the English virgin-

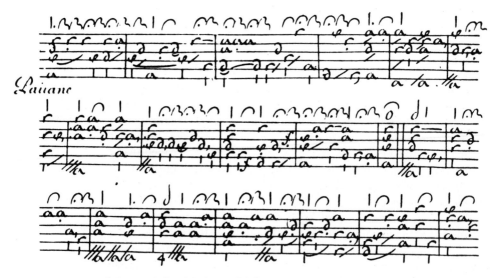

A page of Gaultier's La Rhétorique des dieux; *for a transcription, see* HAM, No. 211.

alists; they also systematically developed the use of little ornaments (*agréments*), sometimes indicated by stenographic signs on the page and sometimes left to the discretion of the player. The French lute style was the source not only of important developments in keyboard music but also of the entire French style of composition in the late seventeenth and early eighteenth centuries.

The earliest important composer in the new keyboard idiom was Jacques Champion de Chambonnières (*ca.* 1602–1672), the first of a long and brilliant line of French clavecinists. The new style was carried to Germany by Froberger, who established the allemande, courante, and sarabande as standard components of dance suites. In Froberger's manuscripts the suites end with a slow dance, the sarabande; in a later, posthumous publication of the suites in 1693, they were revised so as to end with a lively gigue. The fusion of genre pieces and dance rhythms in the mid-seventeenth century keyboard suite is well illustrated in one of Froberger's most famous compositions, a lament on the death of the Emperor Ferdinand IV; this piece, in the pattern and rhythm of an allemande, forms the first movement of a suite.

A different kind of improvisatory composition, already foreshadowed by some Italian keyboard works of the late sixteenth century, occurs in some of the toccatas of Frescobaldi. In contrast to the imposing objective grandeur and virtuosity of the Venetian school, these toccatas are in a reserved, subjective, mystical vein, with sustained harmonies and extraordinary original chord progressions. These works, exemplified by the well known *Toccata for the Elevation* from

A seventeenth-century Italian harpsichord in an elaborately sculptured Baroque case. (Courtesy Metropolitan Museum of Art, Crosby Brown Collection of Musical Instruments, 1889)

the *Fiori musicali*, are the very essence of improvisatory style, although they utterly renounce technical display.

Other keyboard toccatas of Frescobaldi's, however, are related to the Venetian type: they allow scope for virtuosity and in form are a long series of loosely connected sections with great luxuriance of musical ideas. The various sections of these toccatas, the composer states, may be played separately, and the piece may be ended at any appropriate cadence if the player so desires; moreover, Frescobaldi indicates that the tempo is not to be subject to a regular beat but may be modified according to the sense of the music, especially by retarding at cadences.

More solidly formed though less exuberant toccatas were written by Froberger; in these, the free improvisatory passages provide a framework for systematically developed sections in the contrapuntal style of a fantasia. Froberger's pieces were the model for the later Baroque coupling of toccata and fugue, such as occurs in the works of Buxtehude or the familiar *Toccata in D minor* of Bach. Similar pairing of improvisatory and fugal styles was used by many German organ composers of the seventeenth century.

X The Mature Baroque: Vocal Music

Opera, Cantata, Song

In the second half of the seventeenth century, opera spread through Italy and outward to other countries. The principal Italian center was Venice, whose opera houses were famous all over Europe.

The Venetian opera of this period, although by later standards dramatically ridiculous, was scenically and musically splendid. The plots were a jumble of improbable characters and situations, an irrational mixture of serious and comic scenes, and served mainly as pretexts for striking stage effects, pleasant melodies, and beautiful solo singing. Vocal virtuosity had not yet reached the dizzying heights it attained in the eighteenth century, but the way was being prepared. The chorus had practically disappeared, the orchestra had little to do except accompany, and the recitatives were of only slight musical interest: the aria reigned supreme. Composers of the new aria did not entirely disregard the text, but they considered it merely a starting point; they were chiefly interested in the musical construction, the material for which they drew from the rhythms and melodies of popular music—that is, music familiar to the people in general. Motives imitated from trumpet figures were used for martial or vehement arias, often being expanded into brilliant coloratura passages. An example is the aria "Vittrici schieri" ("Victorious hosts") from the opera *Adelaide* (1672) by M. A. Sartorio (*ca.* 1620–*ca.* 1685). The coloratura had not yet become—as it had by the end of the century among second-rate composers—an arbitrary vocal adornment for display of virtuosity; it was still serving a definite expressive function.

Sartorio was one of the last of the Venetians who continued the heroic style of opera established by Monteverdi and Cavalli. In the works of Sartorio's follower Giovanni Legrenzi (1626–1690) a milder, more genial temper prevails. The aria "Ti lascio l'alma impegno" ("I leave my soul imprisoned with thee") from Legrenzi's *Giustino*

(Venice, 1683) shows the combination of graceful nobility of melodic line and natural contrapuntal and constructive skill which is typical of Italian music in the late seventeenth century.

In addition to Sartorio and Legrenzi, the most important Italian opera composers of the late seventeenth and early eighteenth centuries were Francesco Provenzale of Naples (1627–1704), Alessandro Stradella (1644–1682), Carlo Pallavicini (1630–1688), Agostino Steffani (1654–1728), and Alessandro Scarlatti (1660–1725).

Pallavicini and Steffani were two of the many Italian composers who in the late seventeenth and early eighteenth centuries carried Italian opera to the eagerly receptive German courts. Pallavicini worked chiefly in Dresden, Steffani at Munich and Hanover.

In his later works Steffani wrote amply proportioned arias and accompaniments of rich *concertato* texture; he nearly always managed to maintain an equal balance between form and emotional content in his music. One of the best Italian opera composers of his time, his works are important not only for themselves but also historically; they illustrate the transition from the style of the middle Baroque to that of the late Baroque, and they exerted influence on eighteenth-century composers, especially Keiser and Handel.

Steffani's aria "Un balen d'incerta speme" ("A flash of uncertain hope") from the opera *Enrico detto il Leone* (*Henry the Lion*; Han-

Example 71   Aria, "Un balen," from *Enrico detto il Leone*, Steffani

…is the only ray [of hope] that sustains me amidst the clouds of pain.

over, 1689) illustrates his early style. The aria has a da capo form of modest dimensions, with a contrasting middle section. The coloratura passages, though prominent, are neither excessive nor unrelated to the text: they occur on the pictorial words "balen" ("flash") and "raggio" ("ray"), while the passage on "dolor" ("pain") expresses the thought in typically Baroque fashion with chromatic melody and harmonic cross-relations. (Example 71; the complete aria is given in HAM, No. 244.)

In Italy even before the end of the seventeenth century there were distinct tendencies in opera toward stylization of musical language and forms, and toward a simple musical texture with concentration on the single melodic line of the solo voice, supported by ingratiating harmonies. The eventual result was a style of opera which was more concerned with elegance and external effectiveness than with dramatic strength and truth; but the dramatic weaknesses were often redeemed by the beauty of the music. This new style, which became dominant in the eighteenth century, was apparently developed in its early stages principally at Naples, and hence is sometimes known as the *Neapolitan* style.

The Neapolitan style

One type of aria often found in Italian opera of this period is the *Siciliana*. Derived from folksong, it consists of a rather melancholy, languid melody in 6/8 or 12/8 meter, usually in the minor mode; frequently at cadences the supertonic (the second degree of the scale) is flatted, thus producing the chord called the *Neapolitan sixth* (see Example 72, measures 5 and 8).

Another notable feature of eighteenth-century Italian opera was the emergence of two distinct types of recitative. One type—which later was given the name *recitativo secco* ("dry recitative") and was accompanied only with the harpsichord and a sustaining bass instrument—was used chiefly to get through long stretches of dialogue or monologue as quickly as possible with a minimum of musical interference. The second type—*recitativo accompagnato* ([orchestrally] "accompanied recitative")—was used for especially tense dramatic situations; the rapid changes of emotion in the dialogue were reinforced by the orchestra, which both accompanied the singer and punctuated his phrases by brief instrumental outbursts. There was also a type of melody which was neither so rhythmically free as the recitative nor so regular as the aria, but stood somewhere between the two; this kind of melody is called *arioso*, that is, "aria-like."

The struggle between the seventeenth-century Baroque opera and the newer style is evident in the works of Alessandro Scarlatti. Scarlatti's earliest operas were similar to those of Legrenzi and Stradella. In many of his later works, notably in *Mitridate* (Venice, 1707), *Tigrane* (Naples, 1715), and *Griselda* (Rome, 1721), the broad dramatic conception of the arias and the importance of the orchestra evidence Scarlatti's devotion to a serious musical ideal; but pressure from his patrons and the demands of his audiences sometimes induced him to write in a simpler, more immediately attractive idiom. An example of the lighter Italian style is the comic duet from *Gl'inganni felici (The Lucky Stratagems)*, an opera performed at Naples in 1699.

By the beginning of the eighteenth century, Italian opera had been accepted by every country in Western Europe save France. Although a few Italian operas had been played at Paris toward the middle of the seventeenth century, the French for a long time would neither accept the Italian opera nor create one of their own. However, in the 1670's a national French opera was finally achieved under the august patronage of Louis XIV. With special features that distinguished it from the Italian form, it remained essentially unchanged until past the middle of the eighteenth century. Tentative experiments in French opera were made by Robert Cambert (*ca.* 1628–1677) beginning in 1659; but the first important composer was Jean-Baptiste Lully (1632

Example 72   Aria, "Ricordati ch'io t'amo," from *L'Eraclea*, A. Scarlatti

cor - da - ti ch'io t'a - - mo, e ser - vo e ta - cio

ri - cor - da - ti ch'io t'a - mo, e ser - vo e ta -

cio.

Remember that I love you and serve you and am silent.

213

−1687), who succeeded in blending elements from the ballet and the drama in a form which he called a *tragédie lyrique* ("tragedy in music") .

Lully was an Italian who came to Paris at an early age, and who by astute business management and the favor of the king made himself virtually the musical dictator of France. His opera music, monotonous in harmony and almost totally unrelieved by any flash of spontaneous feeling, is most immediately attractive to modern ears in the massive spectacular choruses and in the rhythmical dances of the ballet scenes,

Jean-Baptiste Lully

Jean-Baptiste Lully (*1632–1687*).

for example the Chaconne from *Roland*. Dances from Lully's ballets and operas eventually became widely popular in arrangements as independent instrumental suites, and many composers in the late seventeenth and early eighteenth centuries wrote dance suites in imitation of Lully's.

An important and original contribution of Lully was the devising of a kind of recitative suitable to the French language. On the whole, the difference between recitatives and more melodic passages for solo voice was far less marked in French than in Italian opera. Fairly often

Example 73

Air from *Alceste*, Lully

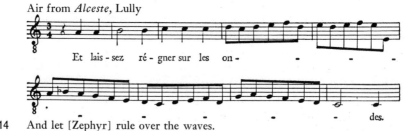

Et lais - sez ré - gner sur les on -

And let [Zephyr] rule over the waves.

des.

Lully writes a recitative which is periodically interrupted by a recurring melodic phrase, as in the lament "O mort! venez finir mon destin déplorable" ("O death, come and put an end to my unhappy fate") from *Persée*.

Lully's operas contain many short songs in the graceful rhythm of the minuet or some other dance. In contrast to the Italian composers, Lully avoids coloratura writing, except for the purpose of briefly illustrating some pictorial detail (see Example 73; the entire song is in HAM, No. 225).

Other airs, less numerous but of greater musical interest, are poetical depictions of quiet scenes and of the contemplative feelings aroused by them. An example is "Bois épais" ("Dark forest") from the opera *Amadis* (1684; Example 74). Musical mood-paintings of this kind— serious, restrained, elegantly proportioned, full of aristocratic yet sensuous charm—were much admired and frequently imitated by later composers.

Even before he began to write operas Lully had established the musical form of the *ouverture*, the "French overture." In the late seventeenth and early eighteenth centuries, instrumental pieces in this form not only introduced operas and other large composite works, but also appeared as independent compositions and sometimes con-

Air, "Bois épais," *Amadis*, Lully

Example 74

Thick forest, redouble your shadows: you cannot be dark enough, you cannot sufficiently conceal my unhappy love.

stituted the opening movement of a suite, sonata, or concerto. The French overture has two parts. The first section is homophonic in style, slow in movement, majestic, with persistent dotted rhythm. The second section is more contrapuntal in texture (or at least usually starts out with some semblance of fugal imitation) and is comparatively fast-moving, though without ever sacrificing a certain grave and serious character; this section often ends with an *allargando*, which sometimes includes a reference to the characteristic rhythm and perhaps to the actual musical material of the first section. Each section is marked to be repeated. Some later opera overtures and other instrumental pieces begin in this way, then continue with a number of additional movements. The original aim of the *ouverture* was to create a festive atmosphere for the opera that was to follow; Venetian overtures of the early seventeenth century had served the same purpose. By the end of the century, the Italian opera composers were beginning to write overtures (which they called *sinfonie*) of a quite different type, but the French remained faithful to their traditional form.

English opera

Opera in England had a short career in the second half of the seventeenth century. John Blow's (1649–1708) *Venus and Adonis*

John Blow

(1684 or 1685) is an unpretentious pastoral opera, containing some charming and even moving music, in which the influences of the Italian cantata as well as of both the native English and the fashionable French styles of the period are discernible. The overture and prologue are obviously modeled on those of French opera; many of the airs and recitatives adapt the emotionally expressive curves of Italian *bel canto* to English words; other songs have more purely English rhythms and melodic outlines. The final threnodic chorus "Mourn for thy servant" is typically English in its simple, truthful interpretation of the text, its grave rhythms, flawless declamation, lucid part writing, and frequent harmonic audacities.

Henry Purcell

Henry Purcell, the finest English musical genius after William Byrd and the last great English composer before the twentieth century, was a pupil of Blow; he served as organist of Westminster Abbey from 1679 and held other posts in the official musical establishments of London. In addition to many odes for chorus and orchestra, cantatas, songs, catches, anthems, Services, fancies, chamber sonatas, and keyboard works, he wrote incidental music for forty-nine plays, the largest and most important part of this theatre music being composed during the last five years of his life.

His opera *Dido and Aeneas* (1689) is a masterpiece of opera in miniature; the orchestra consists of strings and continuo, there are only four principal roles, and the three acts, including dances and choruses, take only about an hour to perform. The music shows that Purcell was able to incorporate in his own style both the achievements of the English school of the seventeenth century and the influences on that school from Continental sources. The overture is of the

John Blow (1649–1708).

French type, and the homophonic choruses in dance rhythms suggest, although they surpass in tunefulness, the choruses of Lully. The minuet rhythm $\frac{3}{4}$ ♩ ♩ | ♩ ♫ | ♩ ♩ | ♩ of the chorus "Fear no danger to ensue" is especially reminiscent of French models. The closing chorus "With drooping wings" must certainly have been suggested to Purcell by the final chorus in Blow's *Venus and Adonis;* equally perfect in workmanship, it has a larger scale and a profounder depth of

Henry Purcell (ca. 1659–1695).

217

elegiac sorrow, the sentiment being supported by the musical suggestion of "drooping" and the impressive pauses after the word
"never." The recitatives are neither the rapid chatter of the Italian
recitativo secco nor the stylized rhythms of French operatic recitative,
but free plastic melodies flexibly molded to the accents, pace, and
emotions of the English text. Three of the arias are built entirely over
a ground bass; the last of these—and one of the greatest arias in all
opera—is Dido's lament "When I am laid in earth." In its perfect
adaptation of technique to expression this song is one of the landmarks
of seventeenth-century music.

Apart from *Dido and Aeneas*, Purcell's output of dramatic music
was all incidental music for plays. In four or five of these the musical
portions are so extensive as to make them in effect operas within the
seventeenth-century English meaning of the word—that is, dramas in
spoken dialogue but with overtures, entr'actes, and long ballets or
other musical scenes. Purcell's principal operas of this sort were
Dioclesian (1690), *King Arthur* (1691), *The Fairy Queen* (1692; an
adaptation of Shakespeare's *Midsummer Night's Dream*), *The Indian
Queen* (1695), and *The Tempest* (1695).

Unfortunately for English music, no composer appeared after
Purcell who had sufficient stature to maintain the national tradition
against the overwhelming popular preference for Italian opera at the
beginning of the eighteenth century. For two hundred years English
opera remained a stepchild while English audiences lavished their
enthusiasm on the productions of Italian, French, or German composers.

German opera

Despite the prevailing fashion for Italian opera at the German
courts in the seventeenth century, a few cities supported German
companies and gave operas in German by native composers. The most
important center was the northern free city of Hamburg, where the
first public opera house in Europe outside Venice was opened in 1678.
The Hamburg opera existed until 1738, by which time the changed
public taste would no longer support native opera on any considerable
scale. During these sixty years, however, a number of German opera
composers were active, and a national school of opera arose. Many
librettos of German operas in this period were translated or imitated
from the Venetian poets, and the music of the German composers was
influenced by both Venetian and French models.

The foremost German opera composer was Reinhard Keiser (1674
–1739), who wrote over one hundred works for the Hamburg stage

*Reinhard
Keiser*

between 1696 and 1734. Keiser's operas at their best represent a successful union of Italian and German qualities. In subject matter and
general plan the librettos are like those of the Venetian operas, and
the virtuoso arias even surpass their Italian counterparts in vigor and
brilliance. The slower melodies, though lacking the suave perfection
of the Italian *bel canto*, are serious and sometimes profoundly expressive; the harmonies are well organized in broad, clear structures.

Keiser was no slave to the current Italian fashion of casting practically every aria in the da capo form; when he uses this pattern it is often with modifications, and in addition he introduces free arioso melodies not bound strictly to any rhythmic or formal scheme, as well as songs in purely German style. His accompaniments are of special interest, for Keiser shared the preference of most German Baroque composers for a comparatively full polyphonic texture in contrast to the Italian tendency to concentrate everything in the melody. Thus his arias abound in interesting basses and varied combinations of orchestral instruments which "concertize" or "compete" with the voice in independent melodic figures.

Another of Keiser's traits, which may be due to his German background, is his feeling for nature. In his most famous opera, *Croesus* (Hamburg, 1710), and in other works, there are pastoral scenes which the composer has handled with a freshness and naturalism rare in Italian opera of the time; the opening scene of the second act of *Croesus*, for example combines the effect of rustic instruments with a melodic line realistically suggesting bird songs.

Along with opera, the other important Italian form of vocal composition in the second half of the seventeenth century was the cantata. After the early years of the century, the cantata had developed from monody with strophic variation to a form consisting of many short contrasting sections; in the second half of the century it finally settled into a more clearly defined pattern of alternating recitatives and arias —normally two or three of each—for solo voice with continuo accompaniment, on a text usually of amatory character in the form of a dramatic narrative or soliloquy, the whole taking perhaps ten to fifteen minutes to perform. Thus in both its literary and its musical aspects the cantata resembled a detached scene from an opera; it differed from opera chiefly in that both poetry and music were on a more intimate scale. Designed for performance in a room, without stage scenery or costumes, and for smaller and more discriminating audiences than those of the opera houses, the cantata kept always a certain elegance and refinement of workmanship that would have been out of place in opera. Because of its intimate character, also, it offered more opportunity than opera for experimental musical effects.

Practically all the Italian opera composers of the seventeenth century were prolific composers of cantatas. In quantity as well as in quality the years from 1650 to about 1720 were astoundingly productive ones in Italy; but as is true of the operas, only a tiny fraction of these works is accessible in modern editions.

The most noted cantata composers after Carissimi, L. Rossi, and Cesti were Legrenzi and Stradella. A climax was reached toward the end of the century with the more than six hundred cantatas of Alessandro Scarlatti. His cantata *Lascia, deh lascia* (Cease, O Cease) has many characteristics typical of the form. It begins with a short section of *arioso* (see Example 75a; the entire cantata is given in GMB, No.

260). The ensuing recitative is typical of the mature style of Scarlatti in its wide harmonic range: notice the modulation to the remote key of E-flat minor at the words "inganni mortali" ("deceptions of mortal life"; Example 75b). Then follows a full da capo aria with long, supple melodic phrases over a bass in stately eighth-note rhythm, organized partly by the help of sequences and containing likewise some unusual harmonic progressions and chromatics expressive of the word "tormentar" ("torment"; Example 75c).

A second brief recitative, leading in rapid succession through various keys from F major to B minor, introduces a second da capo aria in E minor, the key of the opening movement. Although the middle sections of both arias end in the dominant minor, the general tendency of the modulations throughout is toward the subdominant. The mood of tender melancholy, the elegant melodic lines, and the refinement of the harmonic workmanship are thoroughly characteristic of Scarlatti.

A form midway between cantata and opera was the *serenata*, a semidramatic piece usually written for some special occasion, which frequently had allegorical texts and typically was performed by a small orchestra and several singers. Stradella was one of the first composers of serenatas; his example was followed by Scarlatti, Handel, and most other composers of the late seventeenth and eighteenth centuries.

Example 75a   Cantata: *Lascia, deh lascia*, Alessandro Scarlatti

a. Cease, O cease to torment me.

b.

Example 75b

[fie - le] d'un i - dol trop-po in - gra - to tra - gl'in - gan - ni mor -

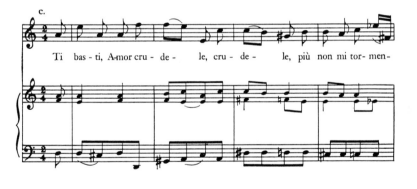

ta - li; se sco-po all' i - re d'un av - ver - so fa - to:

b. ... [bitterness] of an adored one too ungrateful, among the deceptions of mortal life; if it is the purpose of the wrath of adverse fate [only to make me die]....

c.

Example 75c

Ti bas - ti, A-mor cru - de - le, cru - de - le, più non mi tor - men -

tar, più non mi tor - men - tar ch'io vuò mo - ri - re,

c. Enough, cruel Love; torment me no more.

221

X. The
Mature
Baroque:
Vocal Music

Song in other
countries

The Italian chamber cantata was imitated or adapted in other countries, though to a lesser extent than Italian opera. In France Marc-Antoine Charpentier (1634–1704), a pupil of Carissimi, composed both secular cantatas and sacred oratorios in the Italian style. Italian influence remained strong on most of the French cantata composers of the early eighteenth century; thus Louis Nicolas Clérambault (1676–1749), who published five books of cantatas between 1710 and 1726, alternated recitatives in the manner of Lully with arias in Italian style, sometimes even with Italian words. In France there was also a modest but steady production throughout the seventeenth century of *airs* of various types, some attaching to the older tradition of courtly vocal music and others of a more popular cast.

The situation in Germany was similar; Keiser, Telemann, and others in the early eighteenth century wrote cantatas on Italian as well as on German texts. Among the many seventeenth-century German composers of solo songs the most notable was Adam Krieger (1634–1666) of Dresden, a pupil of Scheidt; his *Neue Arien* (*New Airs*), published in 1667 and 1676, were for the most part strophic melodies in a charmingly simple popular style with short five-part orchestral ritornellos, though occasionally he approached the form of the cantata with through-composed text in contrasting movements. The use of orchestral accompaniments and ritornellos with solo songs was more common in Germany than in other countries, and many German composers also wrote songs and arias on sacred texts. Toward the end of the seventeenth century in Germany the song as a type of independent composition practically disappeared, being absorbed into composite forms—the opera or the cantata. Occasional songs in collections around the turn of the century are similar in style, if not in form, to opera arias.

England was of all western European nations the most remote from Italian influence in the seventeenth century. There were some attempts to imitate the new monodic recitative during the Commonwealth, and after the Restoration English musicians became acquainted with the works of Carissimi and Stradella; but the best song productions of English composers owed little to foreign models. In this genre as in all others the outstanding composer was Henry Purcell. In addition to the many songs written as theatre music, he wrote a large number of vocal solos, duets, and trios.

Church Music and Oratorio

The separation, so characteristic of the Baroque era, between conservative or "strict" style and progressive or "free" style is nowhere more vividly illustrated than in the music of the Roman Catholic Church during the later seventeenth and early eighteenth centuries. Hundreds of Masses and other liturgical compositions were written

in the manner of the Roman school of Palestrina, many of them employing the Renaissance techniques of parody and *cantus firmus*.
Frequently such works included canons and other learned contrapuntal artifices; they were sung by unaccompanied voices, or with
instruments merely doubling the vocal parts. But the new musical
resources of the seventeenth century—solo singing, the basso continuo, multiple choirs, the *concertato* treatment of voices and instruments—were also eagerly taken up by church composers, and on the
basis of the works of Monteverdi, Carissimi, Schütz, and other
masters of the early and middle Baroque a further evolution of style
occurred in the late seventeenth and early eighteenth centuries.

Viennese church music in this period was the product of a union of
Italian and South German characteristics, and sums up many of the
principal stylistic achievements of the Baroque. The Mass and other *Church music at Vienna*
liturgical texts were set to music on a magnificent festive scale with
choruses and solo ensemble sections freely intermingled, supported by
full orchestral accompaniment as well as orchestral preludes and ritornellos. Especially elaborate choruses were written for the "Amen" of
the Gloria and Credo in the Mass. Sequential repetitions became a
common constructive device within a clearly outlined harmonic
major-minor system.

Church composers who worked at Vienna include Johann Heinrich
Schmelzer (*ca.* 1623–1680), Johann Kaspar Kerll (1627–1693), Antonio Draghi (1635–1700), and Marco Antonio Ziani (ca. 1653–1715),
as well as Johann Josef Fux (1660–1741), who in addition to works
in the old Palestrina style also composed Masses and motets with
orchestral accompaniment.

In the Masses of Antonio Caldara (1670–1736), a pupil of Legrenzi,
there are not only solo or ensemble sections within predominantly
choral movements but also independent, self-contained solo arias and
duets with concertizing instruments and orchestral ritornellos; these
Masses thus have somewhat the aspect of a series of separate musical
numbers, like an opera—although the operatic recitative was never
used in liturgical compositions, and the full da capo aria form appeared but seldom.

The originators of the peculiarly plaintive early eighteenth-century
chromaticism, which of course affects the melody as well as the harmony, were Italian—Antonio Legrenzi and Antonio Lotti (*ca.* 1667– *Pergolesi and Hasse*
1740), and especially Alessandro Scarlatti and the younger Giovanni
Battista Pergolesi (1710–1736). Pergolesi's *Stabat Mater*, written only
ten years later than Caldara's, exemplifies the fragile texture, the
admirably balanced phrasing, and the lyrically sentimental tone of
much Italian religious music of the eighteenth century. German and
Italian traits also meet in the works of Johann Adolf Hasse (1699–
1783), a composer who studied and lived many years in Italy and who
in addition to some one hundred operas also wrote many oratorios,
Masses, and other church compositions.

The oratorio, although on sacred subjects, was not bound by the conventional limitations of purely liturgical music, being intended rather for performance in what might be called sacred concerts, and thus often serving as a substitute for opera during Lent or at other seasons when the theatres were closed. After Carissimi's time, the Latin oratorio with choruses was largely abandoned in favor of the *oratorio volgare*. Practically all Italian opera composers of the Baroque also wrote oratorios, and as a rule there was little if any difference in musical style between the two. The chorus was retained to a slight extent in the oratorio, but most of the oratorio music was written as solos and duets, as in opera. The close connection between the two forms is suggested by the fact that most of the oratorios in the Catholic centers of South Germany in this period were, like the operas, on Italian texts.

The favorite church composer of the early eighteenth century at Paris was Michel-Richard Delalande or de Lalande (1657–1726), some of whose motets for chorus and orchestra are worthy examples of the grand style in ecclesiastical music of this period. Another eminent name in this field is that of François Couperin (1668–1733); his *Leçons de ténèbres* (1714), on texts from the Offices of Matins and Lauds for Holy Week for one or two solo voices with accompaniment in a spare *concertato* style, are uniquely impressive works.

The principal forms of Anglican church music after the Restoration were the same as those of the early part of the century, namely anthems and Services. Among the many English church composers, John Blow and Henry Purcell were outstanding. Since Charles II favored solo singing and orchestral accompaniments, many anthems of the verse type were produced, such as Pelham Humfrey's (1647–1674) *O Lord my God*. Anthems for coronation ceremonies were, of course, especially elaborate works; examples are Purcell's *My heart is inditing* or the splendid coronation anthems of Blow. Not a few of the composers of English Restoration verse anthems descended to triviality in their efforts to mimic the attractions of theatre music. A more even level of musical excellence was maintained in the less pretentious "cathedral" or "full" anthems for chorus without soloists, of which Purcell's earlier four-part *Thou knowest, Lord, the secrets of our hearts* is a beautiful example. Some of the best of Purcell's sacred music is found in his settings of nonliturgical texts, pieces for one or more solo voices usually in a rhapsodic arioso style with continuo accompaniment, evidently designed for private devotional use.

The Baroque era, particularly the period from 1650 to 1750, was the Golden Age of Lutheran music. Its development was affected by two conflicting tendencies within the church. The Orthodox party, holding to established dogma and public institutional forms of worship, favored using all available resources of choral and instrumental music in the services. Opposed to Orthodoxy was the widespread movement known as Pietism, which emphasized the freedom of the individual believer; Pietists distrusted formality and high art in worship, and preferred the expression of personal feelings of devotion in music of more simple character.

The enormous increase in production of devotional songs in the latter part of the seventeenth century was accompanied by a general decline in both poetic and musical quality. Many of the Pietistic texts expressed self-centered and sentimental religious attitudes in extravagantly emotional language, while attempts to give the music a simple folklike quality too often resulted only in mediocrity. Not until after 1700 did the opposing currents of Pietism and Orthodoxy arrive at a mutually beneficial union. In the meantime developments of importance took place in Orthodox centers where the environment was favorable and the material resources adequate for the maintenance of high artistic standards. Three basic musical elements were involved in the developments: the chorale, the solo song, and the *concertato* style as established in Germany by Schein, Scheidt, Schütz, and other composers of the early and middle seventeenth century. These elements were combined by later composers in many different ways, so that within the prodigious amount of Lutheran church music from the late seventeenth and early eighteenth centuries they exist in almost every conceivable combination. Three examples must suffice to show some of the wide range and variety of forms in this period.

Schütz's tradition of concerted music for chorus, solo voices, and orchestra without reference to chorale melodies may be illustrated by a chorus "Die mit Tränen säen" ("They that sow in tears") from a larger work by his pupil the Hamburg organist Matthias Weckmann (1619–1674). Weckmann's treatment of the words "They that sow in tears shall reap in joy" is typically Baroque in the contrast between the two opposite moods suggested by the text.(Example 76; the entire chorus is given in GMB, No. 212.) *Concerted church music*

Another example of the concerted style, but for a smaller performing group, is a setting of the chorale *Wachet auf* (*Wake, awake*) for solo voice, strings, and continuo by Franz Tunder (1614–1667) of Lübeck (Example 77; the chorale appears in HAM, No. 214).

More subjective in mood, and showing some influence of Pietist sentiment, were the influential "Dialogues between God and a Believing Soul" by Andreas Hammerschmidt (1612–1675), published in 1645 (Example 78; the entire piece appears in HAM, No. 213). This work is remarkable for the skilful use of a trombone obbligato in the tenor register.

An important line of development toward the eighteenth-century church cantata was marked out by those concerted compositions that incorporated both text and melody of a familiar chorale. Tunder was one of the pioneers in this form.

One of the principal Lutheran composers of the late seventeenth century was Dietrich Buxtehude (*ca.* 1637–1707), Tunder's son-in-law and his successor at Lübeck. Although the majority of Buxte-

hude's works were of the free *concertato* type he also wrote *chorale
variations,* a form in which each stanza of a chorale in turn serves as a
basis for elaboration by voices and instruments. *Wachet auf* is written
this way; its form consists of a short festive instrumental prelude or
sinfonia, the outline of which seems to have been suggested by the first
two phrases of the chorale melody; a first stanza of the chorale for
soprano voice and orchestra (strings, bassoon, continuo), in 3/2 and
4/4 time, each phrase slightly ornamented in the voice and the vocal
phrases separated by brief orchestral interludes, the whole being
considerably extended by repetition of the last half of the chorale
tune; a second stanza, bass voice with orchestra, treated similarly to
the first stanza, but in brisk 3/4 rhythm; a third stanza, for two
sopranos and bass, in 3/2, which is more compact, with short points
of imitation on several of the chorale phrases, and which broadens out
at the end to a sonorous climax. All movements are in the same key,

Example 76   Chorus from Cantata: *Wenn der Herr die Gefangenen zu Zion,* Matthias
Weckmann

D major, so that contrast is achieved mainly through change of texture and rhythm.

The variation form, so common in the Baroque period, is frequently found in chorale-based concerted compositions of the late seventeenth century. When a chorale melody was not used, composers felt free to employ a more flexible arrangement, alternating short solo arioso

Cantata: *Wachet auf*, Franz Tunder   Example 77

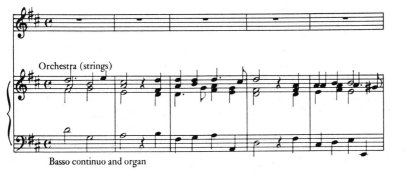

Basso continuo and organ

Example 77
(cont.)

Wa- chet auf, ruft uns die
Mit- ter- nacht heisst die - se

Stim - - me der Wäch- ter sehr hoch
Stun - - de, sie ru- fet uns mit

auf der Zin - ne: wach auf, wach auf, du
hel - lem Mun - de: wo seid, wo seid ihr

Awake! the voice calls to us, the voice of the watchers high up on the tower; awake, thou city of Jerusalem! Midnight is this hour; it calls to us with a clear voice: Where are ye, wise maidens?

sections with ensemble and choral parts. Toward the end of the century a somewhat standardized pattern of concerted church music developed, consisting of a "motet-like opening chorus on a Bible verse, a solo movement or movements (aria or arioso) . . . and a final chorus setting a stanza of a chorale."[1] Free concertato without chorale prevails in the vocal works of Johann Pachelbel (1653–1706), most famous of a long line of composers working at or in the vicinity of Nuremberg. Like many of the composers in southern Germany, where Venetian influence remained powerful, Pachelbel frequently wrote for double chorus.

Until the end of the seventeenth century the texts of Lutheran compositions consisted chiefly of passages from the Bible or the

Dialogue: *Wende dich, Herr*, Andreas Hammerschmidt

Example 78

229

X. The
Mature
Baroque:
Vocal Music

Example 78
(cont.)

Alto: Turn thee, O Lord, and be merciful unto me.
Bass: Is not Ephraim my dear son and my beloved child? Because I remember
well [what I have said to him]. . . .

*The Lutheran
church cantata*
church liturgy, together with verses taken from or modelled on
chorales or other hymns. In 1700 Erdmann Neumeister (1671–1756)
of Hamburg, an Orthodox theologian but a poet of decidedly Pietist
leanings, introduced a new kind of sacred poetry for musical setting,
in a form which he designated by the Italian term "cantata." Neumeister (and, after him, several other Lutheran poets of the early
eighteenth century) wrote cycles of cantatas, intended to be used

systematically throughout the church year. The characteristic feature of these church cantatas was the employment, in connection with the prescribed Biblical passages or hymns, of original poetic insertions which sought to expound the given basic text and to bring its meaning home to the individual worshipper through devout meditations of a subjective character. Each of the added poetic texts was designed to be composed either as an arioso or else as an aria, usually in da capo form and frequently with an introductory recitative. Neumeister and his imitators favored the free fancy of the composer by writing their poetry in the so-called "madrigal" style, that is in lines of unequal length with the rhymes irregularly placed; many of Bach's cantata texts and the arias in the *St. Matthew Passion* are in this madrigal style.

The widespread acceptance of this new cantata type was of cardinal importance for Lutheran church music. Its poetic scheme reconciled Orthodox and Pietistic tendencies in a satisfactory blend of objective and subjective, formal and emotional elements; its musical scheme incorporated all the great traditions of the past—the chorale, the solo song, the concerted style—and added to these the dramatically powerful elements of operatic recitative and aria. Strictly speaking, the designation "cantata" is applicable only to compositions of the sort described above; concerted church compositions of the seventeenth and early eighteenth centuries in Lutheran Germany usually had no special designation. However, as in the case of the word "motet," a somewhat loose practice now exists of applying "cantata" indiscriminately to nearly all types of concerted Lutheran church music of the Baroque period, both before and after Neumeister's innovations.

J. S. Bach was the greatest master of the church cantata. His most important immediate forerunners were Johann Philipp Krieger of Weissenfels, who also composed operas; Johann Kuhnau (1660–1722), Bach's predecessor at Leipzig; and Friedrich Wilhelm Zachow (1663–1712) of Halle. Zachow's cantatas have a great variety of forms: recitatives and da capo arias are intermingled with choruses, which sometimes make use of chorale melodies. The writing for both solo and chorus is brilliant in sonority and strong in rhythm; instruments are prominently used in *concertato* fashion. His works point directly and unmistakably to the cantatas of Bach, with which they have many characteristics in common.

Among the contemporaries of Bach notable for their church compositions should be mentioned Christoph Graupner (1683–1760) of Darmstadt; Johann Mattheson (1681–1764) of Hamburg, who wrote Passions and oratorios, but who was mainly important as a theorist; and Georg Philipp Telemann (1681–1767), who worked at Leipzig, Eisenach, Frankfurt, and Hamburg. Telemann's immense production included forty operas, twelve complete cycles of cantatas and motets (about 3000 pieces altogether), forty-four Passions, and a large number of oratorios and other church compositions as well as hundreds of orchestral and chamber works.

The Passion

Among the forms of church music in Lutheran Germany the *Passion* was of especial importance. Plainsong settings of the Gospel accounts of the suffering and death of Christ had existed since early medieval times. After about the twelfth century it was customary to have the story recited in semidramatic form, with one priest singing the narrative portions, another the words of Christ, and a third the words of the crowd (*turba*), all with appropriate contrasts of range and tempo. (The Passion is still sung in this way in Catholic churches.) After the late fifteenth century, composers made polyphonic settings of the *turba* portions in motet style, contrasting with the plainsong solo parts; this type of setting was known as the "dramatic" or "scenic" Passion. Johann Walter adapted the dramatic Passion to Lutheran use with German text in his *St. Matthew Passion* of 1550, and his example was followed by many subsequent Lutheran composers, including Heinrich Schütz. Often, however, the entire text would be set as a series of polyphonic motets—called the *motet Passion*. Motet Passion settings were made by various Catholic composers from about the middle of the fifteenth century; the most celebrated Lutheran motet Passions were those of Joachim a Burck (1568), Leonhard Lechner (1594) and Christoph Demantius (1631).

The rise of the concerted style in the seventeenth century led to a new type of Passion which approximated the form of the oratorio and hence is called the *oratorio Passion;* this setting employs recitatives, arias, ensembles, choruses, and instrumental pieces, all of which lend themselves to a dramatic presentation, as in opera. Schütz's *Seven Last Words* is an early approach to this kind of musical treatment, although its text is a composite of all four Gospels instead of being taken, as was customary in the Passion, from one Gospel exclusively.

In the second half of the seventeenth century the Gospel text was expanded by the addition of, first, poetic meditations on the events of the story, which were inserted at appropriate points and set to music usually as a solo aria, sometimes with a preceding recitative; and second, by chorales traditionally associated with the story of the Passion, which were usually sung by the choir or congregation.

XI The Mature Baroque: Instrumental Music

Up to now instrumental music has been discussed on the basis of musical forms derived from compositional procedures: the ricercare and other fugal forms; the canzona and sonata; variations and other pieces based on a *cantus firmus;* dances and the suite; the toccata and related improvisatory forms. However, instrumental composition in the later seventeenth and early eighteenth centuries will be discussed on a different basis, namely, the medium of performance: music for a keyboard instrument (organ, harpsichord, or clavichord); and music for an ensemble of instruments, whether a small (chamber) group or one of larger size.

The principal types of compositions associated with each of these media are:

Keyboard: toccata (prelude, fantasia); fugue; arrangements of Lutheran chorales or other liturgical material (chorale prelude, verset, etc.); variations, passacaglia, chaconne, and other compositions on a *cantus firmus;* suite; sonata (after 1700).

Ensemble: sonata (*sonata da chiesa*), sinfonia, and related forms; suite (*sonata da camera*) and related forms; concerto.

Organ Music

The greatest development of organ music took place in Germany during the late seventeenth and early eighteenth centuries. In the north, continuing the tradition established in the early part of the century by Sweelinck and Scheidt, the chief figures were Georg Böhm (1661–1733) at Lüneburg and Buxtehude at Lübeck. A central group in Saxony and Thuringia (the Bach region) included Zachow and Kuhnau, as well as Johann Christoph Bach (1642–1703) of Eisenach. One of the most notable of the German organ composers was Johann Pachelbel of Nuremberg. There were many other organists in the south (at Munich, Vienna, and other cities), but their contributions to the literature of the instrument were less imposing than those of their northern colleagues because in the Catholic service the organ functioned mostly as an instrument of accompaniment.

Two principal species of organ compositions were perfected in the late Baroque in Germany: the *toccata* and the *organ chorale*. Each of these designations stands for a general class of compositions, and, as usual in this period, the nomenclature is unstable.

The toccata

The toccata was orginally and always remained essentially a style of music which aimed to suggest the effect of an improvised performance. To this end it used many devices: irregular or free rhythm in contrast with a propulsive unceasing drive of sixteenth-notes; phrases deliberately kept indistinct or wilfully irregular; sudden sharp changes of texture. But mostly the effect of improvisation was maintained by means of a contrived uncertanty in the harmonic flow of the music: by quick erratic changes of direction or (at the opposite extreme) a slow-paced movement involving long, harmonically inert stretches marked usually by extended pedal points. The naturally capricious, exuberant character of toccatas was often intensified by making them vehicles for displaying a performer's skill at the keyboard and on the organ pedals; the demand made for virtuosity in playing the pedals was a feature that especially distinguished the German composers from all other organ composers of the time.

Toccatas best exhibit the outthrusting, fantastic, dramatic aspects of the Baroque spirit in music. It was equally characteristic of the Baroque, however, to discipline the freedom of the toccata, and in the most dramatic manner possible, by yoking it with the ricercare in a union of musical opposites. Composers early began to incorporate in their toccatas well-defined sections of imitative counterpoint which contrasted with the otherwise prevailing rhapsodic style. These contrasting sections were especially necessary in long toccatas. Moreover, the desire for clearly articulated and symmetrical phrases became stronger as the seventeenth century wore on; and even in short toccatas without fugal interludes some measure of order was brought into the rhapsodic flow of sound by means of the two most common crystallizing devices of late Baroque music, the melodic sequence and sequential imitation. The Toccata in E minor by Pachelbel is a good example of this usage.

Works which illustrate on a grand scale the Baroque conflict between impulse and order are the monumental organ compositions of the north German masters, above all those by Buxtehude. Buxtehude's toccatas are made up of sections in free toccata style which alternate regularly with as long or longer sections of imitative counterpoint. The toccatas have a wonderful sense of movement and climax, with great variety in the figuration, and they take full advantage of the idiomatic qualities of the organ. Yet the soaring fantasy of the composer is held in balance by the architectural plan of the whole work.

The opening is always in free toccata style, ending with a solid ca-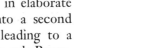
dence; then follows a fugue, always on a subject of salient melodic
outline and with well-marked rhythm, fully developed in elaborate
contrapuntal style; this merges at length gradually into a second
toccata-like section, shorter than the first, and again leading to a
cadence. At this point the composition may close; but as a rule Buxte-

Varied Forms of a Fugal Subject, Dietrich Buxtehude   Example 79

hude goes on to a second and sometimes a third fugue, with brief
interludes and a closing climactic section in toccata style. When there
is more than one fugue, the subjects in the majority of cases are
variants of a basic musical idea (see Example 79, the three fugue subjects from the toccata printed in HAM, No. 234). This use of the
variation principle in a fugal type of composition is derived from the
early seventeenth-century keyboard fantasies of Sweelinck and
Scheidt, as well as from the variation canzona of Frescobaldi and the
toccatas of Froberger.

The class of compositions described above are called by the generic
word "toccata," which is in accord with seventeenth-century usage.
Buxtehude himself used the term only four times; most of his works
in this form, including all the longer ones, were probably originally
called "Praeambula" or "Praeludia." Eighteenth-century musicians
preferred to call such a composition a "Praeludium et fuga," or "Prelude and Fugue," and this is the designation generally used today. The

simple coupling of two contrasted movements, a prelude in free or homophonic style and a fugue in contrapuntal style, is found only in the late Baroque; most seventeenth-century compositions called "Prelude and Fugue" by later editors show a relationship to the simpler Buxtehude type of toccata, that is, a toccata with one comparatively long fugal section in the middle.

The fugue

Fugues were also written as independent pieces. By the end of the seventeenth century the fugue had almost entirely replaced the old ricercare. The essential differences between the two are apparent in late seventeenth-century works (HAM, No. 249a–b) by Johann Krieger (1652–1735). The fugue subject has a more definite melodic character and a livelier rhythm than the ricercare subject; the ricercare develops in a placid, abstract manner without much variety or any marked climax, but the fugue drives ahead energetically to its close; the fugue has some short episodes (passages where the subject is not being heard in any voice) which are set off by a little lightening of the texture and sometimes also by the use of sequences; whereas the ricercare has fewer such passages and those few not sequential nor in any way different in texture from the rest of the piece. Moreover, the fugue has a tonal organization with a clear dominant-tonic relationship, while the conservative ricercare tends to stay closer to the old modal system.

Neither the fugues of Krieger, however, nor the ninety-four short fugues which Pachelbel wrote for use in the church service as preludes to the singing of the Magnificat give much more than a hint of the potentialities that were realized in the next generation. The final perfection of the fugue, as well as of all the other large musical forms characteristic of the late Baroque, was inseparable from the full development of the major-minor system of tonality with its hierarchy of keys, which made possible a systematic use of key relationships in the musical design of long movements.

Corollary to this development was the gradual extension of the system of *equal temperament* to the tuning of keyboard instruments. In this tuning, the octave is divided into twelve exactly equal semitones, so that an instrument sounds equally in tune in any one of the twelve keys. Formulated by many theorists after the early sixteenth century, and apparently in actual use for lutes, viols, and other fretted instruments during the sixteenth and seventeenth centuries, the system or some practical approximation to it began to be generally applied to keyboard instruments on the Continent by the early years of the eighteenth century. J. K. F. Fischer's (*ca.* 1665–1746) *Ariadne musica* of 1715, a collection of keyboard preludes and fugues using nineteen different major and minor keys, was the principal forerunner of Bach's *Well-Tempered Clavier* (Book I, 1722), which uses all twenty-four keys.

The other principal class of organ composition of the late seventeenth and early eighteenth centuries was works based on a chorale

melody. Organ composers in the seventeenth century used the chorale
in three fundamental ways: as a theme for variations, as a subject for
a fantasia, or as a melody to be presented with appropriate embellishment and accompaniment. These three ways of treating a chorale
melody gave rise to three important types of composition: the *chorale
partita*, the *chorale fantasia*, and the *chorale prelude*. The chorale
partita, a set of variations on a chorale tune, was initiated early in the
century by Sweelinck and Scheidt, and was continued, although with
modifications in the technique, by later organ composers to the time
of Bach and after. The chorale fantasia, also dating from the early part
of the century, gradually moved away from the severe contrapuntal
style of the fantasias of Scheidt. At the hands of Reinken, Buxtehude,
and other north German composers the form became extended. The
treatment of the material became freer; each phrase of the chorale was
worked out in turn and a great variety of figuration and texture was
introduced, always with strong emphasis on brilliant virtuoso effects.

Chorale prelude, a term often loosely applied to any organ composition based on a chorale melody, will be used here in a somewhat
more restricted sense to denote relatively short pieces in which the
entire melody is presented once in readily recognizable form. This
form of the chorale prelude did not appear until after the middle of
the seventeenth century. As the name implies, such pieces probably
originated as functional liturgical music: the organist played through
the tune, with accompaniment and ornaments *ad libitum*, as a prelude
to the singing of the chorale by the congregation or choir; later on,
when pieces in this same general style were written down, they were
called "chorale preludes" whether or not they were intended to serve
the original liturgical purpose. Naturally, many varieties of treatment
are found. (1) Each phrase of the melody in turn may serve as the
subject of a short fugal development, the whole piece thus taking on
the form of a chain of fughettas. This form has an obvious resemblance to the chorale fantasia, but is more concise and more consistent
in style. (2) In one type of chorale prelude, chiefly associated with
the name of Pachelbel, the first phrase receives a fairly extended fugal
treatment, after which this and all the following phrases in turn
appear, usually in the top voice, in long notes with relatively little
ornamentation; each such appearance is preceded by a short antici-
patory imitative development of its characteristic melodic motive
in short notes (that is, in diminution) in the other voices. Sometimes
the opening fugal development is shortened and the first phrase
introduced in the same manner as the ones following. (3) More
numerous are chorale preludes in which the relation between melody
and accompaniment is less exact. The accompaniment, while still
borrowing many of its motives from the chorale tune, is treated much
more freely and with greater variety from phrase to phrase; the
melody, which usually begins at once without any introductory imitative material, is ornamented in an imaginative, unstereotyped manner,

and sometimes extended in a long melismatic phrase at the final cadence. The masters of this subjective and often highly poetic form of
the chorale prelude were Buxtehude and Georg Böhm. (4) Finally,
there are chorale preludes in which the melody, unornamented, is
accompanied in the other voices by a continuous rhythmic figure not
related motivically to the melody itself. This type is not common in
the seventeenth century, but is often found in Bach.

A distinctive French Baroque school of organ music produced some
attractive settings of popular airs and pieces resembling the overtures
and expressive recitatives of French opera, as well as more learned,
contrapuntal works and antiphonal "dialogues" for the three or four
divisions of a large organ. This music has the typically French ornaments (*agréments*); many pieces were designed to exploit particular
color possibilities on the organ, and the stops were often specified.
Among the finest French organ music of this age are the "Masses"
(versets and interludes to be played in the Mass) of François Couperin,
which include specimens of all the distinctive types mentioned above.
Couperin's noble organ music is one of the glories of the Baroque era
in France, as was Buxtehude's in Germany.

*Organ
Masses*

The passacaglia or chaconne was another common form of composition in the late Baroque. In general it retained the same characteristics as in the early part of the seventeenth century: its basis was a
simple four- or eight-measure harmonic pattern indefinitely repeated;
on this rigid framework the composer exercised his ingenuity to
provide continuity, variety, and a sense of progression to climax in
the movement as a whole. Some passacaglias had a definite recurring
bass melody; more often, however, the only recurring factor was the
harmonic pattern, which itself might be somewhat varied in detail

*Passacaglia and
chaconne*

*François Couperin (1668–1733).
(Courtesy Metropolitan Museum
of Art)*

although it always preserved the original four- or eight-measure length with regularly periodic cadences.

The term *clavier* is used to denote both the clavichord and the harpsichord. It is not always possible in the Baroque period, especially in Germany, to tell which of the two a composer intends in a given piece; sometimes it is even uncertain whether a clavier or an organ is the desired instrument. Though all the types of composition described in the preceding section were also used in clavier music, the two important forms of clavier music were the *theme and variations* and the *suite*.

As has already been mentioned, variation of a given musical subject was one of the most widely used techniques in Baroque composition. This basic arrangement of a theme (air, dance, chorale, or the like) followed by a series of variations goes back to the early history of instrumental music. No essential change occurred in the late Baroque, although there was a tendency to abandon the earlier *cantus firmus* type of variation, except in chorale partitas. Many composers after 1650 preferred to write an original song-like melody (often called an *aria*) for the theme rather than borrow a familiar tune as earlier composers had commonly done.

A large proportion of the clavier music of the late seventeenth and early eighteenth centuries is in the form of the *suite*. Two distinct varieties existed. In France, the *ordres* of François Couperin published between 1713 and 1730 consist each of a loose aggregation of many—sometimes as many as twenty or more—miniature pieces. Most of these are in dance rhythms, such as courante, sarabande, gigue and so on, highly stylized and refined. Their transparent texture and delicate melodic lines decorated with many embellishments, as well as their conciseness and humour, are typical of French music of the early eighteenth century.

In Germany before the end of the seventeenth century the clavier suite had assumed a definite order of four dances: allemande, courante, sarabande, and gigue. To these might be added an introductory movement or one or more optional dances placed either after the gigue or before or after the sarabande. The dances, each distinguished by its characteristic rhythm and tempo, were all in the same key and cast in the same formal mould: a first section, modulating to the dominant (or relative major) and ending with a full cadence in the new key; a second section, usually somewhat longer than the first, beginning in the dominant (or relative major) and modulating through one or two closely related keys back to the tonic. Each section was to be repeated. Sometimes the closing measures of the second section would be a (transposed) recapitulation of those of the first section. This feature, but even more the standard modulation scheme of the dances, foreshadows the sonata-form of the Classical period.

The most important composers of the German keyboard suite, besides Froberger, were Pachelbel, Alessandro Poglietti (d. 1683) at

Vienna, Johann Krieger, J. K. F. Fischer, Johann Kuhnau, and Georg
Böhm. A contemporary of Bach and Handel was Gottlieb (= Theo-
phil) Muffat (1690–1770), whose suites are examples of the pre-
Classical style of the eighteenth century. In England, the charming
harpsichord suites of Henry Purcell are the only notable representatives of this form.

*The keyboard
sonata*

The sonata, which in the Baroque period was primarily a type of
composition for instrumental ensemble, was first transferred to the
clavier by Kuhnau in 1692. His *Frische Klavierfrüchte* (*Fresh Clavier-
fruits*), published in 1696, consists entirely of sonatas. More interesting
than these rather experimental pieces are the six sonatas Kuhnau published in 1700, which represent in music stories from the Old Testament, with titles such as "Saul's Madness Cured by Music." "The
Combat between David and Goliath," or "Hezekiah's Illness and
Recovery." These Biblical sonatas are attractive and well-constructed
pieces, as well as amusing musical renditions of the stories. Instrumental program music was not unknown to the seventeenth and early
eighteenth centuries; there are examples in the Fitzwilliam Virginal
Book, as well as numerous battle pieces scattered among the works of
keyboard composers of the period. Heinrich Ignaz Franz Biber (1644
–1704) also wrote Biblical sonatas; and the picturesque titles of Couperin's keyboard and orchestral works are part of this tradition.

Ensemble Music

By the beginning of the eighteenth century Italian musical pre-
eminence had been challenged by the achievements of the French
clavecinists and the north German organists; but in the realm of instrumental chamber music, as in the opera and cantata, the Italians
reigned as undisputed masters and teachers of Europe. The age of the
great violin makers of Cremona—Niccolò Amati (1596–1684), Antonio Stradivari (1644–1737), and Giuseppe Bartolomeo Guarneri
"del Gesù" (1698–1744)—was also the age of great string music in
Italy.

*The ensemble
sonata*

In the most general sense, the independent instrumental sonata of
the Baroque period is a composition for a small group of instruments
—usually two to four—having a basso continuo and consisting of
several sections or movements in contrasting tempos and textures.
Within this general scheme, of course, there may be any amount of
diversity. Two main types or classes of sonatas begin to be clearly
distinguished after about 1660: the *sonata da chiesa* (the "church
sonata," usually designated simply as "sonata"), the movements of
which are not obviously in dance rhythms and do not bear the names
of dances; and the *sonata da camera* (chamber sonata), which is a
suite of stylized dances. So goes the definition, but in practice the two
types do not always appear unmixed: many church sonatas end with

Violin made of maple, pine, and ebony by Antonio Stradivari (1644–1737) of Cremona. (Courtesy Metropolitan Museum of Art, Bequest of Annie Bolton Matthews Bryant, 1934)

one or more dance movements (not always so designated), while many chamber sonatas have an opening movement which is not a dance. The most common instrumentation after 1670 for both church and chamber sonatas is two violin parts with continuo. A sonata written in this way is called a *trio sonata*, even though for performance it requires four players (since the basso continuo line is played on a violoncello or similar instrument while the harpsichordist or organist fills in the implied harmonies). The texture exemplified in the trio sonata—two high melody lines over a bass—appears frequently in many other types of Baroque music, and persists even beyond the Baroque era.

Less numerous than trio sonatas in the seventeenth century, although more numerous after 1700, are sonatas for solo violin with continuo (the so-called *solo sonata*). Larger groups, up to six or eight instrumental parts with continuo, are also used in the Baroque, and there are a few sonatas (or like pieces under a different designation) for a single stringed instrument without accompaniment.

With respect to its external form, the evolution of the canzona-sonata in the seventeenth century may be summarized as a progressive reduction in the number of movements and a progressive increase in the length of each movement. The order of the movements did not become standard until toward the end of the seventeenth century, but complete thematic independence of the various movements became increasingly the rule.

It is significant that the trio sonata, not the solo sonata, was especially favored by Italian composers of the seventeenth century. The instrumentation of the trio sonata made possible an ideal balance of lyrical melody and limpid polyphony. The two high singing violins could interweave their contrapuntal patterns (in which the distant bass as well might join), but the texture, held together by the unobtrusive harmonies of the harpsichord, was sufficiently open so that there was no danger of obscuring the lines or making the sonority too thick. Also, the solo sonata was fatally prone to excesses of virtuosic

241

Arcangelo Corelli (1653–1713).

display; but the trio sonata subordinated the individual to the ensemble in a regulated disposition of forces which directed attention to the substance rather than to the outward show of the music.

Arcangelo Corelli

The perfect examples of the serene, balanced, classical phase of Baroque musical art are the violin sonatas of Arcangelo Corelli (1653–1713). His works include trio sonatas, solo sonatas, and concertos.

Corelli's trio sonatas

In his trio sonatas Corelli summed up the achievements of Italian chamber music in the late seventeenth century; in his solo sonatas and concertos he initiated developments that were followed for the next fifty years and more. He was exceptional among Italian composers of his time in that he apparently wrote no vocal music whatever; he transferred the national genius for song to the violin, the instrument that most nearly approaches the expressive lyric quality of the human voice.

A fundamental technical device in all of Corelli's music is the sequence. It is no coincidence that Corelli, the first Baroque composer to make extensive and systematic use of this means of construction, was also the first to write music in which we hear the full realization of the major-minor tonality practically free from any trace of modality. The sequence, whether carried out diatonically within one key or modulated downward in the circle of fifths, is one of the most powerful agents in establishing tonality. Corelli's modulations within a movement—most often to the dominant and (in minor keys) the relative major—are always logical and clear; he established the principles of tonal architecture which were elaborated and extended by Handel, Vivaldi, Bach, and all other composers of the next generation. Corelli's music is almost completely diatonic; chromaticism is limited virtually to a few diminished seventh chords and an occasional flatted second (Neapolitan sixth) at a cadence.

Many of the Corelli's trio church sonatas consist of four movements in the order slow-fast-slow-fast, similar to the order of the four move- ments in the cantata of this period. The same order of movements was often used by other composers of the late seventeenth and early eighteenth centuries, so that some music historians regard it as "the" type of Baroque sonata—a slightly over-simplified view, as there are so many exceptions to the general rule. Corelli's chamber sonatas, both trio and solo, usually begin with a *preludio*, which is followed by two or three of the conventional dances of the suite in the normal order; but the final gigue may be replaced by a gavotte.

As a rule, all four movements are in the same key. There are no contrasting or "secondary" themes within a movement. The subject of the whole musical discourse to come is stated at once in a complete sentence with a definite cadence; from then on the music unfolds in a continuous expansion of this subject, with sequential treatment, brief modulations cadencing in nearby keys, and fascinating subtleties of phraseology. This steady unfolding or "spinning out" (the Germans call it *Fortspinnung*) of a single theme is highly characteristic of the late Baroque.

Corelli's solo sonatas have the same order and character of movements as the corresponding types of trio sonatas, though in his solo church sonatas an additional fast movement of contrasting texture is always coupled with one or the other of the regular two. Naturally, the solo sonatas have a larger proportion of homophonic movements than do the trio sonatas. Corelli's most conspicuous innovation, however, is the technical treatment of the violin. Although the third position is never exceeded, there are difficult double and triple stops, fast runs, arpeggios, cadenzas, and étude-like movements in *moto perpetuo*.

All in all, these solo sonatas give us a comprehensive idea of what Corelli expected in the way of technique from his students. His teaching was the foundation of most of the violin schools of the eighteenth century; it was as influential on later generations of players as his music was on later generations of composers. Some of his contemporaries and many of his followers surpassed him in *bravura*, but none in the understanding of the *cantabile* qualities of his instrument nor in the good taste with which he avoided mere displays of virtuosity unjustified by musical content. His most difficult (at least as far as bowing technique is concerned) as well as his most enduringly popular composition is the masterly set of twenty-four variations which concludes his Opus 5. The theme is the *Follia* (or *Folia*, known also as *les Folies d'Espagne* and by other titles), a well-known tune of probably Portuguese origin dating from the early sixteenth century, with a bass similar to that of the romanesca (see Example 67), and like the romanesca a favorite subject for variations in the seventeenth century.

Performers in the Baroque era were always expected to add notes to those the composer had written. The realization of a figured bass,

XI. The
Mature
Baroque:
Instrumental
Music

*Improvisation
in Baroque
musical
performance*

for example, was worked out by the player. Vocal and instrumental solo melodic lines were dependent on performers' skill, taste, and experience for their proper completion by means of ornaments.

Melodic ornamentation has a long history going back to the Middle Ages. Ornaments probably always originated in improvisation; and although they might at some later stage be partially or even wholly written out, still they kept a certain coloring of spontaneity. For us, the word *ornamentation* is liable to carry misleading connotations, to suggest something unessential, superfluous, a mere optional adjunct to the melody. This was not the Baroque view. The ornaments were not merely decorative; they had a definite expressive function as means of conveying affections. Moreover, some of the more common ornaments—especially the trill and the appoggiatura—incidentally added a spice of dissonance, of which the notated version of the music gives no hint.

In general, there were two ways of ornamenting a given melodic line: (1) small melodic formulas (such as trills, turns, appoggiaturas, mordents) attached to one or two of the written notes. These were sometimes, though not always, indicated by special signs; and (2) longer ornaments, which included the smaller formulas and also scales, runs, leaps, arpeggios, and the like, by means of which the notes of a melody were broken down into a multitude of smaller notes to produce a free and elaborate paraphrase of the written line. The longer ornamentation (called *division, diminution, figuration, graces* and other names) was, of course, most appropriate to melodies in slow tempo. Graces for the slow movements of Corelli's solo sonatas have been preserved from an eighteenth-century edition (printed in HAM, No. 252), one of the few instances in Italian compositions where such ordinarily improvised decorations were written out. Whether or not the graces as we now have them are Corelli's own, they undoubtedly represent the general character of such melodic embellishments as practiced in the late Baroque.

Still another species of ornamentation, common in late Baroque opera and found also in some of the instrumental music of Corelli and his contemporaries, was the *cadenza*, an elaborate extension of the six-four chord of a final cadence. The cadenza at the end of the second movement of Corelli's solo sonata Opus 5, No. 3 is a foreshadowing of the long cadenzas in the concertos of the Classical and Romantic periods.

Performers in the Baroque thus had the liberty to add to the composer's written score; they were equally free to subtract from it or change it in various other ways. Arias were omitted from operas, or different arias substituted, practically at the whim of the singers. Frescobaldi permitted organists to dismember his toccatas or end them at any point they pleased. Composers of variations, suites, and sonatas took it for granted that the players would omit movements *ad libitum.*

Very many title pages of instrumental ensemble music collections allow not only for different kinds of instruments, but also for an optional number of them; for example, sonatas were issued for violin and basso continuo with an additional violin or two "if desired."

The Italian trio sonatas were imitated or adapted by composers in all countries. Purcell in his two sets of trio sonatas published in 1683 and 1697 "endeavor'd a just imitation of the most fam'd Italian masters"; some traces of French influence may be discerned in his rhythms and melodies, but many passages are profoundly English and Purcellian. Handel's trio sonatas are mostly in the same four-movement form and general style as those of Corelli.

In Germany, sonatas for trio or larger combinations were written by Georg Muffat (*Armonico tributo, A Harmonic Tribute;* 1682), Reinken (*Hortus musicus, The Garden of Music,* 1687), Buxtehude (1696), Fux, Caldara, Christoph Graupner, and others. The sonatas of Fux and Graupner contain some remarkable examples of intricate fugal writing which combines the German fondness for counterpoint with a form and style derived from Italian composers.

The earliest as well as the most important trio sonatas in France were those of Couperin. Some of these works were composed probably as early as 1692, although not published until many years later. A collection of 1726, entitled *Les Nations Sonades et Suites de Simphonies en Trio*, contains four "ordres," each consisting of a *sonata da chiesa* (the "sonade") in several movements followed by a suite of dances (the "*suite de simphonies*"). The style, though obviously influenced in the *sonades* by that of Corelli and the other Italians, is distinguished throughout by the same refinement of melody and the same exquisite taste in ornaments that mark Couperin's clavecin pieces. Couperin's chamber music also includes a series of twelve "concerts" for harpsichord and various combinations of instruments, each consisting of a prelude and a number of dance movements; the first four are generally known as the *Concerts royaux* (having been played before Louis XIV in 1714 and 1715), and the last eight were published in 1724 under the collective title *Les Goûts-réunis*, "the united [French and Italian] styles."

The solo violin sonata had always been a prime vehicle for experiments in special bowings, multiple stops, and all kinds of difficult passage work. This early Baroque tradition lived on in Germany in the works of Johann Jakob Walther (1650–1717?), whose collection of twelve sonatas published in 1676 under the title *Scherzi* outdid in these respects anything previously known. Likewise a virtuoso player, but a composer of broader interests, was Heinrich Johann Franz Biber. Although Biber composed church music and instrumental ensemble works, he is remembered chiefly for his fifteen violin sonatas composed around 1675 which represent for the most part episodes in the life of Christ. These ingenuous examples of Baroque program music make considerable use of *scordatura*, unusual tunings of the violin strings to facilitate the playing of particular chords.

Both Walther and Biber often interspersed rhapsodic movements or sections analogous to a toccata in their sonatas, and both wrote many of their longer movements in the form of a theme and variations or a passacaglia. Biber's passacaglia for unaccompanied solo violin which is appended to the collection of Biblical sonatas is perhaps the most important precursor of Bach's great Chaconne in D minor. Most German violin composers after Biber and Walther came under the influence of the Italian schools and developed a cosmopolitan style on that foundation.

A pupil of Corelli was Francesco Geminiani (1687–1762), who had a long career as virtuoso and composer in London. He published there, in 1751, a violin method which undoubtedly embodies the principles of technique and interpretation that were taught by Corelli and the other Italian masters of the early eighteenth century. Geminiani's solo sonatas and *concerti grossi* are founded on the style of Corelli, which is intermingled with progressive traits. Some characteristics of the Baroque still remain in the compositions of two other famous early eighteenth-century violinists, Francesco Maria Veracini (1690–ca. 1750) and Pietro Locatelli (1695–1764), the latter another Corelli pupil. Most celebrated of all the Italian virtuosi was Giuseppe Tartini (1692–1770); but his solo sonatas and concertos are predominantly in the pre-Classical style of the mid-eighteenth century.

The principal French composer of violin sonatas was Jean-Marie Leclair (1697–1764). His music seems to combine the Classical purity of Corelli with a peculiarly French grace and sweetness of melody, and perfect clarity of texture and form with abundant tasteful decoration; his rondeau movements have a particular charm.

The trio and solo instrumentations, although they were the most common, were not the only sonorities to be employed for sonatas (or similar pieces under whatever name) in the Baroque period. In Italy, from the days of Giovanni Gabrieli on through the first half of the seventeenth century, there was a steady production of canzonas, dance suites, sonatas, and sinfonias for groups of three or more melody instruments in addition to a basso continuo.

*Works for
larger
ensembles*

The sonata and more especially the suite for an ensemble of instruments had a particularly long life in Germany. The most notable (though not the most typical) works in this form after Schein's *Banchetto musicale* were the chamber sonatas of Johann Rosenmüller (*ca.* 1620–1684), published in 1670. Each of the eleven sonatas in this collection consists of a "sinfonia" followed regularly by an allemande, courante, ballo (a short, light-humored, sharply rhythmic movement in 4/4 time), and sarabande. The instrumentation is for five strings ("or other instruments") and basso continuo. The sinfonias, which were evidently inspired by the Venetian opera overtures (Rosenmüller spent a large part of his life in Venice), are most remarkable: their principal section is a songful, expressive movement in moderate or slow triple meter, which is repeated da capo after a contrasting faster section. This movement has an introduction which may consist either of imposing block harmonies with dramatic pauses between the phrases, or of short vivid alternations of solemn Grave with agitated Allegro; and as a rule a brief recall of the impressive introductory material both follows the main movement and precedes its da capo repetition.

Toward the end of the seventeenth century a generally recognized distinction of style began to be made between *chamber* music and *orchestral* music—that is, between ensemble music with only one instrument to a part and ensemble music with more than one instrument playing the same part. In a large proportion of seventeenth-century ensemble works it is not clear if composers had any preference in this regard; the choice could depend on circumstances. For instance, a trio *sonata da chiesa*, though presumably conceived for two solo violins, might be played in church by an orchestral ensemble if the size of the auditorium made it desirable or if the occasion were festive. Conversely, neither the designation "sinfonia" nor the presence of three, four, or more melodic parts above the bass necessarily called for an orchestral rather than a chamber group of players. When parts were to be reinforced the usual procedure in the seventeenth century was to increase the number of chord-playing instruments for the continuo and add more melody instruments on the soprano line. Beyond the use of the basso continuo and the predominance of the stringed instruments, there was no common standard that regulated either the makeup of an ensemble or the number of instruments to a part.

Opera houses of course maintained orchestras; consequently the opera overture in both Italy and France, as well as the numerous dances that formed an indispensable part of French opera, were always conceived as specifically orchestral music, and were written in a style suited to orchestral rather than chamber performance. The most famous orchestra in Europe was that of the Paris Opéra, which under the severe regime of Lully had been brought to a pitch of technical perfection hitherto unknown for so large a group of instrumental performers.

German disciples of Lully introduced French standards of playing, along with the French musical style, into their own country. One result was a new type of *orchestral suite* which flourished in Germany from about 1690 to 1740. The dances of these suites, patterned after those of Lully's ballets and operas, did not appear in any standard number or order. From the fact that they were always introduced by a pair of movements in the form of a French Overture, the word *ouverture* soon came to be used as a designation for the suite. Among the early collections of orchestral suites was Georg Muffat's *Florilegium* (1695 and 1698), the second part of which included an essay with much information about the French system of bowing, the playing of the *agréments*, and other matters. Another important

XI. The
Mature
Baroque:
Instrumental
Music

The concerto

collection was J. K. F. Fischer's *Journal de Printemps* (1695). *Ouverture* suites were written also by Fux, Telemann, and a host of other German composers, including J. S. Bach.

A new kind of orchestral composition, the *concerto*, appeared in the last two decades of the seventeenth century, and became the most important type of Baroque orchestral music after 1700. The concerto was the supreme synthesis in purely instrumental music of four fundamental Baroque practices: the *concertato* principle; the texture of a firm bass and a florid treble; musical organization based on the major-minor key system; and the device of building a long work out of separate autonomous movements.

Three different kinds of concertos were being written around 1700. One, the *orchestral concerto* (called also *concerto-sinfonia* or *concerto-ripieno*), was simply an orchestral work of several movements in a style that emphasized the first violin part and the bass, and that usually avoided the more complex contrapuntal texture characteristic of the sonata and sinfonia. More numerous and important at this time were the other two types, the *concerto grosso* ("grand concerto") and the *solo concerto*, both of which systematically contrasted sonorities: in the concerto grosso, a small group of solo instruments, in the solo concerto a single instrument, were set against the main mass of orchestral sound. The "orchestra" was almost always a string orchestra, usually divided into first and second violins, viola, and violoncello with basso continuo. The solo instruments also were usually strings: violin in the solo concerto; two violins, or two violins and viola, or violins plus viola and violoncello in the concerto grosso; but solo wind instruments might be added or substituted. *Concerto grosso* originally signified the "large consort," that is, the orchestra, as opposed to the *concertino* or "little consort," the group of solo instruments. Later, the term *concerto grosso* was applied to the composition which used these opposed groups. In both the solo concerto and the concerto grosso, the usual designation for full orchestra is *tutti* ("all") or *ripieno* ("full").

The concerti grossi of Corelli, which are among the earliest examples of the form, employ the principle of solo-tutti contrast; but Corelli did not differentiate in style between the solos and the tutti portions, and these concertos are in effect merely church sonatas or chamber sonatas divided between a small and a larger group of instruments, although the comparative prominence of the first violin part occasionally suggests the texture of the later solo concerto.

The composer who contributed most to the development of the concerto around the turn of the century was Giuseppe Torelli (1658–1709), the leading figure in the last years of the Bologna school. A significant stage of evolution is apparent in the violin concertos from Torelli's last publication (1709), a collection of six concerti grossi and six solo concertos. Most are in three movements (fast-slow-fast), an arrangement which became general with later concerto composers.

Giuseppe Torelli (1658–1709).

The Allegros as a rule are in fugal style, while the middle movement is made up of two similar Adagios framing a brief Allegro. Torelli's vigorous, dynamic Allegro themes are characteristic of the early eighteenth century. Equally significant is the distinction in style between the tutti and the solo passages: the latter blossom forth with lively, diversified, idiomatic figuration, contrasting brightly with the solid thematic quality of the ripieno.

The most important achievement is the form of Torelli's Allegro movements: each begins with a complete exposition of the theme by the full orchestra; alternating with solo episodes, the material of this tutti exposition recurs once or twice, slightly modified and in different keys; the movement is rounded off and brought to a close with a final tonic tutti practically identical with the opening one. A tutti which recurs in this way in a concerto is called a *ritornello;* this structure is typical for all first and last movements of late Baroque concertos. The form is something like that of the rondeau, with the important exception that in a concerto all the ritornellos except the first and last are in different keys. The concerto therefore combines the principle of recurrence with the equally important principle of key relationship. An outline of the structure of the finale of Torelli's Opus 8, No. 8 illustrates the scheme:

Ritornello I: Theme, C minor (10 measures) with sequential extension and cadence in the dominant minor (6 measures).

Solo I: $9\frac{1}{2}$ measures with prominent sequential patterns, beginning in the dominant minor and modulating to the relative major.

Ritornello II: 8 measures, similar to Ritornello I, in the relative major, modulating to the subdominant.

Solo II: 12 measures, modulating to the tonic and concluding with four nonthematic measures of dominant preparation for:

Ritornello III: same as Ritornello I but cadencing in the tonic and with the last four measures repeated *piano* by way of coda.

A similar but slightly more complex scheme is found in the finale of Torelli's D minor Concerto Opus 8, No. 7. Here there are four ritornellos; the second is in the dominant, the third modulates from the subdominant to the relative major, and the last is, after four initial modulating measures, identical with the first. Each solo episode is in faster rhythm than the preceding one; this arrangement contributes markedly to a sense of growing animation as the movement proceeds. The first movement of this concerto uses a version of the chromatic passacaglia bass; the tutti intervenes briefly from time to time in the midst of the solo passages, a common practice in later concertos.

The achievements of Torelli in the realm of the concerto were matched and extended by other Italian composers, especially the Venetian Tomaso Albinoni (1671–1750) and the Italian-German Evaristo Felice dall'Abaco (1675–1742). The concerti grossi of Geminiani and Locatelli are generally conservative, but Locatelli's solo concertos introduce virtuoso passages which foreshadow the importance of this element in the concertos of the Classical period. The greatest Italian master of the concerto was Antonio Vivaldi, whose works we shall study in the following chapter.

XII The Early Eighteenth Century

The overlapping of style periods was seldom if ever so extensive as in the first half of the eighteenth century. All around the late Baroque masters a new style of music was growing up. We have already discussed the first half of the eighteenth century under its aspect as a late stage of the Baroque; in the chapter that follows this one, we shall discuss it as an early stage of the Classical era. But the composers working during these years were not consciously, or at any rate not primarily, concerned with either the historical past or the possible historical future; they were living in the present. In this chapter we shall try to achieve a fuller understanding of the music of the first half of the eighteenth century by surveying the life and works of its four most important composers: Vivaldi, Rameau, Bach, and Handel.

All these four composers were successful and eminent in their own time; all wrote music which, by virtue of its craftsmanship, integrity, and imaginative content, is still significant today. All came to terms with the contemporary conflict between contrapuntal and homophonic styles; all were competent in both instrumental and vocal composition. All were aware of the new currents in musical thought, though none was a deliberate revolutionary in his own music. All worked within the established forms and styles of the late Baroque, and their originality consisted chiefly in doing the accepted things in a uniquely excellent way. Bach brought to consummation all forms of late Baroque music except opera. Vivaldi, Rameau, and Handel excelled in opera; Vivaldi, in addition, perfected the Italian Baroque concerto; Handel created—out of Baroque elements—a new kind of oratorio; and Rameau, in his theoretical writings, developed a new conception of harmony and tonality that proved valid not only for the music of his own time but also for that of many succeeding generations.

Pianoforte dated 1720, one of two surviving instruments built by its inventor, Bartolomeo Christofori (1655–1731). (Courtesy Metropolitan Museum of Art, The Crosby Brown Collection of Musical Instruments, 1889)

Antonio Vivaldi

Antonio Vivaldi (*ca.* 1678–1741), son of one of the leading violinists of St. Mark's chapel, was educated both for music (under Legrenzi) and for the priesthood. He began his priestly duties in 1703, but because of ill health was excused from active service a year later and thenceforward devoted himself wholly to music. From 1704 to 1740 Vivaldi was continually employed as conductor, composer, teacher, and general superintendent of music at the Conservatory of the Pietà in Venice, with frequent leaves of absence to compose and conduct operas and concerts in other Italian cities and elsewhere in Europe.

The conservatories of eighteenth-century Naples and Venice were pious institutions founded originally to shelter orphans and illegitimate children—of whom there must have been a considerable number. The organization of the conservatories was like that of a convent, but as a rule musical training formed an important part of the curriculum. The teaching was thorough and the results important for the musical life of the entire country. Instruction was efficiently organized and pursued without stinting either energy or expense. The resulting

Antonio Vivaldi (ca. *1678–1741*);
from an engraving by F. M. de la
Cave, 1725.

throng of enthusiastic young amateurs, their natural emulation
spurred by special rewards in privileges and stimulated always by the
presence of a few outstandingly gifted individuals, must have provided a highly favorable environment for any composer. Vivaldi was
expected to furnish new oratorios and concertos for every recurring
festival at the Pietà. For these he wrote concertos, the form of instrumental music commonly used at church festival services. About 450
concertos of his are extant, in addition to twenty-three sinfonias,
seventy-five solo or trio sonatas, forty-nine operas, and many cantatas,
motets, and oratorios.

As an opera composer, Vivaldi was certainly successful in his day;
during the years in which he was writing operas (1713–1739) the
theatres of Venice staged more works of his than of any other com- *Vivaldi's vocal*
poser, and his fame was by no means limited to his own city and *works*
country. The few accessible specimens of his church music show
that in this realm also Vivaldo was a composer of real stature. The fact
that many solo and choral passages in his works sound as though they
might have been written by Handel proves merely that both composers used the international musical language of the early eighteenth
century.

Vivaldi's instrumental works, and especially the concertos, are
perennially attractive because of the freshness of their melodies, their
rhythmic verve, their skilful treatment of solo and orchestral string *Vivaldi's*
color, and the balanced clarity of their form. Many of the sonatas, as *concertos*
well as some of the early concertos, are in the seventeenth-century
contrapuntal style of Corelli. However, in his first published collection of concertos (Opus 3, *ca.* 1712) Vivaldi already showed that he
was fully aware of the modern trends toward distinct musical form,
vigorous rhythm, and idiomatic solo writing exemplified by Torelli
and Albinoni. 253

About two-thirds of Vivaldi's concertos are for one solo instrument with orchestra—usually, of course, a violin, but with a considerable number also for violoncello, flute, or bassoon.

Vivaldi's usual orchestra at the Pietà probably consisted of twenty to twenty-five stringed instruments, with harpsichord or organ for the continuo; this is always the basic group, though in many of his concertos he also calls for flutes, oboes, bassoons, or horns, any of which may be used either as solo instruments or in ensemble combinations. The exact size and makeup of Vivaldi's orchestra varied, of course, depending on the players that might be available on a particular occasion. Vivaldi's writing is always remarkable for the variety of color he achieves with different groupings of the solo and orchestral strings; the familiar *Primavera* (*Spring*) concerto—first of a group of four concertos in Opus 8 (1725) representing programmatically the four seasons—is but one of many examples of his extraordinary instinct for effective sonorities in this medium.

Most of Vivaldi's concertos are in the usual eighteenth-century pattern of three movements: an Allegro; a slow movement in the same key or a closely related one (relative minor, dominant, or subdominant); and a final Allegro somewhat shorter and sprightlier than the first. Though a few movements are found in the older fugal style, the texture is typically more homophonic than contrapuntal—but homophonic in the late Baroque sense, with much incidental use of counterpoint and with particular emphasis on the two outer voices. Typical of the late Baroque, also, is Vivaldi's constant use of sequential patterns.

The formal scheme of the individual movements of Vivaldi's concertos is the same as in Torelli's works: ritornellos for the full orchestra, alternating with episodes for the soloist (or soloists). Vivaldi differs from Torelli and all earlier composers not by virtue of any innovation in the general plan of the concerto but because his musical ideas are more spontaneous, his formal structures more clearly delineated, his harmonies more assured, his textures more varied, and his rhythms more impelling. Moreover, he establishes between solo and tutti a certain dramatic tension; he does not merely give the soloist contrasting idiomatic figuration (which Torelli had already done) but makes him stand out as a dominating musical personality against the ensemble as the solo singer does against the orchestra in opera—a relationship inherent in the ritornello aria (the precursor and model of the concerto form), but one which Vivaldi first brought to full realization in a purely instrumental medium. "The tutti announces the propositions that are to be debated in the course of the movement; and the arguments which these provoke give rise to a musical contest between soloist and orchestra, ending in a reconciliation or synthesis of emotions and ideas."[1]

All of Vivaldi's opening themes are so constructed as to define the tonality of the movement with the utmost precision: they consist of

*A page from one of Vivaldi's manuscripts—a tutti section from the finale
of the Concerto in A for solo violin and four-part string ensemble.*

emphatically reiterated primary triads, triadic melodies, scales, or
combinations of these elements. So stark a harmonic vocabulary could
result in monotony; but this danger is avoided thanks to an unflagging
vitality that drives the music onward in an ever varied but never
ceasing rhythmic torrent from the beginning of a movement to its
very last measure. Moreover, once the main tonality is firmly established, the harmony is varied not only by the usual cycle of modulations but also by devices such as the use of minor thirds and sixths
in a major key, or of chromatic chords to signal the approach of a
cadence. Triplet division of the beat is common. The phraseology of
themes and sections is often irregular and sometimes quite subtle.

Vivaldi was the first composer to give the slow movement of a
concerto equal importance with the two Allegros. His slow movement
is usually a long-breathed expressive cantabile melody, like an *adagio*
operatic aria or arioso, to which the performer was of course expected
to add his own embellishments. The slow movements show a predilection for minor keys, especially E minor. There is no standard
formal scheme for these middle movements; many of them have
particularly interesting sonorities in the accompaniments, which usually are lightly scored in contrast to the two Allegros. In his program
music, such as the widely admired *Seasons* concertos and a dozen or
so others of similar cast, Vivaldi shared the half-serious, half-playful
attitude of the eighteenth century toward the naïve realism implied in
such musical depictions.

Vivaldi's influence on instrumental music in the middle and later eighteenth century was equal to that of Corelli a generation earlier. Vivaldi was one of the most important figures in the transition from late Baroque to early Classical style; the assured economy of his writing for string orchestra was a revelation; his dramatic conception of the role of the soloist was accepted and developed in the Classical concerto; above all, the concise themes, the clarity of form, the rhythmic vitality, the impelling logical continuity in the flow of musical ideas, all qualities so characteristic of Vivaldi, were transmitted to many other composers, and especially directly to J. S. Bach. Bach copied at least nine of Vivaldi's concertos, arranging six of them for harpsichord, two for organ, and one (originally for four violins) for four harpsichords and string orchestra. Vivaldi's influence is apparent both in the general scheme and in the details of many of Bach's original concertos, as well as in those of his German contemporaries. Finally, Vivaldi, more than any other single composer, through his concertos impressed on the eighteenth century the idea of an instrumental sound in which the effect of solo-tutti contrast was important, an idea that prevails not only in concertos of the period but in much of the other orchestral music and keyboard music as well.

Vivaldi's influence

Jean-Philippe Rameau

Jean-Philippe Rameau (1683–1764), the foremost French musician in the eighteenth century, had a career unlike that of any other eminent composer in history. Practically unknown until the age of forty, he attracted attention first as a theorist and only afterward as a composer. He produced most of the musical works on which his fame depends between the ages of fifty and fifty-six. Attacked then as an innovator, he was assailed twenty years later even more severely as a reactionary; in favor with the French Court and reasonably prosperous during the later years of his life, he remained always a solitary, strict, and unsociable person, but a conscientious and intelligent artist.

Rameau's career

Rameau's importance for the history of music rests chiefly on his theoretical writings and his operas. Throughout his life Rameau was interested in the theory or, as it was called at that time, the "science" of music; he is one of the rare instances in history of a composer of genius who reflected constantly and systematically on theoretical matters. His writings in this field differ from those of practically all previous Baroque theorists in that he sought to explain the essential nature of musical phenomena on a scientific basis; most other so-called theoretical works of the seventeenth and early eighteenth centuries were little more than codifications of the rules for realizing a figured bass and practical guides for players of keyboard instruments. Not all of Rameau's ideas were original; some, in fact, go back to the writings of the famous sixteenth-century theorist Zarlino, and others had been

Rameau's theoretical works

256

touched upon incidentally by more recent authors. But Rameau seized upon the central issues and stated them in such definitive form that for over two hundred years his principles remained the foundation of music theory and are even yet important for the study of harmony. His system is expounded in his *Treatise on Harmony Reduced to its Natural Principles* of 1722, although he introduced some additions, refinements, and modifications in later books.

Rameau considers the chord the primal element in music—not the single tone, and not melodic lines or intervals. The major triad he eventually derived from the overtone series; he had more difficulty in accounting for the minor triad on "natural principles," though he did establish the so-called melodic minor scale. He posited the building of chords by thirds (upward and downward), whereby the triad was expanded to a chord of the seventh or ninth. Rameau's recognition of the identity of a chord through all its inversions had far-reaching consequences, as did the corollary idea of the *basse fondamentale*, or, as we would say, the root-progressions in a succession of harmonies. Moreover, Rameau established the three chords of the tonic, dominant, and subdominant as the pillars of tonality, and related other chords to these, thereby creating the concept of functional harmony; he also stated the conception that modulation might result from the change of function of a chord (in modern terminology, a pivot chord). The fundamental nature of all these ideas is obvious.

Less widely significant were Rameau's theory of the derivation of all melody from harmony (expressed or implied) and his views on the peculiar quality of specific chords and keys. It is an interesting historical coincidence that Rameau's *Treatise on Harmony* and the first book of Bach's *Well-Tempered Clavier* appeared in the same year. Bach's work gathers up the past, definitively presenting the outcome of centuries of polyphony; Rameau's theories sum up and clarify the

Jean-Philippe Rameau (1683–1764).
(Courtesy Metropolitan Museum of Art)

257

XII. The
Early
Eighteenth
Century

*Rameau's
musical style*

methods of composers of the immediately preceding generations, but they also presage the future—a musical style which was to achieve its full realization through harmony, not counterpoint.

The entire development of French opera after Lully was toward increasing the already large proportion of decorative elements—scenic spectacle and ballet, with descriptive orchestral music, dances, choruses, and songs. More and more the drama, even in works called *tragédies lyriques,* had deteriorated in both importance and quality, and eventually opera-ballet had frankly come to be nothing but ballet and spectacle on a huge scale with only the thinnest thread, or none at all, of dramatic connection between the various scenes. Rameau's "heroic ballet," *Les Indes galantes* (The Gallant Indies, 1735), is a finished example of an opera-ballet: each of its four *entrées* or acts has a self-contained plot, and each takes place in a different quarter of the globe, thus giving opportunity for a variety of decorations and dances which gratified the early eighteenth-century French public's interest in exotic scenes and peoples. The *entrées* are entitled respectively "The Generous Turk" (the scene is laid in "an island of the Indian Ocean" and the plot is similar to that which Mozart later used for his *Abduction from the Seraglio*), "The Incas of Peru," "The Flowers, a Persian Festival," and "The Savages" (the locale is "a forest of America" and the plot introduces Spanish and French characters as well as Indians). Rameau's music, especially in the *entrée* of the Incas, is far more dramatic than the libretto would lead one to expect.

As far as musical features are concerned, Rameau's theatre works are obviously similar to Lully's. Both show the same minute interest in appropriate declamation and exact rhythmic notation in recitatives; both intermingle recitative with more formally melodic aria sections, choruses, or instrumental interludes; both follow the tradition of introducing frequent long *divertissement* scenes; and (in Rameau's early operas) the form of the overture is the same. But within this general frame, Rameau introduced many important changes, so that in reality the resemblance between his music and Lully's is superficial rather than substantial.

Perhaps the most notable contrast is in the nature of the melodic lines. Rameau the composer constantly put into practice the doctrine of Rameau the theorist that all melody is rooted in harmony. Many of his melodic phrases are plainly triadic and none leave room for any uncertainty as to the harmonic progressions that must underlie them. Moreover, the harmony is of the eighteenth-century sort, with an orderly relationship, within the major-minor tonal system, of dominants, subdominants, and all secondary chords and modulations. Rameau uses purely harmonic means for expressive purposes in a way that is completely lacking in Lully's style. Rameau's harmonies are for the most part diatonic, but on occasion he uses chromatic and enharmonic modulations most effectively: in the trio of the Fates in the fifth scene of Act II of *Hippolyte et Aricie* (1733: Example 80)

he modulates rapidly by a descending chromatic sequence through
five keys in as many measures, underlining the import of the words
"Où cours-tu, malheureux? Tremble, frémis d'effroi!" ("Where dost
thou flee, miserable one? Tremble, shudder with terror!")

Modulations in *Hippolyte et Aricie*, Rameau

Example 80

In his treatment of form also Rameau was an innovator. Even when
he maintained Lully's pattern of the French *ouverture*, as he did in
Castor and Pollux (1737) and *Les Indes galantes*, the second movement, particularly, was expanded and deepened. Some of the formal
plans of the overtures are evidently experimental (for example, that
of *Les Fêtes d'Hébé*, 1739) and in his last works Rameau freely
adapted the three-movement form of the Italian sinfonia. Quite often
his overture introduces a theme that is used later in the opera, and
occasionally (as in *Zoroastre*, 1749) the overture becomes a kind of
symphonic poem, depicting the course of the drama to follow.

As with Lully and other French composers, Rameau used less contrasting melodic styles for recitative and aria than did the Italian composers of this period. Rameau's vocal airs, despite their variety of
dimensions and types, can for the most part be classified into two basic
formal patterns: the relatively short two-part form *AB;* and the longer
form with repetition after contrast, either *ABA* as in the Italian da
capo aria or with more than one repetition as in the usual French
rondeau. Nearly always, whatever their form or size, Rameau's airs
preserve a certain coolness and restraint in contrast to the intensity
and abandon of the Italian opera aria. Elegance, picturesqueness, pi-
quant rhythms, fullness of harmony, and melodic ornamentation by
means of *agréments* are their outstanding traits.

This is not to say that Rameau's music lacks dramatic force; the
opening scenes of Act I of *Castor et Pollux* and the closing scenes of
Act IV of *Hippolyte et Aricie* have a tragic grandeur not surpassed
in eighteenth-century French opera. However, the most powerful
effects in his operas are achieved not by solo voice, but by the joint
use of solo and chorus. Choruses, which remained prominent in
French opera long after they had passed out of use in Italy, are numerous throughout Rameau's works. The invocation to the sun ("Brillant
soleil") in Act II of *Les Indes galantes* is an excellent example of the
effectiveness of his predominantly homophonic choral writing.

On the whole, Rameau's most original contributions were made in the instrumental portions of his operas—the overtures, the dances, and the descriptive symphonies that accompany the stage action. In all these, his invention is inexhaustible; themes, rhythms, and harmonies have an incisive individuality and an inimitable pictorial quality. The French valued music especially for its depictive powers and Rameau is their leading tone-painter. His musical pictures range from graceful miniatures to broad representations of thunder (*Hippolyte*, Act I), tempest (*Les Surprises de l'Amour* [1757], Act III), or earthquake (*Indes galantes*, Act II).

The pictorial quality of Rameau's music is often enhanced by his novel orchestration. He was apparently the first composer to introduce clarinets in the orchestra of the Paris Opéra (in *Zoroastre*, 1749, and *Acanthe et Céphise* [1751]); his use of the bassoons and horns, and the independence of the woodwinds in his later scores are in accordance with the most advanced orchestral practice of his time. In this respect, as well as in some features of his melodic style and general texture, Rameau must be counted, like Vivaldi, among the precursors of the Classical symphony.

Rameau's clavecin pieces have the fine texture, the rhythmic vivacity, elegance of detail, and picturesque humor that appeared also in the works of Couperin. In his third and last collection (*Nouvelle Suites de Pièces de clavecin, ca.* 1736), Rameau experimented with virtuoso effects in somewhat the same manner as Domenico Scarlatti. Rameau's only publication of instrumental ensemble music was a collection of trio sonatas entitled *Pièces de clavecin en concerts* (1741); in these, the harpsichord is not treated simply as accompaniment but shares equally with the other instruments in the presentation and working out of the thematic material.

The work of Rameau may be summed up under three aspects. In the heroic, grand style of his early operas and opera-ballets he is a representative figure of the late Baroque, comparable to Bach and Handel. His heroic qualities are always accompanied, and sometimes supplanted, by the characteristic French traits of clarity, grace, moderation, and elegance, and by a constant striving toward the picturesque; in these respects he may be compared with his contemporary, Watteau. Finally, and equally typical of his period and country, he is a *philosophe* as well as a composer, an analyst as well as a creator; and in this respect he may be compared to his contemporary, Voltaire. These three aspects cannot be separated if we are to understand Rameau's achievements fully. He was one of the most complex as well as one of the most fecund musical personalities of the eighteenth century.

Johann Sebastian Bach

The uneventful external career of Johann Sebastian Bach (1685–1750) was similar to that of many successful musical functionaries of his time in Lutheran Germany. Bach served as organist at Arnstadt (1703–07) and Mühlhausen (1707–08); as court organist and later Concertmaster in the chapel of the Duke of Weimar (1708–17); as Music Director at the court of a prince in Cöthen (1717–23); and finally as Cantor of the St. Thomas school in Leipzig (1723–50), a position of considerable importance in the Lutheran world. He enjoyed some reputation in Protestant Germany as an organ virtuoso and writer of learned contrapuntal works, but there were at least a half-dozen contemporary composers who were more widely known in Europe. He regarded himself as a conscientious craftsman doing a

Johann Sebastian Bach (1685–1750) in 1746, a painting by E. G. Hauss-mann done when Bach became a member of the Society of the Musical Sciences. In Bach's hand is the triple canon which, with a portrait, was required of all new members. (Bettmann Archive)

job to the best of his ability for the satisfaction of his superiors, for the pleasure and edification of his fellowmen, and to the glory of God. Doubtless he would have been astonished if he had been told that two hundred years after his death his music would be performed and studied everywhere and his name more deeply venerated by musicians than that of any other composer.

Bach's Instrumental Music

Bach was trained as a violinist and organist, and organ music first attracted his interest as a composer. As a youth he visited Hamburg to hear the organists there, and while he was at Arnstadt he made a journey on foot to Lübeck, where he was so fascinated by the music of Buxtehude that he overstayed his leave and was duly reproved by his superiors.

Bach's earliest organ compositions include chorale preludes, several sets of variations (partitas) on chorales, and some toccatas and fantasias which in their length, diffuseness, and unbridled exuberance of ideas recall the toccatas of Buxtehude. Then, while he was at the court of Weimar, Bach became interested in the music of Italian composers, and with his usual diligence set about copying their scores and making arrangements of their works; thus he arranged several of Vivaldi's concertos for organ or harpsichord, writing out the ornaments, occasionally strengthening the counterpoint, and sometimes adding inner voices. He also wrote fugues on subjects by Corelli and Legrenzi. The natural consequence of these studies was an important change in Bach's own style: from the Italians, especially Vivaldi, he learned to write more concise themes, to clarify and tighten the harmonic scheme, and above all to develop subjects by a continuous rhythmic flow into lucid, grandly proportioned formal structures. These qualities were combined with his own prolific imagination and his profound mastery of contrapuntal technique to make the style which we consider typically "Bachian," and which is in reality a fusion of Italian and German characteristics.

As has already been noted, one of the characteristic large musical structures of the late Baroque was the combination of a prelude (or

Bach's preludes and fugues

toccata, fantasia) and a fugue. Most of Bach's important compositions in this form date from the Weimar period, though a few were written at Cöthen and Leipzig. Perfectly idiomatic to the instrument, technically difficult but never parading empty virtuosity, Bach's preludes and fugues sum up all the striving of the Baroque toward pure, balanced tonal architecture on a monumental scale.

The Toccata in D minor (? 1709; BWV 565)[2] is an example of the form established by Buxtehude, in which the fugue is interspersed with sections of free fantasia. The Passacaglia in C minor (?1717; BWV 582) serves as prelude to a double fugue, one of whose subjects is identical with the first half of the passacaglia theme. Some of the preludes are extensive compositions in two or three movements; that of the great Fantasia and Fugue in G minor (Cöthen, 1720; BWV 542) glorifies the Baroque conception of a richly colored, passionately expressive fantasia or toccata with contrapuntal interludes. The variety of types and the incisive melodic and rhythmic outline of Bach's fugue subjects are especially remarkable; see Example 81.

From the later years of Bach's life comes the gigantic Prelude in E-flat major, and the Fugue ("St. Anne's") in the same key (BWV 552), published in 1739; these two are respectively the opening and closing sections of Part III of the *Clavier Übung* (literally, *Keyboard Practice*, a title Bach used for four different collections of his keyboard pieces). The central portion of Part III of the *Clavier Übung* is a series of chorale preludes on the hymns of the Lutheran Catechism. In symbolic recognition of the dogma of the Trinity there expounded, Bach writes for conclusion a triple fugue with a key signature of three flats; each of the three sections of the fugue has its own subject, with increasing rhythmic animation, and the first subject is combined contrapuntally with each of the other two. The multi-sectional fugue goes back to the practice of Buxtehude and other earlier masters; Bach had used it in his early Toccata in E major (BWV 566).

Less spectacular than the preludes and fugues, but equally important, are the six Trio Sonatas (BWV 525–530) which, according to Forkel, Bach wrote at Leipzig for his eldest son Wilhelm Friedemann. These works show the way Bach adapted the Italian ensemble trio sonata as a piece for a solo performer. They are written in a contrapuntal texture of three equal independent voices, one for each

Organ Fugue Subjects, J. S. Bach   Example 81

Example 81
(cont.)

manual and one for the pedals, but the order of movements (mostly fast-slow-fast) and the general character of the themes show the influence of their Italian prototypes.

Bach, as an organist and a devout Lutheran, was naturally concerned with the chorale. Among the approximately 170 chorale settings he made for the organ, all types known to the Baroque are represented; moreover, as with other forms of composition, Bach brought the organ chorale to a summit of artistic perfection. Short chorale preludes comprise the collection called the *Orgelbüchlein* (*Little Organ Book*), which Bach compiled at Weimar and during his first years at Cöthen. The arrangement and intention of this collection illustrate several things important for an understanding of Bach. He originally planned to include settings for the chorale melodies required by the liturgy for the entire church year, 164 in all, though he actually completed only 45. However, the plan is characteristic of Bach's desire to fulfil thoroughly the potentialities of a given undertaking, to realize all the suggestions inherent in any musical situation. This is the reason that in the maturity of his life his compositions often are devoted to single aspects of one large unified design—for example, the complete circle of keys in *The Well-Tempered Clavier*, the cycle of catechism chorales in the *Clavier Übung*, the systematic order of the *Goldberg Variations*, the exhaustive working out of a single subject in *The Musical Offering*, or the exemplification of all types of fugue in *The Art of Fugue*.

With one exception (a set of chorale variations), all the numbers of the *Orgelbüchlein* are chorale preludes in which the tune is heard once through, generally in the soprano, in complete, continuous, and readily recognizable form; a few treat the melody in canon, and three present it with fairly elaborate *agréments*. Quite often the accompanying voices are not derived from motives of the chorale melody but each is constructed throughout on a single independent motive. In some instances the accompaniment exemplifies the practice—common to all composers of the Baroque, but carried out by Bach with surpassing poetic ingenuity—of recognizing, by means of pictorial or symbolic motives, the visual images or underlying ideas of the text of the chorale. Thus in *Durch Adams Fall ist ganz verderbt* (*In Adam's*

Bach's chorale preludes

fall the world was lost) *fall* is depicted by a jagged falling motive in the pedals, while the tortuous chromatic lines of the inner voices suggest at once the ideas of sin and sorrow and the sinuous writhing of the serpent (Example 82).

Similar pictorial or symbolic suggestions abound in Bach's organ chorales, as well as, of course, in his vocal works; however, he never uses pictorial devices as mere superficial adornments, but always as a way to present the inner, musical significance of a passage. One of the finest examples of the poetic transfiguration of an external suggestion is the final cadence of the chorale prelude *O Mensch, bewein' dein' Sünde gross* (*O man, bewail thy grievous sin*) from the *Orgelbüchlein,* in which the long-drawn-out *adagissimo* reflects the word "länge" ("long") in the closing phrase of the chorale text (see illustration, page 270).

Chorale Prelude: *Durch Adams Fall,* J. S. Bach

Example 82

Three collections of organ chorales were compiled during Bach's Leipzig period. The six *Schübler* chorales (BWV 645–650) are transcriptions of movements from cantatas. The *Eighteen Chorales* (BWV 651–668) that Bach collected and revised between 1747 and 1749 were composed at earlier periods of his life; they include all varieties of organ chorale settings: variations, fugues, fantasias, trios, and extended chorale preludes of various types. The catechism chorales in Part III of the *Clavier Übung* (BWV 669–689) are grouped in pairs, a longer and a shorter (usually fugal) setting of each hymn, corresponding symbolically to the "longer" and "shorter" catechism. All these later organ chorales of Bach are conceived with larger proportions than those of the *Orgelbüchlein;* they also are less intimate and subjective, replacing with a more formal symbolism or a purely musical development of ideas the vivid expressive details of the earlier works. An example of the difference between Bach's early and late organ chorales may be found in two settings of *Wenn wir in höchsten Nöten sein* (*When we are in deepest need*). In the *Orgelbüchlein* version (BWV 641) the melody appears with luxuriant ornamentations over an accompaniment whose principal motive is derived from the first four notes of the tune. In a later setting (BWV 668) the same

melody is used with the title "Vor deinen Thron tret' ich hiermit"
("Before Thy throne I now appear"); in this version Bach reverts to
the old Pachelbel form of chorale prelude. The melody is almost bare
of ornaments, and each phrase is introduced by a short fugato on its
leading motive in the three lower voices. Another example of the
organ chorales of Bach's late period is a set of five canonic variations
(BWV 769) on the Christmas hymn *Vom Himmel hoch* (*From high
heaven*) which he wrote in 1747 on the occasion of his election to a
learned musical society.

*Bach's clavier
music*

Bach's music for the clavier, like that for the organ, includes masterpieces in every form known to the late Baroque: preludes, fantasies,
and toccatas; fugues and other pieces in fugal style; dance suites; and
variations. In addition there are early sonatas and capriccios, miscellaneous short works (including many teaching pieces), and clavier
concertos with orchestra. A large proportion of Bach's clavier music
was written at Cöthen, although many important works were produced in the Leipzig period. In general, the clavier compositions—
which were not bound, like the organ works, to a local German tradition or to a liturgy—show prominently the cosmopolitan or international features of Bach's style, the intermingling of Italian, French,
and German characteristics. The Chromatic Fantasia and Fugue in D
minor (BWV 903) is Bach's greatest clavier work in that form, a
worthy companion to the organ Fantasia and Fugue in G minor.

*The Well-
Tempered
Clavier*

Undoubtedly the best known of Bach's clavier works is the famous
set of preludes and fugues called *The Well-Tempered Clavier*. Part I
was completed at Cöthen in 1722, and Part II was collected at Leipzig
in 1744. Each part consists of twenty-four preludes and fugues, one
prelude and one fugue in each of the twelve major and minor keys.
Part I is more unified in style and purpose than Part II, which includes
compositions from many different periods of Bach's life. In addition
to demonstrating the possibility, with the then novel tempered tuning,
of using all the keys, Bach had particular didactic intentions in Part I.
In most of the preludes a single specific technical task is given the
player; thus they might be called, in the terminology of a later age,
"*études*," for which some of Bach's little preludes (BWV 933–943)
as well as all the two-part inventions and the three-part sinfonias may
be regarded as preliminary studies. The teaching aims of *The Well-
Tempered Clavier* go beyond mere technique, however, for the preludes exemplify different types of keyboard composition of the late
Baroque. The fugues, wonderfully varied in subjects, texture, form,
and treatment, constitute a compendium of all the possibilities of concentrated, monothematic fugal writing.

Bach's suites

Bach's clavier suites show the influence of French and Italian as well
as of German models. There are three sets of six suites each: the *French*
and *English Suites*, composed at Cöthen, and the six Partitas published
separately between 1726 and 1730 and then collected in 1731 as Part I
of the *Clavier Übung*. Part II of the *Clavier Übung* also contains a

large Partita in B minor, entitled "Overture in the French style for a harpsichord with two manuals."

The designations *French* and *English* for the suites composed at Cöthen are not Bach's own, and have no descriptive significance. The suites in both sets consist of the standard four dance movements (allemande, courante, sarabande, gigue) with additional short movements between the sarabande and gigue; each of the *English Suites* opens with a prelude.

In one clavier work Bach summarized another characteristic species of Baroque keyboard music, the theme and variations. The *Aria with (thirty) Different Variations*, published (probably) in 1742 as Part IV of the *Clavier Übung* and generally known as the *Goldberg Variations*, is organized in the monumentally complete fashion of many of the compositions from the latter part of Bach's life. The theme, which may not have been original with Bach, occurs in the second little clavier book for Anna Magdalena (1725); it is a sarabande in two balanced sections, the essential bass and harmonic structure of which are preserved in all thirty variations. The form of the whole, therefore, is that of a chaconne or passacaglia. The variations are grouped by threes, the last of each group being a strict canon, with the canons at successive intervals from the unison to the ninth. The thirtieth and last variation, however, is a *quodlibet*, a mixture of two popular song melodies combined in counterpoint above the fundamental bass; and after this the theme is repeated da capo. The non-canonic variations are of many different types, including inventions, fughettas, a French *ouverture*, ornamental slow arias, and, at regular intervals, sparkling *bravura* pieces for two keyboards. The diverse moods and styles in these variations are unified not only by means of the recurring bass and harmonies but also by the symmetrical order in which the movements are arranged; the entire piece is a perfectly organized structure of magnificent proportions.

Bach wrote six sonatas and partitas for violin alone (BWV 1001–1006) and six suites for violoncello alone (BWV 1007–1012). In these works he demonstrated his ability to create the illusion of a full harmonic and contrapuntal texture by means of multiple stops and single melodic lines which outline or suggest an interplay of independent voices—a technique going back to the lute composers of the Renaissance and related to the style of the French lutenists and clavecinists of the middle and late Baroque. The chaconne from Bach's solo violin Partita in D minor is one of the most famous works in this form.

In the ensemble forms of chamber music Bach's chief compositions include sonatas for violin and harpsichord (BWV 1014–1019), for viola da gamba and harpsichord (BWV 1027–1029), and for flute and harpsichord (BWV 1030–1035). Most of these works have four movements in slow-fast-slow-fast order, like the *sonata da chiesa;* and moreover, most of them are actually trio sonatas, since often the right-hand part of the harpsichord is written as a single melodic line which forms a duet in counterpoint with the melody of the other instrument.

The amalgamation of Italian and German styles is most fully exemplified in Bach's six concertos composed at Cöthen in 1721 and dedicated to the Margrave of Brandenburg (BWV 1046–1051). In these Bach adopted the usual three-movement, fast-slow-fast order of the Italian concertos; the triadic themes, the steadily driving rhythms, and the ritornello form of the Allegro movements are also of Italian derivation. But Bach, as usual, transfigured all these elements, and in addition provided his concertos with such wealth of counterpoint and such variety of instrumental color as to make them unique in the literature of this form.

Concertos

The four *Ouvertures* or orchestral suites (BWV 1066–1069) are likewise masterly examples of this favorite type of Baroque composition, and contain some of Bach's most exuberant and attractive music. The third and fourth suites, which have trumpets and drums added to the strings and winds, were undoubtedly intended for performance out-of-doors. The piece popularly known as *Air for the G String* is an arrangement of the slow movement of the third suite.

Bach's orchestral suites

Bach also wrote three concertos for solo violin with orchestra, and he was probably the first composer to write concertos for the harpsichord. He wrote seven concertos for solo harpsichord with orchestra, three for two harpsichords, two for three harpsichords, and one for four harpsichords, this last being an arrangement of a Vivaldi concerto for four violins. Most if not all of the harpsichord concertos, in fact, are arrangements of violin compositions either by Bach himself or by other composers.

Concertos for solo instruments with orchestra

Two late instrumental works of Bach are in a class by themselves: *Musikalisches Opfer* (*A Musical Offering*) and *Die Kunst der Fuge* (*The Art of Fugue*). The former is based on a theme proposed by Frederick the Great of Prussia on which Bach improvised when he was visiting that monarch at Potsdam in 1747. On returning to Leipzig, Bach wrote out and revised his improvisations, dedicating the finished work to the king. It is a cycle of canons, together with two *ricercari* and a trio sonata in three movements for flute (King Frederick's instrument), violin, and continuo. *The Art of Fugue*, composed in 1749–50 and left unfinished at Bach's death, is a systematic didactic demonstration of all types of fugal writing; it consists of eighteen canons and fugues in strictest style, all based on the same subject or one of its transformations, and arranged in a general order of increasing complexity, in the course of which the most difficult and abstruse contrapuntal devices are handled with masterful ease.

Other works

Bach's Vocal Music

In 1723 Leipzig was a flourishing commercial city with about 30,000 inhabitants, noted as a center of printing and publishing, and the seat of an ancient University. There were five churches in addition to the University chapels; most important were the churches of St. Nicholas and St. Thomas, in which Bach was responsible for the music.

St. Thomas's school was an ancient foundation which took in both day and boarding pupils. It provided fifty-five scholarships for boys and youths who were obliged in return to sing or play in the services of four Leipzig churches as well as to fulfil other musical duties, and who consequently were chosen on the basis of musical as well as general scholastic ability. As Cantor of the school Bach ranked third in the academic hierarchy.

His duties included four hours of teaching each day (he had to teach Latin as well as music), and also preparing music for the church services. He and his family lived in an apartment in one wing of the school, where his study was separated by a thin partition from the home room of the second-year schoolboys.

Altogether the Leipzig churches required fifty-eight cantatas each year, in addition to Passion music for Good Friday, Magnificats at Vespers for three festivals, an annual cantata for the installation of the City Council, and occasional music such as funeral motets and wedding cantatas for which the Cantor received an extra fee. Bach undertook to provide new works for the church services from his own pen as frequently as possible; about two hundred of these works have been preserved. No generalized description can possibly suggest

The Square of St. Thomas, Leipzig, with St. Thomas's Church and School. (Bettmann Archive)

Bach's manuscript of the closing measures of the chorale prelude, O Mensch, bewein'.

the infinite variety, the inconceivable wealth of musical invention, technical mastery, and religious devotion in Bach's cantatas. Two or three examples will serve as an introduction to this vast treasure of music.

Cantata No. 21

Cantata No. 21,[3] *Ich hatte viel Bekümmernis* (*My heart was deeply troubled*), was composed at Weimar in 1714. It consists of a sinfonia, four choruses on Biblical texts, three arias, two recitatives, and a duet. The cantata is divided into two parts, one of which presumably was sung before the sermon and the other after. Part I depicts the sorrow and distress of the sinful soul, Part II its rejoicing in the salvation brought through Christ. The contrast of moods is announced in the first chorus by the sharply contrasted musical settings of the two phrases of text: "When the cares of my heart are many,/Thy consolations cheer my soul" (Psalms, xciv:19). The soul's distress is further depicted in a short soprano aria and in an eloquent accompanied recitative and aria for tenor. The texts of these numbers are typical examples of German Baroque religious poetry, with subjective feelings expressed in fervid—not to say extravagant—terms: the tenor aria likens the lost soul to a ship being driven to destruction in a storm,

270

a favorite comparison in opera arias; and the music, a full da capo form in F minor, is no less operatic in the vehemence of its expression and the vividness of its pictorial details. Part I closes with a chorus of consolation: "Why art thou cast down, O my soul?" (Psalms, xlii: 5), each phrase of which has its own musical motive, ending with a fugue on the words "my help and my God." The tonality throughout Part I is (except for the tenor aria) C minor.

Part II opens with a tender accompanied recitative for soprano and bass in E-flat major, leading into a duet in the same key. Here the soprano allegorically represents the soul and the bass the Saviour. The following chorus, in G minor, introduces the text "Return, O my soul, to thy rest; for the Lord has dealt bountifully with thee" (Psalms, cxvi: 7) in a peacefully flowing stepwise theme in triple measure, which is developed contrapuntally in three voices. Against this background are intoned two stanzas from the chorale "If thou dost suffer God to guide thee." The chorale melody is heard in long notes, the first stanza in the tenor and the next in the soprano, with the stepwise theme in the other three parts always accompanying and furnishing interludes between the phrases of the chorale; the whole thus has the form of an extended organ chorale prelude, a form Bach often employed for choruses in his cantatas. A short cheerful tenor song in F major, with da capo, voices the soul's gladness, and the final chorus, in C major, brings the cantata to a stirring climax. This chorus begins with a setting of the words "Worthy is the Lamb that was slain" which is strikingly similar to Handel's setting of the same text in *Messiah;* equally Handelian is the brilliance of the choral writing in the concluding fugue, reinforced by the full orchestra with three trumpets and timpani on the words "Praise and honor and glory and power be to our God forever and ever, alleluia, amen." (Rev. v: 12–13.) This chorus is to Bach's choral style what the early fugue in D major (BWV 532) is to his organ style: both show what he could do, when he chose, in the way of virtuosity and splendor of effect.

Bach used chorale melodies in a multitude of different ways in his cantatas. Cantata No. 4, *Christ lag in Todesbanden* (*Christ lay in death's dark prison*), refashioned from an earlier version and sung at Leipzig in 1724, is exceptional in that it goes back to the old form of chorale variations. A more usual scheme in the Leipzig cantatas is that used in No. 80, *Ein' feste Burg* (*A mighty fortress*), first composed perhaps in 1724 and later revised. The opening chorus in D major is a towering fantasia on the melody and words of the first stanza of the chorale. The vocal lines, freely adapted from the chorale tune, introduce each phrase in turn fugally, leading to a simple climactic statement of the phrase by the trumpet in its high clarino register, answered in strict canon by the bass instruments. In this way the melody, phrase by phrase, is expanded into a vast architectural structure of 223 measures. The next number is a duet, also in D, for soprano and bass. The soprano sings the words of the second chorale stanza to an ornate version of the tune while the bass, in an even more ornate but completely independent line, has a separate text appropriately commenting on that of the soprano; they are accompanied by a steady vigorous sixteenth-note figure in the strings *unisono* and the continuo bass moving in eighth notes. The texture is one of four independent contrapuntal parts, of which the highest, the soprano solo, is doubled and further embellished by the oboe. Then follow a recitative and arioso for bass and an aria (B minor) for soprano, both on inserted poetic texts. The third stanza of the chorale is set in the form of a chorale prelude, the tune being proclaimed by the chorus in unison while each phrase is introduced and accompanied by the full orchestra in an energetic 6/8 rhythm. A recitative-arioso for tenor and a quietly moving duet for tenor and alto (G major) follow, and the cantata is concluded by the fourth and final stanza of the chorale, now in a straightforward four-part harmonic setting for full chorus (in which the congregation also may have joined) with instruments doubling the vocal parts.

Bach's secular cantatas, most of which he titled "dramma per musica," were composed for various occasions, and not infrequently he used some of the same music for a sacred text: eleven numbers of the *Christmas Oratorio*, for example, appear also in secular cantatas. Among the best of the musical dramas are *Phoebus and Pan* (BWV 201) and *Schleicht, spielende Wellen* (*Glide gently, ye waters;* BWV 206) which was written to celebrate the birthday of Augustus III in 1733; the *Coffee Cantata* and the burlesque *Peasant Cantata* (BWV 211 and 212) are delightful specimens of Bach's lighter music.

The word *motet* at Leipzig in Bach's time signified a composition for chorus, generally in contrapuntal style, without obbligato instrumental parts, and with a Biblical or chorale text. The motets sung in the Leipzig churches were relatively short, and were used as musical introductions to the service; apparently they were chosen from a traditional repertoire of old works, and the Cantor was not expected to furnish new motets. The six surviving motets of Bach (BWV 225–230) were written either for particular occasions (such as funerals) or perhaps for special church services. They are long works, and four of them are for double chorus. The voice parts are always complete in themselves, but it is an open question whether in Bach's time they were sung *a cappella* or with instrumental doubling—as was, for example, the opening chorus of Cantata No. 38, which is in motet style. Many of the motets incorporate chorale melodies; the five-voice *Jesu meine Freude* (*Jesus, my joy*) uses the chorale in six of its eleven movements.

The great Magnificat (BWV 243), for five-part chorus and orchestra, is one of Bach's most melodious works, more Italian in style than most of his church music. The *Christmas Oratorio* (BWV 248), produced at Leipzig in 1734, is in reality a set of six cantatas for the festivals of the Christmas and Epiphany season. The Biblical narratives

(Luke ii: 1–21; Matt. ii: 1–12) are presented in recitative; appropriate arias and chorales are added to reflect or comment on the various episodes of the story. The designation of "oratorio" is justified by reason of the narrative element, which is not present in the usual cantata.

The culmination of Bach's work as a church musician was reached in his settings of the Passion according to St. John and St. Matthew. These two works, essentially similar in structure, are the crowning examples of the north German tradition of Gospel Passion settings in oratorio style. For the *St. John Passion*, in addition to the Gospel story (St. John xviii and xix, with interpolations from St. Matthew) and fourteen chorales, Bach also borrowed words, with some alterations, for added lyrical numbers from a popular Passion poem of B. H. Brockes. Bach's musical setting, which was, probably, first performed at Leipzig, in 1724, was subjected later to numerous revisions.

The *St. Matthew Passion*, for double chorus, soloists, and orchestra, first performed in 1729, is a drama of epic grandeur, "the most noble and inspired treatment of its subject in the whole range of music." The text is from St. Matthew's Gospel, chapters xxvi and xxvii; this is narrated in tenor solo recitative and choruses, and the narration is interspersed with chorales, a duet, and numerous arias, most of which are preceded by arioso recitatives. The "Passion Chorale" (see Example 56) appears five times, in different keys and in four different four-part harmonizations. The author of the added recitatives and arias was C. F. Henrici (1700–1764; pseudonym, Picander), a Leipzig poet who also provided many of Bach's cantata texts. As in the *St. John Passion*, the chorus sometimes participates in the action and sometimes, like the chorus in Greek drama, is an articulate spectator introducing or reflecting upon the events of the narrative. The opening and closing choruses of Part I are huge chorale fantasias; in the first, the chorale melody is given to a special ripieno choir of soprano voices.

Nearly every phrase of the *St. Matthew Passion* affords examples of Bach's genius for merging pictorial musical figures with expressive effects. Of the many beautiful passages in this masterpiece of music, four may be singled out for special mention: the alto recitative "Ah, Golgotha"; the soprano aria "In Love my Saviour now is dying"; the last setting of the Passion Chorale, after Jesus' death on the Cross; and the stupendous three measures of chorus on the words "Truly this was the Son of God."

The *Passion According to St. Matthew* is the apotheosis of Lutheran church music: in it the chorale, the concertato style, the recitative, the arioso, and the da capo aria are perfectly united under the ruling majesty of the central religious theme. All these elements, save the chorale, are equally characteristic of Baroque opera. The dramatic, theatrical qualities of both the *St. Matthew* and the *St. John Passions* are obvious. While it is true that Bach never wrote an opera, nevertheless the language, the forms, and the spirit of opera are fully present in the Passions.

The *Mass in B minor* is, necessarily, more general in content and more contemplative in viewpoint than the Passions, and hence less dramatic in detail. Choruses (mostly in five parts) take a far larger proportion of the work than they do in the Passions. The Kyrie and Gloria were presented in 1733 to Frederick Augustus, the Catholic King of Poland and Elector of Saxony, together with Bach's petition for an honorary appointment to the Electoral Chapel—a petition which was not granted until three years later. The remaining movements—some newly composed, others adapted—date from various periods in Bach's life; the work was not completed before 1747 or 1749. Bach probably never heard it performed in entirety, though parts were sung at Leipzig, where an abbreviated form of the Latin Mass still had a place in the liturgy.

Several numbers of the B-minor Mass are rearrangements from cantatas, for example, the "Gratias agimus" and the "Dona nobis pacem" (both of which use the same music) from the first chorus of Cantata No. 29, and the "Crucifixus" from the first chorus of Cantata No. 12. This Mass is not liturgical music; it is too long and too elaborate to be used in any church service. It is rather a work which, like Beethoven's *Missa solemnis*, transcends denominational limits and rises to the height of a universal statement of Christian faith. Bach symbolized the continuity of the Christian tradition by using Gregorian *cantus firmi* in the Credo and in the "Confiteor" choruses. The "Crucifixus" is perhaps the most wonderful example in all music of the use of an ostinato bass. The music was written originally in 1724, to different words, as the opening chorus of a cantata. Bach altered the original ending to depict Christ's descent into the grave by the low register of the voices and at the same time, by a modulation to G major, to suggest the hope of the resurrection, which bursts forth in the next chorus like a dance of joy.

Burial and resurrection might well describe the history of Bach's music. Very few of his works were published during his lifetime, and he was all but forgotten by the generation which followed his death. A few musicians toward the end of the eighteenth century were familiar with *The Well-Tempered Clavier* and some other keyboard works; Mozart heard and studied the motets on a visit to Leipzig in 1789, and they came to him as a revelation. The rediscovery of Bach which occurred in the nineteenth century was marked in 1802 by the publication of the first biography (by J. N. Forkel), by Zelter's revival of the *St. Matthew Passion* and its performance at Leipzig under Mendelssohn's direction in 1829, and in 1850 by the foundation of the Bach Society, whose authoritative edition of Bach's works was completed by 1900.

We can begin to understand the central position Bach has in the history of music when we realize, first, that he absorbed into his music

the multiplicity of styles and forms current in the early eighteenth
century and developed hitherto unsuspected potentialities in every
one; and second, that in his music the opposed principles of harmony
and counterpoint, melody and polyphony, are maintained in a tense
but satisfying equilibrium found in no other composer. The continuing vitality of his music is not, of course, due to its historical
significance as a summation of the late Baroque, but to the qualities of
the music itself: the concentrated and individual themes, the copious
musical invention, the balance between harmonic and contrapuntal
forces, the strength of rhythm, the clarity of form, the grandeur of
proportion, the imaginative use of pictorial and symbolic figures, the
intensity of expression always controlled by a ruling architectural
idea, and the technical perfection of every detail.

George Frideric Handel

Handel (1685–1759) was a typical international composer of the
eighteenth century. As a boy in his native town of Halle he became
an accomplished organist and harpsichordist, studied violin and oboe, *Handel's*
received a thorough grounding in counterpoint, and became familiar *instrumental*
with the music of contemporary German and Italian composers by *music*
the usual and effective method of copying their scores. After a year
at the University he went to Hamburg, where his first opera, *Almira*,
was performed in 1705. From some time in 1706 until the middle of
1710 Handel was in Italy, where he was soon recognized as one of the
coming young composers and where he associated with the leading
patrons and musicians of Rome, Florence, Naples, and Venice. In
1710 he was appointed Music Director at the Electoral Court of

George Frideric Handel (1685–
1759); a portrait by Bromley.
(Courtesy Metropolitan Museum
of Art)

Hanover but almost immediately obtained a leave of absence for a visit to England. In 1712 he returned to London; while he was there his master, the Elector of Hanover, was proclaimed King George I of England. Enjoying the patronage of the royal family, the Duke of Chandos, and other influential personages, Handel settled down to a long and prosperous career in London, becoming a naturalized British subject in 1726.

Oratorios and operas form the most important part of his work, though he also wrote pieces for keyboard instruments and for ensembles both vocal and instrumental.

Handel's keyboard works include three sets of concertos for harpsichord or organ, two collections of suites for harpsichord published respectively in 1720 and 1733, and a number of miscellaneous pieces. The suites contain not only the usual dance movements but also specimens of most of the keyboard forms of the time. The popular set of variations called *The Harmonious Blacksmith* (the title was bestowed in the nineteenth century) is the air (with variations) from the fifth Suite of the first collection. Handel composed nineteen solo sonatas and an equal number of trio sonatas, for various chamber music combinations. In most of these the dominant influence is obviously that of Corelli, but the sophistication of the harmonies and the smooth, easy assurance of the musical movement (particularly in the Allegros) mark a later stage of the Italian style.

The most significant of Handel's instrumental works are those for full orchestra, including the overtures to his operas and oratorios, the two suites known as the *Fireworks Music* (1749) and the *Water Music* (?1717), and above all the concertos. There are six concertos for woodwinds and strings, usually called the "oboe concertos," and twelve *Grand Concertos* Opus 6, for two solo violins, string orchestra, and continuo, composed in 1739.

On the whole, the concertos of Opus 6 show a combination of retrospective and modern elements, with the former predominating. The ruling conception is the same as that in Corelli's work, namely, a *sonata da chiesa* for full orchestra. The framework is the usual order of four movements (slow-fast-slow-fast), with one of the Allegros fugal; but this scheme is usually expanded by an additional movement or two, which may be in dance rhythm. The common designation of *concerto grosso* does not strictly suit these works, since as a rule the solo parts are not markedly set off from the tuttis: in fact, in a majority of the movements the concertino instruments either merely play throughout in unison with the ripieno or else appear by themselves only for brief trio-like interludes; and when there are extended passages for the solo violins, these usually differ neither in thematic material nor in style from the tutti passages. Only rarely and, as it were, incidentally, does Handel imitate Vivaldi in giving decorative figuration to a solo violin (as in Nos. 3, 6, and 11). Moreover, the serious, dignified bearing and the prevailingly full contrapuntal texture of this music are less characteristic of the 1730's than of the earlier part of the century when Handel was forming his style in Italy. But, conservative or no, the concertos are fascinating music, original and abundantly varied.

To the general public Handel is known almost exclusively as a composer of oratorios; nonetheless, for thirty-five years of his life his principal occupation was composing and conducting operas. The subjects of his operas are the usual ones of the time: tales of magic and marvelous adventure, or, more often, episodes from the lives of heroes of antiquity, freely adapted to get the maximum number of intense dramatic situations. The musical scheme is likewise that of the early eighteenth century: development of the action in *recitativo secco*, interrupted periodically by solo da capo arias. Each aria is intended to give musical expression to a single specific mood or affect, so that the opera as a whole consists of a series of isolated arias which are strung like pearls on the thread of the plot. From our point of view an opera of this sort is not so much a drama in music as a concert in costume.

Handel's operas

These operas were written so that every singer had arias that favorably displayed the scope of his vocal and histrionic powers; furthermore, the arias had to be distributed according to the importance of each member of the cast. Within the limits of these essential requirements the composer might work with as much freedom as he chose or as his inventive powers allowed. Handel, like most eighteenth-century composers, could turn out an opera any time that would be good enough to satisfy expectations and enjoy the usual brief success; but he could also on occasion create a masterpiece like *Ottone* (1723), which teems with beautiful melodic writing. His scores are remarkable for the wide variety of aria types, a variety that eludes strict classification. Arias range from brilliant virtuoso coloratura effects to sustained, sublimely expressive pathetic songs, such as the "Cara sposa" from *Rinaldo* (1710); arias of Baroque grandeur with rich contrapuntal accompaniments alternate with simple folklike melodies or arias *all'unisono*, in which the strings play in unison with the voice throughout; still other songs are in dance rhythms, and others in the fashionable light melodic manner of the Italian school. The pastoral scenes are especially noteworthy examples of eighteenth-century musical nature painting. Not all of Handel's arias are in da capo form, and occasionally he presented two contrasted affects in the same aria.

Transcending all mastery of technique is Handel's power of incarnating in music the essence of a mood or affect, with overwhelming poetic depth and suggestiveness. This is a quality that cannot be adequately analyzed or described in words, but can only be sensed from the experience of the music itself. It is because of this power that some of the personages in Handel's operas loom as figures of heroic, superhuman grandeur, like the great characters in the tragedies of Corneille and Racine.

In addition to the ordinary *recitativo secco* Handel sometimes, for scenes of particular poignancy or rapidly shifting affects, used the more weighty and more melodic *recitativo accompagnato*. For these accompanied recitatives—as indeed for many other features of his operas—Handel found splendid models in the works of Alessandro Scarlatti. Sometimes both types of recitative are freely combined with short arias or ariosos (short songs flexible in form and rhythm, syllabic in style, and without text repetition) to make large scene-complexes that recall the freedom of seventeenth-century Venetian opera and at the same time foreshadow the methods of Gluck and other composers of the later eighteenth century. Examples of such scene-complexes occur at the end of Act II in *Orlando* (1733) and, on a smaller scale, in Act I, Scene 7 and Act III, Scene 4 of *Giulio Cesare* (1724) and elsewhere.

Handel's operas, typically for his time, consist almost entirely of solo singing. There are occasional descriptive sinfonias and, in a few works, ballets. Duets or other ensembles are rare, as are also the choruses which, strictly speaking, are ensembles in chordal style with only one singer to a part.

Beginning in the 1730's Handel, finding his kind of operas no longer so popular, turned his attention increasingly to composing oratorios. These works, of which there are twenty-six in all, laid the foundations of Handel's immense and long-continued influence on English musical life. Among his principal oratorios are *Saul, Israel in Egypt* (both 1739), *Messiah* (1742), *Judas Maccabaeus* (1746), and *Jephtha* (1751).

*Handel's
oratorios*

The Italian Baroque oratorio was hardly anything other than an opera on a sacred subject, presented in concert instead of on the stage. This conception is an essential element of Handel's oratorios. Most of the arias in these works differ in no essential respects—neither in form, musical style, nature of the musical ideas, nor technique of expressing affects—from the arias in his operas. As in the operas also, the mood of each aria is usually prepared, and the aria introduced, by a preceding recitative. But there are important alterations and additions which transform the oratorios into something different from the conventional eighteenth-century opera.

Fundamental is the fact that Handel's oratorio librettos were in English. The Italian used in opera undoubtedly had snob appeal for London listeners most of whom, if pressed, could hardly have translated a dozen words of that language without help. The use of English was gratifying to the middle class; it also meant that at least some of the absurdities and artificial conceits which were part of the tissue of the usual opera libretto must be renounced, since they could no longer be decently concealed under the cloak of a foreign tongue. Even more important, a new kind of subject matter had to be found. Classical mythology and ancient history were all very well for upper-class audiences who, whatever the actual state of their education, felt obliged to pretend some acquaintance with such matters.

The entire storehouse of both history and mythology known to middle-class Protestant England in the eighteenth century was the Bible, or, more accurately, the Old Testament, including the apocryphal books. Most of Handel's oratorios, and especially his most popular ones, are based on Old Testament stories (even *Messiah* has more text from the Old than from the New Testament, except in its third part). Moreover, such subjects as *Saul, Israel in Egypt, Judas Maccabaeus,* and *Joshua* had an additional appeal based on something besides familiarity with the ancient sacred narratives: it was impossible for English audiences in an era of prosperity and expanding empire not to feel a kinship with the chosen people of old whose heroes triumphed by the special favor of Jehovah. Handel more than once was chosen to be the official musical spokesman on occasions of national moment, as with his four anthems for the coronation of George II (1727), the Funeral Anthem for Queen Caroline (1737), the *Te Deum* in thanksgiving for an English military victory at Dettingen in 1743, and the *Fireworks Music* of 1749 celebrating the Peace of Aix-la-Chapelle; the oratorio *Judas Maccabaeus,* like the *Occasional Oratorio* of the preceding year, was designed to honor the Duke of Cumberland for his victory over the Jacobite rebels at Culloden. But even where there was no immediate connection with a particular occasion, many of Handel's oratorios struck a responsive patriotic note with the British public.

The oratorios are not to be regarded as church music. They are intended for the concert hall, and are much closer to the theatre than to the church service. Not all are even on sacred subjects: some, like *Semele* and *Hercules* (1744) are mythological; others, like *Alexander's Feast,* the *Ode for St. Cecilia's Day* (1739), and Handel's last composition, *The Triumph of Time and Truth* (1757, rearranged from a youthful Italian work), are allegorical. The arrangement of the libretto varies: *Susanna* (1748), *Theodora* (1749), and *Joseph* (1743) are practically straight operas; most of the Biblical oratorios are close to the original narrative, but the Biblical text was rewritten in recitatives (sometimes prose, sometimes rhymed verse), arias, and choruses; *Israel in Egypt,* on the other hand, tells the story of the exodus of the Israelites entirely in the words of Scripture. *Messiah* also has a purely Scriptural text, but is the least typical of all Handel's oratorios in that it tells no story; it is a series of contemplations of the Christian idea of redemption, starting with Old Testament prophecies and going through the life of Christ to His final triumph.

Beyond question the most important innovation in the oratorios was Handel's use of the chorus. To be sure, the chorus had had its place in the Italian oratorios of Carissimi, and Handel's early training had made him familiar with the Lutheran choral music of Germany as well as with the characteristic combination of the chorus with orchestra and soloists in the southern German Catholic centers; but the English choral tradition impressed him most profoundly. His conquest of this English musical idiom was fully achieved in the *Chandos*

XII. The
Early
Eighteenth
Century

*Handel's choral
style*

anthems, written for the Duke of Chandos between 1718 and 1720—masterpieces of Anglican Baroque church music from which the composer frequently borrowed in his later works.

The monumental character of Handel's choral style was particularly appropriate to oratorios in which emphasis is on communal rather than individual expression as in the opera aria. Handel often used choruses in the oratorios where in opera an aria would appear—that is, as appropriate commentary or reflection on a situation that has arisen in the course of the action. Inevitably the collective nature of the choral group tends to endue such places with a remote impersonality, a quality akin to the choruses of Greek drama: one of the best of many examples from the Handel oratorios is the chorus "How dark, O Lord, are Thy decrees" in *Jephtha*. Handel's chorus also participates in the action, for instance in *Judas Maccabaeus;* is an element in incidental scenes, as in *Solomon;* or even narrates, as in *Israel in Egypt,* where the choral recitative "He sent a thick darkness" is remarkable equally for its unusual form, its strange modulations, and its pictorial writing.

Pictorial and affective musical symbolism is one of the most conspicuous and endearing features of Handel's choral writing. Of course word painting and descriptive figures—the musical language of the affections—were universal in the Baroque, but Handel often uses these devices in especially felicitous ways. Many examples may be found in *Israel in Egypt:* the somewhat literal representation of frogs, flies, lice, hail, and the other plagues of Egypt is amusing rather than impressive; but the profound, subtle, and moving symbolism of "The people shall hear" lifts this chorus to an eminence hardly equalled elsewhere even by Handel himself. In *Messiah* there is a half-playful use of word painting, the appositeness of which is surprising in view of the fact that the music, up to the last few measures, was adapted from a rather frivolous Italian duet of Handel's composed shortly before. The chorus in *Messiah* sings: "All we like sheep have *gone astray* [diverging melodic lines]; we have *turned* [a rapidly twisting, turning figure that never gets away from its starting point] every one *to his own way*" [stubborn insistence on a single repeated note]; but the point is revealed suddenly, with incomparable dramatic force, at the solemn coda: "and the Lord hath laid on Him the iniquity of us all." A parallel though less striking dramatic contrast is heard in the chorus "For unto us a child is born." This music is taken from another part of the same Italian duet; the carefree roulades that celebrate the birth of the Redeemer lead up to the mighty Handelian hammerstrokes on the words "Wonderful, Counsellor, the Mighty God."

Passages such as these vividly reveal Handel the dramatist, the unerring master of grandiose effects. He is one of the comparatively few among the great composers who knew how to write well for a chorus. His style is simpler than Bach's, less finely chiseled, less subjective, less consistently contrapuntal. He alternates passages in open fugal texture with solid blocks of harmony, sets a melodic line in sustained notes against one in quicker rhythm. Everything is planned so as to lie well within the most effective range of the voices; at points where he designs the maximum fullness of choral sound, especially, Handel brings the four parts tightly together, the basses and tenors high, the sopranos and altos in the middle register. This grouping is often used in the characteristically Handelian closing cadences: an *allegro* chorus climaxing on an inconclusive chord; a tense moment of silence; and then the final cadential chords in three or four splendid sonorous *adagio* harmonies, in which the chorus, in one great outburst of sound, gathers up the whole meaning of everything that has come before.

Handel, like most eighteenth-century composers, occasionally incorporated in his compositions themes, sections, or even whole movements from other works, sometimes literally but more often with changes and improvements. Most of his borrowings were from his own earlier works, but a considerable number were from other composers; three duets and eleven of the twenty-eight choruses of *Israel in Egypt*, for example, were taken in whole or in part from the music of others, while four choruses were arrangements from earlier works by Handel himself. Further borrowings, although not on such an extensive scale, have been traced in many of Handel's compositions written after 1737. It has been suggested that he resorted to borrowing as a means of overcoming the inertia that sometimes afflicted him when he was beginning a new work, particularly after 1737, when he had suffered a paralytic stroke and nervous collapse. In any event, Handel cannot be criticized as a modern composer might be for plagiarism; if he borrowed, he more often than not repaid with interest, clothing the borrowed material with new beauty and preserving it for generations that otherwise would scarcely have known of its existence.[4]

Handel's greatness and historical significance rest on two achievements: his contribution to the musical treasure of the late Baroque and his anticipation of many elements that became important in the new style of the mid-eighteenth century. As a choral composer in the grand style he is without peer. He is a consummate master, not only in choral music but in all fields, of the basic Baroque principle of contrast. At the same time, Handel's emphasis on melody and harmony, as compared to the more strictly contrapuntal style of Bach, links him with the progressive elements of his time. His deliberate appeal to a middle-class audience in the oratorios was one of the first manifestations of a social change which continued throughout the latter half of the century, and which had far-reaching effects on the evolution of music. In some details it might be said that Handel anticipated even the Romantics—the descriptive music of the pastoral scenes in *Giulio Cesare;* the dramatic scene-painting in the "Witch of Endor" episode in *Saul;* the use of clarinets in the opera *Tamerlano* (1724—thus antedating Rameau by twenty-five years); or the four horns in *Giulio Cesare.* The vast intellect of this lord of music seems to have embraced both the past and the future in one superb and comprehensive grasp.

Summary

281

XIII Sources of Classical Style: The Sonata, Symphony, and Opera in the Eighteenth Century

The Background

Four aspects of eighteenth-century life and thought are especially important for understanding the music of this period. In the first place, the eighteenth century was a *cosmopolitan* age. National differences were minimized in comparison with the common humanity of men. Quantz, writing at Berlin in 1752, postulates as the ideal musical style one made up of the best features of the music of all nations: "A music that is accepted and recognized as good not by one country only . . . but by many peoples . . . must, provided it is based as well on reason and sound feeling, be beyond all dispute the best."[1] Chabanon, in 1785, declared "Today there is but one music in all of Europe . . . this universal language of our continent."[2]

The Enlightenment was *humanitarian* as well as cosmopolitan. Rulers not only patronized arts and letters but also busied themselves with programs of social reform. Humanitarian ideals, longings for universal human brotherhood, spread over Europe. Mozart's *Magic Flute*, Schiller's *Ode to Joy*, and Beethoven's Ninth Symphony were among the outgrowths of the eighteenth-century humanitarian movement.

With the rise of a numerous middle class to a position of influence, the eighteenth century witnessed the first steps in a process of *popularization* of art and learning. A new market was appearing for the productions of writers and artists, and not only the subject matter but also the manner of presentation had to be shaped to the new demands. The popularizing trend found powerful support with the growth of the "back to nature" movement and the exaltation of sentiment in literature and the arts.

Music was also, of course, affected along with everything else. Patronage was on the wane and the modern musical public was coming into being. Public concerts designed for mixed audiences began to rival the older private concerts and academies. Music printing increased enormously; the bulk of the publication was directed at amateurs, and much music was issued in magazines. An amateur public naturally demanded and bought music that was easy to understand and to play, and the same public was interested in reading about and discussing music. Musical journalism began; after the middle of the century magazines sprang up which were devoted to musical news, reviews, and criticism. The first histories of music were written and the first collection of medieval musical treatises published.

Finally, the Enlightenment was a *prosaic* age. Its best literature was prose, and it valued in all the arts the virtues of good prose writing: clarity, animation, good taste, proportion, and elegance. Rational rather than poetic, the age had little liking for Baroque mysticism, gravity, massiveness, grandeur, and passion, and its critical temper inhibited great poetry in large forms. Early eighteenth-century aesthetics held that the task of music, like that of the other arts, was to imitate nature, to offer to the listener pleasant sounding images of reality; music was an imitative, hence a decorative art, "an innocent luxury," as Dr. Charles Burney called it in his *General History of Music* (1776).

Moreover, music of the Enlightenment was supposed to meet the listener on his own ground, and not compel him to make an anxious effort to understand what was going on; it must please (by agreeable sounds and rational structure) and move (by imitating feelings), but not too often astonish (by excessive elaboration) and never puzzle (by too great complexity). Music, as "the art of pleasing by the succession and combination of agreeable sounds,"[3] must eschew contrapuntal complexities, which could only be appreciated by the few learned in such abstruse matters. Quantz felt that "the old composers were too much absorbed with musical 'tricks' [contrapuntal devices] and carried them too far, so that they neglected the essential thing in music, which is to move and please."[4] Such opinions were shared by most critics in the second half of the eighteenth century, and the expressive qualities of the music of the time are often sentimental and childlike, bound up as they are with this artificial striving for naturalness.

The ideal eighteenth-century music

The ideal music in the eighteenth century, then, might be described as follows: its language should be universal, not limited by national boundaries; it should be noble as well as entertaining; it should be

XIII. Sources
of Classical
Style:
The Sonata,
Symphony,
and Opera
in the
Eighteenth
Century

expressive within the bounds of decorum; it should be natural, that is, free of needless technical complications and capable of immediately pleasing any normally sensitive listener. The music that most nearly realized these ideals was written in the Classical period, approximately the years 1770 to 1800, and its masters were Gluck, Haydn, Mozart, and the young Beethoven.

Because Gluck, and more especially Haydn and Mozart, over-shadow their predecessors and contemporaries in much the same way that Bach and Handel overshadow theirs, it is easy to fall into the error of viewing the late seventeenth-century composers merely as the forerunners of Bach and Handel, and the mid-eighteenth-century composers merely as the forerunners of Gluck, Haydn, and Mozart. It is especially easy in the latter instance because so little is yet known about either eighteenth-century opera or the origins of the Classical symphony. This area is one of the comparatively blank spots in music history, and until more information about it is available any endeavor to deal with it in a comprehensive way must be regarded as tentative.

Instrumental Music: Sonata and Symphony

Two general styles or manners can be distinguished within the so-called pre-Classical period beginning around 1720: the *rococo* and the *expressive*. The former was cultivated especially in France, and the French term *style galant* (gallant style) is often used as a synonym for rococo. The expressive style, which arose somewhat later and was chiefly associated with German composers, is often designated by the equivalent German phrase *empfindsamer Stil* (literally, "sensitive" style). Both may be regarded as outgrowths of the Baroque tendency to concentrate all musical interest in the two outer voices; but in these newer styles the bass loses all vestiges of leadership and contrapuntal independence, and becomes merely a background for the melody, while the inner voices hardly exist at all.

Rococo and expressive styles

The rococo or gallant style arose in courtly, aristocratic circles; it was elegant, playful, easy, witty, polished, and ornate. *Rococo* origi-nally described the elaborately ornamental decoration of interiors and furnishings fashionable in France during the age of the Regency; *galant* was a catchword of the same period, applied to everything that was thought to be modern, smart, chic, smooth, easy, and sophisti-cated. The rococo is Baroque decorativeness without grandeur. The expressive style, on the other hand, was an affair of the middle class; it was the *style bourgeois*. Instead of being ornate, it is sometimes ostentatiously plain. It domesticates the Baroque affections, turning them into sentiments of the individual soul. The ease and elegance of the rococo, as well as some of its decorative charm, were combined with the expressive quality of the *style bourgeois* in most compositions

284

by the middle of the eighteenth century, and both styles are completely absorbed into the music of the Classical period.

The change from Baroque to the new kind of eighteenth-century music included among other things a change in the conception of melody and melodic development. The new composers of the eighteenth century, while retaining the late Baroque method of constructing a movement on the basis of related keys, gradually abandoned the older idea of the one basic affection and began to introduce contrasts between the various parts of a movement or even within the theme or themes themselves. Moreover, instead of the Baroque spinning-out technique and complex phraseology, the melodies were organized into more distinct phrases of regular two- or four-bar length, resulting in a periodic structure.

The harmonic vocabulary and tonal system of the middle and late eighteenth century were substantially the same as those of the late Baroque, but the harmonic rhythm of most of the new music is slower and the harmonic progressions less weighty than in the older style. A great deal of bustling melodic activity goes on over relatively slow-moving and conventional harmonies, and important harmonic changes almost always coincide with the strong accents indicated by the barlines. The thorough subordination of the bass and harmonies to the role of mere accompaniment to the melody is symbolized by one of the most widely used devices of eighteenth-century keyboard music, the *Alberti bass*, named for the Italian composer, Domenico Alberti (*ca.* 1710–*ca.* 1740). This device consists in breaking each of the underlying chords into a simple pattern of short notes incessantly repeated, thus producing a discreet undulation in the background which sets off the melody to best advantage. The Alberti bass was extremely useful; it was not disdained by Haydn, Mozart, and Beethoven, and lasted well into the nineteenth century.

The chief Italian keyboard composer of the eighteenth century, and one of the most original geniuses in the history of music, was Domenico Scarlatti (1685–1757). Son of the famous Alessandro Scarlatti, born in the same year as Bach and Handel, Domenico Scarlatti produced no works of lasting importance before his first collection of harpsichord sonatas (called on the title page *essercizi*, "exercises" or "diversions") which was published in 1738. In 1720 or 1721 Scarlatti left Italy to enter the service of the King of Portugal. When his pupil the Infanta of Portugal was married to Prince Ferdinand of Spain in 1729, Scarlatti followed her to Madrid, where he remained for the rest of his life in the service of the Spanish courts and where he composed most of his 550 sonatas.

Scarlatti's music is idiomatic for the harpsichord as Chopin's or Debussy's is for the piano. Every imaginable shading of harpsichord sonority, every resource of harpsichord technique, may be found in the sonatas. Some are virtuoso pieces of formidable difficulty, others quiet pastorale-like movements; variegated moods, reminiscences of

XIII. Sources
of Classical
Style:
The Sonata,
Symphony,
and Opera
in the
Eighteenth
Century

popular song and of Italian, Portuguese, and Spanish dance rhythms pervade them. A basic two-voice homophonic texture is alternately filled and thinned with an infallible ear for shape of the phrase and the right sound on the instrument. Rhythmic vitality is combined with an exuberant flow of thematic invention. Because his sonatas absorb and transfigure so many of the sounds and sights of the world, and because he treats texture and harmony freely with a view to sonorous effect, Scarlatti's music may be termed "impressionistic"; but it has none of the vagueness of form we are apt to associate with that word.

All the Scarlatti sonatas are organized by means of tonal relationships into the standard late Baroque binary pattern used for dance pieces and other types of composition: two sections, each as a rule repeated, the first cadencing in the dominant or relative major (rarely some other key), the second modulating further afield and then returning to the tonic. This is the basic scheme from which nearly all the forms of instrumental and solo vocal music in the eighteenth century stem. In Scarlatti's sonatas the closing part of the first section invariably returns, but in the tonic key, at the end of section two. Within each section there is a contrast between the tense, rapidly modulating central portion and the broad, relaxed, cadential closing periods.

Sonata form

The Classical sonata, as exemplified in Haydn, Mozart, and the early works of Beethoven, is a composition in three or four movements of contrasting mood and tempo. The first movement, and sometimes also the second and the last, is typically organized in a pattern called *sonata form* or *first movement form*, consisting of three main divisions: exposition, development, and recapitulation.

The essential factor in this form is the key scheme, the creation of tension by modulating away from the tonic and the resolution of tension by returning to the tonic. The return to the tonic usually coincides with a restatement of some of the thematic material of the first part of the movement. But the other features of standard Classical sonata form—contrasting themes (or even the existence of themes at all, in the sense of distinctive musical entities), a distinct development section, a complete recapitulation, and a coda—are all optional. It is erroneous to suppose that a sonata movement which lacks any of these accessories is somehow imperfect or primitive. The eighteenth-century sonata form did not develop by the mere mechanical annexment of one feature after another until the final full-fledged Classical sonata form appeared. Many individual composers and schools, with different styles, different aims, and different kinds of musical ideas, made use of a common basic pattern, modifying or expanding or adding to it as their purpose and the nature of their musical material required.

*Pre-Classical
symphonies and
chamber music*

Both keyboard sonatas and orchestral compositions of similar form of the early part of the eighteenth century were influenced by the Italian opera overture (*sinfonia*), which about 1700 assumed a structure of three movements in the order fast-slow-fast, that is, an Allegro, a short lyrical Andante, and a finale in the rhythm of a minuet or a gigue. Inasmuch as such overtures as a rule had no thematic or other connection with the opera to follow, they could be played as independent pieces in concerts. Hence it was natural, around 1730, for Italian composers to begin to write concert symphonies using the general plan of the opera overtures. One of the first to do this was G. B. Sammartini or San Martini (1701–1775) of Milan. Other Italians whose works were important in the history of the symphony were the opera composers Rinaldo di Capua (*ca.* 1710–*ca.* 1780), Baldassare Galuppi (1706–1785), and Niccolò Jommelli (1714–1774). The lead of the Italians was soon followed by composers in Germany, Austria, and France, so that after about 1740 the symphony replaced the concerto as the leading form of concerted instrumental music.

Chamber music in this new style did not begin to have a separate history until after the middle of the eighteenth century; many works called "trios" and "quartets" in the pre-Classical era could be performed by either solo instruments or full orchestra. The trio sonatas attributed to G. B. Pergolesi (1710–1736), written in 1732–33, exemplify the new formal principles, which often appear side by side with the fugal and ostinato bass patterns of the late Baroque; the melodies are cheerful, sensitive, and imbued with a lyrical quality which resembles that of vocal arias. The violin concertos and sonatas of Giuseppe Tartini (1692–1770) indicate that the new style gradually penetrated and transformed these types of composition also in the mid-eighteenth century.

The entrance of the expressive style (*empfindsamer Stil*) into instrumental music toward the middle of the century, though not exclusively the achievement of German composers, may be most clearly illustrated in their works. Two of the sons of J. S. Bach are important in this connection. The eldest, Wilhelm Friedemann (1710–1784), was an extraordinarily gifted organist and composer whose life ended in failure and poverty because he was not able to adjust himself to the contemporary requirements for a successful musical career. Some of his works are conservative in style, like those of his great father and teacher; others pay tribute to the fashionable *style galant;* but the outstanding features of his music are a certain freedom, even capriciousness, in the details of harmony, melody, and rhythm; sudden contrasts of mood; and, on occasion, an intensely personal, almost Romantic emotion, which presages the nineteenth century. A kindred spirit to W. F. Bach was Johann Schobert (*ca.* 1720–1767), one of the many German musicians resident in Paris around the middle of the eighteenth century. Schobert is credited with having introduced orchestral effects into keyboard writing, a technique which was taken up by later composers.

Carl Philipp Emanuel Bach (1714–1788), one of the most influential composers of his generation, has been called the founder of Classical style. Trained in music by his father, he was in service at the court

XIII. Sources
of Classical
Style:
The Sonata,
Symphony,
and Opera
in the
Eighteenth
Century

Carl Philipp Emanuel Bach (1714–1788), son of J. S. Bach. (Bettmann Archive)

of Frederick the Great in Berlin from 1740 to 1768 and then became music director of the five principal churches in Hamburg. His compositions include oratorios, songs, symphonies, and chamber music, but most numerous and important are his works for clavier. In 1742 he published a set of six sonatas (the *Prussian* sonatas) and in 1744 another set of six (the *Württemberg* sonatas). These sonatas, especially those of 1742, were quite revolutionary in style, and exerted a strong influence on later composers. C. P. E. Bach's favorite keyboard instrument was not the harpsichord but the softer, more intimate clavichord, with its capacity for delicate dynamic shadings. The clavichord enjoyed a spell of renewed popularity in Germany around the middle of the eighteenth century before both it and the harpsichord were gradually supplanted by the pianoforte; the last five sets of C. P. E. Bach's sonatas (1780–87) were written for the pianoforte, as were many of the later keyboard pieces of Wilhelm Friedemann Bach.

The principal technical characteristics of the *empfindsamer Stil*, of which C. P. E. Bach was one of the chief representatives, may be summarized as follows. The aim to express feeling naturally was realized through two devices, used either separately or in combination: the melodic *sigh*, a motive ending *portamento* on a weak beat—usually the resolution of an appoggiatura and often including also an anticipation of the note of resolution; and *chromaticism*, which might affect both melody and harmony.

Simplicity or naturalness must be understood in the eighteenth-century sense: the ideal did not by any means preclude ornamentation, but composers did endeavor to keep the ornaments within appropriate proportions and to assimilate them into the entire expressive content of a passage. The expressive style often exploited the element of surprise, with abrupt shifts of harmony, strange modulations, unusual turns of melody, expectant pauses, changes of texture, sudden *sforzando* accents, and the like. The subjective, emotional qualities of the *Empfindsamkeit* reached a climax during the 1760's and 1770's; the style is sometimes described by the same term *Sturm und Drang*— storm and stress—which is also applied to German literature of the same period. The Classical composers later brought this emotionalism under control by imposing unity of content and form. The entire development will be traced in the discussion of Haydn, in the following chapter.

C. P. E. Bach's movements in sonata form as a rule have two distinct themes and usually recapitulate the whole exposition. Seldom, however, is there a real contrast in character between the two themes. As is usual with the north German composers, Bach's ruling ideal is unity of mood and material; consequently, themes usually begin to be developed as soon as they have been stated; and the section immediately after the double bar, the development section of the standard Classical symphony, is relatively short. In this concept of thematic unity within sonata form, as well as in his general musical language, C. P. E. Bach is closer to Haydn and Beethoven than to Mozart. Most of his sonatas have the usual three movements—Allegro (or Allegretto), Andante, Allegro—though in some of the later ones the Andante was shortened to a mere bridge between the two fast movements. Some of Bach's most ingenious and charming music is found in the rondos which alternate with the sonatas and fantasias of the last five sets of the *Sonatas for Connoisseurs* published from 1780 to 1787.

Not the least of C. P. E. Bach's contributions to music was his *Essay on the True Art of Playing Keyboard Instruments* (1753–62), the most important treatise on ornamentation in the middle eighteenth century and a work which, like Quantz's essay on flute playing, includes much information about the musical thought and practice of the period.

The principal German centers of symphonic composition from 1740 onward were Mannheim, Vienna, and Berlin. The founder of the Mannheim school was Johann Stamitz (1717–1757); under his leadership the Mannheim orchestra became renowned all over Europe for its virtuosity (Burney called it "an army of generals"), for its hitherto unknown dynamic range from the softest *pianissimo* to the loudest *fortissimo*, and for the thrilling sound of its crescendo. The exploitation of the orchestral crescendo and of abrupt contrasts between *forte* and *piano* were manifestations of the same desire for flexibility and variety of musical effects that was responsible for the adoption of the pianoforte as successor to the harpsichord.

German symphonic composers

Stamitz was one of the first composers regularly to use a contrasting, lyrical second theme in his Allegro movements in sonata form and to expand the symphony from three movements to four (the standard number in the Classical period) by adding a fast finale after the minuet, which had formerly served as the closing movement. Despite such premonitions of later forms, however, his music, like that of all the early German symphony composers, is still in the rococo-expressive style of the middle eighteenth century; at the hands of his successors many of his tricks of style degenerated into mannerisms. One of the best of the later Mannheim symphonists was Christian Cannabich (1731–1798).

The Vienna school is of especial interest because it was the immediate background of the work of Haydn, Mozart, and Beethoven. Georg Matthias Monn (1717–1750) was one of the earliest of the Viennese composers, but a more important figure was Fux's pupil Georg Christoph Wagenseil (1715–1777). In his music, as also in that of the later Austrian composers Florian Leopold Gassmann (1729–1774) and Michael Haydn (1737–1806), we find the pleasant, typically Viennese lyricism and good humor that is such an important feature in Mozart's style. The Viennese composers for the most part favored contrasting theme-groups in their movements in sonata form.

The principal symphonic composers of the Berlin or north German group were Johann Gottlieb Graun (1703–1771) and C. P. E. Bach. The north Germans were conservative, in that they held consistently to three-movement structure for the symphony and were chary of introducing sharp thematic contrasts within a movement. On the other hand, it was they chiefly who initiated the technique of thematic development in a dynamic, organically unified, serious, and quasi-dramatic style, and at the same time enriched symphonic texture with contrapuntal elements.

An important composer of symphonies, as well as of chamber music, keyboard music, and operas, was Johann Christian Bach (1735–1782), youngest of the sons of Johann Sebastian Bach.

Paris became an important center of composition and publication toward the middle of the eighteenth century; a considerable number of German and other foreign composers lived there. Works of the French school included symphonies and, particularly after 1770, a form known as the *symphonie concertante*, that is, a symphonic work employing two or more solo instruments in addition to the regular orchestra. One of the most noted composers of symphonies in France was a Belgian, François Joseph Gossec (1734–1829), who came to Paris in 1751.

Another noteworthy eighteenth-century composer of symphonies was the Englishman, William Boyce (1710–1779). His symphonies are conservative in form, but fresh and engaging in their melodies and rhythms.

In the last quarter of the eighteenth century the symphony and other forms of ensemble music gradually discarded the basso continuo as all the essential voices were taken over by the melody instruments. With the final disappearance of the harpsichord from the orchestra, toward the end of the century, the responsibility of conducting the group fell on the leader of the violins.

The eighteenth-century symphony orchestra was much smaller than the orchestra of today. In the symphonies of the middle of the century the usual orchestration gave all the essential musical material to the strings, and used the winds only for doubling, reinforcing, and filling in the harmonies. Sometimes in performance woodwinds and brasses might be added to the orchestra even though the composer had written no parts for them. Later in the century the wind instruments came to be entrusted with more important and more independent material.

The types of chamber music in the 1770's and 1780's included the sonata for clavier and violin, with the violin usually in a subsidiary role; but the principal medium eventually became the string quartet. A distinguished composer of chamber music was Luigi Boccherini (1743–1805), whose output includes about 125 string quintets, 91 quartets, 54 trios, and 20 symphonies.

A different type of music, designed primarily for out-of-doors or for informal occasions, was the Viennese serenade, which like the divertimento, cassation, and notturno was a cross between the Baroque orchestral suite and the Classical symphony; it consisted usually of five or more movements, many of them in dance rhythms, but in no regularly prescribed order. Such pieces were written for wind instruments alone, or strings alone, or a combination of the two; they kept a certain popular flavor in their tunes and rhythms, and were not without influence on the style of the Viennese Classical symphony. Historically they were important because they accustomed composers to the sound of ensemble music without basso continuo, the elimination of which was an essential step in the evolution of the Classical string quartet.

Opera, Song, and Church Music

As with the sonata and symphony, so with the opera: new forms and styles were emerging from and gradually supplanting the old during the first quarter of the eighteenth century. The French *tragé-*
die lyrique was resistant to change in this period, and the general style of Venetian Baroque opera maintained itself for a long while in Germany; but a strong progressive current was emanating from Italy. The new Italian opera that eventually dominated the stages of Europe in the eighteenth century was a product of the same forces that were reshaping all other forms of music in the age of the Enlightenment. It aimed to be clear, simple, rational, faithful to nature, of universal appeal, and capable of giving pleasure to its audiences without causing them undue mental fatigue. The artificialities which it soon acquired, and for which it was roundly condemned by critics in the latter part of the century, were in part merely outmoded conventions of an earlier period and in part accidental accretions.

XIII. Sources
of Classical
Style:
The Sonata,
Symphony,
and Opera
in the
Eighteenth
Century

The aria

The musical interest of the Italian opera was centered in the arias, which were created by eighteenth-century composers in astounding profusion and variety. The most common form in the earlier part of the century was the da capo aria, a basic scheme that permitted infinite variation in detail. After about the middle of the century it became more common to write arias in a single movement, usually an expanded version of the first part of a da capo aria, with a key-scheme like that of the sonata and with orchestral ritornellos as in a concerto.

Concentration upon the aria as almost the only significant musical ingredient in opera opened the way to abuses. The scheme of regularly alternating recitatives and arias came to be treated too rigidly. Singers, including the famed Italian *castrati* (male sopranos), made arbitrary demands on the poets and composers, compelling them to alter, add, and substitute arias without respect for dramatic or musical propriety. Moreover, the melodic embellishments and cadenzas which the singers added at will were all too often mere tasteless displays of vocal acrobatics. A famous satire on the opera and everything connected with it, entitled *The Fashionable Theatre* (*il Teatro alla moda*), was published anonymously by Benedetto Marcello in 1720, but not until about 1745 did Italian composers attempt any important reforms. The beginning of operatic reform coincided with the rise of the expressive style, and, like that style, was a sign of the growing influence of middle-class ideas on the narrowly aristocratic standards of the early part of the century.

Among the leading composers of Italian opera were Handel, Pergolesi (whose serious operas, however, were unsuccessful and practically without influence), Nicola Porpora (1686–1768)—and a German, Johann Adolph Hasse (1699–1783), who became thoroughly Italian in his musical style. He was the most popular and successful opera composer of Europe around the middle of the century, and Burney's remarks about his music reveal the qualities that endeared him to the connoisseurs:

> . . . the most natural, elegant, and judicious composer of vocal music . . . now alive; equally a friend to poetry and the voice, he discovers as much judgment as genius, in expressing words, as well as in accompanying those sweet and tender melodies, which he gives to the singer. Always regarding the voice, as the first object of attention in a theatre, he never suffocates it, by the learned jargon of a multiplicity of instruments and subjects; but is as careful of preserving its importance as a painter, of throwing the strongest light upon the capital figure of his piece.[5]

Beginnings of opera reform

When certain Italian composers began seriously to try to bring the opera into harmony with changing ideals of music and drama, their efforts were directed toward making the entire design more natural—that is, more flexible in structure, more deeply expressive in content, less laden with coloratura, and more varied in other musical resources. The da capo aria was not abandoned but it was modified, and other forms were used as well; arias and recitatives were alternated more flexibly so as to carry on the action more rapidly and realistically; greater use was made of accompanied recitative; the orchestra became more important both for its own sake and for adding harmonic depth to accompaniments; choruses, long disused in Italian opera, reappeared; and there was a general stiffening of resistance to the arbitrary demands of the solo singers.

The consummation of the international style of opera was the work of Christoph Willibald Gluck (1714–1787). He began by writing operas in the conventional Italian style, but was strongly affected by the movement of reform in the 1750's. Spurred on by the more radical ideas of the time, he collaborated with the poet Raniero Calzabigi (1714–1795) to produce at Vienna *Orfeo ed Euridice* in 1762 and *Alceste* in 1767. In a dedicatory preface to the latter work Gluck summarized his aims: to remove the abuses that had hitherto deformed Italian opera, "to confine music to its proper function of serving the poetry for the expression and the situations of the plot" without regard either to the outworn conventions of the da capo aria or the desire of singers to show off their skill in ornamental variation; furthermore, to make the overture an integral part of the opera, to adapt the orchestra to the dramatic requirements, and to lessen the contrast between aria and recitative. "I believed that my greatest effort should be directed to seeking a beautiful simplicity . . . and there is no accepted rule that I have not thought should be gladly sacrificed in favor of effectiveness."

Christoph Willibald Gluck

The beautiful simplicity which Gluck professed to seek is exemplified in the celebrated aria "Che farò senza Euridice?" ("What shall I do without Euridice?") from *Orfeo*, and in other airs, choruses, and dances of the same work. *Alceste* is a more monumental opera, in contrast to the prevailingly pastoral and elegiac tone of *Orfeo*. In both, the music is plastically molded to the drama, with recitatives, arias, and choruses intermingled in large unified scenes. Gluck

Christoph Willibald Gluck (1714–1787), a portrait by Duplessis. (Bettmann Archive)

XIII. Sources
of Classical
Style:
The Sonata,
Symphony,
and Opera
in the
Eighteenth
Century

achieved his mature style in these operas, assimilating Italian melodic grace, German seriousness, and the stately magnificence of the French *tragédie lyrique*. He was ready for the climax of his career, which was ushered in with the successful production of *Iphigénie en Aulide* (*Iphigenia at Aulis*) at Paris in 1774. Revised versions of *Orfeo* and *Alceste* (both with French texts) swiftly followed. In a mischievously instigated rivalry with the popular Neapolitan composer Niccolò Piccinni (1728–1800), Gluck composed in 1777 a five-act opera, *Armide*, on the same libretto of Quinault that Lully had set in 1686. Gluck's masterpiece, *Iphigénie en Tauride* (*Iphigenia in Tauris*), was produced in 1779. It is a work of large proportions, having an excellent balance of dramatic and musical interest, and utilizing all the resources of opera—orchestra, ballet, solo and choral singing—to produce a total effect of Classical tragic grandeur.

Gluck's operas were models for the works of his immediate followers at Paris, and his influence on the form and spirit of opera was transmitted to the nineteenth century through such composers as his erstwhile rival Piccinni, Luigi Cherubini (1760–1842), Gasparo Spontini (1774–1851), and Hector Berlioz (1803–1869).

The term *comic opera* denotes works that are lighter in style than serious opera; they present familiar scenes and characters rather than *Comic opera* heroic or mythological material, and require relatively modest performing resources. Comic opera took different forms in different countries, although everywhere it represented an artistic revolt against the *opera seria*, the "serious" or tragic Italian opera. Comic opera librettos were always in the national tongue, and the music likewise tended to accentuate the national musical idiom. From humble beginnings the comic opera grew steadily in importance after 1760, and before the end of the century many of its characteristic features had been absorbed into the main stream of operatic composition. Its historical significance was twofold: it responded to the universal demand for naturalness in the latter half of the eighteenth century, and it was the principal early channel of the movement toward musical nationalism which became prominent in the Romantic period.

The Italian *opera buffa* originated early in the eighteenth century from the custom of presenting short comic musical *intermezzi* between the acts of a serious opera. An early master was Pergolesi, whose *Italy* *La serva padrona* (*The Maid Mistress*, 1733) is still popular. Written for only bass and soprano (there is a third character who is mute) with a string orchestra, the music is a paragon of the nimble, spirited comic style at which Italian composers surpass the rest of the world.

One of the achievements of the *opera buffa* was its exploitation of the possibilities of the bass voice, either in straight comedy or in burlesque of other styles. In the comic operas of Nicola Logroscino (1698–*ca.* 1765) and Baldassare Galuppi another feature appeared, the *ensemble finale:* for the ending of an act all the characters are gradually brought on to the stage while the action continues with growing animation until it reaches a climax in which every singer in the cast takes part. These ensemble finales were unlike anything in the serious opera, and in writing them composers were forced to follow the rapidly changing action of the scene without losing coherence in the musical form. The challenge was well met by two Neapolitan composers of *opere buffe*, Piccinni and Giovanni Paisiello (1740–1816); but perfect success in this difficult task was reserved for Mozart.

Meanwhile, beginning about the middle of the century, largely owing to the Italian dramatist Carlo Goldoni (1707–1793), a refinement of the *opera buffa* libretto took place; plots of a serious, sentimental, or pathetic character began to appear, as well as the traditional comic ones. An example of this new type was Piccinni's *La buona figliuola* (*The Good Girl*) of 1760, adapted by Goldoni from Richardson's novel *Pamela* which had appeared twenty years before. Paisiello's *Barbiere di Siviglia* (*The Barber of Seville;* 1782), from Beaumarchais's drama, was a semiserious treatment of current political issues, while his *Nina* (1789) had an out-and-out sentimental plot. All in all, the *opera buffa* came a long way, both dramatically and musically, in the course of the century; Mozart made good use of its mingled heritage of comic, serious, and sentimental drama and live, flexible, and widely acceptable musical style.

The national French form of light opera was known as *opéra comique*. It began around 1710 as a lowly form of popular entertainment, and until the middle of the century relied almost entirely on popular tunes (*vaudevilles*), or simple melodies in imitation of such tunes, for its music. The visit of an Italian opera troupe at Paris in 1752 stimulated the production of *opéras comiques* in which original airs (called *ariettes*) in a mixed Italian-French style were introduced along with the old vaudevilles; gradually the ariettes replaced the vaudevilles until by the end of the 1760's the latter were completely discarded and the entire score was newly composed. *France*

The French *opéra comique* (like all the national forms of light opera except the Italian *opera buffa*) used spoken dialogue instead of recitative. Following the general European trend in the second half of the century, the *opéra comique* took on a romantic tinge, and some of the librettos furthermore dealt quite boldly with the burning social issues that were agitating France during the pre-Revolutionary years. The principal composers were François André Danican-Philidor (1726–1795; also famous as a chess master), Pierre-Alexandre Monsigny (1729–1817), and above all the Belgian-born André Ernest Modeste Grétry (1741–1813), whose *Richard Coeur-de-Lion* (*Richard the Lion-Hearted;* 1784) was a forerunner of numerous "rescue" operas around the turn of the century—Beethoven's *Fidelio* was one—in which the hero, after lying for two and a half acts in imminent danger of death, is finally saved through the devoted heroism of a friend. Grétry's music in his fifty or more operas is never profound, but it is melodious, singable, and quite effective, with occasional moments of

XIII. Sources
of Classical
Style:
The Sonata,
Symphony,
and Opera
in the
Eighteenth
Century

moving dramatic expression. The *opéra comique*, with its alternation of spoken dialogue and musical numbers, was extremely popular in France. It flourished through the Revolution and the Napoleonic era and took on even greater musical significance during the Romantic period.

The English *ballad opera* rose to popularity with the extraordinary success of *Beggar's Opera* at London in 1728. This piece broadly satirized the fashionable Italian opera; its music, like that of the early *opéra comique*, consisted for the most part of popular tunes—ballads —with a few numbers parodied from familiar operatic airs. The immense popularity of ballad operas in the 1730's was one sign of a general reaction in England against foreign opera, that "exotic and irrational entertainment," as Dr. Johnson called it—a reaction which, as we have already noticed, had among its consequences that of turning Handel's energies from opera to oratorio in the latter part of his life. The only notable composer of English opera in the eighteenth century was Thomas Augustine Arne (1710–1778); many comic operas on sentimental or romantic subjects were produced by him and lesser composers throughout the century.

In Germany a form of comic opera called the *Singspiel* arose about the middle of the eighteenth century. The principal early singspiel composer was Johann Adam Hiller (1728–1804) of Leipzig. In northern Germany the singspiel developed along romantic lines, its history eventually merging with that of early nineteenth-century German Romantic opera. In the south, particularly at Vienna, the fashion was for farcical subjects and treatment, with lively music in popular style, influenced to some extent by the idioms of the Italian *opera buffa*. A typical Viennese singspiel composer was Carl Ditters von Dittersdorf (1739–1799), who was also notable for his instrumental music. The German singspiel was as important as the Italian *opera buffa* in the historical background of Mozart's works for the theatre.

Solo songs, cantatas, and other types of secular vocal music outside opera were produced in every country during the eighteenth century, but special artistic importance attaches to the rise of the German *Lied*. The principal center of song composition after the middle of the century was Berlin, with J. J. Quantz (1697–1773), K. H. Graun, and C. P. E. Bach the chief composers. The professed ideals of the Berlin school required that *Lieder* should be in strophic form with melodies in a natural, expressive style like folk song, having but one note to a syllable; only the simplest possible accompaniments, held completely subordinate to the vocal line, were permitted. These principles, which were in accord with the philosophy of the expressive style, were generally accepted in the eighteenth century; but their effect eventually was to impose artificial restrictions on the Lied, and composers of imagination gradually transcended them, particularly in the direction of making the form more varied and giving more significance to

Lied: *Erlkönig*, J. F. Reichardt

Who rides so late through night and wind? It is the father with his child. He has the boy within his arm, he holds him fast, he keeps him warm. "My son, why do you hide your face in fear?" ... "You dear child, come, go with me; lovely games I'll play with you."

XIII. Sources
of Classical
Style:
The Sonata,
Symphony,
and Opera
in the
Eighteenth
Century

the accompaniment. The leading Berlin composers toward the end of the century were Johann Abraham Peter Schulz (1747–1800) and Johann Friedrich Reichardt (1752–1814); the latter's 700 *Lieder* included many on poems by Goethe (see Example 83). Among the best German songs of the eighteenth century are Gluck's settings of seven of Klopstock's odes, published at Vienna in 1785.

Singspiele

Over 750 collections of *Lieder* with keyboard accompaniment were published in Germany during the second half of the century, and this figure does not include the numerous *Singspiele* of the same period, which consist for the most part of songs exactly similar to *Lieder*. Practically all composers of *Singspiele*, in fact, also wrote *Lieder* in large quantities. The production continued steadily into the nineteenth century; when Schubert began composing songs in 1811 he was entering into a long and rich tradition, of which his own work was the consummation.

Church music

The secular, individualistic temper of the eighteenth century had the effect of making sacred music less distinctive, and bringing it into conformity with the style of secular music, particularly that of the theatre. The dominant trend was to introduce into the church the musical idioms and forms of opera, with orchestral accompaniment, da capo arias, and accompanied recitatives. The list of the leading eighteenth-century Italian church composers is almost identical with the list of the leading opera composers of the same period. Even more than the Mass and motet, the oratorio in Italy grew to be almost indistinguishable from opera, especially when, as happened occasionally at Rome and Naples after 1780, oratorios were staged and acted in costume. At the same time some composers, particularly in northern Italy and southern Germany and Austria, effected a compromise between conservative and modern elements, and this mixed style— influenced also by the instrumental symphonic forms of the Classical period—was the background of the sacred compositions of Haydn and Mozart.

Lutheran church music rapidly declined in quality and importance after the death of J. S. Bach. The principal achievements of the north German composers were in the half-sacred, half-secular form of the oratorio; oratorios written after 1750 show some reaction against the excesses of operatic style. The best oratorios of this period were those of C. P. E. Bach. Karl Heinrich Graun's *Der Tod Jesu* (*The Death of Jesus*), a mediocre work which was first performed at Berlin in 1755, remained popular in Germany up to the end of the nineteenth century.

In England, the overpowering influence of Handel operated to discourage originality, and the generally low level of church music is relieved only by the works of a few composers such as Maurice Greene (1695–1775) and Samuel Wesley (1766–1837). Wesley, incidentally, was one of the first musicians of his time to recognize the greatness of J. S. Bach and did much to stimulate performance of

Bach's organ music in England. The latter half of the eighteenth century was not by any means a period of musical stagnation in England; there was an active concert life, and much intelligent appreciation of foreign musicians, notably Haydn, who wrote several of his most important symphonies for London audiences.

XIV The Late Eighteenth Century

The two outstanding composers of the late eighteenth century are Haydn and Mozart. Together they represent the Classical period in much the same sense that Bach and Handel represent the late Baroque, using the accepted musical language of their time and creating in that language works of unsurpassed perfection. Haydn and Mozart have much more in common than mere contemporaneity and similarity of idiom; they were close personal friends, and each admired and was influenced by the music of the other. Haydn was born in 1732, Mozart in 1756; Mozart died in 1791 at the age of 35, Haydn in 1809 at the age of 77. Haydn's growth to artistic maturity was much slower than Mozart's, who was a child prodigy. Had Haydn died at 35 he would hardly be remembered today; in fact, most of his best-known works were not produced until after Mozart's death. In personality the two men were utterly different: Mozart was a precocious genius, of roving disposition and unsettled habits, a born showman, a virtuoso pianist, a consummate musical dramatist, but helpless in most of the practical affairs of life; Haydn was largely self-taught, a patient and persistent worker, modest, an excellent conductor but no virtuoso soloist (thought he occasionally played viola in string quartets), precise and regular in the conduct of his affairs, and one who on the whole lived contentedly under the patronage system—the last eminent composer to do so.

Franz Joseph Haydn

Haydn entered the service of the wealthy and noble Esterházy family in 1761 and remained under their patronage to the end of his life. He lived on his patrons' remote country estate of Eszterháza, where he found ideal conditions for composing. In 1790 he settled in his own house in Vienna, where, except for two long visits to London in the early 1790's, he lived most of the time for the rest of his life.

His output includes over 100 symphonies and 83 string quartets; many overtures, divertimentos, serenades, baryton trios, string trios, piano trios, and other chamber works; a few concertos; 52 piano sonatas; songs, arias, cantatas, Masses and other settings of liturgical texts, 23 operas, and 4 oratorios. Most important are the symphonies and quartets, for Haydn was above all an instrumental composer and the symphonies and quartets are his finest achievements in this field. Of his vocal music, the most important works are the last six Masses and the two oratorios *The Creation* and *The Seasons;* all these were written during the last years of his life, and all are permeated to some extent by the spirit and technique of the symphony.

The Symphonies Nos. 2–92 were written between 1760 and 1788, most of them of course for Prince Esterházy's orchestra; Nos. 82–87 were composed on commission in 1785–86 for a concert series in Paris (and hence are known as the *Paris Symphonies*); Nos. 88–92 were commissioned by private individuals. No. 92 is called the *Oxford Symphony* because it was played on the occasion when Haydn received the honorary degree of Doctor of Music from Oxford University in 1791. Many of the other symphonies (as well as many of the quartets) have been given special names for one reason or another, but hardly any of these designations are the composer's.

The symphonies written during Haydn's first ten years at Eszterháza are all quite short, and many of them are obviously experimental. Those of the 1760's progress toward more serious and meaningful musical content (No. 35) and more subtle use of form (finale of No. 38). The symphonies in minor keys (Nos. 26, 39, and 49) have an intensity of feeling that is a harbinger of the music written in the early 1770's. No. 26 (*Lamentatione*) incorporates a Gregorian melody from an old plainsong Passion drama as thematic material in the first two movements.

Franz Joseph Haydn (1732–1809), from a portrait by Thomas Hardy, London, 1792.

The work of Haydn's "romantic" period shows him as a composer of ripe technique and fervent imagination. The symphonies of the years 1771 to 1774 are among his best works. We may take as representative of this period Nos. 44, 47, and 56. All are on a larger scale than the symphonies of the previous decade. Themes are more broadly laid out, those of the fast movements often beginning with a bold unison proclamation followed immediately by a contrasting idea, with the whole theme then restated. Development sections, which use motives from the themes, become more propulsive and dramatic. Dramatic also are the unexpected changes from *forte* to *piano*, the crescendos and *sforzati* that are a part of this style. Counterpoint appears, not awkwardly, as a foreign element contrasting with homophonic texture, but as a natural concomitant of the musical ideas. Regularly periodic four-measure phrases are the norm, with occasionally an artful extension to six measures (as in the second part of the minuet of Symphony No. 56) to avoid a too perfect regularity. The harmonic palette is richer than in the early symphonies; modulations range more widely and the harmonic arches are broader.

The symphonies of 1771–1774

The slow movements have a romantically expressive warmth. Symphony No. 44, in E minor, known as the *Trauersinfonie* (*Symphony of Mourning*), has one of the most beautiful Adagios in all Haydn's works; the Adagio of No. 56 is equally moving, and shows what effects Haydn can draw from the introduction of the minor mode into a movement in a major key. Most of the slow movements are in sonata form, but with such leisurely, freely drawn-out progression of the thought that a listener is hardly conscious of the structure. The slow movement of No. 47, however, is a theme with variations, a favored form for slow movements in Haydn's later works; the first period of the theme is constructed in double counterpoint at the octave, so that the last period of the theme (and of each of the four variations) is the same as the first but with the melody and the bass interchanged.

No. 56 is one of Haydn's twenty symphonies in C major. All except the very earliest of the symphonies written in this key form a special group, being uniformly festive in spirit, and require the addition of trumpets and drums to the normal orchestra. The first movement of No. 56 gains additional pomp from the timbre of the high horns and trumpets; the Minuet is in Haydn's best popular, hearty vein, while the finale sounds like a brilliant, capricious tarantella, with sharp dynamic contrasts and tremendous rhythmic energy. Each of the fast movements of this symphony is in sonata form and has a contrasting second theme, something by no means common with Haydn.

The quartets of 1760–1781

Haydn's string quartets of the early 1770's testify as eloquently as do the symphonies to his arrival at full artistic stature. Especially in the six Quartets of Op. 20 (composed in 1772 and known as the *Sun* quartets), he achieved a union of all stylistic elements and a perfect adaptation of form to musical content; by doing so, he definitely established both his contemporary fame and his historical position as the founder of the Classical string quartet. The four instruments have individuality and equality, and the texture is free from any suspicion of dependence on a basso continuo; at the same time, counterpoint rises to importance: three of the finales in Op. 20 are actually in fugue, and everywhere contrapuntal writing enriches the texture, as in the symphonies of this same period. The movements in sonata form approach full three-part structure, with the development section enlarged so that all three parts—exposition, development, and recapitulation—are more nearly equal in length than they are in the earlier quartets; moreover, development of the announced themes is spread over the entire movement, a procedure typical of Haydn's later works in sonata form. A favorite device of Haydn makes its appearance in the first movement of Op. 20, No. 1, namely the *fausse reprise* or false recapitulation: the opening theme appears in the main key, in the midst of the development section, as though the recapitulation had already been reached—but this is a deception, for the theme is only a starting point for further development and the real recapitulation comes later. There is much variety of mood in the quartets of Op. 20, from the sombre F minor of No. 5 to the serene joyousness of No. 4 in D major. Marks of dynamics and expression are frequent and explicit, showing the composer's care for details of interpretation.

The six quartets of Op. 33, known as the *Russian* quartets, were composed in 1781, after Haydn had met Mozart and had been strongly impressed by the latter's music. Haydn's statement that these quartets had been composed "in a new and special manner" may refer to the fact that in them he applied the technique of development by means of thematic motives even more thoroughly than in his previous works. The *Russian* quartets are on the whole lighter in mood than those of 1772, less romantic, but more witty and popular. Only the first movements are in sonata form; the finales are either rondos or variations. The minuets, although entitled "scherzo" or "scherzando" (whence the alternative name *Gli Scherzi* for this set), are not essentially different from Haydn's other minuets except that they require a slightly faster tempo in performance. The finest of this group is No. 3, in C major, known as the *Bird* quartet from the trills in the trio of the Minuet. In the Adagio Haydn wrote out the repeat of the first section in order to vary the melodic ornaments—a device possibly borrowed from C. P. E. Bach, whose ideas on music had influenced Haydn over many years. The finale is an excellent specimen of Haydnesque humor.

In comparison with the symphonies of 1770–74, those of the late 1770's and early 1780's are less impressive, perhaps because at this time Haydn was chiefly concerned with other kinds of composition, particularly opera. The finale of No. 77 (*ca.* 1782) is one of the earliest examples in Haydn's work of the sonata-rondo form, which combines features of the sonata (key scheme, systematic development of motives) with those of the rondo (multiple recurrence of the principal

The symphonies of 1775–1788

theme). This form was frequently used for finales in Haydn's subsequent works, and was a favorite with Beethoven.

The six *Paris Symphonies* (Nos. 82 to 87) of 1785–86 and the five next following (Nos. 88 to 92) of 1787–88 introduce the culmination of Haydn's symphonic achievements. In these works of the late 1780's, Mozart's influence on Haydn is most noticeable, evidenced in the *cantabile* character of the themes and in the emotional depth of the entire symphony, especially the slow movement. No. 85 (called *La Reine* and said to have been especially loved by Queen Marie Antoinette) is a model of Classical style; Nos. 88 and 92 (*Oxford*) are two of the most popular of Haydn's symphonies. All the works of this period have ample dimensions, incorporating significant and expressive musical ideas in a complex but thoroughly unified structure and making always appropriate use of many different and ingenious technical resources.

A new feature of the first movements of these symphonies is the slow introduction, themes of which are sometimes related to those of the following Allegro. Haydn still avoids or at least minimizes contrasting subjects in movements in sonata form; thematic development, instead, pervades all parts of the movement. Many of the slow movements have a quiet introspective coda featuring the woodwind instruments and using colorful chromatic harmonies (as in No. 92). The wind instruments are prominent also in the trios of the minuets; indeed, Haydn gives to the winds in all his symphonies much more responsibility than the average listener is likely to realize, for the large size of the string section in a modern symphony orchestra tends to overwhelm the sound of the flutes, oboes, and bassoons and thus destroy the balance of timbres that the composer intended.

For his minuet trios Haydn often chooses themes that suggest Austrian folk songs; indeed, the use of Austrian, Hungarian, or Croatian folk tunes, or of melodies, harmonies, and rhythms suggestive of such tunes, is fairly common in all of Haydn's symphonies and quartets; the theme of the variations in the *Romanza* of Symphony No. 85 is an old French folk song.

The finales of Symphonies Nos. 82–92 are either in sonata form or, more characteristically, sonata-rondo form. Unlike Haydn's earlier finales, these make great use of contrapuntal texture and contrapuntal devices—for example, the canon in the last movement of No. 88. By such means Haydn perfected closing movements that at the same time had popular appeal and sufficient weight to balance the rest of the symphony; the finale of No. 88 is a particularly fine example.

The quartets of the late 1780's are on an equally high level of inspiration with the symphonies. The opus numbers are 42 (one quartet, *The quartets of* 1785), 50 (the six *Prussian* quartets, 1784–87), 54, 55 (three each, *the 1780's* 1789) and 64 (six quartets, 1790). Technique and forms are like those of the symphonies of the same period, except that the first movements do not have a slow introduction. Many of the slow movements have the form of theme and variations, and among these we find some special types: the Andante of Op. 50, No. 4 is a set of double variations, using two themes in alternation, one in major and the other in minor, so that the pattern becomes *A* (in major) *B* (in minor) *A'B'A''*. The slow movement of Op. 55, No. 2 (in this instance the first movement of the quartet) is a full set of double variations, alternately minor and major, with a coda. The double variation form was frequently employed by Haydn in his later works, as in the Andante of Symphony No. 103 (*Drum Roll*) and the beautiful pianoforte Variations in F minor, composed in 1793.

An invitation from the impresario J. P. Salomon in 1790 to compose and conduct six, and later six more, symphonies for the highly sophisticated, cosmopolitan, and exacting audiences of London *The* London
symphonies spurred Haydn to supreme efforts. Hailed by the British as "the greatest composer in the world," he was determined to live up to what was expected of him. The *London* symphonies are consequently the crown of his achievements. Everything he had learned in forty years of experience went into them. While there are no radical departures from his previous works, all the elements are brought together on a grander scale, with more brilliant orchestration, more daring conceptions of harmony, and an intensified rhythmic drive. The apparently high proportion of folksong melodies among the themes of the *London* symphonies is another evidence of Haydn's desire to make the basis of appeal in these works as broad as possible. He always aimed to please both the ordinary music lover and the expert; and it is one of the measures of his greatness that he succeeded.

The orchestra of the *London* symphonies includes trumpets and timpani, which (contrary to Haydn's earlier practice) are used in most of the slow movements as well as in the others. Clarinets make their appearance in all but No. 102 of the second set of *London* symphonies. Trumpets sometimes have independent parts instead of doubling the horns as previously, and likewise the violoncellos are often used independently of the basses. In several of the symphonies solo strings are featured against the full orchestra. Woodwinds are treated even more independently than hitherto, and the whole sound of the orchestra achieves a new spaciousness and brilliance.

Even more striking than the orchestration, however, is the expanded harmonic range of the *London* symphonies and other works of the same period. Between the various movements, or between minuet and trio, the mediant relationship is sometimes exploited instead of the conventional dominant or subdominant. Within the single movements there are sudden shifts (sometimes one can hardly call them modulations) to remote keys, as at the beginning of the development section of the Vivace of No. 97; or wide-ranging modulations, as in the recapitulation of the same movement, where the music passes quickly through E-flat, A-flat, D-flat, and F minor to reach the dominant of the principal key, C major.[1] An illustration of Haydn's expansion of the harmonic frontiers, a foretaste of Romantic harmony, is found in the Adagio, entitled "Fantasia," of the Quartet Op. 76, No. 6 (1797), which begins in B major and wanders through C-sharp minor, E major and minor, G major, B-flat major and minor, back to B major (Example 84), then through C-sharp minor, G-sharp minor, and A-flat major, finally settling down in B major for the second half of the movement.

Harmonic imagination is an important factor also in the slow introductions to the first movements of Haydn's *London* symphonies. These opening sections have a portentous quality, a purposive dramatic suspense which prepares the listener for the Allegro to follow. The first movements themselves are in sonata form with a second contrasting theme. Haydn came to accept real thematic contrast in these last works, partly because their length seemed to require it; but he still seldom makes much of the second theme. The slow movements are either in the form of theme and variations (Nos. 94, 95, 97, 103) or in a free adaptation of sonata form; one common feature is a contrasting minor section. The minuets are no longer courtly dances, but rather *allegro* symphonic movements in minuet-and-trio pattern; like the

Example 84 Adagio ("Fantasia") Quartet Op. 76 No. 6, Haydn

bb: N6=I⁶ in B:

corresponding movements of the late quartets, they are already scherzos in everything but name. Some of the finales are in sonata form with two themes, but the favored pattern is the sonata-rondo—a general formal concept that admits the utmost variety and ingenuity in actual practice.

The last quartets
The quartets of Haydn's last period include Opp. 71, 74 (three each, 1793), 76 (six, 1797), 77 (two, 1799, of which the second is probably Haydn's greatest work in this form), and the two-movement torso, Op. 103 (1803). Of the relatively familiar late quartets,

a few details should be mentioned: the interesting modifications of sonata form in the first movement of Op. 77, No. 1 and the wonderful coda of the slow movement; the lovely variations on Haydn's own melody, the Austrian national hymn, in the slow movement of Op. 76, No. 3; the romantic character of the Largo (in F-sharp major) of Op. 76, No. 5; and the apotheosis of the Haydn finale in all these quartets, especially perhaps in Op. 76, Nos. 4 and 5 and Op. 77, No. 1.

Haydn's piano sonatas, which he wrote in every period of his creative life, consist for the most part of three movements, and in general follow the same course of evolution as the symphonies. The largest of *The sonatas* the sonatas is No. 49 in E-flat, composed in 1789 or 1790; all three movements are of full Classical dimensions, and the Adagio, Haydn himself declared, has "deep significance." From the London period there are three sonatas (Nos. 50–52, composed in 1794), of which No. 52, in E-flat, is the best; its slow movement is in the remote key of E major (prepared for by a passage in that key in the development of the first movement), and has an almost Romantic quality with its Chopinesque ornaments.

Haydn's Vocal Works

Haydn's operas were fairly successful in his lifetime, but he did not possess the genius for dramatic composition which enabled Handel and Mozart to breathe life into the artificial and often ridiculous librettos of the eighteenth century. Haydn fully realized this; and in 1787 he declined a commission to compose an opera for Prague on the ground that he was not familiar with the conditions there and that in any event "scarcely any man could stand comparison with the great Mozart"—who by that time had written *Figaro* and *Don Giovanni.*

Haydn's songs, though numerous, were distinctly a side issue with him. In addition to original songs with German or English texts, he also arranged about 450 Scottish and Welsh airs for various English publishers.

Most important among Haydn's church music are the last six Masses. Composed for Prince Nicholas Esterházy between 1796 and 1802, they show the influence of Haydn's recent preoccupation with *Haydn's church* the symphony. All are on the large scale of festival Masses, using or- *music* chestra, chorus, and four solo vocalists. Haydn's Masses, like those of Mozart and most other Austrian composers of the eighteenth century, have a certain flamboyant, theatrical character that goes well with Austrian Baroque church architecture. The fact that these Masses employ a full orchestra, including drums and trumpets, and are written in a musical idiom not unlike that of the opera and the symphony does not mean that they are either insincere or inappropriate. Haydn was occasionally criticized for writing music that was too cheerful for church; he replied that at the thought of God his heart "leaped for joy" and he did not think God would reproach him for praising Him "with a cheerful heart."

True to the Viennese tradition, in his late Masses Haydn inter-changed solo voices with chorus; what is new in these Masses is the leading position given to the orchestra, and the pervasion of the entire work by symphonic style and even by symphonic principles of form. Yet traditional elements are retained: the generally contrapuntal style of the writing for solo voices, for instance, and the customary choral fugues at the conclusion of the Gloria and the Credo. Probably the best known of Haydn's late Masses is the *Missa in angustiis*, known also as the *Lord Nelson* or *Imperial Mass*, in D minor, composed in 1798. Among the many impressive features of this magnificent work, the beautiful setting of the "Incarnatus" and the electrifying close of the "Benedictus" are moments of particularly high inspiration. On an equal level with the *Nelson Mass* are the *Missa in tempore belli* (*Mass in Time of War*) of 1796, the *Theresienmesse* of 1799, and the *Harmoniemesse* (*Wind-band Mass*) of 1802.

One important consequence of Haydn's sojourn in London was that he became acquainted with Handel's oratorios. At a performance of *Messiah* in 1791 at Westminster Abbey, Haydn was so deeply moved by the Hallelujah Chorus that he burst into tears and exclaimed "He is the master of us all." The results of Haydn's discovery of Handel are apparent in all the choral parts of his late Masses, and above all in his oratorios *The Creation* and *The Seasons*.

*Haydn's
oratorios*

The text of *The Creation* is based on the book of Genesis and Milton's *Paradise Lost;* that of *The Seasons* is distantly related to James Thomson's poem of the same name, which had been published between 1726 and 1730. Both oratorios are religious in concept, but a large part of their charm consists in their naïve and loving depiction of Nature and of man's innocent joy in the simple natural life. Both the devotional and the pastoral implications of the texts are reflected in Haydn's music, and the instrumental introductions to the various divisions of these oratorios are among the finest examples of late eighteenth-century program music. The "Depiction of Chaos" at the beginning of *The Creation* introduces Romantic harmonies that fore-shadow Wagner, while the transition in the following recitative and chorus, climaxed by the superb choral outburst on the C major chord at the words "and there was light," is one of Haydn's great strokes of genius. The choruses "The Heavens are telling," and "Achieved is the glorious work" from *The Creation* and the chorus "But who shall dare these gates to pass?" at the end of *The Seasons* have a truly Handelian breadth and power. No music more perfectly captures the mood of pure delight in nature than the arias "With verdure clad" and "Rolling in foaming billows" from *The Creation*, or the mood of awe before nature's grandeur than the choruses "Behold on high he mounts" and "Hark the deep tremendous voice" from *The Seasons*. The accompanied recitative "Straight opening her fertile womb" in *The Creation*, describing the creation of the animals, is a charming example of humorous musical depiction, while the chorus "Joyful the liquor flows" and the air and chorus "A wealthy lord, who long had loved" from *The Seasons* reflect Haydn's profound sympathy with the pleasures of simple people. As in the Masses, in these two oratorios Haydn effectively combines solo voices with the chorus. These works are among the most extraordinary instances in history of a composer's manifestation of an advanced age of unimpaired youthful freshness and vigor.

In forming an estimate of Haydn's historical position, it is necessary to avoid extremes. In the first place, he is not the naïve, amiable composer of pretty tunes that the nickname "Papa Haydn" has unfortunately connoted to so many generations; nor, on the other hand, is he a devout mystic like Bach, or a heaven-storming Titan like Beethoven. His achievement was original and complete; he was not merely a forerunner of Beethoven or of Romanticism. During the course of a long and laborious personal evolution, he assimilated many of the stylistic elements of the eighteenth century—the late Baroque, the Rococo, the expressive, the *Sturm und Drang*, and folk music—and out of these elements forged his own musical language. The perfected Classical style of the late eighteenth century owes more to Haydn than to anyone else, and owes most of all to his genius for pure instrumental form, for in this area Haydn was one of the most sophisticated of all composers. His art is characterized by the union of sophistication with honest craftsmanship, humility, purity of intention, and a never-failing spiritual contact with the life of the common people from whom he had sprung.

Summary

Wolfgang Amadeus Mozart

Wolfgang Amadeus Mozart (1756–1791) was born at Salzburg in western Austria, the seat of an archbishopric and a lively provincial center of music. His father, Leopold Mozart, was assistant director of the archbishop's chapel, a composer of some ability and reputation, and the author of a celebrated treatise on violin playing. From earliest childhood Wolfgang showed such a prodigious talent for music that his father dropped all other ambitions and devoted himself to educating the boy—and to exhibiting his accomplishments in a series of journeys that eventually took them to France, England, Holland, and Italy, as well as to Vienna and the principal cities of Germany.

Mozart's career

Young Mozart was thus on tour and on show over half of his time between the ages of six and fifteen. By 1762 he was a virtuoso on the clavier, and soon became a good organist and violinist as well. His public performances as a child included not only the playing of prepared pieces, but also reading concertos at sight and improvising variations, fugues, and fantasias. Meanwhile he was composing: he produced his first minuets at the age of six, his first symphony just before his ninth birthday, his first oratorio at eleven, and his first opera at twelve. His more than 600 compositions are listed and numbered in the thematic catalogue first compiled by L. von Köchel in 1862 and since brought up to date in the light of recent scholarship by Alfred Einstein; the Köchel or "K." numbers are universally used to identify a Mozart composition.

Thanks to his father's excellent teaching, and even more to the many trips made during his formative years, young Mozart was brought into contact with every kind of music that was being written or heard in contemporary western Europe. Moreover, he absorbed all that was congenial to him with uncanny aptitude. He imitated, but in imitating he improved on his models; and the ideas that influenced him not only were echoed in his immediate productions but also continued to grow in his mind, sometimes bearing fruit many years later. His work thus is a synthesis of the ideas of the late eighteenth century, a magic mirror in which was reflected the music of the whole period, illumined by his own transcendent genius. In this quality of universality Mozart surpasses Haydn, for unlike Haydn he is equally great in both instrumental and vocal composition. On the other hand Mozart's universe is wholly one of art music; he cared nothing for natural scenery, and he had little sympathy for the music of the common folk. Nowhere in his works do we find either the musical landscapes or the robust, wholehearted acceptance of folklike tunes and rhythms that are present in Haydn.

Mozart's personal and aristocratic quality is related to another characteristic which we may call *absolute musicality*. It is useless to try to connect his music with particular biographical events. The vicissitudes of Mozart's life left no immediate or obvious traces in his works, which seem to come out of an ideal realm undisturbed by the accidents of common life. Mozart's real existence—like that of all

Wolfgang Amadeus Mozart (1756–1791); an unfinished portrait by Joseph Lange, 1782. (Bettmann Archive)

artists, but to a greater degree than with most—was in this inner ideal realm, to which the happenings of his everyday existence were but a troubled and shadowy parallel; and only his inner life is reflected in his music.

Furthermore, Mozart did not have to struggle with composing. He had been taught systematically and thoroughly from infancy, and he learned instantaneously from each new musical impression. Working out his ideas probably involved for him the minimum of conscious effort necessary for such a complex operation. Haydn always found composition a labor, and he was always experimenting with the machinery. He set himself to compose at regular hours; when ideas did not come at once he prayed for them, and when they came he worked them out with conscious and unremitting industry. One cannot imagine Mozart having to pray for musical ideas; they must always have been there, and he was able to transmute them into sound with a facility at once childlike and godlike. Given a satisfactory initial phrase, the process of composition went on without hesitation or interruption to the end, in a perfectly logical if essentially mysterious flow. There is something miraculous about Mozart's apparently effortless perfection, and it was perhaps this miraculous quality that made him, rather than Haydn, the musical hero of the early Romantic generation.

One monumental study of Mozart distinguishes in his life and work no fewer than thirty-five style periods. For our purposes a broader and simpler division will suffice: (1) childhood and early youth, to 1774; (2) the period of the first masterworks, 1774–81; and (3) the years in Vienna, 1781–91.

Mozart's Childhood and Early Youth

The first period may be considered Mozart's apprentice and journeyman years. During all this time he was under the tutelage of his father—completely as far as practical affairs were concerned, and to a considerable extent also in musical matters. Other important early influences were those of Johann Schobert, whose music Mozart heard at Paris in 1764, and Johann Christian Bach, from whom the boy received lessons at London in 1765. The spirit of Italian music and especially the Italian style in opera, to which Mozart was first introduced by Bach, became a fundamental and permanent factor in his work.

Mozart's early works

A visit to Vienna in 1768 led, among other things, to the composition by the precocious twelve-year-old of an Italian *opera buffa*, *La finta semplice* (*The Pretended Simpleton;* not performed until the next year at Salzburg) and the attractive German singspiel *Bastien und Bastienne*. The years 1770 to 1773 were largely occupied with travels in Italy, where Mozart studied counterpoint with the famous

teacher and composer Padre Giambattista Martini (1706–1784) and
had two operas performed at Milan. From these journeys Mozart returned more thoroughly italianized than ever and profoundly discontented with his limited prospects in Salzburg. A new influence,
that of Joseph Haydn, becomes apparent in some symphonies of this
period, particularly K. 133 (composed in July, 1772). Another sojourn at Vienna in the summer of 1773 brought Mozart a renewed
understanding and feeling for the characteristic qualities of southern
German music; from this time onward Haydn's works became a
constant factor in Mozart's creative life, and their influence was reinforced by a warm personal friendship with the older composer.

The two most important national musical idioms in Europe after
1760 were those of Italy and Germany. The differences between them

may be summed up as follows: Italian music aimed at entertainment
and German music at expression; hence, by comparison, Italian music
was light and German music serious. The Italians' natural medium was
vocal and their natural forms the opera and cantata; the Germans'
natural medium was instrumental and their natural forms the symphony and the sonata. The natural Italian musical texture was homophony, the German polyphony; to charm and please through melody was the Italian goal, whereas the Germans were not averse to some
display of the science of counterpoint. All these statements, of course,
are over-simplifications, for neither in theory nor in practice were the
two styles so utterly different; and although the Italians were little
disposed to learn from the Germans, the latter were strongly influenced by the Italian style. Haydn expressed an enlightened view
and at the same time uttered a profound judgment of Mozart's genius
when he said to Leopold Mozart: "Before God and as an honest man
I tell you that your son is the greatest composer known to me either
in person or by name. He has taste and, what is more, the most
profound knowledge of composition."[2] Those were the two essentials:
taste, the instinct for what is appropriate, the awareness of limits; and
knowledge, the technique to say what one has to say fully, clearly,
and persuasively. Broadly speaking, taste was the specialty of the
Italians and knowledge that of the Germans. Mozart, an Austrian,
combined the two in his own style.

Mozart's First Masterworks

Late in 1773 and early in 1774 Mozart composed two symphonies
which were his first real masterworks in this form. The one in G
minor (K. 183) is a product of the same mood that was finding expression in the contemporary symphonies of Haydn. It is remarkable
not only for its intense, serious quality but also for its thematic unity
and for the expansion of the entire form as compared with Mozart's
earlier symphonies. Similar dimensions and formal characteristics are

found in the A major Symphony (K. 201), the mood of which is robust and cheerful; the finale has a particularly long and well worked out development section. On the whole, Mozart was much less adventurous than Haydn in the matter of formal experiments, preferring to take the patterns as he found them and to concentrate on weaving into them the richest possible musical content. His themes seldom give the impression, as Haydn's sometimes do, of having been invented with a view chiefly to their possibilities for motivic development; on the contrary, a theme of Mozart usually is complete in itself, and his invention is so profuse that sometimes he will dispense with a formal development section altogether and in its place write a completely new theme (as in the first movement of the String Quartet K. 428). Again unlike Haydn, Mozart nearly always has a contrasting, lyrical second theme (or themes) in his *allegro* movements in sonata form, though he is apt to conclude the exposition with a reminiscence of the opening subject; and, once more unlike Haydn, he seldom surprises the listener by making extensive changes in the order or treatment of his materials in the recapitulation.

From 1774 to 1781 Mozart lived chiefly at Salzburg, where he became more and more impatient with the narrowness of provincial life and the lack of musical opportunities. In a fruitless attempt to better himself he undertook, in September, 1777, in company with his mother, another journey, this time to Munich, Augsburg, Mannheim, and Paris. All his hopes for a good position in Germany came to nothing, and prospects for a successful career at Paris likewise ended in failure. The stay in Paris was further saddened by his mother's death in July, 1778, and Mozart returned to Salzburg early in 1779 more discontented than ever. Nonetheless, he was steadily growing in stature as a composer. Among the important works of this period are the piano sonatas K. 279–284 (Salzburg and Munich, 1774–75), K. 309 and 311 (Mannheim, 1777–78), K. 310 and 330–333 (Paris, 1778), and several sets of variations for piano, including those on the French air *Ah, vous dirais-je maman* (K. 265; Paris, 1778). The variations were probably intended for pupils, but the sonatas were played by Mozart himself as part of his concert repertoire. His custom in the earlier years had been to improvise such pieces as needed, so that few very early Mozart solo piano compositions have survived.

The sonatas K. 279–284 were undoubtedly designed to be published together: there is one in each of the major tonalities in the circle of fifths from D to E-flat, and the six works show a wide variety of form and content. The two Mannheim sonatas have brilliant and showy Allegros and tender and graceful Andantes. The Paris sonatas are among Mozart's best-known compositions in this form: the tragic A minor sonata (K. 310), its light counterpart in C major (K. 330), the A major sonata with the variations and the *rondo alla turca* (K. 331), and two of the most characteristically Mozartean sonatas, those in F major and B-flat major (K. 332 and 333).

Of the chamber music from this middle period we may mention the
Flute Quartet in D major (K. 285), composed in December, 1777, an
excellent example of the light, charming Mozart style; and the Oboe
Quartet (K. 370), an equally representative but more serious work
dating from the early part of 1781.

Most of Mozart's music was composed either on commission or for
a particular occasion; even in those works that do not seem to have
been intended for an immediate performance, he had in mind a definite
type of potential performer or audience, and considered their prefer-
ences. Like all his contemporaries, he was a "commercial composer"
in that he not merely hoped but expected as a matter of course that
his music would be performed, that it would please, and that he would
make money from it. There are, of course, some compositions of his
that have little significance outside their immediate social or commercial occasion—for instance, the many sets of dances that he turned
out for balls at Vienna during the last four years of his life. But there
are other works which, though produced only with the modest aim
of furnishing background music or light entertainment for some
ephemeral occasion, have greater musical importance than their original purpose deserved.

Of this sort are the pieces, dating for the most part from the 1770's

Mozart's manuscript of the first page of the Serenade in B-flat K. 361.
(Library of Congress)

and early 1780's, which Mozart composed for garden parties, sere- Mozart's First
nades, weddings, birthdays, or home concerts for his friends and   Masterworks
patrons, and which he called usually either "serenade" or "divertimento." The most familiar of Mozart's serenades is *Eine kleine Nacht-*   *Serenades*
musik (K. 525), a work for small string orchestra, originally in five
movements, composed in 1787 but for what occasion (if any) is not
known. Elements of the concerto appear in the three Salzburg serenades in D (K. 203, 204, 320), each of which has interpolated two or
three movements where the solo violin is featured. The *Haffner*
Serenade of 1776 is another example of the concerto-symphonic style,
and the *Haffner Symphony* (K. 385) was originally written as a
serenade with an introductory and closing march and an additional
minuet between the Allegro and the Andante.

Among the notable compositions of Mozart's second period are the
violin concertos K. 216, 218, and 219, in G, D, and A respectively, all
from the year 1775, and the piano concerto in E-flat, K. 271 (1777).   *Violin*
The violin concertos are inexpressibly beautiful; nowhere else is the   *concertos*
Mozartean blend of crystalline clarity with sensuously luxuriant sound
more potent than in the Adagio of the G major Concerto, or the
aristocratic Mozartean verve and humor more evident than in the
rondo finale of the same work.

With few exceptions, Mozart's Masses, motets, and other settings of
sacred texts are not to be counted among his major works. His Masses,
like those of Haydn, are for the most part in the symphonic-operatic   *Vocal music*
idiom of the period, intermingled with counterpoint at certain places
in accordance with the current custom, the whole for chorus and
soloists in free alternation, with orchestral accompaniment. An example is the *Coronation Mass* in C (K. 317), composed at Salzburg in
1779. The finest of his Masses is the one in C minor (K. 427), which
Mozart wrote as fulfillment of a vow at the time of his marriage in
1782. Though the Credo and Agnus Dei were never completed, this
Mass nevertheless is one of the few works of its kind in the eighteenth
century worthy to be named along with the B minor Mass of Bach.
It is noteworthy that Mozart wrote it neither on commission nor to
order, but apparently to satisfy an inner need. Equally devout, equally
profound, though brief and in simple homophonic style, is another
church composition, the motet *Ave verum* (K. 618, 1791). In connection with the vocal church music may be mentioned Mozart's
seventeen *Epistle Sonatas*—short pieces for organ and orchestra which
he wrote to be played in the Salzburg Cathedral.

Mozart's last important composition before he moved to Vienna
was the opera *Idomeneo*, first performed at Munich in January of
1781. *Idomeneo* is the best of Mozart's *opere serie*. The music, despite
the rather clumsy libretto, is dramatic and pictorial. Numerous accompanied recitatives, conspicuous use of the chorus, and the presence
of spectacular scenes show the influence of Gluck and the French
tragédie lyrique; but the ruling conception of the work, in which the   315

music wholly dominates and embraces the dramatic movement, is Mozart's own.

The Vienna Period

When in 1781 Mozart decided, against his father's advice, to quit the service of the Archbishop of Salzburg and settle in Vienna, he was sanguine about his prospects. The first years there were, in fact, fairly prosperous. His singspiel, *Die Entführung aus dem Serail* (*The Abduction from the Seraglio*, 1782), was performed repeatedly; he had all the distinguished pupils he was willing to take, he was the idol of the Viennese public both as pianist and composer, and for four or five seasons he led the bustling life of a successful freelance musician. But then the fickle public deserted him, pupils fell off, commissions were few, family expenses mounted, his health declined, and, worst of all, no permanent position with a steady income came his way, except for a trifling honorary appointment in 1787 as Chamber Music Composer to the Emperor with a salary less than half that which Gluck, his predecessor in the post, had received. The most pathetic pages in Mozart's correspondence are the begging letters written between 1788 and 1791 to his friend and brother Mason, the merchant Michael Puchberg of Vienna. To Puchberg's honor, he always responded to Mozart's appeals.

Most of the works which make Mozart's name immortal were composed during the last ten years of his life, in Vienna, when the promise of his childhood and early youth came to fulfillment between the ages of twenty-five and thirty-five. The perfect synthesis of form and content, of the *galant* and the learned styles, of polish and charm on the one hand and of textural and emotional depth on the other, was finally achieved, and equally in every kind of composition. The principal influences on Mozart in this period came from his continuing study of Haydn and his discovery of the music of J. S. Bach. He became acquainted with Bach's *Art of Fugue, The Well-Tempered Clavier*, the trio sonatas, and other works. He arranged several of Bach's fugues for string trio or quartet (K. 404a, 405), and another immediate result of this new interest was his own fugue in C minor for two pianos (K. 426). The influence of Bach was deep and lasting; it is manifested in the increasing use of contrapuntal texture throughout Mozart's later works (for example, in his last piano sonata, K. 576) and in the profoundly serious moods of *The Magic Flute* and the *Requiem*.

Of the piano solo compositions of the Vienna period, the most important is the Fantasia and Sonata in C minor (K. 475 and 457). Other keyboard works of this period are the Sonata in D major for two pianos (K. 448, 1781) and the finest of all Mozart's four-hand sonatas, the one in F major (K. 497, 1786). For chamber music ensembles of various kinds there is an impressive number of masterpieces, of which the following must be mentioned: the Violin Sonata in A major (K. 526), the Piano Trios in B-flat (K. 502) and E major (K. 542), the Piano Quartet in E-flat (K. 493), and the String Trio (K. 563).

In 1785 Mozart published six string quartets (K. 387, 421, 428, 458, 464, 465) which he dedicated to Joseph Haydn as a token of his gratitude for all that he had learned from the older composer. These quartets were, as Mozart said in the dedicatory letter, "the fruit of a long and laborious effort"; they show his mature capacity to absorb the essence of Haydn's achievement without becoming a mere imitator. Closest to Haydn in mood and themes are the opening and closing movements of the Quartet in B-flat (K. 458), while the Adagio has harmonies that may be called Romantic (Example 85a). The D minor Quartet (K. 421) expresses a gloomy, fatalistic mood. The striking cross-relations in the slow introduction to the first movement of the C major Quartet (K. 456) have given this work its name of the *Dissonance Quartet* (Example 85b).

All the *Haydn Quartets* are remarkably unified and concentrated. There are no merely transitional or filling passages; every measure is alive with thematic significance. Contrapuntal texture is ever present, though never obtrusive. Moreover, even in the Allegros the themes

Themes from Quartets, Mozart

Example 85

(a) Mozart: Adagio from Quartet K. 458

(b) Mozart: Introduction of Quartet K. 456

always sing; the instrumental melodies have a vocal allure that reflects the Italian heritage in Mozart's training. Mozart never surpassed these six quartets in his later works for the same medium, which include the *Hoffmeister Quartet* (K. 499) and three others of a projected set of six for the King of Prussia (K. 575, 589, 590). Unlike Haydn and Beethoven, Mozart most fully revealed his genius as a chamber music composer not in his quartets, but rather in his quintets. The best of these are the string quintets in C major (K. 515) and G minor (K. 516), both composed in the spring of 1787, works comparable only with Mozart's last two symphonies, which are in the same keys. Another masterpiece is the Clarinet Quintet in A (K. 581), composed at about the same time as the opera buffa *Così fan tutte*, and similar to it in mood.

Mozart's Vienna symphonies include the *Prague Symphony* in D major (K. 504), the charming *Linz Symphony* in C major (K. 425), and his last and greatest works in this form, the Symphonies in E-flat (K. 543), G minor (K. 550), and C major (the *Jupiter*, K. 551). These three symphonies were composed within a space of six weeks in the summer of 1788. It is not known for what occasion Mozart intended them or indeed whether he ever heard them played at all. Each has its own character; each is a complex but distinct personality, a personality which is defined perfectly by the music but which completely eludes verbal formulation. The three works must be viewed as a summation, unusually complete and clear, of three fundamental aspects of Mozart's musical being and consequently of the whole musical world of the late eighteenth century.

The concertos for piano and orchestra

A very important place among the productions of Mozart's Vienna years must be assigned to the seventeen concertos for piano and orchestra. All were written in order to provide brand-new works for concerts, and the rise and fall of Mozart's popularity in Vienna may be roughly gauged by the number of new concertos he felt it necessary to supply for each year: three in 1782–83, four in each of the next two seasons, three again in 1785–86, one only for each of the next two seasons, and after that no more until the last year of his life, when he played a new concerto (K. 595) in a concert organized by another musician.

The first three Vienna concertos (K. 414, 413, 415) were, as Mozart wrote to his father,[3] "a happy medium between what is too easy and too difficult . . . very brilliant, pleasing to the ear, and natural, without being vapid. There are passages here and there from which connoisseurs alone can derive satisfaction; but these passages are written in such a way that the less learned cannot fail to be pleased, though without knowing why." The next concerto (K. 449, in E-flat), originally written for a pupil, was later played by Mozart with "unusual success," as he reported. Then follow three magnificent concertos, all completed within a month of one another in the spring of 1784: K. 450 in B-flat, K. 451 in D (both, in Mozart's words, "concertos to make the player sweat"), and the more intimate, lovely K. 453 in G. The Vienna Period Three of the four concertos of 1784–85 are likewise works of first rank: K. 459 in F, K. 466 in D minor (the most dramatic and most frequently played of Mozart's concertos), and K. 467 in C, spacious and symphonic. During the winter of 1785–86, when he was at work on *The Marriage of Figaro*, Mozart turned out three more concertos, of which the first two (K. 482 in E-flat and K. 488 in A) are in comparatively lighter style, while the third (K. 491, C minor) is one of his great tragic creations, one of his most "Beethovenish" works. The big C major concerto of December, 1786 (K. 503) may be regarded as the triumphal counterpart of K. 491. Of the two remaining concertos, one is the popular *Coronation Concerto* in D (K. 537), so called because Mozart played it (and probably also K. 459) at a concert in Frankfurt in 1790 during the coronation festivities for the Emperor Leopold II. K. 595, in B-flat, Mozart's last concerto, was completed on the fifth of January, 1791; it is a work of serene, transcendent beauty, the testament of a musician who must have felt himself to be already beyond the passions, the struggles, and the triumphs of this life.[4]

The concerto, particularly the piano concerto, was more important in Mozart's work than in that of any other composer of the second half of the eighteenth century. In the realm of the symphony and the quartet Haydn is his peer, but Mozart's concertos are incomparable. Not even the symphonies reveal such wealth of invention, such breadth and vigor of conception, such insight and resource in the working out of musical ideas. The Classical concerto, in the form definitively established by Mozart in the 1780's, resembles the concerto of Vivaldi in its general scheme of three movements in fast-slow-fast order, and in the relatively greater length and weight of the first movement as compared with the other two. But Mozart's concerto differs from that of Vivaldi and indeed of all preceding composers (including C. P. E. Bach and J. C. Bach) in respect to the relation between the solo instrument and the orchestra: Mozart's orchestra is the symphonic ensemble of the late eighteenth century, and the instruments are used as in a symphony. Moreover, since the piano is fully on a par with the orchestra in range and flexibility, the two are treated as equal protagonists in a symphonic texture, a conception that considerably modifies the older idea of regular alternation of distinct tutti and solo sections.

Although these concertos were show pieces, intended to dazzle and impress an audience, Mozart never allowed the element of display to get out of hand; a healthy balance of musical interest between the orchestral and the solo portions is always maintained, and Mozart's ear was infallible for the myriad combinations of colors and textures that arise from the interplay of the piano with the orchestral instruments. Moreover, the immediate public purpose of his concertos did not prevent his using the form as a vehicle for some of the most profound expressions of his musical thought.

After *Idomeneo* Mozart wrote no more *opere serie*, with the exception of *La clemenza di Tito* (*The Mercy of Titus*), which was commissioned for the coronation of Leopold II as King of Bohemia at Prague and composed in haste during the summer of 1791. The chief dramatic works of the Vienna period were the singspiel, *Die Entführung aus dem Serail* (*The Abduction from the Seraglio*, 1782), three Italian operas, *Le nozze di Figaro* (*The Marriage of Figaro*, 1786), *Don Giovanni* (*Don Juan;* Prague, 1787), and *Così fan tutte* (*Thus Do They All*, 1790)—all three on librettos by Lorenzo da Ponte (1749-1838)—and the German opera *Die Zauberflöte* (*The Magic Flute*, 1791).

Figaro is the epitome of Italian eighteenth-century *opera buffa*, with its lively and amusing libretto, beautiful arias, and masterly ensembles; but it is *opera buffa* transformed from the stock antics of type figures into profound human comedy, in which the characters are real three-dimensional persons, thanks to Mozart's psychological penetration and his genius for characterization in music. It is remarkable that the character delineation takes place not only in solo arias but more especially in duets, trios, and larger ensembles; and the ensemble finales are miraculous combinations of realism, ongoing dramatic action, and superbly unified musical form. *Figaro* had only moderate success in Vienna, but its enthusiastic reception at Prague led to the commission for *Don Giovanni*, which was given in that city the next year. *Don Giovanni* is not an *opera buffa* but a *dramma*

The final scene of **Don Giovanni.** *The Don carouses before the arrival of his guest, the Commandant.* (*Courtesy Metropolitan Opera Company; photo by Louis Melançon.*)

giocoso, a tragi-comedy; there is in it a unique opposition of comic-spectacular elements and grim earnestness, the latter announced at once in the opening measures of the overture and intensified by the sound of the trombones in the cemetery scene and at the apparition of the Commandant's statue at Don Juan's banquet in the last act. *Così fan tutte*, on the other hand, is pure *opera buffa*, glorified by some of Mozart's most sparkling music.

Mozart brought Italian opera to a peak of glory in *Figaro, Don Giovanni*, and *Così fan tutte;* he transfigured the German singspiel in *Die Entführung aus dem Serail* and *Die Zauberflöte. Die Entführung* is a comic story of adventure in an oriental setting, with a plot that had been used by Rameau and Gluck as well as many lesser composers before Mozart. The significance of Mozart's version is that it lifted the humble German singspiel into the realm of high art, without altering in any way its established features.

Die Zauberflöte is another matter. Though outwardly a singspiel —with spoken dialogue instead of recitative, and with some characters and scenes appropriate to popular comedy—its action is full of symbolic meaning and its music so rich and profound that *Die Zauberflöte* must be regarded as the first and one of the greatest of modern German operas. The solemn mood of much of its music is probably due in part to the fact that Mozart felt a relationship between the action of this opera and the teachings and ceremonies of Freemasonry; his Masonic affiliation meant much to him, as is obvious from allusions in his correspondence and especially from the serious quality of the music which he wrote for Masonic occasions in 1785 (K. 468, 471, 477, 483, 484) and the Masonic cantata of 1791 (K. 623), his last completed composition. *Die Zauberflöte* gives the impression that Mozart desired to weave into new designs the threads of all the musical ideas of the eighteenth century: the vocal opulence of Italy; the folk humor of the German singspiel; the solo aria; the *buffo* ensemble, which is given new musical meaning; a new kind of accompanied recitative applicable to German texts; solemn choral scenes; and even (in the duet of the two armed men in Act II) a revival of the Baroque chorale prelude with contrapuntal accompaniment.

In the *Requiem*—Mozart's last work, left unfinished at his death— Baroque elements are still more prominent. The double fugue of the Kyrie has a subject that had been used by both Bach and Handel, and is definitely Handelian in flavor; even more so are the dramatic choral outbursts of the "Dies irae" and "Rex tremendae majestatis." But the "Recordare" is pure Mozart, the Austrian composer who understood and loved the musical tradition of Italy and interpreted it in his own perfect way.

XV Ludwig van Beethoven (1770-1827)

The Man and His Music

Beethoven's character

Beethoven came on the scene at a favorable moment in history. He inherited from Haydn and Mozart a style and certain musical forms which were well developed but still capable of further growth. He lived at a time when new and powerful forces were abroad in human society, forces which strongly affected him and made themselves felt in his work. Beethoven, like Napoleon and Goethe, was a child of the tremendous upheaval which had been fermenting all through the eighteenth century and had burst forth in the French Revolution. It is a curious fact that in all Mozart's correspondence and other records of him there is not one mention of the Revolution. As far as he

Ludwig van Beethoven (1770–1827); a portrait made before 1800. (Bettmann Archive)

322

was concerned, it might never have happened, and much the same may
be said of Haydn; but the music of Beethoven is unthinkable without
it. Historically, then, Beethoven's work is built on the achievements
of the Classical period. Through external circumstances and the
force of his own genius he transformed this heritage and became
the source of much that was characteristic of the Romantic period.
But he himself is neither Classic nor Romantic; he is Beethoven, and
his figure towers like a colossus astride the two centuries.

His works include nine symphonies, eleven overtures, incidental
music to plays, a violin concerto and five piano concertos, sixteen
string quartets, nine piano trios and other chamber music, ten violin
sonatas and five violoncello sonatas, thirty large piano sonatas and
many sets of variations for piano, an oratorio, an opera (*Fidelio*), and
two Masses (one the *Missa solemnis* in D), besides arias, songs, and
numerous lesser compositions of different sorts. There is an obvious
disparity when these figures are compared with the output of Haydn
and Mozart: nine symphonies, for example, to Haydn's hundred or
Mozart's fifty. A partial explanation, of course, is that Beethoven's
symphonies are longer; but a more important reason is that Beethoven
wrote music with great difficulty. Probably no other composer ever
habitually subjected himself to longer or more severe criticism. Beethoven kept notebooks in which he jotted down plans and themes for
compositions, and thanks to these sketchbooks we can sometimes
follow the progress of a musical idea through various stages until it
reaches the final form (Example 86). The sketches for the Quartet
Op. 131 cover three times as many pages as the finished copy of the
work.

Beethoven's music, more than that of any composer before him,
gives the impression of being a direct outpouring of his personality.
To understand the music, therefore, it is helpful to know something
about the man himself. Sir Julius Benedict described his first sight of
Beethoven (1823) in these words:

> ...a short, stout man with a very red face, small, piercing eyes, and
> bushy eyebrows, dressed in a very long overcoat which reached nearly to
> his ankles ... notwithstanding the high color of his cheeks and his general
> untidiness, there was in those small piercing eyes an expression which no
> painter could render. It was a feeling of sublimity and melancholy com-
> bined.... The wonderful impression his first appearance made on me was
> heightened every time I met him. When I first saw him at Baden, his white
> hair flowing over his mighty shoulders, with that wonderful look—some-
> times contracting his brows when anything afflicted him, sometimes
> bursting out into a forced laughter, indescribably painful to his listeners—
> I was touched as if *King Lear* or one of the old Gaelic bards stood before
> me.[1]

The "indescribably painful" sound of Beethoven's laughter may
have been due to his deafness. This most dreadful of all afflictions for
a musician began to manifest itself as early as 1798, and grew steadily

worse until by 1820 it was practically total. In the autumn of 1802 Beethoven wrote a letter, now known as the "Heiligenstadt testament," intended to be read by his brothers after his death; in it he describes in moving terms how he suffered when he realized that his malady was incurable:

> I must live like an exile; if I approach near to people a hot terror seizes me, a fear that I may be subjected to the danger of letting my condition be observed. Thus it has been during the last half year which I spent in the country . . . what a humiliation when one stood beside me and heard a flute in the distance and *I heard nothing* or someone heard *the shepherd singing* and again I heard nothing—such incidents brought me to the verge of despair; but little more and I would have put an end to my life. Only art it was that withheld me, it seemed impossible to leave the world until I had produced all that I felt called upon to produce. . . . O Providence, grant me at last but one day of pure *joy*—it is so long since real joy echoed in my heart. . . .[2]

—yet the same man who thus cried out of the depths had, during that same half year in the country, written the exuberantly joyful Second Symphony!

The outstanding characteristic of Beethoven's music, in comparison with that of his predecessors, is a certain daemonic energy, a quality that is felt most starkly in passages like the close of the first movement of the Fifth Symphony, the coda of the finale of the Sonata Op. 57, or the finale of the Quartet Op. 59, No. 3. The energy breaks forth also as humor—not the witty playfulness of Haydn nor the refined gaiety of Mozart, but something more robust and hearty: for instance, the anxious antics of the double basses in the trio of the Scherzo of the Fifth Symphony, the stuttering halts in the rhythm after the double bar; the metronomic Allegretto of the Eighth Symphony; the apparently premature entrance of the horn in the first movement of the Third Symphony, just before the recapitulation; or the exquisitely comic passage in the coda of the finale of the Eighth Symphony where the entire orchestra starts chasing off after the theme like a puppy after a stick in the impossibly remote key of F-sharp minor—and then, once more safely returned home to F, proceeds to reassure itself by sounding the major third F-A down and back through five octaves of the woodwinds.

Beethoven's music is not always volcanic and exuberant; it may melt into tenderness (second movement of the Sonata Op. 90) or sadness (Adagio of the Quartet Op. 59, No. 1). Abrupt contrasts of mood occur: the Sonata Op. 57 opens with an ominous theme, builds up suspense, hesitates, pauses tentatively, then bursts out in sudden fury, recedes, sighs, and finally soars into a beautiful singing melody in A-flat, which is subtly akin to the first theme (Example 87).

An even more striking contrast occurs in the development section of the first movement of the Third Symphony: after a long, fiercely dissonant *fortissimo* with off-beat *sforzandi* a completely new theme

Characteristics of Beethoven's music

Sketches for Theme of Adagio of Ninth Symphony, Beethoven

First Movement from Sonata Op. 57, Beethoven

Example 87

of tender melancholy appears in the strangely foreign key of E minor. Perhaps the most overwhelming of Beethoven's sudden changes of mood, however, is found in the finale of the Ninth Symphony, at the words "vor Gott." Full chorus and orchestra have reached a stupendous climax on a unison tonic A, to which at the last moment a strident and surprising F-natural has been added; this climax has been preparing steadily for over ninety measures, and it leaves the hearer breathless. What can possibly follow? A very strange thing indeed: after a few random grunts and thumps, all the wind instruments, together with triangle, cymbals, and bass drum, go into a "Turkish March," a little 6/8 tune grotesquely caricaturing the main theme. Beethoven thus introduces a moment of comic relief, just as Shakespeare does with the entrance of the sleepy porter after Duncan's murder in *Macbeth*.

It is customary to divide Beethoven's works into three periods, on the basis of style and chronology. Vincent d'Indy[3] calls them the periods of Imitation, Externalization, and Reflection. Needless to say, the dividing lines are not sharp, but they run approximately as follows: the first period, of Imitation, goes to about 1802, and includes the six string quartets Op. 18, the first ten piano sonatas (through Op. 14), and the first two symphonies. The second period, of Externalization, runs to about 1816, and includes the symphonies III to VIII, the incidental music to Goethe's drama *Egmont*, the *Coriolan* overture, the opera *Fidelio*, the piano concertos in G and E-flat, the violin concerto, the quartets of Opp. 59 (the *Rasumovsky* quartets), 74, and 95, and the piano sonatas through Op. 90. The last period, of Reflection, includes the last five piano sonatas, the *Diabelli* variations, the *Missa solemnis*, the Ninth Symphony, the quartets Opp. 127, 130, 131, 132, 135, and the *Grosse Fuge* (*Grand Fugue*) for string quartet (Op. 133, originally the finale of Op. 130).

First Style Period

The works of the first period naturally show most clearly Beethoven's dependence on the Classical tradition. The first three sonatas published at Vienna (Op. 2, 1796) contain some passages reminiscent

The sonatas

of Haydn, to whom they are dedicated; the Adagio of No. 1, for example, is quite Haydnesque both in themes and treatment. The sonata in E-flat (Op. 7), published in 1797, is especially characteristic of Beethoven in the theme of the Largo with its eloquent pauses and in the mysterious *minore* trio of the third movement. Op. 10, No. 1, in C minor (1798) is a companion piece to the *Sonate Pathétique*, Op. 13, which was published in the following year. Each is in three movements, of which the outer two have the stormy, passionate character associated with the key of C minor, not only in Beethoven but in Haydn and Mozart as well; and each has a calm, profound, and richly scored slow movement in A-flat.

The Quartets of Op. 18 (composed 1798–1800) demonstrate how well Beethoven had learned from Haydn's example the art of developing motives and animating the texture by means of counterpoint; yet these quartets are no mere imitations, for Beethoven's individuality is evident in the character of the themes, the frequent unexpected turns of phrase, the unconventional modulations, and some subtleties of formal structure. Thus the Adagio of the G major Quartet (No. 2) is a three-part ABA structure in C major; its middle section is an Allegro in F, consisting entirely of a development of a little motive from the closing cadence of the Adagio; and this motive, moreover, is related to conspicuous motives in the opening themes of the other three movements (Example 88).

Related Motives from Quartet in G Major Op. 18, No. 2, Beethoven Example 88

(a) Allegro

(b) Adagio cantabile   Allegro

(c) Scherzo: Allegro

(d) Allegro molto quasi Presto

The First Symphony was composed in 1799; it was first played at a concert in April, 1800, on a program that included also a symphony of Mozart, an aria and a duet from Haydn's *Creation*, a piano concerto
and the Septet by Beethoven, and improvisations by Beethoven at the piano. The First is the most Classical of the nine symphonies. Its spirit is that of Haydn, and all four movements are so regular in form that they might serve as Classical models. Yet there are many evidences of Beethoven's originality, such as the unusual prominence of the woodwinds throughout, the character of the third movement—which, though labeled *Menuetto*, is actually a scherzo—and the long and important codas in the other movements. The frequent marking *cresc.* $<p$ is but one example of the careful attention to dynamic shading that is an essential element in Beethoven's style.

The Adagio introduction to the first movement of this symphony is especially noteworthy. The key of the symphony is C, but the introduction begins in F, modulates to G at the fourth measure, and

avoids a definitive cadence in C for the next eight measures, or until
the first chord of the Allegro itself; Beethoven thus converges on the
tonic from two opposite sides, the subdominant and the dominant.
The short introduction to the finale has a Haydnesque wit.

Second Style Period

With the Second Symphony in D major (composed in 1802) we
are at the beginning of Beethoven's second style period. The long
Adagio that introduces the first movement announces a work conceived on a scale hitherto unknown in symphonic music. The rest of
the symphony has correspondingly large dimensions, with a profusion
of thematic material held together in perfect formal balance. The
Larghetto is especially remarkable for the large number of themes,
and for its rich *cantabile* character. The scherzo and finale, like the
first movement, are full of Beethovenian energy and fire. The finale is
written in an enlarged sonata form, with suggestions of rondo in extra
recurrences of the first theme, one at the beginning of the development section and one at the beginning of the coda; the coda itself is
twice as long as the development section, and introduces a completely
new theme.

Within a dozen years after his coming to Vienna Beethoven was
acknowledged throughout Europe as the foremost pianist and composer for the piano of his time, and as a symphonist who ranked
equally with Haydn and Mozart. Such adverse criticisms as were
uttered were directed against his eccentricity, his "frequent daring
shifts from one motive to another, by which the organic connection
of a gradual development of ideas was put aside. Such defects often
weaken his greatest compositions, which spring from a too great
exuberance of conception. . . . The singular and the original seemed
to be his main object in composition." These are the words of J. W.
Tomaschek, pianist and composer, a slightly younger contemporary
of Beethoven, who heard him improvise at Prague in 1795; they are
typical of many later criticisms. Tomaschek's opinions show that
some of the ideas in even the early works of Beethoven, which now
we accept as natural because they have become a part of our common
musical language, disturbed an intelligent musician of the 1790's.

The Third Symphony in E-flat, composed in 1803, is one of the
most important works of Beethoven's second period. This symphony
bears the title *Eroica*, the "heroic symphony," and it stands as an
immortal expression in music of the ideal of heroic greatness. It was a
revolutionary work, of such unprecedented length and complexity
that audiences at first found it difficult to grasp. In place of the usual
slow movement it has a funeral march in C minor with a contrasting
section in C major, of tragic grandeur and pathos. The finale is a set
of variations with fugally developed episodes and coda, in an extreme-

ly complex but thoroughly logical form. The first movement begins, after two introductory chords, with one of the simplest imaginable themes on the notes of the E-flat major triad, a theme which Beethoven subjects to endless variation and development in the course of the movement. Five other themes are presented in the exposition, and the development section brings in still another, which recurs in the coda. Most remarkable, however, in this movement, as in all of Beethoven's, is neither the formal pattern nor the abundance of ideas, but the way in which all the material is propelled constantly along, one theme seeming to unfold out of another in a steady dynamic growth which mounts from one climax to the next, driving with a sense of utter inevitability to the end. This capacity to organize a large amount of contrasting material into a unified musical whole is one of the chief marks of Beethoven's greatness.

The opera *Fidelio* was composed at about the same time as the Third Symphony and is similar to it in character. As far as the libretto is concerned, *Fidelio* is a rescue opera of the kind that was so popular at the turn of the century. Beethoven's music, however, transforms this conventional material, making of the chief character Leonore (after whom the opera was originally named) a personage of sublime courage and self-abnegation, an idealized figure. The whole last part of the opera is in effect a celebration of Leonore's heroism and the great humanitarian ideals of the Revolution. Beethoven wrote four different overtures for the opera. Three of them (those for the performances of 1805 and 1806 and another composed in 1806) are now known as the *Leonore* overtures.

The three quartets of Op. 59 are dedicated to Count Rasumovsky, the Russian Ambassador to Vienna. Rasumovsky was the patron of a quartet of string players said to be the finest in Europe, in which he himself played second violin. As a compliment to the Count, Beethoven introduced a Russian melody as the principal theme of the finale of the first quartet, and another in the third movement of the second quartet. These three quartets, composed in the summer and autumn of 1806, occupy a position in Beethoven's work similar to that of the Quartets Op. 20 in Haydn's: they are the first to exemplify the composer's mature style and characteristic manner of expression in this medium. They are indeed full of the emotional fire, boldness of formal treatment, and striking originality that characterize Beethoven's second period. So great was their novelty that musicians were slow to accept them. When Count Rasumovsky's players first tried over the Quartet in F (No. 1 of the set), they were convinced that Beethoven was playing a joke on them. Clementi, the brilliant London pianist whom Mozart had once described as a "mere mechanician," reported that he had said to Beethoven "Surely you do not consider these works to be music?" to which the composer, with unusual self-restraint, answered, "Oh, they are not for you, but for a later age." The Allegretto movement of the F major Quartet in particular gave rise to charges of "crazy music." It took some time for musicians and audiences to realize that Beethoven's innovations were logical, that the nature of his musical ideas compelled modification of the traditional language and forms.

In the quartets of Op. 59 as well as in the *Eroica Symphony*, the sonata form is expanded to unheard-of proportions by the multitude of themes, the long and complex developments, and the extended codas which take on the dimensions and significance of a second development section. Along with this expansion, Beethoven intentionally conceals the formerly clear dividing lines between the various parts of a movement: recapitulations are disguised and varied, new themes grow imperceptibly out of previous material, and the progress of the musical thought has a dynamic, propulsive character that toys with, if not actually scorns, the neat, symmetrical patterns of the Classical era. These developments continue throughout the whole of Beethoven's second period, but the change is more radical in the quartets and piano sonatas than in the less intimate symphonies and overtures. The two quartets Op. 74 (1809) and Op. 95 (1810) show Beethoven on the way toward the dissolution of traditional form that later marked the last quartets of the third period.

Among the other chamber works of Beethoven's second period, special mention should be made of the Violin Sonatas Op. 47 (the *Kreutzer Sonata*) and Op. 96, and the Trio in B-flat Op. 97. The two Sonatas for Violoncello and Piano, Op. 102 (1815), belong stylistically to the third period.

The Fourth to Eighth Symphonies

The Fourth, Fifth, and Sixth Symphonies were all composed between 1806 and 1808, a time of exceptional productivity. Beethoven seems to have worked on the Fourth and Fifth Symphonies at the same time; the first two movements of the Fifth, in fact, were already in existence before the Fourth was completed. The two works contrast, as though Beethoven wished to express simultaneously two opposite poles of feeling. Joviality and humor mark the Fourth Symphony, while the Fifth has always been interpreted as the musical projection of Beethoven's resolution "I will grapple with Fate; it shall not overcome me." The progress through struggle to victory, as symbolized in this symphony by the succession C minor to C major, has been an implicit subject of many symphonies since Beethoven's, but none other has so caught the popular imagination.

The Sixth (*Pastoral*) Symphony was composed immediately after the Fifth and the two were first played on the same program in December, 1808. Each of the five movements bears a descriptive title suggesting a scene from life in the country. Beethoven adapts his descriptive program to the usual Classical symphonic form, merely inserting after the scherzo ("Merrymaking of the Peasants") an extra movement ("Storm") which serves to introduce the finale ("Thankful feelings after the storm"). In the coda of the Andante ("Scene by the brook"), flute, oboe, and clarinet join harmoniously in imitating bird

calls—the nightingale, the quail, and, of course, the cuckoo. All this
programmatic apparatus is subordinate to the expansive, leisurely
musical form of the Symphony as a whole; the composer himself
warns that the descriptions are not to be taken too literally: he calls
them "expression of feelings rather than depiction." The *Pastoral
Symphony* is one of hundreds of works from the eighteenth and early
nineteenth centuries that aimed to portray natural scenes or suggest
the moods aroused by the contemplation of such scenes (*cf.* Vivaldi's
Seasons concertos); its enduring appeal testifies not to the accuracy
of its landscape painting but to the way in which the emotions of a
lover of nature have been captured in great music.

The Seventh and Eighth Symphonies were both completed in 1812.
The Seventh, like the Second and Fourth, opens with a long slow
introduction with remote modulations, leading into an Allegro dominated throughout by the rhythmic figure♪ ♩. The second movement, in the parallel minor key of A, was encored at the first performance and has always been a favorite with audiences. The scherzo
(not so labeled) is in F major, the lower submediant of the principal
key of the symphony; it is unusual furthermore in that the trio (D
major) recurs a second time, thus expanding this movement to a five-
part form (*ABABA*). The finale, a large sonata-form with coda,
"remains unapproached in music as a triumph of Bacchic fury."[4] By
contrast with the huge scale of the Seventh Symphony, the Eighth
appears miniature—or would, if it were not for the long coda of the
first movement and the still longer one of the finale. This is the most
mercurial of all the nine symphonies, but its humor is sophisticated and
its forms extremely condensed. The second movement is a brisk
Allegretto, while the third, by way of compensation, is a deliberately
archaic Minuet instead of the usual Beethoven Scherzo.

Related in style to the symphonies are Beethoven's orchestral
overtures, which usually take the form of a symphonic first movement. The three *Leonore Overtures* have already been mentioned.
The other most important overtures are *Coriolan* (1807), inspired by
a tragedy of the same name by H. J. von Collin which was performed
occasionally at Vienna after 1802; and *Egmont*, composed, together
with songs and incidental music, for a performance of Goethe's drama
in 1810.

The piano sonatas of the second period show a wide range of styles
and forms. Among the earliest, dating from about 1802, are the Sonata
in A-flat with the funeral march, Op. 26, and the two sonatas *quasi
fantasia* of Op. 27, the second of which is popularly known as the
Moonlight Sonata. The first movement of the D minor Sonata Op. 31,
No. 2 has an introductory *largo* phrase which recurs at the beginning
of the development section and again at the beginning of the recapitulation, each time in expanded form and with increased musical significance; its last appearance leads into an expressive instrumental recitative, of the kind that Beethoven afterward used with effect in some of

*The sonatas and
concertos*

331

his later works. The finale of this sonata is an exciting *moto perpetuo* in sonata-rondo form.

Outstanding among the sonatas of the second period are Op. 53 in C major (called the *Waldstein Sonata* after Beethoven's patron, to whom it is dedicated) and Op. 57 in F minor, commonly called the *Appassionata*. Both were composed in 1804. These two works illustrate what happened to the Classical sonata at Beethoven's hands. Each has the usual Classical three movements in the order fast-slow-fast; each exhibits the patterns of sonata-form, rondo, or variations, with appropriate key-schemes. But their formal order has, as it were, been expanded from within by the resistless force of Beethoven's musical imagination, expressed in themes of elemental power that require a structure of hitherto unknown tension and concentration to support their natural development and completion. When we listen to a sonata by Mozart we rejoice in the composer's constant and willing submission to an accepted order of things musical; when we listen to one of Beethoven's sonatas we rejoice that the revolutionist submits only where he pleases, and that elsewhere he creates a new order, one growing out of the old but resembling it only in externals.

As a concert pianist Beethoven naturally composed concertos for his own use. The two largest works in this form are the Concerto in G major Op. 58, composed in 1805–06 and the one in E-flat, known as the *Emperor Concerto*, which was composed in 1808–09 and first performed at Vienna in 1812 by Carl Czerny. (Czerny [1791–1857] as a young man had studied piano with Beethoven, and subsequently had a successful teaching career at Vienna; he was the composer of many studies and other works for the piano.)

The concertos of Beethoven are related to those of Mozart much as are the symphonies of these two composers: Beethoven retained the division of the concerto into three movements and the general outline of the Classical form; but he expanded the framework, and intensified the content. The virtuosity of the solo part is more marked than in Mozart's concertos, but is not excessive in view of the expanded dimensions. In Beethoven's magnificent Violin Concerto, Op. 61 in D major (composed 1806), the solo part is ideally interwoven with the orchestra.

Third Style Period

The years up to 1815 were, on the whole, peaceful and prosperous for Beethoven. His music was much played in Vienna, and he was celebrated both at home and abroad. Thanks to the generosity of patrons and the steady demand from publishers for new works, his financial affairs were in good order, despite a ruinous devaluation of the Austrian currency in 1811; but his deafness became a more and more serious trial. As it caused him to lose contact with others, he retreated into himself, becoming morose, irascible, and morbidly suspicious even toward his friends.

In 1816 he was appointed guardian of his nephew, the ten-year-old son of his deceased brother Karl. The boy's mother was joint guardian, but Beethoven, convinced that she was not a fit person for the task, took legal measures to have her ousted, and after four years finally succeeded. This whole affair was a source of untold annoyance and suffering to Beethoven, and it was only by a supreme effort of will that he continued composing amidst all these troubles. The last five piano sonatas were written between 1816 and 1821; the *Missa solemnis* was completed in 1822, the *Diabelli* variations in 1823, and the Ninth Symphony in 1824, each after long years of labor; and the last quartets, Beethoven's musical testament, followed in 1825 and 1826. At his death in 1827 he had plans for a tenth symphony and many other new works.

Beethoven's compositions of the third period more and more come to have a meditative character; the former urgent sense of communication is replaced by a feeling of assured tranquillity, passionate outpouring by calm affirmation. The language becomes more concentrated, more abstract. Extremes meet: the sublime and the grotesque side by side in the Mass and the Ninth Symphony, the profound and the apparently naïve side by side in the last quartets. Classical forms remain only as the former features of a landscape remain after a geological upheaval—recognizable here and there under new contours, lying at strange angles underneath the new surface.

One of the characteristics—a concomitant of the meditative quality —in Beethoven's late works is the deliberate working out of themes and motives to the utmost of their potentialities. This is in part a continuation of his earlier technique of motivic development, which he now carries to its extreme limits; more especially, it reflects a new conception of the possibilities of thematic *variation*. *Characteristics of Beethoven's late style*

In Beethoven's works, as in those of Haydn and Mozart, variation occurs in three kinds of situations: (1) as a technique within a larger formal plan, as when in a rondo each recurrence of the principal theme is varied, or in a sonata form the first theme is varied in the recapitulation; (2) a theme-and-variations as an independent composition; and (3) a theme-and-variations as one of the movements of a symphony or sonata. Examples of the first use in Beethoven's late works are the slow movements of the Sonata Op. 106, the Quartet Op. 132, and the Ninth Symphony; the finale of this symphony also begins (after the introduction) as a set of variations.

As for independent compositions in variation form, in all Beethoven wrote twenty sets of these for piano, the majority of them on favorite tunes from contemporary operas; from the last period there is only one independent set, but it is a work that surpasses anything in this form since Bach's *Goldberg Variations:* the *Thirty-three Variations on a Waltz by Diabelli*, Op. 120, which were completed and published in 1823. These differ from other variations of the late eighteenth or early nineteenth centuries in that they are made up not of comparatively straightforward alterations in the physiognomy of the theme, but of transformations in its very character. Diabelli's commonplace little waltz, taken by Beethoven as if contemptuously to show what could be made of it, surprisingly expands into a world of variegated moods—solemn, brilliant, capricious, mysterious—ordered with due regard for contrast, grouping, and climax. Each variation is built on motives derived from some part of the theme, but altered in rhythm, tempo, dynamics, or context so as to produce a new design. Other examples of variations, like the Diabelli set but more concentrated, are the slow movements in Beethoven's Sonata Op. 111 and in the Quartets Opp. 127 and 131. In these, as it were, we overhear the composer while he meditates on his theme, finding with each meditation new depths of insight, and gradually leading us into a realm where the music takes on a luminous and transcendent quality of mystical revelation.

Another feature of Beethoven's late style is a continuity he achieved by intentionally blurring dividing lines: within a musical sentence, by making cadential progressions terminate on a weak beat, by delaying the progression of the lower voices, placing the third or the fifth of the tonic chord in the upper voice at such a resolution, or by otherwise concealing the cadential effect (first theme of the slow movement of the Ninth Symphony); within a movement, by interpenetration of Introduction and Allegro (first movements of Sonata Op. 109 and Quartets Opp. 127, 130, 132) or making the Introduction a part of the Allegro (first movement of the Ninth Symphony); even within a complete work, by interpenetration of movements (Adagio and Fuga in the Sonata Op. 110; recall of the first movement theme after the Adagio of Op. 101). A feeling of vastness comes also from the widespaced harmonic arches and the leisurely march of the melodies in such movements as the Adagio of the Quartet Op. 127 or the "Benedictus" of the Mass in D. At times all motion pauses for long moments of reflection; such passages have the character of improvisation, and may give us some idea of the actual improvisations of Beethoven at the piano which so impressed his hearers. (Similar examples are the slow movement of the Sonata Op. 101 and the Largo introduction to the finale of the Sonata Op. 106; this style was forecast in the slow movement of the *Waldstein Sonata*, Op. 53.) Sometimes these improvisatory passages culminate in instrumental recitative, as in the Adagio of the Sonata Op. 110, and also the recitatives in the Quartets Opp. 131 and 132 and the finale of the Ninth Symphony.

The abstract, suprapersonal quality of Beethoven's late style is symbolized by the increased extent and importance of contrapuntal textures in the compositions of the third period. This increase was in part the fruit of his lifelong reverence for the music of J. S. Bach, but it was also a necessary consequence of the nature of his musical

Beethoven's manuscript of the theme of the variations from the Piano Sonata Op. 109. (Library of Congress)

thought in the last ten years of his life. It is apparent in the numerous canonic imitations and generally contrapuntal voice-leading of all the late works; it is evidenced specifically by fugatos incorporated in development sections (as in the finale of Op. 101) and by complete fugal movements, such as the finales of the Sonatas Opp. 106 and 110, the first movement of the Quartet in C-sharp minor Op. 131, the gigantic *Grosse Fuge* for String Quartet Op. 133, the fugues at the end of the Gloria and Credo of the Mass in D, and the two double fugues in the finale of the Ninth Symphony.

Another, incidental, consequence of the abstract quality of Beethoven's last works was the creation of new sonorities: as the former habits of vertical tone combination were modified by the rigorous logic of contrapuntal lines, or as new ideas required new alignments of sound for their realization, he produced unaccustomed effects. The widely spaced piano sonorities at the end of the Sonata Op. 110, the partition of the theme between the two violins (on the principle of the medieval hocket) in the fourth movement of the C-sharp minor Quartet, and the extraordinary dark coloring of the orchestra and chorus at the first appearance of the words "Ihr stürzt nieder" in the finale of the Ninth Symphony are instances of such new sonorities.   335

Some critics have held that in his late works Beethoven went too far in subjugating euphony and considerations of practicability to the demands of his musical conceptions, and some attribute this alleged fault to his deafness. There are places   the finale of the Sonata Op. 106, the first section of the *Grosse Fuge*, the B major cadenza of the four soloists in the last movement of the Ninth Symphony, the "Et vitam venturi" fugue in the Mass—that almost require a miracle to make them "sound" in performance. The ideas seem too big for human capabilities to express; but whether one approves or condemns these passages, there is not the slightest reason to suppose that Beethoven, even had his hearing been perfect, would have altered a single note, either to spare tender ears among his auditors or to make things easier for the performers.

As with Classical texture and sonority, so with Classical form in the works of Beethoven's third period: two of the last quartets and two of the last sonatas retain the external scheme of the usual four movements, but the rest dispense with even this obeisance to tradition. The Sonata Op. 111 has only two movements, an Allegro in compact sonata form and a long set of variations, *Adagio molto*, so eloquent and so perfect that nothing further seems to be required. The Quartet Op. 131 has seven movements: (1) A fugue in C-sharp minor, *adagio*, 4/4. (2) *Allegretto molto vivace*, D major, 6/8, in something vaguely like sonata form. (3) Eleven measures, *allegro moderato*, in the spirit of a *recitativo accompagnato*, functioning as an introduction to the following movement and modulating from B minor to E major, which becomes the dominant of (4) *Andante*, A major, 2/4: theme of two double periods, with six variations and a seventh variation incomplete, merging with a coda which itself embodies still one more variation of the first and fourth periods of the theme. (5) *Presto*, ₵, E major: four themes, rapidly chasing one another around in the order Abcd-
  Coda
AbcdA̅b̅c̅dA. (6) Adagio, G-sharp minor, 3/4: 28 measures in the form *ABB* with coda, introducing (7) Allegro, C-sharp minor, ₵, sonata form. All this could be forcibly equated with the Classical sonata scheme by calling 1 and 2 an introduction and first movement, 3 and 4 an introduction and slow movement, 5 a scherzo, and 6 and 7 an introduction and finale; a similar arbitrary adjustment would also be possible with the Quartet Op. 132, but not with Op. 130, which in the number and order of movements is more like a serenade than anything else. In any event, in all Beethoven's late sonatas and quartets both the musical material and its treatment are so different from those of Haydn and Mozart that resemblances to Classical patterns are at most incidental.

The Mass in D   The most imposing works of the last period are the Mass in D (the *Missa solemnis*) and the Ninth Symphony. The former is, with the possible exception of Bach's Mass in B minor, the greatest musical setting ever made of this text. It is a deeply personal and at the same time universal confession of faith. Like Bach's Mass, Beethoven's is too long and elaborate for ordinary liturgical use; it is rather a huge vocal and instrumental symphony using the text of the Mass as its fabric. The choral treatment owes something to Handel, whose music Beethoven revered equally with that of Bach; one theme of the "Dona nobis pacem" is adapted from Handel's melody to the words "And He shall reign forever and ever" in the Hallelujah Chorus, and the lofty style of the whole is quite in the spirit of Handel. The form, however, is radically different. Handel's oratorios and Bach's Mass were conceived, in accordance with the Baroque practice, as a series of independent numbers, without interconnecting themes or motives and usually without any very definite plan of musical unity in the work as a whole. Beethoven's Mass is a planned musical unit, a symphony in five movements, one on each of the five principal divisions of the Ordinary of the Mass. In this respect it is like the late Masses of Haydn, and like them also it freely combines and alternates solo voices and chorus in each movement.

Within the framework of the symphonic structure there is abundant variety of detail. Beethoven seizes upon every single word that offers him a possibility for dramatic musical expression; to realize the contrast in this respect between Beethoven's treatment of the text and that of Bach, one should compare their respective settings of the words "judicare vivos et mortuos" ("to judge both the quick and the dead") in the Credo. (Beethoven's effective pause after the word "et," here and elsewhere in the Credo, had been anticipated in Haydn's *Missa in tempore belli*.) The threefold interruption of the "Dona nobis pacem"—the "prayer for inward and outward peace"—by threatening interludes with martial motives in trumpets and drums (an idea also anticipated by Haydn) is another superbly theatrical touch. But neither this nor any of the other vivid details of the score is theatrical in a bad sense; all are gathered into and made part of the vast and wonderfully organized structure of the Mass.

The Ninth Symphony was first performed on May 7, 1824, on a program with one of Beethoven's overtures and three movements of the Mass (the Kyrie, Credo, and Agnus Dei). The large and distinguished audience applauded vociferously after the symphony. Beethoven did not turn around to acknowledge the applause because he could not hear it; one of the solo singers "plucked him by the sleeve and directed his attention to the clapping hands and waving hats and handkerchiefs. . . . he turned to the audience and bowed."[5] The receipts at the concert were large, but so little remained after expenses had been paid that Beethoven accused his friends who had managed the affair of having cheated him. A repetition two weeks later before a half-full house resulted in a deficit. Thus was the Ninth Symphony launched into the world.

The Ninth Symphony

Its most striking novelty is the use of chorus and solo voices in the finale. Beethoven had had the thought as early as 1792 of composing a setting of Schiller's *Ode to Joy*, but his decision to make a choral finale on this text for the Ninth Symphony was not reached before the autumn of 1823. It is significant of Beethoven's ethical ideals that in choosing the stanzas to be used he selected those that emphasize two ideas: the universal brotherhood of man through joy, and its basis in the love of an eternal heavenly Father. Beethoven was troubled by the apparent incongruity of introducing voices as the climax of a long instrumental symphony. His solution of this aesthetic difficulty determined the unusual form of the last movement: a brief tumultuous dissonant introduction; a review and rejection (by instrumental recitatives) of the themes of the preceding movements; suggestion of the joy theme and its joyful acceptance; orchestral exposition of the theme in four stanzas, *crescendo*, with coda; again the tumultuous dissonant opening measures; bass recitative: "O friends, not these tones, but let us rather sing more pleasant and joyful ones"; choral-orchestral exposition of the joy theme in four stanzas, varied (including the Turkish March), and with a long orchestral interlude (double fugue) before a repetition of the first stanza; new theme, orchestra and chorus; double fugue on the two themes; and a complex, gigantic coda, in which the "heaven-descended flame" of Joy is hailed in strains of matchless sublimity. The first three movements of the symphony are on a comparably grand scale. The scherzo, in particular, is an outstanding example of Beethoven's ability to organize an entire movement in sonata form around a single rhythmic motive.

Beethoven and the Romantics

Only a few of his contemporaries understood Beethoven's late works, which in any event were so personal that they could hardly be imitated. His influence on later composers came mostly from the works of the middle period, especially the *Rasumovsky Quartets*, the Fifth, Sixth, and Seventh Symphonies, and the piano sonatas. Even in these works it was not the Classical element in Beethoven's style—not the overruling sense of form, unity, and proportion that always dominated even his most subjective creations—but rather the revolutionary element, the free, impulsive, mysterious, daemonic spirit, the underlying conception of *music as a mode of self-expression*, that fascinated the Romantic generation. As E. T. A. Hoffmann wrote, "Beethoven's music sets in motion the lever of fear, of awe, of horror, of suffering, and awakens just that infinite longing which is the essence of romanticism. He is accordingly a completely romantic composer...."[6] Romantic or not, Beethoven was the most powerful disruptive force in the history of music. His works opened the gateway to a new world.

XVI Romanticism: Vocal Music

The Nature of Romanticism

In music history, the Romantic period is generally regarded as equivalent to the nineteenth century, with the understanding that certain Romantic traits are evident in the music of the latter part of the eighteenth century and others persist in various guises into the twentieth century. In accepting this concept, our first task must be to define as clearly as possible what we mean by *Romantic* with reference to music of the nineteenth century; having done this, we shall examine the principal types of vocal, instrumental, and operatic compositions of the period. In the course of our survey it will become clear that "Romantic" includes a great variety of styles and that within it are many contradictions and countercurrents.

In a very general sense, all art may be said to be Romantic; for, though it may take its materials from actual life, it transforms them and thus creates a new world which is necessarily to a greater or lesser degree remote from the everyday world. From this point of view, Romantic art differs from Classic art by its greater emphasis on the qualities of remoteness and strangeness, with all that such emphasis may imply as to choice and treatment of material. Romanticism, in this general sense, is not a phenomenon of any one period, but has occurred at various times in various forms. Thus it is possible to see in the history of music, and of the other arts, alternating periods of Classicism and Romanticism.

Another fundamental trait of Romanticism is boundlessness, in two different though related senses. First, Romantic art aspires to transcend immediate times or occasions, to seize eternity, to reach back into the past and forward into the future, to range over the expanse of the world and outward through the cosmos. As against the classic ideals of order, equilibrium, control, and perfection within acknowl-

Traits of Romanticism

339

edged limits, Romanticism cherishes freedom, movement, passion, and endless pursuit of the unattainable. And just because its goal can never be attained, Romantic art is haunted by a spirit of longing, of yearning after an impossible fulfillment.

Second, the Romantic impatience of limits leads to a breaking down of distinctions. The personality of the artist tends to become merged with the work of art; Classical clarity is replaced by a certain intentional obscurity, definite statement by suggestion, allusion, or symbol. The arts themselves tend to merge; poetry, for example, aims to acquire the qualities of music, and music the characteristics of poetry.

If remoteness and boundlessness are Romantic, then music is the most Romantic of the arts. Its material—ordered sound and rhythm—is almost completely detached from the concrete world of objects, and this very detachment makes music most apt at suggesting the flood of impressions, thoughts, and feelings which is the proper domain of Romantic art. Obviously only instrumental music—pure music free from the burden of words—can perfectly attain this goal of communicating emotion. Instrumental music, therefore, is the ideal Romantic art. Its detachment from the world, its mystery, and its incomparable power of suggestion which works on the mind directly without the mediation of words, made it the dominant art of the Romantic period. "All art constantly aspires towards the condition of music," wrote Pater.

The Romantic dualities

At this point we come upon the first of several apparently opposing conditions that beset all attempts to grasp the meaning of *Romantic* as applied to the music of the nineteenth century. We shall endeavor to deal with this difficulty by summarizing the conflicting tendencies that affected the music of the time and noting in what way the musicians of the Romantic period sought to harmonize these oppositions in their own thought and practice.

The first opposition involves the relation between music and words. If instrumental music is the perfect Romantic art, why is it that the acknowledged great masters of the symphony, the highest form of instrumental music, were not Romantics, but were the Classical composers, Haydn, Mozart, and Beethoven? Moreover, one of the most characteristic Romantic forms was the Lied, a vocal piece, in which Schubert, Schumann, Brahms, and Hugo Wolf attained a new and intimate union between music and poetry. Even the instrumental music of most Romantic composers was dominated by the lyrical spirit of the Lied rather than the dramatic-epic spirit of the symphony.

Music and words

The conflict between the ideal of pure instrumental music as the supremely Romantic mode of expression on the one hand, and the strong literary orientation of Romantic music on the other, was resolved in the conception of *program music*. Program music, as the nineteenth century used the term, was instrumental music associated with poetic, descriptive, or even narrative subject matter—not by means of conventional musical figures (as in the Baroque era) or by imitation of natural sounds and movements (as in the eighteenth century), but by means of imaginative suggestion. Program music aimed to absorb and transmute the imagined subject, taking it wholly into the dimension of music in such a way that the resulting composition, while it includes the "program," nevertheless completely dominates it and is in a certain sense independent of it. Instrumental music thus becomes a vehicle for the utterance of thoughts which, though they may be hinted in words, are ultimately beyond the power of words to express. Practically every composer of the Romantic era was, to a greater or lesser degree, writing program music, whether or not he publicly acknowledged it; and one reason why it is so easy for listeners to connect a scene or a story or a poem with a piece of Romantic music is that often the composer himself, perhaps unconsciously, was working from some such idea. Romantic writers on music projected their own conceptions of the expressive function of music into the past, and read Romantic programs into the instrumental works not only of Beethoven but also of Mozart, Haydn, and Bach.

Another area of conflict involved the relationship between the composer and his audience. The Romantic composers, if they were to succeed, somehow had to reach a vast, new, and relatively uncultured audience; their struggle to be heard and understood had to occur in an incomparably larger arena than at any previous epoch in the history of music. Yet it is the Romantic period more than any other that offers us the phenomenon of the unsociable artist, one who feels himself to be separate from his fellow-men and who is driven by isolation to seek inspiration within himself. These Romantic musicians did not compose, as did their eighteenth-century forebears, for a patron or for a particular function, but for infinity, for posterity, for some imaginable ideal audience which, they hoped, would some day understand and appreciate them; either that, or they wrote for a little circle of kindred spirits, confessing to them those inmost feelings considered too fragile and precious to be set before the crude public of the concert halls. Partly in sheer self-defense they were driven to the conception of the composer as an exalted combination of priest and poet, one to whom it was given to reveal to mankind the deeper meaning of life through the divine medium of music. The artist was a "genius" who wrote under "inspiration," a prophet even though his message might be rejected.

The crowd and the individual

It is remarkable that the great virtuoso performers of the nineteenth century were dominating, heroic individuals—for example, Paganini and Liszt. They were instrumental soloists, as opposed to the typical eighteenth-century virtuoso, the operatic singer, who was the most conspicuous member of a group, and the typical twentieth-century virtuoso, the conductor, who is the dictator of a group. This accent on the individual is present everywhere in Romanticism: the best vocal music of the period is for solo voice, not for chorus. This conception of the composer as a prophet, a lone heroic figure struggling against a hostile environment, also served to lend the music a quality of excitement, an emotional tension by means of which the audience was stimulated and uplifted.

Man and nature

Partly because of the industrial revolution, the population of Europe increased tremendously during the nineteenth century. Most of the increase occurred in cities: the populations of both London and Paris quadrupled between 1800 and 1880. Consequently, the majority of people, including the majority of musicians, no longer lived in a community, a court or town, where everybody knew everybody else and the open countryside was never very far away; instead, they were lost in the huge impersonal huddle of a modern city.

But the more man's daily life became separated from Nature, the more he became enamored of Nature. From Rousseau onward, Nature was idealized, and increasingly so in its wilder and more picturesque aspects. However, for the Romantic composer Nature was not merely a subject to be depicted. A kinship was felt between the inner life of the artist and the life of Nature, so that the latter became not only a refuge but also a source of strength, inspiration, and revelation. This mystic sense of kinship with Nature, counterbalancing the artificiality of city existence, is as prevalent in the music of the nineteenth century as it is in the contemporary literature and art.

Science and the irrational

The nineteenth century saw a rapid expansion in exact knowledge and scientific method. Simultaneously, as though in reaction, the music of the Romantic era is constantly thrusting beyond the borders of the rational into the unconscious and the supernatural. It takes its subject material from the dream (the individual unconscious), as in Berlioz's *Symphonie fantastique*, or from the myth (the collective unconscious), as in Wagner's music dramas. Even Nature itself is haunted in the Romantic imagination by spirits and is fraught with mysterious significances. The effort to find a musical language capable of expressing these new and strange ideas led to new worlds of harmony, melody, and orchestral color.

Materialism and idealism

The nineteenth century was in the main a secular and materialistic age, though there was an important movement of revival in the Catholic Church. But the essential Romantic spirit, once again in conflict with an important trend of its time, was both idealistic and nonchurchly. The most characteristic Romantic musical settings of liturgical texts were, like Beethoven's *Missa solemnis*, too personal and too big for ordinary church use: the gigantic *Requiem* and the *Te Deum* of Berlioz and the *Requiem* of Verdi. The Romantic composers also gave expression to generalized religious aspiration in nonliturgical settings, such as the *German Requiem* of Brahms, Wagner's *Parsifal*, and Mahler's Eighth Symphony. Furthermore, a great deal of Romantic music is infused with a kind of idealistic longing that might be called "religious" in a vague pantheistic sense.

Another area of conflict in the nineteenth century was political: it was the conflict between the growth of nationalism and the beginning of supranational socialist movements outlined by the *Communist Manifesto* of Marx and Engels (1848), and Marx's *Capital* (1867). Nationalism was an important influence in Romantic music. Differences between national musical styles were accentuated and folk song came to be venerated as the spontaneous expression of the national soul. Musical Romanticism flourished especially in Germany, not only because the Romantic temper was congenial to German ways of thinking, but also because in that country national sentiment, being for a long time suppressed politically, had to find vent in music and other forms of art. Supplementary to the concentration on national music was a delight in exoticism, the sympathetic use of foreign idioms for picturesque color. The music of the great Romantic composers was not, of course, limited to any one country; what it had to say was addressed to all humanity. But its idioms were national when compared with the eighteenth-century ideal of a cosmopolitan musical language in which national peculiarities were minimized.

The Romantic movement had from the beginning a revolutionary tinge, with a corresponding emphasis on the virtue of originality in art. Romanticism was seen as a revolt against the limitations of Classicism. With respect to the immediate past, however, the revolutionary aspect was overshadowed by the conception of Romanticism as the fulfillment of Classicism. Beethoven and, to some extent, Mozart also were viewed by the Romantic composers as having marked out the path which they themselves were to follow. Thus arose the concept of music as an art that had a history—moreover, a history which was to be interpreted, in accord with the dominant philosophical ideas of the time, as a process of evolution.

The past was manifested in Romantic music by the persistence of the Classical tradition. Composers still wrote in the Classical forms of sonata, symphony, and string quartet; the Classical system of harmony was still the basis of Romantic music. Moreover, not all the Romantic composers went the whole way in adopting Romantic innovations; there were conservatives and radicals within the general movement.

One of the most striking aspects of the Romantic movement is its affinity with Bach and Palestrina, its conscious preoccupation with the remote past—an attitude previously unknown in the history of music. The rapid rise of historical musicology in the nineteenth century was an outgrowth of the Romantic interest in the music of former ages, while the discoveries of musicologists further stimulated such interest. The Romantics, of course, romanticized history; they heard in the music of Bach, Palestrina, and other older composers what it suited them to hear, and adopted such things as they wanted for their own purposes. It was not the least of the many contradictions within the Romantic movement that its subjectively motivated reach into the past should have opened the way to the objective discipline of historical research in music.

The Nature of Romanticism

Nationalism and internationalism

Tradition and revolution

343

Haydn's *Creation* and *Seasons*, Mozart's *Don Giovanni* and *Magic Flute*, and Beethoven's Fifth and Ninth Symphonies were the immediate sources of musical Romanticism. From Haydn came its pleasure in depicting the world of nature, from Mozart its preoccupation with the inner life of the individual human being, and from Beethoven its Faustian aspirations and storming assaults on the Ideal.

The most remarkable Romantic achievements lay in the development of harmonic technique and instrumental color. There was a continuous increase of harmonic complexity throughout the nineteenth century. Chromatic harmonies, chromatic voice leading, distant modulations, complex chords, freer use of nonharmonic tones, and a growing tendency to avoid distinct cadences on the tonic, all operated to extend and blur the outlines of tonality. Romantic harmony as a means of expression went hand in hand with an ever-expanding palette of color. New sonorities were discovered in piano music; new instruments were added to the orchestra, and older instruments were redesigned to be more sonorous and more flexible; above all, new combinations of instruments in the ensemble were invented to produce new color effects. Harmony and color were the principal means whereby the nineteenth-century composers sought to express in music the Romantic ideals of remoteness, ardor, and boundless longing.

The Lied

The pitifully short life of Franz Peter Schubert (1797–1828) illustrates the tragedy of genius overwhelmed by the petty necessities and annoyances of everyday existence. Without wide public recognition, sustained only by the love of a few friends, constantly struggling against illness and poverty, he composed ceaselessly. His works include nine symphonies, twenty-two piano sonatas, and a multitude of short piano pieces for two and four hands, about thirty-five chamber compositions, six Masses, seventeen operatic works, and over six hundred *Lieder*.

The songs reveal Schubert's supreme gift for making beautiful melodies, a power which few even of the greatest composers have possessed so fully. Many of his melodies have the simple artless quality of folk song; others are suffused with an indescribable romantic sweetness and melancholy; still others are declamatory, intense, and dramatic; in short, there is no mood or nuance of Romantic feeling but finds spontaneous and perfect expression in Schubert's melody. This wonderful melodic stream flows as purely and as copiously in the instrumental works as in the songs.

Along with melody went a sensitive feeling for harmonic color. Schubert's modulations, often far-flung and complex, sometimes embodying long passages in which the tonality is kept in suspense, powerfully underline the dramatic qualities of a song text. Masterly use of chromatic coloring within a prevailingly diatonic sound is another characteristic of Schubert's harmony. His modulations tend characteristically to move from the tonic toward flat keys, and the minor submediant is a favorite relationship.

Equally diverse and ingenious are the piano accompaniments in Schubert's *Lieder*. Very often the piano figuration is suggested by some pictorial image of the text; such pictorial features are never merely imitative, but are designed, in the best Romantic fashion, to

Franz Peter Schubert (1797–1828).

contribute toward the mood of the song. Thus the accompaniment of *Gretchen am Spinnrad*—one of the earliest (1814) and best of the *Lieder*—suggests not only the whirr of the spinning wheel but also the agitation of Gretchen's thoughts as she sings of her lover. The rushing octave triplets of *Erlkönig* depict at the same time the galloping of the horse and the frantic anxiety of the father as he rides "through night and storm" with his frightened child clasped in his arms. This song, composed in 1815, is one of Schubert's relatively few ballads. Goethe's poem is more compact than the usual early Romantic ballad, and is all the more effective because of the speed of its action. Schubert has characterized in an unforgettable manner the three actors in the drama—the father, the wily Erlking, and the terrified child with his cries rising a tone higher at each repetition; the cessation of movement and the final line in recitative make a superbly dramatic close. An entirely different style of accompaniment is found in another of Schubert's *Lieder, Der Doppelgänger:* here are only long, somber chords, with a recurrent sinister melodic motif in low triple octaves, below a declamatory voice part which rises to an awesome climax before sinking in a final despairing phrase. Nothing could better suggest the ghostly horror of the scene than the heavy, obsessive dark chords, revolving fatally about the tonic of B minor except for one brief, lurid flash of D-sharp minor near the end.

345

Many of Schubert's *Lieder* are in strophic form, with either literal repetition of the music for each stanza or repetition with slight variation. Others, particularly those on longer texts, alternate between declamatory and arioso style, the whole unified by recurring themes and evidencing a carefully planned scheme of tonalities. The form, however complex, is always suited to both poetic and musical requirements. Schubert drew on the works of many different poets for his texts; from Goethe alone he took fifty-nine poems, and he wrote five different solo settings for "Nur wer die Sehnsucht kennt" from *Wilhelm Meister*. Some of the finest of Schubert's *Lieder* are found in the two cycles on poems by Wilhelm Müller, *Die schöne Müllerin* (1823) and *Winterreise* (1827). The *Schwanengesang* (1828), not intended as a cycle but published as such posthumously, includes six songs on poems by Heinrich Heine. On the whole, Schubert's texts are excellent material for musical treatment, though naturally uneven in literary quality; but his music is able to glorify even commonplace poetry.

Schumann's Lieder

Lieder were written by most of the Romantic composers, but the first important successor of Schubert in this field was Robert Schumann (1810–1856). Schubert, though his music is Romantic in its lyrical quality and harmonic color, nevertheless always maintained a certain Classical serenity and poise. With Schumann we are in the full restless tide of Romanticism. His first collection of songs appeared in 1840, all his previously published works having been for piano. Although his melodic lines are warm and expressive, Schumann's *Lieder* lack the spontaneous charm of Schubert's; the accompaniments, however, are of unusual interest. Indeed, many of Schumann's *Lieder* are really duets for voice and piano. The preluding piano phrases, the interludes, and especially the sometimes quite extended postludes (as in the *Dichterliebe* cycle) often seem to sum up in concentrated and poignant form the essence of an entire song.

An excellent example of perfect union between voice and piano is found in the beautiful *Mondnacht* (1840), on words by J. von Eichendorff, one of Schumann's favorite poets. With simpler accompaniment, but equally permeated with the quintessence of Romantic feeling and harmony, is the setting of Heine's *Die Lotosblume* (1840). Schumann's most famous song of the ballad type is *Die beiden Grenadiere* (1840), which incorporates the melody of *La Marseillaise* at the climax. Some of the finest of Schumann's *Lieder* are the love songs; in 1840, the year of his long-delayed marriage to his beloved Clara Wieck, he produced over one hundred *Lieder*, including the two cycles *Dichterliebe* (Heine) and *Frauenliebe und Leben* (A. von Chamisso). In these works the Romantic genius of Schumann appears in perfection.

Brahms's Lieder

The principal successor to Schumann was Johannes Brahms (1833–1897), for whom the Lied was a congenial medium and whose works in this form (over 260 altogether) come from every period of his life. Brahms declared that his ideal was the folk song, and many of his own songs, as for example the familiar *Wiegenlied*, are exactly in this style.

Schubert was Brahms's model in song writing, and a considerable proportion of his *Lieder* are, like Schubert's, in a more or less freely treated strophic form. Among them are *Vergebliches Ständchen*, one of the few Brahms songs of a humorous and outrightly cheerful nature. For the most part, however, Brahms's tone is serious. His music is Romantic in harmony and texture, but it has not the soaring, ardent, impulsive character of Schumann's; restraint, a certain classic gravity, an introspective, resigned, elegiac mood are predominant. Within this fundamentally reflective style, however, there is room for the expression of passion, expression all the more effective because it avoids excess and is felt to be always under control. Among all German *Lieder* there are no finer love songs than some of the Romances of the *Magelone cycle* (Op. 33) on poems by Ludwig Tieck, or such songs as *Wie bist du meine Königin* and *Meine Liebe ist grün*.

The essential elements of Brahms's *Lieder* are the melody and bass, the tonal plan and form. The accompaniments are rarely pictorial, and there are not many of the instrumental preludes and postludes which are so important in Schumann's songs. Yet the piano parts are marvelously varied in texture, frequently using extended arpeggio figuration and syncopated rhythms. Perhaps the greatest—certainly the most typically Brahmsian—of the *Lieder* are those concerned with reflections on death, particularly the *Vier ernste Gesänge*, the "four serious songs" (Op. 121, 1896) on Biblical texts, the supreme achievement of Brahms's last years.

Photograph of Johannes Brahms (1833–1897) taken during his twenties. (Bettmann Archive)

347

Choral Music

In considering the choral music of the nineteenth century, it is necessary to make a distinction between works (for example, operas) in which the chorus is used as a part of a larger apparatus and those in which the choral writing is intended to be a principal focus of interest. It is significant that the two composers of this period who best understood how to write idiomatically for chorus—Mendelssohn and Brahms—were precisely the two who were most strongly resistant to the extreme tendencies of Romanticism. The chorus is less suited to express typically Romantic sentiments than the symphony orchestra, and indeed, many nineteenth-century composers treated the chorus primarily as a division of the orchestra, to supply picturesque touches and supplementary colors.

Nineteenth-century choral music is of three main classes: (1) part songs (that is, songs in homophonic style for a small vocal ensemble, with the melody in the topmost voice) or other short choral pieces, usually on secular words, to be sung either *a cappella* or with accompaniment of piano or organ; (2) music on liturgical texts or intended for use in church services; (3) oratorios and cantatas for chorus (often with one or more solo vocalists) and orchestra, on texts of dramatic or narrative-dramatic character, but intended for concert rather than stage performance.

Part songs and cantatas

The composition of part songs, which had begun before the end of the eighteenth century, received impetus in the Romantic period from the rise of national sentiment and the awakening of interest in folk song. The multiplication of singing societies and the institution of festivals in Germany and France during the first half of the nineteenth century were a further stimulus to choral composition. Practically every composer in Europe produced part songs and choruses for men's, women's, or mixed voices, accompanied and unaccompanied, on patriotic, sentimental, convivial, and every other imaginable kind of verse. This music served its purpose and has been for the most part forgotten. Of more permanent interest are some of the Romantic cantatas, such as Mendelssohn's *Erste Walpurgisnacht* (1832, revised 1843) and Schumann's *Paradise and the Peri* (1843) and *Scenes from Goethe's "Faust"* (1844–53). The master in this field was Johannes Brahms, whose works include many short, usually unaccompanied songs for women's, men's, or mixed voices, as well as a number of larger compositions for chorus with orchestra. Among these are some of the most beautiful choral works, not only of the nineteenth century but of all time—the *Rhapsody* for alto solo and men's chorus (1870), the *Schicksalslied* (*Song of Fate*, 1871) and *Nänie* (song of lamentation on verses by Schiller, 1881) for mixed chorus, and *Gesang der Parzen* (*Song of the Parcae, i.e.*, the Fates, 1883), for six-part mixed chorus.

348   The nineteenth century was not one of the great ages of church

music. The best Catholic church music in the early part of the century came from Luigi Cherubini at Paris and Franz Schubert at Vienna. Schubert's Masses in A-flat and E-flat (D. 678, 950) are among the finest settings of this text in the nineteenth century. The Masses and other sacred music of the Parisian Charles Gounod (1818–1893) were highly regarded in their time, but his peculiar blend of piety and mild Romanticism had the misfortune to be so assiduously (though unintentionally) parodied by later composers that it has lost whatever validity it may have possessed.

A dazzling conflagration was set off by the collision of Romantic musical energy with sacred themes in the *Grande Messe des Morts* (*Requiem*) and the *Te Deum* of Hector Berlioz (1803–1869). These are magnificent religious works, but they are not music for the church service. Their nature is wholly original and Romantic. They are dramatic symphonies for orchestra and voices which use poetically inspiring texts that happen to be liturgical. The tradition to which they belong is not ecclesiastical but secular and patriotic; their historical forebears are the great popular musical festivals of the French Revolution. Both works were associated with solemn national emotions, the *Requiem* (1837) being originally intended to honor the heroic dead of the July Revolution and the *Te Deum* (first heard in 1855) to commemorate the victories of Napoleon in Italy. Both are of appropriately vast dimensions—vast not only in length and number of performers, but in grandeur of conception and brilliance of execution. Too much has been said about the orchestra of one hundred and forty players, the four brass choirs, the four tam-tams, ten pairs of cymbals, and sixteen kettledrums that Berlioz requires for the "Tuba mirum" chorus of the *Requiem*—and too little about the superb musical effect he obtains in the comparatively few places where all these are sounding. Berlioz's orchestra, like the Emperor Gordianus's twenty-two concubines,[1] is "designed for use rather than ostentation." There are a hundred other strokes of genius in the orchestration of the *Requiem:* one may take for examples the chords for flutes and trombones alternating with men's chorus in the "Hostias," and the further development of this kind of sonority at the beginning of the "Agnus Dei"; the stark lines of the English horns, bassoons, and low strings in combination with unison tenor voices in the "Quid sum miser"; or the return of the wonderful long tenor melody of the "Sanctus," where the five-measure responsive phrases of soloist and chorus are punctuated by *pianissimo* strokes of the bass drum and cymbals. The *Te Deum* is less replete with striking orchestral experiments than the *Requiem*, but it is in a more mature style, and its final number ("Judex crederis") is certainly one of the most thrilling movements ever written for chorus and orchestra.

What Berlioz did outside the church Franz Liszt (1811–1886) tried to do within it. His Festival Mass for the consecration of the cathedral at Gran (Hungary) in 1855, as well as his Mass for the coronation of the King of Hungary in 1867, are on a scale and in a style corresponding to Liszt's own ideal of Romantic sacred music, which he expressed thus in 1834:

> For want of a better term we may call the new music Humanitarian. It must be devotional, strong, and drastic, uniting on a colossal scale the theatre and the church, at once dramatic and sacred, splendid and simple, ceremonial and serious, fiery and free, stormy and calm, translucent and emotional.[2]

Two Italian composers, Gioacchino Rossini (1792–1868) and Giuseppe Verdi (1813–1901), made important contributions to church music in the nineteenth century. Rossini's *Stabat Mater* (1832, 1841) is a serious, sincere, and well-made composition, containing some excellent choral writing (especially in the opening and closing numbers) along with arias in operatic style. Verdi's *Requiem* (1874) is an immense work, deeply moving, vividly dramatic, and at the same time thoroughly Catholic in spirit—unlike the *Requiem* of Berlioz, to which Verdi's is musically indebted in many respects.

The most important church composer of the later nineteenth century was Anton Bruckner (1824–1896), whose choral and symphonic compositions are today most unjustly ignored outside the Germanic countries of Europe. A solitary, simple, and profoundly religious soul, thoroughly schooled in counterpoint, organist of the Cathedral at Linz and from 1867 Court Organist at Vienna, Bruckner succeeded as no one before him in uniting the spiritual and technical resources of the nineteenth-century symphony with a reverent and liturgical approach to the sacred texts. His Masses and his symphonies have many qualities and even some musical themes in common.

The Mass in D minor was composed in 1864, that in F minor (the larger of the two) in 1867. The happiest fusion of neo-medieval and Romantic elements is heard in his Mass in E minor (1866) for eight-part chorus and fifteen wind instruments.

The Romantic oratorio

The Romantic oratorio is now remembered chiefly through Mendelssohn's *St. Paul* (1836) and *Elijah* (1846) and Liszt's *Legend of St. Elizabeth* (1857–1862). Berlioz's *Enfance du Christ* (*The Infant Christ;* 1854) is charming and picturesque rather than churchly.

Brahms's *German Requiem* (1868), for soprano and baritone solos, chorus, and orchestra, is one of the outstanding choral works of the nineteenth century. It has for its text not the liturgical words of the Latin Requiem Mass but Biblical passages of meditation and solace in German, admirably chosen by the composer himself. Brahms's music, like that of Schütz and Bach, is inspired by a deep concern with man's mortal lot and his hope of Heaven; but in the *German Requiem* these solemn thoughts are expressed with the peculiar intensity of Romantic feeling and clothed with the opulent colors of Romantic harmony, regulated always by spacious formal architecture and guided by an unerring judgment for choral and orchestral effect.

XVII Romanticism: Instrumental Music

Music for Piano

The piano of the nineteenth century was quite a different instrument from the one for which Mozart had written. Reshaped, enlarged, and mechanically improved, it had been made capable of producing a full, firm tone at any dynamic level, of responding in every way to Romantic demands for both expressiveness and overwhelming virtuosity. The piano was the supreme Romantic instrument.

General features

The piano works of Carl Maria von Weber (1786–1826) include four sonatas, two concertos, and the better known *Concertstück* in F minor for piano and orchestra (1821), as well as many short pieces of which the *Invitation to the Dance* (1819) has remained popular. His style is rhythmic, picturesque, full of contrast, and technically brilliant, but without profound content.

The early Romantic composers

A distinctive school of pianists and composers flourished in Bohemia in the early nineteenth century. Johann Ladislaus Dussek (1760 –1812) was especially noted for his sonatas. Johann Wenzel Tomaschek (1774–1850) and Johann Hugo Woržischek (1791–1825) wrote short lyrical piano pieces with the titles *eclogue, rhapsodie,* or *impromptu.* The music of these Bohemian composers embodied many of the characteristics of early Romanticism, and Woržischek, who lived in Vienna after 1813, exerted considerable influence on Schubert.

Schubert wrote for the piano, in addition to innumerable marches, waltzes and other dances, fourteen short pieces to which he gave the modest titles of *impromptu* or *moment musical.* His most important larger works for the piano are the eleven completed sonatas and a Fantasia in C major (1822) on a theme adapted from his song, *Der Wanderer.* Important also are his many duets, particularly the *Grand Duo* (D. 812), the Fantasia in F minor (D. 940), and the Rondo in A major (D. 951). He wrote no concertos. The six *Moments musicaux* (D. 789) and the eight *Impromptus* (D. 899, 935) are for the piano

Franz Schubert

what his *Lieder* are for the voice. Abounding in Schubertian melodies and harmonies, perfect in form and detail, each one quite distinctive in mood, these works became the model for every subsequent Romantic composer of brief, unpretentious, intimate piano pieces. The *Wanderer* fantasia (D. 760) stands almost alone among Schubert's piano compositions in making considerable demands on the player's technique. It is in four movements like a sonata; the movements are linked together and the whole is centered around the Adagio and Variations, the theme of which also appears, variously transformed, in the other three movements of the work.

In his sonatas Schubert seems to have been influenced more by Haydn and Mozart than by Beethoven. Their external form never departs from the standard Classical patterns, but their atmosphere is more lyric than dramatic; instead of concentrated thematic development or surging Romantic emotions Schubert gives us expansive melodies and shimmering harmonic progressions. Some of the slow movements might well have been published as impromptus or *moments musicaux*—for example, those of the sonatas in B major Op. 147 (D. 575) and A major Op. 120 (D. 664). The last of his sonatas (D. 960) is undoubtedly Schubert's greatest work for the piano. A long singing melody begins the first movement; hovering modulations are featured in the subsidiary theme section and the development; the sonorities are perfectly spaced throughout. The slow movement is in C-sharp minor (the enharmonic minor mediant key), with a middle section in A major; the delicately varied ostinato rhythm of this movement is typical of Schubert, as are also the expressive harmonic suspensions and the unexpected shifts between major and minor in the coda.

*Felix
Mendelssohn-
Bartholdy*

Felix Mendelssohn-Bartholdy (1809-1847) was himself a virtuoso pianist. His piano music requires a fluent technique, but in general the style is elegant and sensitive, not given to violence or excess bravura.

*Felix Mendelssohn-Bartholdy
(1809-1847).*

His finest large work for piano is the *Variations sérieuses* in D minor, Op. 54 (1841). A certain elfin lightness and clarity in scherzo-like movements, a quality unique in Mendelssohn's music, is evident in the familiar *Andante and Rondo Capriccioso*, Op. 14. The most popular piano works of Mendelssohn were the forty-eight short pieces issued at intervals in six books under the collective title *Songs without Words* —a title itself typical of the Romantic period. Mendelssohn's harmony has few of the delightful surprises that one encounters in Schubert, nor do his melodies, rhythms, and forms introduce many unexpected features. His music, like his life, flowed serenely and harmoniously; it is essentially Classical in outline, imbued with Romantic color and sentiment but never more than lightly touched with Romantic pathos or passion.

Mendelssohn's three preludes and fugues and six sonatas for organ are among the few distinguished contributions of the Romantic period to the literature of that instrument. Notable features in the sonatas are the frequent fugal writing and the use of Lutheran chorale melodies.

All of Schumann's published compositions (Opp. 1–23) up to 1840 were for piano, and these include most of his important works for that instrument with the exception of his one concerto (1845). This con- *Robert* certo, the Fantasia in C major Op. 17 (1836), and the set of variations *Schumann* entitled *Symphonic Études* (1834) are his chief longer works for piano, though he wrote also several other sets of variations and three sonatas. The remainder of his production consists of short character pieces, which he often grouped in loosely organized cycles with names such as *Papillons, Carnaval, Fantasiestücke, Kinderscenen, Kreisleriana, Novelletten, Nachtstücke, Faschingsschwank aus Wien.* Charming little pieces for children are gathered in the *Album for the Young* (published 1848).

The titles of both the collections and the separate pieces suggest that Schumann intended his music not only to be considered as pat-

Robert Schumann (1810–1856).

terns of sound but in some manner to suggest extra-musical poetic fancies. This is a typical Romantic attitude and its significance is not at all diminished by the fact that Schumann, on his own admission, usually wrote the music before he thought of the title. His music embodies more fully than that of any other composer the depths, and the contradictions and tensions of the Romantic spirit; it is by turns ardent and dreamy, vehement and visionary, whimsical and learned. Schumann's piano music, while far from easy to play, never aims to impress the listener by sheer bravura. It is thoroughly idiomatic for the instrument, and the virtuoso element is always subordinate to the poetic idea.

The compositions of Frédéric Chopin (1810–1849) are almost exclusively for piano. The principal works are: two concertos and a few other large pieces for piano with orchestra, three sonatas, thirty études, four scherzos, four ballades, twenty-four preludes, three impromptus, nineteen nocturnes, numerous waltzes, mazurkas, and polonaises, a *Barcarole* in F-sharp, a *Berceuse* in D-flat, and a *Fantasia* in F minor.

Frédéric Chopin

Although Chopin lived in Paris from 1831, he never ceased to love his native Poland or to be afflicted by her misfortunes. His mazurkas, impregnated with the rhythms, harmonies, forms, and melodic traits of Polish popular music (though without any direct quotation from Polish folk songs) are among the earliest and best examples of the Romantic music inspired by national idioms. To some extent his polonaises may also be regarded as a national manifestation.

Many of Chopin's pieces have an introspective character and, within clearly defined formal outlines, contrive to suggest the quality of improvisation. Although he was a concert pianist, he was not an overwhelming, theatrical performer, and it is probable that other virtuosos have projected the heroic side of his music more emphatically than he himself was able to do, and perhaps more emphatically than he would have desired. All his works, however, demand of the player not only a flawless touch and technique but also an imaginative use of the pedals and a discreet application of *tempo rubato*, which Chopin himself described as a slight pushing or holding back within the phrase of the right-hand part while the left-hand accompaniment continues in strict time.

The nocturnes, impromptus, and preludes are Chopin's most obviously intimate works. Both the name and the general idea of the nocturnes were taken from the Irish pianist and composer John Field (1782–1837), those of the impromptus presumably from Schubert. The Nocturne in D-flat (Op. 27, No. 2) and the Impromptu in F-sharp (Op. 36) are examples of Chopin's *cantabile* melodic style—influenced probably by the Italian opera composer, Bellini—his sensitive treatment of widely spaced accompaniment figures, and his inimitable creative fancy in pianistic ornamentation, by the use of which he produces some effects that forecast Impressionism. Such piano

sonorities had been unknown before Chopin. The preludes were composed at a time when Chopin was immersed even more deeply than
usual in the music of Bach. Like the preludes in the *Well-Tempered
Clavier*, these brief, sharply defined mood pictures go through all the
major and minor keys, though the succession Chopin uses is by the
circle of fifths (C major—A minor—G major—E minor, and so on).
Chopin's music was an important source of later Romantic developments in harmony; his extraordinarily original genius for chromatic
harmonies and modulations is evident in many of the preludes.

*Frédéric Chopin (1810–1849); after
a daguerreotype in the Warsaw
Museum.*

The fundamental traits of Chopin's style are displayed on a larger
canvas in the ballades and scherzos. He was apparently the first composer to use the name *ballade* for an instrumental piece; his works in
this form capture the Romantic narrative charm of the literary ballads,
and combine it with that indefinable spontaneity, those constantly
fresh turns in the harmony and form, that are a distinctive mark of
Chopin. The principal scherzos are those in B minor (Op. 20) and
C-sharp minor (Op. 39). Chopin's scherzos have no trace of this
form's original connotation of playfulness; these are wholly serious,
virile, and passionate works, organized—as are the ballades—in compact forms that grow naturally out of the musical ideas. On an equally

large scale but even more varied in content is the great *Fantasia* in F minor (Op. 49), a worthy companion to the like-named Romantic works of Schubert and Schumann.

Chopin's études (twelve in each of Opp. 10 and 25 and three without opus numbers) are important landmarks in the history of piano music. An *étude* is, as the name indicates, a study primarily for the development of technique. Chopin's études are transcendent studies in technique and at the same time intensely concentrated tone poems; they are all the more definite in meaning because the composer carefully avoided any clues that could serve as a pretext for attaching descriptive labels.

Franz Liszt (1811–1886); a portrait by Henry Lehmann. (Bettmann Archive)

Franz Liszt

The life of Franz Liszt was one of the most brilliant of the Romantic era. His piano style was based on Chopin's, from whom he took the latter's repertoire of pianistic effects—adding new ones of his own —as well as his lyrical melodic qualities, his manner of *rubato* playing, and his harmonic innovations, which Liszt further extended. Some of the late works, in particular, contain strikingly advanced chords and modulations.

A considerable proportion of Liszt's piano music consists of transcriptions or arrangements—fantasies on operatic airs, transcriptions of Schubert's songs and Berlioz's and Beethoven's symphonies, Bach's organ fugues, excerpts from Wagner's music dramas, and the like. Related to these are the compositions which make free use of national tunes; chief among these are the nineteen *Hungarian Rhapsodies*.

For piano and orchestra Liszt wrote two concertos (E-flat major, A major), a *Hungarian Fantasia* (expanded from the fourteenth Rhapsody), and the *Totentanz* (*Dance of Death*), a paraphrase on the plainsong *Dies irae*. His piano studies include the terrific twelve

Études d'exécution transcendante, published in their finally revised version in 1852 with titles (No. 4 is the frequently played *Mazeppa*); six studies transcribed from Paganini's caprices for solo violin, published in final shape in 1851 (among them *La Campanella*); and three *Études de concert* (1848).

The variety of Liszt's poetic imagination is displayed in many of his short separately published piano pieces and in several collections of tone pictures, of which the chief are *Années de pèlerinage* (three books; the first two composed before 1850 and the third in 1867–77), *Consolations* (1850), and *Harmonies poétiques et religieuses* (1852). These collections contain some of his best compositions, which negate the all too common impression of Liszt as concerned only with bravura effects. An important large work is the Sonata in B minor (1853), in which four themes are worked out in one extended movement, although with subdivisions analogous to the sections of a Classical sonata movement.

Liszt also wrote about a dozen works for organ, the most important of which are a big *Fantasia and Fugue* (1850) on a chorale theme ("Ad nos, ad salutarem undam") from Meyerbeer's opera *Le Prophète*, and a Prelude and Fugue on the name of Bach—that is, on a theme beginning with the chromatic motif *B* (the German symbol for B-flat), *A*, *C*, *H* (the German symbol for B-natural).

The piano style of Brahms has neither the elegance and sentiment of Chopin nor the extreme brilliance and romantic rhetoric of Liszt. Its models are Schumann and Beethoven. Technically it is character- ized by fullness of sonority, broken chord figuration, frequent doubling of the melodic line in octaves, thirds, or sixths, and considerable use of cross-rhythms. It has the harmonic richness and emotional warmth of Romanticism, but the language is governed by basic conceptions that are essentially more Classical than Romantic. Brahms's works for the piano include two concertos, three sonatas, several sets of variations, and some thirty-five shorter pieces with titles such as ballade, rhapsody, capriccio, or intermezzo. Chief among the larger works are the concertos, the Sonata in F minor (1853), the *Variations and Fugue on a Theme of Handel* (1861), and the difficult étude-like *Variations on a Theme of Paganini* (1863). Brahms is the great conservative of the Romantic era. A direct link with the past is found in his eleven chorale preludes for the organ, written during the last years of his life—the finest compositions in this form since Bach.

Among the piano music of Brahms's contemporaries must be noted Mussorgsky's *Pictures at an Exhibition* (1874) and three works by the Belgian César Franck, namely a *Prelude, Chorale, and Fugue* (1884), a *Prelude, Aria, and Finale* (1887), and the *Symphonic Variations* for piano and orchestra (1885). The *Variations* are based on two themes, and the structure is a synthesis of variation and sonata form. Franck studied in Paris and made his home there after 1844; like Brahms, he sought to incorporate the achievements of Romanticism

César Franck (1822–1890). (Bett-mann Archive)

in an essentially Classical framework, with a harmonic idiom influenced to some extent by the chromaticism of Liszt and Wagner. His compositions for organ include several sets of short pieces and three so-called *Chorales* (1890), which actually are skilfully developed fantasias on original themes.

Chamber Music

The style of chamber music was not congenial to many Romantic composers; on the one hand it lacked the intimate personal expressiveness of the solo piano piece or the Lied and on the other the glowing colors and overpowering sound of orchestral music. The best works in this medium in the nineteenth century came from those composers who had the closest affinity with the Classical tradition—Schubert and Brahms pre-eminently, Mendelssohn and Schumann to a lesser degree.

Schubert's first quartets, modeled after Mozart and Haydn, were written primarily for the pleasure of his circle of friends. The most popular work from his earlier period is the *Forellen* or *Trout Quintet* for piano and strings (1819), so called because between the scherzo and the finale there is an additional movement (*andantino*) consisting of variations on his own song *Die Forelle*. Three important works of his maturity are the quartets in A minor (D. 804, 1824), D minor (D. 810, 1824–26), and G major (D. 887, 1826).

Schubert's chamber music

The A minor quartet is an outpouring of sadness, elegiac in the first movement and minuet, full of Schubertian melody and beautiful modulations, but with a cheerful finale in Hungarian style. The Quartet in D minor is more grimly serious and more consistent in feeling. It is built around the second movement, a set of variations on Schubert's own song, *Death and the Maiden*. Within the sustained

unity of the quartet as a whole each movement offers variety of
thematic ideas, developed with great skill and contrapuntal ingenuity.
The G major quartet is on a larger scale than either of the other two;
its form is as perfect as that of the D minor quartet, but it is even more
abundant in musical content. It opens with one of the most remarkable
instances of Schubert's device of alternating major and minor forms
of the triad, reversed and differently colored at the recapitulation (see
Example 89), and the whole is full of harmonic boldness.

First Movement, Quartet in G Major (D. 887), Schubert   Example 89

Undoubtedly Schubert's masterpiece of chamber music is the String
Quintet in C major (D. 956), written during the last year of his life.
As in Boccherini's quintets, the added instrument is a second violoncello, and Schubert obtains from this combination some of the most
exquisite sound effects in all Romantic music. The Quintet has the
profound lyricism, the unobtrusive contrapuntal mastery, the long
melodic lines (for example, the first fifteen measures of the Adagio),
and the wealth of harmonic invention that characterize the late piano
sonatas. The finale, like that of the Quartet in A minor, is in a more
popular style, releasing the tension built up by the first three movements.

Mendelssohn's published chamber music comprises six string quartets, two quintets, an octet, a sextet for piano and strings, and two
piano trios, as well as a sonata for piano and violin, two sonatas for
piano and violoncello, and a few lesser works and arrangements. Very
few of these pieces are as interesting as his symphonic productions.
Mendelssohn writes smoothly, if diffusely, in the Classical forms; but
his Romantic feeling for descriptive tone color finds relatively little
scope in the medium of chamber music. An exception, however, is the
early Octet (1825), particularly the scherzo, which is a fine example
of Mendelssohn's inimitable style in this type of movement. The two   359

piano trios (D minor, Op. 49 and C minor, Op. 66) are among the
most popular of Mendelssohn's chamber works and well display both
the excellences and the weaknesses of the composer in this field—
tuneful, attractive themes, vigorous idiomatic writing, but occasional
looseness of form and repetitiousness in the development of the
material.

Schumann's string quartets reveal the influence of Beethoven not
only in general aim but also in some details: developments are frequently contrapuntal, and the *Andante quasi variazioni* of the second
Quartet, a movement in A-flat major, is reminiscent of the Adagio of

*Schumann's
chamber music*

*Mendelssohn's autograph of the second page of the String Octet Op. 20.
(Library of Congress)*

Beethoven's Op. 127. Schumann's third quartet, in A major, is a deeply
Romantic work, with a particularly beautiful slow movement. The
Piano Quartet, Op. 47, is less successful than the Piano Quintet, Op.
44, which is a splendid example of the mature style of this most
romantic of all the Romantic composers.

Brahms is the giant among composers of chamber music in the
Romantic era, the true successor of Beethoven in this field as in that
of the symphony. Not only is the quantity of his production impressive—twenty-four works in all—but it includes at least a half-dozen
masterpieces of the first rank. His first published chamber work was
a Piano Trio in B (Op. 8, 1854), which he issued again in a thoroughly
rewritten version in 1891. Two string sextets—Op. 18 in B-flat (1862)
and Op. 36 in G (1867)—make an interesting contrast. The B-flat
Sextet is a hearty work of ample dimensions, combining humor and
Classical poise; the slow movement is a set of variations in D minor
and the finale is a Haydn-like rondo form with a big coda. The Sextet
in G has a more serene mood, with widely spaced transparent sonorities in the opening Allegro and a quietly vivacious finale; the second
movement, labeled Scherzo, is a semi-serious moderate Allegro in
2/4 time in G minor—a type of movement that Brahms also employed,
with modifications, in his symphonies—and the Adagio, in the form
of a theme in E minor with five variations, may be considered an
epitome of some of Brahms's most individual harmonic and rhythmic
procedures.

Two piano quartets, Op. 25 in G minor and Op. 26 in A major, date
from the late 1850's. The first is one of the most original and most
popular of Brahms's chamber works with its mysterious, Romantic
second movement (called Intermezzo) and lively Hungarian rondo
finale on a theme of three-measure phrases. These two quartets contrast with each other much as do the first two string sextets. The third
Piano Quartet (Op. 60, C minor) was given its final form in 1874; it
is a grandly tragic composition, with the concentration of material
characteristic of Brahms's later works.

The "climax of Brahms's first maturity" is the great Piano Quintet
in F minor, Op. 34A. Brahms originally composed this in 1862 as a
string quintet with two violoncellos; he later arranged it for two
pianos, and then, still unsatisfied, combined the string and pianoforte
sonorities for the final version (1864). The first movement is a powerful, closely knit Allegro in sonata form, with a second theme group in
C-sharp minor, a well integrated development section, and a coda that
begins *pianissimo* with a quiet contrapuntal improvisation on the
principal theme above a tonic pedal and then rises to end in the
stormy mood of the beginning. The slow movement (A-flat) is a
beautiful Schubertian three-part *Andante un poco adagio* with a
middle section in E major. Both the spirit and the themes of the
Scherzo recall those of the corresponding movement in Beethoven's
Fifth Symphony. The rousing Finale is preceded by a broad *poco*

sostenuto which is like a sketch for the even broader introduction to the last movement of Brahms's First Symphony.

The Trio Op. 40 for piano, violin, and waldhorn (the natural horn, without valves) is another successful example of the union of a sonorous, expressive Romantic idiom with forms well grounded in Classical practice. The Trio was composed in 1865; it brings to an end what may be called, by analogy with Beethoven, Brahms's second period. After a pause of eight years came the two string quartets in C minor and A minor, Op. 51; then in 1876 (the year of the First Symphony) the String Quartet in B-flat, Op. 67. The eloquent *Grave ed appassionato* of the String Quintet in F major, Op. 88 (1882) is combined with the scherzo in a single movement—a device used by César Franck seven years later in his Symphony.

Outstanding among Brahms's later works are the two piano trios Op. 87 in C major (1882) and Op. 101 in C minor (1886), the String Quintet in G major Op. 111 (1890), and the profound Clarinet Quintet in B minor, Op. 115 (1891). All these have something of the same character as Beethoven's later quartets and piano sonatas: the musical ideas are pure, with a purity that is sometimes thoughtlessly called abstract because it is so concretely musical as to be undefinable in any

Brahms's autograph of the first page of the Piano Quintet Op. 34. (Library of Congress)

other medium; textures are smoothly contrapuntal; and forms are
handled with a freedom that is the result of logic in movement and
conciseness in statement.

A special category of Brahms's chamber music consists of sonatas
for a single instrument with piano. There are three such sonatas for
violin, two for violoncello, and two for clarinet. All except the first
violoncello sonata (1862–65) are late works. The first two violin
sonatas (G major, Op. 78, 1878; A major, Op. 100, 1886) contain some
of Brahms's most lyric and melodious writing; the third (D minor,
Op. 108, 1887) is on a more symphonic scale. The clarinet sonatas
Op. 120 (F minor and E-flat major), written in 1894, may be grouped
with the piano pieces Opp. 116–119, the Clarinet Quintet, the *Four
Serious Songs,* and the organ chorale preludes as among the ripest
achievements of the composer whose music demonstrated, more clearly than that of any other nineteenth-century composer, that the flower
of Romanticism had deep roots in the Classical tradition.

The founder of modern French chamber music was César Franck;
his chief works in this field are a Piano Quintet in F minor (1879), a
String Quartet in D major (1889); and the well-known Violin Sonata
in A major (1886). All these works employ cyclical themes—that is,
themes that recur identically or transformed in two or more different
movements.

Music for Orchestra

The two main tendencies in orchestral music of the first half of the
nineteenth century may be roughly designated as conservative (represented by Schubert, Mendelssohn, and Schumann) and radical (represented by Berlioz and Liszt). Generally speaking, the conservative
composers were those whose musical imagination worked naturally
within the formal structures, themes, harmonies, and orchestrations
that had been inherited from the Classical period; if these composers
gave descriptive titles to their works they did so incidentally and
without emphasis. The radicals were those whose creative imagination
was less apt to be stimulated by a strictly musical idea than by a
literary or some other extra-musical impulse; and precisely because
the impulse came from outside the conventional domain of music,
the resulting composition was likely to be unconventional in some
respects—in form, for instance—although in other respects it might
adhere to Classical usage.

The most important symphonies of Schubert—the *Unfinished* in
B minor of 1822 and the great C major Symphony of 1828—exemplify
the harmonic originality which has already been noted as a feature of
his style. A new element, related to Schubert's harmonic sensitivity, is
his Romantic feeling for orchestral tone color. The *Unfinished* may
be called the first truly Romantic symphony. In the C major Sym-

phony Schubert has expanded his material almost to the breaking point; the "heavenly length" which Schumann admired in this work would be less heavenly if it were not for the beauty of Schubert's melodies.

*Mendelssohn's
symphonies*

With Mendelssohn we enter the realm of Romantic landscapes. His two most important symphonies carry geographical subtitles—the *Italian* (1833) and the *Scotch* (1842). In these works Mendelssohn records some typical German Romantic impressions of the south and the north. In both symphonies Mendelssohn's writing is, as always, impeccable, and he has skilfully fitted his melodious Romantic themes into the regular Classical forms. The four divisions of the *Scotch Symphony* are linked by the use of portions of the slow introduction

Sketch of introduction and beginning of first movement of Schumann's First Symphony. (Library of Congress)

to the first movement as introductions to the following two move-
ments, as well as by subtle similarities of melodic outline among many of the themes throughout the work.

to the first movement as introductions to the following two movements, as well as by subtle similarities of melodic outline among many
of the themes throughout the work.

Mendelssohn's peculiar genius for musical landscapes is especially
evident in his overtures *The Hebrides* (or *Fingal's Cave;* 1832) and
Calm Sea and Prosperous Voyage (1828–32), while *Melusine* (1833)
is a symphonic incarnation of the early Romantic spirit of the fairy
tale. Among his incidental music for plays, the overture for Victor
Hugo's *Ruy Blas* (1839) is excelled only by the incomparable *Midsummer Night's Dream* overture, written at the age of seventeen—
a work that set the standard for all subsequent concert overtures of
the Romantic period. All this music, while it may be called program-

*Page 1 of the autograph score of Schumann's First Symphony. (Library
of Congress)*

matic (in the same sense as Beethoven's *Pastoral Symphony*), and while it is certainly Romantic in the quality of its imagination and its treatment of the orchestra, is nonetheless Classical in outline (most of the overtures, for example, are in sonata form), and Classical moreover in that it avoids extremes of feeling and never allows the extramusical inspiration to disturb the musical balance. The program is no more than a faint mist about the structure, lending charm to the view but not obscuring the outlines. Essentially the qualities of Mendelssohn's symphonies and overtures are not different from those of his Violin Concerto (1844), one of his masterpieces and one of the greatest of all violin concertos.

Schumann's symphonies

Schumann's first two published symphonies were composed in 1841. The first, in B-flat major, is called the *Spring Symphony*, from some indications given by the composer himself and from his intention at one time to prefix a descriptive title to each movement.

The Symphony in D minor was originally called a symphonic fantasia. We do not know whether Schumann had any program in mind in connection with this symphony, but the fantasia element is present in the irregular form of the first Allegro and in the fact that each movement contains themes derived from motives announced in the slow introduction to the first. Schumann did not allow his D minor Symphony to be published until 1851, after he had made extensive revisions; in consequence this symphony, though second in order of composition, was fourth in order of publication, and is so numbered.

The Second Symphony (again, the second to be published), in C major (1846), is the most severely Classical of Schumann's symphonies, but except for the Adagio its musical interest is less than that of the two earlier works. The *Rhenish Symphony* in E-flat (1850) is vaguely programmatic and contains some characteristically vigorous themes, though on the whole it is less spontaneous than the First Symphony. Apart from the symphonies and the piano concerto, Schumann's chief orchestral work is the overture from his incidental music to Byron's *Manfred* (1849). His orchestral style in general has been criticized as pianistic, and on the whole he failed to achieve the long lines and the organic unity of Classical symphonic style. The beauty of Schumann's symphonies lies in their details and in the ardor of their Romantic spirit.

Berlioz's symphonies

The diffused scenic effects in the music of Mendelssohn and Schumann seem pale indeed when compared with the feverish and circumstantial drama which is commonly supposed to constitute the story of Berlioz's *Symphonie fantastique* (1830). Partly out of compliance with the fashion of the time and partly because his imagination always tended to run in parallel literary and musical channels, Berlioz provided a program for this symphony. It is unfortunate that he did so, and doubly unfortunate that he once subtitled the work "Episode in the Life of an Artist"; for ever since, commentators have insisted on

regarding this symphony as a highly colored musical autobiography and have also ignored Berlioz's direction that at concert performances the program need not be given out, since the composer hoped that the symphony would "of itself, and irrespective of any dramatic aim, offer an interest in the musical sense alone."

There is nothing revolutionary about the main formal outlines of the *Symphonie fantastique*. The principal novelty is the recurrence of the opening theme of the first Allegro (the *idée fixe*, the obsessive image of the hero's beloved, according to the program) in all the other

Hector Berlioz (1803–1869).

movements. One salient aspect of Berlioz's originality is his orchestration; he had no textbooks and few models to help him, but his extraordinary aural imagination and restless inventiveness in the realm of orchestral sonorities is evident in practically every measure of the *Symphonie fantastique*. To mention but one example: in the coda of the Adagio there is a passage for solo English horn and four kettledrums intended to suggest "distant thunder"—a marvelously poetic and evocative twenty-two measures, and no more an example of realism (if by that word is meant mere literal imitation of natural noises) than the bird songs in the slow movement of the *Pastoral Symphony*.

Berlioz's second symphony, *Harold in Italy* (1834), is a set of four scenes suggested by his reading of Lord Byron's *Childe Harold*. As with the *Symphonie fantastique*, the movements are in a conventional Classical order. There is a connecting recurrent theme, given chiefly to a solo viola, and this instrument is featured throughout somewhat in the manner of a concerto; but the soloist is less dominant than in an ordinary concerto, and in fact much of the symphony is scored so lightly as to suggest chamber music.

Five years after *Harold in Italy* Berlioz produced his "dramatic symphony," *Romeo and Juliet*, for orchestra, soloists, and chorus, in seven movements. In adding voices to the symphonic orchestra, he was following the example of Beethoven; but in this work the voices enter in the first movement (after an instrumental introduction) and are used in three of the remaining ones as well, so that the entire symphony, although the scheme of the Classical order of movements can still be traced, begins to approach the form of the "dramatic legend" which the composer later perfected in his *Damnation of Faust* (1846). Nonetheless, *Romeo and Juliet* is essentially a symphonic work, and may be understood as an extension of the idea of the *Symphonie fantastique*. Only the finale is decidedly operatic in character.

Among Berlioz's other symphonic works are several overtures (including the familiar *Roman Carnival*, 1844) and the *Funeral and Triumphal Symphony*, composed for a national ceremony in 1840. But his importance for the history of nineteenth-century instrumental music rests chiefly on his first three symphonies, especially the *Symphonie fantastique*. Even though his conception of the relation between music and program was widely misunderstood, these works made Berlioz the first leader of the radical wing of the Romantic movement, and all subsequent composers of program music—including Strauss and Debussy—were indebted to him. His orchestration initiated a new era: by example and precept he was the founder of modern orchestral conducting; he enriched Romantic music with new resources of harmony, color, expression, and form; his use of a recurrent theme in different movements (as in the *Symphonie fantastique* and *Harold in Italy*) was an important step in the development of the cyclical symphonic forms of the later Romantic period; and his symphonies, particularly *Romeo and Juliet*, were among the sources upon which Wagner drew in establishing the form of his own music dramas.

The foremost composer of program music after Berlioz was Franz Liszt, twelve of whose symphonic poems were written between 1848 and 1858; a thirteenth was written in 1881–82. The name *symphonic poem* is significant: these works are symphonic but Liszt did not call them symphonies presumably because they are relatively short and are not divided into separate movements in a conventional order. Instead, each is a continuous form with various sections more or less contrasting in character and tempo, and a few themes which are developed, repeated, varied, or transformed in accordance with the particular design of each work. *Les Préludes*, the only one of them that is still much played, is well designed, melodious, and effectively scored; but its idiom, like that of some of Liszt's other compositions, seems rhetorical, in a bad sense. The form of the symphonic poem was imitated by such composers as Smetana (*Má Vlast*), Franck (*Psyché*), Saint-Saëns (*Le Rouet d'Omphale, Danse macabre*), and Tchaikovsky (*Romeo and Juliet*).

Liszt's symphonic poems

Liszt's two symphonies are as programmatic as his symphonic poems. His masterpiece, the *Faust Symphony* (1854), was dedicated to Berlioz; it consists of three movements entitled respectively "Faust," "Gretchen," and "Mephistopheles," with a finale (added later) which is a setting, for tenor soloist and chorus of men's voices, of the *chorus mysticus* which closes Goethe's drama. The first three movements correspond to the Classical plan: introduction and Allegro (in sonata form), Andante (three-part form), and Scherzo (three-part form, followed by a long additional development and coda).

It is a far journey from Liszt's seething Romanticism to the Olympian realm of Brahms's four symphonies. The Classical reaction of the second half of the nineteenth century is epitomized in these works. The First Symphony, in C minor, was finished after many years of work in 1876, when the composer was forty-three; the second, in D major, appeared in 1877, while the last two (F major and E minor) were composed in 1883 and 1885 respectively. To the works already mentioned are to be added the Violin Concerto in D major (1878), which ranks with Beethoven's concerto in the literature of this instrument, and the Double Concerto in A minor for violin and violoncello, Op. 102 (1887).

The Brahms symphonies are Classical in several respects: they are laid out in the customary design of four movements, each of which has a form recognizably close to the Classical pattern; they make use of the Classical techniques of counterpoint and motivic development; and they have no specified program—that is, they are absolute music in the same sense as Brahms's chamber works. At the same time the symphonies are Romantic in their harmonic idiom, in their full, multi-colored orchestral sound, and in other general features of their musical language. Yet they are no mere synthesis of Classicism and Romanticism; Brahms's style is consistent and individual, and various elements may be distinguished within it—among them a profoundly expressive, Schubertian, lyrical breadth of melodic line, a ballad-like quality of Romantic strangeness, and a fundamental respect for tradition as against the individualistic approach to music of Berlioz and Liszt. For Brahms, inspiration was not enough: craftsmanship was equally important; ideas had to be soberly thought out and brought to a finally perfect form. In this regard Brahms, whether he realized it or not, was responding to a general tendency of his time. The childlike freshness and the youthful ardor of Romanticism were alike spent by the middle of the century, and the wild oats period was over; a return to discipline, a revival of order and form, is apparent in the late works of Schumann and Berlioz, and even in those of Liszt and Wagner. Brahms's symphonies illustrate the trend even more clearly.

The First is the most Romantic. In key and general construction it takes its departure from Beethoven's Fifth; it is the only one of Brahms's symphonies which uses the Romantic formula of struggle (in minor) leading to triumph (in major).

The Second Symphony, in contrast to the First, has a peaceful, pastoral character, though not without serious undertones. Its third movement (like the corresponding movement in the First and Third Symphonies) has the lyrical rhythmic grace of an intermezzo rather than the daemonic intensity of the Beethoven scherzo; it is of the type that Brahms had created in the G major Sextet of 1867.

The Third Symphony has been called Brahms's *Eroica*. Its opening measures afford a particularly good illustration of one characteristic trait in his harmonic usage, the cross-relation of the minor and major

Example 90

Outline of First Theme of Third Symphony, Brahms

forms of the tonic triad (see Example 90); the rising F–A-flat–F motive of the bass is conspicuous again in the last movement of this symphony, which begins in F minor and does not settle in F major until the coda.

First page of the autograph score of Brahms's Third Symphony. (Library of Congress)

Anton Bruckner (1824–1896).

The Andante of the Fourth Symphony is one of Brahms's ballades-que movements, the mood being suggested by the modal (Phrygian) tinge of the introduction and principal theme. The finale of this symphony is written in an unusual form: a passacaglia or chaconne, consisting of thirty-two variations and a brief coda on an ostinato eight-measure theme.

César Franck's only symphony (1888) shows some trace of Liszt in its chromatic harmonies and cyclical treatment of themes. But it is nonprogrammatic, and its stylistic elements are welded into a highly individual work, the influence of which was strongly felt by the following generation of composers in France. *Franck's symphony*

Bruckner's symphonies may perhaps best be understood as the ex-pression of a profound religious spirit, which is revealed not only by quotation of themes from his Masses and *Te Deum,* but also by the prevailing serious, weighty mood of the symphonies as a whole; it is especially evident in the combination of mystic ecstasy and tonal splendor of the chorale-like themes that are the climaxes of his finales (and sometimes also of the first movements). Bruckner's symphonies begin, like Beethoven's Ninth, with a vague agitation in the strings, out of which the theme emerges and builds up in a *crescendo.* These first themes have what may be called an elemental character; they begin with conspicuous emphasis on the notes of the tonic triad, ex-tended usually over an octave or more, and set the tonality of the movement in most positive terms; the favorite rhythmic formula is the pattern $\left(\begin{smallmatrix} 4 \\ 4 \end{smallmatrix}\right)$ ♩ ♩ ♩ ♩ ♩. The finales open in the same way and usually with the same kind of theme, which may even so closely resemble that of the first movement as to suggest cyclical recurrence. The first- *Bruckner's symphonies*

371

theme complex is followed by the "song-theme group" (as Bruckner called it), and this in turn by a lengthy closing section in which a chorale-like theme may be introduced. The movement continues with development and recapitulation (sometimes merged) and a coda which often presents a grand apotheosis of the preceding themes. Both the first and last movements, though in *allegro* tempo, give the effect of moving slowly because of their intentionally static harmonic rhythm and block-like structure. The slow movements, usually cast in a broad sonata-like form with extended coda, are devout and solemn; those of the last three symphonies are especially impressive. The Scherzos reveal a different aspect of Bruckner's musical personality. Their energy is like Beethoven's, but the melodies and rhythms of their trios reflect the spirit of Austrian popular songs and rustic dances.

Bruckner had the misfortune to live in Vienna under the shadow of Brahms and to be continually attacked by critics as a disciple of Wagner. His symphonies received little acclaim during his lifetime; even today only two of them—the Fourth and Seventh—are played often outside Vienna and a few other European cities. No doubt their length and their monumental and solemn character have worked against their popular acceptance. Bruckner's importance rests on the integrity of his work, its significance as a personal resolution of the basic musical issues of the late nineteenth century, and its influence on the later Viennese composers, Mahler and Schoenberg.

Other composers

The only remaining symphonists to be mentioned are the Bohemians Bedřich Smetana (1824–1884) and Antonin Dvořák (1841–1904) and the Russian, Peter Ilyich Tchaikovsky (1840–1893). They have a place in this chapter because, although their music is in some respects an outgrowth of nationalist ideas, their symphonies are essentially in the line of the German Romantic tradition. Smetana was chiefly a disciple of Liszt, Dvořák of Brahms. Dvořák is the more important of the two in this context since his best works are his chamber music and symphonies—particularly the Fourth and the Fifth (*From the New World*)—whereas Smetana, except for the six symphonic poems collectively entitled *Má Vlast* (*My Fatherland*) and the string quartet *From My Life*, is most distinguished as an opera composer.

Tchaikovsky's principal orchestral works are his last three symphonies (No. 4, F minor, 1877; No. 5, E minor, 1888; No. 6 [*Pathétique*], B minor, 1893), the symphonic fantasia, *Francesca da Rimini* (1877), the symphonic poem *Romeo and Juliet* (1869, 1880), the First Piano Concerto in B-flat minor (1875), and the Violin Concerto (1878). The immense popularity of the symphonies is due to their tunefulness, brilliant orchestration, and somewhat theatrical exhibition of Romantic emotion. In the programmatic tone poems Tchaikovsky was not plagued with the necessity of fitting his ideas into the conventional mold of the symphony. The symphonies themselves are program music thinly disguised, but only the Sixth approaches the

*Peter Ilyich Tchaikovsky (1840–
1893), as he appeared in his student
days. (Bettmann Archive)*

symphonic ideal of a musical content really suited to the form.
Tchaikovsky is at his best in less pretentious music, particularly his
ballets *Swan Lake* (1876), *The Sleeping Beauty* (1890), and *The
Nutcracker* (1892).

XVIII Nineteenth-Century Opera and Music Drama

France

The combined influences of Gluck, the Revolution, and the Napoleonic Empire made Paris the operatic capital of Europe during the first half of the nineteenth century, and favored the rise there of a certain type of serious opera that is exemplified in *La Vestale* (1807). The composer of this work was Napoleon's favorite musician, Gasparo Spontini (1774–1851), an Italian who had come to Paris in 1803 and who had a second career after 1820 as Court Music Director at Berlin. In *La Vestale* Spontini united the heroic, statuesque character of the late Gluck operas with the heightened dramatic tension of the then popular rescue plot, and clothed the whole in a grand display of solo, choral, and orchestral magnificence.

Grand opera

With the rise of a numerous and influential middle class after 1820, a new kind of opera came into being, designed to appeal to the relatively uncultured audiences who thronged the theatres in search of excitement and entertainment. The leader of this school of *grand opera*, as it came to be known, was Giacomo Meyerbeer (1791–1864), whose two operas *Robert le diable* (*Robert the Devil*, 1831) and *Les Huguenots* (1836) definitely established the style.

Meyerbeer's music was thoroughly eclectic and included the most popular elements of both the Italian and the French styles. It differed from Spontini's *Vestale* and other operas of the Napoleonic period not so much in externals as in the efficiency with which it set about achieving its main purpose, which was to give people what they wanted. For a public which presumably cared above all for sentiment and sensationalism, librettists and composers seemed willing to sacrifice both dramatic and musical integrity wherever necessary to produce an effect. Nevertheless, Meyerbeer was an expert craftsman, and his treatment of the orchestra, in particular, influenced Verdi and many other later composers; moreover, it must be acknowledged that some of his works—notably *Dinorah* (1859) and his two later grand operas *Le Prophète* (1849) and *L'Africaine* (first performed in 1865)—were less beset by the artistic shortcomings that marred *Robert* and *Les Huguenots*. Other composers of grand opera around 1830 were Rossini (*Guillaume Tell;* 1829) and Jacques Fromental Halévy (1799–1862), whose masterpiece, *La Juive* (*The Jewess;* 1835), deservedly outlasted Meyerbeer's works. *La Juive* and *Guillaume Tell* are the best of the grand operas of this period because they best incorporate the essential grandeur of the form—grandeur of structure and of style —in music that effectively serves more than the externals of the action.

Side by side with the grand opera in France, the *opéra comique* pursued its course during the Romantic period. As in the eighteenth century, the technical difference between these two was that the *opéra comique* used spoken dialogue instead of recitative. Apart from this, the principal differences were those of size and subject matter. The *opéra comique* was less pretentious than grand opera, required fewer singers and players, and was written in a much simpler musical idiom; its plots as a rule presented straightforward comedy or semiserious drama instead of the huge historical pageantry of grand opera. Two kinds of *opéra comique* may be distinguished in the early part of the nineteenth century, namely the romantic and the comic; it is not possible to maintain this distinction too rigidly, however, since many works possessed characteristics of both types. Predominantly romantic in plot, melodious, graceful, and sentimental in music, was the extremely popular *La Dame blanche* (*The White Lady*) by François Adrien Boieldieu (1775–1834), which was first performed at Paris in 1825. A romantic *opéra comique* was *Zampa* (1831) by Ferdinand Herold (1791–1833).

A more mordant Parisian style is evident in the work of Daniel François Esprit Auber (1782–1871), who in *Fra Diavolo* (1830) and his many other comic operas mingled romantic and humorous elements in tuneful music of considerable melodic originality. A new genre, the *opéra bouffe*, which emphasized the smart, witty, and satirical elements of comic opera, appeared at Paris in the 1860's. Its founder was Jacques Offenbach (1819–1880), whose *Orphée aux enfers* (*Orpheus in the Underworld;* 1858) and *La Belle Hélène* (1864) may be taken as typical. Offenbach's work influenced developments in comic opera elsewhere: the operettas of Gilbert and Sullivan in England (*The Mikado*, 1885) and those of a Viennese school whose best-known representative is Johann Strauss the Younger (*Die Fledermaus* [*The Bat*]; 1874).

The romantic type of *opéra comique* developed toward a form for which the designation "lyric opera" seems appropriate. Lyric opera lies somewhere between light *opéra comique* and grand opera. Like the *opéra comique*, its main appeal is through melody; its subject matter is Romantic drama or fantasy, and its general scale is larger than that of the *opéra comique*, although still not so huge as that of the typical grand opera.

The most famous lyric opera is Gounod's *Faust*, which was first given in 1859 as an *opéra comique* (that is, with spoken dialogue) and later arranged by the composer in its now familiar form with recitatives. Gounod wisely restricted himself to Part One of Goethe's drama, dealing chiefly with the tragic love affair of Faust and Gretchen, for which his musical gifts were adequate. The result is a work of just proportions, in an elegant lyric style, with attractive melodies, sufficiently expressive but without Romantic excess.

A landmark in the history of French opera was Georges Bizet's (1838–1875) *Carmen*, first performed at Paris in 1875. Like the original version of *Faust*, *Carmen* was classified as an *opéra comique* because it contained spoken dialogue (later set in recitative by another composer); but the fact that this stark, amoral drama could ever be called "*comique*" is simply an indication that by this time the distinction between opera and *opéra comique* had become a mere technicality. The music of *Carmen* has an extraordinary rhythmic and melodic vitality; it is spare in texture and beautifully orchestrated, obtaining the utmost dramatic effect always with the most economical means.

Hector Berlioz contributed more than any other composer to the glory of French Romantic opera. His *Damnation of Faust* may be included here, although strictly speaking it is a "dramatic legend" rather than an opera and is not intended for stage performance. Nonetheless, it is one of the most diversified and most inspired of Berlioz's works; the familiar orchestral excerpts (including the Hungarian "Rákóczy" March) give but a faint and partial impression of its riches.

The opera *Benvenuto Cellini* (1838) in another example of this composer's new way with traditional forms. Its general plan is, like that of *The Damnation of Faust*, a chain of broadly conceived episodes rather than a plot completely and minutely developed. The score is notable for the vigor and variety of its music and for the treatment of the crowd scenes, which foreshadow those of Wagner's *Meistersinger*. The crown of Berlioz's dramatic works is the great five-act opera *Les Troyens*, composed in 1856–1858. *Les Troyens* is unlike any other opera. The text, by Berlioz himself, is based on the second and fourth books of Vergil's *Aeneid*; as with *Cellini* and *Faust*, only the essential stages of the action are presented, in a series of mighty scene-complexes. The drama preserves the antique, suprapersonal, epic quality of Vergil's poem, and the music speaks in the same accents. Not a note is there for mere effect; the style is severe, almost ascetic by comparison with some of Berlioz's earlier works. At the same time every passion, every scene and incident, are brought to life on a heroic scale. *Les Troyens* is the Romantic consummation of the French opera tradition in the line of descent from Rameau and Gluck.

Italy

The history of Italian opera in the nineteenth century may be understood as the orderly evolution of an established tradition, healthily grounded in the life of the nation. Italy was less susceptible than northern countries to the seductions of the Romantic movement, and her composers were therefore less quickly tempted to try new and radical experiments. Romantic elements permeated Italian opera only gradually, and never to the same degree as in Germany and France. Moreover, opera was the only important Italian musical outlet in this period, so that the genius of the nation was largely concentrated on this one form; and such a situation also tended to encourage a conservative attitude.

Gioacchino Rossini (1792–1868), the principal Italian composer of the early nineteenth century, was endowed with a pronounced gift for melody and a flair for stage effect that brought him quick success.

Gioacchino Rossini

Gioacchino Rossini (1792–1868).

Between the ages of eighteen and thirty he produced in Italy thirty-two operas and two oratorios, in addition to a dozen cantatas, two symphonies, and a few other instrumental works.

Opera buffa was congenial to Rossini, and many of his works in this genre sound as fresh today as when they were first written. His masterpiece, *Il Barbiere di Siviglia* (*The Barber of Seville*, Rome; 1816), ranks with Mozart's *Figaro* and Verdi's *Falstaff* among the supreme examples of Italian comic opera.

Rossini's style combines a spontaneous and inexhaustible flow of melody with pungent rhythms, clear phraseology, well-shaped and sometimes quite original structure of the musical period, a spare texture, clean and discriminative orchestration, and a harmonic scheme which, though not complex, is by no means always conventional. He is a master of comic delineation, both of characters and situations—comic, not merely witty, for at his best he is able, like Mozart and

Verdi, to make us feel the hint of pathos that underlies all high comedy. Rossini's ensembles, that type of scene so characteristic of the *opera buffa*, are managed with sparkle and gusto.

Although Rossini wrote no more operas after 1829, his influence dominated Italian opera through the first half of the century. As far as the bulk of his work is concerned, Rossini represented the deep-rooted Italian conviction that an opera is in essence the highest manifestation of an intensely cultivated art of song, and that its primary purpose is to delight and move the hearer by music that is melodious, unsentimental, spontaneous, and, in every sense of the word, popular. This national ideal was important in the Romantic period as a counter-balance to the different conceptions of opera that were held in France and Germany.

Gaetano Donizetti

One of the most prolific Italian composers of the second quarter of the century was Gaetano Donizetti (1797–1848), who in addition to some seventy operas composed about a hundred songs, several symphonies, oratorios, cantatas, chamber music, and church music. Donizetti had some of Rossini's instinct for the theatre and his talent for melody, and in *Don Pasquale* (1843) he created a work that can well endure comparison with *Il Barbiere*. On the whole his comic operas stand the test of time better than his serious ones. The rough, impulsive character of his music is well adapted to the representation of crude, melodramatic situations, but his works—composed for the most part very rapidly and with a view to immediate success—are all too often marred by monotony of harmony, rhythm, and orchestration; yet much of *Lucia di Lammermoor* (1835) and *Linda di Chamounix* (1842), and some scenes in his other operas must be excepted from this criticism.

Vincenzo Bellini

Vincenzo Bellini (1801–1835) may be called the aristocrat of his period. Of his ten operas (all serious) the chief are *La Sonnambula* (*The Sleepwalker*; 1831), *Norma* (1831), and *I Puritani e i Cavalieri* (*The Puritans and the Cavaliers*, Paris; 1835). The style is one of the utmost lyric refinement; the harmony is sensitive, and the intensely expressive melodies have a breadth, a flexibility of form, a certain elegance of curve, and an elegiac tinge of feeling that are often reminiscent of Chopin's nocturnes. Bellini is a master of psychological expression in recitative, of which a splendid example is afforded by the opening number of the second act of *Norma*.

Giuseppe Verdi

The career of Giuseppe Verdi (1813–1901) practically constitutes the history of Italian music for the next fifty years after Donizetti. Except for the *Requiem* and a few other settings of sacred texts, a few songs, and a string quartet, all Verdi's works were written for the stage. The first of his twenty-six operas was produced in 1839, the last in 1893. At no point did Verdi break with the past or experiment radically with new theories; his evolution was toward refinement of aim and technique, and in the end he brought Italian opera to a peak of perfection never since surpassed.

Giuseppe Verdi (1813–1901). Photograph dated Genoa, February 18, 1897.

The only basic Romantic issue that much affected Italian music was nationalism, and in this respect Verdi was uncompromising. He believed wholeheartedly that each nation should cultivate the kind of music that was natural to it; he maintained a resolute independence in his own musical style and deplored the influence of foreign (especially German) ideas in the work of his younger compatriots. Many of his early operas contain choruses that were thinly disguised inflammatory appeals to the patriotism of his countrymen struggling for national unity and against foreign domination during the stirring years of the *Risorgimento;* and Verdi's popularity was further increased when his name became a patriotic symbol and rallying-cry: *"Viva Verdi!"* to Italian patriots stood for *"Viva Vittorio Emanuelo Rè D'Italia!"*— Long live Victor Emanuel, King of Italy.

A profoundly national trait in Verdi was his unswerving adherence to an ideal of opera as human drama—in contrast to the emphasis on romanticized Nature and mythological symbolism in Germany—to be conveyed primarily by means of simple, direct, vocal solo melody —in contrast to the complicated orchestral and choral luxuriance of French grand opera.

Verdi's creative life may be divided into three periods, the first culminating with *Il Trovatore* and *La Traviata* (1853), the second *Early works* with *Aïda* (1871), and the last comprising only *Otello* (1887) and *Falstaff* (1893). With the exception of *Falstaff* and one unsuccessful early work, all Verdi's operas are serious. His main requirements of a libretto were strong emotional situations, contrasts, and speed of action; plausibility was no object. Consequently most of the plots are violent blood-and-thunder melodramas, full of improbable characters

379

and ridiculous coincidences, but with plenty of opportunity for the exciting, lusty, ferocious melodies and rhythms which are especially characteristic of Verdi's early style.

A change in Verdi's style began to be evident with *Luisa Miller* (1849); here, and increasingly henceforward, personages are depicted with finer psychological distinction, and emotion in the music becomes less raw than in the early operas. Characterization, dramatic unity, and melodic invention unite in the masterpiece *Rigoletto* (1851). *La Traviata* (*The Lost One;* 1853) is in a more intimate vein than heretofore, and is remarkable for the appearance of a new kind of melody, a flexible, expressive, semideclamatory arioso which Verdi developed still further in *Otello*.

Two experiments in grand opera were *I Vespri siciliani* (*The Sicilian Vespers;* 1855) and *Don Carlo* (1867), both of which were first performed at Paris. *Don Carlo* is the more successful of the two; its revised version (1884) contains powerful dramatic scenes, as well as some interesting orchestral and harmonic effects typical of Verdi's late style. *Un Ballo in Maschera* (*A Masked Ball;* 1859) and *La Forza del Destino* (*The Power of Destiny*, 1862; revised, 1869) make use of a device fairly common in the nineteenth century and one with which Verdi had experimented already in *Rigoletto* and elsewhere: the recurrence of one or more distinctive themes or motives at crucial points which serves to produce both dramatic and musical unity. All the advances of the second period are gathered up in *Aïda* (1871), which unites the heroic quality of grand opera with sound dramatic structure, subtle character delineation, pathos, and a wealth of melodic, harmonic, and orchestral color.

Sixteen years elapsed before Verdi came before the public with *Otello*, produced at Milan in 1887. The libretto, skilfully adapted

Late works

from Shakespeare's play by the Italian poet and composer Arrigo Boïto (1842–1918), sets forth a powerful human drama which the music penetrates, sustains, and glorifies at every turn. The harmonic language and the orchestration are fresh and vital, yet transparent, never usurping the expressive function of melody or obscuring the voices. A summary idea of these features, as well as of the evolution of Verdi's style in general, can be obtained by comparing the beautiful love duet at the end of the first act of *Otello* with some duets from his earlier operas: *Nabucco* (Act III, "Donna, chi sei?"), *Rigoletto* (end of Act II, "Piangi, fanciulla"), and *Aïda* (end of Act IV, "O terra addio").

Otello was the consummation of Italian tragic opera, *Falstaff* (1893) of *opera buffa*. As *Otello* transfigured dramatic lyrical melody, so *Falstaff* transfigured that characteristic element of *opera buffa*, the ensemble. Carried along over a nimble, fine-spun, endlessly varied orchestral background, the comedy speeds to its climaxes in the great finales of the second and third acts. At times Verdi seems to be satirizing the entire Romantic century, himself included. The last scene culminates in a fugue to the words "tutto nel mondo è burla"— "all the world's a joke, all men are born fools."

In all Verdi's operas, from *Nabucco* to *Falstaff*, one trait is constant: a combination of primitive, earthy, elemental emotional force with directness, clarity and—beneath all its refinement of detail—fundamental simplicity of utterance. Verdi is essentially more Classical than Romantic in spirit; his Classicism is attained not by triumphing over Romanticism, as Brahms did, but rather by almost ignoring it. His relation to the Romantic movement might be suggested by the contrast between his attitude and that of the northern Romantics toward Nature. The depiction of the natural background in Verdi's operas is concise, suggestive, almost formalized, like the landscapes in Renaissance Italian paintings—the storm music in *Rigoletto* and *Otello*, for example, or the exotic atmosphere in *Aïda*. His attitude toward Nature is completely unsentimental. All his interest is in humanity; Nature is there to be used, not worshiped. Verdi is the only eminent composer in history who was also a successful farmer.

German Romantic Opera

One of the distinguishing marks of the nineteenth century, as we have seen, was the strong mutual influence between music and literature. The composite art form of opera is well adapted to display the effects of such influences; and since Germany was the country in which Romanticism flourished most intensely, some of the most far-reaching developments and ramifications of the whole Romantic movement are exhibited in German opera. The definitive work that established German Romantic opera was Weber's *Der Freischütz*, first performed at Berlin in 1821.

Carl Maria von Weber (1786–1826).

Weber Der Freischütz

There is no intelligible brief English equivalent for the title. The story revolves about a situation common in folklore and immortalized in Goethe's *Faust:* a man has sold his soul to the devil in return for earthly favors—in this instance, for some magic bullets which will enable him to win a contest of marksmanship and with it the hand of the lady he loves. As usual, the devil is cheated; the hero is redeemed by his lady's pure love from the consequences of his bargain, and all ends well. The sombre forest background is depicted idyllically by the melody for horns at the beginning of the overture and diabolically in the eerie midnight "Wolf's Glen" scene of the casting of the magic bullets (finale of Act II). Rustic choruses, marches, dances, and airs mingle in the score with full-bodied arias in Italian style. The quintessence of mysterious Romantic suggestion through orchestration and harmony is in the twelve measures at the end of the Adagio introduction to the overture; likewise, it is the orchestration and the strange harmonic scheme (contrast of F-sharp minor and C minor) that chiefly contribute to the musical effectiveness of the Wolf's Glen scene, a model of Romantic depiction of supernatural horror. The overture to *Der Freischütz* is not, like so many opera overtures of the early nineteenth century, a simple medley of tunes; rather, like the overtures of Beethoven, it is a complete symphonic first movement in sonata form with a slow introduction.

The immense popular success of *Der Freischütz*—a success based on its appeal to national sentiment as well as on the beauty of the music—was not repeated either by Weber's later works or by those of his successors. Most of Schubert's operas and *Singspiele*—a half dozen of each, and several others uncompleted—never reached the stage during his lifetime, and have remained without influence, though they contain a great deal of excellent music. In his best opera, *Fierrabras* (1823), there are some interesting anticipations of the leitmotif technique. German opera for twenty years after Weber was carried on by a number of estimable second-class composers, chief of whom were Heinrich Marschner (1795–1861) and Albert Lortzing (1801–1851). Marschner specialized in Romantic *Singspiele* of a semipopular sort; his most important work, *Hans Heiling* (1833), derives from Weber and at the same time looks forward to Wagner in both its plot and its musical style. Lortzing's *Zar und Zimmermann* (*Czar and Carpenter*; 1837) is a good example of the comic genre in which he excelled.

Richard Wagner: The Music Drama

The outstanding composer of German opera, and one of the crucial figures in the history of nineteenth-century music, was Richard Wagner (1813–1883). Wagner's significance is threefold: He brought

Richard Wagner (1813–1883).

German Romantic opera to its consummation, in much the same way that Verdi brought Italian opera; he created a new form, the *music drama;* and the harmonic idiom of his late works carried to the limit the Romantic tendencies toward the dissolution of Classical tonality, becoming the starting point for developments still active to the present day. In addition, Wagner's writings had considerable influence on nineteenth-century thought, not only about music, but also about literature, drama, and even political and moral issues.

For Wagner, the function of music was to serve the ends of dramatic expression; his only important compositions are those for the theatre. His first triumph came with *Rienzi*, a five-act grand opera performed at Dresden in 1842. In the following year, also at Dresden, appeared *Der fliegende Holländer (The Flying Dutchman)*, a Romantic opera in the tradition of Weber and Marschner. In *Der fliegende Holländer* the lines of development that Wagner was to follow in his later works are established. The libretto—written, like those of all his operas, by the composer himself—is based on a legend; the action takes place against a background of the stormy sea, and the drama is resolved with the redemption of the hero through the unselfish love of the heroine Senta. Wagner's music is most vivid in the depiction of the storm and of the contrasted ideas of curse and salvation, which are clearly set forth in the central number of the opera, Senta's ballad. The themes of the ballad are also those of the overture, and they recur elsewhere throughout the opera, although this technique was not so thoroughly and systematically applied as it was in Wagner's later works.

Earlier works

Tannhäuser (Dresden; 1845) is a brilliant adaptation of the substance of the German Romantic libretto to the framework of grand opera. *Lohengrin*, first performed under Liszt's direction at Weimar in 1850, is the last important German Romantic opera and at the same time embodies several changes prophetic of the music dramas of

383

Wagner's next period. Its orchestration is at once fuller and more subdued than that of *Tannhäuser;* the music flows more continuously, with less marked traces of division into separate numbers; the well-written choruses are combined with solo singing and orchestral background into long, unified musical scenes. Greater use is made of a new style of declamatory, arioso melody; the technique of recurring themes is further developed and refined; tonality becomes important in dramatic as well as musical organization. The style on the whole is diatonic, with modulations usually toward the mediant keys.

As a result of the political troubles of 1848–49, Wagner emigrated to Switzerland, and this country became his home for the next ten years. Here he found leisure to formulate his theories about opera and to publish them in a series of essays, the most important of which is *Opera and Drama* (1851). At the same time he was writing the poems of a cycle of four dramas with the collective title *Der Ring des Nibelungen (The Ring of the Nibelung)*. The music of the first two

Tannhäuser, *Act II: In the great hall of the Wartburg the Landgraf receives the song contestants. (Courtesy Metropolitan Opera Company; photo by Sedge LeBlang.)*

—*Das Rheingold (The Rhine Gold)* and *Die Walküre (The Valkyrie)*—and part of the third, *Siegfried*, was finished by 1857; the entire cycle was completed with *Götterdämmerung (The Twilight of the Gods)* in 1874, and the first complete performance took place two years later in a theatre especially built according to Wagner's specifications at Bayreuth. In the meantime he had composed *Tristan und Isolde* (1857–59) and *Die Meistersinger von Nürnberg (The Mastersingers of Nuremberg,* 1862–67). His last work was *Parsifal* (1882).

Wagner's conception of the music drama is illustrated most clearly in the *Ring*. Its subject matter is drawn not from legend or fairy tale, but from Norse mythology; Wagner regarded the myths as suitable not only because they offer plentiful opportunities for effective theatre but also because they embody, in a concentrated, poetic, and picturesque fashion, certain philosophical issues that are of fundamental importance in human life. The ruling ideal of Wagner's form is the absolute oneness of drama and music; the two are organically connected expressions of a single dramatic idea—unlike conventional opera, in which song predominates and the libretto is merely a framework for the music. The action of the drama is considered to have an inner and an outer aspect; the former is the province of instrumental music, that is, of the orchestra, while the sung words make clear the particular events or situations that are the outer manifestations of the action. Consequently, the orchestral web is the primary factor in the music and the vocal lines are part of the polyphonic texture, not arias with accompaniment. The music is continuous throughout each act, not formally divided into recitatives, arias, and other set numbers; in this respect Wagner carried to its logical end a steadily growing tendency in the opera of the first half of the nineteenth century. Even so, the continuity is not completely unbroken; broad scene divisions remain, and within the scenes a distinction is still evident between recitative-like passages with orchestral punctuation and others of arioso melody with continuous orchestra. Moreover, the unfolding of the drama is occasionally interrupted, or adorned, with skilfully interwoven scenes of decidedly operatic character that are not always strictly necessary to the plot.

Within the general continuity of the action and music Wagner uses two principal means for achieving articulation and formal coherence. The first is the leitmotif. A leitmotif is a musical theme or motive associated with a particular person, thing, or idea in the drama. The association is established by sounding the leitmotif (usually in the orchestra) at the first appearance or mention of the object of reference, and by its repetition at each subsequent appearance or mention. Thus the leitmotif is a sort of musical label—but it is more than that: it accumulates significance as it recurs in new contexts; it may serve to recall the thought of its object in situations where the object itself is not present; it may be varied or developed in accord with the development of the plot; similarity of motifs may suggest an underlying connection between the objects to which they refer; motifs may be contrapuntally combined; and, finally, repetition of motifs is an effective means of musical unity, as is repetition of themes in a symphony.

About twenty leitmotifs appear in all four of the *Ring* dramas; some thirty others are also used quite extensively. A similar system prevails in *Tristan*, *Die Meistersinger*, and *Parsifal* (see Example 91). The principle of the leitmotif did not originate with Wagner, but his use of it differs from that of such composers as Verdi and Weber.

First, Wagner's motifs themselves are for the most part short, concentrated, and (in intention, at least) so designed as to characterize
their object at various levels of meaning. Another and more important
difference, of course, is that Wagner's leitmotifs are the essential
musical substance of the work; they are used not as an exceptional
device, but constantly, in intimate alliance with every step of the
action.

A system of leitmotifs, however ingeniously applied, cannot of itself produce musical coherence. To this end, Wagner wrote his acts

*Formal
structure*

in sections or "periods," each of which is organized in some recognizable musical pattern, most often *AAB* (*Bar* form) or *ABA* (three-
part, or *Bogen* [arch] form). This structural framework, it must be
said, is revealed only by analysis. The forms are not intended to be
obvious to the listeners, and their essential outlines are modified by
transitions, introductions, codas, varied repetitions, and many other
devices. Periods are grouped and related so as to form a coherent
pattern within each act, and each act in turn is a structural unit in the

Example 91   Leitmotifs, Richard Wagner

From the *Ring*:

From *Tristan:* (Lento)

From *Die Meistersinger:*

pp staccato

From *Parsifal:*

shape of the work as a whole. This formidable complex of forms within forms was perhaps not entirely a matter of deliberate planning on the composer's part, but it exists nevertheless.

Tristan is in many respects the quintessence of Wagner's mature style. Few works in the history of music have exerted so potent an influence on succeeding generations of composers. The system of leitmotifs is happily subordinated to a flow of inspiration, an unbroken intensity of emotion, that effectively conceals and transcends mere technique. In contrast to the tragic gloom and the extremely chromatic idiom of *Tristan* are the sunny human comedy and predominantly diatonic harmony of *Die Meistersinger*. Here Wagner suc-

Isolde's costume for the original production of Tristan und Isolde *at Munich in 1865.*

ceeded most fully in fusing his conceptions of the music drama with the forms of Romantic opera, and in combining a healthy nationalism with universal appeal. *Parsifal*, by comparison, is somewhat less assured, less unified both in content and musical form, but abounds (as does *Die Meistersinger*) in beautiful choral scenes and instrumental numbers.

In the harmony of his later works, and especially in *Tristan*, Wagner carried out an evolution in his personal style that had been stimulated by his acquaintance in the 1850's with the chromatic idiom of Liszt's symphonic poems. The complex chromatic alterations of chords in *Tristan*, together with the constant shifting of key, the telescoping of resolutions, and the blurring of progressions by means of suspensions and other nonharmonic tones, produces a novel, ambiguous kind of tonality, one that can be explained only with difficulty in terms of the harmonic system of Bach, Handel, Mozart, and Beethoven. This departure from the Classical conception of tonality in such a conspicuous and musically successful work can today be viewed historically as the first step on the way toward new systems of harmony which have marked the development of music since 1890. The evolution of harmonic style from Bruckner, Mahler, Reger, and Strauss to Schoenberg, Berg, Webern, and contemporary twelve-tone composers can be traced directly back to the *Tristan* idiom.

Wagner's influence

Wagner's work affected all subsequent opera. His peculiar use of mythology and symbolism could not be successfully imitated; but his ideal of opera as a drama of significant content, with words, stage setting, visible action, and music all working in closest harmony toward the central dramatic purpose—the ideal, in short, of the *Gesamtkunstwerk* or "universal art-work"—was profoundly influential. Almost equally influential was his technical method of continuous music ("endless melody") which minimized divisions within an act and assigned to the symphonic orchestra the function of maintaining continuity with the help of leitmotifs while the voices sang in nonperiodic, arioso lines rather than in the balanced phrases of the traditional aria. As a master of orchestral color Wagner had few equals, and in this respect also his example was fruitful. Above all, his music impressed itself on the late nineteenth century because it was able, by its sheer overwhelming power, to suggest or arouse or create in its hearers that all-embracing state of ecstasy, at once sensuous and mystical, toward which all Romantic art had been striving.

XIX The End of an Era

Late Romanticism

One of the foremost German composers of the late nineteenth century was Hugo Wolf (1860–1903). His compositions include instrumental works and an opera, but he is chiefly important for his 250 *Lieder*, which ably continue the German Romantic tradition of the solo song with piano accompaniment. Most of Wolf's songs were produced in short periods of intense creative activity during the ten years from 1887 to 1897.

Hugo Wolf

Wolf's literary taste in the selection of texts was more uncompromising than that of earlier German song writers. He concentrated on one poet at a time, and placed the name of the poet above that of the composer in the titles of his collections—indicating a new conception of the relation between words and music in the Lied, derived from Wagner's music dramas, an ideal of a particular kind of equality between poetry and music, and of particular technical means for achieving such equality. Wolf adapted Wagner's methods with discrimination; the fusion of voice and instrument is achieved without sacrificing either to the other. Wolf's piano accompaniments, even in the most "symphonic" of his songs, seldom suggest either an orchestral texture

Hugo Wolf (1860–1903) at the age of 29. (Bettmann Archive)

or the predominance of instrumental over vocal sound which is common in Wagner. Likewise, the singer's line, though it often is written in a declamatory or arioso style rather than being organized into periodic melodic phrases, always preserves a truly vocal character.

Some passages in Wolf's songs are clearly inspired by the idiom of *Tristan* with its chromatic voice-leading, appoggiaturas, and rapid modulations (Example 92); but equally beautiful effects are obtained in a sensitive diatonic style. Wolf's treatment of pictorial images is always restrained but at the same time highly poetic and original; one instance among many is the suggestion of distant bells in the piano part of *St. Nepomuks Vorabend* (Goethe). It is impossible to convey an adequate idea of the infinite variety of fine psychological and musical details in Wolf's songs. Study of the scores brings continuous discovery of new delights.

The last of the great German post-Romantic symphony composers was the Viennese, Gustav Mahler (1860–1911). His works, composed for the most part in the summer between busy seasons of conducting, include nine symphonies (a tenth remained uncompleted) and four song-cycles for solo voices with orchestra, of which the chief is *Das Lied von der Erde* (*Song of the Earth,* composed in 1908).

Gustav Mahler

Mahler's symphonies are typical post-Romantic works: long, formally complex, programmatic in nature, and demanding enormous performing resources. Thus the Second Symphony, first performed in 1895, requires, along with a huge string section, 4 flutes (two

Example 92   *Anakreons Grab,* Hugo Wolf

390   What grave is this which all the gods have planted and adorned with life?

*Gustav Mahler (1860–1911) in 1885,
at a time when he was directing
Wagner's operas at Prague. (Bettmann Archive)*

interchangeable with piccolos), 4 oboes, 5 clarinets, 3 bassoons and a
contrabassoon, 6 horns and 6 trumpets (plus four more of each, with
percussion, in a separate group), 4 trombones, tuba, 6 kettledrums and
numerous other percussion instruments, 3 bells, 4 or more harps, and
organ, in addition to soprano and alto soloists and a chorus. The
Eighth, composed in 1906–07 and popularly known as the *Symphony
of a Thousand,* calls for an even larger array of players and singers.
But the size of the orchestra is not the whole story. Mahler is one of
the most adventurous and most fastidious of composers in his treatment of instrumental combinations, comparable in this respect perhaps
only with Berlioz; his natural genius for orchestration was reinforced
by his constant activity as a conductor, which gave him opportunity
to perfect details of scoring in the light of practical experience.
Instances of his felicity in orchestral effects, ranging from the most
delicate to the most overwhelmingly gigantic, occur abundantly in
all the symphonies (compare, for example, the ending of the third
movement of the First Symphony or the beginning of the second
movement of the *Song of the Earth* with the tremendous opening of
the Eighth Symphony). Mahler's instrumentation, as well as his extremely detailed indications of phrasing, tempo, and dynamics and his
occasional use of unusual instruments (such as the mandolin in the
Eighth Symphony and the *Song of the Earth*), are not mere displays
of ingenuity, but are intrinsically part of the composer's musical ideas.
For instance, the *scordatura* solo violin—all the strings tuned one full
tone higher than normally—in the scherzo of the Fourth Symphony
is intended to suggest the sound of the medieval *Fiedel* (fiddle) in a
musical representation of the Dance of Death, a favorite subject in
old German paintings.

Although the programmatic content is not always expressly indi-   391 cated, in most of his symphonies Mahler probably had in mind generalized extra-musical ideas similar to those illustrated in the Third and Fifth Symphonies of Beethoven. Thus Mahler's Fifth and Seventh move steadily from funereal gloom to triumph and joy; the Sixth, on the contrary, is his "tragic" symphony, culminating in a colossal finale in which heroic struggle seems to end in defeat and death. The Ninth, Mahler's last completed symphony (composed 1909–10), flows in a mood of resignation, of indescribably strange and sad farewell to life, symbolized by deliberate reference to the "Lebe wohl" ("Farewell") theme of the opening of Beethoven's Sonata Op. 81a. This motif, or reminiscences of it, pervades the first and last movement

Example 93   "Farewell" Motives

d. Dark is life, is death

e. The lovely earth everywhere blossoms in the new green of spring.

(both in slow tempo) of the Ninth Symphony, as well as that other "farewell" work of Mahler's last years, the *Song of the Earth* (Example 93).

Mahler the symphonist cannot be separated from Mahler the song composer. Themes from his early *Lieder eines fahrenden Gesellen* (*Songs of a Wayfarer;* composed 1883–84) appear in the opening and closing movements of the First Symphony; the Second, Third, and Fourth Symphonies incorporate melodies from the cycle of twelve songs on folk poems from the early nineteenth-century collection *Des Knaben Wunderhorn* (*The Boy's Magic Horn*) which Mahler composed between 1888 and 1899. Following the example of Beethoven, Berlioz, and Liszt, Mahler uses voices as well as instruments in four of his symphonies. The last movement of the Fourth has a soprano soloist, while soprano and alto soloists join with women's and boys' choruses in the fourth and fifth movements of the Third. The most extensive use of singing, however, occurs in the Second and Eighth Symphonies.

The Second, one of Mahler's most frequently played works, is known as the *Resurrection Symphony*. Like Beethoven, Mahler brings in voices for the final climax of the work. After a long, agitated, and highly developed first movement there follows an Andante in the easy, swinging, folksong-like rhythm of an Austrian *Ländler*, or slow waltz. The third movement is a symphonic adaptation of one of the *Wunderhorn* songs, and the brief fourth movement is a new setting, for contralto solo, of still another poem from this collection. This serves to introduce the finale which, after a vivid and dramatic orchestral section depicting the day of Resurrection, leads to a monumental setting for soloists and chorus of a Resurrection ode by the eighteenth-century German poet, Klopstock. The Eighth Symphony consists of two huge choral movements, on the texts respectively of the plainsong hymn *Veni creator spiritus* and the whole closing scene of Part II of Goethe's *Faust*. The second movement is practically a complete secular oratorio in itself, resembling in many ways Liszt's *Faust Symphony* and *St. Elizabeth*, or Wagner's *Parsifal*.

The *Song of the Earth* is based on a cycle of six poems translated from the Chinese by Hans Bethge under the title *The Chinese Flute*. The texts alternate between a frenzied grasping at the fleeting dream-like whirl of life and a resigned sadness at imminent parting from all its joys and beauties. As Mahler called on the human voice in the symphonies to complete his musical thought with the language of words, so here he calls on the orchestra to sustain and supplement the tenor and contralto solos with all its resources, both in accompaniment and in extensive connecting interludes. The exotic atmosphere of the words is lightly suggested by details of instrumental color and the use of the pentatonic scale. The *Song of the Earth* is deservedly Mahler's best-known work, one that epitomizes all the traits of his genius. Nowhere else did he so perfectly define and bring into balance that peculiar dualism of feeling, that ambivalence of ecstatic pleasure underlaid with deadly foreboding, that seems to characterize not only the composer himself but also the whole autumnal mood of late Romanticism. At no other time in history, perhaps, could the insistently recurring phrase "Dark is life, dark is death" (Example 93d) have been given such poignant musical expression.

Summary

The most general clue to Mahler's style is just this dualism, which extends to every feature of his work. In his symphonies he attempted —not always with success—to join sophistication with simplicity, to juxtapose the most lofty, wide-ranging cosmic conceptions and struggles with lyricism, Austrian folk song, nature painting, popular dance rhythms, chorale themes, marches, elements of parody, the spooky, and the grotesque. In his own phrase, each symphony was to be "a world." In this striving to be all-inclusive, Mahler was at one with the Romantic spirit, which he embodied most clearly in the Second Symphony. The Third, on the other hand, suffers from a too apparent dichotomy of styles. A vast, full-blown symphonic first movement is followed by five relatively short ones, diverse in character: a minuet with trio featuring a posthorn, a *scherzando* based on one of Mahler's early songs, a contralto solo on a text from Nietzsche's *Zarathustra*, a soprano solo with boys' and women's chorus on a gay strophic song from *Des Knaben Wunderhorn*, and, for conclusion, a broadly expressive orchestral adagio. The Fourth Symphony likewise mirrors a variegated "world," but one better unified in musical form, shorter, more lightly orchestrated, and altogether more easily accessible; this symphony and the Second have always been more popular than any of Mahler's works except the *Song of the Earth*.

With the composition (1900–1904) of ten songs for solo voice and small orchestra on poems of Friedrich Rückert, Mahler had forecast the change of style which is evident in his Ninth and (unfinished) Tenth Symphonies and the *Song of the Earth*. The typically full, crowded textures of the earlier works were often replaced by a more austere idiom, with clearer contrapuntal lines in an instrumentation of almost chamber-music style and proportions. At the same time, some of Mahler's techniques contributed to the steadily weakening sense of traditional tonal organization and furnished suggestions of procedure which later composers took up and developed. Mahler was thus, in a way to which there seems to be no real parallel in previous musical history, a transitional composer. He fell heir to the whole Romantic tradition—Berlioz, Liszt, Wagner—and particularly to the Viennese branch—Beethoven, Schubert, Brahms, and above all Bruckner. Restlessly experimenting, all-devouring in his interests, he expanded the Romantic Symphony and symphony-oratorio to their point of final dissolution; still experimenting, he foreshadowed a new age and became a prime influence on the later Viennese composers, Schoenberg, Berg, and Webern.

Richard Strauss

A quite different historical significance must be assigned to the most
famous of the German post-Romantic composers, Richard Strauss
(1864–1949). He wrote some 150 *Lieder*, of which not more than a
dozen or so—mostly from his early period—are commonly known
outside Germany and Austria; but he is important mainly for his
symphonic poems and operas. Most of the symphonic poems were

Richard Strauss (1864–1949). (Bett-
mann Archive)

produced before 1900, while all but one of the operas came after that
date.

There are two kinds of program for a symphonic poem: one, which
we may call the "philosophical," lies in the realm of general ideas and
emotions, unattached to particular incidents; the other, which we may
call the "descriptive" type of program, requires the composer to
render or attempt to illustrate in music particular nonmusical events.
The two types cannot be strictly set apart, since philosophical programs often include descriptive elements and descriptive programs
usually have also a more general significance; the distinction rests only
on the relative conspicuousness of the descriptive details. Strauss wrote
symphonic poems to both philosophical and descriptive programs. His
best works of the former type are *Tod und Verklärung (Death and
Transfiguration;* 1889) and *Also sprach Zarathustra (Thus Spake
Zarathustra;* 1896); of the latter, *Till Eulenspiegels lustige Streiche
(Till Eulenspiegel's Merry Pranks;* 1895) and *Don Quixote* (1897).
Among his principal other orchestral works are the symphonic poems
Don Juan (1889) and *Ein Heldenleben (A Hero's Life;* 1898), and
the *Sinfonia domestica* (1903).

Tod und Verklärung embodies a program similar to that of many
symphonies and operas of the nineteenth century: the progress of the

*Strauss's
symphonic
poems*

soul through suffering to self-fulfillment. This is a general, philosophical program, though Strauss later admitted that he had had in mind
certain descriptive details. The music is worked out with genuine
warmth of emotion in themes and harmonies of spontaneous power,
with strong dramatic contrasts. Its musical form can best be understood as an Allegro in free sonata form with a slow introduction and a
hymnlike epilogue; the principal themes occur in cyclical fashion in
all three parts.

The program of *Zarathustra* is philosophical in a double sense: the
work is a musical commentary on the philosophy of the brilliant,
erratic Friedrich Nietzsche, whose doctrine of the superman was
agitating all Europe at the end of the century (a choice of subject
typical of Strauss's highly developed sense for the value of publicity).
Although a part of Nietzsche's prologue stands at the head of the
score and the various divisions are furnished with titles from the book,
the music cannot be regarded as an attempt to depict a philosophical
system in tones; Nietzsche's ideas served merely as a stimulus to
Strauss's musical imagination. The only obviously artificial touch is the
construction of a fugue theme which uses all twelve notes of the
chromatic scale (Example 94) to symbolize the all-embracing but
dark and cloudy realm of *Wissenschaft* (science, learning, knowledge)
—the symbolism being reinforced by the low-lying thick sound of the
fugal exposition, which is given to the double basses and violoncellos,
each divided in four parts. One unifying feature of *Zarathustra* is the
motive C-g-c (first measure of Example 94), which is heard recurrently throughout, even in the final cadence; another consistent feature is the constant play of contrast between the tonalities of C and B,
a contrast that remains unreconciled even in the closing measures
where, under the sustained B-major chords of the woodwinds and
high strings, the unresolved appoggiatura C-natural still sounds in the
pizzicato of the double basses and violoncellos.

Example 94

Fugue Subject from *Also sprach Zarathustra*
Very slow

In *Till Eulenspiegel,* the popular favorite among his symphonic
poems, Strauss developed a comic program in music of unfading
freshness and melodic attractiveness. The realistic details of Till's
adventures (specified by a few marginal notes that the composer
added to the printed score) are so thoroughly blended with the musical flow that the work could easily be heard simply as a character
sketch of a particularly appealing rascal, or even more simply as a
piece of unmediated musical humor, reminiscent of Haydn. A further
suggestion of Haydn lies in Strauss's indication that *Till* is "in rondo
form." Rondo it is not in the Classical sense, but rondo-like by reason

of the many recurrences of the two "Till" themes, which appear in an endless variety of guises, enlivened by shrewd touches of instrumentation. In no other work does Strauss seem so unconstrained, so spontaneously himself, as in this merry musical tale.

Strauss leaped into fame as an opera composer first in 1905 with *Salome* and from that time on the powers of depiction and characterization that had formerly gone into symphonic poems were utilized almost exclusively in opera.

Strauss accepted the Wagnerian principles of continuous music, the primacy of the polyphonic orchestra, and the systematic use of leitmotives. *Salome* is a setting of Oscar Wilde's one-act play in German translation. The music, by its orchestral splendor, novel rhythms, and keenly descriptive harmonies, captures with such expressive force the macabre tone and atmosphere of the drama as to lift it to a plane where artistry prevails over perversion. *Elektra* (1909) began the long and fruitful collaboration between Strauss and the Viennese dramatist, Hugo von Hofmannsthal (1874–1929). For von Hofmannsthal's rather one-sided version of Sophocles' play, which dwells throughout its long single act on the emotions of insane hatred and revenge, Strauss conceived music that in sharpness of dissonance and apparent harmonic anarchy outdid anything previously known.

Salome and *Elektra* scandalized the respectable public of the 1900's, the former chiefly by its subject and the latter by its music. Time has tempered the criticisms, and the once fearful dissonances sound common enough. What remains, and is to be esteemed, is Strauss' amazing virtuosity in the invention of musical ideas and instrumental sonorities to characterize both persons and actions.

Der Rosenkavalier (*The Rose Cavalier*, 1911), on an excellent libretto in three acts by von Hofmannsthal, takes us into a sunnier world, a world of elegant, stylized eroticism and tender feeling, the aristocratic wig-and-powder milieu of eighteenth-century Vienna. *Der Rosenkavalier* is Strauss's operatic masterpiece. The sultry harmonies of *Salome* and the cacophonies of *Elektra* are softened to a mature synthesis of the elements in the earlier operas and symphonic poems. The ultra-Romantic, sensuous melodic curves, the sophisticated chromatic harmonies, the magical orchestral colors, tumultuous rhythms, robust sense of comedy, and speciously simple diatonic style derived from South German dances and folk songs, are held together in poise and given depth of meaning by an overruling humane sympathy that never quite slips over the verge into irony. Consistent with this turn toward Classicism is the fact that in *Der Rosenkavalier* the human voice once again becomes prominent; woven into the orchestral background and alternating with much cleverly wrought *parlando* dialogue are melodious arias, duets, trios—not really separate numbers as in the Classical opera, but still significant as departing from the Wagnerian (and earlier Straussian) rule of purely declamatory or, at most, arioso singing subordinated to the orchestra. The whole score, with its mingling of sentiment and comedy, is pervaded with the light-hearted rhythms and melodies of Viennese waltzes.

Ariadne auf Naxos (*Ariadne at Naxos*, 1912) was originally set, with other incidental music, in the framework of von Hofmannsthal's adaptation of Molière's *Bourgeois gentilhomme*. It has survived in revised form (1916) as an independent work, half *opera buffa* and half mythological drama. Its delightful music, in a modernized Mozartean idiom and using a small orchestra, includes recitatives, ensembles, and arias in Classical forms; it is, in short, a model of neo-Classical chamber opera.

Strauss's Der Rosenkavalier: *Octavian arrives to present the silver rose to Sophie.* (*Henry Rapisarda, Cosmo Sileo, Inc.*)

In his subsequent operas Strauss remained comparatively unaffected by the progressive currents of his time, preferring to continue along the lines he had laid down in *Der Rosenkavalier* and *Ariadne*. Of special interest are the comic opera *Intermezzo* (1924) and the lyrical comedy, *Arabella* (1933), the last of Strauss' seven operas on librettos by von Hofmannsthal.

Nationalism, Old and New: Russia

Nationalism was an important force in nineteenth-century music. A distinction must be made, however, between early Romantic nationalism and the nationalism which appeared after 1860. The results of the early nineteenth-century German folk song revival were so thoroughly absorbed into the fabric of German music as to become an integral part of its style, which in the Romantic period was the nearest thing to an international European musical style. The new nationalism, in contrast to the old, flourished exclusively in countries that had no great or unbroken musical tradition of their own but had long been musically dependent on other nations, chiefly Germany. Nationalism was one of the weapons by which composers in those countries sought to free themselves from the domination of foreign music. As a movement, it was self-conscious and sometimes aggressive. One of its consequences was the rise of new styles through fertilization of orthodox Germanic music by tonal, melodic, harmonic, rhythmic, and formal characteristics of the national idioms. This development took place earliest in Russia.

The first important landmark of Russian nationalism was the patriotic opera *A Life for the Tsar* (1836) by Michael Glinka (1804–1857). Although nationalism was more evident in the libretto than in the music, this work gave impetus to a movement that culminated with a group of composers known as "the Mighty Five": César Cui (1835–1918), Mily Balakirev (1837–1910), Alexander Borodin (1833–1887), Modest Mussorgsky (1839–1881), and Nicolas Rimsky-Korsakov (1844–1908).

All these men save Balakirev were amateurs—a fact important for the growth of Russian music. Russian musicians trained in German conservatories—and practically no other professional training was available—naturally tended to perpetuate the German style of music. But the nationalist composers' comparative ignorance of conservatory harmony and counterpoint became a positive asset in their struggle to create an all-Russian style: it forced them to discover their own ways of doing things, and in the process they used the materials nearest at hand, namely folk songs.

Balakirev made effective use of folksong melodies in his symphonic poem *Russia* (1887) and his piano fantasia *Islamey* (1869). Borodin's principal works are the Second Symphony in B minor (1876), the second String Quartet in D major (1887), a symphonic sketch *In the Steppes of Central Asia* (1880), and the four-act opera *Prince Igor*, completed after Borodin's death by Rimsky-Korsakov and Glazunov and first performed in 1891. Borodin seldom quotes folk tunes but his melodic style is permeated with their spirit. His talent, like Mendelssohn's, was primarily lyrical and descriptive, and *Prince Igor* is less a drama than a series of picturesque tableaus. The familiar "Polovetzkian Dances," which occur in Act II of the opera, illustrate the iridescent harmonies, bright colors, graceful melodic lines, and the refined, exotic oriental flavor that characterize much Russian music in this period.

Mussorgsky, the greatest of the Mighty Five, was also the one least well-equipped with the techniques of composition. A militant nationalist, he earned a painful living as a clerk in the civil service, and received most of his musical training from Balakirev. His principal works were: a symphonic fantasy *Night on Bald Mountain* (1867); the set of piano pieces *Pictures at an Exhibition* (1874); the song cycles *Without Sun* (1874), *Songs and Dances of Death* (1875), and

*Modest
Mussorgsky*

The Nursery (1872); and the operas *Boris Godunov* (first performed in 1874) and *Khovanshchina* (completed by Rimsky-Korsakov and produced in 1885). Mussorgsky's individuality is evident in every aspect of his music. His treatment of texts aims at the closest possible adherence to the accents of natural speech; hence in his vocal music

Modest Mussorgsky (1839–1881).

he generally avoids lyrical melodic lines and symmetrical phrasing. His songs are among the finest of the nineteenth century. Although Mussorgsky only occasionally quotes actual folk tunes (as in the Coronation Scene of *Boris*), it is evident that Russian folk song is rooted in his musical nature even more deeply than in Borodin's.

Russian folk tunes tend to move within a narrow range and to be made up either of obsessive repetition of one or two rhythmic motives or of phrases in irregular rhythm constantly sinking to a cadence, often by the interval of a descending fourth. Another prominent feature of Russian folk songs, and of Mussorgsky's melodies, is their modal character, and this modality affected Mussorgsky's harmonic style, as well as that of all the Russian nationalists. It was the Russians first of all who were responsible for introducing modality into the general musical language of Europe, and their influence in this respect on the music of the early twentieth century is important. In his harmony Mussorgsky is one of the most original and indeed revolutionary of all composers. Unfettered by traditional habits of thought and unpracticed in the manipulation of standard formulas, he was obliged to work out laboriously at the piano his "bold, crude, but always curiously 'right' harmonies"[1]—for which, as well as for his rhythms, he may have been indebted to his memories of polyphonic folk singing. His harmonic vocabulary is seldom advanced (except for some use of the whole-tone scale), but his apparently simple progressions convey precisely the effect he wants, and often resist

a. Fast

b. Slow

c. Allegretto   Mussorgsky—Song, *The Magpie*

d. Andantino   Mussorgsky—*Boris Godunov*, End of Act II
(Vocal line omitted)

any attempt made to explain them by analysis on normal textbook principles (see Example 95).

The work of Rimsky-Korsakov forms a link between the first generation of nationalists and the Russian composers of the early twentieth century. His compositions include symphonies, chamber music, choruses, and songs, but his most important works are symphonic poems and operas. His music, in contrast to the intense dramatic realism of Mussorgsky's, is distinguished by lively fantasy and a superb gift for bright orchestral colors. The *Capriccio espagnol* (1887), the symphonic suite *Scheherezade* (1888), and the *Russian Easter Overture* (1888) are outstanding manifestations of his genius for orchestration; his teachings on this subject were systematized in a treatise published in 1908. In the two most important of his fifteen operas—*Sadko* (1897) and *The Golden Cockerel* (first performed in 1910)—he alternates a diatonic, often modal style with one lightly chromatic, fanciful, and most apt at suggesting the fairytale world in which the action of these pieces takes place.

Rimsky-Korsakov

401

A quite unclassifiable Russian composer of the post-Romantic period, one whose music has no connection whatever with the nationalist movement, was Alexander Scriabin (1872–1915). A concert pianist, Scriabin began by writing nocturnes, preludes, etudes, and mazurkas in the manner of Chopin. Influenced by the chromaticism of Liszt and Wagner, and to some extent also by the methods of Impressionism, he gradually evolved a complex harmonic vocabulary peculiar to himself; the growth of this language can be followed step by step in his ten piano sonatas, of which the last six, composed between 1908 and 1913, dispense with key signatures and attain a harmonic vagueness amounting at times to atonality. Traditional tonal structures were replaced by a system of chords built on unusual intervals (particularly fourths, with chromatic alterations; see Example 96); traditional formal articulations were dissolved in a stream of strange, colorful, and sometimes magnificent sound. All this was intended to express vast

Example 96   Chord Forms, Alexander Scriabin

conceptions of an extraordinary, mysterious, theosophical cast; Scriabin eventually developed a theory of an ultimate synthesis of all the arts for the sake of inducing states of unutterable mystic rapture. His most typical compositions, apart from the late sonatas, are two orchestral works, the *Poem of Ecstasy* (1907) and *Prometheus* (1910); the latter requires colors to be projected on a screen during the playing of the music.

Other Nations

Bedřich Smetana and Antonín Dvořák, the two principal Czech composers of the nineteenth century, have already been mentioned in connection with the symphonic and chamber music of the Romantic period. Bohemia had for centuries been an Austrian crown land, and thus, unlike Russia, had always been in contact with the main stream of European music; her folk songs do not differ from those of western nations nearly so much as the Russian. Nor was the Czech nationalist movement marked from the outset, as was the Russian, by self-conscious efforts to avoid western influence. The nationalism of Smetana and Dvořák is chiefly apparent in the choice of national subjects for program music and operas, and in an infusion of their basic musical language (Smetana's derived from Liszt, Dvořák's more

*Czech
composers*

like Brahms's) with a melodic freshness and spontaneity, a harmonic and formal nonchalance, together with occasional traces of folklike tunes and popular dance rhythms. The most prominent national traits of both composers are found in some of their operas—Smetana's *Bartered Bride* (1866) above all, but also in his later opera *The Kiss* (1876)—and in some works in small forms, such as Dvořák's *Slavonic Dances*.

A Czech composer with thoroughly national tendencies was Leos Janáček (1854–1928), a more important figure in early twentieth century music than his as yet limited fame would indicate. Unlike Smetana and Dvořák, Janáček after 1890 consciously renounced the styles of western Europe. Like Bartók but even earlier, he was a diligent scientific collector of folk music, and his own mature style grew out of the rhythms and inflections of Moravian peasant speech and song. Recognition came late, beginning only with the performance of his opera *Jenufa* (1902) at Prague in 1916. Janáček's creative power continued unabated to the end of his life. Later operas were *Káta Kabanová* (1921), *The Vixen* (1924), *The Makropulos Case* (1925), and *From a Death-House* (1928). Janáček composed much choral music, among which the *Glagolitic Mass* of 1926, on a text in Old Slavic, is an outstanding work. His chamber music includes two quartets and a violin sonata; for orchestra the chief works are the symphonic rhapsody *Taras Bulba* (1918) and a *Sinfonietta* (1926).

Nationalism in Norway is represented by Edvard Hagerup Grieg (1843–1907), whose best works are his short piano pieces, songs, and incidental orchestral music to plays. Among his larger compositions *Norway* are the well-known Piano Concerto in A minor (1868, revised 1907), a piano sonata, three violin sonatas, a violoncello sonata, and a string quartet (1878) that apparently provided Debussy with a model for his own work in the same form fifteen years later.

The weaknesses in these works stem from Grieg's tendency to think always in two- or four-measure phrases and his inability to achieve rhythmic continuity and formal unity in long movements; such national characteristics as they possess are superimposed on an orthodox style which Grieg learned in youthful studies at the Leipzig Conservatory. His essential nationalism is more clearly apparent in the songs on Norwegian texts, the choruses for men's voices Op. 30, the four Psalms for mixed chorus Op. 74, many of his *Lyric Pieces* for piano (ten collections), the four sets of piano arrangements of folk songs, and especially the *Slåtter* (Norwegian peasant dances arranged by Grieg for the piano from transcripts of country fiddle playing). His piano style, with its delicate grace notes and mordents, owes something to Chopin, but the all-pervading influence in his music is that of Norwegian folk songs and dances; this is evidenced particularly in modal turns of melody and harmony (Lydian raised fourth, Aeolian lowered seventh, alternative major-minor third), frequent drone basses (suggested by old Norwegian stringed instruments), and 403 such details as the fascinating combination of 3/4 and 6/8 rhythm in the *Slåtter*. These national characteristics blend with Grieg's sensitive feeling for Romantic harmony in a personal, poetic music that has not lost its freshness.

Musical nationalism in the European countries could be defined as the rise of an important body of art music under the impetus of

United States patriotic feeling, in a style whose distinctive features result from the composers' more or less conscious use of folk elements as material or models for compositions. In this sense there was no continuity of musical nationalism in the United States of America in the nineteenth century. The materials lay ready—Indian music, Negro spirituals, ragtime, blues, religious and secular folk songs—in profusion. But all the serious music the American public could take was being imported —Italian opera, English oratorio, and German symphony—while Gottschalk's pieces in Creole rhythms were looked down on and dismissed as claptrap. The handful of American composers in the nineteenth and early twentieth centuries who were capable of writing in large forms had learned their craft in German conservatories and were interested exclusively in producing more of the European kind of music. Dvořák's enthusiastic interest in the Negro spirituals and the songs of Stephen Foster (1826–1864), which he heard when he visited the United States in 1892–95, suggested to a few composers—among them Arthur Farwell (1872–1952) and Henry Gilbert (1868–1928)— the possibility of using national materials in symphonic works; but the composers of this group, chiefly active in the first two decades of the twentieth century, lacked both the genius and the social encourage- ment to do for the United States what Glinka, Balakirev, and Mus- sorgsky had done for Russia.

Specific national traits are not prominent in the music of the two most celebrated American composers of the post-Romantic era. Hora- tio Parker (1863–1919), whose output included songs, choruses, and two prize-winning operas, is best known for his cantatas and oratorios, especially the oratorio *Hora novissima* (1893). Edward MacDowell (1861–1908) lived and studied for ten years in Germany, where he became known as a pianist and where many of his compositions were first played and published. From 1896 to 1903 he held the first profes- sorship of music at Columbia University. His compositions include songs, choruses, symphonic poems, orchestral suites, many piano pieces and studies, four piano sonatas, and two piano concertos. His best large works are the Second Piano Concerto, in D minor, and the last Piano Sonata (the *Keltic*, dedicated to Grieg).

MacDowell's melodies have a peculiar charm; his harmony, late Romantic in color but without modality, is handled in a distinctly personal way. A fine sensitiveness for the sonorous effects of spacing and doubling is evident in his short piano pieces, which are his most characteristic works. Most of them were issued in collections—*Wood-*
404 *land Sketches,* the *Sea Pieces,* the *New England Idyls*—and the in-

dividual pieces are furnished with titles or poems suggesting musical moods and pictures of the sort common in Grieg, to whose general style MacDowell's bears some resemblance. One of his finest works, and the only one that uses American folk material (Indian melodies), is the second (*Indian*) suite for orchestra.

The first important distinctively American composer was the New Englander, Charles Ives (1874–1954), a pupil of his father and of Horatio Parker. Like the early Russian nationalists, Ives was not a musician by profession. Public recognition of his achievements came

Charles Ives (1874–1954), a photograph taken about 1915 in Battery Park, New York. (Courtesy Mrs. Charles Ives)

only in the 1930's, many years after he had, in isolation and without models, created works that anticipated some of the most radical developments of twentieth-century music (dissonance, polytonality, polyrhythm, and experimental form). His compositions, most of which were written between 1890 and 1922, include some two hundred songs, five violin sonatas and other chamber music, two piano sonatas, five symphonies, and other orchestral music. Conventional and unconventional elements stand side by side in his works, or are mingled—in John Kirkpatrick's phrase—"with a transcendentalist's faith in the unity behind all diversity"; fragments of folk songs, dance tunes, or gospel hymns emerge from a complex, rhapsodic, uniquely ordered flow of sound. The many movements based on hymn tunes offer a parallel to the use of Lutheran chorales by German composers.

Ives's technical procedures, which he would have scorned to designate as a system, were dictated by an uncompromising idealism in the pursuit of his artistic aims, coupled with an extraordinary musical imagination and a mordant sense of humor. Like Erik Satie's work in France, his has been of incalculable importance to younger generations of American musicians.

The great Finnish composer, Jean Sibelius (1865–1957), is national- *Finland* istic only in a limited sense. His mind was steeped in the literature of his country, particularly the *Kalevala*, the Finnish national epic, from which he chose texts for vocal works and subjects for symphonic

*Jean Sibelius (1865–1957), during
his early twenties, when he was
studying in Vienna.*

poems; and it is easy to imagine much of his music—"somber,"
"bleak," and "elemental" are favorite adjectives for it—as having
been inspired by his profound love of nature and the particular aspects
of nature characteristic of northern countries. On the other hand, he
does not quote or imitate folk songs and there is small evidence of
direct folk song influence in his works, the best of which depend little,
if at all, on qualities that can be concretely defined as national.

Although Sibelius lived until 1957, he published no important works
after 1925. The first of his seven symphonies appeared in 1899, the
last in 1924. Three symphonic poems—*En Saga, The Swan of Tuone-
la,* and the familiar *Finlandia*—were works of the 1890's (all revised
about 1900); the principal later symphonic poems were *Pohjola's
Daughter* (1906) and *Tapiola* (1925). The programs of these poems,
except for *Pohjola's Daughter,* are very general; the symphonies have
no expressed programmatic suggestions.

Sibelius's originality is not of a sensational order. Except in the
Fourth Symphony his conception of tonality and his harmonic vocabulary are close to common practice; he makes no conspicuous use of
chromaticism or dissonances, though modality is a basic factor. Sibelius
remained aloof from the disturbing experimental movements in European music in the first quarter of the century, and in his late works,
particularly the Seventh Symphony and *Tapiola,* he arrived at a final
synthesis in a style of Classical tranquillity.

Though the movements of his symphonies can usually be analyzed
with reference to Classical formal schemes, such schemes—particularly in his later works—are felt to be wholly subordinate, incidental
to the organic development of the musical ideas. Long ostinato passages, sometimes in the form of a subdued *agitato* rustling of strings
under fragments of solo woodwind melody, are a common connective
device; pauses, brief ejaculatory phrases, sudden contrasts of timbre,
are incidental features. The Fourth Symphony is the quintessence of
Sibelius—a model of concision, intensity, and thematic unity, exploiting in every movement the tritone interval C-F-sharp of the
opening phrase (Example 97).

Example 97

Nationalism in English music came comparatively late. Sir Edward Elgar (1857–1934) was the first English composer in more than two hundred years to obtain wide international recognition; but his music is not in the least touched by folk song nor has it any technical characteristics that seem to derive from the national musical tradition. His oratorio *The Dream of Gerontius* (1900) and the *Enigma Variations* (1899) for orchestra are his most important works.

England

The English musical renaissance signalized by Elgar took a nationalist turn in the twentieth century. Folk song collections by Cecil Sharp (1859–1924), Ralph Vaughan Williams (1872–1958), and others led to the use of these melodies in compositions such as Vaughan Williams's *Norfolk Rhapsodies* for orchestra (1907) and the *Somerset Rhapsody* by Gustav Holst (1874–1934). These two com-

407

posers became the leaders of a new English school which will be dealt
with in the following chapter.

In Spain a nationalist revival somewhat like the English was initiated
by Felipe Pedrell (1841–1922) with his editions of sixteenth-century
Spanish composers. Further nationalist impetus came from the works
of Isaac Albéniz (1860–1909), whose piano suite *Iberia* (1909) used
Spanish dance rhythms in a colorful virtuoso style. The principal
Spanish composer of the early twentieth century, Manuel de Falla
(1876–1946), collected and arranged national folk songs, and his
earlier works—for example, the opera *La Vida breve* (*Life is Short;*
composed 1905) and the ballet *El Amor Brujo* (*Love, the Sorcerer;*
1915)—are imbued with the melodic and rhythmic qualities of Spanish
popular music. *Nights in the Gardens of Spain,* three "symphonic
impressions" for piano and orchestra (1916), testify both to national
sources and the influence of Debussy. Falla's finest mature works are
the concerto for harpsichord with five solo instruments (1926) and
the little stage piece *Master Peter's Puppet Show* (1923), based on an
episode from *Don Quixote.* Both are profoundly Spanish in inspiration, but the specific national elements are transmuted into a translu-
cent, delicately colored musical fabric of classic serenity.

New Currents in France

Three main lines of development—interdependent, naturally—may
be traced in the history of French music from 1871 to the early years
of the twentieth century. Two of these are best defined by their
historical background: first, the cosmopolitan tradition, transmitted
through César Franck and carried on by his pupils, especially d'Indy;
and second, the specifically French tradition, transmitted through
Saint-Saëns and continued by his pupils, especially Fauré. The third
development, later in inception but more far-reaching in results, was
rooted in French tradition, but was distinguished by a new technique
of composition; this was Impressionism, whose chief representative
was Debussy.

Vincent d'Indy's (1851–1931) principal compositions are: the First
Symphony, "on a French mountain air" (1886), the Second Symphony, in B-flat (1903), the symphonic variations *Istar* (1896), the symphonic poem *Summer Day on the Mountain* (1905), the Violin Sonata
(1904), and the opera *Fervaal* (1897). The First Symphony is exceptional for a French work because it uses a folk song as its principal
subject; both this and the Second Symphony exhibit to the highest
degree the process of cyclical transformation of themes that d'Indy
learned from Franck. The quasi-programmatic *Istar* variations are
remarkable as an inversion of the usual plan: the set begins with the
most complex variation and progresses to the simple statement of the
theme at the end. *Istar* and the First Symphony are the most spontaneous and attractive of d'Indy's compositions.

The specifically French tradition is something essentially Classical: it rests on a conception of music as sonorous form, in contrast to the Romantic conception of music as expression. Order and restraint are fundamental. Emotion and depiction are conveyed only as they have been entirely transmuted into music. That music may be anything from the simplest melody to the most subtle pattern of tones, rhythms, and colors; but it tends always to be lyric or dancelike rather than epic or dramatic, economical rather than profuse, simple rather than complex, reserved rather than grandiloquent; above all, it is not concerned with delivering a Message, whether about the fate of the cosmos or the state of the composer's soul. A listener will fail to comprehend such music unless he is sensible to quiet statement, nuance, and exquisite detail, able to distinguish calmness from dullness, wit from jollity, gravity from portentousness, lucidity from emptiness. This kind of music was written by two French composers as remote in time and temperament as Couperin and Gounod. Berlioz did not write such music; and Berlioz was not a success in France.

In Camille Saint-Saëns (1835–1921) this French inheritance was coupled with high craftsmanship, facility in managing Classical forms, and the ability to adopt at will any of the fashionable tricks of Romanticism. This eclectic, hedonistic trait also runs through the many successful operas of Jules Massenet (1842–1912), which also exhibit that composer's talent for suave, sensuous, charming, and often sentimental melody. The music of Gustave Charpentier's opera *Louise* (1900) is in a style not greatly different from Massenet's.

Gabriel Fauré (1845–1924) was one of the founders of the National Society for French Music and first president of the Independent Musical Society which branched off from the parent association in 1909. His refined, highly civilized music embodies the aristocratic qualities of the French tradition. Except for a few songs,[2] his works have never become widely popular, and many foreigners, even musicians, cannot understand why he is so highly regarded in France. Primarily a composer of lyric pieces and chamber music, his few compositions in larger form include the *Requiem* (1887), incidental music to Maeterlinck's *Pelléas et Mélisande* (1898), and the operas *Prométhée* (1900) and *Pénélope* (1913). His music is not remarkable for color; he was not skilled at orchestration, and published no symphonies or concertos. His characteristics are most fully revealed in his songs and piano pieces, which were written during all periods of his creative life. The principal chamber compositions are three late works: the second Violin Sonata (1917), the second Piano Quintet (1921), and the String Quartet (1924).

Modality is a prominent feature of Fauré's harmonic style; especially characteristic is the free succession of seventh chords, usually associated with suspensions and other nonharmonic tones; sequential passages may involve enharmonic modulations (illustrated in Example 98), but with all his darting excursions into remote keys Fauré never

Enharmonic Modulations in the Eleventh Nocturne, Fauré

allows us to lose the sense of a definite tonal center. His apparently
Wagnerian chromatic progressions lack the feeling of emotional
unrest that Wagner's progressions have; the combination of chromaticism and repose is very characteristic of Fauré. His music has been
often described as "Hellenic" in recognition of the qualities of clarity,
balance, and serenity that recall the spirit of ancient Greek art.

The most conspicuous and influential development in French music
in the late nineteenth and early twentieth centuries is incarnate in a
Impressionism: single composer, Claude-Achille Debussy (1862–1918). *Impressionism*
Claude Debussy is a term that was first applied to a school of French painting which
flourished from about 1880 to the end of the century; its chief representative is Claude Monet (1840–1926). In relation to music, the word
is thus defined in Webster's Dictionary: "A style of composition
designed to create descriptive impressions by evoking moods through
rich and varied harmonies and timbres." Impressionism is thus a kind
of program music. It differs from most Romantic program music in
that, first, it does not seek to express feeling or tell a story, but to
evoke a mood, an "atmosphere," with the help of suggestive titles and
occasional reminiscences of natural sounds, dance rhythms, characteristic bits of melody, and the like; second, impressionism relies on
allusion and understatement instead of the more forthright or strenu-
ous methods of the Romantics; and third, it employs melodies, harmonies, colors, rhythms, and formal principles which, in their totality,
make a musical language sharply different from that of the German
Romantic tradition.

The chief element in that language is color: color not only in the
narrow sense of timbre, but in the broader sense as rising from
harmonic, melodic, and rhythmic factors as well. Melodies are likely
410 to be short motives of narrow range, freely combined to make a

Claude-Achille Debussy (1862–1918) in 1882. (Bettman Archive)

musical mosaic of irregular, varicolored pieces. Pentatonic, wholetone, or pseudo-modal scales may furnish the material of melodies and chords. Rhythm, in the kind of music one most often thinks of as "impressionistic," is nonpulsatile, vague, concealed by syncopations and irregular subdivisions of the beat; but in some compositions by Debussy, the rhythm is a rapid, animated pulsation (often continued in ostinato fashion), or is patterned on some exotic or imagined dance. Outlines of phrases and the formal structure as a whole are deliberately blurred and indistinct, though in many impressionistic pieces a general three-part (*ABA*) form is discernible.

The principal means by which Debussy achieved his impressionistic color effects was harmony. One basic factor in his harmonic idiom is the use of chords in a largely "nonfunctional" manner: that is, chords are not used to shape a phrase by tension and release through a conventional series of progressions and resolutions; instead, each chord is conceived as a sonorous unit in a phrase whose structure is determined more by melodic shape or color value than by the movement of the harmony. Such a procedure does not negate tonality, which indeed Debussy was careful to preserve by pedal points or periodic frequent returns to the primary chords of the key; but the tonal relationships within the phrase may be so complex or willful that it is impossible to hear a given chord or series of chords as being in the key of the phrase in which they occur. The structure of chords is also veiled by abundance of figuration and, in the piano works, by the blending of sounds with the use of the damper pedal. The chords employed are chiefly sevenths and ninths (often with chromatic alterations and non-harmonic tones), sometimes triads, augmented fifths, or irregular types built on fourths or seconds. A very common device is the "chord stream," a succession of chords with organum-like parallel movement of all the voices.

Instances of all these devices may easily be found in Debussy's piano music, which—along with Ravel's—constitutes the most important

Debussy's harmony

addition made to the literature of that instrument in the early twentieth century. No mere listing of technical features can suggest the coruscating play of color, the ravishing pianistic effects, the subtle poetic fancy these pieces reveal. The principal impressionistic piano works of Debussy occur in collections published between 1903 and 1913: *Estampes*, two books of *Images*, and two books of *Préludes*. The earlier *Suite bergamasque* (1893), the suite *Pour le piano* (1901), and the delightful *Children's Corner* (1908) are not particularly impressionistic, although they do include some features of that style. The Quartet (1893) fuses Debussy's harmonic and coloristic traits with Classical forms and cyclic treatment of themes.

Impressionism in the orchestral works begins with the celebrated *Prélude à l'après-midi d'un faune* (*Prelude to the Afternoon of a Faun*; 1894), and is continued in the *Nocturnes* (1899) and the symphonic sketches, *La Mer* (1905). Debussy's orchestration, like his piano writing, is admirably suited to the musical ideas. A large orchestra is required, but it is seldom used to make a loud sound. Strings are frequently divided and muted; harps add a distinctive touch; among the woodwinds, the flute (especially in the low register), oboe, and English horn are featured in solos; horns and trumpets, also often muted, are heard in short pianissimo phrases; percussion of many types —kettledrums, large and small drums, large and small cymbals, tam-tams, celesta, glockenspiel, xylophone—is still another source of color.

The one successful application of impressionism to opera is Debussy's setting of Maeterlinck's symbolist play *Pelléas et Mélisande* (1902). The veiled allusions and images of the text are perfectly matched by the strange (often modal) harmonies, subdued colors, and restrained expressiveness of the music. The voices, in plastic recitative, are supported but never dominated by a continuous orchestral background, while the instrumental interludes connecting the scenes carry on the mysterious inner course of the drama. In Debussy's late works the impressionism of the 1900's gave way to a more austere, almost neo-Classical style, evident in the Villon songs, the settings of poems by Charles d'Orléans (1908), the four-hand piano *Epigraphes* (1914), the piano *Études* (two books; 1915), the suite *En blanc et noir* for two pianos (1915), and—with some diminution of creative power—the *Sonates pour divers instruments* (violoncello and piano; flute, viola, and harp; piano and violin) of 1915–17.

Pelléas et Mélisande

The impressionism of Debussy is best regarded as a late and very special offshoot of Romanticism, shaped by French ideals but embodying the Romantic predilection for mood, color, and harmonic opulence in a homophonic texture with relaxed treatment of rhythm and form. Nevertheless the changes that Debussy introduced, particularly those in the harmonic system, link him with a later epoch. His work is distinctly a bridge between Classical and twentieth-century conceptions of tonality. Moreover, even though impressionism itself did not become a school, its effects were felt everywhere. To name

Debussy's influence

the composers who at one time or another came under the influence of Debussy would be to name nearly every composer of the early twentieth century.

The most important composer after Debussy was Maurice Ravel (1875–1937); the titles of his first and last compositions for piano— *Menuet antique* (1895) and *Le Tombeau de Couperin* (1917)—give a hint of the direction in which his work diverged from that of Debussy. Although Ravel adopted some of the impressionist technique, this never overcame his basic affinity for the clean melodic contours, distinct rhythms, and firm structures of Classicism. Moreover, his harmonies, while complex and sophisticated, are functional, not only pictorial and impressionistic like some of Debussy's. Ravel's Classical orientation is most clearly apparent, of course, in such works as the piano *Sonatina* (1905) and the chamber music. His most mark-

Maurice Ravel (1875–1937).
(Bettmann Archive)

edly impressionistic works for piano are the *Jeux d'eau* (1901), the five pieces entitled *Miroirs* (1905), and the three entitled *Gaspard de la nuit* (1908). Impressionist also to some extent are the orchestral suite *Rapsodie espagnole* (1907) and the ballet *Daphnis et Chloé* (1909–11).

Ravel was able to absorb ideas from everywhere, adapting them to his own use with as much assurance as he adapted impressionism. He used jazz elements in the piano *Concerto for the Left Hand* (1931), and Spanish idioms in the *Rapsodie*, the comic opera *L'Heure espagnole* (1910), and the rousing *Bolero* (1928), which became the musical equivalent of a best-seller. One of his most charming works is *Ma Mère l'Oye* (*Mother Goose*), a set of five little piano duets for children written in 1908, children's music comparable to Mussorgsky's *Nursery* songs, Debussy's *Children's Corner*, and the children's piano pieces of Satie.

Among Ravel's songs are many settings of folk melodies from various countries; his important original songs are the five humorous and realistic characterizations of animal life in the *Histoires naturelles* (1906) and the *Chansons madécasses* (*Songs of Madagascar;* 1926), 413 for voice, flute, violoncello, and piano; and three poems of Mallarmé set for voice, piano, string quartet, two flutes, and two clarinets (1913), suggested to Ravel by Schoenberg's *Pierrot Lunaire*.

A composer whose significance extends beyond the first decade of the century is Albert Roussel (1869–1937), whose three symphonic *Evocations* (1911) and the opera-ballet *Padmâvatî* (composed 1914, first performed 1923) exemplify the French Romantic musical treatment of exotic subjects. Roussel's postwar works show the contemporary trend toward neo-Classicism, evident particularly in the orchestral *Suite in F* (1926), the Third Symphony, in G minor (1930), and the *Sinfonietta* for string orchestra (1934).

Impressionism produced a reaction in France, which was spearheaded by the eccentric genius Erik Satie (1866–1925). In some of his early piano pieces (for example the three *Gymnopédies* of 1888), Satie anticipated the unresolved chords and quasi-modal harmonies of impressionism in an ostentatiously plain texture. His piano works between 1900 and 1915 specialize in caricature, an activity particularly congenial to the French temperament. Satie's caricature takes outward form in surrealistic titles: *Trois Morceaux en forme de poire* (*Three Pieces in the Form of a Pear*), *Embryons desséchés* (*Dried Embryos*), *Danse maigre* (*Lean Dance*), with a running commentary and directions to the player in the same style: *pp en un pauvre souffle* (pianissimo in a poor whisper), *avec beaucoup de mal* (with much illness), *léger comme un oeuf* (light like an egg), *ralentir avec politesse* (slow down politely) printed along with the music. All this obviously satirizes the impressionistic titles and directions of Debussy. But the comic spirit lives also in the music itself—notated without barlines, spare, dry, capricious, brief, repetitive, parodistic, witty in the highest degree. Most of Satie's compositions are for piano. Among his works

Erik Satie (1866–1925).
(Bettmann Archive)

for other media are the stylized "realistic ballet" *Parade* (1919) and the "symphonic drama" *Socrate* (1918)—three songs for soprano voice and a small orchestra on texts translated from Plato—which, particularly in the last scene, "The Death of Socrates," attains a poignancy that is intensified by the very monotony of the style and the studied avoidance of direct emotional appeal.

Satie's biting antisentimental spirit, together with his miraculous economy of texture, brevity, rhythmic vitality, and severity of harmony and melody, marked the first really complete break with musical Romanticism in France; his personality and work became the symbol of a movement that extended far into the twentieth century with the work of Milhaud, Honegger, Poulenc, Stravinsky, and others.

Peripheries

One of the lesser musical "isms" of the late nineteenth century was *verism* (*verismo*) in Italian opera. The word means literally "truthism"; it is sometimes translated as "realism" or "naturalism." *Italian opera* Its first sign is the choice of a libretto that presents everyday people in familiar situations acting violently under the impulse of primitive emotions. Its second sign is a musical style appropriate to such a libretto. The veristic opera is the innocent grandfather of the television shock drama. It was just as typical of the post-Romantic period as dissonance, hugeness, and the other musical devices which were used to titillate jaded sensibilities. The veristic operas par excellence are *Cavalleria rusticana* (*Rustic Chivalry;* 1890) by Pietro Mascagni (1863–1945) and *Pagliacci* (*The Clowns;* 1892) by Ruggiero Leoncavallo (1858–1919). Verism was shortlived, though it had some parallels or repercussions in France and Germany.

The most important Italian opera composer of the late nineteenth and early twentieth centuries was Giacomo Puccini (1858–1924), like Massenet a successful eclectic whose works reflect in turn the late Romantic taste for sentiment (*Manon Lescaut;* 1893), sentiment with realism (*La Bohème;* 1896), verism (*Tosca;* 1900), and exoticism (*Madama Butterfly*, 1904; *Turandot*, 1926) in music of lyric intensity, discreetly incorporating modern touches of harmony, and managed with a sensational flair for theatrical effect.

Running through all the musical developments of the later nineteenth century was the steady trend toward the dissolution of Classical tonality, a trend already perceptible in Schubert and Chopin, con- *Summary* tinued in Liszt and Wagner, accentuated with the harmonic experiments of Mussorgsky, Mahler, Strauss, Fauré, Debussy, and Ravel, and climaxed to some extent in the prewar works of Scriabin, Ives, Schoenberg, Bartók, and Stravinsky. Chromaticism, complex and unorthodox chords, national folk song, exoticism, modality, the use of pentatonic, whole-tone, or other non-Classical scales, chord-streams,

XIX. The
End of
an Era
polytonality—all have had a part. To a large extent the task of composers in the first half of the twentieth century was to work out new
concepts of, or find an adequate substitute for, tonality and to reconcile with new harmonic idioms the other musical elements of instrumentation, counterpoint, rhythm, and form.

XX The Twentieth Century

Introduction

In this final chapter we shall survey the work of a few composers who were leading figures in music from the beginning of the First to the end of the Second World War (1914–1945). Since some of these composers were active as early as the turn of the century, we must still be somewhat concerned with that momentous decade, 1900 to 1910—not in its aspect as the end of the Romantic period, but as the beginning of a new era. No attempt will be made to continue systematically beyond 1945, because the most recent musical events are still too close to allow us to make anything but a subjective interpretation of their historical significance.

General features

Three main directions or tendencies may be traced in the music of the twentieth century, which correspond to the three main lines of development of the post-Romantic period: first, the continuing growth of musical styles which employed significant elements from national folk idioms; second, the rise of neo-Classicism and related movements, which involved a conscious return to aesthetic principles, forms, and techniques of Western art music of the pre-nineteenth-century past and the expression of these principles in a contemporary musical language; and third, the transformation of the German post-Romantic idiom into the *dodecaphonic* or twelve-tone styles of Schoenberg, Berg, Webern, and their followers.

These are three "directions" or "tendencies," not "schools"; for (except for the group around Schoenberg) none of these movements acknowledged a single central authority, each included many diverse practices, and more than one of them often was evident in a single composer or even a single composition; moreover, traces of Romanticism, exoticism, impressionism, and other influences were often mingled with them in one way or another.

Musical Styles Related to National Idioms

Consistent with the diversity of the musical scene in the first half of the twentieth century, national differences continued to be emphasized; indeed, speedier communication and the annihilation of distance only accentuated contrasts between cultures. The nationalist musical activities of the twentieth century differed in several respects from those of the Romantic period. The study of folk material was undertaken on a much wider scale than previously, and with rigorous scientific method. Folk music was collected not by the clumsy process of seeking to transcribe it in conventional notation but with the accuracy made possible by the use of the phonograph; and collected specimens were analyzed objectively, by techniques developed in the new science of ethnomusicology, so as to discover the actual character of folk music instead of ignoring its "irregularities" or trying to adjust them to the rules of art music, as the Romantics had often done. More realistic knowledge led to more profound respect for the unique qualities of folk music. Composers, instead of trying to absorb folk idioms into more or less traditional styles, used them to create new styles, and especially to extend the realm of tonality.

Central Europe was the scene of some of the earliest extensive scientific study of folk music. Janáček's pioneer work in the Czecho-Slovak region was soon followed by that of two Hungarian scholar-composers, Zoltán Kodály (born 1882) and Béla Bartók (1881–1945).

Bartók's importance is threefold. He published nearly two thousand folk tunes, chiefly from Hungary and Rumania, these being only a *Béla Bartók* part of all that he had collected in expeditions ranging over Central Europe, Turkey, and North Africa. He wrote five books and innumerable articles on folk music, made settings of or based compositions on folk tunes, and developed a style in which he fused folk elements with highly developed techniques of art music more intimately than had ever been done. Second, he was a virtuoso pianist and a teacher of piano at the Budapest Academy of Music from 1907 to 1934; his *Mikrokosmos* (1926–37)—153 piano pieces in six books of graded difficulty—is not only a work of great pedagogical value but also a summary of Bartók's own style and of many aspects of the development of European music in the first half of the twentieth century. Third and finally, he was one of the four or five composers active between 1910 and 1945 whose music is likely to endure for several generations to come.

The earliest works that begin to manifest Bartók's individual style were composed about 1908, shortly after he had become interested in Hungarian folk song. Compositions of this period include the First Quartet (1908), the one-act opera *Duke Bluebeard's Castle* (1911), and the *Allegro barbaro* for piano. The last is frequently cited as an example of "primitivism," that is, the stylized imitation of primitive music by means of pounding frenetic rhythms, limited melodic range with much repetition of motives, and pungent percussive harmonies. Bartók, like many twentieth-century composers, often treats the piano more as an instrument of percussion, in a class with the celesta or

xylophone, than as a producer of cantabile melodies and arpeggiated

Béla Bartók (1881–1945). (Photo Hackett)

chords, as the Romantics had conceived it. By 1917, early influences from late Romanticism and impressionism had been thoroughly absorbed into the characteristic rhythmic vigor, exuberant imagination, and elemental folk qualities of Bartók's style; in that year he wrote the Second Quartet. Compositions of the next ten years show him pushing toward the limits of dissonance and tonal ambiguity, reaching the furthest point with the two violin sonatas of 1922 and 1923. Other works of this decade were the pantomime *The Marvelous Mandarin* (1919), the *Dance Suite* for orchestra (1923), the Piano Sonata (1926), the first Piano Concerto (1926), and the Third Quartet (1927).

The later works of Bartók are the most widely known. The most popular Quartet is No. 4 (1928). In the *Cantata profana* (1930; for tenor and baritone soloists, double chorus, and orchestra) is distilled the spirit of all Bartók's many vocal and instrumental works specifically based on folk songs or folklike themes. A second Piano Concerto dates from 1931. The Violin Concerto (1938) and the Concerto for Orchestra (1943) are masterpieces in large form. Other works of the late period are the Fifth and Sixth Quartets (1934, 1939), the *Divertimento* for string orchestra (1939), the *Mikrokosmos*, the *Music for Strings, Percussion, and Celesta* (1936), the Sonata for Two Pianos and Percussion (1937), and the Third Piano Concerto (1945; his last completed composition).

Bartók's ideal was to express, in twentieth-century terms, Bach's texture of contrapuntal fullness, Beethoven's art of thematic development, and Debussy's discovery of the sonorous (as distinct from the functional) value of chords. The elements of his style are: melodic   419

lines derived or sublimated from East European folk music; powerful
"motoristic" rhythms, characteristically subtilized by irregular meters
and offbeat accents; an intense expressionistic drive, regulated by
strong formal control embracing everything from the generation of
themes to the comprehensive design of an entire work. His textures
may be prevailingly homophonic or be made up of contrapuntal lines
carried on with secondary regard for vertical sonorities (*linear* counterpoint), depending largely on the medium. The polyphony may
include free use of imitative, fugal, and canonic techniques (No. 145
of the *Mikrokosmos*, the first movement of the *Music for Strings,
Percussion, and Celesta,* or the two outer movements of the Concerto
for Orchestra; and frequently one or more of the interweaving lines
is enriched by parallel-moving voices in chord streams.

*Bartók's
harmony*

Bartók's harmony is partially an incidental result of the contrapuntal movement; it grows out of the character of the melodies,
which may be based on pentatonic, whole-tone, modal, or irregular
scales (including those found in folk music) as well as the regular
diatonic and chromatic scales. All kinds of chords appear, from triads
to combinations built on fourths (quite frequent) and other construc-
tions more complex. Bartók often gives pungency to a chord by
adding dissonant major or minor seconds (as in the final A-flat triad
of the *Allegretto pizzicato* movement of the Fourth Quartet: see
Example 99a); sometimes seconds are piled up in tone clusters (as in
the Piano Sonata, the first Piano Concerto [Example 99b], or the slow
movement of the Second Concerto). But on the whole, especially in
the Quartets, both the construction and the progressions of chords are
extremely complex and difficult to analyze. Bartók's music—although
it is essentially Western, not exotic—nonetheless has a great deal of
the strange, unpredictable violence of barbaric impulses in its harmonies as well as in its rhythms.

Most of his music is tonal in the sense that a fundamental key center

Example 99

Examples of Chords with Seconds and Tone Clusters, Béla Bartók

is recurrently present, though it may be effectually obscured for considerable stretches. Occasionally, and especially in the works of the nineteen twenties, Bartók writes on two or more simultaneous harmonic planes (so-called *polytonality*), but he does not aim systematically at negating tonality. Moreover, though he sometimes writes a theme that includes up to twelve different tones in a row (as in the first movement of the Violin Concerto, measures 73–75 and finale at 129–134), or otherwise uses all the notes of the chromatic scale in a single phrase (opening of the Third and Fourth Quartets), he never uses a technique systematically based on this device. In some of Bartók's late works tonality is defined by relatively familiar procedures—particularly so in the last two Piano Concertos and the Concerto for Orchestra. More commonly, however, the tonal field is less definite and the relations within it harder to grasp. In the Quartets, tonality is

... handled so freely that one is justified only in saying that they are "on" —not "in"—this or that tonality. So the First and Second Quartets are on A, the Third on C♯, the Fourth on C, the Fifth on B♭, and the Sixth on D. By this it is understood that these key-notes serve as orientation points: that the music is organized around them, modally or chromatically, freely fluctuating, using the key-notes as points of departure and points of repose, effecting modulations from and back to them.[1]

In the *Music for Strings, Percussion, and Celesta* the main tonality of the first and last movements is A with an important secondary center at the augmented fourth D-sharp (substituting for the conventional dominant E); the second movement is in C, with a similar tritonic subcenter on F-sharp; the Adagio is indeterminate, fluctuating in the region C-F-sharp (the two keys equidistant on either side from the principal tonality of the work). Some of the principal themes and all of the final cadences bring out clearly this tritone relationship (Example 100), which is common in Bartók, Schoenberg, and many other twentieth-century composers.

Bartók is as individual in his treatment of form as in his harmony. Typically, themes are evolved out of two or three germinal motives (first movement of the Second Quartet), and often the same motives serve to generate themes in more than one movement of a work *Bartók's form* (Fourth Quartet, *Music for Strings, Percussion, and Celesta*). With all this unification of material, however, Bartók usually maintains the principle of contrast, and most movements are articulated in distinct sections. In the main, the formal outlines are those of the Classical tradition; but in some of the late works a symmetrical arch pattern is superimposed, as in the Violin Concerto, where the first and third movements correspond in both thematic materials and formal structure. A similar pattern occurs in the Adagio of the *Music for Strings, Percussion, and Celesta:* of the six sections, the first and sixth correspond, while the fifth is a variant of the second but in the sonorities of the third, so that the fourth becomes the keystone of the arch.

Music for Strings, Percussion, and Celesta, Béla Bartók

Example 100

Brilliant, imaginative sonorities are amply evident in any of Bartók's scores: examples are the colorful orchestration of *The Marvelous Mandarin*, the *Dance Suite*, and the Concerto for Orchestra. The percussive piano style is transfigured and etherealized in the *Music for Strings, Percussion, and Celesta*, and virtuosity in the treatment of percussion is especially notable in the Sonata for Two Pianos and Percussion. The Quartets are full of arresting sonorities, in some of which multiple stops, glissandos, different types of pizzicato, *col legno*, and the like play a part.

The range of Bartók's style is summarized not only in the *Mikro-kosmos* but also—and even more thoroughly—in the Quartets, which constitute probably the most important large addition to the repertoire of this medium since Beethoven. The guiding thread through all Bartók's work is the variety and skill with which he integrated the essence of his national folk music heritage with the highest forms of Western art music. Bartók was not primarily an innovator; rather, like Handel, he gathered up the achievements of the past and present in an individual synthesis and expressed them eloquently in the language of his own day. It is a sign of the difference between their worlds—and certainly of the changed relationship between composer and public—that, unlike Handel, Bartók was very little understood during his lifetime.

Russian folk songs and rhythms appear to some extent in the early compositions of Igor Stravinsky (b. 1882). National influences of various sorts are of course prominent in much Soviet music, as for example the cantata *Alexander Nevsky* (1938) and the opera *War and Peace* (1947) by Sergei Prokofiev (1891–1953), the folk song quotations in the opera *Lady Macbeth* (1934) by Dmitri Shostakovich (born 1906), and the same composer's Seventh Symphony, inspired by the heroic defense of Leningrad against the German armies in 1941. The large amount of film music, mass choruses, and similar popular music by Soviet composers may also be related to nationalistic aims.

Neither Prokofiev nor Shostakovich, however, is a nationalist in the narrower meaning of the word. Prokofiev lived outside Russia from 1918 to 1934, and his compositions of these years are only sporadically touched by national influences. The *Scythian Suite* for orchestra (1916) represents an early nationalistic stage in his music. The *Classical Symphony* (1918), the third Piano Concerto (1921), and some of the music from the opera *The Love of Three Oranges* (1921) are the best known of his early works; the symphonic suite *Lieutenant Kije* (1934; arranged from music for a film) and the "symphonic fairy tale" *Peter and the Wolf*, for narrator and orchestra (1936), have become widely popular. Prokofiev's other works include chamber music, piano sonatas and other piano pieces, operas, ballets, concertos, and symphonies, among which the second Violin Concerto (1935) and the Fifth Symphony (1944) are outstanding. In general, Prokofiev's style is spiced by a sufficient admixture of national and modern features to save it from banality without endangering its chances for wide popular acceptance. Much the same may be said of Shostakovich, whose principal compositions, in addition to those already noted, are the Fifth Symphony (1937) and the Piano Quintet (1940). His music assimilates the national heritage (coming largely through Tchaikovsky) to the main European tradition, with particular influences from Mahler and Hindemith; but although it is undeniably Russian in sound, it shows few traces of specific folk song elements.

England

The foremost English composer of our period is Ralph Vaughan Williams, whose productions include nine symphonies and other orchestral pieces, songs, operas, and a great many choral works. Amid all the variety of dimensions and forms, Vaughan Williams's music was constantly motivated from three main sources: English folk song, English hymnody, and English seventeenth-century literature. But the essential national quality of his music is deeper than any enumeration of influences can suggest; his works exemplify his own saying that "the composer must not shut himself up and think about art, he must live with his fellows and make his art an expression of the whole life of the community."[2] The national quality of Vaughan Williams's art, therefore, is not a matter of merely quoting or imitating British folk tunes or writing "modal harmonies" after the manner of the Elizabethans; it is an expression of his natural way of life.

Ralph Vaughan Williams (1872–1958). (The Bettmann Archive)

The *London Symphony* (1914; revised 1920), a loving evocation of the sounds and atmosphere of the city, is a program symphony in the same sense as Mendelssohn's *Italian* or Schumann's *Rhenish*. It has the regular four movements—the third is called "Scherzo (Nocturne)"—and dies away at the end in an Epilogue on the theme of the *lento* introduction to the first movement. Similar epilogues are found in the later symphonies, and many of Vaughan Williams's large compositions end *pianissimo*. The *London* was his second symphony. The first, the *Sea Symphony* (1910) for orchestra and voices on texts from Walt Whitman, is less important than another early work, the *Fantasia on a Theme of Thomas Tallis* (1909) for double string orchestra and string quartet, in which are heard the antiphonal sonorities and the rich texture of ascetic triads in parallel motion within a modal framework that also characterized many of his later compositions.

The *Pastoral Symphony* (1922) is less definitely programmatic than the *London*. A single mood prevails throughout; there are few strong contrasts of melodic character, dynamics, or tempo among the four movements, but many changing instrumental colors. A wordless melisma in unbarred free rhythm for solo soprano is heard at the

Examples of Themes by Vaughan Williams   Example 101

beginning and (in shortened form) the close of the last movement
(Example 101b); it exemplifies a type of melody with gapped scales
(here of pentatonic character) that often occurs in Vaughan Williams's music. Equally characteristic and folksong-like is the trumpet
tune in the trio of the third movement (Example 101c). Especially
effective use is made of the chord-stream texture in this symphony
(Example 101d).

Other works nearly contemporary with the *Pastoral Symphony* are
the neo-modal *Mass in G minor* (1922) for small *a cappella* chorus,
one of Vaughan Williams's few liturgical compositions; *Flos campi*
(1925) for solo viola, small wordless chorus, and chamber orchestra,
each of the five movements headed by a quotation from the Song of
Solomon, the whole a marvel of sensuous musical imagery; and the
oratorio *Sancta Civitas* (*The Holy City;* 1925) for two soloists, three
choruses, and orchestra, on English texts (despite the Latin title)
from the book of Revelation—one of the composer's "mystical out-
pourings," of which other examples are the *Five Mystical Songs* of
1911 on poems of George Herbert, the "morality" *The Pilgrim's
Progress* (1949), and *Job* (1931), a "Masque for Dancing" based on
the drawings of William Blake.

Vaughan Williams's works for the theater include a "romantic
ballad opera" *Hugh the Drover* (1914, performed 1924) and a larger
opera *Sir John in Love* (1929 with later additions; from Shakespeare's
Merry Wives), both of which appropriately make use of folk songs
actual or invented; a setting of J. M. Synge's *Riders to the Sea* (1927)
in moving semimelodic recitative over a subdued continuous orchestral background; and a comic opera with spoken dialogue, *The
Poisoned Kiss* (1928, performed 1936). Humor is the keynote of the
choral suite *Five Tudor Portraits* (1936) on poems of John Skelton
(1460–1529).

The Fourth Symphony in F minor (1934) has a dissonant idiom
and a vehemence in strong contrast to the *Pastoral*. The F minor
Symphony and its two successors in D major (1943) and E minor
(1947) have been interpreted as reflecting Vaughan Williams's concern with world events—the Fourth as prophesying the war, the Sixth
as describing the nature of war, and the Fifth as a vision of peace—
although no warrant for a programmatic interpretation of any kind is
given by the composer himself. On the other hand, each movement of
the *Sinfonia antartica* has a brief superscription that suggests its underlying reference; the symphony is a tribute to the heroism of Captain
Scott and his men and, by extension, to all men's in the struggle against
overwhelming forces of nature.

Vaughan Williams was on the whole a conservative composer,
sharing the Englishman's typical distrust of theories, especially theories pushed to extremes in practice. Even his most dissonant passages
never outrage the national instinct for euphonious sound present also
in the *Sumer* canon and the works of Dunstable and Byrd; and al-

though his field of tonality is broad, as befits a composer of the twentieth century, it does not extend to regions of obscurity. Fundamental simplicity, a sense of humor, and a horror of Romantic rhetoric are compatible with strong ethical, even mystical, emotions; the eloquence of their musical expression rises unsolicited from the substance of the musical thought.

The United States

Nationalism has played only a subsidiary part in the musical scene of twentieth-century United States of America. The composer who hoped to bridge the gulf between popular music and the concert hall audience in the 1920's was George Gershwin (1898–1937), whose *Rhapsody in Blue* (1924) was an attempt to combine the languages of jazz and Lisztian Romanticism. More spontaneous expression of his natural gifts came in the musical comedies (*Of Thee I Sing;* 1931) and especially in the "folk opera" *Porgy and Bess* (1935).

An example of integration of national American idioms in the music of a composer of high endowment and thorough technical training is found in the work of Aaron Copland (born 1900). Copland was the first of many American composers of his generation who studied at Paris under Nadia Boulanger. Jazz idioms and dissonance are prominent in some of his earlier works, such as the *Music for the Theater* (1925) and the Piano Concerto (1927). These were followed by a number of compositions of a more reserved and harmonically complex style, represented by the Piano Variations of 1930. The felt need to appeal to a larger audience motivated a turn toward simplicity, diatonic harmonies, and the use of folk song material—Mexican folk songs in the brilliant orchestral piece *El Salón México* (1936), cowboy songs in the ballets *Billy the Kid* (1938) and *Rodeo* (1942). The school opera *The Second Hurricane* (1937) and scores for a number of films (including *Our Town*, 1940) are examples of music specifically "for use" in this period. The apex of this trend was reached in *Appalachian Spring* (1944), first written as a ballet with an orchestra of thirteen instruments but better known in the arrangement as a suite for symphony orchestra. *Appalachian Spring* is in Copland's work what the *Pastoral Symphony* is in Vaughan Williams's. Unlike the English composer, Copland incorporates an actual folk tune (the Shaker hymn *The Gift to Be Simple*) as well as suggestions of folk dance music; but the material is subtly transfigured and its essence absorbed in a work that sincerely and simply expresses the pastoral spirit in authentically American terms.

Aaron Copland

On the technical side, Copland uses the *pandiatonic* principle, according to which any or all notes of the diatonic scale may be regarded as consonant with one another for vertical combinations: the opening chord of *Appalachian Spring*, with its derivations and amplifications, serves as a unifying device, a characteristic sonority with divided strings and soft woodwinds that returns from time to time throughout the work (see Example 102).

Example 102 · · · · · · Pandiatonic Chord Forms in *Appalachian Spring*, Copland

A new synthesis on a large scale appeared with the Third Symphony (1946), which has no overt programmatic significance (though some of its tunes are suggestive of folk songs), and well exemplifies Copland's characteristic combination of "leanness and grandiosity."[3] A more finely wrought chamber music idiom, a further evolution from the style of the Piano Variations, is found in the Piano Sonata (1941) and the Violin Sonata (1943). In the songs on *Twelve Poems of Emily Dickinson* (1950), and more markedly in the Piano Quartet (1950) and the Piano Fantasy (1957) Copland adopts some features of the twelve-tone technique. Despite the various influences reflected in the range of styles in his works, Copland retains an unmistakable personal quality. His music preserves the sense of tonality, though not always by traditional means; his rhythms are live and flexible, and he is adept at obtaining new sounds from simple chords by instrumental color and spacing. His work and counsel have influenced many younger American composers.

A more self-conscious nationalist is Roy Harris (born 1898), whose music at its best (as in the Third Symphony, 1939) suggests something of the rugged simplicity of Walt Whitman; many of his works embody actual folk themes, as for example the choral *Folk Song Symphony* (1941).

*Other
American
composers*

Self-conscious nationalism, however, as represented by Harris and by the exploitation of Negro spirituals and cowboy tunes, is by now a thing of the past. So also is the neo-primitive movement represented by Virgil Thomson (born 1896) in his opera *Four Saints in Three Acts* (1934) on a libretto by Gertrude Stein, and in many of his symphonic and choral works. The genuinely national element in this country's music is not easily isolated or defined, blended as it is with cosmopolitan style features which it shares with European music of the period. Obvious external traits are, of course, the choice of American subjects for operas, vocal works, or symphonic poems, but in the music itself nationalism is a more subtle ingredient; it may be detected, perhaps, is a certain forthright, optimistic character, a reticence about the expression of deep emotion, or a fast-driving rhythmic energy, such as that of Robert Palmer's Piano Quartet (1947). Some of the most eminent contemporary American composers, however, write habitually in a language that cannot be called national in any limiting sense of the word: for example, Walter Piston (born 1894), Roger Sessions (born 1896), and Howard Hanson (born 1896). Piston's style is that of a sturdy and sophisticated neo-Classicism, as may be heard from his chamber music and symphonies (No. II, 1943; No. III, 1947; No. IV, 1951; Nos. V and VI, 1956). Sessions' speech is more intense, dissonant, and chromatic (Second Symphony, 1946; Third Symphony, 1957; *Idyll of Theocritus*, 1954). Hanson is an avowed neo-Romantic with a style influenced by Sibelius. A larger proportion of specifically American elements appears in the work of William Schuman (born 1910).

The principal representatives of nationalism in Latin American music are Heitor Villa-Lobos (1887–1959) of Brazil and Carlos Chavez (born 1899) of Mexico. Villa-Lobos's best-known works are a series of compositions for various vocal and instrumental combinations under the general designation "*choros*," which make use of Brazilian rhythms and sonorities. Chavez is particularly notable for the *Sinfonia India* (1936) and the Piano Concerto (1940).

Neo-Classicism

"*Les Six*" was the name given to a group of young French composers who gathered around Erik Satie about 1917. In association with other artists, including the poet Jean Cocteau, they proposed a program for freeing music from impressionism, primitivism, and other modern "isms" by turning for models to the realistic style of the dance hall and cabaret, to jazz and to other manifestations of actual popular taste. The ballets produced in immediate pursuit of this program in the early twenties are of only passing interest; but the idea of *actualité*, of an art divorced from preciosity and Romantic dreaming, stripped of meaningless ornamentations, clear in outlines, and close to real life of the present, was injected into French music and produced results of some importance in the works of composers like Milhaud and Poulenc, as well as Stravinsky, who, though living in Paris at the time, was not one of the *Six*. Moreover, the atmosphere created by these ideas—an eager acceptance of the new and experimental and a wholesale emphatic rejection of the Romantic and impressionist traditions—was one of the factors that prepared the way for the rise of neo-Classicism.

The most important of the *Six* were Arthur Honegger and Darius Milhaud. Honegger (1892–1955), of Swiss parentage but born in France and resident in Paris after 1913, soon departed from the ideals of the *Six*. He excels in music of dynamic action and graphic gesture, expressed in short-breathed melodies, strong ostinato rhythms, bold colors, and sharply dissonant harmonies. The French composer to

Arthur Honegger

whose style his is most nearly related is Florent Schmitt. Honegger's "symphonic movement," *Pacific 231*, in which he aimed not to imitate the sound, but to translate into music the visual and physical impression, of a speeding locomotive, was hailed as a sensational piece of modernistic program music in 1923. The same violent energy, in more tightly organized musical form, was manifested in the "mimed symphony," *Horace Victorious* (1921); a lighter touch marked the orchestral *Pastorale d'été* (*Summer Pastorale;* 1920) and the sparkling *Concertino* for piano and orchestra (1925). His principal orchestral works are the five symphonies (1931–51).

Honegger became world famous after the appearance in concert form (1923) of his oratorio *King David*, which had been first presented in an original stage version two years before. This work marks the beginning of the rise of an important new form in the second quarter of the twentieth century, a compound of oratorio and opera. *King David* has become popular because the choruses are easy to sing (they were written in the first place for amateurs), the rhythmic and formal patterns are conventional, the few harmonic audacities are mingled with familiar consonant diatonic writing, and the unified action—the scene connections, in the concert version, being effected by means of a narrator—is illustrated by music of pictorial vividness and spontaneous melody.

On a grander scale—with five speaking parts, five soloists, mixed chorus (which both sings and speaks), children's chorus, and large orchestra—is *Jeanne d'Arc au Bûcher* (*Joan of Arc at the Stake;* 1938), an elaborate oratorio-drama by Paul Claudel, with music in which Gregorian chant, dance tunes, and modern and medieval folksongs are mingled with Honegger's dissonant, highly colored idiom; this work is held together more by dramatic power than by musical architecture. Of Honegger's operas the finest is *Antigone* (1927); the text is a condensed modernized version of Sophocles done by Jean Cocteau, and the composer has achieved a particularly realistic, rapid, and forceful declamation in recitatives. The *opéra comique, Les Aventures du Roi Pausole* (*The Adventures of King Pausole;* 1930) was a popular success, and Honegger also wrote music for no fewer than thirty-five films. Of all the so-called *avant-garde* composers of his time, Honegger was the first to persuade the public at large to give modern music a hearing.

Darius Milhaud was born at Aix in Provence in 1892. He created a gracious memorial of his native region in the *Suite Provençal* for orchestra (1937), which incorporates melodies of the early eighteenth-century composer André Campra. Milhaud has produced an immense quantity of music. He seems to compose with a facility rare in the twentieth century, which recalls the days of Haydn and Mozart. His works include piano pieces, chamber music (the eighteen string quartets are especially notable), suites, sonatas, symphonies, film music, ballets, songs, cantatas, and operas. There is a contrast between

Darius Milhaud

the frivolity, the mockery and satire of the ballets *Le Boeuf sur le toit* (*The Ox on the Roof;* 1919) or *Le Train bleu* (*The Blue Train;* 1924) and the cosmic earnestness of the opera-oratorio *Christophe Colomb* (1928) or the religious devotion of the music for the Jewish *Sacred Service* (1947). Milhaud is an artist of Classical temperament, not given to theories or systems, but infinitely receptive to many kinds of stimuli which are spontaneously converted to musical expression: Brazilian folk melodies and rhythms, for example, in the orchestral dances (later arranged for piano) *Saudades do Brasil* (*Souvenirs of Brazil;* 1920–21); saxophones, ragtime syncopations, and the blues third in the ballet *La Création du monde* (*The Creation of the World;* 1924). Milhaud's music is essentially lyrical in inspiration, blended of ingenuousness and ingenuity, clear and logical in form, and addressed to the listener as objective statement, not personal confession.

A technical device used recurrently in his works is *polytonality*—one of those terms that are easier to use than to define. Of course we can say that polytonality is the property of music written in two or more keys at once. But is it really possible to *hear* more than one tonality at a time? If it is not, we must conclude that "polytonal" music means no more than music in which one can discern by analysis (usually visual) that two or more lines of melody or planes of harmony, each in a distinct and different key, are sounding simultaneously. A simple instance is given in Example 103a.

Extension of the polytonal principle produced the complex dissonances of *Christophe Colomb* and of the closing scene of the opera *Les Euménides* (1924); in the latter Milhaud builds up to six simultaneous different keys, reduces them gradually to two, and finally resolves on the single key of C major. A similar piling up of tonalities occurs in the first movement of the Fourth Symphony (1948). Of course no listener hears the two tonalities B major and G major in

Polytonality in Works of Milhaud

Example 103

a. *Saudades do Brasil,* I, No. 4

b. String Quartet No. 12

Theme:

First vln and viola (muted)

Cello muted

Coda:

Excerpt of the String Quartet No. 12 by Darius Milhaud used by permission of Editions Salabert, publishers and © owners. *Saudades do Brazil,* © 1922, renewed 1950, by Editions Max Eschig.

Example 103a. What he hears is G major with a few dissonant notes which he probably interprets as passing tones or nonresolving appoggiaturas; in *Les Euménides* and similar passages he hears a mass of undifferentiated dissonance in which the direction of the musical movement is defined by rhythms and melodic lines, while the arrival at the final goal is made climactic by the resolution of dissonance into consonance. Milhaud offers a simple explanation of his use of polytonal chords: "The sound of them satisfied my ear; a polytonal chord when soft is more subtly sweet and when forceful is more violent than the normal kind." And he adds that he used such chords "only to support a diatonic melody"—an important qualification, to which another may be added, namely that the various polytonal planes are distinguished by different instrumental timbres in orchestral writing, and this incidentally diminishes their dissonant effect.

To illustrate this aspect of Milhaud's style, we may take (Example 103b) two passages from the slow movement of the Twelfth Quartet (1945). The opening motives of the movement, exploiting the sonority of parallel thirds against a dominant pedal in A major, form the subject of the coda: two polytonal measures (A-G-D-E-flat) followed by a pandiatonic passage in A with the Lydian sharped fourth, and final cadence with momentary clash of minor and major third.

The gamut of Milhaud's style is disclosed in his operas. In addition to the music for Claudel's translations of three plays from Aeschylus (composed between 1913 and 1924), these include *Les Malheurs d'Orphée* (*The Misfortunes of Orpheus*, 1924), *Le Pauvre Matelot* (*The Poor Sailor*, 1926) on a libretto by Jean Cocteau; three *opéras minutes*, running about ten minutes each, on parodies of classical myths (1927); the huge oratorio-opera *Christophe Colomb* (1928; text by Paul Claudel); the formally more conventional *Maximilien* (1930), *Médée* (1938), and *Bolivar* (1943); and the Biblical opera *David*, commissioned to celebrate the 3,000th anniversary of Jerusalem as the capital of David's kingdom, and first performed in concert version at Jerusalem in 1954. All Milhaud's operas, in contrast to the symphonic music dramas of Wagner, are organized in distinct scene complexes with arias and choruses, and the singing voices are the center of interest rather than the orchestra.

Another member of *les Six*, Francis Poulenc (1899–1963), held more closely to the original ideals of this group than did Honegger or Milhaud. Poulenc's compositions are for the most part in small forms. *Francis Poulenc* He combines the grace and wit of the Parisian popular *chansons* with a gift for satirical mimicry—of Puccini, Massenet, and Debussy in his comic opera *Les Mamelles de Tirésias* (*The Breasts of Tiresias;* 1940), for example—and natural fluent melody with an ingratiating harmonic idiom. By no means are all his works frivolous. His *Concert champêtre* (*Pastoral Concerto*) for harpsichord or piano and small orchestra (1928) is neo-Classical in the spirit of Rameau and Scarlatti; among his compositions are a Mass in G for chorus *a cappella* (1937), several motets, and other choral works. He is very highly regarded as a composer of songs. His three-act serious opera *Dialogues des Carmélites* (*Dialogues of the Carmelites;* 1956) is a most effective setting of an unusually fine libretto by Georges Bernanos.

Of other French composers we shall mention only Olivier Messiaen (born 1908), a neo-Romantic and Catholic mystic whose musical resources include Hindu rhythmic patterns, Balinese instrumental sonorities, bird song motives, plainchant, and electronic instruments. His method of composition involves the building of musical sentences by paraphrasing given motives according to elaborately constructed rhythmic and scale formulas; his aesthetic principles are markedly similar to those of Scriabin. Messiaen is one of the leading teachers of younger composers. His compositions include works for the piano, a *Quatuor pour la fin du temps* (*Quartet for the End of Time;* 1941), songs, a cantata *Trois Petites Liturgies de la Présence Divine* (*Three Short Liturgies of the Divine Presence;* 1942) for orchestra and unison chorus of women's voices, and several works for his own instrument, the organ, among them a set of nine "meditations" on *La Nativité du Seigneur* (*The Nativity of the Lord;* 1935).

We come now to a composer whose works exemplify nearly every significant musical tendency of the first half of the twentieth century, whose career might almost by itself serve as an epitome of that changeful epoch, and whose influence on two generations of composers has been as great as, if not greater than, Wagner's influence between 1870 and 1910: Igor Stravinsky. Born in Russia in 1882, he came to Paris in 1911, lived in Switzerland after 1914, in Paris again after 1920, and has lived in California since 1940.

His principal early compositions were three ballets commissioned by Sergei Diaghilev (1872–1929), the founder and director of the Russian Ballet, which for twenty years after its first season at Paris in

Igor Stravinsky (born 1882); a drawing by Picasso, 1920. (Bettmann Archive)

1909 was a European institution that attracted the services of the leading artists of the time. For Diaghilev and Paris Stravinsky wrote *The Fire Bird* (1910), *Petrushka* (1911), and *Le Sacre du printemps* (*The Rite of Spring*, subtitled *Pictures of Pagan Russia;* 1913). The *Fire Bird* stems from the Russian nationalist tradition, and has the exotic orientalism and rich sensuous orchestration of Stravinsky's teacher, Rimsky-Korsakov. *Petrushka* brings a touch of *verismo* in its circus scenes and characters, while the alert rhythms, bright raw orchestral colors, and leaner contrapuntal texture indicate realms that later were further explored by Stravinsky. The *Sacre* is undoubtedly the most famous composition of the early twentieth century; it had the effect of an explosion that so scattered the elements of musical language that they could never again be put together as before. In the long run this work, along with *The Fire Bird* and *Petrushka*, has enjoyed more public favor than Stravinsky's later compositions.

The *Sacre* was the culminating point of primitivism; Cocteau called it "a pastorale of the pre-historic world." Its novelty consisted not only in the rhythms but even more in the hitherto unheard orchestral effects and chordal combinations, and in the ruthless logic and elemental power with which all these were carried out to the ultimate consequences.

The forced economy of wartime, together with Stravinsky's inner impulsion toward new goals, led to a change of style that became evident in the years 1913 to 1923. Compositions of this period include chamber music, short piano pieces, and songs; the ballets *L'Histoire du Soldat* (*The Soldier's Tale;* 1918), *Les Noces* (*The Wedding,* 1917–23), and *Pulcinella* (1919); and the *Octet for Wind Instruments* (1923). The first feature of the new style which strikes one is the replacement of a large orchestra by small combinations: for *L'Histoire*, solo instruments in pairs (violin and double bass, clarinet and bassoon, cornet and trombone) and a battery of percussion—seven players in all; for *Les Noces*, four pianos and percussion; for *Pulcinella*, a small orchestra with strings divided into concertino and ripieno groups. *L'Histoire* and *Les Noces*, with the *opera buffa, Mavra* (1921), were the last of Stravinsky's Russian works. The *Ragtime* and *Piano Rag Music* were early examples (followed by many others, such as the *Ebony Concerto* of 1945) of his interest in jazz, an interest reflected also in the instrumentation and rhythms of *L'Histoire*. *Pulcinella* is a prelude to Stravinsky's neo-Classical period, of which the *Octet* is the standard early example. The latter was followed by a Concerto for Piano and Wind Instruments (1924), a piano Sonata (1924), and the *Suite in A* for piano (1925).

Neo-Classical is the tag usually attached to Stravinsky's style from the time of the *Octet* to that of the opera *The Rake's Progress* (1951). The word may more broadly also designate a general tendency of this period, one best exemplified perhaps in Stravinsky and largely inspired by him, but evident also to a greater or lesser degree in the majority of other contemporary composers. In this sense neo-Classicism may be defined as adherence to the Classical principles of balance, coolness, objectivity, and absolute (as against Romantic program) music, with the corollary characteristics of economy, predominantly contrapuntal texture, and (usually) diatonic tonal harmonies; it sometimes involves also imitation or quotation of, or allusion to, specific melodies or style traits of older composers—as in Stravinsky's *Pulcinella*, which is built on themes attributed to Pergolesi, or the ballet *Le Baiser de la Fée* (*The Fairy's Kiss;* 1928), based on themes from Tchaikovsky.

Of course the idea of renewing an art by turning to principles and models of an earlier time was not new; it was one of the basic ideas of the Renaissance, and composers of all periods have on occasion deliberately made use of older styles. But the neo-Classicism of the twentieth century had two special features: first, it was a symptom of a search for principles of order, for some way other than Schoenberg's out of the pitfalls of Romanticism and the seeming chaos of the years between 1910 and 1920; and second, composers as never before had a detailed knowledge of many past styles and were aware of the uses they were making of them. The aim was not to revive archaic idioms, but to acknowledge tradition in the sense that Stravinsky defined it: "a living force that animates and informs the present. . . . Far from implying the repetition of what has been, tradition presupposes the reality of what endures. It appears as an heirloom, a heritage that one receives on condition of making it bear fruit before passing it on to one's descendants."[4]

It was difficult for critics and the public, who thought of Stravinsky as the revolutionary composer of the *Sacre,* to comprehend the apparent reversal implied by *L'Histoire, Pulcinella,* and the *Octet.* With our perspective we can see that the change was not so radical as it at first seemed. However, each new work by Stravinsky continued to cause some reaction of surprise, because in each he elaborated a particular generative idea in forms, timbres, and harmonies appropriate to that idea and to no other. Merely to label all of his compositions written between 1923 and 1951 as neo-Classical would be—as always with classifications but especially so here—to overlook the variety in these productions, the individuality of each composition, and the continuity that underlies not only this period but the whole of his work from *The Fire Bird* on.

Stravinsky contributed two large compositions to choral literature: the opera-oratorio *Oedipus Rex* (*Oedipus the King;* 1927) on a Latin translation of Cocteau's adaptation of Sophocles, for soloists, narrator, men's chorus, and orchestra; and the *Symphony of Psalms* (1930) for mixed chorus and orchestra on Latin texts from the Vulgate. Stravinsky used Latin because the language's being conventionalized, like a ritual, left him free to concentrate, as he said, on its "phonetic" qualities. *Oedipus* is statuesque, static, blocklike, intense within its stylized form. The *Symphony of Psalms* is one of the great works of the twentieth century, a masterpiece of invention, musical architecture, and religious devotion.

In line with Stravinsky's attraction to Classical subjects are the ballet *Apollon musagète* (*Apollo Leader of the Muses;* 1928) and the melodrama *Perséphone* (1934), the former for string orchestra and the latter for a normal orchestra with reciter, tenor soloist, mixed chorus, and children's chorus. Chamber music works include, besides the *Octet,* a *Duo Concertant* for violin and piano (1932), a concerto for two pianos (1935), the *Dumbarton Oaks Concerto* in E-flat (1938), and the *Basle Concerto* in D (1946), both for chamber orchestra. Normal orchestral forces are employed in the *Capriccio* for piano and orchestra (1929) and the Violin Concerto (1931). The *Symphony in C* (1940) is a model of neo-Classical clarity and compact form. The *Symphony in Three Movements* (1945) is more agitated and dissonant, and recalls some features of the *Sacre.*

The subject of the opera, *The Rake's Progress,* was suggested by Hogarth's engravings; the libretto is by W. H. Auden and Chester Kallman. In this work Stravinsky adopts the eighteenth-century division into recitatives, arias, and ensembles, organizes the entire opera on the basis of key relationships, and achieves in the final scenes a climax of pathos without sentimentality.

A setting of the Mass (1948) for mixed chorus with double woodwind quintet and brasses exhibits an austere "neo-Gothic" style that places this work transitionally between the *Symphony of Psalms* and the *Canticum sacrum* for tenor and baritone soloists, chorus, and orchestra, composed "in honor of St. Mark" and first sung in St. Mark's Cathedral at Venice in 1956. In parts of the *Canticum sacrum* and other compositions of the 1950's (including the Septet, 1953; the song *In memoriam Dylan Thomas,* 1954; the ballet *Agon,* 1954–57; and the *Threni,* 1958, for voices and orchestra on texts from the Lamentations of Jeremiah), Stravinsky judiciously and most effectively adapts for his own purposes the techniques of the Schoenberg-Webern school.

An analysis of Stravinsky's style that would do justice to both the diversity of its manifestations and the unity that underlies it throughout would require a book. Here we can only call attention to a few characteristic features, emphasizing as we do that Stravinsky's rhythms, harmonies, colors, and all other details are inseparate from a living body of music; the student should hear and study these features in their context, in the works themselves, and in so doing he will sharpen his perception for all the details in Stravinsky's music.

Rhythm: One of the steps of the present century has been the liberation of rhythm from the "tyranny of the barline," that is, from the regularity of constant two- or three-unit groups of strong and weak accents in which the strong accents regularly coincide with changes of harmony. Stravinsky often denies the barline by introducing an irregular pattern of rhythm after a regular one has been

established, and by returning to the regular pattern from time to time
(Example 104a). The regular beat may be maintained in one part
against a conflicting irregular pattern in another (Example 104b); or
two different rhythms may be combined (Example 104c). A rhythmic
motive may be shifted from place to place in the measure (Example
104d). The rhythm at the beginning of the last movement of the *Sacre*
looks very irregular but sounds orderly; as a matter of fact it is
organized rather symmetrically around the motive 𝄾 ♫, which
appears eight times (Example 104e). Patterns of the subtlety of
Example 104f may be found in practically any of Stravinsky's compositions of the neo-Classical period. Particularly fascinating is the
way in which he thickens and then opens out the harmonies, dislocates
and relocates the rhythms, in a long pulsation of tension and release
before an important cadence: the endings of the *Octet*, the third and
fourth movements of the *Symphony in C*, and the Sanctus in the *Mass*.

Another important detail in Stravinsky's rhythm is his use of silences
—sometimes merely a lift between chords, sometimes a breath on the
downbeat before the beginning of a phrase, sometimes a rhetorical
pause that accumulates tension in the progress toward a climax (the
Interlude between the second and third movements of the *Symphony
in Three Movements* and many places elsewhere in this symphony,
the Symphony in C, and other works).

Harmony: Stravinsky's music is organized around tonal centers.
Ambiguous chords like the one in the second movement of the *Sacre*
(Example 105a) and the notorious bitonal C–F-sharp in *Petrushka*
(Example 105b), however they may be explained, are certainly not to
be interpreted in their context as atonal. One type of ambiguity common in Stravinsky's work results from his use of both the major and
minor third of a triad either simultaneously or in close juxtaposition
(Examples 105c and d; in the latter example, other degrees of the scale
are also present in simultaneously conflicting forms).

A more subtle use of the major-minor third relationship is shown in
Example 105e: here the conflict between the keys of C and E-flat
major (the minor third of C) is resolved to C major at measure seven.
This chord marks at the same time a resolution of the tonal tendencies
of the two preceding movements which centered respectively on the
notes E and E-flat, the major and minor thirds of C.

The pandiatonic passage in A major (with a chromatic F-natural)
of Example 106a contrasts with the more linear texture of Example
106b (notice the motive marked by brackets). This passage is in D
and predominantly modal (Dorian). It is an instrumental phrase that
recurs identically twice as a ritornello; at the end (Example 106c)
Stravinsky takes B-sharp = C-natural as a pivot note for a modulation
back from the dominant A, then recapitulates in condensed form the
harmonies of the ritornello and adds a cadential echo, using only
modal tones and leaving the seventh of the mode (C-natural) with its
fifth (G) unresolved in the final chord.

Orchestration: A high proportion of Stravinsky's works is written for unusual groups of instruments. This is another respect in which each new composition is a law to itself; the particular color is part of the particular musical conception in each instance. The odd combination of L'Histoire is ideally suited to—is inseparable from—the kind

Stravinsky Rhythms Example 104

a. *Sacre (Augures printaniers)*

b. *Histoire du Soldat*, Scene 1

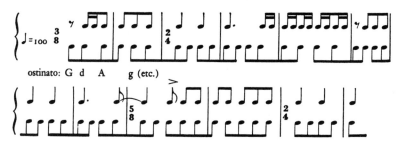

ostinato: G d A g (etc.)

c. *Petrushka*, Pt. I

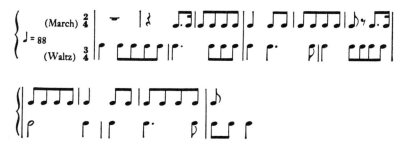

d. *Symphony of Psalms*, last movement

Example 104
(cont.)

e. *Sacre (Danse sacrale)*

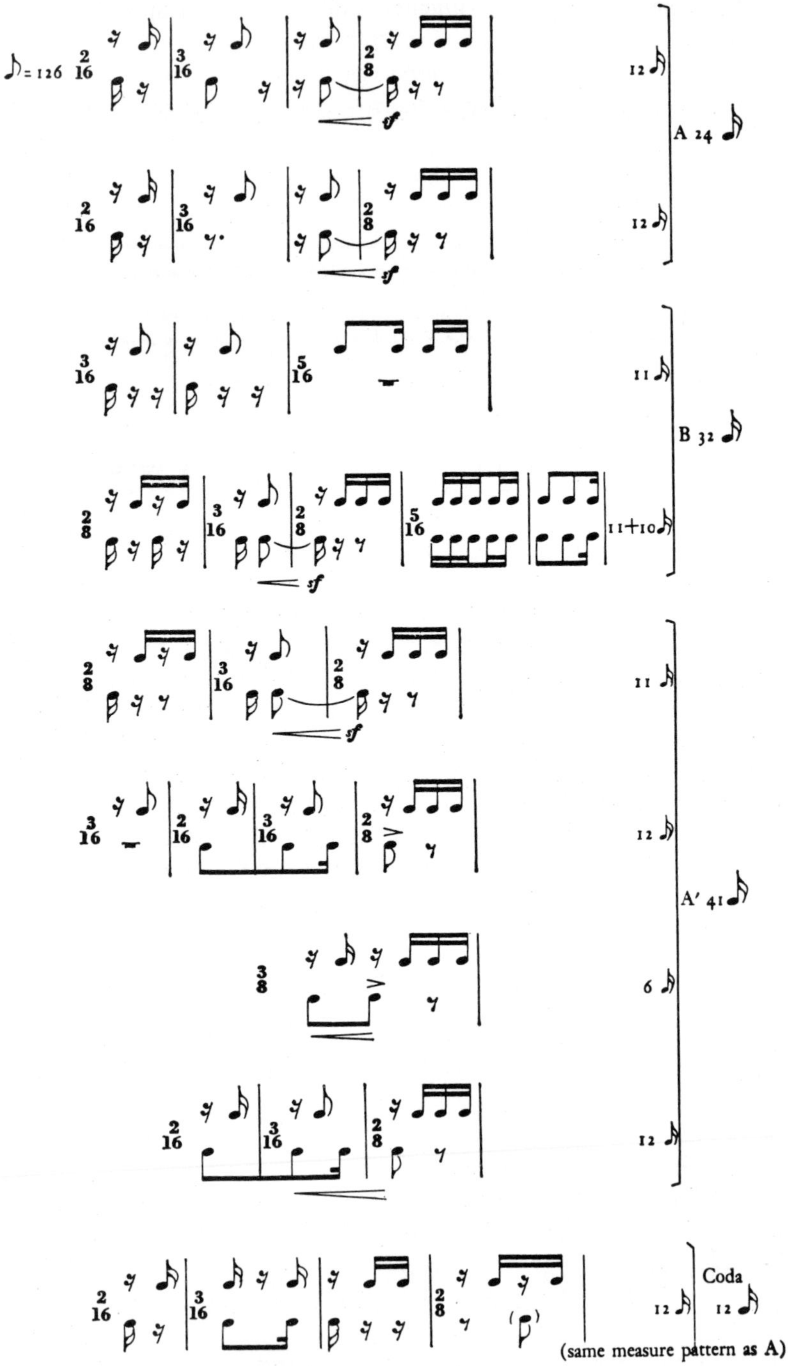

(same measure pattern as A)

of music that the piece is; so equally are the serene strings of *Apollon musagète*, the dark solo woodwinds at the opening of the *Sacre*, and the Mozartean clarity of the orchestra of the *Symphony in C.*

The piano is used conspicuously and effectively in *Petrushka;* it contributes to the orchestral color (usually in conjunction with the harp) in many later works, notably *Oedipus*, the *Symphony of Psalms*, *Perséphone*, and the *Symphony in Three Movements*. Several works of the years around 1920 use no stringed instruments (*Ragtime, Les Noces, Octet, Piano Concerto, Symphonies for Wind Instruments*); it is as though Stravinsky distrusted their color as associated with sentimentality. The warm tones of the violins, violas, and clarinets are avoided in the *Symphony of Psalms*. In some of the late works the instruments are grouped antiphonally. In the Mass two oboes, English horn, and two bassoons are balanced against two trumpets and three

Examples of Stravinsky's Harmony   Example 105

Example 105
(cont.)

trombones; the instrumentation of the *Canticum sacrum* is similar
though somewhat larger (seven woodwinds and eight brasses), and
harp, organ, violas, and double basses are also added to the antiphony.
The tenor voice in the Dylan Thomas song is accompanied sparely by
solo strings with short ritornellos for string quartet, and the song is
framed by a prelude and postlude in which the strings alternate with a
quartet of trombones in chorale-like dirge canons.

Of innumerable special orchestral effects in Stravinsky we cite: the

442

a. *Symphony in Three Movements*

Example 106

b. Agnus Dei from *Mass:* beginning

c. Agnus Dei from *Mass:* conclusion

Mass, © 1948 by Boosey & Hawkes Inc.; reprinted by permission.

ravishing duet and trio combinations with their arabesques and open-work accompaniment in the first and last sections of the slow movement of the *Symphony in C;* the heterophony of the strings in the finale of the same symphony; the accompaniment of upward-rushing scales at the "Divum Jocastae caput" monologue in *Oedipus Rex* (compare the opening of the *Symphony in Three Movements*); and the device of doubling a legato melodic line by another instrument playing staccato, which gives a peculiar percussive accent to each note (finale of the *Symphony in Three Movements*).

Stravinsky clearly defined his attitude toward composition in the *Poetics of Music* as the acceptance of limits as a means to freedom: 443

The creator's function is to sift the elements he receives from [imagination], for human activity must impose limits on itself. The more art is controlled, limited, worked over, the more it is free.

As for myself, I experience a sort of terror when, at the moment of setting to work and finding myself before the infinitude of possibilities that present themselves, I have the feeling that everything is permissible to me....

Will I then have to lose myself in this abyss of freedom? To what shall I cling in order to escape the dizziness that seizes me before the virtuality of this infinitude? ... Fully convinced that combinations which have at their disposal twelve sounds in each octave and all possible rhythmic varieties promise me riches that all the activity of human genius will never exhaust ... I am always able to turn immediately to the concrete things that are here in question. I have no use for a theoretic freedom. Let me have something finite, definite—matter that can lend itself to my operation only insofar as it is commensurate with my possibilities. And such matter presents itself to me together with its limitations. I must in turn impose mine upon it....

My freedom thus consists in my moving about within the narrow frame that I have assigned myself for each one of my undertakings.

I shall go even farther: my freedom will be so much the greater and more meaningful the more narrowly I limit my field of action and the more I surround myself with obstacles. Whatever diminishes constraint diminishes strength. The more constraints one imposes, the more one frees oneself of the chains that shackle the spirit.[5]

The conditions Stravinsky imposed on himself were different for each work and he made no attempt to formulate a general system of composition. Such an attempt was made, however, by the German composer Paul Hindemith (1895–1963) in his music, his writings, and his teaching—at the Berlin School of Music 1927–37, Yale University 1940–53, and the University of Zurich from 1953.

Hindemith was first of all a practical musician. An experienced solo, orchestral, and ensemble player on the violin and viola, he learned

Paul Hindemith (1895–1963). (BMI Archives)

to play many other instruments as well. Unlike Schoenberg, Bartók, and Stravinsky, he did not go through any early important Romantic or impressionist stage but plunged at once with his first published compositions into the seething, confused world of the new music in Germany of the 1920's. It is noteworthy that in the light of changed conceptions of tonality the composer some twenty-five years later revised the three principal large works of this decade. These were a song cycle for soprano voice and piano on poems of R. M. Rilke, *Das Marienleben* (*The Life of Mary;* 1923), the tragic expressionist opera *Cardillac* (1926), and the comic opera *Neues vom Tage* (*News of the Day;* 1929). Four string quartets and a large quantity of other chamber music are also among Hindemith's works of this period.

In the late 1920's and early 1930's, Hindemith, disturbed by the cleavage between composers and public, undertook the works that caused his name to be associated with *Gebrauchsmusik*—that is, "music for use," as distinguished from "music for music's sake." Among such works were a musical playlet for children entitled *Wir bauen eine Stadt* (*Let's Build a Town;* 1930) and a number of pieces of the sort known in Germany as *Sing- und Spielmusik,* a term for which there is no convenient English equivalent. It means "music for singing and playing" by amateurs who do it for fun; it is "play" music in a double sense of the word. It is necessarily not too difficult, and must be attractive for the performers without being vulgar. *Spielmusik* occupies an important place both in Hindemith's works and in his teachings about the social obligations of a composer.

Less dissonant linear counterpoint, more systematic tonal organization, and a new quality of almost Romantic warmth became evident in the 1930's (compare Examples 107a and 107b). Compositions of this decade include the opera *Mathis der Maler* (*Matthias the Painter;* 1934), based on the life and works of the sixteenth-century German artist Matthias Grünewald; the orchestral suite of excerpts from this opera is probably the best known of all Hindemith's works. Also from the 1930's come the three Piano Sonatas (1936); a sonata for piano four hands (1938); the ballets *Nobilissima visione* (1938; on St. Francis of Assisi) and *The Four Temperaments* (1940); and the *Symphony in E-flat* (1940).

A great deal of Hindemith's music was composed for use in the sense that it was written for particular players, or to add to the repertoire of certain instruments for which little literature existed: among his numerous sonatas are some for such comparatively neglected solo instruments as the viola d'amore, horn, trumpet, English horn, double bass, and tuba, as well as the more usual ones (flute, oboe, clarinet, viola, violin, organ). There are concertos for orchestra and various instrumental groups (string quartet with piano, brass, and two harps; woodwinds and harp; trumpet, bassoon, and strings) and for solo instruments (piano, violin, violoncello, clarinet, organ); and there is a *Symphony for Concert Band* (1951).

Examples of Hindemith's Harmony

Quartet No. 4, © 1924, renewed 1952, by B. Schott's Soehne, Mainz. *Mathis der Maler,*
© 1935 by B. Schott's Soehne, Mainz.

Another kind of music for use was written for teaching purposes.
The title *Klaviermusik: Übung in drei Stücken* (*Piano Music: Three
Practice Pieces;* 1925) is reminiscent of Bach's *Clavier Übung.*
Analogous to *The Well-Tempered Clavier* is Hindemith's *Ludus
tonalis* (*Game of Tonalities;* 1942) for piano: subtitled "Studies in
Counterpoint, Tonal Organization, and Piano Playing," it consists of
twelve fugues (one in each key) with modulating interludes, a Prelude
(C ➔ F-sharp), and Postlude (F-sharp ➔ C).

Compositions after 1940 include the Fifth and Sixth Quartets (1943,
1945) the *Symphonic Metamorphoses* on themes of Weber (1943), a
"requiem" on words of Whitman ("When lilacs last in the dooryard
bloom'd"), and other choral works; the new version of the *Marienleben* (1948); and the opera *Die Harmonie der Welt* (*The Harmony*

of the Universe; 1957), parts of which had already appeared as a three-movement orchestral symphony in 1951.

For Hindemith, tonality in music was as inevitable as the law of gravity in the physical world, and he held that attempts to ignore it not only are ineffective but result in chaos. The various possible combinations of intervals within the twelve tones of the scale have a naturally ordered relationship both to each other and to fundamental central tonalities, and such natural relationships must be observed in all musical composition. Hindemith's statement does not imply a return to the particular method of tonal organization that prevailed in the eighteenth and nineteenth centuries, but is a much more inclusive synthesis.

A practical result of his theories was the 1948 revision of the *Marienleben* songs, which involved, among other things, changes in the vocal line to integrate the melodies more closely with the harmony, and the introduction of a general scheme of precise tonal interrelationships connected with expressive or symbolic purposes. Some typical changes of detail are illustrated in Example 108, the first eight measures of the second song. Hindemith altered both the passacaglia bass theme and the vocal melody, and the result is a line that is more natural to sing and more consistent with the harmony (for instance, the circled nonchord tones resolve downward by step), while the phrase as a whole is tonally better organized around C, with a climax of tension (most remote keys) at measures five to seven.

Hindemith's work was as versatile and nearly as large in amount as Milhaud's. He was a mid-twentieth-century representative in the German cosmopolitan line of Schumann, Brahms, and Reger; important additional influences in his work came from Bach, Handel, Schütz, and the German sixteenth-century polyphonic song composers. His writing evolved from a dissonant, contrapuntal, impersonal style to one compounded of neo-Romantic feeling and Baroque-Classical formal structures, in a harmonic idiom based on a reasoned extension of tonal principles.

Schoenberg and His Followers

The twentieth-century movement that because of its radical nature has attracted most attention grew out of the music of post-Romanticism in Germany. The earliest important work of Arnold Schoenberg (1874–1951), the symphonic string sextet *Verklärte Nacht* (1899), is in a chromatic idiom clearly derived from that of *Tristan,* while the symphonic poem *Pelleas und Melisande* (1903) is reminiscent of Strauss. With the huge symphonic cantata *Gurre-Lieder* (*Songs of Gurre*) for five soloists, narrator, four choruses, and large orchestra (1901, orchestration finished 1911) Schoenberg outdid even Mahler and Strauss in size and complexity of the score and Wagner in Romantic violence of expression.

447

Changes Made in *Das Marienleben*, Hindemith

Marienleben (old version) © 1924, renewed 1951, by B. Schott's Soehne, Mainz.
Marienleben (new version) © 1948, Schott & Co., Ltd., London.

A new direction is evident in the works of Schoenberg's second period, which include the first two Quartets (D minor and F-sharp minor, 1905 and 1908), the first *Kammersymphonie* (*Chamber Symphony;* 1906) for fifteen instruments, the *Five Orchestral Pieces* Op. 16 (1909), two sets of short piano pieces (Op. 11, 1908 and Op. 19, 1911), a cycle of songs with piano accompaniment, *Das Buch der hängenden Gärten* (*Book of the Hanging Gardens;* 1908), a monodrama for soloist and orchestra *Erwartung* (*Expectation;* 1909), and a dramatic pantomime *Die glückliche Hand* (*The Lucky Hand;* 1911–13). In these works Schoenberg turns away from post-Romantic gigantism either to small instrumental combinations or, if he uses a large orchestra, to soloistic treatment of instruments or swift alternation of colors (as in the *Five Orchestral Pieces* and *Erwartung*) rather than massive blocks of sound. Concurrent with this is an increasing rhythmic and contrapuntal complexity and fragmentation of the melodic line, together with greater concentration: for example, the First Quartet, which is in a one-movement cyclical form, evolves all its themes from variations and combinations of a few germinal motives and uses hardly any material, even in the subsidiary voices, that is not derived from the same motives. Historically significant also is the fact that between 1905 and 1912 Schoenberg moved from a chromatic style on a tonal basis to something that is commonly called *atonality*.

Atonal means literally "not tonal." Roughly speaking, atonal music is music in which the person who is using the word cannot hear tonal centers. More precisely, atonal music is that in which the composer

Arnold Schoenberg (1874–1951).

systematically avoids reference to tonal centers by avoiding harmonic and melodic formulas—for instance, dominant-tonic progressions and melodic phrases implying such progressions—which suggest the traditional system of chords organized about a fundamental tonic or key note. It is unfortunate that the negative term has become fixed in usage instead of Schoenberg's own word *pantonal*, meaning "inclusive of all tonalities." But since *atonal* seems to be permanently lodged in the musical vocabulary, we shall use it, bearing in mind that, like *dissonance*, it is a relative term and that its exact signification varies with the context.

To illustrate: the phrase of Example 109a is from a piece by Schoenberg that is always called atonal. The atonal effect in this instance is due partly to the obscurity of the roots and partly to the "illogical" root movements; but the impression of atonality is reinforced by three factors that are not part of the harmonic scheme at all, namely, the

449

Possible Harmonic Analysis of Passage of Op. 23, No. 5, Schoenberg

fast tempo, the subdivision of beats, and the octave displacement of two melody and two bass notes. If we slow down the pace, smooth out the rhythm, and bring most of the notes within a single octave range, we obtain a phrase that could conceivably—if irrelevantly—be analyzed as shown in Example 109b. The atonal quality of Webern's Symphony Op. 21 (see Example 113) is much more pronounced, owing partly to the numerous major and minor seconds in the harmony and the conspicuous melodic leaps of a minor ninth, as well as to the discontinuous lines and the distribution of the melody notes among different instruments.

The whole course of late Romantic music, especially in Germany, tended toward atonality. Chromatic melody lines and chord progressions, even in Wagner's work and more markedly in Strauss', had resulted in passages in which no tonal center could be perceived; but these passages had been exceptional, relatively short, and anchored within a tonal context.

The close relationship between the late Romantic and the Schoenbergian melodic styles may be seen in Example 110; extreme ranges and wide leaps are characteristic of both. Schoenberg explored the extreme possibilities of chromaticism within the limits of tonality in the *Gurre-Lieder* and *Pelleas*. After that, it was a natural move to cut loose altogether from a key center and treat all twelve notes of the octave as of equal rank instead of regarding some of them as chromatically altered tones of a diatonic scale. Corollary to this was another step—already foreshadowed by the nonfunctional harmonies of Debussy—which Schoenberg called "the emancipation of the dissonance," meaning the freedom to use any combination of tones what-ever as a chord not requiring resolution. The change from tonality obscured by extreme chromaticism to atonality with free dissonance was a gradual process with Schoenberg. The piano pieces Op. 11 are

Relationships of style between Schoenberg and Late Romantic Composers

Example 110

Heldenleben, © 1899, renewed 1927, by F. E. C. Lauckart. *Gurre-Lieder,* © 1920, re-newed 1948, by Universal Edition, Vienna. *Pierrot-Lunaire,* © 1914, renewed 1941, by Universal Edition, Vienna

in a transitional style; the last movement of the Second Quartet (except for the final cadence in F-sharp) and the piano pieces of Op. 19 are more nearly atonal.

Pierrot Lunaire (*Moonstruck Pierrot;* 1912), Schoenberg's best-known composition of the prewar era, is a cycle of twenty-one songs on rather decadent surrealist French poems in German translation, for contralto soloist with a chamber ensemble of five players and eight instruments: flute (interchangeable with piccolo), clarinet (bass clarinet), violin (viola), violoncello, and piano. Each song is accompanied by a different instrumental combination in textures of crystalline clarity. One feature of *Pierrot Lunaire* which accentuates the atonal impression is the use of *Sprechgesang* (speech-song) or *Sprechstimme* (speaking voice): the voice, instead of singing tones of fixed pitch, only suggests the pitches and then immediately moves away from them. This stylized musical declamation partakes of the character of both speaking and singing; the rhythm is notated strictly, while the approximate or initial pitch is indicated by the sign ↗.

Schoenberg and his pupil Alban Berg are the chief representatives in music of a movement called *expressionism*. This word, like *impressionism*, was first used in connection with painting. Expressionism emphasized a contrasting approach, however; whereas impressionism sought to represent objects of the external world as perceived at a given moment, expressionism, proceeding in the opposite direction, sought to represent *inner* experience, using whatever means seemed best suited to the purpose. By virtue of its subjective starting point expressionism is an outgrowth of Romanticism; it differs from Romanticism in the kind of inner experience it aims to portray, and in the means chosen to portray it. The subject matter of expressionism is man as he exists in the modern world and is described by twentieth-century psychology: isolated, helpless in the grip of forces he does not understand, prey to inner conflict, tension, anxiety, fear, and all the elemental irrational drives of the subconscious, and in irritated rebellion against established order and accepted forms.

Hence, expressionistic art is characterized both by desperate intensity of feeling and revolutionary modes of utterance: both characteristics are illustrated by Schoenberg's *Erwartung*, which has tremendous emotional force and is written in a dissonant, rhythmically atomistic, melodically fragmentary, strangely orchestrated, nonthematic musical idiom. *Erwartung, Die glückliche Hand*, and *Pierrot Lunaire* are all expressionist works. They are devoted, down to the last detail, not to being pretty or realistic, but to using the most penetrating means imaginable, no matter how unusual—subject, text, scene design and lighting (in the operas), as well as music—to communicate the particular complex of thought and emotion which Schoenberg wanted to express. Form, of course, they must have. At this period of his development Schoenberg was depending mostly on the text to establish unity in long works; the early atonal piano pieces of Op. 19 are so short—models of concise, epigrammatic style—that the difficulties of formal unity inherent in long instrumental compositions are avoided.

By 1923, after six years during which he published no music, Schoenberg had formulated a "method of composing with twelve tones which are related only with one another." The essential points of the theory of this *twelve-tone* (dodecaphonic) or *serial* technique may be summarized as follows. The basis of each composition is a *row* or *series* consisting of the twelve tones of the octave arranged in any order the composer decides. The tones of the series are used either successively (as melody) or simultaneously (as harmony or counterpoint), in any octave and with any desired rhythm; but, in theory at least, all twelve should be heard before any one recurs (see Example 109). The row may also be used in inverted, retrograde, or retrograde inverted form, and in transpositions of any of the four forms. No note may be used in the composition that does not occur in a succession identical with that of one or another of the forms of the row.

In practice, all sorts of modifications, refinements, complications, and compromises are made. Using the same tone row for an entire composition is a means of unity analogous to using one main key for a composition in tonal style; at the same time the serial technique permits and indeed requires much variety of rhythm, texture, dynamics, and timbre. In a sense, a work using this method may be called a perpetual variation of the basic row.

The first works in which Schoenberg deliberately used tone rows were the five piano pieces Op. 23 (1923), of which however only the last has a complete row of twelve tones. The technique was perfected over the next few years (Suite for Piano, Op. 25; Wind Quintet, Op. 26) and the twelve-tone method appears completely developed in the Third Quartet (1926) and the *Variations for Orchestra* (1928). It is employed also for most of the works Schoenberg wrote after coming to America in 1933, particularly the Violin Concerto (1936) and the Fourth Quartet (1937). "In olden [and tonal] style" he wrote a Suite for String Orchestra (1934), while in the *Ode to Napoleon* and the Piano Concerto (both 1942) he approached a synthesis of his own system with some elements of orthodox tonality.

In 1931–32 Schoenberg composed the first two acts of a three-act opera for which he had written his own libretto, entitled *Moses and Aaron*. The music was never completed, and the score remains a magnificent torso. Against the Old Testament background Schoenberg presents the tragic conflict between Moses as mediator of the word of God and Aaron as Moses' interpreter to the people: conflict, because Moses is unable himself to communicate his vision, and Aaron, who can communicate, cannot rightly understand; tragic, because the flaw of separation is intrinsic and not to be overcome by good will, being rooted in the nature of the philosopher-mystic on the one hand and the statesman-educator on the other. (Aaron says to Moses [Act III, Scene 1], "I was to discourse in images, you in concepts; I to the heart, you to the mind.") Symbolically, Moses speaks (*Sprechstimme*) but does not sing: the Word is not incarnate in music save for one moment only (Act I, Scene 2) as Moses warns Aaron, "Purify your thought: set it free from earthly things, dedicate it to Truth." The solemn alliteration of the German text is reminiscent of Wagner (see Example 111) and throughout Schoenberg employs vowel and consonant sounds in symbolic connection with the music and the dramatic ideas.

Example 111   *Moses and Aaron*, Act I, Scene 2, Schoenberg

Rei - ni- ge dein Den-ken,   lös es von Wert-lo - sem,   wei - he es

Wah - rem:

Moses and Aaron is as much oratorio as opera. The choruses of the people of Israel have a large part in the action; a group of six solo voices (in the orchestra, not on the stage) represents the Voice of God—again, like Moses himself, in *Sprechstimme* with orchestral accompaniment. Undoubtedly the most picturesque part of the score is the complex of solos, choruses, and dances in the big scene of the worship of the Golden Calf (Act II), where rhythm, instrumental color, and sudden contrasts combine in a spectacle of oriental gorgeousness and dramatic effect. The entire opera is based on a single tone row, one form of which is represented in Example 111. In *Moses and Aaron* a profound philosophical conception embodied in appropriate dramatic form unites with the penetrating expressive power of the music and a towering unity of construction to make this work its composer's masterpiece and to give it, along with Berg's *Wozzeck*, a place among the great operas of its time.

Expressionism, and atonalism as a musical style closely associated with it, were in tune with a state of mind prevalent in western Europe in the 1920's, and are therefore significant as a social phenomenon of the period. The Schoenberg followers must be regarded, as far as the first half of the twentieth century is concerned, as a school existing side by side with others which still maintain an allegiance to Classical tonal principles. The music of Berg, some of the late works of Schoenberg, and recent experiments by other composers with serial methods indicate a potential synthesis, which still remains to be achieved.

Schoenberg's most famous pupil, Alban Berg (1885–1935), adopted most of his master's methods of construction; but he used them with freedom and often chose tone rows that allowed for tonal-sounding chords and progressions in the harmony. Moreover, Berg combined

Schoenberg's influence

Alban Berg

454

the technique with a warmth of Romantic feeling so that his music is more readily accessible than that of many twelve-tone composers. His chief works are a *Lyric Suite* for string quartet (1926); a Violin Concerto (1935); and two operas, *Wozzeck* (composed 1917–21, first performed 1925) and *Lulu* (composed 1928–35, the orchestration not quite completed at Berg's death).

Wozzeck is the outstanding example of expressionist opera as well as an impressive historical document. The libretto, arranged by Berg from fragments of a drama by Georg Büchner (1813–1837), presents the soldier Wozzeck as a symbol of "wir arme Leut'" ("we poor people"), a blind and hapless victim of his environment, despised, betrayed in love, driven finally to murder and suicide. The music is continuous throughout each of the three acts, the changing scenes (five in each act) being connected by orchestral interludes as in Debussy's *Pelléas*. Berg's music is unified partly by the use of a few leitmotives but chiefly by being organized in closed forms adapted from those of Classical music (suite, rhapsody, song, march, passacaglia, rondo, symphony, inventions) and by other subtle means. In the vocal parts Berg flexibly alternates ordinary speech and *Sprechgesang* with conventional singing. The many passages of stylized realism (snoring chorus, gurgling of water, a tavern orchestra with an out-of-tune piano caricaturing a waltz motive from *Der Rosenkavalier*) are skilfully employed for expressionistic purposes. The grim, ironical, symbolical action, the wealth of musical invention, the ever-varied, ingenious, and appropriate orchestration, the constant formal clarity and concentration, the pictorial quality and dramatic force of the music cumulate in an effect of unforgettable poignancy.

Lulu is a more abstract, complex opera, equally expressionistic but with more involved symbolism than *Wozzeck;* its music is organized more strictly on twelve-tone lines, though not without some tonal implications. The *Lyric Suite* and the Violin Concerto, like the two operas, are typical of Berg's constant tendency to show the connection between the new style and that of the past. Both the Suite and the Concerto are partially written according to the twelve-tone method; both display Berg's inventive genius and his easy mastery of contrapuntal technique. The basic row of the Concerto is designed in such a way that tonal combinations become practically inevitable (Example 112); in the finale also the tone row forms a link to introduce the melody of a chorale that Bach had harmonized to the words of the hymn *It is Enough* (Cantata No. 60)—an allusion to the death of Manon Gropius, to whose memory the Concerto is dedicated.

Berg represents the Romantic potential of Schoenberg's teaching; Schoenberg's other celebrated pupil, Anton von Webern (1883–1945) represents the Classical potential—atonality without Romanticism. Webern wrote no opera and he never used the device of *Sprechstimme*. The ruling principles in his work are economy and extreme concentration. In his mature style each composition is evolved by

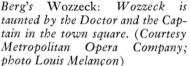
Berg's Wozzeck: Wozzeck *is taunted by the Doctor and the Captain in the town square.* (*Courtesy Metropolitan Opera Company; photo Louis Melançon*)

imitative counterpoint (often strictly canonic); he uses devices such as inversion and rhythmic shifts, but avoids sequences and (for the most part) repetitions. The melodic outline of the generating "cells" usually involves intervals like major sevenths and minor ninths which exclude tonal implications. Textures are stripped to bare essentials; rhythmic patterns are complex, often based on simultaneous duple and triple divisions of all or a part of the measure; and the sound, with all its fine gradation of dynamics, seldom rises above the level of a *forte*.

Most remarkable is Webern's instrumentation. A melodic line **may** be distributed among different instruments somewhat in the manner of medieval hocket, so that sometimes only one or two—seldom more than four or five—successive tones will be heard in the same timbre. The result is a texture made up of sparks and flashes of sound blending in a unique balance of color (see Example 113). A good illustration of this kind of orchestration applied to a more familiar kind of music is Webern's arrangement of the Ricercare from Bach's *Musical Offering*. Special effects—pizzicato, harmonics, tremolo, muting, and the like—are common in all of Webern's music. His sensitiveness for color and clarity often leads him to choose unusual combinations, as in the Quartet Op. 22 for violin, clarinet, tenor saxophone, and piano, or the three songs Op. 18 for soprano, E-flat clarinet, and guitar.

456   It is natural that in a style of such concentration the compositions

Chorale melody

should be short. Not all are so brief as the *Six Bagatelles* for string quartet, Op. 9, or the *Five Pieces* for orchestra, Op. 10 (both 1913), which average respectively about 36 and 49 seconds for each movement (No. 5 of Op. 10 runs only 19 seconds); but even "larger" works like the Symphony (1928) and the String Quartet (1938) take only eight or nine minutes' playing time, so intensely compressed is the language. This compression, together with the unfamiliarity of the idiom, requires an unusual degree of attention from the listener. With respect to dissonance (the effect of which is largely mitigated by skilful use of contrasting timbres) and harmonic complexity in general, Webern's music is considerably easier to hear than that of Schoenberg, Berg, and many other twentieth-century composers.

In his development, Webern, like Schoenberg, passed through the stages of late Romantic chromaticism, free atonality, and organization by tone rows, the last beginning with the three songs of Op. 17 (1924). With few exceptions his works are in chamber style; they are about equally divided between instrumental and vocal compositions. The principal instrumental works are the Symphony Op. 21, the String Quartet Op. 28, the Concerto for nine instruments Op. 24 (1934), and the Piano Variations Op. 27 (1936). For voices there are numerous collections of solo songs—some with piano, others with different small ensembles—and a few choral pieces, notably *Das Augenlicht* (*Light of the Eyes;* 1935) and two cantatas (1939, 1943) for soloists, chorus, and orchestra. These cantatas, and also the Variations for Orchestra Op. 30 (1940), are in a somewhat more relaxed and expressive style than Webern's previous works; in them he applied the serial technique but included homophonic as well as contrapuntal texture.

The Symphony Op. 21 is for nine solo instruments. Some idea of Webern's use of the serial technique may be obtained from Example 113 (the beginning of the first movement). What may be called the "original" form of the tone row is designated by the numbers 1, 2, etc. (note that the second half of the row is the retrograde of the first half and that consequently the retrograde form of the entire row is a duplicate of its original form); the numbers 1′, 2′, etc. designate an

inversion (or a retrograde inversion) of the original form, beginning
a major third lower; 1″, 2″, etc. designate an inversion (or retrograde
inversion) beginning at the original pitch. The C-sharp in measure
four begins a statement of the original form of the row (or its retrograde) transposed a major third upward.

Webern's output was relatively small: his complete works have
been recorded on eight long-playing record sides. Though his achievement received hardly any acclaim during his lifetime, recognition of

Example 113   First Movement, Symphony Op. 21, Anton Webern

his work has grown steadily in the years since the Second World War, and his music has launched interesting new developments in Italy, Germany, France, and the United States.

The twelve-tone technique has proved its adaptability to many different styles of composition. Older established composers (for example, Copland, Sessions, and Stravinsky) have adopted, either wholly or in part, the methods of dodecaphony; very many younger composers are working in this technique, with results which it is too soon yet to assess. Altogether, it seems likely that the movement begun by Schoenberg—either in some synthesis with traditional methods or in other ways that cannot be predicted—will be a dominating force in the music of the coming years.

Conclusion

To recapitulate: the three main directions of music in the first half of the twentieth century were: (1) toward absorption of folk elements into structures organized on a broadly tonal basis; (2) toward continuous extension of musical practices of the past; and (3) toward new methods of musical organization not conditioned by tonality. Each direction represents something valuable and indeed essential to the continuing vitality of art as we know it in western culture. These essentials are: (1) the ultimately democratic foundation of and sanction for art; (2) the continuity of tradition; and (3) freedom for the individual to search out and try new things and to have a fair hearing. No one of the three essentials that these directions represent is independent of the others; fruitful interaction and tension among all produce the only condition by which art can live.

The tension has been exceptionally sharp in the twentieth century. The ideal of art for everyone has degenerated to dictatorial regulation of style or the production of huge masses of cheap commercial entertainment music. Continuity of tradition has been menaced by both the passivity of its defenders and the intransigence of its attackers; Schoenberg and Webern acknowledged tradition but some of their younger disciples seem determined to annihilate the last vestiges of it. Individual freedom has been pushed to the point where composers have become alienated from the majority of potential listeners, and consequently have written music of a subjective or esoteric nature capable of being understood only by a little circle of initiates.

However, the conflicts that are now apparent in twentieth-century musical practice and theory will doubtless eventually be resolved or transformed, just as the conflicts of the *ars nova*, the *nuove musiche*, and the Brahms-Wagner era were. Every period of music has had its currents and countercurrents. Every composer has had to take from his environment what he needed, reject what he could not use, and restate to his contemporaries the eternal truth of music as he himself has been able to comprehend it.

Glossary

Accidental. A sign used to change the pitch of a note by raising it one semitone (sharp, ♯), lowering it one semitone (flat, ♭), or cancelling the effect of a previous sharp or flat (natural, ♮).

Alteration. Changing the pitch of a note by means of an accidental (♯, ♭, or ♮) to raise or lower it by one halfstep from its normal pitch in the scale.

Appoggiatura. A nonharmonic tone, sounded on a strong beat and resolved (regularly by step) to a harmonic tone on a following weaker beat (see also *suspension*).

Atonality (atonal). The absence of tonality.

Bar. (1) A vertical line (barline) through the staff(s) marking the division into measures; (2) a measure (not used in this sense in this book); (3) a form, *AAB*, common in medieval monophonic music, polyphonic ballades of the fourteenth century, Lutheran chorales, and other music.

Cadence. The melodic and/or harmonic formula that marks the end of a musical phrase, section, or composition. The most common harmonic final cadence is the progression Dominant-Tonic (V-I).

Canon, canonic imitation. (1) Exact imitation, continued for more than one phrase, of the melody of one voice by another voice or voices: the imitating voice(s) may begin on the same note as the leading voice (canon at the unison), or on another note (canon at the fifth above, at the fourth below, etc.); (2) a rule or direction specifying the way in which such imitation is to be carried out; (3) a composition in which two or more voices proceed throughout in canonic imitation (see also *round*).

Chord. A simultaneous combination of three or more notes of different pitch forming an entity than can be used for the analysis of harmony (see also *triad*).

Chromaticism (chromatic). (1) The use of tones not in the regular diatonic scale of the composition or passage in which such tones occur; (2) a quality of harmonic styl₂ marked by the frequent use of such tones.

Circle of fifths. The arrangement of keys by ascending fifths (C-G-D, etc.), each key having one more sharp or one less flat in its signature; or by descending fifths (C-F-B♭, etc.), each key having one more flat or one less sharp in its signature. *Circle* refers to the fact that at the twelfth step the series returns to its point of beginning: in the equal-tempered tuning B♯ or D♭♭ = C.

Clavier. A keyboard instrument of the harpsichord or clavichord type.

Clavier music. Music for harpsichord, clavichord, or pianoforte.

Coda. A concluding section of a composition, particularly of a fugue or a movement of a sonata or symphony.

Codetta. Literally, a "small coda"; particularly, the closing passage of one section of a piece, for example, the exposition of a movement in sonata form.

Color. (1) The quality of a musical sound (as the color of the clarinet tone) or of sounds in combination (as

461

the color of Debussy's orchestration); (2) the quality of the sound of a composition or passage (see also *texture, timbre*).

Consonance (*consonant*). An interval or chord which produces an agreeable or satisfactory effect, or an effect of repose.

Contrary motion. Movement of two simultaneous voices in opposite directions, one upward and the other downward.

Counterpoint (*contrapuntal*). A musical texture consisting predominantly of two or more simultaneous melodic lines, with or without additional material.

Cross-relation. The use of a note and its chromatic alteration in different voices, either simultaneously or in immediate or close juxtaposition.

Diatonic. (1) Pertaining to a major, minor, or modal scale of eight tones to the octave; (2) the quality of music marked by infrequent use of chromatic tones.

Dissonance (*dissonant*). An interval or chord which produces a disagreeable ("discordant") or unsatisfactory effect, or an effect which requires completion (see also *resolution*).

Dominant. In harmonic practice, the fifth degree or note of the scale (see also *cadence*).

Drone. (1) A note or notes, usually in the bass, sustained throughout an entire piece or section; (2) a string, pipe, or mechanism for producing such notes.

Duet, duo. A composition, or section of a composition, having two equally important melodic lines, with or without accompaniment; or a composition written for two performers of equal importance, on the same or different instruments.

Enharmonic. In Greek music, intervals less than a semitone; in Western music, notes which are identical in sound in the equal-tempered scale (as F♯-G♭).

Equal temperament. A method of tuning in which the octave is divided into twelve equal semitones.

Form patterns. The arrangement of material within a composition. In this book form patterns are designated by italic letters thus: *aba, ABA,* etc. The mark ' after a letter (*A'*) indicates a modified repetition of the formal unit.

Free rhythm. Rhythm in which the durations of the notes and rests are not fixed fractions or multiples of a common unit of duration (see *metrical rhythm*).

Fuga (Latin, "flight"). In medieval and renaissance usage, a canon; after 1600, the meaning is usually the same as *fugue.*

Fugato. A short fugal passage or fugal exposition.

Fughetta. A short fugue.

Fugue (*fugal*). A type or style of contrapuntal composition based on the development of (usually) a single short theme or *subject* in imitation.

Harmonic. (1; adj.) A musical texture consisting predominantly of chords or of melody accompanied by chords; (2; noun), a high flute-like tone produced by lightly touching the string of a violin at 1/2, 1/3, etc. of its length.

Harmonic rhythm. The movement of music as marked by the succession of changing harmonies.

Harmony. (1) Any simultaneous combination of sounds; a chord; (2) the chordal or "vertical" aspect of a musical composition as contrasted with melodic, contrapuntal, rhythmic, coloristic, or other aspects; (3) the style of a composition considered with respect to the chords employed and the principles governing their succession (see also *harmonic*).

Hemiola (literally, "one and one-half"). A mensural device in the notation of the fifteenth and sixteenth centuries which in effect alters the movement from |♩.♩.| to |♩♩♩|. Hence, in Baroque music, a common cadential formula in triple meter, by which two measures of 3/4 time are made to sound like one measure of 3/2 time: |♩♩|♩♩|

Heterophony. The sounding of a melody simultaneously in a simple and an ornamented form.

Homophony. A texture in which all the voice parts move in the same or nearly the same rhythm.

Imitation. The closely following restatement of a melody or phrase by another voice or voices in a contrapuntal texture. If the restatement is exact, it is called *strict* imitation; if similar, but not exact, *free* imitation.

Interval. The distance in pitch between two tones, simultaneous or successive. Intervals are measured by scale degrees or steps, counting both the first and last tones; thus, C-E is a third, D-G is a fourth, and so on.

Inversion. Substitution of a higher for a lower note. An interval is inverted when its higher note is placed below its originally lower note: a chord is inverted (or *in inversion*) when any of its notes other than the root is in the bass; a melody is inverted when an equal descending interval is substituted for every ascending interval and *vice versa;* two or more melodic lines in counterpoint are inverted when one of them, originally higher, is placed in the bass.

Key, keynote. A tone (including its duplication in any octave) to which the other tones of the octave stand in subordinate relation.

Key signature. Sharp(s) ♯ or flat(s) ♭ placed on line(s) or space(s) at the beginning of each staff; all notes on the lines or spaces so indicated are to be raised or lowered respectively one semitone (unless the effect of the sharp or flat is cancelled by a natural ♮). A particular combination of sharps or flats may also indicate the key of a composition.

Keyboard music. Music for a keyboard instrument (organ, harpsichord, clavichord, piano).

Line. A melody or part of a melody, considered either by itself or as a constituent in a polyphonic (especially a contrapuntal) texture.

Measure. (1) A unit of time, usually comprising two to six smaller units (*beats*); (2) the space between two bar lines.

Melody. A succession of tones perceived as an entity.

Metrical rhythm. Rhythm in which the duration of every note and rest is a fixed multiple or fraction of a common unit of duration.

Mixture. An organ stop by which certain higher tones ("harmonics") are artificially made to sound along with the fundamental tone.

Modality. The quality of music written more or less definitely in accordance with the system of the modes of medieval music instead of the major or minor scales.

Modulation. Harmonic movement from one key to a different key in the course of a composition.

Monophony (monophonic). A musical texture consisting of single line of melody without accompaniment; opposite of *polyphony.*

Motive, motif. The smallest unit of a musical idea (see also *phrase, theme*).

Musette. (1) A form of bagpipe; (2) a piece in pastoral style and light dance-like rhythm, with a drone bass.

Nonharmonic tone. A tone foreign to, and therefore dissonant with, the basic harmony or chord with which it is sounding.

Note. (1) A graphic sign directing a performer to produce a tone of a certain pitch and duration; (2) the tone represented by such a sign.

Note designation. A note referred to without regard to its octave position is designated by a capital letter (A). A note in a particular octave is designated by a letter according to the following scheme:

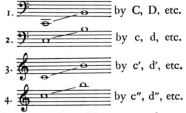

1. by C, D, etc.
2. by c, d, etc.
3. by c', d', etc.
4. by c", d", etc.

Oblique motion. Movement of two voices in which one remains at the same pitch while the other moves to a different pitch.

Ornament, ornamentation. Decorative notes added to a melodic line.

Ostinato. A short melodic figure persistently repeated, usually in the same voice and at the same pitch, throughout a composition or section of a composition.

Parallel motion. Two or more voices moving constantly at the same interval from one another.

Part. (1) A section of a composition; (2) a voice in contrapuntal texture.

Partial signature. A signature applied to fewer than all the voices of a polyphonic composition.

Phrase. A musical unit made up of one or more motives and corresponding to a sentence in speech.

Pivot chord. In modulation, the chord which is heard as common to both the initial key and the new key.

Polyphony (polyphonic). "Many-voiced"; a musical texture consisting of two or more lines of melody (see *counterpoint*), or melody and accompaniment, or chords. In this book *polyphonic* is used in contrast to *monophonic*, as a general term including both contrapuntal and harmonic textures (see also *monophonic, counterpoint, harmony*).

Principal. An organ stop controlling the pipes which produce the basic, characteristic tone color of the instrument.

Recitative. A style of vocal writing based on imitating the rhythms and inflections of speech, with a minimum of symmetrical musical structure.

Resolution. The movement of a dissonant interval or chord to a more consonant one, producing an effect of completion or of comparative repose.

Root. The lowest note of a chord considered as a combination of tones built up by successive thirds (see also *root position, triad, inversion*).

Root position. A chord is in root position when its root is the lowest sounding note (compare *inversion*).

Round. A canon, usually vocal, in which each voice continues to repeat its part as many times as desired (see *canon*).

Rubato. A slight modification of the regularity of the beat, introduced by the performer for the purpose of musical expression.

Shawms. Double-reed instruments of the oboe family, of various sizes, in use from the thirteenth to the seventeenth centuries.

Signature, see *key signature, time signature.*

Stop. A mechanism of the organ enabling the player to bring on or shut off different ranks of pipes at will.

Stretto. (1) A portion of a fugal composition in which imitations of the subject occur at closer time intervals than in the original presentation of the subject; (2) a closing portion, in quicker time, of a movement in fast tempo.

Subject. The theme of a fugue.

Suspension. A nonharmonic tone held over (*suspended*) on a strong beat from a previous harmony in which it was a harmonic tone, and then resolved (regularly by step downward) to a harmonic tone on a weaker beat (compare *appoggiatura*).

Syncopation. Displacement of the normal accent by transferring it from a strong to a weak beat, or from a strong to a weak part of a beat.

Tempered, see *equal temperament.*

Texture. The character of a musical composition in terms of its density, tone colors, and relative levels of activity in the different voice parts. With regard to the last criterion, textures range from those in which the level of activity is the same in all voices (*homophony*) to those in which the levels of activity are markedly distinct while the voices retain equal melodic importance (*counterpoint*).

Theme. A characteristic musical idea which serves as the basis for development of a composition or section of a composition.

Thirds, see *interval.*

Timbre. The characteristic color or quality of a musical sound as produced by various instruments—as the timbre of the clarinet, oboe, and so on (see also *color*).

Time signature. A sign placed at the beginning of a composition to indicate either (a) the proportion according to which longer time values are to be divided into shorter ones; or (b) the number of beats in each measure and the kind of note that represents a single beat: a time signature of 3/4 means three beats in a measure, a quarter note representing one beat.

Tonality (*tonal*). (1) The quality by virtue of which a musical composition, or a part of a composition, is organized harmonically around a constant central tone (compare *atonality, modality*); (2) the central tone or key of a composition.

Tone. A musical sound of definite pitch.

Tonic. The first note of the scale; the key note.

Triad. A chord consisting of three notes: one, the root, and two others respectively a third and a fifth above the root (see also *root position, inversion*).

Trio. (1) A composition, or section of a composition, in three voices; (2) a composition for three performers; (3) in Classical sonatas and symphonies, a second two-part section following a minuet or scherzo, and followed by a repetition of the minuet or scherzo.

Tritone. The interval of the augmented fourth, which contains three whole tones, as F-B♮, C-F♯, B♭-E′. In strict contrapuntal writing this interval may not occur harmonically between the bass and an upper voice, or melodically as two successive notes in any voice.

Vibrato. A slight fluctuation of pitch, used especially by singers and by players of bowed string instruments to make the tone more expressive.

Voice. A melodic line, especially in contrapuntal texture.

Abbreviations

CDMI   *I Classici della Musica Italiana*, Milan, 1918–21 (36 vols.).

CMI   *I Classici Musicali Italiani*, Milan, 1941–42.

DdT   *Denkmäler deutscher Tonkunst*, Leipzig, 1892–1931 (65 vols.).

DTB   *Denkmäler deutscher Tonkunst: Denkmäler der Tonkunst in Bayern*, Braunschweig, 1900–38 (38 vols., many of which are subdivided).

DTOe   *Denkmäler der Tonkunst in Oesterreich*, Wien, 1894– (91 vols. to 1956). Numbered by volume and also, up to Vol. 83, by years (*Jahrgänge*). Many of the yearly designations are subdivided; for example, Vol. 39 is *Jahrgang* 19/2.

EE   Alfred Einstein, Appendix to *A Short History of Music*, New York, 1947. Contains notes, some translations, and many musical examples which are referred to in these Appendixes.

EP   R. Eitner, ed., *Publikationen älterer praktischer und theoretischer Musikwerke, vorzugsweise des XV und XVI Jahrhunderts*, Berlin, 1873–1905 (29 vols. in 33 *Jahrgänge*).

EM   Harold Gleason, ed., *Examples of Music before 1400*, New York, 1946. No notes or translations; piano reductions; some pieces transposed; some form designations and performance indications questionable.

GMB   Arnold Schering, ed., *Geschichte der Musik in Beispielen* [*History of Music in Examples*], Leipzig, 1931; reprint, New York, 1950. Notes and translations in German; indications for performance frequently arbitrary.

HAM   Archibald T. Davison and Willi Apel, eds., *Historical Anthology of Music*, Cambridge, 1950. Vol. I: Oriental, Medieval, and Renaissance Music; Vol. II: Baroque, Rococo, and Pre-Classical Music. Notes and translations.

JAMS   *Journal of the American Musicological Society*, 1948–.

MM   Carl Parrish and John F. Ohl, eds., *Masterpieces of Music Before 1750*, New York, 1951. Good editorial notes; translations.

MMA   Gustave Reese, *Music in the Middle Ages*, New York, 1940.

MQ   *The Musical Quarterly*, 1915–.

PAM   *Publikationen älterer Musik . . . der Deutschen Musikgesellschaft*, 1926–40.

RMAW   Curt Sachs, *The Rise of Music in the Ancient World*, New York, 1943.

SR   Oliver Strunk, *Source Readings in Music History*, New York, 1950.

TEM   Carl Parrish, *A Treasury of Early Music*, New York, 1958. Supplements, without duplicating, MM; good notes and translations.

WM   Johannes Wolf, *Music of Earlier Times*, New York. The American edition of Wolf's *Sing- und Spielmusik aus älterer Zeit*, 1926. No notes or translations.

Bibliography

General Bibliography

In addition to the anthologies of musical examples listed below by chapters, the following series will be found useful: *Das Musikwerk; eine Beispielsammlung zur Musikgeschichte*, K. G. Fellerer, ed., Cologne, 1951–; each volume is devoted to examples of music in a particular form or from a particular period.

Composers and compositions can be located with the help of *Historical Sets, Collected Editions and Monuments of Music*, compiled by Anna Harriet Heyer, Chicago, American Library Association, 1957.

There are recordings to accompany MM and TEM. Other historical anthologies are: RCA Victor's *History of Music in Sound*, ten volumes; *Archiv Production*, issued by the History of Music Division of the Deutsche Grammophon Gesellschaft and distributed in the United States by MGM Records; *L'Anthologie Sonore*, Haydn Society, 1954–, originally recorded at Paris in seventeen albums of 78 r.p.m. records; and *Music of the Bach Family*, Boston Records, 1957, a recording of the music in the anthology of the same title edited by K. Geiringer, Cambridge, 1955.

Music Anthologies

Willi Apel, *Harvard Dictionary of Music*, Cambridge, 1944.
Baker's Biographical Dictionary of Musicians, 5th ed., rev. N. Slonimsky, New York, 1958.
Georg Kinsky, *A History of Music in Pictures*, New York, 1951.
Curt Sachs, *The History of Musical Instruments*, New York, 1940.

Reference Works

Chapter I (Pp. 1-13)

Transcriptions of extant Greek melodies and fragments are given in HAM, Nos. 7, 8; GMB, No. 1; EE, No. 2.

Examples of Hebrew and Byzantine music are given in HAM, Nos. 6, 8; EM, p. 1.

For the music of Gregorian Chant, see Appendix to Chapter II. Examples of chants from other Western liturgies are given in TEM, Nos. 1–3; HAM, Nos. 9 and 10.

Music

Books and articles listed under this heading are not offered as bibliography, but are simply suggested readings (mostly in English) which will be profitable to a student beginning the study of music history. Under no circumstances should this reading be regarded as a substitute for the listening or playing experience, or for the study of the music itself.

A basic book is SR. For Chapter I, read the selections in the first chapter, "The Greek View of Music," and in the second chapter, "The Early Christian View of Music."

Also see RMAW; and MMA, Chapters 1 through 4.

On Greek music: Plato, *Republic*, Book III, 395–403; Aristotle, *Politics*, Book VIII.

For Further Reading

Bibliography   *On Hebrew music:* A. Z. Idelsohn, *Jewish Music in Its Historical Development,*
New York, 1929.
For the influence of Byzantine music, see Egon Wellesz, *Eastern Elements in
Western Chant,* Oxford, 1947.

Music   *Chapter II* (Pp. 14-35)

Collections   *Antiphonale Sacrosanctae Romanae Ecclesiae pro diurnis horis,* Paris, 1949.
                     Graduale Sacrosanctae Romanae Ecclesiae, Paris, 1948.
                     The Liber Usualis with Introduction and Rubrics in English, New York, 1956.
Examples in the   Syllabic Chant: MM, No. 3; melismatic chant: MM, No. 2; HAM, Nos. 12, 13.
Anthologies   Psalm Tones, with antiphons: MM, No. 1; HAM, No. 11.
                     Tracts: *Graduale,* pp. 208, 232.
                     Graduals: HAM, No. 12; *Graduale,* p. 75**.
                     Alleluias: MM, No. 2; HAM, No. 13; EE, No. 2.
                     Kyrie: HAM, No. 15a.
                     Gloria and Sanctus: GMB, No. 2.
                     Other chants of the Ordinary of the Mass: *Liber Usualis,* pp. 16–94.
                     Tropes: HAM, No. 15b; compare HAM No. 33a and TEM, No. 14.
                     Sequences and proses: HAM, No. 16; MM, No. 3; GMB, Nos. 4–6; EE, No. 5.
                     Liturgical dramas: TEM, No. 5; GMB, No. 8.
                     Goliard songs: EM, p. 7. The reconstruction of the rhythm in this example is
                     conjectural.
                     Monophonic conductus: HAM, No. 17, EM, p. 7.
                     Songs from Adam de la Halle's *Robin et Marion:* EM, pp. 16–19.
                     Troubadour songs: TEM, No. 6; HAM, No. 18; GMB, Nos. 11, 13; EE, No. 7.
                     Trouvère songs: MM, No. 4; HAM, No. 19; GMB, No. 14.
                     Minnesongs: MM, No. 5; HAM, No. 20; GMB, Nos. 12, 21; EM, pp. 20–21.
                     Meistersongs: TEM, No. 22; HAM, No. 24; GMB, Nos. 78, 79; EE, No. 8.
                     Other monophonic songs: TEM, Nos. 7, 8; HAM, Nos. 21, 22, 23; GMB, No.
                     25; EM, pp. 22–23.
                     Instrumental pieces: MM, No. 12; HAM, Nos. 40, 41, 58, 59; GMB, No. 28;
                     EM, pp. 55–57.

For   Willi Apel, *Gregorian Chant,* Bloomington, 1958. This book is the most recent
Further   full-scale scholarly study, historical and stylistic, of the subject.
Reading   Rev. Dom Dominic Johner, *A New School of Gregorian Chant,* New York,
                 1925. A practical introduction to the subject of Gregorian Chant, with much
                 historical and liturgical information.

Music   *Chapter III* (Pp. 36-63)

Examples in the   Early organum: MM, No. 6; HAM, No. 25; EM, pp. 26, 27.
Anthologies   Eleventh-century counterpoint: MM, No. 7; HAM, No. 26; GMB, No. 9; EM,
                     p. 28.
                     St. Martial organum: MM, No. 8; HAM, No. 27; EM, pp. 30, 33.
                     Notre Dame organum (period of Leonin): TEM, No. 9; HAM, Nos. 28 c-e,
                     29.
                     Clausulae: HAM, No. 30.
                     Notre Dame organum (period of Perotin): MM, No. 9; HAM, No. 31; EM,
                     p. 36.
                     Conductus: MM, No. 11; HAM, Nos. 38, 39; GMB, No. 16; EM, pp. 41, 43, 44,
                     49; EE, No. 6.
                     Conductus style: HAM, No. 32c; EM, pp. 29, 31, 35, 47, 48.
                     Interchanged voices (*Stimmtausch*): MM, No. 10; HAM, Nos. 32c, 33a.
                     Motet: TEM, Nos. 10, 12; MM, No. 10; HAM, Nos. 28f-i, 32–35; GMB, Nos.
          468   18–20; EM, pp. 58, 60, 62, 63, 65, 67; EE, No. 9; WM, No. 3.

Miscellaneous cantilena types: HAM, No. 36; EM, pp. 74, 76.
Hocket: TEM, No. 11; EM, p. 70.
Rota (*Sumer* canon): HAM, No. 42; GMB, No. 17; EM, p. 45.
Rondellus: EM, p. 46.

For details of the notation of twelfth- and thirteenth-century polyphonic music, see Carl Parrish, *The Notation of Medieval Music*, New York, 1957, Chapters 3–5; and Willi Apel, *The Notation of Polyphonic Music*, Cambridge, 1949, 310ff.

Chapter IV (Pp. 64-80)

Motets from the *Roman de Fauvel:* HAM, No. 43; EM, pp. 77, 79.
Works of Guillaume de Machaut:
  Chansons balladées: HAM, No. 46; GMB, No. 26b; EM, p. 80.
  Motets: HAM, No. 44; GMB, No. 27; EM, p. 88; WM, No. 5.
  Rondeau: EM, p. 81.
  Ballades: HAM, No. 45; GMB, No. 26a; EM, p. 85; EE, No. 11.
  Mass: MM, No. 13 (Agnus Dei I, also in EM, p. 97).
Church music of the fourteenth and early fifteenth centuries: TEM, Nos. 13, 14;
  HAM, Nos. 55, 56; GMB, No. 29.
Late fourteenth-century secular French music: TEM, No. 17; HAM, Nos. 47, 48;
  GMB, No. 24.
Italian music of the fourteenth century:
  Madrigals: HAM, Nos. 49, 50; GMB, No. 22; EM, p. 99.
  Cacce: TEM, No. 16; HAM, No. 52; EM, p. 100; WM, No. 7.
  Ballata: HAM, No. 51 (also in EE, No. 10).
Works of Francesco Landini:
  Madrigals: HAM, No. 54; EM, pp. 106, 108, 113.
  Ballate: MM, No. 14; HAM, No. 53; GMB, No. 23; EM, pp. 103, 104;
  WM, No. 6.
Instrumental music: TEM, No. 15; HAM, Nos. 58, 59.

Selections from fourteenth-century treatises in SR: Marchetto da Padua, 160–71; Jean de Muris, 172–79; and Jacob of Liège, 180–90.
  On Guillaume de Machaut: George Perle, "Integrative Devices in the Music of Machaut," *MQ* 24 (1948), 169–76; Otto Gombosi, "Machaut's *Messe Notre-Dame*," *MQ* 36 (1950), 204–24.
  The original Latin text of Pope John XXII's decree of 1324 concerning church music is in Vol. I of *The Oxford History of Music*, London, 1929, 294–95. For some other pronouncements on this subject see MMA, 321, 390; and P. H. Lang, *Music in Western Civilization*, New York, 1941, 140, 163.

Chapter V (Pp. 81-98)

English music of the fourteenth and early fifteenth centuries, other than Dunstable: HAM, Nos. 57, 63, 64 (compare also HAM, Nos. 25c, 33a, 37, 42 and EE, No. 6).
  Dunstable: TEM, No. 18; HAM, Nos. 61, 62; GMB, No. 35; WM, No. 11.(The transcriptions of GMB, Nos. 32 and 34 are not reliable.)
  The Burgundian School: *Chansons:* MM, No. 16; HAM, Nos. 67, 68, 69, 70, 71, 72; GMB, Nos. 40, 41, 42. *Motets:* HAM, No. 65; GMB, Nos. 38, 43; WM, No. 12. *Masses:* MM, No. 15; HAM, No. 66 (and compare Nos. 73, 92); GMB, No. 39; EE, No. 12.

Frank Ll. Harrison, *Music in Medieval Britain*, London, 1958. An excellent study of the period from the eleventh century to the Reformation; it deals not only with musical style but also with the institutions under whose patronage the music was composed and performed.

Bibliography

For
Further
Reading

Manfred F. Bukofzer, *Studies in Medieval and Renaissance Music,* New York, 1950. The first four essays in this volume are concerned with English music of the fourteenth and early fifteenth centuries. The seventh essay ("*Caput:* a Liturgico-Musical Study") deals with the origins of the cyclic Mass and contains an analysis of three Masses based on the *Caput cantus firmus.*

Manfred F. Bukofzer, "John Dunstable: A Quincentenary Report," *MQ* 40 (1954), 29–49. Biography, musical sources, style, and significance, in brief and attractive form.

Richard Leighton Greene, *The Early English Carols,* Oxford, 1935. The fundamental work on the form of the carol; includes a collection of all extant carol texts to 1550.

Music

Chapter VI (Pp. 99-119)

Examples in the Anthologies

(The following is only a partial list; for additional examples, consult the anthologies.)

Ockeghem: MM, No. 17; HAM, Nos. 73 (the very strict treatment of the *cantus firmus* in this example is exceptional in Ockeghem), 74, 75.

Canonic devices in Netherlands music: MM, No. 17, with introductory commentary; HAM, Nos. 66c, 89, 91, 92, with commentary on pages 223, 225–226.

Obrecht: MM, No. 18; HAM, Nos. 77, 78.

The Netherlands chanson in the early sixteenth century: HAM, Nos. 68, 69, 70, 72, 74, 75, 79 (an exceptional type, the motet chanson), 91; GMB, No. 53. For instrumental pieces in vocal collections dated around 1500, see HAM, Nos. 78, 83; GMB, Nos. 56, 62b, 67, 68.

Josquin des Prez: MM, No. 19; HAM, Nos. 90, 91. The motet *Absalon fili mi* is in the *Oxford History of Music,* Vol. II, 77–83. The Mass *Pange lingua* is Vol. I of Blume, *Das Chorwerk.*

Contemporaries of Obrecht and Josquin: HAM, Nos. 88, 92.

For
Further
Reading

The indispensable starting point for any detailed study of this period is Gustave Reese, *Music in the Renaissance,* New York, 1959, a comprehensive, concrete, and accurate account of every phase of musical activity from 1400–1600. Very full bibliographical references are included.

Chapters V, VI, and VII of Manfred Bukofzer's *Studies in Medieval and Renaissance Music* deal chiefly with the period 1450–1550.

Music

Chapter VII (Pp. 120-151)

Examples in the Anthologies

(The following is a partial list; for additional examples, consult the anthologies.)

Netherlands composers 1520–*ca.* 1550: HAM, Nos. 106, 109, 113, 114, 125; EE, No. 15; WM, No. 27; GMB, No. 118.

National schools of the early sixteenth century: *Italy:* TEM, Nos. 20, 21; HAM, Nos. 94 (the use of an antiphon melody [see MM, p. 63] in this lauda is exceptional, as are likewise the antiphonal two-voice phrases and, to a lesser degree, the imitations in measures 29 to 37), 95; WM, Nos. 20–23; GMB, Nos. 69–72. *France:* HAM, No. 107; EE, No. 16. *Germany:* TEM, No. 32; HAM, Nos. 81, 82, 87, 93, 110; GMB, No. 87; Quodlibets: TEM, No. 31; HAM, No. 82; GMB, No. 111; Ode, GMB, No. 73; *Spain:* HAM, Nos. 97, 98, 128; TEM, Nos. 19, 23; GMB, No. 96. *England:* HAM, Nos. 86, 112, 127.

Instrumental music:

  Organ pieces on a *cantus firmus:* HAM, Nos. 100, 101, 120, 133.

  Vocal compositions transcribed: GMB, Nos. 62b, 63a; from a later date, but illustrative of the technique of trancription, are the compositions in MM, Nos. 20, 21; HAM, No. 145.

  Ricercare (imitative): HAM, Nos. 115, 116; GMB, Nos. 105, 113; EE, No. 22.

Canzona: HAM, No. 118 (also compare No. 91).

Dances: HAM, No. 137; MM, No. 22; GMB, Nos. 90, 91.
Improvisatory pieces: HAM, Nos. 84, 99, 121; GMB, Nos. 63b, 93.
Variations: HAM, Nos. 122, 124, 134; compare No. 103 (ostinato pattern).
Secular vocal music of the late sixteenth century:
Italy: TEM, No. 33; MM, No. 27; HAM, Nos. 129–131, 155, 158, 161, 188; GMB, Nos. 98, 100, 101, 106, 140, 165 (the lower voices arbitrarily edited for instruments), 167; EE, Nos. 18, 20; WM, Nos. 38, 46, 47.
Germany and France: HAM, Nos. 138, 142, 145a, 146a, 147, 165, 168; GMB, Nos. 124, 125, 139, 141, 144, 152.
England: TEM, No. 34; MM, No. 28; HAM, Nos. 159, 162, 163, 170; GMB, Nos. 145, 146.

R. B. Lenaerts, "The 16th-Century Parody Mass in the Netherlands," *MQ* 36 (1950), 410–21.
Edward Lowinsky, *Secret Chromatic Art in the Netherlands Motet* brilliantly presents a theory which, although controversial in some details, is well established in essentials. A related article is Lowinsky's "The Goddess Fortuna in Music." *MQ* 29 (1943), 45–77.
Alfred Einstein, *The Italian Madrigal*, Princeton, 1949 (3 vols.), is the definitive work on this subject, a rare combination of scholarly accuracy, wide knowledge, and attractive presentation. Chapter I deals with the frottola and other fore-runners of the madrigal in Italy.
On improvisation in Renaissance music, see E. Ferand, "'Sodaine and Unex-pected' Music in the Renaissance," *MQ* 37 (1951), 10–27.
For examples of Italian madrigal poetry in accurate but inelegant translation, see HAM, Vol. I, 251ff and MM, No. 27. On madrigal poetry in general, see Walter Rubsamen, *Literary Sources of Secular Music in Italy (ca.* 1500), Berkeley, 1943; Einstein, *The Italian Madrigal*, Vol. I, 166–212; and E. H. Fellowes, *English Madrigal Verse*, Oxford, 1929.
On the life and music of Gesualdo, see Cecil Gray and Philip Heseltine, *Carlo Gesualdo, Prince of Venosa, Musician and Murderer*, London, 1926; on Monte-verdi: Leo Schrade, *Monteverdi, Creator of Modern Music*, New York, 1950.
For information about English music of the early sixteenth century: John Stevens, *Music & Poetry in the Early Tudor Court*, Lincoln, Nebr., 1961; of the Elizabethan age: E. H. Fellowes, *The English Madrigal Composers*, Oxford, 1921; Peter Warlock (pseudonym for Philip Heseltine), *The English Ayre*, London, 1926; Ernest Walker, *A History of Music in England*, Oxford, 1952, Ch. IV; Walter L. Woodfill, *Musicians in English Society*, Princeton, 1953; and Charles Kennedy Scott, *Madrigal Singing*, London, 1931; and Joseph Kerman, *The Elizabethan Madrigal*, American Musicological Society, 1962.
Morley's *A Plaine and Easie Introduction to Practicall Musicke* (1597) has been published in an excellent modern edition, with the spelling brought up to date and the musical examples transcribed in modern notation, by R. Alec Harman, New York, 1952. See also SR Nos. 29 (Morley) and 37 (Henry Peacham).

For
Further
Reading

Chapter VIII (Pp. 152-179)

Music

Protestant church music: *Lutheran:* TEM, No. 24; HAM, Nos. 108, 111, 167a; GMB, Nos. 77, 80, 84, 108–110, 123, 143, 159–162; WM, No. 35. *Calvinist:* TEM, Nos. 25, 26; HAM, Nos. 126, 132; GMB, No. 142. *Anglican:* TEM, No. 27; HAM, Nos. 151, 169, 171, 172.
Catholic church music of the late Renaissance: MM, Nos. 23–25; HAM, Nos. 139–141, 143, 144, 146b, 148–150, 152, 156, 164, 166; GMB, Nos. 120–122, 126–129, 131, 179; WM, No. 41.
Instrumental music of the late Renaissance: TEM, Nos. 29, 30, 35, 36; MM, No. 29; HAM, Nos. 135–137, 145b, 153, 154, 160b, 167b, 173–180; GMB, Nos. 134–138, 147–151, 153, 155–157, 174; EE, Nos. 22, 25, 26; WM, Nos. 39, 40, 43, 56, 57.
The Venetian School: TEM, No. 28; HAM, Nos. 157, 173; GMB, Nos. 130, 148; EE, No. 19.

Examples in the Anthologies

Bibliography   SR, Nos. 28, 29, 34–36, 38, 40, 43–45.

Waldo S. Pratt, *The Music of the Pilgrims,* Boston, 1921, contains a description of the Bay Psalm Book; see also Irving Lowens, "The Bay Psalm Book in 17th-Century New England," *JAMS* 8 (1955), 22–29.

For
Further
Reading

Palestrina's music is subjected to detailed analysis in Knud Jeppesen's *The Style of Palestrina and the Dissonance,* London, 1927. Some counterpoint textbooks based on the Palestrina style are: R. O. Morris, *Contrapuntal Technique in the Sixteenth Century,* Oxford, 1922; K. Jeppesen, *Counterpoint,* tr. G. Haydon, New York, 1929; A. T. Merritt, *Sixteenth Century Polyphony,* Cambridge, 1939.

Edmund H. Fellowes, *William Byrd,* London, 1948.

Wilfrid Mellers, "John Bull and English Keyboard Music," *MQ* 40 (1954), 364–83, 548–71.

Music   *Chapter IX* (Pp. 180-208)

*Examples in the
Anthologies*

The opera and its forerunners: MM, No. 31; HAM, Nos. 182, 186, 187, 206, 208, 209, 221, 230; GMB, Nos. 164, 166, 171, 175–178, 199–204; EE, No. 24; WM, No. 48.

Vocal chamber music: MM, No. 30; HAM, Nos. 184, 189, 203–205; GMB, Nos. 170, 172, 173, 187, 193, 194, 197; WM, Nos. 49, 53, 65, 66.

Catholic church music and oratorio: TEM, No. 37; MM, No. 32; HAM, Nos. 183, 185, 207; GMB, Nos. 168, 169, 180, 198; WM, No. 52.

Lutheran church music in Germany: TEM, No. 38; MM, No. 33; HAM, Nos. 201, 202, 213; GMB, Nos. 188–192; EE, No. 27.

Instrumental music: TEM, No. 39; MM, Nos. 26, 34, 35; HAM, Nos. 190a, 191–199, 210–212, 215–217, 229, 230, 256; GMB, Nos. 153, 155–158, 181–185, 196, 205, 207 (compare 206), 215, 216, 218; EE, No. 26; WM, Nos. 54–56, 63, 64.

For
Further
Reading

SR, Nos. 46–56.

Manfred F. Bukofzer, *Music in the Baroque Era,* New York, 1947. A comprehensive survey of the entire Baroque, with music examples and bibliographies.

On the interrelation of music and the other arts in general, see Curt Sachs, *The Commonwealth of Art,* New York, 1946.

Frank Arnold's *The Art of Accompaniment from a Thorough-Bass as Practiced in the XVIIth and XVIIIth Centuries,* London, 1931, is the basic work on this subject, with copious quotations and examples from the sources.

On the opera, in the Baroque and later periods, see D. J. Grout, *A Short History of Opera,* New York, 1947 (2 vols.); Joseph Kerman, *Opera as Drama,* New York, 1956. Egon Wellesz, *Essays on Opera,* London, 1950, deals for the most part with seventeenth-century works.

On the Florentine Camerata and Italian vocal chamber music, see Claude Palisca, "Girolamo Mei," *MQ* 40 (1954), 1–20; *idem, Girolamo Mei, Letters on Ancient and Modern Music,* American Institute of Musicology, 1960; Nino Pirrotta, "Temperaments and Tendencies in the Florentine Camerata," *MQ* 40 (1954), 169–89; Nigel Fortune, "Italian Secular Monody from 1600 to 1635; an Introductory Survey," *MQ* 39 (1953), 171–95.

Other aspects of Baroque music are treated in Curt Sachs, *A World History of the Dance,* New York, 1937; Leo Schrade, *Monteverdi,* New York, 1950; Gotthold Frotscher, *Geschichte des Orgel-Spiels und der Orgel-Komposition,* Berlin, 1935–36 (2 vols.); William S. Newman, *The Sonata in the Baroque Era,* Chapel Hill, 1959.

Music   *Chapter X* (Pp. 209-232)

Modern editions

Examples of French opera overtures may be found in MM, No. 36 and HAM, Nos. 223 and 224; examples of the same form in other contexts are EE, No. 30 and GMB, Nos. 278 and 292. Some other examples are: J. S. Bach, the four Suites (*Ouvertures*) for orchestra, and the opening movements of the cantatas Nos. 61, 97, 119; Handel, Overture to *Messiah* and first movements of the *Concerti Grossi* Nos. 10 and 12.

The following examples of the passacaglia form in Baroque music may be
compared with Purcell's aria "When I am laid in earth" from *Dido and Aeneas:*
HAM, Nos. 222, 238; GMB, Nos. 230, 231, 233; and the "Crucifixus" from Bach's
Mass in B Minor.

Some examples of vocal chamber duets in the manner of Steffani are the
"Christe eleison" from Bach's *Mass in B Minor;* and the duets in Vol. 32 of the
Händelgesellschaft edition of the works of Handel.

Some modern editions of Italian vocal chamber music of the seventeenth and
eighteenth centuries are: CDMI, Vols. 2 (G. B. Bassani), 17 (Marcello), 30 (A.
Scarlatti); CMI, Vol. 2 (Marcello); K. Jeppesen, ed., *La Flora.* For others, see
Bukofzer, *Music in the Baroque Era,* 462–463.

Opera: TEM, Nos. 44, 46; MM, No. 36; HAM, Nos. 222–225, 241, 243, 244,
255, 267, 281; GMB, Nos. 195, 222–224, 226, 227, 231, 232, 233, 234, 236, 247, 250,
258, 259, 261, 266, 268–270, 272, 274, 293; EE, No. 30.

Cantata and song: TEM, No. 49; HAM, Nos. 228, 254, 258, 273 (by Francesco
Durante, 1684–1755; a *tour de force* of chromatic harmonies and remote modulations; compare also GMB, No. 197 and TEM, No. 49); GMB, Nos. 209, 210, 217,
235, 242, 248, 254, 256, 260, 262, 287; EE, No. 28.

Roman Catholic and Anglican church music: TEM, Nos. 42, 43; HAM, Nos.
218, 226, 242, 257, 266, 268; GMB, Nos. 225, 230, 246, 271, 273, 275, 310.

Lutheran church music: HAM, Nos. 213, 214, 235, 272; GMB, Nos. 208, 211,
212, 267, 290.

SR, Nos. 57–64.

Beekman C. Cannon, *Johann Mattheson, Spectator in Music,* New Haven, 1947;
an account of the famous theorist of the early eighteenth century, a contemporary of Bach and Handel.

On Venetian opera in the second half of the seventeenth century, see Simon
Towneley Worsthorne, *Venetian Opera in the Seventeenth Century,* Oxford,
1954.

The books listed in the Appendix to Chapter IX should also be consulted for
supplementary reading for the material in Chapter X.

Chapter XI (Pp. 233-250)

Music for organ: TEM, No. 41; MM, No. 37; HAM, Nos. 190b,c,d, 215, 231,
234, 237, 239, 247, 249a,b, 251; GMB, Nos. 243, 249, 263, 265, 291; EE, No. 35.

Music for lute, harpsichord, and clavichord: TEM, No. 40; MM, Nos. 38, 40;
HAM, Nos. 212, 232, 233, 236, 240, 248, 250, 261, 265a, 265b, 280; GMB, Nos. 215,
216, 218, 244, 253, 264. The keyboard suite by J. K. F. Fischer in HAM, No. 248
has for its second movement a "passacaille"; in this passacaglia the theme, instead
of being continuously repeated, recurs like a refrain, with contrasting interludes.
The movement thus assumes the form of a rondeau (compare HAM, No. 265b).
The French clavecinists used the terms *chaconne* or *passacaglia* for pieces of this
kind (compare HAM, No. 212; HAM, No. 240 combines the regular passacaglia
with the rondeau form).

Solo sonatas with basso continuo: HAM, Nos. 219, 238, 252, 253, 275, 278;
GMB, Nos. 238, 245, 294, 295; EE, No. 32.

Trio sonatas: MM, No. 39; HAM, Nos. 245, 263, 269; GMB, Nos. 240, 241; EE,
No. 29.

Works for larger ensembles: TEM, No. 45; HAM, Nos. 220, 223; GMB, Nos.
214, 220, 221, 224, 233, 252.

Orchestral suites and concertos: HAM, Nos. 246, 260; GMB, Nos. 251, 257, 277.

Henry Mishkin, "The Solo Violin Sonata of the Bologna School," *MQ* 29
(1943), 92–112.

Ernst H. Meyer, *English Chamber Music,* London, 1946.

Johann Josef Fux, *Steps to Parnassus,* tr. Alfred Mann, New York, 1943. Includes pages 41–139, 279, and the preface of the original edition of 286 pages;
includes "that part of the *Gradus ad Parnassum* ... which has survived as the
essence of Fux's teaching: the study of counterpoint."

Bibliography   Marc Pincherle, *Corelli, His Life, His Music,* New York, 1956.
William S. Newman, *The Sonata in the Baroque Era,* Chapel Hill, 1959.
Arthur Hutchings, *The Baroque Concerto,* New York, 1961.

Chapter XII (Pp. 251-281)

**Music
Catalogue**

Wolfgang Schmieder, ed., *Thematisch-systematisches Verzeichnis der musikalischen Werke von Johann Sebastian Bach (BWV),* Leipzig, 1950. A complete systematic-thematic index of Bach's works, with references to the Bach Society edition and also to other standard modern editions.

*Examples in the
Anthologies*

Vivaldi: TEM, No. 47; HAM, No. 270; GMB, No. 276.
Rameau: MM, No. 41; HAM, Nos. 276, 277; GMB, Nos. 296, 297.
Bach: MM, Nos. 46–50; HAM, No. 190d; GMB, Nos. 283–285, 286[?]; EE, No. 33.
Handel: MM, Nos. 43–45; GMB, Nos. 278–280.

**For
Further
Reading**

Vivaldi: Marc Pincherle, *Vivaldi,* New York, 1957.
The general structure of the Vivaldi concerto is so clearly reflected in J. J. Quantz's *Essay on How to Play the Flute* of 1752 (see SR, 583–88) that we may suppose the author to have had Vivaldi's works in mind as a model.

Rameau: The best comprehensive study in English is Cuthbert Girdlestone, *Jean-Philippe Rameau, His Life and Work,* London, 1957.

Bach: The standard work is Philipp Spitta, *Johan Sebastian Bach,* 4th ed., Leipzig, 1930 (2 vols.). An English translation in three volumes, published at London in 1885, has recently been reissued: *Johann Sebastian Bach, His Work and Influence on the Music of Germany,* New York, 1951.

An invaluable book is Hans David and Arthur Mendel, *The Bach Reader,* New York, 1945; it contains (in English translation) "all the surviving sources of any importance from which our knowledge of Bach's life and reputation has been drawn," as well as essays on Bach's life and music and on the history of his fame.

A detailed account of Bach's life is given in Charles Sanford Terry, *Bach, a Biography,* London, 1928; the same author's *Bach, the Historical Approach* is semipopular in style but sound in substance. Albert Schweitzer, *J. S. Bach,* first published in 1908 (English translation, 1911; reissued, 1923) has been a valuable and influential book, but its historical conclusions and treatment of Bach's musical symbolism can no longer be accepted uncritically.

Handel: The two standard biographies in English are those by R. A. Streatfeild, New York, 1909, and Newman Flower, New York, 1948. An excellent short biography is E. J. Dent, *Handel,* London, 1934.

Otto Erich Deutsch, *Handel, a Documentary Biography,* New York, 1954, is a "collection of all known and many hitherto unknown or overlooked documents referring to Handel's life"; it contains also a large bibliography.

The long chapter entitled "Origin of the Italian Opera in England and its Progress There during the Present Century" in Burney's *General History of Music* (Book IV, Ch. 6) includes a detailed account of Handel's operas in London and many observations on the music. This chapter is found in the second edition of Burney's work, F. Mercer, ed., New York, 1935 (2 vols.), II, 651–904.

On *Messiah,* see Robert Manson Myers, *Handel's* Messiah, *a Touchstone of Taste,* New York, 1948; and Jens Peter Larsen, *Handel's* Messiah; *Origins, Composition, Sources,* New York, 1957. See also Winton Dean, *Handel's Dramatic Oratorios and Masques,* London, 1959.

Chapter XIII (Pp. 282-299)

*Examples in the
Anthologies*

For one aspect of the contrast between Baroque and Classic, compare the complex phrase structure of Vivaldi's Concerto Grosso in A minor (HAM, No. 270) with the regular two- and four-measure phrases of Stamitz's Symphony in D (HAM, No. 294).

Examples of Classical melodic styles: *Chord outlining*, GMB, No. 304, Pt. 2;
HAM, Nos. 294, 304. *Parlando*, HAM, No. 284 (compare No. 287). *Singing allegro*, HAM, No. 303. *Momentary shifts to minor*, GMB, Nos. 282 (Pt. 2) and 303. For the *Alberti bass*, see HAM, No. 304.

Sonatas by Domenico Scarlatti are in MM, No. 42; HAM, No. 274; GMB, No. 282. The sonata movement in F-sharp minor by Manuel Blasco de Nebra, HAM, No. 308, has some of the qualities of rhythmic alertness, coloristic dissonances, and use of repeated phrases characteristic of Scarlatti.

HAM, No. 284, is the last movement of a sonata by Giovanni Platti (1690–1763), composed probably about 1740. On the basis of its resemblance to the concerto form, this movement may be analyzed as follows (the sign ≅ means "equivalent to"):

Ritornello I (C): measures 1–12
Solo I (C-G): 12–43
    Sequential extension leading to V of G: 14–19
    V of G: 21–28
    Cadential closing section, reiterated I-V-I- G *: 29–43
Ritornello II (G): 44–55 (≅ 1–12)
Solo II (G-*a*); 55–82
    Sequential extension in *a*: 60–66 (motive from m. 25) 66–74 ≅ 35–43 with interrupted cadence in *a*
    Close in *a*: 74–82 (motives in 75–80 from 25–28)
Ritornello III (C) = Ritornello I (1–12): 83–94
Solo III (C): 94–124 (≅ 12–43)
    Sequential extension leading to V of C: 95–101 (≅ 14–19)
    V of C: 102–9 (≅ 21–28)
    Cadential closing section I-V-I- in C: 110–124 (≅ 29–43)
Ritornello IV (C), shortened (first motive of Ritornello I, with cadential phrase): 124–130

* Grouping of measures 29–43: 29–31 32–34 35–36 37–38 39–40 41–43

If we prefer to think of this piece in terms of Classical sonata-form we may subdivide it in this way:

Exposition: 1–43
    First theme group in C (two themes): 1–12
    Transition to dominant (three [or two] themes): 12–29
    Second theme group in G (two themes): 29–43
First theme group in G: 44–55
"Development" section: 55–82
Recapitulation: 83–124, and cadential close: 124–130

The sonata movement by G. M. P. Rutini (1723–1797) printed in HAM, No. 302, which was written about 1760, sounds rather like the gigue finale of a Baroque suite, although the consistent two-voice homophonic texture, the many repeated phrases, and the Alberti bass are Rococo features. There is a very slight thematic contrast between the opening material and what might be called the second theme (measures 9 ff.). The section after the double bar begins with the opening material in the dominant key. There is no recapitulation of this material in the tonic, but the closing eight measures of both sections are identical except in key.

The two movements of a sonata by Tartini in GMB, No. 295, are from an early, not really representative work. The *Presto assai* in HAM, No. 275, from a set of twelve sonatas published at Rome in 1745, though typical in form and texture for its period, is of little interest as far as its musical content is concerned. A more adequate idea of Tartini's work can be obtained from the two concertos published in the *Smith College Music Archives*, Vol. 9, Northampton, 1948.

Additional examples:

The *empfindsamer Stil;* C. P. E. Bach: HAM, Nos. 288, 289, 296, 297; GMB, Nos. 303, 304 (Pt. 1).

Symphony and chamber music: HAM, Nos. 271, 283, 294, 295, 304, 307; GMB, Nos. 305–307; EE, No. 31.

Italian *opera seria:* HAM, Nos. 262, 282; GMB, No. 298.

Gluck: HAM, Nos. 292, 293; GMB, No. 313; EE, No. 39.

Bibliography	Comic opera: TEM, No. 50; HAM, Nos. 264, 285–287, 291, 300, 301, 305, 306; GMB, Nos. 281, 309; EE, No. 36.

The Lied: GMB, Nos. 287, 289, 299–301.

Church music and oratorio: HAM, Nos. 272, 279, 281, 298, 299; GMB, Nos. 308, 310.

For Further Reading

SR, Nos. 65–77.

C. P. E. Bach's *Versuch über die wahre Art, das Clavier zu spielen* was first published in 1753 (Part One) and 1762 (Part Two). An English translation by William J. Mitchell, *Essay on the True Art of Playing Keyboard Instruments*, New York, 1949, combines the original and revised editions of the eighteenth century. Excerpt in SR, No. 67.

The *Versuch einer Anweisung, die Flöte traversiere zu spielen* [*Essay on the Method of Playing the Transverse Flute*] by Johann Joachim Quantz (1697–1773), another important treatise of this period, was first published in 1752. Excerpts in SR, No. 65.

On the sonata, see William S. Newman, *The Sonata in the Classic Era*, Chapel Hill, 1963.

The best book about Scarlatti is Ralph Kirkpatrick, *Domenico Scarlatti*, Princeton, 1953, a model of scholarly authority and musical insight.

For an account of the life and music of J. S. Bach's sons, see Karl Geiringer, *The Bach Family*, New York, 1954. The standard biography of Johann Christian Bach is by Charles Stanford Terry, London, 1929.

Marcello's *Teatro alla moda*, in an annotated English translation by R. G. Pauly, is in *MQ* 34 (1948), 371–403; and 35 (1949), 85–105.

Important sources of information about eighteenth-century musical life are Dr. Charles Burney's *General History of Music* and his two travel books: *The Present State of Music in France and Italy*, London, 1771, and *The Present State of Music in Germany, The Netherlands, and the United Provinces*, London, 1775 (2 vols.), as well as his *Memoirs of the Life and Writings of the Abate Metastasio, in Which Are Incorporated Translations of His Principal Letters*, London, 1796 (3 vols.). Excerpts from *The Present State of Music in France and Italy* are in SR, No. 74. Brief excerpts from the travel books and Burney's journals, with connecting summaries by the editor, are found in Cedric Howard Glover, *Dr. Charles Burney's Continental Travels 1700–1772*, London, 1927. See also Percy A. Scholes, *The Great Dr. Burney; His Life, His Travels, His Works, His Family and His Friends*, London, 1948 (2 vols.). Mr. Scholes has also edited Burney's two travel books under the titles *An Eighteenth-Century Musical Tour in France and Italy* and *An Eighteenth-Century Musical Tour in Central Europe and the Netherlands*, both London, 1959.

On the *symphonie concertante* see Barry S. Brook, *La Symphonie française dans la seconde moitié du XVIIIe siècle*, Paris, 1962 (3 vols., including one volume of musical examples).

Martin Cooper, *Gluck*, New York, 1935, and Alfred Einstein, *Gluck*, New York, 1936, are comprehensive studies of the life, works and musical environment of this composer.

Chapter XIV (Pp. 300-321)

Haydn

Thematic catalogue: Anthony van Hoboken, *Joseph Haydn, thematisch-bibliographisches Werkverzeichnis*, Mainz, 1957–. Vol. 1 lists the instrumental works. In our Chapter XIV the symphonies are numbered according to van Hoboken's listing, which is the same as that of the Breitkopf & Härtel collected edition and of Robbins Landon's *Symphonies of Joseph Haydn;* the sonatas are also numbered according to van Hoboken, but the quartets are referred to by the more familiar opus numbers.

The best general biographies and studies of Haydn in English are: Karl Geiringer, *Haydn, a Creative Life in Music*, New York, 1946; and Rosemary Hughes, *Haydn*, London, 1950, reprinted 1956 (Appendix B gives a convenient conspectus of Haydn's works). A basic study is H. C. Robbins Landon, *The Symphonies of Joseph Haydn*, London, 1955.

On the quartets, see the article "Haydn" by D. F. Tovey in *Cobbett's Cyclo-* *pedic Survey of Chamber Music*, London, 1929–30 (2 vols.), Vol. 1, 515–45; on the symphonies, D. F. Tovey, *Essays in Musical Analysis*, Vol. 1, London, 1935. This last book is a mine of entertainment, information, and enlightenment about the late Haydn symphonies, as well as symphonies of Mozart, Beethoven, Schubert, and Brahms.

Ludwig Köchel, *Chronologisch-thematisches Verzeichnis sämtlicher Tonwerke Wolfgang Amade Mozarts;* rev. A. Einstein, Leipzig, 1937.
The most important book about Mozart's life and music is Hermann Abert, *W. A. Mozart*, Leipzig, 1956 (2 vols.). This is a revision of Otto Jahn's *Mozart*, which was first published in four volumes in 1856–59; an English translation in three volumes appeared at London in 1882.
Useful books about Mozart in English are Eric Blom, *Mozart*, New York, 1949, Alfred Einstein, *Mozart: His Character, His Work*, tr. A. Mendel and N. Broder, New York, 1945. A. Hyatt King, *Mozart in Retrospect*, New York, 1955; H. C. Robbins Landon, ed., *The Mozart Companion*, London, 1956.
Important and interesting material is found in *The Letters of Mozart and His Family*, Emily Anderson, ed., London, 1938 (3 vols.).
Leopold's Mozart's *Gründliche Violinschule* (1756) is published in facsimile, Leipzig, 1956, and in an English tr. by E. Knocker as *A Treatise on the Funda-mental Principles of Violin Playing*, London, 1951.

Bibliography

Mozart

Chapter XV (Pp. 322-338)

Thematic index: Georg Kinsky and Hans Halm, *Das Werk Beethovens; Ver-zeichnis seiner sämtlich vollendeten Kompositionen*, Munich, 1955.
The Letters of Beethoven, translated and edited by Emily Anderson, New York, 1961 (3 vols.).
The best biography is Alexander Wheelock Thayer, *Life of Ludwig van Beethoven*, New York, 1921 (3 vols.).
John N. Burk, *The Life and Works of Beethoven*, New York, 1943, is a con-venient, concise, and accurate handbook.
Beethoven; Impressions of Contemporaries, New York, 1926, is interesting and useful for a knowledge of Beethoven's personality; about his music, see Sir Donald F. Tovey, *Beethoven*, London, 1945, the unfinished last work of one of the most perceptive musicians of the twentieth century.

Beethoven

Chapters XVI and XVII (Pp. 339-373)

SR, Nos. 78–82, 85, 86.
Alfred Einstein, *Music in the Romantic Era*, New York, 1947. A useful general survey.
Logan Pearsall Smith, *Four Words: Romantic, Originality, Creative, Genius*, London, 1924. A beautifully written, illuminating essay of 48 pages which traces the history of the ideas that have been denoted at various periods by these words.
On the social history of the piano, see Arthur Loesser, *Men, Women, and Pianos*, New York, 1954; on its mechanical history, Rosamund E. M. Harding, *The Piano-Forte: Its History to the Great Exhibition of 1851*, Cambridge, 1933; the best historical survey of piano music is Walter Georgii, *Klaviermusik*, Zürich, 1956.

Berlioz: Jacques Barzun, *Berlioz and the Romantic Century*, Boston, 1950 (2 vols.); a perceptive, detailed study of the composer's environment, life, and works. Many of Berlioz's writings are published in English translation; see especially his *Memoirs*, with annotations by Ernest Newman, New York, 1935.
Brahms: Walter Niemann, *Brahms*, tr. C. A. Phillips, New York, 1945; Arnold Schoenberg, "Brahms the Progressive," in *Style and Idea*, New York, 1950, 52–

For
Further
Reading

General

Composers

Bibliography   101; Edwin Evans, *Handbook to the Chamber and Orchestral Music of Johannes Brahms,* London, 1933–35 (2 vols.).

Bruckner: Hans F. Redlich, *Bruckner and Mahler,* London, 1955. An excellent brief biography and style study, with list of works and bibliography.

Chopin: Gerald Abraham, *Chopin's Musical Style,* London, 1939; also André Gide, *Notes sur Chopin,* Paris, 1948; English tr., New York, 1949.

Dvořák: Letters and Reminiscences, Otaker Sourek, ed., Prague, 1954; Alec Robertson, *Dvořák,* New York, 1949.

Franck: Vincent d'Indy, *César Franck,* New York, 1910; Norman Demuth, *César Franck,* London, 1949.

Liszt: Humphrey Searle, *The Music of Franz Liszt,* London, 1954.

Mendelssohn: Philip Radcliffe, *Mendelssohn,* London, 1954.

Paganini: G. I. C. de Courcy, *Paganini the Genoese,* Norman, Oklahoma, 1957 (2 vols.).

Schubert: Otto Erich Deutsch, *Schubert: Thematic Catalogue of All His Works,* New York, 1951. Since the publication of this catalogue, any work of Schubert may be identified by a "D" number. Deutsch has also edited *The Schubert Reader,* New York, 1947, "a life of Franz Schubert in letters and documents"; and *Schubert: Memoirs by His Friends,* New York, 1958. The best biography is Maurice J. E. Brown, *Schubert; a Critical Biography,* New York, 1958. See also Alfred Einstein, *Schubert, a Musical Portrait,* New York, 1951; Gerald Abraham, ed., *The Music of Schubert,* New York, 1947; and Richard Capell, *Schubert's Songs,* New York, 1957.

Schumann: Schumann's essays were published under the title *Gesammelte Schriften über Musik und Musiker,* Leipzig, 1891 (2 vols.); an abridged English edition called *Music and Musicians, Essays and Criticisms* was published in two volumes at London in 1880. On Schumann, see also G. Abraham, ed., *Schumann, a Symposium,* New York, 1952, and Marcel Brion, *Schumann and the Romantic Age,* tr. G. Sainsbury, London, 1956.

Tchaikovsky: Gerald Abraham, ed., *Tschaikovsky, a Symposium,* London, 1945.

Chapter XVIII   (Pp. 374-388)

For Further Reading   SR, Nos. 83, 84, 87.

Rossini: Francis Toye, *Rossini; a Study in Tragi-Comedy,* London, 1954, is the best critical biography and survey in English. Stendhal's *Life of Rossini* (1824), New York, 1957, gives delightful insights into the way the composer was regarded by a worshipping contemporary who considered factual accuracy negligible for a biography.

Verdi: Francis Toye, *Giuseppe Verdi, His Life and Works,* New York, 1946, is an excellent introduction.

Wagner: Ernest Newman, *The Wagner Operas,* New York, 1949; Newman's *The Life of Richard Wagner,* New York, 1933–46 (4 vols.) is the standard biography.

Weber: The standard biography is by the composer's son, Max von Weber; an English adaptation, under the title *Weber: the Life of an Artist* was published at London in 1865 (2 vols.). See also L. and R. Stebbins, *Enchanted Wanderer,* New York, 1940.

Chapter XIX   (Pp. 389-416)

An excellent survey of the period covered in this chapter will be found in Gerald Abraham, *A Hundred Years of Music;* Neville Cardus, *A Composers Eleven,* London, 1958, contains good though nontechnical essays on Schubert, Wagner, Brahms, Bruckner, Mahler, Richard Strauss, César Franck, Debussy, Elgar, Delius, and Sibelius.

Late Romanticism: On Wolf, see Frank Walker, *Hugo Wolf, a Biography*, London, 1951.

Mahler: H. F. Redlich, *Bruckner and Mahler*, London, 1955; Bruno Walter, *Gustav Mahler*, New York, 1941; Alma Maria Mahler, *Memories and Letters*, London, 1947; Dika Newlin, *Bruckner, Mahler, Schoenberg*, New York, 1947; and Arnold Schoenberg, "Gustav Mahler," in *Style and Idea*, New York, 1950.

Strauss: The composer's own *Recollections and Reflections*, London, 1953. Of the published correspondence, two volumes are available in translation: with von Hoffmansthal, in English translation under the title *A Working Friendship*, New York, 1961; and with von Bülow (London, 1953).

Nationalism Old and New: On Russian music in general, see Gerald Abraham, *Studies in Russian Music*, New York, 1939; M. D. Calvocoressi and G. Abraham, *Masters of Russian Music*, New York, 1936; and Rosa Newmarch, *The Russian Opera*, New York, 1914.

The two best books in English on Mussorgsky are *The Mussorgsky Reader*, ed. J. Leyda and S. Bartensen, New York, 1947, and M. D. Calvocoressi, *Modest Mussorgsky*, London, 1956.

The subject of modality in Western music is well covered in John Vincent, *The Diatonic Modes in Modern Music*, Berkeley, 1951; on Russian music, see especially Ch. 28.

Rimsky-Korsakov's *Memoirs* were first published in 1908, and in English translation as *My Musical Life*, New York, 1923. The composer's *Principles of Orchestration*, with musical examples drawn from his own works, was published in English translation, New York, 1933.

On Grieg, see *Grieg: a Symposium*, Gerald Abraham, ed., Norman, Oklahoma, 1950; biography by David M. Johansen (in English translation), Princeton and New York, 1938.

For the music of the United States of America in this period, see Gilbert Chase, *America's Music*, New York, 1955, Chapters 10–14 and 19–22. MacDowell's Columbia University lectures are published under the title *Critical and Historical Essays*, Boston, 1912; see also Marian MacDowell, *Random Notes*, Boston, 1950.

On Ives, see Henry and Sidney Cowell, *Charles Ives and His Music*, New York, 1955.

Sibelius: Gerald Abraham, ed., *The Music of Sibelius*, New York, 1947; Karl Ekman, *Jean Sibelius, His Life and Personality*, New York, 1938; Cecil Gray, *Sibelius*, London, 1934; id., *Sibelius: the Symphonies*, London, 1935; H. E. Johnson, *Jan Sibelius*, New York, 1959; Simon Parmet, *The Symphonies of Sibelius*, London, 1959.

For English musical nationalism in the early twentieth century, see Ch. 13 of Ernest Walker, *History of Music in England*, Oxford, 1952.

Elgar: Diana McVeagh, *Edward Elgar: His Life and Music*, London, 1955; Percy Young, ed., *Letters of Elgar and Other Writings*, London, 1956.

Falla: Jaime Pahissa, *Manuel de Falla: His Life and Works*, London, 1954.

New Currents in France: Martin Cooper, *French Music from the Death of Berlioz to the Death of Fauré*, London, 1951.

d'Indy: Norman Demuth, *Vincent d'Indy*, London, 1951.

Fauré: Norman Suckling, *Fauré*, London, 1946, is an excellent study of the life and music of this composer.

Debussy: Léon Vallas, *Claude Debussy*, London, 1933; Edward Lockspeiser, *Debussy;* New York, 1952; Rollo H. Myers, *Debussy*, London, 1948. Debussy's essays were published at Paris in 1923 under the title *Monsieur Croche, anti-dilettante;* in translation, *Monsieur Croche, the Dilettante Hater*, New York, 1928.

Ravel: Norman Demuth, *Ravel*, London, 1947; Roland-Manuel, *Maurice Ravel*, London, 1947.

Satie: Rollo H. Myers, *Erik Satie*, London, 1948. There are two excellent chapters on Satie in Roger Shattuck, *The Banquet Years*, New York, 1958.

Chapter XX (Pp. 417-460)

1900–1950 in general: Nicolas Slonimsky, *Music since 1900*, New York, 1949; Adolfo Salazar, *Music in Our Time*, New York, 1946; Wilfred Mellers, *Studies in Contemporary Music*, London, 1947; Allen Forte, *Contemporary Tone Structures*, New York, 1955; Humphrey Searle, *Twentieth Century Counterpoint*, London, 1954; William Austin, "The Idea of Evolution in the Music of the Twentieth Century," *MQ* 39 (1953), 26–36; Edward T. Cone, "Music: a View from Delft," MQ 47 (1961), 439–53; George Perle, *Serial Composition and Atonality*, Berkeley and Los Angeles, 1963.

Bartók: Halsey Stevens, *The Life and Music of Béla Bartók*, New York, 1953.

Soviet composers: Gerald Abraham, *Eight Soviet Composers*, New York, 1943; Nicolas Slonimsky, "The Changing Styles of Soviet Music," *JAMS* 3 (1950), 236–55; Israel Nestyev, *Sergei Prokofiev: His Musical Life*, New York, 1946; Ivan Martynov, *Dmitri Shostakovich, the Man and His Work*, New York, 1947.

Vaughan Williams: Hubert Foss, *Ralph Vaughan Williams, a Study*, London, 1950; Percy Young, *Vaughan Williams*, London, 1953; Frank Howes, *The Music of Ralph Vaughan Williams*, London, 1954; A. E. F. Dickinson, *Vaughan Williams*, London, 1963; and the composer's own writings including *National Music*, London, 1934, and especially his "Musical Autobiography," Ch. 3 of Foss's book.

Holst: Imogen Holst, *The Music of Gustav Holst*, London, 1951; Edmund Rubbra, *Gustav Holst*, Monaco, 1947.

Copland: Arthur Berger, *Aaron Copland*, New York, 1953; and the composer's own writings, especially *Our New Music*, New York, 1941; and *Music and Imagination*, Cambridge, 1952.

Thomson: His own writings, especially *The Art of Judging Music*, New York, 1948; and *Music, Right and Left*, New York, 1951.

Milhaud: His autobiography, *Notes without Music*, London, 1952.

Messiaen: Olivier Messiaen, *The Technique of My Language*, Paris, 1956; and articles on him by David Drew in *The Score* (London), December, 1954 and September and December, 1955.

Stravinsky: Igor Stravinsky: a Complete Catalogue of His Published Works, London, Boosey & Hawkes, 1957; *Stravinsky, an Autobiography*, New York, 1936; Stravinsky, *Poetics of Music*, New York, 1956; Eric White, *Stravinsky*, New York, 1948; Alexandre Tansmann, *Igor Stravinsky, the Man and His Music*, New York, 1949; Théodore Strawinsky, *The Message of Igor Stravinsky*, London, 1953; Igor Stravinsky and Robert Craft, *Conversations with Igor Stravinsky*, New York, 1959; Roman Vlad, *Stravinsky*, London, 1960.

Busoni: Ferruccio Busoni, *Sketch of a New Esthetic of Music*, New York, 1911; id., *The Essence of Music*, London, 1957; see also Edward J. Dent, *Ferruccio Busoni, a Biography*, London, 1933.

Hindemith: Catalogue of Published Works and Recordings, London, Schott, 1954; Hindemith, *The Craft of Musical Composition*, New York, 1945; id., *A Composer's World*, Cambridge, 1952.

Schoenberg: Egon Wellesz, *Arnold Schoenberg*, New York, 1924; Dika Newlin, *Bruckner, Mahler, Schoenberg*, New York, 1947; Josef Rufer, *Composition with Twelve Notes*, London, 1954; Alban Berg, "Why Is Schoenberg's Music So Hard to Understand?" *The Music Review*, 13 (1952), 187–96; Schoenberg's collected essays, *Style and Idea*, New York, 1950; see also the excellent brochure by Allen Forte and Milton Babbitt which accompanies the recording of *Moses and Aaron* (Columbia K3L–241).

Berg: H. F. Redlich, *Alban Berg, the Man and His Music*, New York, 1957; W. Reich, "A Guide to *Wozzeck*," MQ, 38 (1952), 1–21.

Webern: Die Reihe, Heft II, ed., H. Eimert and K. H. Stockhausen, Bryn Mawr, 1958.

References

1 Aristotle, *Politics*, Book VIII, 6, 1341 ᵃ 10, tr. B. Jowett; in R. McKeon, ed., *The Basic Works of Aristotle*, New York, 1941, 1313. Cf. also Plato, *Laws*, II, 669E, 770A.
2 P. Wagner, *Einführung in die grego-* *rianischen Melodien*, Leipzig, 1911, I, 42.
3 St. Augustine, "In Psalmum xcix enarratio, sermo ad plebem"; pr. Migne, *Patrologiae cursus completus, Series Latina*, XXXVII, 1272.

Chapter I, *pp. 1–13*

1 From an account by a fourteenth-century Florentine chronicler, Filippo Villani.

Chapter IV, *pp. 64–80*

1 *Song of Solomon* (King James version) vii:6–7, 5, 4, 11–12. The text in the order used by Dunstable is found in the *Antiphonale Sarisburiense*, facsimile ed., London, 1901–25, 528–529.

Chapter V, *pp. 81–98*

1 The *soggetto cavato* is not peculiar to the sixteenth century. One need only recall the many pieces written on the theme B-A-C-H (*b-flat, a, c, b-natural*)—for instance, Liszt's organ fantasia. The supplement to a special number of the Paris *Revue Musicale* for October, 1922, is entitled: "*Hommage à Gabriel Fauré; Sept pièces de piano sur le nom de Fauré: F fa, A la, U sol, R ré, E mi, par Louis Aubert, Georges Enesco, Charles Koechlin, Paul Lad-* *mirault, Maurice Ravel, Roger-Ducasse, Florent Schmitt.*"
2 Wolfgang Boetticher, *Orlando di Lasso*, I, 249. The passage refers to the *Penitential Psalms* of Orlando di Lasso, which were written about 1560 and published in 1584. The author was Samuel Quickelberg, a Dutch scholar and physician residing at the court of Munich; the date of his description is 1565.
3 *Dodecachordon*, 1547, III, xxiv.

Chapter VI, *pp. 99–119*

1 *The Sonnets of Petrarch, translated by Joseph Auslander* (1931); quoted by permission of the publishers, Messrs. Longmans, Green & Co.

Chapter VII, *pp. 120–151*

1 Psalms 6, 32, 38, 51, 102, 130, 143 in the King James version of the Bible; 6, 31, 37, 50, 101, 129, 142 of the Vulgate.

Chapter VIII, *pp. 152–179*

1 To appreciate the subtleties of the relationship of music to text, the use of ornaments, and the manner of performance desired by the composer, examples from *Le nuove musiche* (MM, No. 30; HAM, No. 184; GMB, Nos. 172 and 173; WM, No. 49) should be studied in connection with Caccini's preface, which itself contains many musical illustrations (SR, 377–92). The ornamental version in GMB, No. 173 is not Caccini's, but the editor's.

Chapter IX, *pp. 180–208*

References

Chapter X,
pp. 209–232

1 Henry Woodward, "A Study of the Tenbury Manuscripts of Johann Pachelbel," Harvard doctoral dissertation (typescript), 29.

1 Brijon, *Réflexions sur la musique et sur* *la vraie manière de l'exécuter sur le violon*, Paris, 1763, 2–3; paraphrased from the quotation in Pincherle, *Vivaldi*, I, 163.

Chapter XII,
pp. 251–281

2 BWV stands for *Thematisch-systematisches Verzeichnis der musikalischen Werke von Johann Sebastian Bach* (*Thematic-Systematic List of the Musical Works of J. S. Bach*), ed. Wolfgang Schmieder, Leipzig, 1950.

3 The numbering of the Bach cantatas follows the Bachgesellschaft edition, which is also that of BWV. The order is not chronological.

4 Apropos the question of originality in art are these words of William Ivins. He is speaking particularly of drawing, but his conclusions are equally relevant to music: " 'Originality' in art is very much like originality in sin, for we should always bear in mind that 'original sin' is the sin, or at least the kind of sin, about which we poor mortals can do nothing at all. We have it simply because we are descended from Adam and Eve. In the same way, draughtsmen who are original are so no matter how much they may attempt to copy or emulate something that someone else has done before them.... 'Copies' and imitations made by men who have this ineradicable quality of originality are infinitely more original than 'original drawings' made by men who lack it.... The best way to find out how much originality a man has is to see what he can do with another man's idea. I believe it is something of this kind that explains why the great masters—the most original men, that is—have always come out of long lineages of other great artists, on whose shoulders and triumphs they stand." William M. Ivins, Jr., "Some Disconnected Notes about Drawing," *Harpers Magazine* (December, 1949), 84–85. (Quoted by permission of the publishers.)

Chapter XIII,
pp. 282–299

1 J. J. Quantz, *Versuch*, XVIII, in SR, 597–98.

2 Michel Paul Gui de Chabanon, *De la musique considerée en elle-même et dans ses rapports* [etc.], Paris, 1785, 97.

3 Burney, "Essay on Musical Criticism," introducing Book III of his *General History of Music.*

4 Quantz, *op. cit.*, Introduction, § 16.

5 C. Burney, *The Present State of Music in Germany*, London, 1775, I, 238–39. Dr. Burney's—or his editor's—punctuation has been preserved.

Chapter XIV,
pp. 300–321

1 No. 97, the finest of all Haydn's symphonies in C, may have been in the back of Beethoven's mind when he wrote the first movement of his *Eroica:* the triadic outline of the principal theme of Haydn's first movement, the opening of his development section, the fast triple meter, the rhythmic figure ♫ ♪, the displaced accents at the unison triplet passage in both exposition and recapitulation—all are suggestive.

2 Leopold Mozart, letter to his daughter, Vienna, February 14th–16th, 1785; pr. in Emily Anderson, ed., *The Letters of Mozart and His Family*, London, 1938, III, 1321.

3 Letter dated December 28, 1782; Anderson, *op. cit.*, No. 476.

4 A. Einstein, *Mozart*, 314.

Chapter XV,
pp. 322–338

1 Quoted in Thayer, *Life of Beethoven*, III, 138–39.

2 Thayer, *op. cit.*, I, 353–54.

3 *Cobbett's Cyclopedic Survey of Chamber Music*, "Beethoven," London, 1926.

4 D. Tovey, *Essays in Musical Analysis*, New York, 1935, I, 60.

5 Thayer, *op. cit.*, III, 166.

6 From an essay on "Beethoven's Instrumental Music," 1813; in SR, 777.

Chapter XVI,
pp. 339–350

1 E. Gibbon, *The Decline and Fall of the Roman Empire*, Book I, Ch. VII.

2 Reprinted in Liszt, *Gesammelte Schriften*, Leipzig, 1881, II, 55–57.

Chapter XIX,
pp. 389–416

1 Abraham, *A Hundred Years of Music*, 178.

2 He is *not* the composer of *The Palms*. That song was perpetrated by Jean-Baptiste Faure (1830–1914).

1 Halsey Stevens, *The Life and Music of Béla Bartók*, 172. Quoted by permission of the publishers, Oxford University Press.
2 From an essay, "Who Wants the English Composer?", 1912, pr. in Hubert Foss, *Ralph Vaughan Williams*, 200.

3 Arthur Berger, *Aaron Copland*, 40.
4 Stravinsky, *Poetics of Music*, 58–59.
5 *Poetics of Music*, Lesson Three ("The Composition of Music"). Quoted by permission of the publisher, Harvard University Press.

References

Chapter XX, pp. 417–460

Chronology

This chronology is intended to provide a background for the history of music, and to enable the reader to see the individual works and composers in relation to their times.

Entries fall into three categories, each listed in a separate paragraph under the given date:

(M) Significant musical events.
(H) Concurrent events in political, social, and intellectual history.
(A) Representative works and events in the other arts.

The first time a writer's or artist's name appears it is given in full, together with dates of birth and death. Thereafter, unless there is a chance of confusion, it appears in the surname form alone.

800–461 B.C.
(H) Rise of city states in Greece.

753 B.C.
(H) Traditional date of founding of Rome.

586 B.C.
(M) Sakadas of Argos wins Pythian Games with *Nomos Pythicos.*

500 B.C.
(M) Pythagoras (d. *ca.* 497).
(H) Establishment of early Roman Republic.

461–429 B. C.
(H) Age of Pericles.

431–404 B. C.
(H) Peloponnesian War.

429 B. C.
(H) Death of Pericles.
(A) Sophocles (446–406), *Oedipus Rex.*

401 B. C.
(A) Xenophon (434–255), *Anabasis.*

400 B. C.
(H) Athens defeated by Sparta; decline of democracy in Greece.

399 B. C.
(H) Death of Socrates.

380 B. C.
(A) Plato (427?–347), *Republic.*

350 B. C.
(A) Aristotle (384–322), *Politics.* Praxiteles 4th c. B. C.), *Hermes with Infant Dionysos.*

338–337 B. C.
(H) Macedonian conquest of Greece.

336–323 B. C.
(H) Conquests of Alexander the Great and subsequent division of his Empire.

330 B. C.
(M) Aristoxenus (b. *ca.* 354), *Harmonic Elements.*

150 B. C.
(M) Delphic *Hymn to Apollo.*

146 B. C.
(H) Greece under Roman rule.

60 B. C.
(A) Lucretius (*ca.* 96–55), *De Rerum Natura.*

58–51 B. C.
(H) Julius Caesar (100–44) invades Gaul and Britain.

27 B. C.
(H) Augustus Caesar (63 B. C.–14 A. D.) first Emperor of Rome; Principate or Early Empire (27 B. C.–284 A. D.).
(A) Vergil (70–19), *Aeneid;* Horace (65–8), *Ars Poetica;* Ovid (43 B. C.–17 A. D.), *Metamorphoses.*

4 B. C.
(H) Birth of Jesus.

Ca. 33 A. D.
(H) The Crucifixion.

65
(H) First persecution of Christians in Rome.

70
(H) Temple at Jerusalem destroyed.
(A) Colosseum begun at Rome.

100
(M) Plutarch (50–120), *On Music*.
(H) Germanic migrations and invasions begin (to *ca.* 600).

112
(M) Pliny the Younger (62–113) reports hymn singing by Christians.

150
(M) Ptolemy, *Harmonics*.

284
(H) Diocletian becomes Emperor; beginning of Late Roman Empire (284–476).

285
(M) Oxyrhynchos hymn fragment.

330
(H) Constantinople established as new capital of Roman Empire.

374
(H) St. Ambrose (340–397) consecrated as Bishop of Milan.

395
(H) Separation of Eastern and Western Roman Empires.

410
(H) Sack of Rome by Alaric the Visigoth; invasion of Britain by Angles and Saxons.

413
(A) St. Augustine (354–430), *City of God*.

Ca. 450
(A) Establishment of seven liberal arts as course of study.

452
(H) Invasion of Italy by Attila the Hun; Venice founded.

476
(H) Romulus Augustulus deposed; traditional date of end of Roman Empire.

481
(H) Merovingian dynasty in France established (till 751).

500
(M) Boethius (480–524), *De institutione musica*.

527
(H) Justinian becomes Emperor of Eastern Roman Empire.
(A) Construction started on Hagia Sophia, Constantinople (finished 565).

529
(H) Benedictine order founded.

568
(H) Lombard invasion of northern Italy.

590
(H) Election of Pope Gregory the Great (*ca.* 540–604).

622
(M) Isidore of Seville (*ca.* 560–636), treatise on the arts.
(H) Hegira of Mohammed (*ca.* 570–632).

650
(H) Rise of monasteries (to *ca.* 700); Arab conquests in Asia and North Africa.

700
(H) Irish and Anglo-Saxon missionaries on Continent; monastic schools flourish.

750
(H) Arabic science brought to Europe.

768
(H) Charlemagne (742–814) King of the Franks.

800
(M) Cultivation of music in the monasteries.
(H) Charlemagne crowned Emperor by Pope at Rome; Arabic culture appears in Europe; Viking raids and conquests begin.

871
(H) Alfred the Great (849–899) King of England.

900
(M) Arabic musical instruments introduced into Europe; tropes and sequences; *Musica enchiriadis*.

962
(H) Otto the Great (912–973) crowned first Emperor of the Holy Roman Empire.

987
(H) Hugh Capet (*ca.* 940–996) elected King of France.

1025
(M) Guido of Arezzo's (*ca.* 995–1050) first writings on music.

1050
(A) *Chanson de Roland*.

1054
(H) Final separation of Eastern and Western Churches.

1066
(H) Norman invasion of England; Battle of Hastings.

1073

(M) Winchester Tropes.

1094

(A) St. Mark's Cathedral, Venice, begun.

1096

(H) First Crusade (till 1099).

1100

(M) Beginnings of St.-Martial organum.

1145

(A) Chartres Cathedral begun.

1150

(M) Troubadours flourish in Provence; Notre Dame School assumes musical leadership; liturgical dramas appear.
(A) Cathedrals at Sens, Senlis, and Noyen begun.
(H) Rise of universities throughout Europe; high point of Scholasticism.

1163

(A) Cornerstone of Notre Dame at Paris laid.

1167

(H) Beginning of Oxford University.

1170

(H) Beginning of the University of Paris.

1175

(M) Leonin, master of Notre Dame School (fl. after 1150), *Magnus liber organi.*
(A) Canterbury Cathedral begun.

1183

(M) Perotin active at Notre Dame.

1189

(H) Richard Coeur de Lion (1157—1199) King of England.

1200

(M) Trouvères flourish in France, Minnesingers in Germany.
(A) Reims Cathedral begun.

1209

(H) St. Francis of Assisi (1182—1226) founds the Franciscan Order. Cambridge University founded.

1213

(A) The Alhambra begun (completed 1388).

1215

(H) Magna Charta signed by King John.

1240

(M) Motet becomes important type of polyphonic composition.
(A) Chartres Cathedral rebuilt.

1248

(M) Sequence *Dies irae,* attributed to Thomas of Celano.
(A) Cologne Cathedral begun; Sainte-Chapelle, Paris, built.

1250

(M) Period of *ars antiqua.*

1260

(M) Franco of Cologne (active 1250—1280), *Ars cantus mensurabilis.*

1270

(M) Cantigas de Santa Maria; Petrus de Cruce active; Motets of Bamberg Codex.
(A) Roger Bacon (*ca.* 1214—1294), *Opus maius;* St. Thomas Aquinas (1225—1274), *Summa theologica.*
(H) Start of Louis' Second Crusade; Sicilian Vespers.

1284

(M) Adam de la Hale (*ca.* 1230—1288), *Robin et Marion.*

1297

(A) Marco Polo (*ca.* 1254—*ca.* 1324), *Book of Various Experiences.*

1300

(M) Beginning of French *Ars nova* (to *ca.* 1370).

1305

(A) Arena chapel frescoes by Giotto (1266—1337).
(H) The papacy in exile at Avignon.

1307

(A) Dante (1265—1321), *The Divine Comedy.*

1318

(M) Marchetto da Padua, *Pomerium artis musicae mensurabilis.*

1319

(M) Jean de Muris (*ca.* 1290—*ca.* 1351), *Ars novae musicae.*

1325

(M) Philippe de Vitry (1291—1361), *Ars nova;* Robertsbridge Codex.

1327

(A) Petrarch (1304—1374) meets Laura.

1330

(M) Italian *Ars nova* (till 1410); Jacob of Liège (fl. 14th c.), *Speculum musicae.*

1337

(H) Outbreak of the Hundred Years' War.

1348

(H) The Black Death.

1353

(A) Boccaccio (1313—1375), *Decameron.*

1360

(M) Guillaume de Machaut (*ca.* 1300—1377), *Messe de Notre Dame.*

1362

(A) William Langland, *The Vision of Piers Plowman.*

1376

(A) Wycliffe's (*ca.* 1320—1384) translation of the Bible.

1378
(H) Start of Papal schism.

1385
(H) Heidelberg University chartered.

1386
(A) Chaucer (*ca.* 1340–1400), *The Canterbury Tales.*

1405
(H) Duchy of Burgundy (till 1477).

1415
(H) Battle of Agincourt; Council of Constance.

1420
(M) Squarcialupi Codex; Old Hall Manuscript; Trent Codices (to 1480).

1425
(A) Giovanni da Prato, *Paradiso degli Alberti.* Ghiberti (1378–1455) begins *Gates of Paradise* for Baptistry at Florence.

1426
(A) Jan (*ca.* 1366–1426) and Hubert (*ca.* 1370–*ca.* 1440) Van Eyck begin the Ghent Altarpiece.

1431
(A) Lucca della Robbia (*ca.* 1400–1482) starts work on *Cantoria.*
(H) Jeanne d'Arc executed.

1434
(H) Medici powerful in Italy (till 1494).

1435
(A) Donatello (*ca.* 1386–1466), *David.*

1436
(M) Guillaume Dufay (*ca.* 1400–1474), *Nuper rosarum flores.*

1440
(M) Meistersinger in Germany; Canonici Manuscript.

1447
(H) Pope Nicholas V elected (till 1455); Vatican Library founded.
(A) Humanism rises in Italy.

1450
(M) White notation introduced.

1452
(H) Emperor Frederic III (till 1493), last Holy Roman Emperor to be crowned at Rome.
(A) Fouquet (*ca.* 1420–1481), *Book of Hours of Etienne Chevalier.*

1453
(H) End of Hundred Years' War; Constantinople conquered.

1454
(H) Gutenberg (1398–1468) invents printing from movable metal type.
(A) Andrea Mantegna (1431–1506), *St. James Led to Martyrdom.*

1455
(M) Lochamer *Liederbuch.*
(H) Beginning of War of the Roses (till 1485).

1456
(H) Gutenberg prints the Mazarin Bible.

1460
(M) Dufay, Mass *Se la face ay pale;* first Doctor of Music degree awarded at Oxford.

1478
(H) Lorenzo de' Medici (1449–1492; the "Magnificent") ruler in Florence.
(A) Sandro Botticelli (*ca.* 1444–1510), *La Primavera.*

1480
(M) Jacob Obrecht (1452–1505), first Masses.

1481
(A) Andrea del Verrocchio (1435–1488), *Colleoni.*

1484
(M) Josquin des Prez (1450–1521) at Milan.
(A) Sir Thomas Malory, *Morte d'Arthur,* printed by Caxton.

1485
(H) Tudor dynasty in England (till 1603).

1492
(M) Obrecht at Antwerp (till 1504).
(H) Unification of Spain; first voyage of Columbus; Alexander VI (Borgia) elected Pope.

1495
(A) Hieronymus Bosch (*ca.* 1450–1560), *Temptation of St. Anthony;* Leonardo da Vinci (1452–1519), *Last Supper.*

1496
(M) Franchino Gafori (1451–1522), *Practica musicae.*

1497
(H) Voyage of John Cabot (1450–1498); Vasco da Gama (*ca.* 1469–1524), voyage to India; first voyage of Amerigo Vespucci.

1498
(M) License to print music granted to Ottaviano dei Petrucci, Venetian music publisher; first to print complete song collections from movable type.
(H) Execution of Savonarola (1452–1498) at Florence.

1501
(M) Petrucci publishes *Odhecaton,* first book of Josquin's Masses, first book of frottole.

1503
(M) Obrecht Masses printed by Petrucci.
(A) Henry VII's chapel, Westminster; Leonardo da Vinci (1452–1519), *Mona Lisa.*

1504
(A) Michelangelo Buonarotti (1475–1564), *David.*

1506

(A) St. Peter's begun at Rome, under Bramante's direction.

1507

(A) Albrecht Dürer (1471–1528), *Adam and Eve.*
(M) Petrucci issues first printed lute tablature.

1508

(A) Michelangelo begins Sistine Chapel ceiling.

1509

(A) Raphael (1483–1520), *School of Athens.*
(H) Henry VIII King of England.

1511

(M) Sebastian Virdung, *Musica getutscht.*
(A) Desiderius Erasmus (1466–1536), *The Praise of Folly.*

1513

(H) Balboa (1475–1517) discovers the Pacific Ocean; election of Pope Leo X (Giovanni de' Medici).
(A) Matthias Grünewald (1485–1530), Isenheim Altarpiece.

1514

(A) Dürer, *St. Jerome in His Study;* Niccolò Machiavelli (1469–1527), *The Prince.*

1516

(A) Raphael, *Sistine Madonna;* Sir Thomas More (1478–1535), *Utopia;* Lodovico Ariosto (1474–1533), *Orlando Furioso.*

1517

(H) Martin Luther (1483–1546), ninety-five theses.

1518

(H) Conquest of Mexico by Cortes.

1519

(H) Ferdinand Magellan (*ca.* 1480–1521) circumnavigates the globe; Charles V (1500–1558), Holy Roman Emperor (till 1556).

1520

(A) Michelangelo, sculpture for Medici tombs.

1524

(M) Johann Walter (1496–1570), *Geystliche Gesangk Buchleyn.*

1526

(A) Luther, *Deudsche Messe.*

1527

(M) Pierre Attaingnant's (d. 1552) first publication, *Breviarium noviomense.*
(H) Sack of Rome.

1528

(A) Conte Baldassare Castiglione (1478–1529), *The Courtier.*

1530

(A) Nicolaus Copernicus (1473–1543), *De Revolutionibus Orbium Coelesticum.*

1532

(A) François Rabelais (1494?–1553), *Gargantua.*

1533

(M) First Italian madrigals.
(A) Hans Holbein the Younger (1497–1543), *The Ambassadors.*

1536

(M) First music publications of Gardano (Venice) and Petreius (Nuremberg).
(A) Library at Venice founded.

1538

(A) Titian, *Venus of Urbino.*

1539

(M) Jacob Arcadelt (*ca.* 1505–*ca.* 1560), first book of five-part madrigals.
(H) Statute of the Six Articles.

1540

(H) Society of Jesus founded.

1541

(H) Hernando de Soto (1500–1542) discovers Mississippi River.
(A) Michelangelo, *Last Judgment* in Sistine Chapel.

1542

(M) Cipriano de Rore (1516–1565), first book of madrigals.
(H) Ireland made a kingdom.

1545

(H) Council of Trent (till 1563).

1547

(M) Glareanus (1488–1563), *Dodecachordon.*
(A) Benevenuto Cellini (1500–1571), *Perseus.*

1549

(M) Adrian Willaert (*ca.* 1490–1562), *ricercari.*

1551

(M) Claude Goudimel (1505–1572), *First Book of Psalms.*

1554

(M) Giovanni Palestrina (*ca.* 1526–1594), first book of Masses; Philippe de Monte (1521–1603), first book of madrigals.

1555

(M) Orlando di Lasso (*ca.* 1532–1594), first book of madrigals.
(H) Peace of Augsburg.

1558

(M) Gioseffo Zarlino (1517–1590), *Istitutioni harmoniche;* Willaert, *Musica nova.*
(H) Elizabeth I, Queen of England (till 1603).

1561

(M) Palestrina, *Improperia.*

1562

(H) Religious wars of the French Huguenots.

1563

(H) Establishment of the Church of England.

1565

(M) Lasso, *Penitential Psalms.*

1566

(A) Pieter Brueghel the Elder (*ca.* 1525–1569), *The Wedding Dance.*

1568

(H) Revolt of the Netherlands.

1569

(M) Palestrina, first book of motets.

1571

(H) Naval battle of Lepanto.

1572

(H) Massacre of Protestants in Paris.

1575

(M) William Byrd (1543–1623) and Thomas Tallis (*ca.* 1505–1585), *Cantiones sacrae.*

1576

(A) Tintoretto (1518–1594), *Ascension of Christ.*

1577

(M) Monte at Prague.
(H) Sir Francis Drake (1540–1596) starts voyage around the world.

1580

(A) Michel Eyquem de Montaigne (1533–1592), *Essays.*

1581

(M) Vincenzo Galileo (*ca.* 1520–1591), *Dialogo della musica antica e della moderna.*

1582

(H) Calendar reform by Pope Gregory XIII.

1587

(M) Claudio Monteverdi (*ca.* 1567–1643), first book of madrigals.

1588

(M) Nicholas Yonge (d. 1619) issues *Musica transalpina.*
(H) War between Spain and England; defeat of the Spanish Armada.
(A) Christoper Marlowe (1564–1593), *Doctor Faustus.*

1589

(M) Byrd, *Cantiones sacrae, Songs of Sundrie Natures.*

1590

(A) Edmund Spenser (1552–1599), *The Faerie Queene.*

1592

(A) Tintoretto, *The Last Supper.*

1594

(M) Thomas Morley (1557–1602) *The First Book of Ballets for Five Voices;* Orazio Vecchi (1540–1603), *Amfiparnaso;* Carlo Gesualdo (*ca.* 1560–1613), first book of madrigals.
(A) William Shakespeare (1564–1616), *Romeo and Juliet.*

1597

(M) Morley, *A Plaine and Easie Introduction to Practicall Musicke;* Jacopo Peri (1561–1633), *Dafne;* John Dowland (1562–1626), *First Book of Songs or Ayres;* Giovanni Gabrieli (*ca.* 1554–1612), *Symphoniae sacrae.*

1600

(M) Jacopo Peri (1561–1633), *Euridice;* Giulio Caccini (1546–1618), *Euridice;* Emilio de' Cavalieri (1550–1602), *La Rappresentazione di anima e di corpo.*
(H) Henry IV marries Marie de' Medici; Giordano Bruno (1548–1600) burned at stake.
(A) Annibale Carracci (1560–1609), *Polyphemus Hurling Rocks at Acis.*

1601

(M) *The Triumphes of Oriana;* Caccini, *Le Nuove Musiche.*
(A) Shakespeare, *Hamlet.*

1602

(M) Ludovico Viadana (1564–1645), *Cento concerti ecclesiastici.*
(H) Galileo Galilei (1564–1642), discovers law of falling bodies; Dutch East India Company founded.

1603

(H) James I of England (James VI of Scotland) crowned (till 1625).

1604

(A) Shakespeare, *Othello.*

1605

(M) Monteverdi, *Fifth Book of Madrigals;* Michael Praetorius (1571–1621), *Musae Sioniae;* Thomas Luis de Victoria (*ca.* 1549–1611), *Requiem;* John Dowland (1562–1626), *Lachrymae.*
(H) Gunpowder plot.
(A) Miguel de Cervantes (1547–1616), Part I of *Don Quixote;* Francis Bacon (1561–1626), *On the Advancement of Learning;* Ben Jonson (*ca.* 1573–1637), *Volpone.*

1606

(A) Shakespeare, *Macbeth.*

1607

(M) Monteverdi, *Orfeo;* Marco da Gagliano (*ca.* 1575–1642), *Dafne;* Agostino Agazzari (1578–1640), *Del sonare sopra il basso.*
(H) Founding of Jamestown Colony.

1608

(M) Monteverdi, *Arianna;* Girolamo Frescobaldi (1583–1643), organist at St. Peter's.
(H) Quebec founded by Champlain.

1609

(M) Heinrich Schütz (1585–1672) and G. Gabrieli at Venice; Peri, *Le varie musiche.*
(H) Henry Hudson (d. 1611) explores Hudson River; Johannes Kepler (1571–1603), *Astronomia nova.*

1610

(H) Louis XIII crowned (till 1643).

1611

(M) *Parthenia* published.
(A) King James version of Bible.

1612

(A) Bacon, *Novum organum.*
(H) Louvre begun (till 1690).

1613

(M) Domenico Cerone (*ca.* 1560–1626), *The Art of Music and Instructor;* Monteverdi at San Marco.

1614

(M) *Medicean Gradual* published at Rome.
(A) Peter Paul Rubens (1577–1646), *The Descent from the Cross.*

1615

(M) G. Gabrieli, *Canzoni e sonate, Symphoniae sacrae II.*

1617

(M) Biagio Marini (1595–1665), *Affetti musicali;* Schein, *Banchetto musicale;* Schütz at Dresden.

1618

(H) Start of Thirty Years' War.

1619

(M) Praetorius, *Syntagma musicum.*

1620

(H) Pilgrims arrive at Cape Cod; Mayflower Compact.

1624

(M) Jakob Böhme (1572–1624), *Der Weg zu Christo;* Monteverdi, *Il Combattimento di Tancredi e Clorinda;* Samuel Scheidt (1587–1654), *Tabulatura nova.*
(H) Cardinal Richelieu in power in France (till 1642).
(A) Franz Hals (*ca.* 1580–1666), *The Laughing Cavalier.*

1625

(M) Schütz, *Cantiones sacrae.*
(H) Charles I crowned King of England (till 1649).

1626

(H) Manhattan Island bought by Peter Minuit.

1628

(M) Orazio Benevoli (1605–1672), *Salzburg Festival Mass.* Gagliano and Peri, *La Flora;* Schütz, *Psalms of David;* Carissimi at San Apollinare in Rome.
(A) William Harvey (1578–1657), *Essay on the Motion of the Heart and the Blood.*
(H) La Rochelle captured; end of Huguenot power in France.

1630

(H) Puritans establish Boston.

1631

(H) Battle of Lützen; Galilei, *Dialogo dei due massimi sistemi del mondo.*
(A) Rembrandt van Rijn (1606–1669), *The Anatomy Lesson.*

1634

(M) Stefano Landi (*ca.* 1590–1655), *Il Sant' Alessio;* Henry Lawes (1596–1662), *Comus.*
(A) Taj Mahal begun (till 1653).

1635

(H) Académie Française founded.
(A) Diego Valesquez (1599–1660), *Surrender of Breda.*

1636

(M) Marin Mersenne (1588–1648), *Harmonie Universelle.*
(H) Founding of Harvard College; Roger Williams's first settlement in Rhode Island.
(A) Pierre Corneille (1606–1684), *Le Cid.*

1637

(M) Johann Froberger (1616–1667), organist at court chapel, Vienna; first public opera theatre (Venice).
(A) René Descartes (1596–1650), *Discourse on Method;* Anthony van Dycke (1599–1641), *The Children of Charles I.*

1638

(M) Heinrich Albert (1604–1651), first arias; Monteverdi, *Madrigali guerrieri et amorosi;* Pier Francesco Cavalli (1602–1676), second organist at San Marco.

1639

(M) Virgilio Mazzocchi (1597–1646) and Marco Marazzoli (1600–1662) compose first comic opera, *Chi soffre, speri.*
(A) Nicolas Poussin (1594–1665), *Shepherds in Arcadia.*

1640

(H) *The Bay Psalm Book,* first book printed in English colonies.

1642

(M) Monteverdi, *L'incoronazione di Poppea.*
(A) Rembrandt, *The Night Watch.*

1643

(H) Louis XIV King of France at age of five (till 1715).

1644

(A) Giovanni Lorenzo Bernini (1598–1680), *The Ecstasy of St. Teresa.*

1645

(M) Andreas Hammerschmidt (1612–1675), *Dialogues;* Schütz, *Seven Last Words.*

1647

(M) Luigi Rossi's (1597–1653) *Orfeo* staged in Paris; Johann Crüger (1598–1662), *Praxis pietatis melica.*

1648

(M) Schütz, *Geistliche Chormusik.*
(H) Treaty of Westphalia; end of Thirty Years' War.

1649

(M) Cavalli, *Giasone;* Marc' Antonio Cesti (1623–1669), *Orontea.*
(H) King Charles I beheaded; Commonwealth established (till 1660).

1650

(M) Carissimi (1605–1674), *Jephtha;* Athanasius Kircher (1602–1680), *Musurgia universalis.*
(A) Descartes, *Musicae compendium.*

1651

(A) Thomas Hobbes (1588–1679), *Leviathan.*

1653

(M) Jean-Baptiste Lully (1632–1687) court composer at Paris.
(H) Oliver Cromwell (1599–1658) dissolves Parliament.

1656

(A) Velasquez, *The Maids of Honor.*

1660

(M) Cavalli, *Serse.*
(H) Restoration of Charles II in England (till 1685).
(A) Samuel Pepys (1633–1703), *Diary.*

1661

(M) Cesti, *Dori.*
(H) Absolute reign of Louis XIV (till 1715).

1662

(M) Cavalli, *Ercole amante.*
(A) Molière (1622–1673), *École des Femmes.*

1664

(M) Schütz, *Christmas Oratorio.*
(H) New Amsterdam becomes New York.

1665

(H) Charles II of Spain crowned (till 1700); plague in London.
(A) Baruch Spinoza (1632–1677), *Ethics.*

1666

(H) Great fire of London.

1667

(M) Johann Rosenmüller (*ca.* 1620–1684), *12 Sonate de camera a 5 stromenti.* Cesti, *Il pomo d'Oro.*
(A) John Milton (1608–1674), *Paradise Lost;* Bernini, colonnade of St. Peter's.

1668

(A) La Fontaine (1621–1695), *Fables.*

1669

(M) Paris Academy of Music founded.
(A) Claude Gellée Lorrain (1600–1682), *Egeria.*

1670

(M) Jacques Chambonnières (*ca.* 1602–1672), clavecin pieces.
(A) Blaise Pascal (1623–1662), *Pensées;* Molière; *Le Bourgeois Gentilhomme.*

1674

(A) Nicolas Boileau-Despreaux (1636–1711), *L'Art Poétique.*

1675

(M) Lully, *Thésée.*
(A) Sir Christopher Wren (1632–1723) begins St. Paul's Cathedral.

1677

(A) Jean Baptiste Racine (1639–1699), *Phèdre.*

1678

(A) Bartolomé Murillo (1617–1682), *Mystery of the Immaculate Conception;* John Bunyan (1628–1688), *Pilgrim's Progress.*

1681

(M) Arcangelo Corelli (1653–1713), first trio sonatas.

1682

(H) Reign of Peter the Great (till 1725); La Salle explores the Mississippi; Philadelphia founded by William Penn.

1685

(M) Giovanni Legrenzi (1626–1690) at San Marco; John Playford (1623–1686), *The Division Violist.*
(H) James II of England crowned (till 1688); revocation of the Edict of Nantes.

1686

(M) Lully, *Armide.*

1687

(A) Isaac Newton (1642–1727), *Principia mathematica.*

1689

(M) Agostino Steffani (1654–1728), *Enrico detto il Leone;* Henry Purcell (*ca.* 1659–1695), *Dido and Aeneas;* Johann Kuhnau (1660–1722), Clavier Sonatas.
(H) William III and Mary rulers of England (till 1725).

1690

(A) John Locke (1632–1704), *An Essay Concerning Human Understanding.*

1692

(H) Salem witchcraft trials.

1695

(M) Georg Muffat (1653–1704), *Florilegium I;* Reinhard Keiser (1674–1739) director of Hamburg opera.

1697

(M) André Campra (1660–1744), *L'Europe galante.*
(A) John Dryden (1631–1700), *Alexander's Feast.*

1698

(M) Giuseppi Torelli (1658–1709), Violin Concertos Op. 5.

1700

(M) Johann Sebastian Bach (1685–1750) at Lüneburg.
(H) Philip V of Spain crowned (till 1746).

1701

(M) Muffat, *12 Concerti Grossi.*
(H) Frederick I of Prussia crowned; Detroit founded; Yale College founded.

1702

(H) Queen Anne of England crowned; war of the Spanish Succession (till 1714).

1703

(M) George Frideric Handel (1685–1759) at Hamburg.
(H) St. Petersburg founded.

1704

(M) Handel, *St. John Passion;* first Bach cantatas. Georg Telemann (1681–1761) founds Collegium musicum at Leipzig.

1706

(M) Jean-Philippe Rameau (1683–1764), first book of clavecin pieces; Handel in Italy.

1707

(M) Alessandro Scarlatti (1660–1725), *Mitridate eupatore.*

1708

(M) Bach at Weimar.

1709

(M) First pianoforte built; *opera buffa* in Italy.
(A) *The Tatler* and *The Spectator* founded.

1710

(M) Handel in England.
(A) George Berkeley (1685–1753), *A Treatise Concerning the Principles of Human Knowledge.*

1711

(M) Keiser, *Croesus;* Handel, *Rinaldo.*
(A) Alexander Pope (1688–1744), *Essay on Criticism.*

1712

(M) Antonio Vivaldi (*ca.* 1676–1741), Concertos, Op. 3. Handel settles in London.
(H) Toleration Act, London.
(A) Pope, *Rape of the Lock.*

1713

(M) François Couperin (1668–1733), *Pieces de Clavecin,* I.
(H) Peace of Utrecht.

1714

(M) Bach, *Ich hatte viel Bekümmernis;* Silbermann's organ at Freiberg.
(H) George I of England (Handel's patron).
(A) Gottfried Leibnitz (1646–1716), *Monadologie.*

1715

(M) First *opéra comique* founded.
(H) Louis XV of France crowned (till 1774).
(A) Alain Lesage (1668–1747), *L'Histoire de Gil Blas de Santillane.*

1717

(M) Bach at Cöthen—*Orgelbüchlein.*
(H) Triple Alliance.
(A) Jean Watteau (1684–1721), *Embarkation for Cythera.*

1719

(H) Herculaneum and Pompeii rediscovered.
(A) Daniel Defoe (*ca.* 1659–*ca.* 1731), *Robinson Crusoe.*

1720

(M) Benedetto Marcello (1686–1739), *Il teatro alla moda.*
(H) South Sea and Mississippi bubbles.

1721

(M) Bach: *Brandenburg Concertos; French and English Suites.*
(A) Baron de Montesquieu (1689–1755), *Lettres Persanes.*

1722

(M) Bach, *The Well-Tempered Clavier,* I; Rameau, *Traité de l'Harmonie.*

1723

(M) Bach, *St. John Passion.*
(A) François Voltaire (1694–1778), *Henriade.*

1724

(M) Handel, *Giulio Cesare.*

1725

(M) *Concerts spirituels* at Paris; Johann Fux (1660–1741), *Gradus ad Parnassum.*

1726

(M) Vivaldi, *The Seasons;* Rameau, *Nouveau système de musique théorique.*
(A) Jonathan Swift (1667–1745), *Gulliver's Travels.*

1727

(M) Handel, *Coronation Anthem.*
(H) George II of England crowned.

1728

(M) John Gay (1685–1732), *Beggar's Opera.*

1729

(M) Bach, *St. Matthew Passion.*

1730

(M) Bach, cantata, *Ein' feste Burg;* Johann Hasse (1699–1783), *Artaserse.*

1731

(M) Bach, *Klavierübung,* I.
(H) Treaty of Vienna.
(A) Abbé Prévost (1697–1763), *Manon Lescaut.*

1732

(A) Voltaire, *Zaïre;* William Hogarth (1697–1764), *A Harlot's Progress.*

1733

(M) Giovanni Pergolesi (1710–1736), *La Serva padrona.*
(H) Founding of Georgia; War of Polish Succession.

1734

(M) Bach, *Christmas Oratorio;* Giuseppe Tartini (1692–1770), Sonatas, Op. 1.
(A) François Boucher (1703–1770), *Rinaldo and Armida.*

1735

(M) Rameau, *Les Indes Galantes.*
(H) Carolus Linnaeus (1707–1778), *Systema naturae.*
(A) Hogarth, *A Rake's Progress.*

1736

(M) Handel, *Alexander's Feast.*

1737

(M) Rameau, *Castor et Pollux;* Domenico Scarlatti (1683–1757), first published sonatas; San Carlo Opera opens, Naples.
(H) First lodge of Freemasons in Germany.

1738

(M) D. Scarlatti, *Essercizi;* Bach, *Mass in B minor;* Handel, *Saul, Israel in Egypt, Serse.*
(H) Methodist church founded by Wesley and Whitefield.

1739

(M) Handel, *Concerti grossi.*
(A) David Hume (1711–1776), *A Treatise of Human Nature.*

1740

(H) Age of enlightened despots (till 1796); Frederick the Great of Prussia (till 1786).
(A) Giovanni Tiepolo (1696–1770), *Triumph of Amphitrite;* Samuel Richardson (1689–1761), *Pamela.*

1742

(M) Bach, *Goldberg Variations;* Handel, *Messiah* performed at Dublin; C. P. E. Bach (1714–1788), *Prussian Sonatas.*

1743

(M) Handel, *Samson.*
(H) Treaty of Fontainebleau.
(A) Voltaire, *Mérope.*

1744

(M) C. P. E. Bach, *Württemberg Sonatas.*

1745

(M) Johann Stamitz (1717–1757) at Mannheim.

1746

(M) Handel, *Judas Maccabaeus.*
(A) Boucher, *Toilet of Venus.*

1747

(M) Handel, *Joshua.* J. S. Bach, *Musical Offering.*
(A) Sans Souci castle at Potsdam.

1748

(H) End of war of Austrian Succession.
(A) Montesquieu, *Esprit des lois;* Voltaire, *Zadig;* Gottlieb Klopstock (1724–1803), *Der Messias.*

1749

(M) Rameau, *Zoroastre;* J. S. Bach, *Die Kunst der Fuge.*
(A) Henry Fielding (1707–1754), *Tom Jones.*

1750

(A) George Buffon (1707–1788), *Histoire Naturelle.*

1751

(M) Handel, *Jephtha.*
(H) First volumes of *Encyclopédie;* Benjamin Franklin (1706–1790), *Experiments and Observation on Electricity.*
(A) Thomas Gray (1716–1771), *Elegy Written in a Country Churchyard;* Voltaire, *Le Siècle de Louis XIV.*

1752

(M) Johann Quantz (1697–1713), *Versuch einer Anweisung die Flöte traversiere zu spielen;* War of the Buffons in Paris; first German *Singspiel.*

1753

(M) C. P. E. Bach, *Versuch über die Wahre Art.* Jean-Jacques Rousseau (1712–1778), *Lettre sur la musique française.*

1754

(A) Samuel Johnson (1709–1784), *Dictionary;* Thomas Chippendale manufacturing furniture.

1755

(M) Franz Joseph Haydn (1732–1809), first quartets. Karl Graun (1701–1759), *Der Tod Jesu.*
(H) Lisbon earthquake; Moscow University founded.
(A) Gotthold Lessing (1729–1781), *Miss Sara Sampson.*

1756

(H) French and Indian Wars.
(A) Voltaire, *Essai sur les moeurs;* Piranesi engravings of ancient Roman ruins.

1759

(H) Wolfe captures Quebec.
(A) Voltaire, *Candide;* Laurence Sterne (1713–1768), *Tristram Shandy.*

1760

(H) George III of England crowned (till 1820).
(A) Jean Fragonard (1732–1806), Park of the Villa D'Este in Tivoli. James Macpherson (1736–1796), *Ossian.*

1761

(M) Haydn at Eisenstadt; Christoph Gluck (1714–1787), *Don Juan.*

1762

(M) Gluck, *Orfeo ed Euridice.*
(A) Rousseau, *Le Contrat Social, Émile, Pygmalion.*

1763

(H) Beginnings of excavations at Pompeii and Herculaneum; Treaty of Paris; Canada ceded to England.
(A) Charles Bulfinch (1763–1844) designs the Massachusetts State House.

1764

(M) Wolfgang Amadeus Mozart (1756–1791) in London.
(A) Voltaire, *Dictionnaire philosophique;* Johann Winckelmann (1717–1768), *Geschichte der Kunst des Altertums.*

1766

(A) Petit Trianon built. Lessing, *Laokoon;* Oliver Goldsmith (1728–1774), *The Vicar of Wakefield.*

1767

(M) Haydn, Symphonies 35–38; Gluck, *Alceste;* Rousseau, *Dictionnaire de musique.*

1768

(M) Mozart, *Bastien und Bastienne.*
(A) Leonhard Euler (1707–1783), *Lettres à une princesse d'Allemagne;* Sterne, *Sentimental Journey.*

1769

(M) Mozart in Italy.
(H) Watt's steam engine patented.

1770

(H) Beginning of the factory system; James Hargreaves (d. 1778), spinning jenny patented.
(A) Thomas Gainsborough (1727–1788), *The Blue Boy.*

1771

(H) First edition of *Encyclopedia Britannica.*

1772

(M) Haydn, *Sun* Quartets, Op. 20.
(H) First partition of Poland.

1773

(M) Mozart, Symphonies K. 183, 201.
(H) Dissolution of Jesuit order by Clement XIV.

1774

(M) Gluck, *Iphigénie en Aulide, Orphée et Euridice.*
(H) First Continental Congress assembled at Philadelphia; Louis XVI King of France (till 1792); Joseph Priestley discovers oxygen.

1775

(H) Volta's electric battery invented; American Revolution (till 1783).
(A) Pierre Beaumarchais (1732–1799), *Le Barbiere de Séville.*

1776

(M) Sir John Hawkins (1719–1789) and Charles Burney (1726–1814), general histories of music; Gluck, *Alceste.*
(H) Declaration of Independence; discovery of hydrogen.
(A) Thomas Paine, *Common Sense;* Adam Smith (1732–1790), *The Wealth of Nations.*

1777

(M) Gluck, *Armide.*
(H) Articles of Confederation.
(A) Richard Sheridan (1751–1816), *The School for Scandal.*

1778

(M) Mozart, Piano Sonatas K. 310, 330–333, Violin Sonatas K. 296, 301–306; La Scala Opera opens in Milan.

1779

(M) Gluck, *Iphigénie en Tauride.*
(A) Lessing, *Nathan der Weise;* Sheridan, *The Critic.*

1780

(M) Haydn, Quartets, Op. 33.
(H) Cornwallis surrenders at Yorktown.

1781

(M) Mozart, *Idomeneo.*
(A) Immanuel Kant (1724–1804), *Critique of Pure Reason;* Jean Houdon (1741–1828), *Voltaire.*

1782

(M) Mozart, *Die Entführung.*
(A) Johann Schiller (1759–1805) *Die Räuber;* Rousseau, *Confessions.*

1784

(M) Andre Grétry (1741–1813), *Richard Coeur de Lion;* Martin Gerbert (1720–1793), *Scriptores ecclesiastici.*
(A) Beaumarchais, *Le Mariage de Figaro.*

1785

(M) Haydn, *Seven Last Words;* Mozart, *Haydn Quartets.*
(A) Thomas Jefferson (1743–1826), design for Virginia State Capitol.

1786

(M) Mozart, *Le nozze di Figaro;* Haydn, *Paris Symphonies.*
(A) Robert Burns (1759–1796), first edition of poetry; Joshua Reynolds (1723–1792), *The Duchess of Devonshire.*

1787

(M) Mozart, *Don Giovanni,* Quintets K. 515–516.
(H) American Constitutional Convention.
(A) Schiller, *Don Carlo;* Johann Goethe (1749–1832), *Iphigenia.*

1788

(M) Mozart, last three symphonies.
(H) John Fitch's steamboat invented.
(A) Edward Gibbon (1737–1794), *The History of the Decline and Fall of the Roman Empire;* Goethe, *Egmont;* Jacques David (1748–1825), *Paris and Helen.*

1789

(M) Haydn, Quartets, Opp. 54, 55.
(H) French Revolution (till 1794); George Washington first president of United States.
(A) Goethe, *Torquato Tasso.*

1790

(M) Mozart, *Così fan tutte;* Haydn in London.
(A) Kant, *Critique of Judgment.*

1791

(M) Mozart, *The Magic Flute, Requiem;* Haydn, first *London Symphonies.*
(H) Bill of Rights.
(A) James Boswell (1740–1795), *Life of Samuel Johnson.*

1792

(M) Domenico Cimarosa (1749–1801), *Il Matrimonio segreto;* Ludwig van Beethoven (1770–1827) at Vienna.
(H) France declared a republic.

1793

(H) Reign of Terror; Eli Whitney invents cotton gin.
(A) David, *Death of Marat;* William Blake (1757–1827), *Marriage of Heaven and Hell.*

1794

(M) Haydn, second trip to London.
(A) J. G. Fichte (1762–1814), *Über den Begriff der Wissenschaftslehre.*

1795

(M) Beethoven, Trios Op. 1; Paris Conservatory founded.

1796

(M) Haydn, *Missa in tempore belli.*
(H) Jenner's first vaccination; Paul I of Russia (till 1801); Napoleon in Italy; Battle of Lodi.

1797

(M) Luigi Cherubini (1760–1842), *Médée.*
(A) Wilhelm Wackenroder (1773–1798), *Herzensergiessungen.* François Gerard (1770–1837), *Cupid and Psyche.*

1798

(M) Haydn, *The Creation, Imperial Mass.*
(H) Napoleon in Egypt.
(A) Samuel Coleridge (1772–1834) and William Wordsworth (1770–1850), *Lyrical Ballads;* Thomas Malthus (1766–1834), *Essay on the Principle of Population.*

1799

(M) Beethoven, First Symphony, *Sonata Pathétique.*
(H) Napoleon becomes first Consul.
(A) Schiller, *Wallenstein;* Friedrich Holderlin (1770–1843), *Hyperion.*

1800

(M) Haydn, *The Seasons.*
(H) Discovery of ultraviolet rays; Volta invents voltaic pile.
(A) David, *Madame Recamier;* Schiller, *Die Jungfrau von Orleans.*

1802

(M) Beethoven, Second Symphony.
(H) Napoleon made Consul for life.
(A) Chateaubriand, *Génie du Christianisme.*

1803

(M) Beethoven, *Eroica* Symphony.
(H) Louisiana Purchase.

1804

(M) Beethoven, Sonata, Op. 53.
(H) Napoleon crowned Emperor; Lewis and Clark expedition.
(A) Schiller, *Wilhelm Tell;* Jean Paul Richter (1763–1825), *Die Flegeljahre;* Jean Ingres (1780–1867), *Mme. Rivière.*

1805

(M) Beethoven, *Fidelio,* Sonata, Op. 54.
(H) Battle of Trafalgar.
(A) Ludwig Arnim (1781–1831), and Clemens Brentano (1778–1842), *Des Knaben Wunderhorn.*

1806

(M) Beethoven, Fourth Symphony, Violin Concerto, Sonata, Op. 57.
(H) Formal dissolution of the Holy Roman Empire; Lewis and Clark reach Pacific.

1807

(M) Beethoven, Fifth Symphony, *Coriolanus* Overture.
(H) Fulton builds the firts commercial steamboat; London streets lighted by gas.
(A) Wililam Wordsworth, *Intimations of Immortality.*

1808

(A) Goethe, *Faust, Part I.*

1810

(A) Sir Walter Scott (1771–1832), *The Lady of the Lake.*

1811

(M) Franz Schubert (1797–1828), first *Lieder.*
(A) Goethe, *Dichtung und Wahrheit.*

1812

(M) Beethoven, Seventh and Eighth Symphonies, Violin Sonata, Op. 96.
(H) Napoleon retreats from Moscow.
(A) George Byron (1788–1824), *Childe Harold's Pilgrimage;* Jacob (1785–1863) and Wilhelm (1786–1859) Grimm, *Kinder- und Hausmärchen.*

1813

(M) London Philharmonic Society founded.
(H) Napoleon abdicates.
(A) Jane Austen (1775–1817), *Pride and Prejudice.*

1814

(M) Schubert, *Gretchen am Spinnrad.*
(H) Napoleon to Elba; Congress of Vienna.
(A) Sir Walter Scott, *Waverly;* Francisco Goya (1746–1828), *King Ferdinand VII.*

1815

(M) Invention of the metronome; Schubert, *Der Erlkönig,* Third Symphony.
(H) Battle of Waterloo; the Holy Alliance.
(A) Goya, *Witch's Sabbath.*

1816

(M) Gioacchino Rossini (1792–1868), *The Barber of Seville, Otello.*
(A) Percy Bysshe Shelley (1792–1822), *Alastor, or the Spirit of Solitude.*

1817

(M) Muzio Clementi (1752–1832), *Gradus ad Parnassum.*
(A) David Ricardo (1772–1823), *Principles of Political Economy and Taxation;* John Keats (1795–1821), *Endymion;* Byron, *Manfred.*

1818

(M) Beethoven, Sonata, Op. 106; Schubert, Sixth Symphony, Quartet in E.

495

1819

(M) Schubert, *Forellen* Quintet.
(H) First steamship crosses Atlantic; Florida purchased from Spain.
(A) Scott, *Ivanhoe*.

1820

(A) Shelley, *Prometheus Unbound; Ode to the West Wind;* Blake, *Jerusalem.* Alphonse Lamartine (1790–1869), *Méditations Poétiques.*

1821

(M) Carl Maria von Weber (1786–1826), *Der Freischütz;* Beethoven, Sonatas, Opp. 110, 111.
(H) Faraday's electric motor and generator.
(A) John Constable (1776–1837), *The Hay Wain.*

1822

(M) Beethoven, *Missa Solemnis;* Schubert, *Unfinished Symphony.*

1823

(M) Weber, *Euryanthe;* Beethoven, Ninth Symphony; Schubert, *Die schöne Müllerin.*
(H) Monroe Doctrine.

1824

(H) Charles X of France crowned.

1825

(M) Beethoven, Quartets, Opp. 127, 132; Felix Mendelssohn (1809–1847), String Octet.
(H) Erie Canal opened.
(A) Alessandro Manzoni (1785–1873), *I Promessi Sposi.* Alexander Pushkin (1799–1837), *Boris Godunov.*

1826

(M) Beethoven, Quartets, Opp. 130, 135; Schubert, *Die Winterreise;* Mendelssohn, *Midsummer Night's Dream Overture.*
(A) James Fenimore Cooper (1789–1851), *The Last of the Mohicans.*

1827

(M) Beethoven, Quartet, Op. 131.
(H) Mormon church founded.
(A) Heinrich Heine (1797–1856), *Buch der Lieder.*

1828

(M) Schubert, Symphony in C, last three piano sonatas, string quintet; Paganini concerts.
(A) First performance of Goethe's *Faust.*

1829

(M) Hector Berlioz (1803–1869), *Symphonie Fantastique;* Rossini, *Guillaume Tell.*
(H) Independence of Greece.
(A) Honoré de Balzac (1799–1850), *La Comédie Humaine;* Victor Hugo (1802–1885), *Les Orientales;* James Mill (1773–1836), *Analysis of the Mind.*

1830

(M) Daniel Auber (1782–1871), *Fra Diavolo;* Robert Schumann (1810–1856), *Abegg Variations,* Op. 1; Mendelssohn's first *Songs Without Words.*
(H) First railroad, Liverpool to Manchester; July Revolution in France.
(A) Hugo, *Hernani;* Stendhal (1783–1842), *Le Rouge et le Noir.*

1831

(M) Vincenzo Bellini (1801–1835), *Norma;* Schumann, *Papillons.*
(A) Hugo, *Notre Dame de Paris.*

1832

(M) Frédéric Chopin (1810–1849), *Études,* Op. 10, Mazurkas, Op. 6; Mendelssohn, *Hebrides Overture;* Gaetano Donizetti (1797–1848), *L'Elisir d'Amore.*

1833

(M) Wagner, *Die Feen.*
(H) Slavery outlawed in British Empire.
(A) Thomas Carlyle (1795–1881), *Sartor Resartus.*

1834

(M) Berlioz, *Harold in Italy; Neue Zeitschrift fur Musik* founded by Schumann.
(H) McCormick patents mechanical reaper.
(A) Edward Lytton (1803–1873), *The Last Days of Pompeii.*

1835

(M) Donizetti, *Lucia di Lammermoor;* Schumann, Symphonic Etudes, Op. 13, *Carnaval,* Op. 9; Bellini, *I Puritani.*

1836

(M) Giacomo Meyerbeer (1791–1864), *Les Huguenots;* Michael Glinka (1803–1857), *A Life for the Tsar;* Chopin, Ballades, Op. 23.
(A) Charles Dickens (1812–1870), *The Pickwick Papers;* Sir Charles Barry designs Houses of Parliament, London.

1837

(M) Berlioz, *Requiem;* Franz Liszt (1811–1886), *Années de Pèlerinage.*
(H) Morse's telegraph; Queen Victoria crowned.
(A) Carlyle, *The French Revolution.*

1838

(M) Schumann, *Kinderscenen, Kreisleriana;* Berlioz, *Benvenuto Cellini.*
(H) Daguerre (1789–1851) takes first photographs.
(A) Ferdinand Delacroix (1798–1863), *The Capture of Constantinople.*

1839

(M) Chopin, Preludes, Op. 28; New York Philharmonic Society founded; Vienna Philharmonic founded.
(A) Joseph Turner (1775–1851), *The Fighting Temeraire;* Edgar Allan Poe (1809–1849), *Tales of the Grotesque and Arabesque;* Stendhal, *The Charterhouse of Parma.*

1840

(M) Schumann, *Lieder;* Donizetti, *The Daughter of the Regiment.*
(H) First incandescent electric bulb.

1841

(M) Schumann, First and Fourth Symphonies.
(H) Invention of the saxophone.
(A) *Punch* founded.

1842

(M) Wagner, *Rienzi;* Glinka, *Russlan and Ludmilla;* Giuseppe Verdi (1813–1901), *Nabucco.*

1843

(M) Wagner, *Der fliegende Holländer.*
(A) Sören Kierkegaard (1813–1855), *Fear and Trembling.*

1844

(M) Verdi, *Ernani;* Mendelssohn, Violin Concerto.
(H) First telegraph message transmitted.
(A) Alexandre Dumas (1824–1895), *The Three Musketeers.*

1845

(M) Liszt, *Les Préludes,* Wagner, *Tann-häuser.*
(A) Dumas, *The Count of Monte Cristo.*

1846

(M) Berlioz, *The Damnation of Faust;* Mendelssohn, *Elijah.*
(H) First use of ether as an anesthetic; Howe's sewing machine patented; Smithsonian Institution founded.

1847

(M) Verdi, *Macbeth.*

1848

(M) Stephen Foster's (1826–1864) first songs.
(H) Potato famine in Ireland; gold rush in California.
(A) Thomas Macaulay (1800–1859), *History of England;* William Thackeray (1811–1863), *Vanity Fair;* Alexandre Dumas *fils, La Dame aux Camélias;* Karl Marx (1818–1883) and Friedrich Engels (1820–1895), *Communist Manifesto.*

1849

(M) Meyerbeer, *Le Prophète.* Anton Bruckner (1824–1896), *Requiem.*
(A) Gustave Courbet (1819–1877), *The Stone Breaker;* Dickens, *David Copperfield.*

1850

(M) Bachgesellschaft founded; Wagner, *Lohengrin.*
(A) Nathaniel Hawthorne (1804–1864), *The Scarlet Letter;* Henry Wadsworth Longfellow (1807–1882), *Evangeline.*

1851

(M) Wagner, *Oper und Drama;* Schumann, Third Symphony; Verdi, *Rigoletto.*
(H) First successful submarine telegraph cable.
(A) Herman Melville (1819–1891), *Moby Dick;* Jean Millet (1814–1875), *The Gleaners.*

1852

(H) Second Empire under Napoleon III.
(A) Harriet Beecher Stowe (1811–1896), *Uncle Tom's Cabin.*

1853

(M) Verdi, *Il Trovatore, La Traviata.*
(H) Crimean War; Commodore Perry opens Japan to the West.

1854

(M) Liszt, Sonata in B minor.
(A) Henry David Thoreau (1817–1862), *Walden.*

1855

(M) Liszt, *Faust Symphony;* Verdi, *Vespri siciliani.*
(H) Charge of the Light Brigade.
(A) Walt Whitman (1819–1892), *Leaves of Grass.*

1857

(H) Dred Scott decision.
(A) Gustave Flaubert (1821–1880), *Madame Bovary;* Currier and Ives publish prints; Pierre Baudelaire (1821–1867), *Les Fleurs du Mal.*

1858

(M) Berlioz, *Les Troyens;* Verdi, *Un Ballo in Maschera;* Jacques Offenbach (1819–1880), *Orphée aux enfers.*
(H) Covent Garden opera house opens.

1859

(M) Charles Gounod (1818–1893), *Faust;* Wagner, *Tristan und Isolde.*
(H) Charles Darwin (1809–1882), *Origin of Species;* John Brown raids Harper's Ferry.
(A) Millet, *The Angelus;* Alfred Lord Tennyson (1809–1892), *Idylls of the King.*

1861

(M) *Tannhäuser* performed at Paris.
(H) Serfs emancipated in Russia; unification of Italy; Civil War in America (till 1865).
(A) George Eliot (1819–1880), *Silas Marner.*

1862

(M) Verdi, *La Forza del Destino;* Köchel's Mozart catalogue begun.
(H) Bismarck chancellor of Prussia.
(A) Ivan Turgenev (1818–1883), *Fathers and Sons;* Honoré Daumier (1808–1879), *Third Class Carriage.*

1863

(H) Gettysburg Address; Emancipation Proclamation.
(A) Edouard Manet (1832–1883), *Olympia.*

1864

(M) Johannes Brahms (1833–1897), Piano Quintet in F minor; Bruckner, First Symphony; Offenbach, *La Belle Hélène.*
(H) First International founded by Karl Marx; first ascent of the Matterhorn; first transatlantic cable.
(A) Lewis Carroll (1832–1898), *Alice in Wonderland;* Leo Tolstoy (1828–1910), *War and Peace.*

1866

(M) Ambroise Thomas (1811–1896), *Mignon;* Bedřich Smetana (1824–1884), *The Bartered Bride.*
(H) Christian Science founded by Mary Baker Eddy.
(A) Feodor Dostoyevsky (1821–1881), *Crime and Punishment.*

1867

(M) Verdi, *Don Carlo;* Johann Strauss (1825–1899), *On the Beautiful Blue Danube;* first collection of Negro spirituals.
(H) Purchase of Alaska; Franz Joseph I of Austria-Hungary (till 1916).
(A) Henrik Ibsen (1828–1906), *Peer Gynt.* Marx, *Das Kapital.*

1868

(M) Brahms, *A German Requiem*.
(A) Robert Browning (1812–1889), *The Ring and the Book;* Dostoyevsky, *The Idiot*.

1869

(H) Suez Canal opened; first American transcontinental railroad.
(A) Jules Verne (1828–1905), *Twenty Thousand Leagues Under the Sea*.

1870

(M) Wagner, *Die Walküre* performed.
(H) Heinrich Schliemann (1822–1890) excavates the site of Troy; Rome becomes the capital of Italy; Franco-Prussian War; Vatican Council proclaims papal infallibility.

1871

(M) Verdi, *Aïda;* Edvard Grieg (1843–1907), first lyric pieces for piano.
(H) Bismarck chancellor of Germany; Paris Commune, Third Republic.
(A) Ralph Waldo Emerson (1860–1927), *Essays;* Darwin, *The Descent of Man*.

1872

(M) Georges Bizet (1838–1875), *L'Arlésienne;* Bruckner, Mass in F minor.
(A) Whistler, *Portrait of Miss Alexander;* Friedrich Nietzsche (1844–1900), *The Birth of Tragedy*.

1873

(A) Edgar Degas (1834–1917), *Place de la Concorde*.

1874

(M) Modest Mussorgsky (1839–1881), *Boris Godunov, Pictures at an Exhibition;* Verdi, *Requiem;* J. Strauss, *Die Fledermaus*.

1875

(M) New Paris opera house opened; Bizet, *Carmen;* Smetana, *My Fatherland*.
(A) Mary Baker Eddy (1821–1910), *Science and Health;* Tolstoy, *Anna Karenina*.

1876

(M) First Wagner festival at Bayreuth.
(H) Telephone invented by Bell.
(A) Stéphane Mallarmé (1842–1898), *L'-Après-midi d'un Faune;* Mark Twain (1835–1910), *Tom Sawyer;* Pierre Renoir (1841–1919), *Le Bal du Moulin de la Galette*.

1877

(M) Wagner, *Parsifal;* Brahms, First and Second Symphonies.
(H) Edison invents the phonograph.
(A) Claude Monet (1840–1926), *Gare Saint-Lazare*.

1878

(M) Brahms, Violin Concerto.

1879

(M) Tchaikovsky, *Eugen Onegin;* Sir George Grove (1820–1900), *Dictionary of Music and Musicians*.
(H) Edison invents an improved incandescent electric light.
(A) Henry George (1839–1897), *Progress and Poverty;* Ibsen, *The Doll's House;* Dostoyevsky, *The Brothers Karamazov*.

1880

(H) Irish insurrection; Pavlov's experiments on conditioned reflexes.
(A) Émile Zola (1840–1902), *Nana*.

1881

(M) Offenbach, *Tales of Hoffmann;* Boston Symphony founded.
(H) Tsar Alexander II assassinated; President Garfield shot; Panama Canal built.
(A) Renoir, *Luncheon of the Boating Party;* Henry James (1843–1916), *Portrait of a Lady*.

1882

(M) Berlin Philharmonia founded.
(H) Koch discovers tuberculosis germs; Triple Alliance.
(A) Manet, *The Bar at the Folies Bergères*.

1883

(M) Brahms, Third Symphony; Metropolitan Opera opened; Amsterdam Concertgebouw founded.
(H) Gottlieb Daimler (1834–1900) patents automobile motor.
(A) Nietzsche, *Also sprach Zarathustra;* Robert Louis Stevenson (1850–1894), *Treasure Island*.

1884

(M) Jules Massenet (1842–1912), *Manon*.
(H) Pasteur innoculates against rabies.
(A) Auguste Rodin (1840–1917), *The Burghers of Calais;* Georges Seurat (1859–1891), *Sunday Afternoon on Grande Jatte;* Twain, *Huckleberry Finn*.

1885

(M) Brahms, Fourth Symphony; Sir William Gilbert (1836–1911) and Sir Arthur Sullivan (1842–1900), *The Mikado*.
(H) First American electric street railway; Brooklyn Bridge built.
(A) Henry Richardson (1838–1886) designs Marshall Field warehouse; Guy de Maupassant (1850–1893), *Contes et Nouvelles;* Paul Cézanne (1839–1906), *Mont St. Victoire;* William Dean Howells (1839–1920), *The Rise of Silas Lapham*.

1886

(M) César Franck (1822–1890), *Violin Sonata*.
(H) American Federation of Labor organized; Statue of Liberty unveiled in New York Harbor.
(A) Nietzsche, *Jenseits von Gut und Böse;* Henri Rousseau (1844–1910), *Un Soir de carnaval*.

1887

(M) Verdi, *Otello*.
(A) A. Strindberg (1849–1912), *Der Vater*.

1888

(M) Franck, *Symphony in D minor;* Nikolai Rimsky-Korsakov (1844–1908), *Scheherazade;* Erik Satie (1866–1925), *Gymnopédies;* Hugo Wolf (1860–1903), *Mörike Lieder;* Tchaikovsky, Fifth Symphony.
(H) Kaiser Wilhelm II crowned (till 1918).
(A) Vincent van Gogh (1853–1900), *The Sunflowers*.

1889

(M) Richard Strauss (1864–1949), *Don Juan;* Gustav Mahler (1860–1911), First Symphony.
(H) Paris World's Fair opened; Brazil expels emperor, becomes republic.
(A) Eiffel Tower completed; Auguste Rodin (1840–1917), *The Thinker.*

1890

(M) Pietro Mascagni (1863–1945), *Cavalleria Rusticana;* R. Strauss, *Death and Transfiguration;* Tchaikovsky, *Pique Dame;* Alexander Borodin (1833–1887), *Prince Igor* (first performance).
(A) Ibsen, *Hedda Gabler.*

1891

(M) Wolf, *Italienisches Liederbuch.*
(A) Sir Arthur Conan Doyle (1859–1930), *Adventures of Sherlock Holmes;* Augustus Saint-Gaudens (1848–1907), *Adams Memorial.*

1892

(M) Gabriel Fauré (1845–1924), *La Bonne Chanson;* Bruckner, Eighth Symphony; Ruggiero Leoncavallo (1858–1919), *I Pagliacci.*
(A) Cézanne, *The Card Players;* Maurice Maeterlinck (1862–1949), *Pelléas et Mélisande;* Henri de Toulouse-Lautrec (1864–1901), *At the Moulin Rouge.*

1893

(M) Engelbert Humperdinck (1854–1921), *Hansel and Gretel;* Giacomo Puccini (1858–1924), *Manon Lescaut;* Verdi, *Falstaff;* Tchaikovsky, Sixth Symphony.
(A) Stephen Crane (1871–1900), *The Red Badge of Courage;* Oscar Wilde (1856–1900), *Salome;* Louis Sullivan (1856–1924), Transportation Building at World's Columbian Exposition.

1894

(M) Anton Dvořák (1841–1904), *New World Symphony;* Debussy, *Prélude à l'après-midi d'un faune.*
(H) Nicholas II crowned, last Czar of Russia; Dreyfus Affair (till 1905).
(A) Rudyard Kipling (1865–1936), *Jungle Book;* George Bernard Shaw (1856–1950), *Candida.*

1895

(M) R. Strauss, *Till Eulenspiegel.*
(H) Wilhelm Roentgen (1845–1923) discovers X-rays.
(A) Winslow Homer (1836–1910), *Northeaster.*

1896

(M) Brahms, *Vier ernste Gesänge;* Edward MacDowell (1861–1908), *Indian Suite;* Puccini, *La Bohème.*
(A) Paul Gauguin (1843–1903), *Maternity;* A. E. Housman (1859–1936), *A Shropshire Lad.*

1897

(M) R. Strauss, *Don Quixote;* John Philip Sousa (1854–1932), *The Stars and Stripes Forever.*

1898

(M) Rimsky-Korsakov, *Sadko.*
(H) Spanish-American War; Boer War.
(A) Edmond Rostand (1808–1918), *Cyrano de Bergerac.*

1899

(M) Maurice Ravel (1875–1937), *Pavane pour une infante défunte;* Arnold Schoenberg (1874–1950), *Verklärte Nacht;* Jean Sibelius (1865–1957), *Finlandia.*

1900

(M) Edward Elgar (1857–1934), *The Dream of Gerontius;* Puccini, *Tosca;* Gustave Charpentier (1860–1956), *Louise;* Philadelphia Orchestra founded.
(H) Boxer Rebellion; Count Ferdinand Zeppelin constructs first dirigible.
(A) Joseph Conrad (1857–1924), *Lord Jim;* John Singer Sargent (1856–1925), *The Wyndham Sisters.*

1901

(M) Mahler, Fourth Symphony, Schoenberg, *Gurrelieder.*
(H) Edward VII crowned (till 1910); Guglielmo Marconi (1874–1937) transmits telegraph signals across Atlantic Ocean; Max Planck develops quantum theory.
(A) Shaw, *Caesar and Cleopatra;* Aristide Maillol (1861–1944), *Mediterranean.*

1902

(M) Jean Sibelius (1865–1957), Second Symphony; Mahler, Third Symphony; Debussy, *Pelléas et Mélisande.*
(H) Discovery of radium by Pierre (1859–1906) and Marie (1867–1934) Curie.
(A) Maxim Gorky (1868–1936), *Tales;* Claude Monet (1840–1926), *Waterloo Bridge.*

1903

(H) Wilbur (1867–1912) and Orville (1871–1948) Wright, first successful airplane flight; Encyclical *"Motu proprio"* of Pope Pius X.
(A) Shaw, *Man and Superman.*

1904

(M) Puccini, *Madame Butterfly;* London Symphony founded. Ravel, *Quartet in F.*
(H) Russo-Japanese War.
(A) Anton Chekhov (1860–1904), *The Cherry Orchard;* James Barrie (1860–1937), *Peter Pan;* Romain Rolland (1866–1943), *Jean Christophe.*

1905

(M) Debussy, *La Mer;* R. Strauss, *Salome;* Franz Lehár (1870–1948), *The Merry Widow.*
(H) Norway separates from Sweden; First Russian Revolution; Sigmund Freud (1856–1939) founds psychoanalysis.

1906

(M) Schoenberg, *Kammersymphonie.*
(H) San Francisco earthquake and fire.

1907

(M) Alexander Scriabin (1872–1915), *Poem of Ecstasy;* Rimsky-Korsakov, *The Golden Cockerel;* first music broadcast.
(H) Second Hague Conference; Triple Entente.
(A) J. M. Synge (1871–1909), *Playboy of the Western World;* William James, 1842–1910), *Pragmatism.*

1908

(M) Ravel, *Rapsodie Espagnole;* Béla Bartók (1881–1945), First Quartet.
(H) Model "T" Ford produced.
(A) Rainer Maria Rilke (1875–1926), *Neue Gedichte.*

1909

(M) Schoenberg, *Piano Pieces*, Op. 11; Ralph Vaughan Williams (1872–1928), *Fantasia on a Theme of Thomas Tallis;* R. Strauss, *Elektra.*

(H) Robert Peary (1856–1920) reaches North Pole.

(A) Frank Lloyd Wright (1869–1959), Robie House, Chicago; Ferenc Molnar (1878–1952), *Liliom.*

1910

(M) Ravel, *Daphnis et Chloë;* Bartók, *Allegro Barbaro;* Stravinsky, *The Firebird.*

(H) Discovery of protons and electrons; George V crowned (till 1936).

(A) Bertrand Russell (1872–) and Alfred Norh Whitehead (1861–1947), *Principia Mathematica.*

1911

(M) Mahler, *Das Lied von der Erde;* R. Strauss, *Der Rosenkavalier;* Sibelius, Fourth Symphony; Bartók, *Duke Bluebeard's Castle;* Stravinsky, *Petrushka;* Ravel, *L'Heure espagnole.*

(H) Roald Amundsen (1872–1928) reaches the South Pole.

(A) Edith Wharton (1862–1937), *Ethan Frome.*

1912

(M) Schoenberg, *Pierrot Lunaire.*

(H) *Titanic* disaster; Balkan Wars.

(A) Marcel Duchamp (1887–), *Nude Descending a Staircase;* Wassily Kandinsky (1866–1944), *Improvisation.*

1913

(M) Anton von Webern (1883–1945), *Six Orchestral Pieces;* Stravinsky, *Sacre du Printemps;* Manuel de Falla (1876–1946), *La Vida breve.*

(A) D. H. Lawrence (1885–1930), *Sons and Lovers;* Thomas Mann (1875–1955), *Death in Venice;* John Sloane (1871–1955), *Sunday, Women Drying their Hair;* Georges Braque (1881–), *Musical Forms;* Marcel Proust (1871–1922), *Remembrance of Things Past.*

1914

(M) Vaughan Williams, *A London Symphony.*

(H) First World War (to 1918); Panama Canal opened.

(A) Robert Frost (1875–1963), *North of Boston;* Vachel Lindsay (1879–1940), *The Congo and other Poems;* D. W. Griffith, *The Birth of a Nation.*

1915

(M) Charles Ives (1874–1954), *Concord Sonata.*

(A) W. Somerset Maugham (1874–), *Of Human Bondage;* Albert Einstein (1879–1955), *General Theory of Relativity.*

1916

(M) Ernest Bloch (1880–1959), *Schelomo;* Enrique Granados (1894–1928), *Goyescas.*

(H) Bolshevik revolution in Russia. Battle of Verdun.

(A) Wright, Imperial Hotel in Tokyo.

1917

(H) U.S. enters World War I.

(A) Georges Rouault (1871–1958), *Three Clowns;* W. B. Yeats (1865–1939), *Wild Swans at Coole.*

1918

(M) Puccini, *Gianni Schicchi;* Stravinsky, *L'Histoire du Soldat;* Sergei Prokofiev (1891–1952), *Classical Symphony.*

(H) End of World War I.

(A) Willa Cather (1873–1916) *My Antonia;* Oswald Spengler (1880–1936), *Decline of the West.*

1919

(M) Falla, *The Three-Cornered Hat.*

(H) Treaty of Versailles; League of Nations; first Atlantic airplane crossing.

(A) André Gide (1869–1951), *La Symphonie Pastorale;* Fernand Léger (1881–1955), *The City;* Paul Claudel (1868), *Le Père Humilié.*

1920

(M) Gustav Holst (1874–1934), *The Planets;* Ravel, *La Valse.*

(H) First commercial radio broadcast.

(A) Sinclair Lewis (1885–1951), *Main Street.*

1921

(M) Arthur Honegger (1892–1955), *King David;* Prokofiev, *The Love For Three Oranges;* Vaughan Williams, *Pastoral Symphony.*

(A) Pablo Picasso (1881–), *Three Musicians;* Charlie Chaplin, *The Kid.*

1922

(M) Schoenberg, Method of Composing with Twelve Tones.

(H) Fascist revolution in Italy.

(A) John Galsworthy (1867–1933), *The Forsyte Saga;* T. S. Eliot (1888–), *The Waste Land;* James Joyce (1882–1941), *Ulysses.*

1923

(M) Stravinsky, *Les Noces, Octet;* Paul Hindemith (1895–1963), *Das Marienleben;* Honegger, *Pacific 231.*

(H) Hitler-Ludendorff Putsch in Munich.

(A) Paul Klee (1879–1940), *At the Mountain of the Bull.*

1924

(M) George Gershwin (1898–1937), *Rhapsody in Blue;* Schoenberg, *Serenade, Woodwind Quintet;* Puccini, *Turandot.*

(H) Joseph Stalin (1879–1953) becomes dictator in Russia.

(A) Shaw, *Saint Joan;* Mann, *The Magic Mountain;* Franz Kafka (1883–1924), *The Trial.*

1925

(M) Alban Berg (1885–1935), *Wozzeck;* Bloch, *Concerto Grosso.*

(A) Theodore Dreiser (1871–1945), *An American Tragedy;* F. Scott Fitzgerald (1896–1940), *The Great Gatsby.*

1926

(M) First all-sound films; Zoltán Kodály (1882–), *Háry János;* Dmitri Shostakovich (1906–), *First Symphony.*

(A) Ernest Hemingway (1898–1961), *The Sun Also Rises.*

1927

(M) Stravinsky, *Oedipus Rex.*
(H) Charles Lindbergh (1902–) solos across the Atlantic; first television transmission.
(A) Sir Jacob Epstein (1880–1959), *Madonna and Child;* Virginia Woolf (1882–1945), *To the Lighthouse;* Eugene O'Neill (1888–1953), *Strange Interlude.*

1928

(M) Kurt Weill (1900–1950), *Threepenny Opera;* Ravel, *Bolero;* Webern, Symphony, Op. 21.
(H) First all-talking film; Graf Zeppelin crosses Atlantic; first radio broadcast of N. Y. Philharmonic.
(A) D. H. Lawrence, *Lady Chatterley's Lover;* Aldous Huxley (1894–), *Point Counter Point;* Stephen Vincent Benét (1898–1943), *John Brown's Body.*

1929

(M) Hindemith, *Neues vom Tage.*
(H) New York stock market crash.
(A) Mies Van der Rohe (1886–), German pavilion; Jean Giraudoux, (1882–1944), *Amphitryon 38;* Thomas Wolfe (1900–1938), *Look Homeward, Angel;* William Faulkner (1897–1962), *The Sound and the Fury.*

1930

(M) Darius Milhaud (1892–), *Christophe Colomb;* Stravinsky, *Symphony of Psalms.*
(H) Penicillin discovered.
(A) Piet Mondriaan (1872–1944), *Fox Trot;* Edward Hopper (1882–), *Early Sunday Morning;* Grant Wood (1892–1942), *American Gothic;* José Ortega y Gasset (1883–1954), *The Revolt of the Masses.*

1931

(M) William Walton (1902–), *Belshazzar's Feast;* Gershwin, *Of Thee I Sing.*
(H) Japan invades Manchuria.
(A) O'Neill, *Mourning Becomes Electra.*

1932

(M) Ravel, two piano concertos.
(A) Gertrude Stein (1874–1946), *Matisse, Picasso and Gertrude Stein.*

1933

(M) Hindemith, *Mathis der Maler;* R. Strauss, *Arabella;* Stravinsky, *Perséphone;* Shostakovich, First Piano Concerto.
(H) Franklin D. Roosevelt (1882–1945) inaugurated; Adolf Hitler (1889–1945) Chancellor of Germany.
(A) Joan Miró (1893–), *Composition;* Arnold Toynbee (1889–), *A Study of History.*

1934

(M) Virgil Thomson (1896–), *Four Saints in Three Acts.*
(H) Hitler becomes Führer.
(A) Mann, *Joseph and His Brothers.*

1935

(M) Berg, *Violin Concerto;* Gershwin, *Porgy and Bess;* Honegger, *Joan of Arc at the Stake.*
(H) Italy invades Ethiopia.
(A) Eliot, *Murder in the Cathedral;* José Orozco (1883–1949), *Man in Four Aspects.*

1936

(M) Prokofiev, *Peter and the Wolf;* 440 adopted as standard pitch.
(H) Spanish Civil War.
(A) John Dos Passos (1896–), *U.S.A.*

1937

(M) Carl Orff (1895–), *Carmina Burana;* Berg, *Lulu* (first performance); Shostakovich, Fifth Symphony.
(H) Japan invades China.
(A) Picasso, *Guernica.*

1938

(M) Walter Piston (1894–), *The Incredible Flutist;* Bartók, *Violin Concerto.*
(A) Raoul Dufy (1879–1953), *Regatta.*

1939

(M) Bartók, Sixth Quartet; Prokofiev, *Alexander Nevsky;* Roy Harris (1898–), *Third Symphony.*
(H) World War II begins (till 1945).
(A) Joyce, *Finnegans Wake;* C. S. Forester (1899–), *Captain Horatio Hornblower;* John Steinbeck (1902–), *The Grapes of Wrath.*

1940

(M) Stravinsky, Symphony in C major.
(H) First radio broadcast of the Metropolitan Opera; Roosevelt elected to third term.
(A) Hemingway, *For Whom the Bell Tolls.*

1941

(M) Aaron Copland (1900–), *Piano Sonata.*
(H) United States enters war; Atlantic Charter.

1942

(M) Shostakovich, Seventh Symphony; Heitor Villa-Lobos (1887–1959), *Choros No. 11.*
(H) United Nations Alliance.

1943

(M) Vaughan Williams, Fifth Symphony.
(A) Marc Chagall (1887–), *Crucifixion.*

1944

(M) Copland, *Appalachian Spring;* Bartók, *Concerto for Orchestra,* Hindemith, *Ludus Tonalis.*
(H) Roosevelt elected to fourth term. Allies invade Germany.

1945

(M) Benjamin Britten (1913–), *Peter Grimes;* Bartok, *Third Piano Concerto.*
(H) Germany surrenders; atom bomb used against Japan. New York chosen as seat of United Nations.

1946

(M) Britten, *The Rape of Lucretia;* Copland, Third Symphony.
(H) First assembly of United Nations; Nuremberg trials.
(A) Le Corbusier (1887–), Unité d'Habitation, Marseilles; Dylan Thomas (1914–1953), *Deaths and Entrances.*

1947

(M) Prokofiev, *War and Peace;* Piston, Third Quartet.
(H) Marshall Plan; Indian independence; Tennessee Williams (1914–), *A Streetcar Named Desire.*

1948

(M) Piston, Third Symphony; Stravinsky, *Mass;* Vaughan Williams, Sixth Symphony.

1949

(M) Orff, *Antigonae;* Samuel Barber (1910–), *Knoxville: Summer of 1915.*
(H) North Atlantic Defense Pact; China goes Communist.
(A) George Orwell (1903–1950), *1984;* Arthur Miller (1916–), *Death of a Salesman.*

1950

(M) Honegger, Fifth Symphony; Gian Carlo Menotti (1911–), *The Consul.*
(H) Korean War.
(A) Eliot, *The Cocktail Party.*

1951

(M) Menotti, *Amahl and the Night Visitors;* Stravinsky, *The Rake's Progress;* Pierre Boulez (1925–), *Polyphonie X.*
(A) Jacques Lipchitz (1891–), *Birth of Venus.*
(H) NATO formed from North Atlantic Pact.

1952

(A) Alexander Calder (1898–), *Giraffe;* Albert Camus (1913–1960), *L'Homme Revolté;* Eliot, *Complete Plays and Poems.*

1953

(M) Karlheinz Stockhausen (1928–), *Kontra-Punkte.*
(A) Reg Butler, *The Unknown Political Prisoner;* Churchill, *History of Second World War.*
(H) Stalin dies; Malenkov succeeds him.

1954

(A) e. e. cummings (1894–1962), *Poems 1923–1954;* Thomas, *Under Milk Wood.*

1955

(M) Luigi Nono (1924–), *Incontri.*
(A) W. H. Auden (1907–), *The Shield of Achilles.*

1956

(M) Stravinsky, *Canticum sacrum;* Ernst Pepping (1901–) *Te deum;* Stockhausen. *Gesang der Jünglinge.*
(H) Revolt in Hungary.

1957

(M) Stravinsky, *Agon;* Wolfgang Fortner (1907–) *Bluthochzeit;* Francis Poulenc (1899–1963) *Dialogues des Carmélites.*
(H) First "Sputnik" launched; International Geophysical Year begins.

1958

(M) Stravinsky, *Threni;* Witold Lutoslawski (1913–), *Funeral Music;* Olivier Messiaen (1908–) *Catalogue des oiseaux.*
(H) Explorer I (U.S. satellite); Voyage of the *Nautilus;* Khrushchev succeeds Malenkov as premier of U.S.S.R.

1959

(M) Orff, *Oedipus der Tyrann.*
(H) First moon rockets.

1960

(M) Copland, *Nonet for Strings;* Frank Martin (1890–), *Mystère de la Nativité.*
(H) 25 artificial satellites now in orbit.

1961

(M) Elliott Carter (1908–), *Double Concerto.*
(H) Establishment of the Peace Corps; Berlin Wall erected; first manned space flights.

1962

(M) Britten, *War Requiem.*
(H) Vatican Council II convenes.

1963

(H) John F. Kennedy assassinated; succeeded by Lyndon B. Johnson.

Index

503